The BILLBOARD ILLUSTRATED ENCYCLOPEDIA of
JAZZ & BLUES

Publisher and Creative Director: Nick Wells
Commissioning Editor: Polly Willis
Project Editor: Julia Rolf
Consultant Editor: Philip van Vleck
Picture Researchers: Melinda Revesz and Julia Rolf
Designer: Mike Spender
Production: Chris Herbert and Claire Walker

Special thanks to: Howard Cooke, Eric LeBlanc, Sonya Newland, Robin Newton,
Sylvia Pitcher, Sara Robson

First Published in 2005 by Billboard Books
An imprint of Watson-Guptill Publications
A division of VNU Business Medis, Inc.
770 Broadway, New York, New York 10003
www.wgpub.com

Created and produced by
FLAME TREE PUBLISHING
Crabtree Hall, Crabtree Lane
Fulham, London SW6 6TY
United Kingdom
www.flametreepublishing.com

Music information site: www.musicfirebox.com

Flame Tree is part of The Foundry Creative Media Company Limited
© 2005 Flame Tree Publishing

Library of Congress Control Number 2005924576
ISBN 0-8230-8266-0
Library of Congress cataloging-in-publication data for this title can be obtained from the Library of Congress.

Printed and bound in Spain by Bookprint, S.L., Barcelona

The BILLBOARD ILLUSTRATED ENCYCLOPEDIA of JAZZ & BLUES

Ted Drozdowski, James Hale, Todd Jenkins, Kenny Mathieson, John McDonough,

Bill Milkowski, Jim O'Neal, Bob Porter, William Schafer, David Whiteis

GENERAL EDITOR: HOWARD MANDEL

FOREWORD BY JOHN SCOFIELD

Billboard Books

An imprint of Watson-Guptill Publications, New York

Contents

How To Use This Book

Each chapter covers a decade or era and is divided into jazz and blues sections.

WWW Track boxes link to MP3 files with written commentaries on the website www.musicfirebox.com. These specially selected tracks aim to show how, as jazz and blues developed, the new sounds and textures introduced can often be linked back to the music's earlier incarnations.

Quotes from contemporary musicians and critics provide insight into the developments and overall feel of the musical scene dominating each era.

Cross-references pinpoint the interplay of influences between the artists and musical styles of both genres, enabling the reader to follow specific areas of interest into other parts of the book.

Popular Melody boxes highlight a track that summarizes the characteristic sounds and styles of jazz and blues music at that time.

Classic Recordings chronologically highlight important albums, tracks and session line-ups from the artist's career.

Quotes from fellow musicians and contemporary figures provide insight into the playing style and accomplishments of each key artist.

Key Track boxes examine a well-known tune or song that gives a good example of the player's overall sound, delving into the melody, lyrics and instrumentation used.

Cross-references pinpoint the interplay of influences between the artists and musical styles of both genres, enabling the reader to follow specific areas of interest into other parts of the book.

Foreword

Jazz and blues are the most influential, overriding and ultimate musical styles of the twentieth century – I think everyone agrees. Without them, popular music as we know it would not exist. I've always been happy to be part of these hugely important movements. Jazz and blues each make a recognizable and significant contribution to cultures everywhere. I see this in all aspects of my life. Music transcends languages and local culture, ties us together and maintains a powerful thread between the past, present and the future. Who among us does not have a soundtrack to his or her own life?

Believe it or not, I decided to become a professional guitar player before I had ever held one in my hands. After a brief period of begging, my parents (not understanding my sense of true destiny) *rented* me a cheap guitar and I began to practice. I focused on learning to play with a joyful, albeit dogged, enthusiasm that has not waned to this day.

The first music I was interested in was more in the folk tradition. Peter, Paul & Mary and the Kingston Trio were frontline in the American consciousness of the early 1960s. We saw folk music on TV, heard it on the radio and sheet music was readily available. One of the musical styles included in the movement was rural blues. Concurrently, America was experiencing what we called the British Invasion. From my 12-year-old perspective, the Beatles and Stones seemed to be the coolest people on the planet. They played songs by Muddy Waters, Howlin' Wolf and Chuck Berry, so I checked *them* out too.

Folk music and rock'n'roll both forged a link to the blues. Liner notes and word-of-mouth/common knowledge led me from blues to jazz. More importantly, jazz was the music that truly grabbed me, my first love. I can't recall which came first – seeing Barney Kessel on television or hearing a Django Reinhardt record my father bought for me – but I was quickly and permanently swayed in a jazz direction.

My experience in this field is something that I never take for granted. I'm so fortunate that I get to do this, so fortunate that it worked out. Music has given me an international existence that few ever know. I'm continually surprised that I am able to make a decent living doing what I love to do. The travel, the accolades, the personal validation are all benefits but those perks pale next to the thrill of playing with other musicians – learning from them and sharing music with them. I still pinch myself when I think of the opportunities I've had to play with so many of my idols. But it's not only the older ones; I've been equally inspired at times by people half my age.

That being said, my one greatest joy is simply the MUSIC itself. Listening and playing every day of my life, I keep going back to much of the same music that originally inspired me. I still discover performances I have never heard and artists new to me that continue to surface from early eras. Great new music shows up on the scene today too. As much as I've listened to any older piece, if I hear it again after several years away, I usually get something new from it. My own musical development gives me a deeper sense and appreciation of what I hear. Music is never finite!

What you'll find in this book is a history, a celebration of what I love. I am inspired, motivated and intrigued by jazz and blues music every day – and am a better person for it.

John Scofield, 2005

Introduction

Every book, even an illustrated encyclopedia of music, tells a story. Ours concerns 100 years of jazz and blues – enduring, artful, popular musics created by vivid characters during turbulent times.

Our history of these musics, which bear both irrevocable kinship and fundamental differences, begins where they were born: the United States of America. The blues' prime movers were descendants of African-American slaves. They played music for themselves and nearby neighbours, toured lowly venues as restless loners or in barnstorming troupes, and occasionally ascended to a theatre stage. Jazz was engendered by self-taught black American instrumentalists, more formally-trained Creole and Latin American musicians, and odd individuals of general lower, upper and middle, immigrant, laboring and dilettante classes as they jostled together in the burgeoning ports, river cities, labour camps and industrial centers of early-twentieth-century America.

From the start, Europe embraced and forwarded the movement of jazz and blues. African-American globetrotters such as James Reese Europe, Sam Wooding, Josephine Baker, Louis Armstrong,

Sidney Bechet and Duke Ellington captured the fancies of London, Paris, Berlin, St. Petersburg and other cosmopolitan capitols (as well as South America and eventually Africa, the Middle East and Asia), attracting enthusiastic audiences and coteries of adherents. Blues and jazz have always been embraced by aficionados and the uninitiated alike, recognized as universal forms of art capable of expressing all of human experience.

Life's dramas involve love, loss, honour, regret, festivity, commitment, rootlessness, devotion, depravity, setbacks and victory – conditions evoked and enacted, in nuanced detail, by blues and jazz. Furthermore, these musics have evolved to be both flexible and firm. Jazz and blues can accept, celebrate and assimilate the most profound effects of their most singular innovators, yet remain arts unto themselves. Bessie Smith influenced the blues forever, but the blues is not Bessie Smith; Miles Davis will exert an enormous influence on jazz for evermore, but there is jazz besides Miles.

Blues and jazz were ideally suited or readily tailored for the sound recording and broadcast technologies that developed in the twentieth century. They were the first musics disseminated as documents of the spontaneous creativity of charismatic virtuosi, rather than as artifacts of fixed interpretations of printed scores. Jazz and blues records were snatched up, but they merely whetted appetites for live appearances by heroes celebrating the immediate eternal moment. Was it mere coincidence that international interest in jazz and blues tied in with the rise of faster, easier and cheaper international travel?

In truth, blues and jazz are best when they are heard live; live performance demonstrates a music's vitality genuinely, and first-hand witnesses are usually more able transplantors of imported arts. Jazz and blues scattered seeds wherever they landed, and everywhere those seeds took root.

From our perspective, blues and jazz are self-perpetuating gifts to the world coming from deep in the heart of post-slavery America, a historic place and state-of-mind in which rustic and regional traditions are transformed to suit the global digitopolis of today. Musicians well beyond the US and Europe, enthralled with jazz and blues, model songs on the musical styles but with their own unique vocabularies, inflections and dialects. The musics' strains, strategies and structures have been pressed to serve many cultures' and peoples' needs; given the space explorations of artists such as Sun Ra, being beyond the rainbow may be swinging, too.

So other histories of jazz and blues could be, and should be, told – the all-too-often overlooked women; the considerable influences exerted by Hispanola, the Mediterranean and the Caribbean isles; the investigation of the links between concert-hall compositions and sounds shaped by improvisation, the better to fulfil the imperatives of the brothels, street parades, barrooms,

dancehalls and smoky dives from which the music originated.

The Illustrated Encyclopedia of Jazz & Blues touches on those topics, but its focus is elsewhere. We don't claim to be exhaustive, but hope that our selectivity represents breadth and inclusivity. We acknowledge the diverse forces, decade by decade, that shaped all peoples' activities, understanding that blues and jazz musicians are as prey to the influence of circumstance as anyone else. But we highlight, over all, those individuals who made this music.

Here they are, the musicians, year after year, page after page, many captured in the heat of action. Always, their photos and attendant graphic ephemera are illustrative, revealing: even when they've been posed, jazz and blues musicians make their points, directing the narrative. Read all about them. See what they chose to show.

Blues crystallizes images of strength against adversity; jazz expands upon insights, whims and systems of the imagination. Our *Illustrated Encyclopedia* points to a world off the page – go out and hear how the music sounds. And know that the story of jazz and blues has not ended. We believe it has just begun.

Howard Mandel New York, 2005

early years:
the roots and teens

j azz and blues are rooted in the enormous technological and social transformations affecting the USA and Western Europe at the turn of the twentieth century. The most striking changes were the advent of easier and cheaper travel; better communications; electric lighting; improvements in audio recording and moving pictures; increased urbanization; and the rise of the US, concurrent with the fall of the UK, as the world's leading military, economic and cultural power. The budding empowerment of African-Americans, who no longer faced slavery, had more impact on the development of new forms of music than any other engine of change. The abolishment of slavery was the beginning of the end of white performers in blackface impersonating Negroes in minstrel shows. African-Americans in the US still may not have been treated equally, but they could gather more freely, and engage in group amusements without censure. Loose threads of African retentions, Scotch-Irish ballads, Christian hymns, vaudeville themes, Spanish dance rhythms, marching-band fanfares and idiosyncratic expression began to be woven together by musicians who were either seeking their fortunes adrift from their childhood homes, or were immigrants exiled from age-old traditions.

After the First World War, the US tried to regain its isolationist past. But newly efficient production methods and the rapid growth of cities lent the economy unbridled power. Money, speed, relocation and youth were ascendant – blues and jazz sang their anthems. Blues and jazz were themselves flexible enough to adapt to changes that continued at seemingly ever-faster rates, swallowing all prior conventions, throughout the twentieth century.

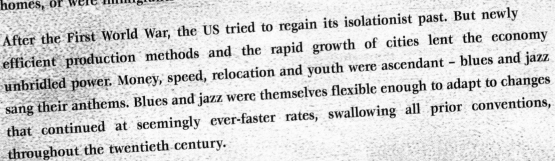

Key Artists: Blues

Charley Patton

Ma Rainey

Key Artists: Jazz

Kid Ory

Clarence Williams

Blues

The blues was shaped by African culture, the experience of slavery and many other influences, but it emerged as a distinct form only around the turn of the twentieth century – some four decades after the abolition of slavery and several generations removed from the mother continent.

of many blues guitarists. The fife and drum music of rural southeast America – a mixture of blues, spirituals and folk pieces played on homemade bamboo-cane fifes and marching drums – can be traced back to black musicians who played in the militia units during and before the Civil War; this genre also has its counterparts in African music.

www

The Rhythmakers
Yellow Dog Blues

*musicfirebox.com
/Yellow*

Echoes Of Distant Cultures

African retentions in timbres, tones and rhythms, and in the functional nature of music in daily life as practiced by people who were not necessarily professional musicians, interacted in America with European musical traditions, including Scotch-Irish fiddle tunes, English ballads, Christian songs and marching bands. Slaves with musical talent learned to entertain whites at plantation dances, balls and parties, performing reels, jigs, waltzes and popular songs of the day. The work songs and hollers of those labouring in the fields often harked back to the chants of their African ancestors, while in the churches Protestant hymns took on an African-American character to emerge as 'Negro spirituals'.

'In the beginning, Adam had the blues, 'cause he was lonesome. So God helped him and created a woman. Now everybody's got the blues.'
Willie Dixon

Africanisms survived in the work and game songs, call-and-response patterns, vocal and instrumental phrasings, syncopations, oral traditions, folk customs and beliefs, pentatonic scales and flattened 'blue notes', as well as in instrumentation. The banjo can be traced back to Africa, along with other bowed or plucked stringed instruments, including the one-string 'diddley bow' – the beginning instrument

Right

Many of the 'plantation songs' performed in the minstrel shows were published as sheet music.

MUSIC-LOVERS LIBRARY

PLANTATION SONGS

WITH PIANOFORTE ACCOMPANIMENT

1/6 NET.

CONTENTS.

Where de Golden Banjoes play
My old Kentucky Home
Dar's one more ribber for to cross
Old Folks at Home
Dat little black face
Massa's in de cold ground
Come where my love lies dreaming
Good news from home
Hard times come again no more
Ring de Banjo
The Yellow Rose of Texas
Come where the moonbeams linger
Belle Mahone
Let me kiss him for his mother
Rosalie, the prairie flower
I'm off to Charlestown
Uncle Ned
Camptown Races
Beautiful Isle of the Sea
Down the River

ASCHERBERG, HOPWOOD & CREW, Ltd.
16, Mortimer Street, London, W.1.
PRINTED IN ENGLAND

Minstrels, Spirituals And Ragtime

After America's Civil War, itinerant songsters, musical roustabouts on the riverboats and travelling minstrel show troupes spread their music far and wide. Early forms of music that would become the blues began to develop not only on the plantations, where former slaves and their descendants now toiled as sharecroppers, but also in towns and cities along the Mississippi and Ohio Rivers and elsewhere. The music makers' repertoires variously included 'jump-ups' (unrelated lines sung over simple chorded accompaniments), ditties, old plantation melodies, breakdowns (uptempo dance pieces), church songs, bad man or folk hero ballads and derogatory 'coon songs' (sung in minstrel shows by blackface performers), as well as popular white music, show tunes and – in some areas, as black musicians acquired formal training – classical works. The jubilee singing of black spiritual ensembles drew national and international attention, and the ragtime craze that swept the country from the 1890s to the First World War established America's fascination with the secular music of African-Americans. The syncopated rhythms of

Above
The beginnings of Delta blues can be traced back to the Mississippi cotton plantations.

ragtime fuelled the sales of pianos, sheet music and piano rolls. Ragtime embodied the spirit of a country liberating itself from Victorian mores (while at the same time, blacks were still subjected to discrimination, oppression and lynch-mob violence).

The blues drew from many sources to give voice to an African-American identity and response in the troubled era of Jim Crow laws, enacted to restrict the rights and opportunities of America's free but unequal black citizens. The lyrics often expressed a desire to move on to a better place or a better mate; songs of lost love and mistreatment sometimes had a double meaning – as codified protests or commentary secretly directed towards the white boss man and his social order. Risqué sexual double-entendres also abounded, as blues inherited the vulgar side of ragtime's early notoriety as low-class and disreputable, denounced by churchgoers as the 'devil's music' played in dens of temptation, violence and evil. It may have been born of sorrow and hardship, consigned to the margins of society, yet blues sought not to wallow in pain and misery but to raise the spirits in cathartic release, often with humour or irony – to get rid of the blues by singing them.

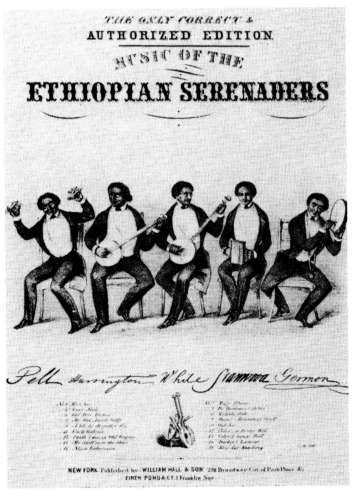

Left
Minstrel troupes such as the Ethiopian Serenaders were popular touring entertainers.

Popular Melody

Traditional – 'Arwhoolie (Cornfield Holler)' (1800s/1900s)
Work songs and field hollers gave rise to the moans of the blues. Library of Congress folksong collectors recorded several of these in the 1930s and 1940s, including one known as 'Arwhoolie (Cornfield Holler)' by Thomas C. Marshall in 1939 in Edwards, Mississippi. The Arhoolie record label took its name from the holler.

The Blues Begins To Spread

Blues took hold in Mississippi, Texas, Georgia, Louisiana, Missouri, the Carolinas and several other southern states. Waves of northward migration would eventually establish Chicago as the blues capital, but in earlier years St Louis and Memphis were more significant urban blues centres. The cotton plantation system of the Mississippi Delta spawned an especially concentrated and prolific blues subculture, as workers sought weekend release from their toils at house parties, juke joints, country suppers, fish fries and picnics, or in the nearest towns' cafés, saloons, barrelhouses, nightclubs and brothels.

A primary function of the blues was as dance music, played by banjoists, mandolinists and guitarists; string bands with fiddles; harmonica blowers and washboard,

fife and drum, and jug bands. In the top rung of entertainers were pianists; the piano remained the dominant instrument in blues for several decades. Most blues performers also worked as fieldhands or labourers, but some made a living from their music, roaming the countryside, playing for workers on plantations and farms or in levee and lumber camps. These went from town to town alone, with companions, or with a minstrel or medicine show, carnival or circus. In towns and cities black musicians were also able to join brass bands, mandolin clubs, singing quartets and dance orchestras, such as the one led by W.C. Handy (1873–1958); this paved the way for jazz, which always bore a strong blues component. Handy drew from his encounters with the blues in the Delta (c. 1903) to write orchestrated versions such as 'Yellow Dog Rag' (later re-christened 'Yellow Dog Blues') and 'Memphis Blues'.

In his autobiography *The Father Of The Blues*, published in 1941, Handy described songs that were apparently blues, which he had heard in St Louis and Evansville, Indiana (c. 1892), and just after that in Henderson, Kentucky, as well as some form of proto-blues in his native Florence, Alabama. Contemporary documentation of turn-of-the-century blues is virtually non-existent; New Orleans was a blues piano centre, by the recollections decades later of Jelly Roll Morton (1890–1941) and Pops Foster (1892–1969). Among the pianists remembered as playing blues at the sporting

Above

In Alabama and other parts of the Deep South, the blues developed as a form of dance music.

Right

Napoleon Strickland, described as the 'fife-blowingest man in the state of Mississippi', with his fife and drum band.

houses were Alfred Wilson, Kid Game and a Creole woman, Mamie Desdunes (Desdoumes), who was playing in New Orleans in 1902, the same year in which Ma Rainey (1886–1939) recalled hearing blues in Missouri. John Jacob Niles later wrote of a blues singer from Louisville, Kentucky named Black Alfalfa (a.k.a. Ophelia Simpson), who in 1898 was performing a song called 'Black Alfalfa's Jail-House Shouting Blues'.

Evidence Of Early Blues Songs

While most such recollections – including those of bluesmen such as Big Bill Broonzy (1893–1958) from Mississippi and Leadbelly (1888–1949) from northwest Louisiana – were published decades after the fact, a few researchers did file more timely reports of early blues or blues-like songs. Charles Peabody, a Harvard archeologist working on an excavation at the Stovall Plantation in the Mississippi Delta in 1901, wrote of the 'autochthonous music' he heard the black workers singing; folklorist Howard Odum collected a number of blues songs in Georgia and Mississippi, from both local musicians and travelling performers between 1905 and 1908, as well as some from North Carolina. Besides this, songs dating back to 1890 were collected by Gates Thomas in Texas. Various

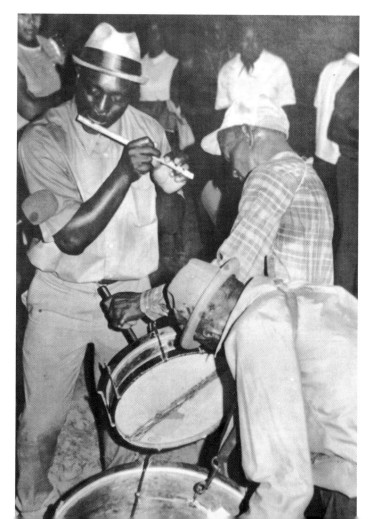

introduction ⊙ 10   jazz roots ⊙ 22

compositions published in the 1890s and early 1900s contained some structural or lyrical resemblance to blues, although the blues form had yet to congeal; 'I Got The Blues' by New Orleans violinist Antonio Maggio – the 1908 instrumental that was perhaps the earliest such number to use blues in the title – was advertised as an 'up-to-date rag'.

Few recordings of black performers were made in the earliest eras of cylinders, piano rolls and 78-rpm discs; of those that were made, most were spirituals, coon songs or comedy routines. The primary dissemination of black music was still done via sheet music (including 'ballits' sold on the streets by itinerant songwriters) and public performances. Blues had yet to make a name for itself and was in fact only just beginning to be called 'blues' – some early bluesmen remembered the songs being called 'reels' or 'reals'. But a folk blues repertoire was forming (although not yet being recorded) from songs such as 'Make Me A Pallet On The Floor', 'Joe Turner Blues', 'East St. Louis', 'Stack O' Lee' and 'John Henry', along with other southern airs noted by Handy.

The earliest secular recordings listed in *Blues And Gospel Records 1890-1943* are cylinders by a banjo duo, the Bohee Brothers (1890–92); another banjo team, Cousins and DeMoss, recorded a one-sided disc in 1897. In London the American singer Belle Davis, one of the first black women to record, provided a taste of the blues to come in her 1902 recording 'The Honeysuckle And The Bee'.

Left

The 'father of the blues', composer and music collector W.C. Handy.

Popular Melody

Traditional – 'Joe Turner Blues' (1893–97, published by W.C. Handy in 1915)
Thought to be one of the oldest blues, 'Joe Turner' originated as a lament for the men sentenced to serve under chain-gang boss Joe Turney, brother of Peter Turney (governor of Tennessee, 1893–97). A number of seminal folk blues songs employed the same melody.

Blues

Charley Patton
*Screamin' And
Hollerin' The Blues*

*musicfirebox.com
/Screamin*

Blues made a leap forward into the public consciousness of America in 1912, when Baby Seals, Hart Wand and W.C. Handy (1873–1958) became the first composers to publish blues sheet music, or at least to register blues with the copyright office. Many more 'blues' were to follow, often from the pens of New York songwriters. Not all compositions named 'blues' were actually blues in structure or feel – many such songs of the era were rags, vaudeville tunes or Tin Pan Alley pop pieces, with 'blues' fashionably attached to the end of the title. The real breakthrough for blues came with Handy's 'St. Louis Blues', which innovatively incorporated traditional folk and blues elements,

'I wrote "St. Louis Blues" in the key of G because colored people can moan better in that key. It has a mournful plaintiveness.' **W.C. Handy**

along with a touch of habañera that Handy had heard in Cuba. In the years following its first publication in 1914, it became one of the most widely recorded compositions of all time and topped the sales lists for sheet music and piano rolls.

The Blues Influence In Vaudeville

Prior to the record industry's discovery that there was a niche market for blues and jazz among black buyers – sparked by the success of Mamie Smith's (1883–1946) recording of 'Crazy Blues' in 1920 – what little black music was recorded was done so with white audiences in mind. The first singers to record any of Handy's blues in 1914 were white, in fact, and so were many other vaudeville

W. C. HANDY
—1873-1958—
"Father of the Blues" composer and family lived at this site 1903-05. In Clarksdale Handy was influenced by Delta blues which he collected and later published as well as his own famous and influential music.

MISSISSIPPI DEPARTMENT OF ARCHIVES AND HISTORY 1981

Right

A memorial to the great W.C. Handy in Clarksdale, Mississippi.

singers who began to incorporate the blues (something of a novelty at the time) into their repertoires, including the young star billed as 'Queen of the Blues', Marion Harris, and even Sophie Tucker. In New York, the most famous of the early black vaudevillians, Bert Williams, was in the nineteenth year of his recording career when he finally waxed 'I'm Sorry I Ain't Got It, You Could Have Had It If I Had It Blues' in 1919, followed by two blues in 1920, both of which preceded 'Crazy Blues'.

Blues On Wax

Another black act, Dan Kildare's string band, featuring two banjos, had recorded 'St. Louis Blues' in 1917 in London, where they were entertaining white Britons at clubs and dance halls; they were billed as Ciro's Club Coon Orchestra. Banjoists also played in the bands accompanying some of the early female blues singers. The guitar would supplant the banjo as blues came to fruition, but even so the record labels were late in bringing Sylvester Weaver, the first recorded blues guitarist, to the studio in 1923, and later still in rounding up the first generation of great blues singer-guitarists such as Blind Lemon Jefferson (*c.* 1897–1929), Lonnie Johnson (*c.* 1894–1970), Blind Blake (*c.* early 1890s– *c.* 1933) and Charley Patton (*c.* 1891–1934). Seminal figures such as Henry 'Ragtime Texas' Thomas (1874–1930), Frank Stokes and banjoists Gus Cannon (1885–1979) and Papa Charlie Jackson (*c.* 1890–1938) only began to record in the 1920s, but their music obviously echoed sounds from the dawn of the blues and before. The most extensive recording of early black ballads, pre-blues, and work and game songs was done by Leadbelly (1888–1949) at the behest of folklorists John (1867–1948) and Alan (1915–2002) Lomax, but not until the 1930s and 1940s; such music held little appeal for commercial recording concerns.

The Early Blues Divas

Even from its emergence, blues was a multi-faceted phenomenon, developing both as a grassroots folk music in local community environments and as a professional entertainment medium on a more commercial level. It also continued to influence and be affected by musicians from other genres, within or outside the African-American culture – from jazz and gospel to old-time country and pop. The blues' first proven stars atop the

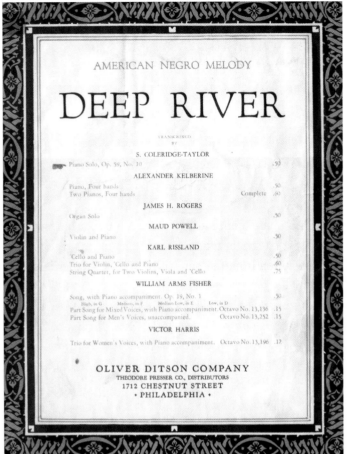

Left

African-American blues songs and spirituals such as 'Deep River' began to be performed in vaudeville shows.

black showbusiness ladder were the divas who travelled the vaudeville circuit co-ordinated by the Theater Owners Booking Association (TOBA, founded in Memphis in 1909). Well before their recording careers began, Ma Rainey (1886–1939), Sara Martin (1884–1955), Ida Cox (1896–1967) and a young Bessie Smith (1894–1937), among others, had years of experience in tent shows and vaudeville revues; women such as Alberta Hunter (1895–1984) also worked their way in to cabarets, supperclubs and white society venues. That they were advertised not just as singers but as 'comediennes' underscored the nature of their art; they could turn tears into laughter and survive in the face of adversity. When the doors to the recording industry opened to them in the 1920s, they were already on centre stage.

Popular Melody

W.C. Handy – 'Memphis Blues' (1912)

Although it would be eclipsed by his 'St. Louis Blues' (1914), 'Memphis Blues' was W.C. Handy's first published work, the first blues to be recorded (by the Victor Military Band, in 1914) and 'the first to make blues a viable popular music form', according to historian Tim Brooks.

Charley Patton

Classic Recordings

1929
'Screamin' And Hollerin' The Blues', 'Down The Dirt Road', 'Pony Blues', 'Banty Rooster Blues', 'Pea Vine Blues', 'Tom Rushen Blues', 'A Spoonful Blues', 'Shake It And Break It', 'High Water Everywhere'

1930
'Dry Well Blues', 'Moon Going Down'

1934
'High Sheriff Blues', 'Stone Pony Blues'

Although not really the 'Founder of the Delta Blues', as one reissue album title touted, Charley Patton more than anyone defined not only the genre but also the image of the hard-living, rambling Delta bluesman, leaving trouble in his wake as he rolled from plantation to plantation and woman to woman. His rough vocal timbre – combined with the poor sound quality of the few surviving Paramount 78s he recorded – may have caused some listeners to regard him as primitive, yet even guitarists such as John Fahey, who wrote the first book on Patton, have been awed by both the power and the complexity of his music.

repertoire drew from traditional black folk songs, white pop tunes, religious songs, dance pieces and frolics, as well as his own creative wellspring as a composer and storyteller. His records are noteworthy for his descriptions of topical events, such as the great Mississippi River flood of 1927, and for the local lore and real-life characters that he worked into songs such as 'Tom Rushen Blues' and 'High Sheriff Blues'. He died in 1934, but his influence persists into the twenty-first century; Bob Dylan included a tribute song – 'High Water Everywhere (For Charley Patton)' – on his 2001 album *Love And Theft*.

A Formidable Bluesman

Under the influence of an older guitarist named Henry Sloan on the Dockery Plantation, Patton, probably born in 1891 in Bolton, Mississippi, developed into the most famous and formidable Delta bluesman of the early twentieth century. By his biographers' accounts, he was leading the way long before his belated recording debut in 1929. Patton, of mixed black, white and Native American ancestry, was an animated performer who clowned with the guitar and beat on the instrument for percussive effects. He taught or influenced guitarists such as Tommy Johnson, Willie Brown, Roebuck 'Pops' Staples and Howlin' Wolf during his stays in the Dockery area, and later, further north in the Delta, added Son House, Robert Johnson and others to the list. Tommy Johnson used some of Patton's themes on his own Victor recording debut in 1928.

> *'If I were going to record for just my pleasure I would only record Charley Patton songs.'*
>
> *Bob Dylan*

Right

Charley Patton, the first great Delta bluesman and a key influence on all who followed.

Patton's Lasting Influence

Patton's first Paramount disc, 'Pony Blues'/'Banty Rooster Blues', was his biggest hit. His recorded

Ma Rainey

Gertrude 'Ma' Rainey, the 'Mother of the Blues', had been singing the blues for some two decades before she commenced her influential series of recordings for the Paramount label in 1923. She even laid claim to naming the music 'the blues' after hearing the singing of a young girl in Missouri in 1902, where Rainey was performing with a tent show.

Assassinators Of The Blues

Born Gertrude Pridgett on 26 April 1886, Rainey began performing in her native Columbus, Georgia as a schoolgirl, before joining a number of travelling revues and minstrel shows, working southern theatres, circuses, carnivals and other venues. She teamed with William 'Pa' Rainey, whom she married in 1904, to perform as 'Rainey and Rainey, Assassinators of the Blues'. Known for her flamboyant stage shows, jewelled attire and colourful lifestyle, she was already one of the best-known blues singers in the South when recruited by Paramount.

A Versatile Performer

Rainey helped to shape the character, style and presentation of blues in its formative years, and her role and stature in the blues genre escalated during her brief but prolific career (1923–28). Her records were noted not only for the powerful majesty of her singing, but also for the variety of outstanding accompaniment by acclaimed jazz, blues and jug band musicians. Ma Rainey possessed an earthier, more downhome southern style than most of the early blues queens, and was effective working

with bluesmen such as Tampa Red, Georgia Tom Dorsey and Blind Blake, as well as with jazz musicians. She retired in 1935 and died four years later, but her influence is evident in the work of her protégé Bessie Smith and many others. Among Rainey's classics were the original version of 'See See Rider', 'Bo-Weavil Blues', 'Moonshine Blues' and 'Ma Rainey's Black Bottom' (also the title of an award-winning play written in the 1990s by August Wilson, with a Rainey studio recording session as its setting).

Classic Recordings

Madame 'Ma' Rainey (with Lovie Austin and her Blues Serenaders) (1923)
'Bad Luck Blues', 'Bo-Weavil Blues', 'Barrel House Blues'

'Ma' Rainey (1924)
'Shave 'Em Dry Blues'

Ma Rainey (with her Georgia Jazz Band) (1924)
'Booze And Blues Blues', 'Toad Frog Blues', 'See See Rider Blues'

'Ma' Rainey (with her Georgia Band) (1925–27)
'Yonder Comes the Blues', 'Stack O' Lee Blues', 'Blues Oh Blues', 'Ma Rainey's Black Bottom'

'Ma' Rainey (1926–28)
'Mountain Jack Blues', 'Daddy Goodbye Blues'

Ma Rainey (with her Tub Jug Washboard Band) (1928)
'Black Cat Hoot Owl Blues', 'Prove It On Me Blues'

Ma Rainey & Papa Charlie Jackson (1928)
'Ma And Pa Poorhouse Blues'

Left
Ma Rainey, a flamboyant blues singer with a powerful voice who mentored others, including Bessie Smith.

A-Z of artists

Gus Cannon

(Vocals, banjo, jug, kazoo, guitar, fiddle, piano, 1885–1979)

A pioneering bluesman who became a central figure in the Memphis jug band scene, Gus Cannon may have been the first blues recording artist, if tales of music he recorded as early as 1898 are true. However, no documentary evidence of Cannon recordings has been retrieved prior to his Paramount sides of 1927; furthermore, if he did record almost 30 years earlier the music may not have been blues at all, for his repertoire also drew from pre-blues black and white folk and minstrel traditions. Cannon performed as Banjo Joe on medicine shows in the teens and 1920s and recorded his first sides under that name.

Inspired by the success of the Memphis Jug Band, Cannon reconfigured his act into Cannon's Jug Stompers and signed with Victor in 1928. Among the Cannon songs reworked by latter-day folk revivalists is 'Walk Right In', which became a number-one pop hit in the US for the Rooftop Singers in 1963. The notoriety enabled Cannon to record an album for Stax Records in 1963, although his participation in the blues revival of the 1960s was limited.

Georgia Tom Dorsey

(Vocals, piano, 1899–1993)

Thomas A. Dorsey earned his greatest fame as the 'Father of Gospel Music' after leaving his blues career behind in 1932, but in his early days he was an important blues performer, songwriter, arranger and studio musician. In his youth in ragtime-era Atlanta and in Chicago from 1916, Dorsey developed his piano-playing skills at barrelhouses and rent parties. He also worked with jazz orchestras and Ma Rainey's band before teaming up with Tampa Red in 1928. Dorsey composed songs for the duo as well as material for Ma Rainey and others, and had a special knack for the risqué double-entendre – ironic for a man best known for religious classics such as 'Precious Lord (Take My Hand)'.

Dorsey achieved his greatest success as a music publisher and was founder of the National Convention of Gospel Choirs and Choruses, Inc. Despite his stature in religious circles, Dorsey continued to give credit to the blues, both as a valid expression of the human condition and as a contributing element in the development and acceptance of gospel music.

Below

The multi-talented Georgia Tom Dorsey (third from left) with Ma Rainey's band.

Mississippi John Hurt
(Vocals, guitar, 1892–1966)

A songster and fingerpicking guitarist from Avalon, Mississippi, John Hurt excelled in the pre-blues black folk ballad tradition as well as in blues, gospel and dance instrumentals. He spent most of his life working on farms and entertaining at local parties and functions for both blacks and whites. His first opportunity to record came

'I saw him at Newport '63 and he just killed me. His voice, his face, his attitude, his gentle innocence, his real profound thoughts; I was just lost, lost into the world of John Hurt.'
Dick Waterman

in 1928, when the white Mississippi fiddle/guitar duo of Narmour and Smith informed OKeh Records of a talented black guitar picker that they knew.

Hurt not only contributed songs such as 'Candy Man' and 'Avalon Blues' to the blues canon, but also reinvigorated the folk legends of Casey Jones, Frankie & Albert and Stack O' Lee. Hurt enjoyed a new career on the folk-blues circuit from 1963 until his death, recording several excellent albums and charming festival and coffeehouse audiences with his gentle nature and warm, captivating music.

Tommy Johnson
(Vocals, guitar, c. 1896–1956)

Johnson was a highly influential early blues artist due to the impact of his three 1928 records for Victor, which earned him a niche as Mississippi's first black recording star. Johnson recorded only three more 78s after that, for Paramount, plus a few unissued sides, but the songs he recorded for Victor (including 'Cool Drink Of Water', 'Big Road Blues', 'Maggie Campbell Blues' and 'Canned Heat Blues') became entrenched in the repertoires of many bluesmen to follow.

Inspired by Charley Patton, Johnson developed a unique approach, employing falsetto accents and hypnotic guitar riffs. He learned from an older brother, LeDell, who later told folklorist David Evans a tale of Tommy selling his soul to the devil at a crossroads – a story associated today with Robert Johnson (no relation). Johnson's reputation as a great bluesman was equalled perhaps only by his notoriety as a drinker, which no doubt contributed to his quick decline. He ceased recording after 1929 and spent his remaining years playing streets and house parties in Mississippi.

Daddy Stovepipe
(Vocals, harmonica, guitar, 1867–1963)

Daddy Stovepipe – a.k.a. Mobile, Alabama native Johnny Watson – is an obscure figure, with only a scattering of recording sessions to his credit, but he represents an important era of blues and pre-blues music. He was not only one of the first downhome blues performers to record (in 1924), but his 1867 birthdate is the earliest yet documented for any artist in the blues discographies: he was, in fact, decades older than the blues genre itself.

His recorded work has much in common with the jug-band melodies of Memphis, a similarity enhanced by the addition of his wife, Mississippi Sarah, on vocals and jug during the 1930s. Watson performed as a one-man band on streets and in medicine shows in Mississippi, Texas and elsewhere, before going to Chicago, where he played for tips on Maxwell Street. He was one of at least three pre-war bluesmen to record using the name Stovepipe, either in reference to the stovepipe hat or a stovepipe used as a musical instrument.

Above
Formidable guitar picker and gentle folk blues narrator Mississippi John Hurt.

Jazz

'Most of the musicians had day jobs.... They had to work at other trades 'cause there were so many musicians, so many bands. [New Orleans] was just 'bout the most musical town in the country.'

Zutty Singleton

Below
Canal Street, New Orleans, c. 1900, as jazz music was developing.

'Jazz started in New Orleans,' Jelly Roll Morton (*c.* 1890–1941) opined solemnly in his monumental 1938 oral autobiography for the Library of Congress. Jazz also started in many other places across America – a new wave of musical sound, melded from turn-of-the-century African-American rivulets of song in the ragtime and the blues styles, reached middle America

by the teens of the twentieth century with the force of revelation. But in New Orleans, the music was fertilized and nurtured by a vibrant culture of many nationalities and ethnic groups: a melting pot of cultures from across the South.

Ragtime And The Blues Join Forces

Ragtime was a jubilant, rhythmically propulsive music in syncopated march time, while the blues was a slow, emotionally forceful expression of personal sorrow as

both public confession and private transcendence. Forged together, these gifts from the African-American soul created a new music that rapidly circled the globe and became a primary expression of the modern American spirit. The world entered a new age, dancing and singing to the sounds of jazz. Ragtime gathered impetus in the American Midwest – Missouri, Arkansas, Kansas, Indiana, Illinois – and the deepest blues emerged from the hot South – Mississippi's Delta region, the Black Belt of Georgia and Alabama, the sharecropping farms and turpentine camps that stretched west to Texas, Oklahoma and Arkansas.

By 1918, the emerging new music had been named 'jass' (a slang term for sex) – or 'jazz', 'jaz', 'jas', even 'jazs' – by listeners galvanized and fascinated by its manic energy and emotional exuberance. It fused the hot rhythms and lively energy of ragtime with the plangent harmonies and lyrical depth of the blues. In a few years, young novelist F. Scott Fitzgerald could truthfully say people were living in a Jazz Age. The new music emerged from differing sources. Ragtime spread as a piano music; affordable, mass-produced pianos had become the latest badge of middle-class prosperity and gentility, and the newly developed player pianos could reproduce ragtime's three-minute syncopated sonatas with eerie perfection. The blues were pronounced on the street by itinerant guitarists and harmonica players.

A Missouri pioneer and entrepreneur named John Stark heard black pianists playing their own works and decided to use his small music-publishing firm to proselytize America with their enticing, melodic music. In 1899, he published a piece by Scott Joplin (1868–1917), an up-and-coming young ragtime pianist who arrived in Missouri by way of Texas and Arkansas. It was named after a rough and ready Sedalia bar, the Maple Leaf Club. Joplin's 'Maple Leaf Rag' was a nationwide sensation, selling upwards of a million copies of Stark's sheet-music score. It was played everywhere by bands

like those of John Philip Sousa and Arthur Pryor, by banjoists and xylophonists, cranked out on player pianos and barrel organs. Vaudevillians such as clarinettist-bandleader Wilbur Sweatman turned classic ragtime into popular music, as in his 'Down Home Rag' (1916). Ragtime was the reveille call for America's golden new twentieth century; we still dance to its bright syncopations.

Popular Melody

Robert Cole, James W. and J. Rosamond Johnson – 'Under The Bamboo Tree' (1902)
This is a dignified and stately piece of exotic utopianism ('two live as one/Under the bamboo tree'), which typifies early African-American musical comedy styles. It has echoed in cultural history, having been quoted by writers as diverse as T.S. Eliot and Paul Theroux.

The Sounds Of New Orleans

Other streams of music flowed as tributaries into the new jazz river. New Orleans had long, fertile traditions preserving all forms of black music. In Congo Square in the nineteenth century, generations of African-Americans gathered to sing, dance and drum, maintaining a lifeline to their homeland traditions. One notable musician to absorb these influences was piano virtuoso and composer Louis Moreau Gottschalk, who grew up mesmerized by the sounds from Congo Square. Strains of Creole music from the gumbo of New Orleans' mixed culture – French, Spanish, American-Indian and African-American – emerged as a spicy remoulade: red hot peppers mixed with the more formal ballroom music from south of the city (Cuban, Caribbean and Latin-American rhythms such as the habañera, the tango, the meringue). Like the city's open-air markets, the music was redolent of tasty, tangy sounds, and in the teens a 'tango craze' hit the city; many tango halls opened and the dance fad reached everyone. Its presence can be heard in the insinuating Spanish tinge of Jelly Roll Morton's music, in his tangos such as 'Mama Nita', 'The Crave' and 'Creepy Feeling'.

At the beginning of the twentieth century, New Orleans was America's most exotic and cosmopolitan city, with a huge variety of cultures, languages, dialects and patois intertwining, especially in song. In the French Quarter, the long-established French Opera was a temple for popular entertainment, its airs mixing on the streets and squares with street vendors' cries and the bluesy honk of brass bands on parade. People might hum or whistle a blues melody, a minstrel tune, a lilting aria from Bizet or Gounod or an excerpt from the wildly popular melodramatic operas of Giacomo Meyerbeer.

**The Charleston
Chasers**
Basin Street Blues

*musicfirebox.com
/Basin*

Right
John Philip Sousa, whose marches were performed by brass bands all over the US.

Following the Civil War (1861–65), America had become a nation of town, village and municipal band music, with thousands of small bands echoing the monumental work of John Philip Sousa, whose many compositions and arrangements redefined and codified the literature for bands as another all-American signature. His marches became national airs, and their steady tempos the vital pulse of the country. After 1870, brass instrumentation was modernized and standardized, and musical instruments became cheaper and as easy to come by as the nearest Sears, Roebuck & Co. catalogue. The hearty sound of brass could be heard in the air everywhere.

Brass Bands Take Over

New Orleans, a hot-weather city of constant, organized festivities teeming with social clubs, fraternal orders and non-stop partying, fairly demanded the brash urgency of brass-band music. Bands were in demand for lawn parties, parades (for Masonic cornerstone-layings and other ceremonial events), holiday celebrations and funerals. The city marched and danced to brass-band music and many citizens eventually went to rest in their crypts heralded by a band. Ensembles such as the Eureka Brass Band, the Excelsior Brass Band, the Onward Brass Band and others had developed over decades and by the teens were known all over New Orleans. Across the river in Algiers, trumpeter Henry Allen Sr. (1877–1952) led a famous brass band that taught many young players, including his son Henry 'Red' Allen (1908–67), the rudiments of the new hot music.

Known generally as 'social aid and pleasure clubs', hundreds of organizations existed to provide burial insurance that paid for a service, a wake, a funeral and a celebratory send-off – 'the end of a perfect death', as Jelly Roll Morton said. A band of 10 or 12 pieces assembled at the church to play hymns, then provided mournful dirges on the march to the burying ground. After the graveside service, the band left consecrated ground, struck up a lively ragtime march and led the mourners back to a funeral supper. Morton illustrated the 'jazz funeral' idea on his 1938 Library of Congress recordings and on a 1939 band recording of 'Oh, Didn't He Ramble', a rollicking and rude song descended from an even older English ditty, 'The Derby Ram'. His version runs the gamut from mourning to jubilation in three short minutes.

Various kinds of band music joined together to create a multicultural tradition. Circuses, travelling minstrel/tent shows, revival meetings, medicine shows and carnivals all featured bands in which New Orleans musicians apprenticed themselves. Trumpeters like William Geary 'Bunk' Johnson (1889–1949) and Ernest 'Kid Punch' Miller (1894–1971) hit the circus-band circuit and brought back more new music to New Orleans. Both men later fuelled the revival of New Orleans-style jazz that took off in the 1940s.

Above

The New Orleans funeral march remains an important part of the city's musical heritage to this day.

Left

Pianist, composer and bandleader Jelly Roll Morton advocated the 'Spanish tinge' element in jazz music.

Above

Basin Street, Storyville, New Orleans; Tom Anderson's café was a major musical centre.

A Swelling Flood Of Music

Various founts of new music fed the surging tide of jazz in the teens. In Storyville, the few square blocks set aside for licensed prostitution (usually just called 'the District' in New Orleans), itinerant piano 'professors' (or 'ticklers') played dance tunes, blues, bawdy songs, bits of Creole badinage and all the latest pop music for customers in the gilded parlours of the big houses. Jelly Roll Morton began his long career near the turn of the century as a kid piano player nicknamed 'Windin' Boy' – already a dedicated keyboard-and-song man whose idol was Tony Jackson, the 'man of a thousand tunes' that Morton called 'the world's greatest single-handed entertainer'. In his own piano jazz, which emerged from the solid roots of ragtime, Morton tried to capture the ebullience and sophistication of Jackson, who perhaps instituted the characteristic ultra-sharp dress of the iconic bordello keyboardist. Jelly Roll said he always tried to make the piano sound like a band, echoing the novel hot music beyond the District, in the dance halls of the city.

Orchestras And Dance Bands

While brass bands, dance bands, ragtime pianists and blues singers retailed new and exciting musical forms, they inevitably traded and reconfigured them, absorbing the harmonies and rhythms heard in the dance halls, on riverboats, in the streets and picnic grounds, and in Lake Pontchartrain resorts (where one rode a quaint little train called *Smoky Mary* up to Milenburg or Spanish Fort for a day's outing, a seafood dinner and dancing into the night). While attending the French Opera, the Lyric Theater or a fine restaurant, one might hear a theatre-pit orchestra or a 'sit-down' dance orchestra, such as the one John Robichaux fronted for many years, playing from printed scores.

These formal sit-down orchestras brought music to New Orleans from across the US, introducing musical comedy numbers such as Bessie McCoy's smash-hit song 'Yama Yama Man'. This number from the Karl Hoschna–Otto Hauerbach musical *Three Twins*, running in New York in 1908, recalled an earlier transplant – the perennial theme song of Mardi Gras 'If Ever I Cease To Love' from *Bluebeard*, a burlesque comedy of 1872. It was a romantic-comic nonsense patter song introduced by Lydia Thompson and adopted as an anthem by the Krewe of Rex (one of the Carnival organizations), because her paramour Grand Duke Alexis Romanoff was that year's Mardi Gras guest of honour. Since then, the ditty has been sung and played as a traditional part of the parades, balls and parties of the pre-Lenten season.

Other music brought in by orchestras from afar included the New Orleans classic 'High Society', written by Yale student Porter Steele for his university's mandolin-guitar club. This lively little march created a sensation when Robichaux's orchestra played it with a piccolo *obbligato* interpolated by New York arranger Robert Recker in 1901. Robichaux's facile Creole clarinettist, Alphonse Picou (1878–1961), transposed the sprightly piccolo tune for clarinet, creating a stirring solo and a basic entrance exam piece for budding jazz clarinettists everywhere. Now, 'High Society' seems a product of spontaneous improvisation, but it was really part of a long tradition of arranged music feeding the developing jazz genre.

The orchestras' music was produced by publishers like John Stark, whose *Red Backed Book of Rags* gathered work by Joplin, James Scott (1885–1938), Joseph Lamb (1887–1960) and other 'classic ragtime' writers into an invaluable folio of arrangements for a 10- or 12-piece wind and string orchestra. Highly skilled teachers such as 'Professor' James Humphrey (1861–1937) of Magnolia Plantation, Creole violinist and trumpeter Peter Bocage (1887–1967) of Armand J. Piron's popular dance band – he taught Bunk Johnson to read music, played with Frankie Duson (1880–1940) and learned trumpet from riverboat bandleader Fate Marable (1890–1947) – and multi-instrumentalist Manuel Manetta (1889–1969) tutored generations of New Orleans' African-American players, including Humphrey's highly talented sons Percy (trumpet) and Willie (clarinet). Other musicians mentored young followers, just as cornet virtuoso Joe 'King' Oliver (1885–1938) took Louis Armstrong (1901–71) under his wing and called him to the big time in Chicago in the 1920s. Throughout his long, amazing career as a world-renowned musician, Armstrong constantly acknowledged his debt to Oliver and the other jazz pioneers.

The Influence Of 'Papa' Jack Laine

As much early jazz derived from musical scores as from invented or overheard music; in the city, musicians distinguished between readers ('musicianers') and illiterate improvisers ('routiners'). They said of untrained players: 'He couldn't read a note as big as a house!' and expressed as much regard for musical literacy and craftsmanship as they did for imagination and inventiveness. There was also a respect for the sort of drive and hustle embodied by Morton, who turned his hand to pool-sharking, confidence games, pimping, and anything else going that would help to make ends meet. One white entrepreneur-agent, hustler and midwife to jazz was 'Papa' Jack Laine (1873–1966), a sometime drummer who ran a stable of brass bands (under the catch-all cognomen of Reliance Brass Band) and dance groups in New Orleans' thriving white jazz community – comprising Irish, Italian, German and Greek families living in the 'Irish Channel' at the back of the Garden District. These white musicians rubbed elbows with African-American players and quickly adopted their musical styles and traditions, bringing with them lyrical strains of Italian and French operas, folk ditties, the sounds of Mediterranean bands and dance music from old Europe, all transposed into jazz time.

Many of the later stars of white 'Dixieland' jazz – cornettist Nick LaRocca, clarinettist Larry Shields and the Brunis brothers, including New Orleans Rhythm Kings trombonist George and his compatriot cornettist Paul Mares, among many others – rose to success through Laine's bands. Here they traded musical ideas and solidified the style that became the first jazz (identified as such) on record – the music of the Original Dixieland Jass Band, whose sensational New York recordings of 1917–18 utterly changed the nation's musical soundscape overnight.

Below
'Papa' Jack Laine – entrepreneur, drummer and bandleader.

both fast stomps and slow-drag blues, and his charisma as a soloist. Bolden's band dominated the scene until his untimely mental collapse in 1907, when trombonist Frankie Duson took over the group.

But the organization that older musicians recalled as the golden standard of music during the years of the First World War was the Oliver-Ory band, which performed both for dancing and as a brass band. It was led by Edward 'Kid' Ory (1886–1973), the first great trombonist in jazz, and by Joe 'King' Oliver, at this stage largely unchallenged for the cornet crown. Veterans remember how vigorous, inventive and solid this band was; it employed many upcoming

Above

The only known photograph of Buddy Bolden (standing second from left), c. 1895.

Jazz Music Comes Of Age

As the teens turned towards the twenties, jazz was maturing in New Orleans. Young players like cornettist Joseph 'Buddie' Petit (*c.* 1890–1931) developed flexible and infectious styles. Petit led bands that included musicians such as master clarinettist Jimmie Noone (1895–1944), among others, and – although unrecorded – was influential on the next generation of

'When you come right down to it, the man who started the big noise in jazz was Buddy Bolden.... I guess he deserves credit for starting it all.'
Mutt Carey

jazzmen. Another unrecorded trumpet king was Chris Kelly, a student of James Humphrey who was known for his soulful blues playing, especially on his signature tune, the traditional blues ballad 'Careless Love'. These younger men recalled the earliest years of jazz in the city, when Charles 'Buddy' Bolden (1877–1931) led what was then called a 'ragtime' band and entranced the city with his powerful tone, his ability to swing

Right

The Mississippi riverboat SS Capitol.

1920s jazz stars – Louis Armstrong, cornet; Johnny Dodds (1892–1940), clarinet; Warren 'Baby' Dodds (1898–1959), drums, and many others destined soon to leave the Crescent City for the big time. By 1918, Oliver had left New Orleans to follow a crowded northern migration to Chicago, and Kid Ory took the other standard way out,

to California and fame in Los Angeles. In the mid-1920s, the two men would team up again in Chicago for a fruitful collaboration in Oliver's big Dixie Syncopators orchestra.

Jazz musicians were also able to find work on the Mississippi riverboats; Fate Marable, the bandleader and pianist for the Streckfus Lines on paddlewheelers SS *J.S.*, SS *Capitol* and SS *Sidney*, had a plethora of sidemen that included such rising young luminaries as Louis Armstrong, Baby Dodds and banjoist Johnny St. Cyr (1890–1966). These musicians spread new hot sounds to points north including St. Louis, Missouri and St. Paul, Minnesota, and were also able to catch welcome glimpses of the world outside New Orleans.

By 1920, New Orleans jazz was moving up the Mississippi River towards Chicago, before heading across the western territories and northeast to the new mecca

of Harlem with its burgeoning renaissance of arts and culture. Jazz was moving full speed ahead into its golden age, bringing an unparalleled army of talent and genius with it. In New Orleans the party was over – the old District was shut down as a public health menace during the First World War, while a new national culture of youth, speed and modernism was fuelled by the energetic sounds of jazz. In the next decade, the roots of jazz would produce the blossoms and fruit by which we now know the music best.

Above

Bandleader Fate Marable (seated at the piano) with his Capitol Revue.

Popular Melody

Jelly Roll Morton – 'Original Jelly Roll Blues' (1915)
Often called the first true jazz tune published, this appeared both as piano music and in a band score. Composed as early as 1905 (by Morton's account), it uses blues harmonies, breaks, a Spanish tinge (habañera beat) and other basic jazz effects. Originally titled 'Chicago Blues', it became Morton's signature piece and established his name.

Jazz

Jelly Roll Morton's
Red Hot Peppers
Dead Man Blues

musicfirebox.com
/Deadman

In America, in the teens of the twentieth century, change was the national keynote. Everywhere, science, industry, technology and commerce were reshaping American culture. Women were within grasp of the vote, temperance forces were starting the country on a vast experiment with Prohibition, troops returning from Europe had seen Paris and were unwilling to return to the farms, and rapidly expanding cities and suburbs absorbed rural communities. Ford's Model T personalized transportation forever, aircraft were becoming familiar sights overhead, dress was changing from Victorian heavy to central-heating lite, women's hair got shorter – and their skirts did too. Popular music was also beginning to shift. America had been singing and dancing to ragtime for a decade, and the new ragtime was faster, staccato and more urgent. White listeners learned blues harmonies for the first time; phonographs and piano rolls delivered more music to more homes. Language loosened and took on an African-American hue.

'Bands in those days fighting all the time. One band get a job in the Love and Charity Hall, another band move right over there and play better through the windows.'
Bunk Johnson

The Castles Hit The Nation

In the mid-teens, new, one-step dances were popularized by Irene and Vernon Castle, a young and attractive dance team who fascinated the nation with wild new dances sporting animal names – the turkey trot, the grizzly bear, the bunny hug, the buzzard lope. Gone were sedate cotillion numbers and even the old reliable two-step ushered in a generation earlier by John Philip Sousa and his 'Washington Post March' in 1889. Young dancers now not only touched each other but took a firm grip for the athletic shenanigans that followed the downbeat.

The Castles travelled widely, taught, made films and tirelessly proselytized the new music. Their house orchestra was led by Harlem maestro James Reese Europe (1881–1919), a highly educated composer, bandleader and entrepreneur who formed the Clef Club in Harlem as a booking agency, talent pool and union for African-American musicians. Europe mentored a generation of geniuses, including Eubie Blake (1883–1983), Noble Sissle (1889–1975), composer Ford Dabney (1883–1958) and other composers and players who shaped both jazz and musical show styles for the following decades. His orchestra was the

clarion for the Harlem Renaissance of the 1920s, and a series of records spread the fast one-step music, with tunes like 'Castle House Rag' and 'The Castle Perfect Trot' of 1914. Europe distinguished himself in the First World War as the leader of the 369th US infantry regiment band, an African-American contingent nicknamed the 'Hell-Fighters'. They were famous in France and spread Europe's brand of syncopated marches and sizzling numbers including 'Memphis Blues', 'St. Louis Blues', 'The Darktown Strutters' Ball' and 'Russian Rag'. They recorded in 1919, just days before Europe was tragically killed by a crazed drummer in the band.

The Original Dixieland Jass Band

The largest landmark of the decade, however, was the 1917 advent of the Original Dixieland Jass Band, a vaudeville-touring quintet of white New Orleanians. The band opened in Reisenweber's Café in New York and cut landmark (and bestselling) records such as 'Livery Stable Blues', 'Tiger Rag', 'Ostrich Walk' and 'Bluin' the Blues', before branching out to tour in England and take London by storm. New Yorkers, trained by Europe and the Castles, knew how to dance to this frenetic, jerky music, and the records immediately swept the rest of the US and the world. Thus, the Jazz Age was launched by a crew of young white men from the rough Irish Channel district of New Orleans.

Above
New York City, c. 1917, where the arrival of the Original Dixieland Jass Band helped to launch the Jazz Age.

Racial Integration In Music

From its founding, New Orleans was notably an 'open city', with segregation only slowly making headway. People of all social and caste groups lived in mixed neighbourhoods and intermingled freely until Jim Crow and the rule of strict segregation tightened after the turn of the twentieth century. Ultimately, the poison of racism infected everything in US culture, but the power and glory of African-American music kept breaching social divides to free hearts and minds. Black and white musical co-operation and collaboration developed throughout the twentieth century until, in the words of a swing song, 'rhythm saved the world'.

Left
Maestro James Reese Europe, who mentored future stars in his band, including Eubie Blake and Noble Sissle.

Far Left
The people of America were soon dancing to the new jazz sounds.

Popular Melody

James Reese Europe – 'Castle House Rag' (1914)
This rag bridges early ragtime and instrumental jazz and includes a drum solo. Historian Gunther Schuller said that Europe showed bands could play the one-step dance music 'as fast as the piano players did'. The effect on listeners and dancers was liberating and exhilarating.

Kid Ory

Classic Recordings

Spikes' Seven Pods of Pepper or Kid Ory's Sunshine Orchestra (1921–22)
'Ory's Creole Trombone', 'Society Blues'

New Orleans Wanderers (1926)
'Gatemouth', 'Perdido Street Blues'

Louis Armstrong's Hot Five (1926)
'Muskrat Ramble', 'Hotter Than That'

Jelly Roll Morton's Red Hot Peppers (1926)
'Smokehouse Blues', 'Doctor Jazz'

King Oliver's Dixie Syncopators (1926–27)
'Snag It', 'Every Tub'

Louis Armstrong's Hot Seven (1927)
'Potato Head Blues'

Kid Ory's Creole Jazz Band (1944–45)
'1919 Rag', 'Ory's Creole Trombone', 'Creole Song'

Kid Ory's Creole Jazz Band (1953)
'Milenberg Joys', 'The Girls Go Crazy'

Edward 'Kid' Ory was born in LaPlace, Louisiana in 1886. He learned trombone and led a group of young musicians, the Woodland Band, which he took to New Orleans around 1908. He played with veteran jazzmen in the following years and gained a reputation as a powerful ensemble player and inspired soloist, especially where the blues were concerned.

From Lala's To LA

In the teens, Ory worked at Pete Lala's Café and developed a partnership with Joe 'King' Oliver, the top trumpet man and leader in the city. The Ory-Oliver bands showcased rising talents, including the Dodds brothers, Jimmie Noone and Bill Johnson. When Oliver left for Chicago, Ory migrated to Los Angeles, where he assembled a group of musicians who followed him throughout his long career – bassist Ed 'Montudie' Garland, guitarist Arthur 'Bud' Scott, trumpeter Thomas 'Mutt' Carey and clarinettist Wade Whaley were all Ory loyalists, even during the periods in which the band was beset by feuds. Later stalwarts included pianist Albert Wesley 'Buster' Wilson and drummer Minor 'Ram' Hall. In 1922, Ory's band made history as the first African-American New Orleans jazz band to record, cutting sides for the tiny Sunshine label in LA; they accompanied blues singers and made instrumentals including a trick trombone speciality, 'Ory's Creole Trombone'.

Chicago Beckons

Ory left for Chicago in the mid-1920s, becoming a star with King Oliver's Dixie Syncopaters and with Louis Armstrong's Hot Five and Hot Seven. With Oliver and Armstrong, Ory became the model for the traditional 'tailgate' players

of the era. Tailgate playing describes a jazz trombone style in which the instrument fulfils a largely rhythmic and riff-tagging role beneath the more melodic cornets and trumpets. This remained the norm until virtuoso players such as Jack Teagarden came along and reinvented the trombone as a lead instrument. The name itself derives from the trombone player's position at the back of the bandwagons, where the instrument's slide would not be in the way of the other musicians.

Ory also recorded with the New Orleans Wanderers and the New Orleans Bootblacks, as well as participating in Jelly Roll Morton's brilliant first Red Hot Peppers recordings. In the 1930s Ory, like many veteran jazzmen, found work too scarce to continue as a musician. He returned to California, where he was traced by Orson Welles in the early 1940s and brought back to prominence via radio and recordings. A central figure in the revival of New Orleans-style jazz in the 1940s–60s, Ory led bands in California, touring and recording prolifically with many old cohorts to the end of his days in 1973.

Right

New Orleans trombonist Kid Ory, with his Original Creole Jazz Band.

Clarence Williams

Clarence Williams was born in 1898 in Plaquemine, Louisiana, migrating to New Orleans in the teens to play piano in the District and begin a long career as a composer, bandleader and musical promoter. He was manager of two early jazz venues – the Big 25 Club and Pete Lala's Café – hiring the best musicians in the city. He opened a publishing business with Armand J. Piron, the leader of a popular dance band operating at the Lake Pontchartrain resorts. In 1919 he partnered with the savvy publisher-writer Spencer Williams (no relation). They gathered, annotated and copyrighted musical numbers that were floating in the air around the dance halls, bars and brothels of the city, publishing such enduring mega-hits as 'None Of My Jelly Roll' and 'Royal Garden Blues'.

> *'He was very important in coaching and teaching and working on our artists. He could somehow manage to get the best out of them, and to this day hasn't received the credit he really deserves.'*
>
> **Frank Walker**

The Blue Five

Williams left for Chicago around 1917, pursuing publishing and becoming an agent for recording companies. In the 1920s he shifted to New York City as it became a hub for hot music. He assembled bands of friends from New Orleans for OKeh and Columbia Records, including the seminal Blue Five group, which united a young Louis Armstrong, just emerging as the most innovative soloist in jazz, and Sidney Bechet, who was beginning his long reign as king of the soprano saxophone. Williams featured his wife, Eva Taylor, as vocalist on many blues and pop numbers. Among important songs he recorded were 'Cakewalking Babies From Home', 'Papa De Da Da', 'Of All The Wrongs', 'Coal Cart Blues' and 'Texas Moaner Blues'. He also cut a series of Washboard Band recordings, including numbers from his ill-fated musical comedy, *Bottomlands* (1927), which he promoted in New York.

In The Studio

In his long career, Williams' gift for spotting fresh talent and potential musical hits was renowned. Among the first-rate musicians he assembled were trumpeters such as King Oliver, Jabbo Smith, Henry Allen, Ed Allen, Bubber Miley and Louis Metcalf. He recorded clarinettists such as Buster Bailey, Arville Harris and Albert Nicholas and trombonists Charlie Irvis and Ed Cuffee. He was the session piano player on many recordings – for example, he can be heard playing piano on Bessie Smith's classic track 'Nobody Knows You When You're Down And Out' – but he was most comfortable as a musical director for OKeh Records, and an arranger and composer of jazz and pop tunes.

With a fine ear for both novelty jazz material and songs that bridged the gap between pure jazz and pure pop, Williams was an important transmitter of New Orleans traditions to the East Coast musicians he met in his recording and publishing roles. In the 1930s, during the squeeze of the Depression, Williams closed his publishing office, turned to radio promotion and went on to run an antique store in Harlem. He died in 1965, having sold his vast catalogue to Decca Records in 1943.

Classic Recordings

Clarence Williams' Blue Five (1923–24)
'Wildcat Blues', 'Kansas City Man Blues', 'Texas Moaner Blues', 'Everybody Loves My Baby', 'Mandy, Make Up Your Mind', 'Cakewalking Babies From Home'

Clarence Williams & his Washboard Band (1927)
'Cushion Foot Stomp', 'P.D.Q. Blues'

Clarence Williams' Orchestra (1928)
'Organ Grinder Blues', 'Wildflower Rag'

Above

Pianist, composer, arranger and musical director Clarence Williams (back left) with one of his bands.

A-Z of artists

Papa Celestin
(Trumpet, vocals, 1884–1954)

Oscar 'Papa' Celestin was a much-loved New Orleans fixture, who started out with the Algiers Brass Band, under Henry Allen Sr., at the turn of the century. In 1910 he founded the Original Tuxedo Jazz Orchestra with trombonist William 'Baba' Ridgley. Celestin recorded with OKeh and Columbia in the mid-1920s, and his recordings of 'Original Tuxedo Rag' and 'Black Rag' stand up well as sizzling hot jazz or dance music in comparison with the recordings that King Oliver made at the time with his Creole Jazz Band.

Unlike many of his peers, Celestin stayed in New Orleans. After the glory days of the Original Tuxedo Jazz Orchestra, he led bands on Bourbon Street, made records and played regularly for radio broadcasts on a national ABC network show, 'Dixieland Jambake'. He was a sweet-toned trumpeter and a frog-voiced singer, vigorously selling sure-fire tunes like 'Li'l Liza Jane', 'Mama Don't Allow' and 'Bill Bailey'. His band featured elders including Alphonse Picou (clarinet), Bill Mathews (trombone), Ricard Alexis (bass) and Christopher 'Black Happy' Goldston (drums).

Will Marion Cook
(Composer, arranger, violin, 1869–1944)

Will Marion Cook was a highly educated musician, studying at Oberlin Conservatory and the Berlin Hochschule für Musik with virtuoso Joseph Joachim (he also studied briefly with Antonín Dvořák). He worked as a composer with Bob Cole's All-Star Stock Company, a seminal force in early African-American musical comedy production. (The group later employed the Johnson brothers – J. Rosamund and James Weldon – to write pioneering all-black musicals such as *The Shoo-fly Regiment*, 1907 and *The Red Moon*, 1909.) At this time, African-American musical comedy was performed on and off Broadway, but only fragments or sections were recorded, despite the popularity of many of the shows.

Cook dreamed of working with the stellar African-American vaudeville team of (Bert) Williams and (George W.) Walker. In 1898, together with poet Paul Lawrence Dunbar, he wrote *Clorindy*, or *The Origin Of The Cakewalk*. This innovative show starred popular singer-composer Ernest Hogan, as well as a cast of 40 singers and dancers. Very successful, *Clorindy* set a new course for black musicals. This success assured Cook of his dream – he worked for Williams and Walker for more than a decade, while continuing to collaborate with Dunbar on *In Dahomey* (1903), *In Abyssina* (1906) and *In Bandanna Land* (1908). In 1918, Cook formed the New York (or American) Syncopated Orchestra, with settings for the

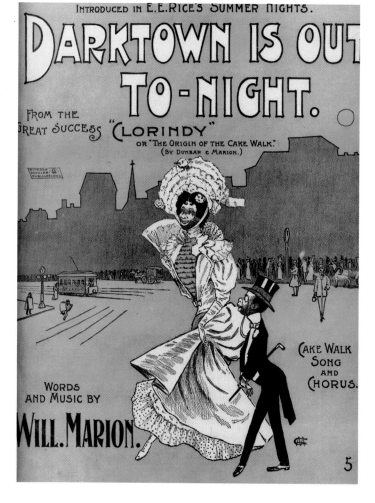

Right

The music for a song from Will Marion Cook's Clorindy, *or* The Origin Of The Cakewalk.

new jazz music. In the 1920s he led Clef Club ensembles and worked with many important musicians, including pioneer big-band leader Fletcher Henderson and singer-actor Paul Robeson. Cook's musical *Swing Along* (1929) displayed his earlier work.

Eagle Band

(Instrumental group, 1900–17)

The Eagle Band, originally led by Buddy Bolden, was an extremely popular and influential New Orleans ensemble. Frankie Duson (or Dusen) (1880–1940), a powerful tailgate trombonist, joined the band in 1906 and went on to take over the band when Bolden suffered a mental collapse the following year. Subsequently, Duson employed various Bolden alumni – guitarists Lorenzo Staulz and Brock Mumford, clarinettist Frank Lewis and cornettist Edward Clem. He also chose younger sidemen who became major jazz stalwarts – Bunk Johnson, Joe Oliver, Sidney Bechet, Johnny Dodds and 'Big Eye' Louis Nelson. Drummers Baby Dodds, Henry Zeno and Abbey 'Chinee' Foster also played with the band.

Duson was associated with the raggy and bluesy music of Bolden, and in the song 'Buddy Bolden's Blues', retailed by Jelly Roll Morton in the 1930s to celebrate the Bolden legend, Duson's name was mentioned: 'I thought I heard Frankie Duson shout,/Gal, give me that money,/Or I'm gonna to beat it out....' The Eagle Band itself sported a simple and catchy motto: 'The Eagles fly high/And never lose a feather./If you miss this dance,/You'll have the blues forever.' Unfortunately for jazz history, Duson's bands never recorded.

Bunk Johnson

(Trumpet, 1889–1949)

William Geary 'Bunk' Johnson, a New Orleans trumpeter with good reading and improvising skills, said that he played in Buddy Bolden's pioneer band before 1900. He was certainly associated with Frankie Duson and other Bolden cohorts, and was famous as a showy, lyrical soloist. Johnson's nickname rose from his loquacity, and he was an inveterate self-promoter (he claimed to have mentored Louis

Armstrong, among others). He played with Adam Olivier's orchestra in the city and then worked mainly in western Louisiana, and on the road with tent shows and other itinerant outfits. Johnson left music in 1933 after an affray in which bandleader Evan Thomas was murdered. He was rediscovered in New Iberia, Louisiana by William Russell and his co-authors of the influential *Jazzmen* (among the first serious jazz histories) in the late 1930s.

After correspondence, in which Johnson claimed he could play again if he were equipped with false teeth and a trumpet, Russell and friends rehabilitated Johnson and set him on the path to a new career with other New Orleans jazz veterans. In the early 1940s, Johnson led bands, recorded steadily for Russell's American Music label and toured, with a long stand in New York City from 1945–46. The band he led continued for decades under the leadership of clarinettist George Lewis, exerting a worldwide impact on the jazz revival.

Johnson generated controversy, epitomizing the acrimony between early jazz advocates ('Mouldy Figs') and zealots for the emerging modern jazz ('Modernists'). His example inspired the jazz revival of ensuing decades, and he joined the pantheon of New Orleans trumpet stars that included Bolden, King Oliver, Louis Armstrong and others. Struggling with alcoholism, Johnson declined in the late 1940s, leaving one final recording session with a hand-picked band of New York musicians which shows his personal concept of hot jazz.

Below

Trumpeter Bunk Johnson, shown here playing with Leadbelly.

Martin was often accompanied by Thomas Morris (cornet) and Charlie Irvis (trombone), both blues specialists. On 'Death Sting Me Blues' (1928), Martin matches Joe Oliver's intensity, and on 'Atlanta Blues' (1923) she delivers the old folk melody with great dignity. Her diction was clear, and she had a good ear for plangent blues that were not over-worn. In 1929, she appeared on film with the immortal Bill 'Bojangles' Robinson in *Hello Bill*. She left show business in the Depression and returned to Louisville.

New Orleans Rhythm Kings
(Instrumental group, 1922–25)

The New Orleans Rhythm Kings (NORK) were one of the major white groups in early New Orleans jazz; after a run at Chicago's Friar's Club in 1922, they recorded with Paul Mares (trumpet), George Brunis (trombone), Leon Roppolo (clarinet), Jack Pettis (alto sax), Elmer Schoebel (piano), Lew Black (banjo), Steve Brown (bass) and Frank Snyder (drums). Mares was a skilful, Oliver-esque lead, Roppolo a highly gifted clarinettist, Schoebel a fine arranger and composer, and Brown a topflight bassist. Sometime associates were drummer (and future bandleader) Ben Pollack, pianist Mel Stitzel and others.

The NORK's sound was different from the Original Dixieland Jass Band (ODJB), with slow blues and relaxed, mid-tempo tunes that swung. They emulated Joe Oliver's style, and recorded some of his music ('Sweet Lovin' Man'), some from the ODJB book ('Tiger Rag') and some basic New Orleans material ('Maple Leaf Rag'). They also recorded standards still played: 'She's Cryin' For Me' and 'Angry'. In 1923 the NORK made history, playing with Jelly Roll Morton on piano to create the first interracial band recording session on sides that included 'Sobbin' Blues'.

Original Creole Orchestra
(Instrumental group, 1912–18)

Freddie Keppard's Original Creole Orchestra toured extensively during the teens as an early harbinger of authentic New Orleans jazz, reaching big-time vaudeville's prestigious Orpheum circuit. Powerful pioneer trumpeter Keppard (1889–1933) had with him Creole clarinettists George Baquet, 'Big Eye' Louis Nelson and Jimmie Noone, pioneer bassist Bill Johnson and multi-instrumentalist Dink Johnson as a drummer.

The band created a sensation among vaudeville audiences well before the ODJB hit New York. Keppard

Above

Trumpeter Freddie Keppard, leader of the Original Creole Orchestra.

Sara Martin
(Vocals, 1884–1955)

Martin, an early classic blues singer, was signed by Clarence Williams for OKeh Records in 1922, at the beginning of the blues craze. While she was a pop-style singer, she was also able to pitch the blues in a rough-and-ready way. She recorded with Williams-led jazz groups, with such illustrious accompanists as King Oliver and Sidney Bechet (on some sessions she sang as 'Margaret Johnson' or 'Sally Roberts').

reputedly refused to record for fear of rival trumpeters 'stealing his stuff'. While the band did not record, Sidney Bechet appropriated a piece of mock-orientalia from Keppard, 'Egyptian Fantasy' (drawn from Abe Olman's 1911 piano rag 'Egyptia'), and recorded the track. The band broke up during 1918 and Bill Johnson set about finding a replacement for Keppard; after contacting Buddy Petit, Johnson settled on King Oliver. Keppard went to Chicago in the 1920s, playing with important orchestras run by Charles 'Doc' Cook. He recorded with the Cook big band and with a small washboard band, demonstrating hot styles from wah-wah to plunger blues to a stirring open horn of startling volume.

Original Dixieland Jass Band
(Instrumental group, 1917–25)

The Original Dixieland Jass (or Jazz) Band were five young white musicians from working-class uptown New Orleans – Nick LaRocca (cornet), Larry Shields (clarinet), Eddie Edwards (trombone), Tony Spargo (real name Sbarbaro, drums) and Henry Ragas (piano). All alumni of 'Papa' Jack Laine's stable of bands, they went to Chicago and then to New York, where their music created a sensation. The word 'jazz' or 'jass' was not spoken in polite circles (it was a slang term for sex), but their frenetic and wild music made it suddenly acceptable.

After making important recordings – including 'Livery Stable Blues'/'Dixie Jass One Step' (1917), the first jazz recording released – and conquering New York society, in 1919 the band went on to a stand in Britain (with Billy Jones on piano), before returning to the US and to further tours and recordings. They disbanded in the mid-1920s but were reunited briefly (with ragtimer J. Russel Robinson on piano) in 1936, making a *March Of Time* short film and cutting new recordings of the ODJB standards, including 'Clarinet Marmalade', 'Skeleton Jangle' and 'Original Dixieland One-Step'. They also recorded with a large swing band backing them.

Below
The Original Dixieland Jass Band c. 1916 with the line-up that preceded their recording career: l–r Tony Spargo, Eddie Edwards, Nick LaRocca, Alcide 'Yellow' Nunez, Henry Ragas.

Victor Records

VOCAL BLUES
RELIGIOUS   SPIRITUALS
RED HOT DANCE TUNES
SERMONS   NOVELTIES

the twenties

The 1920s was, without doubt, the Jazz Age. Workers and the newly burgeoning middle class turned into consumers due to relatively higher wages. The international political advantages that came from having just won a major war buttressed a 'lost generation' of artistic types, who took up residence in Europe. New moral codes, sophistication and cynicism abounded. Some African-Americans benefited from the prosperity, but far from all of them. It was the age of the Harlem Renaissance, of black sports heroes, black revues on Broadway and exotic 'jungle music' in New York and abroad. Yet the Great Migration brought tens of thousands of former farm workers from the southern US to northern industrial areas, seeking jobs and fairer treatment. Although in many ways conditions were better than they had been back home, racist oppression did not end. Corrupt urban governments and landlords exploited the new immigrant population, while employers and labour unions prevented black workers from earning wages equivalent to those of their white counterparts. Meanwhile, back in the South, with the Ku Klux Klan trumpeting white supremacy, it sometimes seemed as if conditions were scarcely better than they had been under slavery.

Against the backdrop of new wealth juxtaposed with poverty and desperation, blues and jazz grew and took root as never before among African-Americans, white Americans and audiences overseas. Advances in the recording industry and radio broadcasts made them fully fledged popular musics. From acoustic guitar pickers on the streets of Texas towns to the 'classic blues' women who sang in well-appointed theatres backed by jazz musicians, from New Orleans orphan trumpeters to would-be Dukes from black Washington, listeners and dancers responded to a newly charged atmosphere of interchange, creativity and inspiration.

Key Artists: Blues

Leroy Carr

Blind Lemon Jefferson

Lonnie Johnson

Bessie Smith

Key Artists: Jazz

Louis Armstrong

Bix Beiderbecke

Duke Ellington

Jelly Roll Morton

King Oliver

Blues

Right

Blind Willie McTell was among the blues musicians based along the Eastern Seaboard.

Although one still often hears the term 'folk music' – a label that implies rustic simplicity, ingenuous lack of artifice and a hand-to-hand passing down of ideas from mentor to student – to describe much of the blues played and recorded during the 1920s, the reality and the music itself were far more complex than that. No doubt there were strong regional and local traditions that might be described as 'folk', some centred around southern plantations like Dockery's, where Charley Patton (*c.* 1891–1934) had learned from older guitarists such as Henry Sloan; others more broadly based, such as along the Eastern Seaboard between Georgia and the Carolinas, where Blind Blake (*c.* early 1890s–*c.* 1933), Blind Willie McTell (1901–59), Blind Boy Fuller (1908–41), Rev. Gary Davis (1896–1972) and others interacted and shared ideas. Certainly, many blues songs' lyrical content, as well as their harmonic and melodic structures, rhythms and even, arguably, the 12-bar form itself, could be traced to traditions that extended back for generations.

'The blues wasn't recognized much until the blues singers got a break, 'til they got a chance, see. And then the blues began to spread.'

Georgia Tom Dorsey

But at the same time, even in remote, rural areas in the 1920s, people were listening to radios and purchasing (or at least hearing) records. One need only listen to the ragtime-influenced guitar patterns played by a 'folk' blues artist such as Blind Blake, or the melange of blues, pop tunes, vaudeville-like comedy routines and novelty songs

Below

Dockery's plantation in Mississippi, where Charley Patton honed his craft.

purveyed by the Mississippi Sheiks to know that these were artists who had a keen ear for 'mainstream' popular entertainment, and who worked diligently and consciously to create music that would please listeners and dancers who shared those tastes. When Gus Cannon (1885–1979) was discovered working as a yard man in Memphis in the early 1960s, his awestruck young admirers asked him where he'd learned his material. 'From the radio,' he answered, instantly shattering virtually all the preconceptions they'd had about him.

The First Blues Recording Session And Its Aftermath

At the very least, the most important event in terms of recorded blues in the 1920s occurred in a decidedly

Left

Banjo player Gus Cannon, whose knowledge of blues music came largely from the radio.

urban, and urbane, context. On 10 August 1920, a vaudeville singer and Harlem nightclub chanteuse named Mamie Smith (1883–1946) entered a New York recording studio and cut a song called 'Crazy Blues', the first recording by an African-American singer to be billed specifically as a 'blues'. Her band was a classy one, anchored by stride piano genius Willie 'The Lion' Smith (1897–1973) and possibly featuring cornettist Johnny Dunn (Willie 'The Lion' remembered the horn man as Addington Major, and many discographers agree with him).

Clearly, songwriter Perry Bradford, who had urged OKeh to do the session and probably also assembled the band, had a pop hit on his mind when he planned the date. But it was Bradford's genius to figure out that a song like 'Crazy Blues', which reflected the vernacular culture, language and tastes of mainstream, working-class African-Americans despite (or alongside) its jazzy uptown setting, might tap into a market of potential listeners that, until then, virtually no one in the recording industry had sought to infiltrate.

'Crazy Blues' sold upwards of a million copies in its first six months, and in its wake a new genre was born. These days that genre is usually referred to as 'classic blues', a name that neither does it justice nor describes it very well. At its best, it combined the sophisticated improvisational musicianship of 1920s-era jazz with the earthy vocal declamations of women singers whose material did, indeed, often invoke 'folk' traditions or portray the day-to-day lives and struggles of urban and rural African-Americans with a hardscrabble, lyric vividness that had never before been heard on record. But the musical context (often a single pianist, but not infrequently an ensemble graced with skilled soloists) was strictly first-class, or was at least staged to look that way.

Popular Melody

Bessie Smith – 'Young Woman's Blues' (1926)

A defiant, taboo-shattering declaration of independence and womanly power, delivered in Smith's patented stentorian yet nuanced blues wail. Proudly proclaiming her lust for moonshine, men and mayhem, the Empress creates a persona that prefigures contemporary hip hop gangsta culture by almost 80 years.

Evolution And Growth

The 'classic blues' sound was no doubt also similar to what these singers had been doing in live performance, especially in the South, for some time. Many if not most of them either got their start or spent significant amounts of time performing in tent shows, minstrel revues and along the rugged Theater Owners' Booking Association (TOBA) African-American vaudeville circuit. The shows that they took out on the road after recording their hits reflected both the sound and style of the records, and the stage acts that they had been honing throughout their professional lives.

These shows, and the records their stars recorded, also had an important (and too often under-recognized) influence on the southern guitarists, pianists and harmonica players who comprise the other half of what might be called the 'blues dialectic' of the 1920s and 1930s. Often, southern acoustic blues and 'classic blues' are portrayed as parallel genres that evolved at the same time but were relatively untouched by each other. Musical evidence, however, suggests that the various blues forms developing during these years were the products of a complex, and still not fully understood, pattern of cross-pollination and influence.

Two-Way Streets And Fuzzy Categories

As already mentioned, ragtime, jazz and/or vaudeville influences can be heard not only in the sophisticated musical backings and well-tempered diction that characterize most of the 'classic blues' singers' recorded output (and, one assumes, their performances), but also in the work of some of the most putatively 'pure' folk bluesmen of the era.

For that matter, some of those 'folk' artists were, in fact, city-born or came of musical age in an urban environment. Even that prototypical 'country' bluesman Blind Lemon Jefferson (*c.* 1897–1929) cut his teeth among the barrelhousers, ragtimers, pimps and hustlers of Dallas's notorious Deep Ellum district. Conversely, even at their most musically refined, 'classic blues' women such as Ida Cox (1896–1967), Victoria Spivey (1906–76) and the various unrelated Smiths often dealt in material with lyrics as nasty and uncompromisingly funk-drenched as anything that might have emanated from a plantation juke (or a backstreet urban gin mill) on a Saturday night.

Blues From The Heart

None of this is to suggest that there is anything inauthentic or faked about the blues recorded and performed in

Right

As the blues grew in popularity, the genre began to dominate 1920s record catalogues.

the 1920s, be it 'classic blues' backed by a single pianist or a full jazz orchestra, or the downhome stylings of a lone Mississippi guitar picker. That records may be recorded and sold as commodities, or that music may be played and sung for profit, does not detract from either's artistic worth or legitimacy – the 'folk'/ 'commercial' dichotomy is, in this context, arbitrary and false. Whether performed in a backwoods shack or a big-city theatre, blues did (and does) express the deepest emotional and aesthetic truths of its purveyors, both as a people and as individuals.

It is the abiding genius of this music that it is also at once culturally specific – rooted in a particular epoch and cultural milieu – and grandly universal, voicing desires, dreams, joys and frustrations common across the human condition. In the 1920s, it evolved to new levels of sophistication as well as artistic and emotional honesty, setting the context and the standards for the developments that would transpire in the decades that lay ahead.

Left
Alberta Hunter, one of the classic blueswomen of the era.

Popular Melody

Blind Lemon Jefferson – 'That Black Snake Moan' (1926)
Jefferson's fretboard filigrees intertwine with his phallic lyric symbolism and moaning vocals to invoke an erotic tension so taut that it attains the level of existential catastrophe. Still stunning today, it must have sounded virtually apocalyptic in its time.

Leroy Carr

Right

Vocalist and pianist Leroy Carr, who died from alcoholism at the age of 30.

Vocalist/pianist Leroy Carr's life and career belie the myth that pre-war acoustic blues artists were necessarily 'rural' or 'primitive'. Carr was born not on a plantation but in Nashville, Tennessee on 27 March 1905. His father worked as a porter at Vanderbilt University. After his parents separated, his mother brought him and his sister to Indianapolis (known in the vernacular as 'Naptown'), which at the time was a major nexus of the US automotive industry.

Carr's Musical Match

Young Leroy taught himself piano and left school at an early age to go out into the world and seek his fortune; he travelled with a circus, he spent time in the military, he worked as a meat packer and as a bootlegger. But by the mid-1920s he was a professional entertainer, performing at private parties and in clubs around Indiana Avenue, Indianapolis's primary black nightlife strip. Some time during these years he met guitarist Francis 'Scrapper' Blackwell (1903–62), who shared his urbane, somewhat wistful musical sensibilities. The two developed an uncanny musical telepathy; they could interweave melodies of pristine delicacy one moment, then charge into a drive-'em-down barrelhouse stomp the next, goading the patrons back on to the dance floor.

'I am in love with Leroy Carr;
I can play his stuff all night and
not give a damn if people like it!'
Barrelhouse Chuck

Key Track

'Motherless Child' (1934)

This obscure track illustrates the blend of aesthetics and emotional shadings that epitomized Carr's and Blackwell's art. Despite the pathos of the lyrics and Carr's melancholy lament, the melody and cadences are almost jaunty – invoking the classic blues fusion of sorrow with belief in better times around the corner.

A Successful Formula

In 1928 the duo had their first recording session for Vocalion. 'How Long, How Long Blues', their debut release, turned out to be their most successful. A melancholy pastiche of images of loss and resignation – lonesome train whistles, departed lovers, desolate mountain vistas – set to a pop-tinged melody line of eight bars, it was sophisticated in feel, yet 'country' enough in its lyric content to strike a familiar chord in listeners down home. In Mississippi, Robert Johnson became a devotee; plenty of others shared his tastes, and the team of Carr and Blackwell quickly became one of the most popular acts in blues. They followed up their first hit with a series of sides, almost all of them featuring Carr's understated yet emotionally rich vocals – 'Naptown Blues', 'Rocks In My Bed', 'We're Gonna Rock', 'Mean Mistreater Mama', 'Blues Before Sunrise' – which may not have sold quite as well as 'How Long ...', but were more than sufficient to maintain their careers for the next seven years or so.

Classic Recordings

1928
'How Long, How Long Blues'

1930
'Sloppy Drunk Blues'

1934
'I Believe I'll Make A Change', 'Blues Before Sunrise', 'Shady Lane Blues', 'Bobo Stomp'

Left

Carr's friend and musical soul-mate, guitarist Scrapper Blackwell.

The Liquor Takes Its Toll

The blues life has never been an easy one, and both Carr and Blackwell (who had also been a bootlegger before he became a bluesman) were heavy drinkers. Their last session together was in February 1935; less than two months later, Carr died from the effects of acute alcoholism. His partner soldiered on for a while, but he was devastated by the loss and eventually dropped out of music. He was 'rediscovered' in 1959, and enjoyed a brief comeback until his death a few years later.

Despite his undeniable influence on Robert Johnson and others (Johnson's 'Love In Vain' carries distinct echoes of both 'How Long ...' and another Carr/Blackwell song, 'When The Sun Goes Down'), and despite the popularity the Carr/Blackwell duo enjoyed in their heyday (among male blues singers, only Blind Lemon Jefferson could claim as many admirers), Leroy Carr is under-recognized today. Perhaps his location in a northern city outside of Chicago or Detroit is a hindrance; maybe his style remains too subtle for those who still insist on associating blues only with sledge-hammer emotions or gutbucket 'primitivism'. But in his own quiet way, Leroy Carr earned himself an honoured place in the pantheon next to Jefferson, Lonnie Johnson, Bessie Smith and the others who helped to codify modern blues in the 1920s.

Blind Lemon Jefferson

Although he is often cited as the first 'folk' bluesman to record, Blind Lemon Jefferson was actually much more than that: he was America's first male blues pop star. On the strength of his recordings for the Paramount label – some of which are said to have sold upwards of 100,000 copies – Jefferson became a celebrity throughout the southern blues circuit and beyond.

'Lemon was fat, dirty, dissolute, but his singing was perhaps the most exciting country blues singing of the 1920s.'
Samuel Charters

Right
Blind Lemon Jefferson, an inventive guitarist and one of the biggest blues stars of his day.

From Couchman To Deep Ellum

Jefferson was born in Couchman, Texas, most likely in 1897. 'Lemmon' was probably his given name. He may have been partially sighted, at least as a youth. He taught himself guitar early on, and by his mid-teens he had travelled as far as Dallas to perform. There he sang on street corners and in the jukes and whorehouses that lined Deep Ellum, the wide-open entertainment district that ran along Elm Street in the city's African-American quarter. He teamed up with Huddie 'Leadbelly' Ledbetter for a while, before Leadbelly went to prison in 1918.

In 1925, someone – possibly pianist Sammy Price – recommended him to a Paramount Records talent scout. For Paramount, Jefferson recorded approximately 100 sides (counting alternate versions), of which 42 were issued. In 1927 he also paid a brief visit to the OKeh label, for whom he cut a version of his already popular '(That) Black Snake Moan', as well as the first incarnation of 'Match Box Blues', which he soon re-cut for Paramount. He became such a celebrity that Paramount adorned some of his discs with a designer label

King of the Country Blues
First in-depth documentary of Blind Lemon Jefferson and his music

featuring that now-famous photo of him, surrounded by bright lemon-yellow trim.

'Don't Play Me Cheap!'

By all accounts, he carried himself like the star he was. He usually travelled alone – or at least without a personal guide – and he comported himself like a dandy, decked out in suits, demanding respect and appropriate remuneration everywhere he went (one of his favourite catchphrases was 'Don't play me cheap!').

Although many of his best-known songs – 'Tin Cup Blues', ''Lectric Chair Blues', 'Match Box Blues' – portrayed a man suffering under oppressive conditions, his musical persona was that of a resolute survivor. His voice was high-pitched and supple, his diction and enunciation crisp and sure. His lyrics expressed the desires, passions and day-to-day struggles of working-class black people with an unadorned yet poetic directness that had never before been captured on disc.

Key Track

'Match Box Blues' (1927)
Although most famous for its signature line 'Sitting here wondering, will a match box hold my clothes', this gem also features a remarkable display of musical impressionism: 'Got a brown across town, she crochet all the time,' Jefferson sings, weaving fretboard figures with the dexterity of a seamstress doing just that.

As a guitarist he was superbly inventive within the confines of the 12-bar form, to which he generally adhered – at least on record (Leadbelly recalled him crooning ballads like 'Careless Love' in performance). Creating separate voices with his basslines and his trademark high-treble arpeggios, and sometimes interrupting the rhythmic flow for a bar or two of unaccompanied single-string solo work, his playing reflected the two-handed contrapuntal attack of the pianists he'd no doubt heard as a young man in the gin mills of Deep Ellum.

'See That My Grave Is Kept Clean'

In December of 1929, Jefferson was found dead on a sidewalk in Chicago, apparently having lost his way in a snowstorm and suffered a heart attack. Pianist Will Ezell took him back to Texas, where he was buried in Wortham Cemetery, not far from where he was born.

Not long afterwards, Rev. Emmet Dickinson recorded what was probably the first 'tribute' record in the history of blues muisc – a sermon entitled 'The Death Of Blind Lemon Jefferson'. That an artist whose recording career spanned less than half a decade would receive such an encomium is remarkable; that a Christian minister would record it is even more so – in those days, church-going Christians were advised to shun the blues. But Dickinson's words eloquently captured the feelings of the many who had listened to Jefferson's records and danced at his shows over the years: 'Blind Lemon Jefferson is dead, and the world today is mourning over this loss ... there is a vacancy in our hearts that will never be replaced.'

Classic Recordings

1926
'Jack O'Diamond Blues', '(That) Black Snake Moan'

1927
'One Dime Blues', 'See That My Grave Is Kept Clean'

1928
'Hangman's Blues'

1929
'Bed Springs Blues'

Below

Deep Ellum – Elm Street in Dallas, Texas – as it would have looked in the days when Blind Lemon Jefferson played there.

Lonnie Johnson

'Lonnie Johnson is one of my favorite guitar players ... he kind of bridged the gap between blues and jazz.'
Catfish Keith

Above
Lonnie Johnson, a highly influential guitarist.

Far Right
New Orleans c. 1900, where Johnson grew up.

Alonzo 'Lonnie' Johnson will probably be forever classified as a 'blues' guitarist, and – at least in his later years – he seemed to accept the label, albeit somewhat gruffly. But in fact he was a consummate musician, deft enough to move between jazz, pop and blues stylings with ease, and inventive enough to imbue everything he touched with new angles of vision and fresh improvisational ideas.

Key Track

'I'm Not Rough' (1927)
In 1927, Johnson played with Louis Armstrong's Hot Five, interweaving his fretboard textures on 'Savoy Blues', 'Hotter Than That' and 'I'm Not Rough'. In his impressive solo on 'I'm Not Rough', he artfully implied a segue into double-time, prodding the ensemble with an all-important (yet understated) propulsive impetus.

A Musical Upbringing

Johnson was born into a musical New Orleans family on 8 February, probably in 1894. At a young age he began performing around town (on violin and piano) with his parents and

siblings. In 1917, the year he purchased his first guitar, he landed an overseas tour with Will Marion Cook's Syncopated Orchestra. When he returned home, he discovered that his entire family, except his brother James, had died in the flu epidemic of 1918. He and James left for St. Louis, where they played in the riverboat bands of Fate Marable and Charlie Creath, with whom Johnson recorded in 1925.

A Prolific Recording Career

Also in 1925, Johnson won a blues contest sponsored by OKeh Records, the first prize for which was a recording contract. He ended up cutting, by his own recollection, 572 sides for the label, many (but not all) of which were 12-bar blues. He also worked, and sometimes recorded, with such jazz stalwarts as Eddie Lang, Louis Armstrong and Duke Ellington.

As a bluesman, Johnson sang in a fluttery, somewhat thin voice, which was nonetheless effective in delivering his sometimes violently misogynistic lyrics. His apparent lack of emotion heightened the threat as he drawled out ultimatums like 'Woman, get out of my face/or I'll take my fist and knock you down' (from 'Cat You Been Messin' Around') with dead-eyed, murderous serenity. Even on ballads such as 'Careless Love' ('I'm goin' to shoot you and shoot you four, five times/And stand over you until you finish dyin''), he sounded like a man hurt beyond all caring. Meanwhile, his lithe guitar lines and horn-like phrasing amplified (and sometimes mercifully tempered) such lyric themes with improvisational *élan* and an ever-present sense of swing.

Echoes Of Johnson's Influence

In 1948 Johnson hit the R&B charts with 'Tomorrow Night', a sentimental ballad that he followed up with several other pop-styled hits. He was nonetheless billed as a 'blues singer' when he toured overseas in 1952. The vicissitudes of the music industry forced him to take a day job shortly

thereafter. In the early 1960s, upon his 'rediscovery', he often found himself playing coffeehouses and being booked on 'folk blues' packages with the likes of Muddy Waters and Big Joe Williams. He is said to have been rather imperious in such settings, but audiences enjoyed his slicked-up versions of traditional blues and pop themes. He made his last recordings for Folkways in 1967.

Following a 1969 automobile accident, Lonnie Johnson suffered a stroke; he died on 6 June 1970. Although he was inducted into the Blues Hall Of Fame in 1997, he is still not often mentioned in the same breath as Blind Lemon Jefferson, Charley Patton or Robert Johnson, yet his influence was at least as important as theirs. Robert Johnson, in fact, was so enamoured of him that it is said he sometimes tried to pass himself off as a relative. Echoes of Lonnie's fusion of blues themes with a jazz-like harmonic and rhythmic sensibility resonate through the work of fretmen such as Charlie Christian, T-Bone Walker and many others, including Walker devotees such as B.B. King. Johnson was undeniably a blues trailblazer and an important figure in the evolution of mainstream American popular music.

Classic Recordings

1927
'Handful O'Keys'

1928
'Careless Love'

1930
'Don't Drive Me From Your Door', 'I Got The Best Jelly Roll In Town, Pts. 1 and 2'

1941
'Chicago Blues'

1948
'Tomorrow Night'

Bessie Smith

Born into crushing poverty in Chattanooga, Tennessee on 15 April 1894, Bessie Smith sang on street corners for tips as a girl, and in her teens she danced in a minstrel show. While honing her craft and expanding her territory, she relocated to several different cities; by the early 1920s she was starring in her own revue, touring the TOBA circuit along the Eastern Seaboard and through the South.

'We had a lot of great singers back then ... Ethel Waters, Ida Cox, Sippie Wallace, Clara Smith, Trixie Smith – they were great singers but they couldn't reach Bessie.'

Little Brother Montgomery

Street Fighting Woman

In 1923 she signed with Columbia Records. Her second session with Columbia resulted in 'Ain't Nobody's Business If I Do', a street-savvy declaration of defiance that became one of her theme songs, and which remains a classic of the genre. On the strength of that record and her subsequent releases, Smith garnered national fame and toured widely, not just in the South but in northern cities where African-American migrants were pouring in, seeking jobs and better living conditions than they had been able to find back home. It was for these audiences that Bessie Smith crafted her music and her persona as a tough-talking, urbane woman of power who nonetheless retained memories of her southern roots.

Right
The 'Empress Of The Blues', Bessie Smith.

The lyrics of the songs Smith recorded dealt uncompromisingly with the harsh realities of African-American life, although their overall themes – love, loss, betrayal, defiance and perseverance in the face of hard times – were universal. Even at her most mournful she undergirded her sorrow with steely resolve, as if determined to shout down suffering with the pure force of will and determination.

Key Track

'St. Louis Blues' (1925)
In this song, from a 1929 film short of the same title, Smith laments her misfortune, while Louis Armstrong's sublime horn weaves in and out of the melody as an extension of Smith's anguished vocals. Despite her melancholy wail, however, there is an underlying glint, reassuring the listener that this streetwise survivor will rise again.

The Empress Of The Blues

Although her vocal range was limited, Smith employed a broad variety of vocal effects – growls, sobs, burnished hollers, church-like ascents and moans – that heightened her appeal for sophisticated jazz aficionados as well as the working-class blues audience that remained her core listenership. In 1925 she recorded some sessions with Louis Armstrong, who responded to her vocal lines on

fearless strutting of her appetites (sexual and otherwise), her defiant refusal to compromise her selfhood or her integrity (at least in public), even her flair for ostentation and conspicuous consumption, she became a role model and heroine for African-American admirers who saw in her success a vision of what 'the race' might some day be able to achieve.

A Tragic End On 'Blues Alley'

In the early morning of 26 September 1937, Smith was travelling along Highway 61, just outside of Clarksdale, Mississippi. The car in which she was riding sideswiped a truck. She was severely injured, with one of her arms torn nearly loose at the elbow. A white physician stopped to help her; after he loaded her into his car, that car was also hit. The ambulance that finally arrived took her to Clarksdale's 'colored' hospital (the legend that she was refused admittance at a 'white' institution has no basis in fact), where she died, primarily from loss of blood.

So ended the life of one of the blues' most monumental talents. Bessie Smith represented not just the crowning glory of the 'classic blues' style, or of 1920s-era African-American popular music, or even of the blues as a whole. She was, and is, an artist against whom all others, male and female, black and white, in all areas of entertainment and popular art, continue to be judged.

Classic Recordings

1923
'Down Hearted Blues', 'Ain't Nobody's Business If I Do'

1925
'You've Been A Good Ole Wagon'

1928
'Empty Bed Blues'

1929
'Nobody Knows You When You're Down And Out'

1930
'New Orleans Hop Scop Blues'

1931
'I Need A Little Sugar In My Bowl'

fare such as 'You've Been A Good Old Wagon' and 'St. Louis Blues' with unerring zest – he obviously treated her as a musical equal, and he riffed off her leads as if she were a fellow horn player.

Eventually she became known as the 'Empress Of The Blues', but even that title doesn't come close to truly reflecting her importance. Like her erstwhile contemporary Ma Rainey, and like other 'race heroes', such as Jack Johnson, Joe Louis, Jesse Owens and Paul Robeson, as well as such latter-day figures as Muhammad Ali, Aretha Franklin and James Brown, she came to symbolize more than mere excellence in her chosen field. With her air of brazen self-confidence, her apparently

Above Left
Janis Joplin, who greatly admired Bessie Smith and helped to finally mark her grave with a tombstone in 1970.

Left
The room where Smith died at the Riverside Blues Hotel, a former hospital near Clarksdale, Mississippi.

A-Z of artists

Texas Alexander
(Vocals, 1900–54)
Alger 'Texas' Alexander's broad-toned, pugnacious vocal delivery recalled older work songs and field hollers, while his themes evoked the hard-travelling lives of migrant workers and hoboes. His recordings on OKeh in the 1920s paired him with sophisticated instrumentalists such as Clarence Williams, Lonnie Johnson and King Oliver. In his later years, he often worked alongside his cousin, vocalist-guitarist Lightnin' Hopkins; the pair recorded for Aladdin in 1947.

Below

Harmonica player Deford Bailey was one of the original stars of the Grand Ole Opry.

Deford Bailey
(Vocals, harmonica, guitar, 1899–1982)
Deford Bailey was a member of the original Grand Ole Opry and was its first big star, until he was dismissed from the troupe in 1941 because allegedly he either could not or would not learn new material. His 'Pan American Blues', a harmonica train imitation, was one of the early Opry's most readily identifiable themes. Bailey recorded for both Brunswick and Victor, and while a member of the Opry he also toured with the show. A drive is currently underway to induct him into the Country Music Hall Of Fame, an institution that seldom, if ever, embraces black artists.

Barbecue Bob
(Vocals, guitar, 1902–31)
Barbecue Bob Hicks was a mainstay of the 1920s Atlanta scene. His 12-string guitar technique featured percussive, banjo-like flailing and sometimes a bottleneck slide, instead of the rag-style fingerpicking often associated with the Southeast. Hicks recorded over 60 sides for Columbia, including his trademark 'Barbecue Blues' (he had a day job at a barbecue stand). He remained a popular entertainer in Atlanta jukes until his death.

Scrapper Blackwell
(Vocals, guitar, 1903–62)
Francis 'Scrapper' Blackwell is best known as Leroy Carr's musical partner, but he was also a gifted artist in his own right. In 1928 he recorded 'Kokomo Blues', which Kokomo Arnold covered as 'Original Old Kokomo Blues', before Robert Johnson retooled it as 'Sweet Home Chicago'. After Carr died in 1935, Blackwell retired from music until 1959, when he was 'rediscovered' by photographer Duncan Scheidt. In the midst of a somewhat tentative comeback, he was shot to death in an Indianapolis alley.

Blind Blake
(Vocals, guitar, c. early 1890s–c. 1933)
Among the most influential instrumentalists in the blues, Blind Blake remains a mystery man in terms of his personal life. Born either Arthur Blake or Arthur Phelps, probably in Florida (Jacksonville or Tampa), he purveyed a ragtime-

influenced, polyrhythmic picking technique that combined jaw-dropping technical virtuosity with an impeccably crafted symmetry. He approached his fretboard like a

'I ain't never heard anybody on a record yet beat Blind Blake on the guitar.'

Rev. Gary Davis

piano or even an entire orchestra, balancing themes, tonal attack, inflections and cadences, yet never losing either his improvisational flair or his seemingly limitless capacity for speed.

He recorded about 80 sides for Paramount (some with jazz clarinettist Johnny Dodds); after the label folded in 1932 he disappeared from sight. He is generally thought to have died about a year later. Generations of guitarists, from Rev. Gary Davis on down, owe much of their inspiration and their art to his genius.

Above

Blind Blake, a virtuoso guitarist whose personal life remains a mystery.

Ida Cox

(Vocals, 1896–1967)

An important figure in the so-called 'classic blues' genre, Ida Cox (née Prather) performed in minstrel and tent shows as a teenager. She had already become a vaudeville star when she began to record for the Paramount label in 1923. Apart from her gifts as a vocalist, she was an independent spirit who wrote much of her own material and managed several touring companies (e.g. Darktown Scandals and Raisin' Cain).

She was one of the relatively few 'classic blues' singers who continued to prosper during the Depression. In 1939 she appeared at John Hammond's landmark Spirituals To Swing concert in Carnegie Hall, but the market for her style of music dwindled in subsequent years and she suffered a stroke in the mid-1940s. Nevertheless, she continued to record and perform, on and off, until her death. Her final recording, from 1961, featured Coleman Hawkins on tenor sax.

Cow Cow Davenport

(Vocals, piano, c. 1894–1955)

Charles Davenport's best-known recording is 1928's 'Cow Cow Blues', a barrelhouse workout that kicks off with a chiming stop-time intro before plunging into a proto-boogie-woogie theme. Davenport recorded over 30 sides for various labels, and he worked in venues ranging from vaudeville theatres to house rent parties. Although slowed by a stroke in 1938, he continued to perform sporadically (sometimes as just a vocalist) until his death almost 20 years later.

Peg Leg Howell

(Vocals, guitar, 1888–1966)

James Barnes 'Peg Leg' Howell, who lost his right leg after being shot when he was about 21 years old, led a three-man band – Peg Leg Howell & his Gang – in Atlanta during the mid- to late 1920s. He recorded for Columbia between 1926 and 1929 and continued to perform locally until the mid-1930s. He was 'rediscovered' in the blues revival of the early 1960s and in 1963 cut an album on Testament.

Left

Ida Cox, who remained a largely independent performer and wrote many of her own songs.

Alberta Hunter
(Vocals, 1895–1984)

Right

*A poster for the musical
Showboat by Jerome
Kern and Oscar
Hammerstein II,
in which Alberta
Hunter appeared.*

Memphis-born Alberta Hunter ran
away to Chicago as a young girl to
seek her fortune as an entertainer.
She survived the cutthroat world
of early-twentieth-century jazz
long enough to establish herself
as a front-line vocalist, albeit in
a somewhat less declamatory style
than that favoured by some of her
contemporaries. She recorded
(sometimes using pseudonyms)
for Black Swan, Paramount and
other labels; she also appeared
in several musical stage revues.

Below

*Blind Willie Johnson
coloured the sacred
music he recorded with
exquisite slide guitar.*

She toured overseas with the play
Showboat (starring Paul Robeson) in the late 1920s, and
in the 1930s she expanded her touring territory to include
both Russia and the Middle East.
Hunter retired in the mid-1950s and
became a registered nurse in New
York, but in the early 1960s she
began to record again. In 1977, at the
age of 82, she returned to performing
and continued as a beloved and still-
potent purveyor of dusky jazz and
blues torch songs and ballads, mostly
in upscale nightclub and concert
settings, until her death.

Papa Charlie Jackson
(Vocals, banjo, c. 1890–1938)

New Orleans-born Charlie Jackson
brought a jazzman's sophistication
to an instrument still too often
overlooked by blues historians. He alternated single-
string solos with percussive chording and dexterous
fingerpicking, allowing him to bridge styles and genres
with rare facility. He released more than 60 sides of his
own, and he also recorded with Freddie Keppard, Tiny
Parham and Kid Ory, as well as both Ma Rainey
and Ida Cox.

Blind Willie Johnson
(Vocals, guitar, c. 1902–47)

Texas-born Willie Johnson, a purveyor of sacred material
who would probably have been appalled at being
categorized as a 'blues' artist, was blinded at the age
of seven when his stepmother threw lye in his face
after being beaten by his father. He sang in a hoarse,
declamatory voice and his fretwork combined tonal purity
and pinpoint accuracy (even when using a pocket-knife
slide) with an emotional intensity unsurpassed by any
acoustic guitarist, regardless of genre.

His masterpiece, the instrumental 'Dark Was The Night
(Cold Was The Ground)', invokes soul-chilling existential
dread, and was once described by guitarist Ry Cooder as
'the most transcendent piece in all American music'. Other
works – 'Jesus Make Up My Dying Bed', 'Keep Your Lamp
Trimmed And Burning' – are testament to his faith and the
resolute certainty with which he held it. Johnson, who
recorded 30 sides for Columbia in 1927–30, died after
contracting pneumonia, having spent a night sleeping
in wet clothes after his house burned down.

Furry Lewis
(Vocals, guitar, 1893–1981)

Born in Greenwood, Mississippi, Walter 'Furry' Lewis played medicine shows as a young man. After moving to Memphis, he recorded 23 sides for Vocalion and Victor between 1927 and 1929. Despite a somewhat chaotic guitar technique, he was an indefatigable entertainer and he became a beloved figure among younger-generation aficionados throughout his post-1959 'rediscovery' period. In 1975 he had a cameo alongside Burt Reynolds in the film *W.W. And The Dixie Dance Kings*.

Blind Willie McTell
(Vocals, guitar, 1901–59)

A skilled purveyor of the ragtime-influenced Piedmont fingerpicking style, Atlanta-based Blind Willie McTell incorporated pop songs and novelty numbers, as well as blues, into his repertoire – befitting an entertainer who got his start in tent shows, medicine shows and carnivals. His voice was unusually tender and expressive for a musician who made his living as a street singer, adding depth and poignancy to deftly crafted meditations on infatuation and loss like his now-standard 'Statesboro Blues'.

His recording career extended (with some significant interruptions) from 1927–56 and his style remained the same throughout. His gift of conveying intense emotion through low-key, intimate vocals rather than flamboyant shouting – as well as his vivid lyric imagery and piano-like, contrapuntal picking artistry on both six- and 12-string guitars (he also played harmonica, accordion and fiddle) – have made him one of the most revered of the south-eastern acoustic blues artists.

Memphis Jug Band
(Vocal/instrumental group, 1927–34)

They did not invent the style, but guitarist/harpist Will Shade (a.k.a. Son Brimmer) and his rollicking aggregation were among the most popular and influential of the jug and string bands that proliferated around Memphis and Louisville, as well as in the Mississippi Delta, during the 1920s and 1930s. With various personnel coming and going, the Jug Band included instruments such as violin, jug, kazoo, piano, mandolin, banjo, guitar, harmonica and washtub bass, and recorded nearly 60 sides for Victor.

Their members over the years included such luminaries as Furry Lewis, harpist Big Walter Horton and

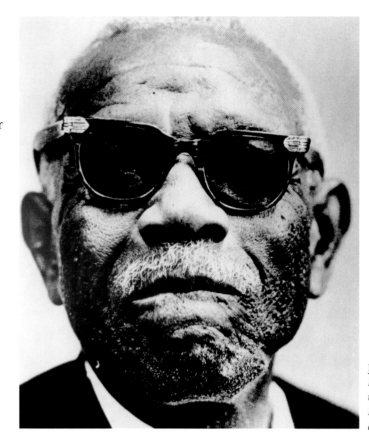

Left

Following a background in medicine shows, Furry Lewis became a popular entertainer.

guitarist Casey Bill Weldon, as well as occasional female guest vocalists. Their repertoire included some blues, but their speciality was tightly arranged pop and novelty numbers, some of which (e.g. 'Stealin', Stealin'') have become standards, and all of which they performed with a theatrical, vaudevillian flair. Although the Jug Band disbanded in the 1930s, Shade himself soldiered on with various reincarnated versions until his death in 1966.

Mississippi Sheiks
(Vocal/instrumental group, 1926–35)

The Mississippi Sheiks were Lonnie Chatmon (guitar, violin) and Walter Vinson (guitar), sometimes joined by Chatmon's brothers Sam (guitar, violin) and Armenter (a.k.a. Bo Carter, guitar), as well as Charlie McCoy (banjo, mandolin); the vocals were shared between the group members. Their repertoire blended blues themes with contemporary pop/novelty tunes, similar to a jug band's but somewhat less hokey in its delivery. According to Sam Chatmon's recollections, they played mostly for white audiences. They recorded for OKeh and Bluebird; their 'Sitting On Top Of The World' has become a standard, subsequently interpreted by Howlin' Wolf and Cream, among many others.

'Hambone' Willie Newbern

(Vocals, guitar, 1899–1947)

A resident of Brownsville, Tennessee, Willie Newbern had only one recording session, for OKeh in Atlanta in 1929. Although he was not widely known outside his area, he influenced quite a few musicians: he recorded the first known version of 'Roll And Tumble Blues' and is said to have taught it to Charley Patton, among others. Allegedly he was killed while serving time in prison.

Mamie Smith

(Vocals, 1883–1946)

Mamie Smith's first recording session, for OKeh in 1920, resulted in a pair of nondescript pop songs, but her manager Perry Bradford then talked the label into recording her as a blues singer. On 10 August 1920, fronting a band dubbed the Jazz Hounds – featuring stride pianist Willie 'The Lion' Smith (no relation) and possibly also cornettist Johnny Dunn – Smith cut the first record ever billed as a 'blues': 'Crazy Blues'. It sold upwards of a million copies, and in support she toured with a flamboyant show that featured trapeze artists, comedians, dancers and other embellishments from her vaudeville past.

Despite her horn-like vocal timbre and emotional delivery, Smith was not really a blues singer: her rhythmic sense was pedestrian, her intonation stiff. But 'Crazy Blues' virtually defined the genre – at least as a recorded popular music – for a generation of women vocalists who followed, each one of whom came in through the door that Mamie Smith had opened.

Trixie Smith

(Vocals, 1895–1943)

Atlanta-born Trixie Smith was a vaudeville trouper when, in 1922, she cut her first records on Black Swan. Although she did not have the vocal prowess of front-line blues stars like Bessie Smith (no relation), she recorded steadily until 1926 – often with top-flight jazz orchestras such as Fletcher Henderson's – and sporadically thereafter. In the 1930s, after her recording career slackened off, she continued in show business, appearing in musical revues and films.

Victoria Spivey

(Vocals, piano, 1906–76)

Houston native Victoria Spivey cut her first sides for OKeh in 1926 and she was soon one of the most popular artists of the 'classic blues' era. An eloquent lyricist alongside her vocal gifts, Spivey worked steadily into the 1940s; in 1962 she emerged from retirement as the head of blues label Spivey Records, on which she recorded herself and other

'rediscovered' blues artists (along with a guest appearance by a youthful Bob Dylan). She continued to record and perform, based in New York City, until her death.

Henry Thomas
(Vocals, quills, guitar, 1874–1930)

A son of former slaves, Henry 'Ragtime' Thomas specialized in the quills, a pan-pipe-like instrument made from hollow reeds. He was itinerant for most of his life, a fact reflected in songs such as 'Railroadin', in which Thomas names train stops from Fort Worth to Chicago. His 'Bull Doze Blues', renamed 'Goin' Up The Country', became a 1960s hit for Canned Heat, who recreated his quills intro note for note.

Ethel Waters
(Vocals, 1896–1977)

Ethel Waters' most significant blues releases, on Cardinal and Black Swan, were recorded in the early 1920s.

Versatile and ambitious, she soon moved into a more pop-oriented direction, and she also began to work in films and theatrical productions. It was in theatre that she eventually made her greatest mark, but after a mid-1950s religious conversion she joined evangelist Billy Graham's crusade, with which she remained until her death.

Rev. Robert Wilkins
(Vocals, guitar, 1896–1987)

Mississippi-born Robert Wilkins' blues style, as evidenced on records he made for Victor, Brunswick and Vocalion from 1928–35, featured vivid lyric imagery couched in eccentrically asymmetrical verses, laid over rudimentary but serviceable strumming. After being ordained in the 1930s, Wilkins quit the blues for religious music. 'Prodigal Son' on the Rolling Stones' *Beggars Banquet* (1968) was a cover of Wilkins' 'That's No Way To Get Along' – ironically, a blues that the Stones recast in a more biblical light.

Below
Ethel Waters surrounded by dancers at the Cotton Club show in Harlem, New York.

Jazz

In the 1920s, with many seminal jazz figures migrating north, the music's epicentre shifted from its birthplace in New Orleans to Chicago. One of the events that caused this mass exodus of pioneering musicians from the Crescent City was the official closing of Storyville, the city's red-light district, in 1917. In 1898, in an attempt to control prostitution, alderman Sidney Story had proposed a city ordinance to confine illegal trafficking to an area of New Orleans bordered on the north by Robertson and on the south by Basin Street. He was determined that such vice would be contained within this area, which became known as Storyville. It flourished as a red-light district for 20 years, providing many musicians with gainful employment in the various sporting houses that flourished there. In 1898, there were about 2,200 registered prostitutes working and advertising their services in Storyville; by 1917, that number had dwindled to 388. Storyville was eventually closed by the Navy on the grounds that it was illegal to operate houses of prostitution within five miles of a military institution.

'Chicago was really jumping around that time [1923]. The Dreamland was in full bloom. The Lincoln Gardens, of course, was still in there. The Plantation was another hot spot at that time. But the Sunset, my boss' place, was the sharpest of them all, believe that.'

Louis Armstrong

Far Right
New Orleans clarinet virtuoso Sidney Bechet.

Right
1920s Chicago, which became the thriving centre of jazz music.

From Crescent City To Windy City

Clarinet great Sidney Bechet (1897–1959) was among the first to leave the Crescent City and head north. In 1917, just as New Orleans' stringent vice laws came into effect, he hooked up with the Bruce & Bruce Stock Company for a whirlwind tour of the Midwest, ending up in Chicago in November of that year. Meanwhile, trombonist and prominent bandleader Edward 'Kid' Ory (1886–1973) went west in 1919 and ended up in Los Angeles, where in 1922 he led the first African-American New Orleans group to make a record (under the name Spike's Seven Pods of Pepper Orchestra). Cornettist Joseph 'King' Oliver (1885–1938), a sideman in Ory's New Orleans group,

Left

A 1926 Charleston competition; the jazz dance craze took 1920s society by storm.

also left for Chicago in February 1919, followed in 1923 by itinerant musician Jelly Roll Morton (1890–1941); both became key figures on the Windy City's hot jazz scene.

The Jazz Age Begins

Chicago held the promise of a new life for the southern black population, which left behind the cotton fields for the blast furnaces, factories and slaughterhouses of the big northern cities; an estimated half million southern blacks arrived in Chicago before 1920. A centrally located transportation link between Los Angeles and New York, Chicago was also an attractive destination for working jazz musicians, many of whom worked in the gangster-owned speakeasies created in reaction to the Volstead Act of 1919 outlawing the manufacture and sale of alcohol in the United States. What followed was the 'Roaring Twenties', a decade marked by a new vitality and spirit of experimentation in the wake of the First World War and underscored by a prevailing air of good times, in spite of the repressive era of Prohibition. The Jazz Age was a time when young, uninhibited people, fuelled by a new permissiveness, sought illegal booze, unregulated revelry and hot music.

In Chicago, jazz matured at the hands of its finest composers and practitioners, including Bechet, Ory, Oliver, Morton, Louis Armstrong (1901–71) and others who held forth on the city's predominantly black South Side, on a nine-block stretch of State Street known as 'The Stroll'. There, jazz lovers could choose between the Lincoln Gardens, Pekin Inn, Dreamland Ballroom, Plantation Café, Elite Café, Vendome, Apex Club, Sunset Café and other spots where hot jazz flowed nightly. It was in this black neighbourhood that the young, white jazz-seeking teenagers who attended Austin High School on Chicago's white, middle-class West Side congregated to hear King Oliver's Creole Jazz Band, featuring Louis Armstrong and Johnny Dodds (1892–1940). By 1923, Chicago had become the centre of the jazz universe.

Popular Melody

Louis Armstrong's Hot Five – 'Muskrat Ramble' (1926)
Kid Ory's raucous, toe-tapping composition, depicting drunken revelry fuelled by muscatel wine, typifies New Orleans-style collective improvisation. There is speculation that the tune was actually written by Louis Armstrong during his apprenticeship in Ory's New Orleans Jazz Band from 1918–22. It became part of the standard jazz repertoire of the early 1920s, and Armstrong later recorded it in 1926 for his Hot Five sessions, featuring Ory on trombone.

The Harlem Renaissance

The mass migration of blacks from the South also fed the growth of population in Harlem, located in uptown New York City. This influx of people helped to create the Harlem Renaissance, a period of unprecedented creative activity among African-Americans in all fields of art. From 1920–30, great works were done by writers and poets such as Langston Hughes, Countee Cullen and Zora Neale Hurston; painters William H. Johnson, Palmer Hayden and Lois Mailous Jones; composer-bandleaders Noble Sissle (1889–1975), Eubie Blake (1883–1983), Duke Ellington (1899–1974) and Fletcher Henderson (1897–1952); and entertainment icons Bill 'Bojangles' Robinson, Paul Robeson, Ethel Waters (1896–1977), Josephine Baker (1906–75) and Bert Williams. Two other geniuses who came up in Harlem during this incredibly rich period in African-American history, and emerged fully fledged stars by the end of the decade, were Thomas 'Fats' Waller (1904–43) and Louis Armstrong. They were good friends whose paths crossed frequently in Chicago and New York, socially and professionally, throughout the 1920s.

Waller And Armstrong

Fats and Louis first met in 1924 while moonlighting with Clarence Williams' Blue Five band at the Hoofer's Club in Harlem. They appeared together on live radio broadcasts and at late-night jams at Connie's Inn (also in Harlem). In 1925, before Armstrong went back to Chicago to record his revolutionary Hot Five sessions, they appeared together on a recording date for Vocalion by Perry Bradford's Jazz Phools. In 1927, the two kindred spirits met up again in Chicago for a series of gigs at the Vendome Theater with Erskine Tate's band. During his brief stay in the Windy City, Waller also sat in on several late-night jam sessions at the Sunset Café with Armstrong's band, which by 1927 included pianist Earl Hines (1903–83).

The Jazz Scene Relocates Again

By the end of the 1920s, the centre of jazz had shifted again, from Chicago to New York. Here, Duke Ellington was leading the way with his sophisticated Cotton Club Orchestra, while Armstrong and Bix

Right
A 1929 poster advertising Duke Ellington's band at the Cotton Club.

www

King Oliver's Creole Jazz Band
Dippermouth Blues
musicfirebox.com /Dippermouth

Below
Louis Armstrong (second from right) with Erskine Tate's Band at Chicago's Vendome Theater.

Left

A typical image of the sudden poverty that followed the 1929 stock market crash.

Beiderbecke (1903–31) were setting the pace for up-and-coming young trumpeters Jabbo Smith (1908–91), Henry 'Red' Allen (1908–67), Jimmy McPartland (1907–91) and Red Nichols (1905–65). Meanwhile, the stock market crash of 29 October 1929 signalled a symbolic end to the raucous, freewheeling, thrill-seeking Jazz Age. As the Great Depression loomed, Americans would soon turn to the ebullient dance music of the Swing Era to heal their woes. While Ellington and Armstrong would spearhead a transition from 'jungle music' and classic jazz into the new Swing Era, others such as Jelly Roll Morton, King Oliver and Kid Ory would fall out of favour in the 1930s, their New Orleans jazz now perceived as archaic and corny by the swing set.

Popular Melody

James P. Johnson – 'Charleston' (1923)

James P. Johnson's syncopated tune from the 1923 all-black musical production Runnin' Wild *became a popular hit and spread like wildfire, sparking a national dance craze and setting the tone for the decadent Jazz Age. Johnson's 'Charleston' was one of the best known and most widely recorded songs of the 1920s.*

Louis Armstrong

An incomparable figure in the history of jazz, Armstrong played with an unprecedented virtuosity and bravura. In the early 1920s, he shifted the emphasis of jazz from ensemble playing to a soloist's art form, while setting new standards for trumpeters worldwide. The sheer brilliance of his playing is best exemplified by his epochal masterworks from the 1920s, such as 'Potato Head Blues', 'West End Blues', 'Hotter Than That', 'Tight Like This', 'Cornet Chop Suey' and 'Weather Bird' – all marked by a passionate, robust attack, dramatic, slashing breaks and a remarkable flexibility and range. As Miles Davis put it, 'You can't play anything on your horn that Louis hasn't already played'.

'What he does is real, and true, and honest, and simple, and even noble. Every time this man puts his trumpet to his lips, even if only to practice three notes, he does it with his whole soul.'
Leonard Bernstein

Satchmo Joins King Oliver

Born in New Orleans on 4 August 1901, Armstrong began playing cornet after being sent to the Colored Waif's Home in 1913. Nicknamed 'Dippermouth' or 'Satchelmouth' (shortened to Satchmo) because of his wide, toothy grin, Armstrong came up playing in parade bands, in bars around Storyville and on steamboat excursions with Fate Marable. In late 1918, he replaced his mentor King Oliver in Kid Ory's band and honed his skills in that oufit for the next few years. On 8 August 1922, Armstrong joined King Oliver's Creole Jazz Band in Chicago, where he caused an immediate stir at Lincoln Gardens. Louis made his recording debut on 6 April 1923 (soloing on 'Chimes Blues'); he remained with Oliver's band throughout that year before moving to New York in early 1924 to join Fletcher Henderson's band during its residency at the Roseland Ballroom.

Right
Perhaps jazz music's most emblematic star, Louis Armstrong.

Key Track

'West End Blues' (1928)
Armstrong's take on this King Oliver piece, featuring the great trumpeter's unmistakeable declamatory tone, rhythmic dash and a stunning introductory cadenza, points to the future of jazz as a soloistic art form.

The Rosetta Stone Of Jazz

After returning to Chicago in 1925, Armstrong recorded the first of his historic Hot Five sessions for OKeh Records with pianist (and Armstrong's second wife) Lil Hardin Armstrong, trombonist Kid Ory, clarinettist Johnny Dodds and banjo player Johnny St. Cyr. There followed some Hot Seven sessions in 1927, featuring Armstrong's hometown friend Warren 'Baby' Dodds on drums, and a second Hot Five session in 1928 with Earl Hines replacing Hardin on piano. Often referred to as 'the Rosetta Stone of Jazz', the Hot Five and Hot Seven recordings are the most exciting and influential in jazz music, if not in the entire twentieth century. Armstrong's all-star ensembles set the ground rules for the direction jazz was to take, establishing it as a basis for improvisation and virtuosic solo playing within a group. He also introduced wordless 'scat' singing and steered jazz towards the more fluid rhythms of swing.

Following these revolutionary recordings, Armstrong began gradually to focus on entertainment at the expense of art. He had already hinted at a more good-humoured direction with his ribald, vaudevillian playfulness on the intro to 'Tight Like This' and in his frisky repartee with pianist Earl Hines to start off 'A Monday Date', both from his Hot Seven recordings of 1928. It was a direction that stern jazzophiles would come to view with increasing indignation over the years.

In 1929, Armstrong gave a crowd-pleasing performance in *Hot Chocolates*, which had its initial run at Connie's Inn in Harlem before moving to the Hudson Theatre on Broadway. It was in that show that Satchmo introduced 'Ain't Misbehavin'', the Fats Waller-Andy Razaf tune that became his first big hit. Armstrong was featured with Leroy Smith's group, at first performing from the pit but eventually taking his spot on stage, to the delight of

audiences. His gravel-throated charisma helped to make *Hot Chocolates* the hottest ticket in town.

Armstrong Follows A New Route

In that same pivotal year of 1929 Armstrong cut the pop song 'I Can't Give You Anything But Love', charting a new course away from the cutting-edge Hot Fives and Hot Sevens, and steering more toward the mainstream entertainment by emphasizing his signature vocals. Armstrong would pursue this direction throughout the 1950s and 1960s with various aggregations of his All-Stars band. By then he had become a beloved yet sometimes controversial icon, a featured player in movies – including *Paris Blues* (in which he appeared with Duke Ellington) and *Hello, Dolly* – and a worldwide ambassador of jazz. After his death in 1971, his home in Queens, New York was preserved as an archive and museum.

Classic Recordings

King Oliver's Creole Jazz Band (1923)
'Chimes Blues', 'Dippermouth Blues', 'Froggie Moore', 'Chattanooga Stomp', 'I Ain't Gonna Tell Nobody'

Fletcher Henderson Orchestra (1924)
'Copenhagen', 'Sugar Foot Stomp', 'Everybody Loves My Baby', 'Shanghai Shuffle'

Louis Armstrong & his Hot Five (1925–28)
'Heebie Jeebies', 'Cornet Chop Suey', 'Muskrat Ramble', 'Big Butter And Egg Man', 'Struttin' With Some Barbecue', 'Hotter Than That'

Louis Armstrong & his Hot Seven (1927)
'Potato Head Blues', 'Wild Man Blues', 'Willie The Weeper', 'Twelfth Street Rag', 'That's When I'll Come Back To You'

Louis Armstrong & his Savoy Ballroom Five (1928)
'West End Blues', 'Tight Like This', 'Beau Koo Jack', 'Save It Pretty Mama', 'Basin Street Blues', 'St. James Infirmary', 'Weatherbird' (duet with Earl Hines)

Louis Armstrong & his Orchestra (1929)
'St Louis Blues', 'After You've Gone', 'Ain't Misbehavin'', 'I Ain't Got Nobody', 'Muggles', 'Rockin' Chair', 'Some of These Days'

Above

The house in Perdido Street, New Orleans in which Armstrong grew up.

Left

The Colored Waif's Home band, featuring Louis Armstrong (back row, indicated by a white arrow).

Bix Beiderbecke

The most strikingly original and authoritative voice on cornet since Louis Armstrong, Leon 'Bix' Beiderbecke set the example for a generation of aspiring white jazz players during the 1920s. His meteoric rise to fame was followed by a dramatic fall from grace that led to his ultimate death from alcoholism at the age of just 28 in 1931.

A Self-Taught Genius

Born in Davenport, Iowa on 10 March 1903, Beiderbecke rebelled against his strait-laced parents and his own upper-middle-class upbringing by becoming a jazz musician, a path that his parents found abhorrent. Inspired by recordings of the Original Dixieland Jass Band from New Orleans (and particularly the playing of the group's trumpeter and bandleader Nick LaRocca), Beiderbecke began playing cornet aged 15. Completely self-taught, he developed a distinctive tone and biting attack along with flawless intonation, a natural sense of swing and an uncanny command of blue notes.

Right

Jazz cornet genius Bix Beiderbecke, who took Chicago by storm.

'Bix's breaks were not as wild as Armstrong's, but they were hot and he selected each note with musical care. He showed me that jazz could be musical and beautiful as well as hot.'

Hoagy Carmichael

Contemporaries such as Hoagy Carmichael later said that the notes coming out of Beiderbecke's horn sounded like they were hit rather than blown, like a mallet striking a chime.

In 1923 Bix joined the Indiana-based

Wolverines (named after Jelly Roll Morton's 'Wolverine Blues'), and in 1924 they cut a series of classic sides for the Gennett label, including 'Tiger Rag', 'Royal Garden Blues', 'Jazz Me Blues', 'Copenhagen' and Hoagy Carmichael's first tune, 'Free Wheeling'. Those recordings were absorbed and analyzed note for note by a group of jazz-hungry young Chicagoans collectively known as the Austin High School Gang, whose ranks included cornettist Jimmy McPartland, saxophonist Bud Freeman, clarinettist Frank Teschemacher, drummer Dave Tough and trombonist Jim Lannigan. It also included other young Windy City players such as trumpeter Muggsy Spanier, drummer Gene Krupa, clarinettist Benny Goodman and banjoist Eddie Condon.

Bix And Tram

In 1925 Beiderbecke moved to Chicago and began sitting in with all the great New Orleans players there, including King Oliver, Jimmy Noone and Louis Armstrong, whom Beiderbecke had first heard playing on a riverboat in 1920 with Fate Marable's band, in his hometown of Davenport. In the early part of 1926, Bix joined a band led by C-melody saxophonist Frankie 'Tram' Trumbauer at the Arcadia Ballroom in St. Louis, and by summer of that year the two were playing in Jean Goldkette's Orchestra at the Graystone Ballroom in Detroit. In late 1927, Bix and Tram were recruited by Paul Whiteman, who led the most

Key Track

'Riverboat Shuffle' (1927)

From the grand, swaggering entrance of his solo to his dazzling triplets and solid command of the swing and blues vernacular, this toe-tapping recording with the Frankie Trumbauer Orchestra showcases Bix at the peak of his powers, and also features great playing by saxophonist Trumbauer and guitarist Eddie Lang.

successful dance band of the day. Though unworthy of his moniker 'King of Jazz', Whiteman did respect the superb artistry that Beiderbecke demonstrated with his horn and featured him frequently on recordings from 1927–29. Bix's brief eight-bar statements within the context of popular Whiteman fare such as 'Marie', 'Louisiana', 'Sweet Sue' and 'Mississippi Mud' were brilliant gems of well-constructed, lyrical improvisation.

At his peak, around 1927–28, Bix was fêted by his fellow jazz musicians, white and black alike. Perhaps his most famous and most widely imitated solo came on a 1927 Trumbauer-led small group recording of Bix's 'Singin' The Blues', which trumpeters of the day studied assiduously. Louis Armstrong refused to record the track himself, believing that Bix's

solo could not be improved upon. Beiderbecke's other famous compositions included 'Davenport Blues' and a Debussy-inspired solo piano piece, 'In A Mist' – one of two such works that he recorded.

The Alcohol Takes Its Toll

In the autumn of 1929, Beiderbecke had a nervous collapse; he was sent back to Davenport and entered a sanatorium to help him with his alcohol problems. Off the Whiteman payroll by the spring of 1930, he tried making a comeback with some recordings as a leader but died of pneumonia, exacerbated by alcoholism, on 6 August 1931. Seven years after his death, Beiderbecke was the inspiration for *Young Man With A Horn*, a novel by Dorothy Baker that was adapted for a 1950 Warner Bros. film starring Kirk Douglas.

*Above
Bix (seated far right)
in his first group –
the Wolverines.*

*Left
Bix (left) with his good
friend and musical
collaborator, saxophonist
Frankie 'Tram'
Trumbauer, in 1928.*

Duke Ellington

Universally acknowledged as one of the twentieth century's emblematic composers, Edward Kennedy 'Duke' Ellington used his longstanding touring orchestra as a tool to create wholly unique tonal colours and a distinctive harmonic language in jazz. From the late 1920s to the early 1970s he composed many tunes that have become standards, as well as exquisite three-minute jazz concertos, dance band repertoire, popular suites, sacred concerts, revues, tone poems and film soundtracks. His most famous titles – including 'Mood Indigo', 'Satin Doll', 'Sophisticated Lady' and 'It Don't Mean A Thing (If It Ain't Got That Swing)' – have become embedded in the English language.

> *'I like any and all of my associations with music – writing, playing, and listening. We write and play from our perspective, and the audience listens from its perspective. If and when we agree, I am lucky.'*
> *Duke Ellington*

The Duke Makes His Name

Born in Washington, DC on 29 April 1899, Ellington was influenced by ragtime piano players and other popular performers of the day, including James P. Johnson, the father of Harlem stride piano. Nicknamed 'Duke' for his dapper appearance, he composed his first pieces – 'Soda Fountain Rag' and the risqué blues 'What You Gonna Do When The Bed Breaks Down?' – as a teenager and in 1919 formed his first group, the Duke's Serenaders. By 1923, Ellington had settled in Harlem in the midst of the area's thriving cultural renaissance. His first gig came as a sideman in the Washingtonians, a sextet led by banjo player and fellow Washington, DC native Elmer Snowden. After a brief stint in 1924 at the Hollywood Club, Ellington took over the band (which featured hot trumpeter James 'Bubber' Miley and drummer Sonny Greer)

Right
Duke Ellington - pianist, composer, bandleader and one of jazz music's most important figures.

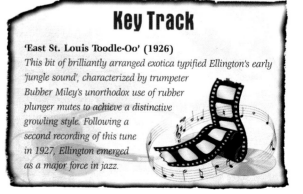

Key Track

'East St. Louis Toodle-Oo' (1926)
This bit of brilliantly arranged exotica typified Ellington's early 'jungle sound', characterized by trumpeter Bubber Miley's unorthodox use of rubber plunger mutes to achieve a distinctive growling style. Following a second recording of this tune in 1927, Ellington emerged as a major force in jazz.

and played at the Kentucky Club in midtown Manhattan. His first recordings with the group in 1924 were 'Choo Choo (Gotta Hurry Home)' and 'Rainy Nights (Rainy Days)'.

A Golden Opportunity In Harlem

A pivotal year in Ellington's career was 1927, when he took over residency at the Cotton Club in Harlem. That same year he also recorded his first masterpieces 'Black and Tan Fantasy' and 'East St. Louis Toodle-Oo' (both composed with Bubber Miley) along with 'Creole Love Call'. In 1928, he recorded 'The Mooche', one of his signature pieces of 'jungle music', marked by Miley's growling trumpet and the plunger-mute trombone work of Joseph 'Tricky Sam' Nanton.

orchestra with new soloists – such as trumpeter Clark Terry, drummer Louie Bellson, trombonist Quentin Jackson and tenor saxophonist Paul Gonslaves – when his longtime sidemen died, retired or moved on. His appearance at the 1956 Newport Jazz Festival led to a *Time* magazine cover, a new contract with Columbia Records and the bestselling *Ellington At Newport*, which featured Gonslaves' fabled 27-chorus solo on 'Diminuendo And Crescendo In Blue'. Ever the open-minded modernist, Ellington recorded with John Coltrane, Max Roach and Charles Mingus in the 1960s. His later masterpieces included 'The Far East Suite' (1966), marked by modal and Asian-inflected motifs, and the 'New Orleans Suite' (1970). Ellington was revered worldwide as a genius and giant of contemporary music long before his death in 1974.

Classic Recordings

Duke Ellington Orchestra (1926–29)
'The Mooche', 'East St. Louis Toodle-Oo', 'Black And Tan Fantasy', 'Jubilee Stomp'

1929–31
'Rockin' In Rhythm', 'Mood Indigo', 'Wall Street Wail', 'Creole Rhapsody'

Left
Harlem's Cotton Club, where Duke Ellington's Orchestra held a three-year residency.

Below
The hugely popular Duke Ellington Orchestra, shown here in Chicago in 1934.

Ellington remained at the Cotton Club until 1930, then took his orchestra to Hollywood to appear in the Amos 'N Andy film *Check And Double Check*. The subsequent decade saw Ellington's flowering, as he produced hundreds of recordings, played countless concerts and broadcasts and became a sophisticated international figure – in his terms, 'beyond category'. Key to Ellington's art was his use of specific musicians – including baritone saxophonist Harry Carney, alto saxophonist Johnny Hodges, trumpeters Cootie Williams and Rex Stewart, trombonist Juan Tizol, bassist Jimmy Blanton, drummer Sonny Greer, and clarinettists Barney Bigard, Jimmy Hamilton and Russell Procope – as individual tones on his compositional palette. He often transformed improvised riffs or half-baked themes into enduring, full-blown works, and in 1938 initiated a remarkable close collaboration with co-composer Billy Strayhorn. In the 1940s Ellington premiered ambitious works, such as 'Black, Brown And Beige' – a musical history of African-Americans – at New York's Carnegie Hall.

A Long And Varied Career

Although not immune from industry-wide downturns and changes in audience tastes, Ellington toured and recorded prolifically throughout the 1950s and 1960s, filling his

Jelly Roll Morton

Ridiculed as a braggart, pimp, card shark and pool hustler, the audacious, self-proclaimed inventor of jazz Jelly Roll Morton was also hailed as a pioneering composer, gifted arranger, dazzling pianist and the greatest entertainer that New Orleans ever produced. He was one of the first jazz musicians to strike a perfect balance between composition and collective improvisation, bridging the gap between ragtime and jazz.

'He was fussy on introductions and endings and he always wanted the ensemble his way but he never interfered with the solo work.... His own playing was remarkable and kept us in good spirits.'

Omer Simeon

Ferdinand Lamothe Becomes Mr Jelly Roll

Born on 20 October 1890, Ferdinand Joseph Lamothe was a Creole of mixed French and African ancestry. He was among the earliest piano players in the bordellos of the Storyville district, where he mixed elements of ragtime, minstrel and marching-band music, foxtrots and French quadrilles, opera and salon music along with Latin American-influenced rhythms, which he called 'the Spanish tinge'.

By 1907, after re-christening himself 'Jelly Roll Morton', he began to travel the black vaudeville circuit around the Gulf Coast. By 1911 his travels had brought him up to New York, and the following year he made trips through Texas and the Midwest. Morton settled in Chicago in 1914 and remained in this new centre of hot jazz until 1917, during which time he composed and published his earliest numbers, including 'Jelly Roll Blues', 'New Orleans Blues' and 'Winin' Boy Blues'.

Right
The multi-talented Jelly Roll Morton.

Morton's Red Hot Peppers

Morton travelled to California during the summer of 1917 and

remained there throughout 1922, working his way up and down the West Coast from Tijuana to Vancouver with pickup bands. By May of 1923 he was back in Chicago and in June made his first recordings – 'Big Fat Ham' and 'Muddy Water Blues' – for the Paramount label. In July, he cut sides with the New Orleans Rhythm Kings ('Sobbin' Blues', 'Mr. Jelly Lord', 'Milenburg Joys' and 'London Blues'), along with some solo piano pieces ('Wolverine Blues', 'New Orleans Joys', 'Grandpa's Spells', 'The Pearls' and 'King Porter Stomp'), for Gennett Records. In 1924, Morton recorded two piano-cornet

Key Track

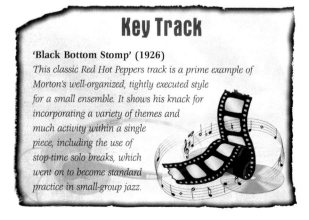

'Black Bottom Stomp' (1926)
This classic Red Hot Peppers track is a prime example of Morton's well-organized, tightly executed style for a small ensemble. It shows his knack for incorporating a variety of themes and much activity within a single piece, including the use of stop-time solo breaks, which went on to become standard practice in small-group jazz.

Classic Recordings

Jelly Roll Morton with the New Orleans Rhythm Kings (1923)
'Milenburg Joys', 'Sobbin' Blues', 'Mr. Jelly Lord'

Piano Solos (1923–26)
'New Orleans Joys', 'Grandpa's Spells', 'King Porter Stomp', 'Wolverine Blues', 'Mr. Jelly Lord', 'The Pearls'

Jelly Roll Morton & his Red Hot Peppers (1926–28)
'Black Bottom Stomp', 'Shreveport Stomp', 'Jungle Blues'

Left

The mid-1920s recordings of Morton's Red Hot Peppers are classics, combining the spirit of New Orleans with the modernism of Chicago Jazz.

duets, 'Tom Cat Blues' and 'King Porter Stomp', with his New Orleans colleague King Oliver. Morton recorded prolifically throughout 1926–27 with two different editions of his Red Hot Peppers, cutting classic New Orleans-flavoured sides such as 'The Chant', 'Black Bottom Stomp', 'Sidewalk Blues', 'Dead Man Blues', 'Jelly Roll Blues' and 'Grandpa's Spells' in 1926 with a group featuring Kid Ory, Omer Simeon and Johnny St. Cyr, and 'The Pearls', 'Jungle Blues' and 'Wild Man Blues' in 1927 with a band that included both Johnny and Baby Dodds.

When the centre of jazz shifted to New York, Morton relocated there and from 1928–30 recorded several sides for the Victor label, including lesser-known tunes such as 'Low Gravy', 'Deep Creek', 'Tank Town Bump' and 'Smilin' The Blues Away'. For these New York sessions, Morton recorded with a new edition of the Red Hot Peppers, featuring trumpeters Henry 'Red' Allen and Bubber Miley, trombonists Geechie Fields and J.C. Higginbotham, clarinettists Omer Simeon and Albert Nicholas, bassist Pops Foster and drummers Paul Barbarin and Zutty Singleton.

A Jazz Musician's Testament

By 1930, Morton's style was considered old-fashioned and his work opportunities declined. He moved to Washington, DC in 1935 – the same year in which Benny Goodman's rendition of Morton's 'King Porter Stomp', arranged by Fletcher Henderson, ushered in the Swing Era – but throughout the decade Morton laboured with little success to regain his earlier status. Although his compositions were performed regularly, he did not receive royalties. In 1938, folklorist Alan Lomax recorded a series of interviews for the Library of Congress in which Morton reminisced about his New Orleans upbringing and his colourful career, while also providing examples of various piano styles. Lomax later used these interviews for an oral biography of Morton, which was released posthumously as *Mister Jelly Lord*. In 1939, Morton recorded eight sides for Bluebird in an all-star session that included New Orleans musicians Sidney Bechet, Sidney de Paris, Zutty Singleton, Henry 'Red' Allen and Albert Nicholas. He made his last recordings in January 1940 and died in poverty and obscurity at the age of 50 in Los Angeles on 10 July 1941.

King Oliver

One of the cornet kings of early New Orleans – along with Buddy Bolden, Freddie Keppard and Bunk Johnson – Joseph 'King' Oliver helped to define the bravura spirit of hot jazz through his work in Chicago during the 1920s with his Creole Jazz Band. He is said to have earned the sobriquet 'King' by besting Keppard in a cutting contest one night in Storyville.

'Joe would stand there fingering his horn with his right hand and working his mute with his left, and how he would rock the place....'

George Wettling

A King And His Mute

Born in Abend, Louisiana on 11 May 1885, Joseph Oliver began working around New Orleans as a cornettist in 1907 with the Onward Brass Band and later with the Eagle Band. By 1917, he became the star cornettist in a popular band led by Kid Ory. One of the early masters of the mute, Oliver created a whole lexicon of vocal effects on his horn during his two-year stint with Ory's band, which influenced a generation of musicians including trumpeter Bubber Miley and trombonist Tricky Sam Nanton – both of whom would play decisive roles in the Duke Ellington Orchestra in the 1930s. When Oliver went north to Chicago in February 1919, Ory hired his 18-year-old protégé Louis Armstrong as his replacement on cornet (Armstrong idolized Oliver and always referred to him as 'Papa Joe').

Right

King Oliver, who taught Louis Armstrong the basics of ensemble cornet playing and improvisation.

Far Right

King Oliver (centre) with his band and assorted musical instruments.

Oliver Rocks Lincoln Gardens

In Chicago, Oliver established himself in Bill Johnson's band at the Dreamland Ballroom. Following a year-long stay in California, he returned to Chicago in June 1922 and started playing regularly with his Creole Jazz Band at the Lincoln Gardens on Chicago's South Side. The original line-up of the Creole Jazz Band included trombonist Honoré Dutrey, bassist Bill Johnson, clarinettist Johnny Dodds, drummer Baby Dodds and pianist Lil Hardin. In July he sent for Louis Armstrong, who joined the group in Chicago on 8 August. Oliver's Creole Jazz Band made its first recordings in April 1923 at the Richmond, Indiana studios of Gennett Records. Included in the batch of Oliver originals that they cut that day were 'Snake Rag', 'Zulu's Ball', 'Just Gone', 'Chimes Blues', 'Canal Street Blues' and 'Dippermouth Blues', which showcases Oliver's wah-wah technique.

Key Track

'Dippermouth Blues' (1923)

This lively tune by King Oliver's Creole Jazz Band, co-written by Oliver and Louis Armstrong, features plenty of freewheeling ensemble interplay between the two trumpets, Johnny Dodds' soaring clarinet and Kid Ory's gutbucket trombone. It is also a brilliant showcase for Oliver's patented muted wah-wah work on lead cornet.

Oliver Loses His Protégé

Lil Hardin and Louis Armstrong were married in February 1924 and Hardin had plans for her new husband, advising him on various matters and ultimately convincing him to leave his mentor's side and join Fletcher Henderson's Orchestra in New York. Shortly after Armstrong's exit, the Creole Jazz Band fell apart; in December 1924 Oliver recorded a pair of piano-cornet duets ('King Porter Stomp' and 'Tom Cat Blues') with Jelly Roll Morton for the Autograph label. In 1925, he took over Dave Peyton's band, which had a residency at the Plantation Café, and renamed it the Dixie Syncopators. From 1927–28, the Dixie Syncopators recorded prolifically for the Vocalion and Brunswick labels, and when the Plantation Café was destroyed by fire in 1929, the band went to New York and worked at the Savoy Ballroom. Oliver unwisely turned down an offer to become the house band at the Cotton Club in Harlem (the gig went to Duke Ellington's Orchestra, which became famous via the club's radio broadcasts) and Luis Russell later took over Oliver's band, renaming it the Luis Russell Orchestra.

Oliver's last recordings as a leader were in 1931 for the Victor, Brunswick and Vocalion labels, although he was suffering from a gum disease and rarely played himself, hiring other cornet players for the sessions. The New Orleans jazz legend spent his last years touring the South and finally settled in Georgia, where he worked as a janitor in a pool hall up until his death in 1938.

Classic Recordings

King Oliver's Creole Jazz Band (1923)
'Dippermouth Blues', 'Chimes Blues', 'Chattanooga Stomp', 'Sobbin' Blues', 'Snake Rag', 'Froggie Moore', 'Canal Street Blues', 'Mabel's Dream'

King Oliver with Jelly Roll Morton (1924)
'Tom Cat Blues', 'King Porter Stomp'

King Oliver's Dixie Syncopators (1925)
'Dead Man Blues', 'Doctor Jazz', 'Snag It', 'Sugar Foot Stomp', 'West End Blues'

A-Z of artists

Josephine Baker

(Vocals, dancer, 1906–75)

Born Freda Josephine McDonald, the St. Louis-born entertainer danced in the 1921 Sissle/Blake musical *Shuffle Along* before gaining a bigger role in their *Chocolate Dandies* in 1924, leading to appearances at the Cotton Club. The following year, she introduced 'le jazz hot' to Paris in *La Revue Négre* (also featuring Sidney Bechet) with her exotic dancing and uninhibited onstage sexuality. After working with the Red Cross and French Resistance during the Second World War – and adopting 12 children – she staged a major comeback in 1973, culminating in a 1975 performance at New York's Carnegie Hall.

Above

Trumpet great Henry 'Red' Allen (second from left) with (l–r) trombonists J.C. Higginbotham and Lou McGarity, and saxophonist Lester Young.

Henry 'Red' Allen

(Trumpet, 1908–67)

The son of bandleader Henry Allen Sr., Henry 'Red' Allen was one of the greatest trumpeters to come out of New Orleans, although he remained eternally in the shadow of Louis Armstrong. He moved to New York in 1927 to join King Oliver's Dixie Syncopators and in 1929 the Victor label signed him as an answer to rival OKeh's Armstrong.

Allen played with Luis Russell's Orchestra from 1929–32, then in 1933 joined Fletcher Henderson's Orchestra for a year, during which he appeared alongside Coleman Hawkins on influential recordings such as 'King Porter Stomp' and 'Down South Camp Meeting'. Following a stint with the Mills Blue Rhythm Band (1934–37), Allen returned to the Russell Orchestra, which by 1937 had become Armstrong's backing band. He then led his own bands through the 1940s and 1950s, participated in the 1957 CBS TV special *The Sound of Jazz* and toured Europe in 1959 with Kid Ory. Allen experienced a renaissance in the 1960s before succumbing to cancer.

Right

Flamboyant stage star Josephine Baker poses on an exotic set in 1933.

Sidney Bechet

(Soprano saxophone, clarinet, 1897–1959)

A child prodigy who left school at the age of 16 and worked with various bands around New Orleans, the Creole clarinettist thrilled audiences and players alike with his soaring tone, forceful attack, penetrating solos, dazzling facility and unusually fast vibrato. In 1917, Bechet and King Oliver played together briefly in Kid Ory's band until Bechet relocated to Chicago. The following year, while on a European tour with Will Marion Cook's Southern Syncopated Orchestra, Bechet discovered the instrument with which he would eventually make jazz history: the unsual straight soprano saxophone.

Bechet made his first recordings in 1923 with the Clarence Williams Blue Five and continued to record prolifically throughout the 1920s and 1930s, scoring a hit in 1938 with his bluesy rendition of George Gershwin's 'Summertime'. The New Orleans revival of the 1940s made him an international star and he lived out his final years in France, where he was feted as a national hero.

Irving Berlin

(Piano, songwriter, 1888–1989)

Born Israel Beilin in Siberia, Berlin's family relocated in 1893 to New York, where he broke into vaudeville. He published his first song in 1907 and in 1911 had his first major hit with 'Alexander's Ragtime Band'. One of America's most prolific melodicists, Berlin wrote hundreds of tunes that became standards, including 'Always', 'Cheek To Cheek', 'White Christmas' and 'There's No Business Like Show Business' from his successful musical *Annie Get Your Gun*. His songs have been interpreted by musicians from Bessie Smith to Charlie Parker to Cassandra Wilson.

Eubie Blake

(Piano, composer, 1883–1983)

A long-surviving link to the ragtime era, James Hubert Blake wrote his first piece, 'The Charleston Rag', in 1899. The Baltimore native started out playing piano in sporting houses and with travelling medicine shows in the early 1900s. He also worked with bandleader-composer James Reese Europe before teaming up on the vaudeville circuit with lyricist Noble Sissle in 1915 – they were billed as 'The Dixie Duo'. In 1921 they collaborated on the first all-black musical, *Shuffle Along*, which produced the hit song 'I'm

Just Wild About Harry' and paved the way for several other all-black productions during the 1920s and 1930s.

After three decades of inactivity, Blake emerged with a triumphant two-record set on Columbia, *The Eighty-Six Years of Eubie Blake* (1969), which sparked a Blake revival and led to the highly successful 1978 Broadway musical revue, *Eubie* (which subsequently travelled to London). Blake continued performing until he was 98.

Garvin Bushell

(Clarinet, bassoon, 1902–91)

Jazz's first double-reed specialist on bassoon, Bushell played with Mamie Smith's Jazz Hounds before a two-year stint with Sam Wooding's Orchestra (1925–27). In 1928 he formed the Louisiana Sugar Babies with Fats Waller and Jabbo Smith, and he later worked with Otto Hardwick (1931), Fess Williams (1933), Fletcher Henderson (1935–36), Cab Calloway (1936–37) and Chick Webb (1938). In 1959 he replaced Omer Simeon in Wilbur de Paris's New Orleans Jazz Band, and in 1961 recorded live in a large ensemble with John Coltrane at the Village Vanguard.

Above
Prolific composer Irving Berlin (left) discusses one of his songs with actor, dancer and singer Fred Astaire.

Eddie Condon
(Banjo, guitar, 1905–73)

Originally from Indiana, Condon became associated with Chicago's Austin High School Gang, a group of white West-Side teenagers who emulated King Oliver's Creole Jazz Band and created their own take on hot jazz. In 1927, Condon co-led a band with William 'Red' McKenzie (which also included Bud Freeman, Frank Teschemacher, Gene Krupa and Jimmy McPartland) that helped to define the driving, freewheeling Chicago jazz sound of the Roaring Twenties. Condon also worked with Red Nichols & his Five Pennies and with McKenzie's Mound City Blue Blowers during the late 1920s.

Condon's considerable wit and charm made him an ideal spokesperson for the 1940s revival of traditional jazz. His all-star concerts in New York's Town Hall were broadcast weekly on the radio from 1944–45. He opened his own club, Condon's, in New York in 1945 and in 1949–50 hosted the first jazz television show, *Eddie Condon's Floor Show*. Condon continued to record, tour, write about and promote jazz until his death.

Johnny Dodds
(Clarinet, 1892–1940)

The premier New Orleans clarinettist of the 1920s, Dodds played in Kid Ory's band from 1912–19 and then alongside Louis Armstrong and his own brother, Warren 'Baby' Dodds, in Fate Marable's riverboat band. Dodds left New Orleans in January 1921 to join King Oliver's Creole Jazz Band in Chicago, taking part in that influential band's classic 1923 recordings for Gennett.

Dodds played a key role in Armstrong's legendary Hot Five and Hot Seven sessions from 1925–27, and his virtuoso solos and distinctive, liquid tone also grace recordings by Jelly Roll Morton's Red Hot Peppers, the New Orleans Wanderers, the Chicago Footwarmers and his own Black Bottom Stompers, featuring Armstrong. He worked regularly in Chicago throughout the 1930s while also running a cab company with Baby Dodds. He led his final session on 5 June 1940, before passing away two months later.

Warren 'Baby' Dodds
(Drums, 1898–1959)

The grandfather of jazz drumming, Baby Dodds played in Fate Marable's riverboat band from 1918–21 before joining King Oliver's Creole Jazz Band and relocating to Chicago. He remained there for the rest of his career, collaborating with Jelly Roll Morton's Red Hot Peppers and Armstrong's Hot Seven, as well as trombonists Kid Ory and Miff Mole, trumpeter Bunk Johnson and clarinettists Jimmie Noone, Sidney Bechet and Dodds' brother Johnny. His soloist style influenced countless drummers, including Gene Krupa, Max Roach and Roy Haynes.

'[Baby Dodds] had a rhythm entirely his own, and I feel that as a drummer he had more personality than any other specialist on any other instrument.... As for Johnny Dodds, his brother, I sincerely believe that he was the greatest clarinettist that ever lived....'
Tommy Brookins

George 'Pops' Foster
(Bass, 1892–1969)

Known for his powerful, slap bass sound and signature solos, Foster worked with the Magnolia Band and A.J. Piron before playing in Fate Marable's riverboat band (1918–21) and collaborating with Kid Ory and others during the 1920s. In 1928 he played with King Oliver's Dixie Syncopators in New York and then joined the Luis Russell Orchestra for an 11-year stint. Foster was in demand during the 1940s New Orleans revival and from 1956–61 he played with Earl Hines in San Francisco. Foster remained active into the mid-1960s.

Bud Freeman
(Tenor saxophone, clarinet, 1906–91)

Freeman was one of the Austin High School Gang, a group of white, jazz-seeking teenagers who were inspired by New Orleans Rhythm Kings records and obsessed with the hot jazz scene on Chicago's South Side. He recorded in 1927 with the McKenzie-Condon Chicagoans, then moved to New York to work with Red Nichols' Five Pennies.

He eventually developed his own style on the tenor saxophone that offered a fresh alternative to Coleman Hawkins and Lester Young, as demonstrated by his masterful showcase on a 1933 Eddie Condon-led recording of 'The Eel'. Freeman became a swing star with the Tommy Dorsey band in 1936 and the Benny Goodman Orchestra in 1938. He was also the house saxophonist at Commodore Records in the 1930s. Freeman reunited with Eddie Condon in 1945 and continued to play freewheeling Chicago-style jazz with the World's Greatest Jazz Band (1968–71) and as a leader into the early 1980s.

Left
A publicity poster for Gershwin's 1935 'folk opera' Porgy & Bess.

George Gershwin
(Piano, composer, 1898–1937)

One of the most enduringly popular composers of the twentieth century, Gershwin composed such enduring melodies as 'Summertime', 'Embraceable You' and 'Let's Call The Whole Thing Off'. His tuneful songs with their rich harmonic progressions are ideal for improvisation and were popular with jazz musicians including Louis Armstrong, Art Tatum, Oscar Peterson, Coleman Hawkins and Miles Davis.

A self-taught pianist, 15-year-old Gershwin was the youngest songwriter on Tin Pan Alley. He and his lyricist brother Ira scored their first big hit in 1919 with 'Swanee' for Al Jolson. From 1919–33 they produced a succession of musicals, including the first Pulitzer Prize-winning musical comedy, *Of Thee I Sing* (1931). In 1924, George wrote *Rhapsody In Blue* as a concerto for piano and the Paul Whiteman Orchestra. His success with this work led to the 1928 tone poem *An American In Paris* and his 1935 'folk opera' *Porgy & Bess*. The Gershwins went to Hollywood in 1936 but George died of a brain tumour the following year. Ira continued to work as a lyricist until retiring in 1960.

Near Left
Johnny Dodds – possibly the finest clarinettist in New Orleans jazz.

Far Left
Eddie Condon was a key figure in the desegregation of jazz and helped to move the music into higher profile venues.

Edmond Hall
(Clarinet, 1901–67)

Raised in a musical family (his father Edward also played clarinet), Hall played around New Orleans during the early 1920s before departing to New York in 1928 to work with Alonzo Ross. He worked with Claude Hopkins, Lucky Millinder, Joe Sullivan and Zutty Singleton in the 1930s; with Teddy Wilson and Eddie Condon through the 1940s; and toured with Louis Armstrong's All-Stars from 1955–58. He reunited with Condon in the 1960s and made his final recording in 1967 at John Hammond's New York Spirituals To Swing concert.

Right

Saxophonist Coleman Hawkins, shown here with Miles Davis in the 1940s.

Lil Hardin Armstrong
(Piano, vocals, arranger, 1898–1971)

Memphis-born pianist Lillian Hardin joined King Oliver's Creole Jazz Band in Chicago during the summer of 1921 and married fellow band member Louis Armstrong in 1924. She played on Armstrong's Hot Five and Hot Seven recordings and also received some composer credits. The couple separated in 1931 and were divorced in 1938. Lil subsequently worked as the house pianist at Decca Records and recorded up until 1961, remaining active on the Chicago club scene. She died during a performance of 'St. Louis Blues' at a Louis Armstrong memorial concert in Chicago.

Below

Jazz pianist Lil Hardin Armstrong, who married Louis in 1924.

Coleman Hawkins
(Tenor saxophone, 1904–69)

'Hawk' played with Mamie Smith's Jazz Hounds in 1922 before joining Fletcher Henderson's band in New York. Louis Armstrong's presence in the band had a major effect on Hawkins' playing; by marrying a swing feel to his heavy tone, informed by his advanced understanding of harmony and chords, Hawkins became a star soloist and the pre-eminent saxophonist of his time.

Returning to the US in 1939 following a sojourn in Europe (during which he worked with Django Reinhardt and Stephane Grappelli), Hawkins recorded 'Body And Soul' – a masterpiece of melodic improvisation and one of the first pure jazz recordings to become a commercial hit. Hawkins was the first prominent Swing era artist to make the transition to bebop, playing with Thelonious Monk, Dizzy Gillespie and Don Byas. In 1948 Hawk made another milestone recording, 'Picasso', a stunning, unaccompanied solo. He recorded prolifically in the 1950s and 1960s with John Coltrane, Roy Eldridge, Duke Ellington, Max Roach, Sonny Rollins and Pee Wee Russell, among others.

Fletcher Henderson
(Piano, arranger, bandleader, 1897–1952)

The Georgia native came to New York in 1920 and worked at a music publishing company owned by Harry Pace and

Left

The Fletcher Henderson Orchestra in 1924. Henderson is seated behind the bass drum; Coleman Hawkins is second from the left with Louis Armstrong behind him, while Don Redman is on the far right.

W.C. Handy. When Pace left in 1921 to form the Black Swan record label, Henderson followed as house pianist and arranger. In 1923 Henderson's session band, which included young talents such as Coleman Hawkins, landed a steady gig at the Club Alabam, and in 1924 began an engagement at the Roseland Ballroom; Louis Armstrong joined the same year.

From 1925–28, Henderson's swinging ensemble was among the finest in jazz, but the Depression took its toll and by 1935 Henderson was writing crack arrangements for the Benny Goodman Orchestra that essentially helped to launch the Swing Era. Henderson led his own small groups during the 1940s and in 1950 co-led a sextet with Lucky Thompson before being sidelined by a stroke.

Jack Hylton
(Piano, bandleader, 1892–1965)

Prominent British bandleader and booking agent Hylton began recreating the 'symphonic jazz' of Paul Whiteman's Orchestra in 1920. His band's popularity grew in England and France through the 1920s and early 1930s. In 1933 Hylton booked the Duke Ellington orchestra to tour Europe for the first time. He toured the US with American musicians in 1935, reformed his British band in 1936 and toured through the 1930s before disbanding in 1940.

James P. Johnson
(Piano, composer, 1894–1955)

The seminal figure among the Harlem stride pianists, Johnson was a mentor to Fats Waller and composer of 'The Charleston', which launched a Jazz Age dance craze. Count Basie, Duke Ellington and Art Tatum were also directly influenced by Johnson's skilful stride and compositions, including 'You've Got To Be Modernistic' – an evolutionary leap from ragtime. His 'Carolina Shout' became proving ground for other stride pianists of the day. Johnson also composed music for the 1923 Broadway show *Runnin' Wild*.

Tommy Ladnier
(Cornet, trumpet, 1900–39)

A stylistic descendant of King Oliver, Ladnier learned under Bunk Johnson and played in various bands around New Orleans. Around 1917 he moved to Chicago, where he became part of the hot jazz scene and worked with Jimmie Noone and King Oliver. In 1925 he toured Europe with Sam Wooding's band and the following year joined Fletcher Henderson in New York. In 1932, Ladnier formed the New Orleans Feetwarmers with Sidney Bechet before dropping off the scene, re-emerging in 1938 with Mezz Mezzrow until his premature death from a heart attack.

Eddie Lang
(Guitar, 1902–33)

Philadelphia native Salvatore Massaro joined the Mound City Blue Blowers in 1924 and by the mid-1920s had become jazz's first in-demand session guitarist, backing various blues and popular singers. A single-note virtuoso, he was also jazz's first guitar hero. In 1926, Lang teamed up with high-school pal Joe Venuti for some classic guitar-violin duet sessions that predated Stephane Grappelli's work with Django Reinhardt. Lang recorded prolifically during 1927, appearing on commercial sessions and also playing in more jazz-oriented settings with Jean Goldkette, Frankie Trumbauer, Red Nichols and Bix Beiderbecke. In 1928 he teamed up with fellow guitarist Lonnie Johnson for some historic duet recordings and in 1929 joined Paul Whiteman's Orchestra, which featured a young Bing Crosby. When Crosby left to launch his solo career in 1932, Lang became his full-time accompanist. The guitarist's career came to an end with his untimely death the following year.

George Lewis
(Clarinet, alto saxophone, 1900–68)

Lewis (born George Louis Francis Zeno) led bands in New Orleans in the 1920s, but he remained in the Crescent City while many of his colleagues headed north to Chicago, where the Jazz Age was being forged on the city's South Side. Lewis did not record until the 1940s (in sessions that teamed him with New Orleans trumpeter Bunk Johnson) and he later became a prominent figure in the New Orleans revivalist movement of the 1950s.

McKinney's Cotton Pickers
(Instrumental group, 1926–34)

Formed in 1926 by drummer Bill McKinney (1895–1969), this Ohio-based big band improved significantly after hiring arranger Don Redman from Fletcher Henderson's band in the summer of 1927. For the next four years, until Redman left in 1931, McKinney's Cotton Pickers rivalled both Henderson's and Duke Ellington's orchestras for ensemble precision. The band's trumpeter and principal soloist John Nesbitt (a close friend of Bix Beiderbecke) also contributed potent arrangements throughout the 1920s.

Jimmy McPartland
(Trumpet, 1907–91)

Part of the Chicago-based Austin High School Gang, along with Bud Freeman, Frank Teschemacher, Jim Lannigan and Dave Tough, McPartland was inspired by recordings of the New Orleans Rhythm Kings and Bix Beiderbecke, who he replaced in the Wolverines in 1925. He joined Ben Pollack's band in 1927 and recorded with the McKenzie-Condon Chicagoans that same year. McPartland worked steadily through the 1930s in Chicago and continued leading Dixieland sessions for the next four decades.

James 'Bubber' Miley
(Trumpet, 1903–32)

A key figure in the Duke Ellington Orchestra of 1926–28, Miley played a lead role on such classic pieces of early Ellingtonia as 'East St. Louis Toodle-Oo', 'Black And Tan Fantasy' and 'Creole Love Call'. His uniquely expressive, growling trumpet style was influenced by the plunger mute approach of King Oliver, and served as one of the signatures of Ellington's 'jungle sound'. Miley formed his own band in 1930 but shortly afterwards died of tuberculosis, aged 29.

Above

McKinney's Cotton Pickers, who recorded some of the tightest ensemble playing in 1920s jazz.

Left

Cornettist Jimmy McPartland was a soldier during the Second World War, and took part in the 1944 D-Day invasion of Normandy.

Far Left

Guitar virtuoso Eddie Lang, who formed a fruitful musical partnership with violinist Joe Venuti.

Punch Miller
(Trumpet, cornet, 1894–1971)

One of the leading New Orleans cornettists during the 1920s, Ernest 'Punch' Miller moved to Chicago in 1926 and found work with fellow New Orleanians Freddie Keppard and Jelly Roll Morton, as well as with Tiny Parham and Albert Wynn's Gutbucket Five. He spent the 1930s in New York before returning to Chicago. In 1956, Miller returned to New Orleans; he recorded his last sessions in the mid-1960s with trombonist George Lewis.

Miff Mole
(Trombone, 1898–1961)

A vital figure of the 1920s, Irving Milfred Mole was among the earliest trombonists with the virtuosity to express fully developed musical lines on an instrument largely still relegated to glissandos and rhythm accents. Mole elevated the instrument to first-chair status on hundreds of records and solos, many recorded with Red Nichols. He left jazz to work in radio after 1929, played in various traditional groups after the Second World War, and was reunited with Nichols in 1956 on the television show *This Is Your Life*.

Sam Morgan
(Trumpet, 1895–1936)

An early practitioner of New Orleans jazz, Morgan travelled the Bay St. Louis-Pensacola-Mobile circuit and played Crescent City venues, including the Savoy on Rampart Street, before suffering a stroke in 1925. He recovered and in 1927 made recordings at the

Far Right
A photo card for Ben Pollack's Park Central Hotel Orchestra, which included Jack Teagarden and Benny Goodman.

Below
The name Red Nichols gave his groups, 'Five Pennies', was a play on his surname (five cents/pennies make a nickel) and often had more than five members.

Werlein's Music Store on Canal Street for the Columbia label, including 'Mobile Stomp', 'Bogalousa Strut' and his vocal feature, 'Short Dress Gal'. Morgan continued to play until he had a second stroke in 1932.

Red Nichols

(Cornet, 1905–65)

As a child, Nichols played in his father's brass band. After moving to New York in 1923 he teamed up with trombone player Miff Mole, and this marked the start of a long musical partnership. With Mole, Nichols recorded various line-ups under different names, the most common of which was Red Nichols & his Five Pennies. He worked prolifically on Broadway and radio as well as on tour and in the studio; a film was made about his life in 1959.

Jimmie Noone

(Clarinet, 1895–1944)

The most fluid and graceful of the classic New Orleans clarinettists, Noone worked with trumpeter Freddie Keppard (1914) and also with the Young Olympia Band (1916) before following Keppard to Chicago in 1917. A member of King Oliver's first Creole Jazz Band (1918–20), he also played in Doc Cooke's Dreamland Orchestra (1920–26) before forming his popular Apex Club Orchestra (featuring Earl Hines) in 1928. Noone led bands throughout the 1930s and joined Kid Ory in 1944.

Ben Pollack

(Drums, 1903–71)

A member of the Chicago-based New Orleans Rhythm Kings, Pollack formed his own band in 1926 and by 1928 was employing such promising young players as Benny Goodman, Jimmy McPartland, Jack Teagarden and Glenn Miller. When Pollack's orchestra disbanded in 1934, its membership became the core group for Bob Crosby's orchestra. Pollack became the musical director for Chico Marx in the early 1940s and continued to play Dixieland music with his Pick-A-Rib Boys into the 1960s.

Ben Pollack
AND HIS PARK CENTRAL HOTEL ORCH

director of McKinney's Cotton Pickers for four years, then led his own big band from 1931–41.

Zutty Singleton
(Drums, 1898–1975)

Arthur 'Zutty' Singleton was one of the first New Orleans drummers, along with Baby Dodds, to develop a melodic approach to the kit and the concept of the extended drum solo. He played in the second configuration of Louis Armstrong's Hot Five, appearing on OKeh recordings cut in 1928 (including the landmark 'West End Blues'), and then moved to New York the following year. In the 1930s he played with Fats Waller, Eddie Condon and Bubber Miley, while also leading his own band.

After moving to Los Angeles in 1943, he demonstrated his versatility by working with a variety of artists including bluesman T-Bone Walker, Dixielander Wingy Manone and jivester Slim Gaillard (appearing on 'Slim's Jam' with bebop icons Charlie Parker and Dizzy Gillespie). He spent the early 1950s in Europe working with Hot Lips Page, and through the 1960s could be found playing drums at Jimmy Ryan's club in New York.

Noble Sissle
(Vocals, composer, bandleader, 1889–1975)

Sissle worked with bandleader James Reese Europe from 1916–19, before teaming up with Eubie Blake; together Sissle and Blake wrote hits for Sophie Tucker and the successful all-black musicals *Shuffle Along* (1921) and *Chocolate Dandies* (1924). Sissle led his own bands in Europe during the late 1920s before returning to America in 1931 and forming a new group that featured singer Lena Horne. Between 1938 and 1950, Sissle's orchestra held forth at Billy Rose's Diamond Horseshoe Club in New York.

Jabbo Smith
(Trumpet, 1908–91)

This Georgia-born trumpeter (real name Cladys Smith) was on the New York scene by the age of 17 in 1925, working with Charlie Johnson's house band at Small's Paradise. In 1927 he played on Duke Ellington's 'Black And Tan Fantasy' and later that year joined James P. Johnson and Fats Waller in Chicago for a production of *Keep Shufflin'*. By 1929, Smith was being touted as competition for Louis Armstrong on the strength of recordings with his Rhythm Aces for Brunswick.

Above

New Orleans drummer Zutty Singleton, whose versatility enabled him to play both traditional and developing styles of jazz, as well as blues music.

Don Redman
(Alto saxophone, clarinet, vocals, composer, arranger, 1900–64)

Renowned for crafting the polished sound of the mid-1920s Fletcher Henderson Orchestra, Redman's innovative arrangements pre-dated the Swing Era by a decade. His sophisticated compositions were significantly affected by the driving, swinging trumpet work of Louis Armstrong, who played in Henderson's Orchestra throughout 1924. The conservatory-trained arranger left Henderson's band in 1927 to become musical

Pine Top Smith

(Piano, vocals, 1904–29)

A seminal figure in the development of boogie-woogie piano, self-taught Clarence 'Pine Top' Smith was raised in Birmingham, Alabama and worked the southern club and vaudeville circuit during the early 1920s. In 1928 he relocated to Chicago, where he roomed with fellow boogie-woogie piano pioneers Meade 'Lux' Lewis and Albert Ammons. Smith recorded his signature 'Pine Top's Boogie-Woogie' for Vocalion in 1928. The following year he was shot in a Chicago dance hall and died aged just 25.

Johnny St. Cyr

(Guitar, banjo, 1890–1966)

Johnny St. Cyr played around New Orleans as a teenager with A.J. Piron and the Superior, Olympia and Tuxedo bands. He joined Kid Ory's band in 1918 and later played in Fate Marable's riverboat band. In 1923 he moved to Chicago, where he joined King Oliver's Creole Jazz Band. He played on Armstrong's historic Hot Five and Hot Seven sessions (1925–27) and also recorded with Jelly Roll Morton's Red Hot Peppers (1926). St. Cyr led a small Dixieland band at Disneyland from 1961 until his death.

Below
Johnny St. Cyr (second from left) in Louis Armstrong's original Hot Five line-up with (l-r) Armstrong, Johnny Dodds, Kid Ory and Lil Hardin Armstrong.

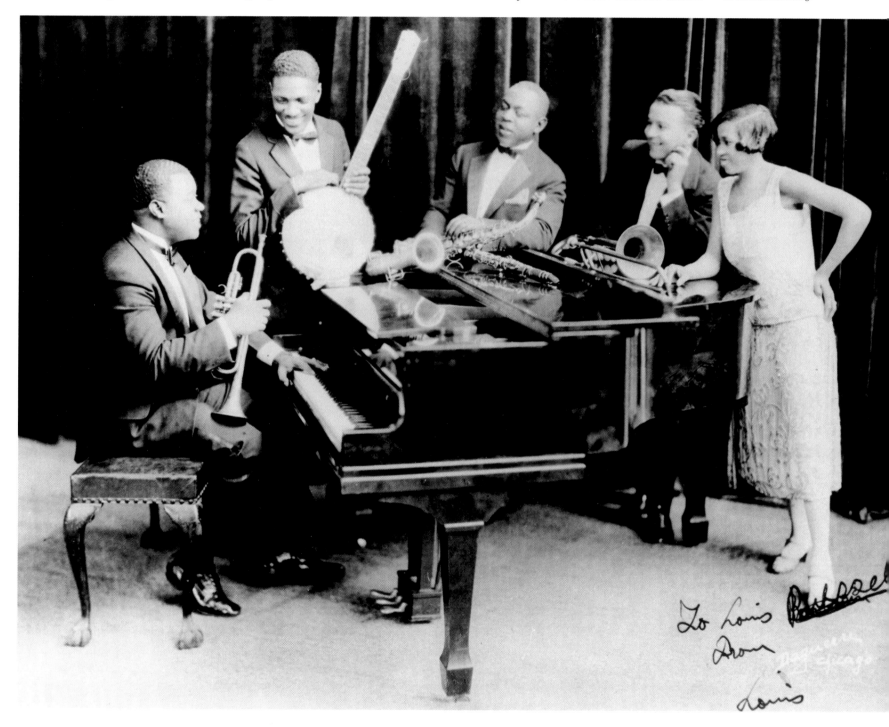

Bix and Tram – the two greatest white instrumentalists of the period – were reunited as star soloists in Paul Whiteman's orchestra in 1927. Trumbauer remained until 1932, during which time he was also on the bandstand with Eddie Lang, Joe Venuti, Andy Secrest, Mildred Bailey and Bing Crosby. His second hitch with Whiteman lasted four years, from 1933–36, and was followed by a stint with the Three Ts, featuring Charlie and Jack Teagarden. Trumbauer continued to record both as a sideman and a leader in the early 1950s.

Joe Venuti
(Violin, 1903–78)

Venuti teamed up with guitarist Eddie Lang in 1926 for some classic duet sessions on OKeh. They reprised their intimate chemistry on 1928 sessions and worked together through the 1920s and 1930s on recordings for Jean Goldkette, Paul Whiteman, Red McKenzie and Roger Wolfe Kahn. In 1933 Venuti led small group sessions and in 1935 fronted a big band. He experienced a major comeback in the 1970s. Venuti was a great practical joker and is fondly remembered in amusing anecdotes from many of his colleagues.

Fats Waller
(Piano, vocals, composer, 1904–43)

Thomas Wright 'Fats' Waller developed his playing style during the early 1920s under the tutelage of Harlem stride pianists James P. Johnson and Willie 'The Lion' Smith. The son of a Baptist preacher, he began playing in the church and by the age of 15 was the house organist at the Lincoln Theatre. He first recorded for OKeh aged 18 and shortly thereafter met lyricist Andy Razaf, who became a key collaborator on popular tunes such as 'Honeysuckle Rose', 'Ain't Misbehavin'' and '(What Did I Do To Be So) Black And Blue' as well as successful musicals *Keep Shufflin'* and *Hot Chocolates*.

'Some little people has music in them, but Fats, he was all music, and you know how big he was.'

James P. Johnson

By 1924 Fats was well known for his piano rolls, radio broadcasts and extroverted, off-the-cuff, jivey performance style. He also flaunted dazzling piano work on many instrumentals, including 'A Handful Of Keys', 'Smashing Thirds' and 'Jitterbug Waltz'. Waller recorded with a sextet in the mid-1930s and by 1940 was a household name.

Above

Harlem-based stride pianist and hugely popular entertainer Fats Waller.

Frankie Trumbauer
(C-melody and alto saxophone, 1901–56)

Known as 'Tram' by his colleagues, Trumbauer was a player of impeccable technique who had a major influence on many saxophonists in the 1920s (notably Benny Carter and Lester Young). He first recorded in 1923 with the popular Benson Orchestra of Chicago and by 1926 was playing alongside cornettist and kindred spirit Bix Beiderbecke in Jean Goldkette's Orchestra at the Graystone Ballroom in Detroit.

Paul Whiteman

(Violin, bandleader, 1890–1967)

Erroneously dubbed 'The King Of Jazz' by press agents, Whiteman led his first dance band in San Francisco in 1918. Arriving in New York in 1920, he assembled some of the city's top musicians and gained popularity with hits such as 'Japanese Sandman' and 'Whispering'. In 1924 his orchestra premiered George Gershwin's *Rhapsody In Blue*. Whiteman's best band (1927–30) included such superb soloists as Frankie Trumbauer, Bix Beiderbecke, Eddie Lang and Joe Venuti, and launched crooner Bing Crosby's career.

Sam Wooding

(Piano, arranger, bandleader, 1895–1985)

Wooding led his Society Syncopators in the early 1920s before travelling to Berlin in 1925 with the *Chocolate Kiddies* revue. One of the first wave of expatriate American jazz musicians to live abroad, he spent the remainder of the 1920s in Europe playing with bands that featured star soloists such as Doc Cheatham and Tommy Ladnier. He returned to the United States in 1935 but had little success swimming against the tide of the Swing Era.

Left

Lyricist Andy Razaf, who collaborated with Fats Waller on a number of songs, including 'Ain't Misbehavin'.

Left

Bandleader Paul Whiteman, whose orchestral line-up at various times included Bix Beiderbecke, Eddie Lang and Bing Crosby.

the thirties

a s if at the convenience of history, the stock market crash in the final weeks of 1929 severed the 1920s from the 1930s. The breach was economic but its consequences were pervasive, sweeping away economic values and social illusions, and affecting all aspects of life for Americans and Europeans alike. America's compliant 1920s middle class became the 1930s 'new poor'. Rural African-Americans were pitched back into conditions akin to servitude; those in the urban North and West after the Great Migration struggled anew to adapt. Poverty's ubiquity lent it unusual moral standing, reflected in movies and songs. Businessmen lost status; the wealthy were subjected to cultural ridicule and liberal reform unleashed by one of their own, President Franklin D. Roosevelt. Clashes over small-town and big-city values were replaced by battles over wages and hours between capital and labour.

Popular culture found easy ways forth. Network radio, paid for by advertisers, took hold; outlets competed for local and niche audiences, hiring bluesmen to host shows aimed at African-American listeners, for example. The record industry almost expired, but live music, especially for dancers, thrived. Movies, combining social realism and romantic fantasy, offered the decade's most iconic imagery. Within 10 years, movies and touring bands displaced theatre and vaudeville as transmitters of a popular culture, available for the first time to millions simultaneously, sea to sea – and beyond. That culture was centred on jazz, steeped in the blues, immersed in transition. In April 1939 the New York World's Fair opened a vision to a future dominated by technology, which 1930s music and art had essentially come to represent. Five months later the decade ended with the beginning of the Second World War. Music and art faced another wild ride.

Key Artists: Blues

Albert Ammons
Big Bill Broonzy
Robert Johnson
Leadbelly

Key Artists: Jazz

Count Basie
Charlie Christian
Roy Eldridge
Benny Goodman
Lester Young

Blues

'Piano dominated blues music in the twenties and thirties and 'til the late forties. See, acoustic blues that original Sonny Boy Williamson was playing, Big Bill Broonzy, and Memphis Minnie, they all used piano.'
Billy Boy Arnold

Above
The shadow of the Great Depression hung over 1930s America.

America. The Depression hung over America like a dark cloud and economic conditions improved very slowly. While the government instituted many reforms and programmes to help the unemployed, it could do only so much. It would take a wartime economy in the next decade to pull the country out of the doldrums.

Political Change

The 1930s also saw a rise in radical political activity. Critics of capitalism found eager followers, workers banded together in labour unions, and artists and intellectuals were drawn to Marxism as a solution to the problems of America. The infamous trials of the Scottsboro Boys in Alabama, involving rape charges by two white women against eight black men, dominated the news pages during 1931–32 and the Communist Party (CP) was in the middle of that battle. The National Association for the Advancement of Colored People (NAACP), founded in 1909, had been working to expose the racial injustice of the country through traditional methods and was moving cautiously; however, it was upstaged by the CP, which organized marches, demonstrations and letter-writing campaigns. Lawyers from the CP-controlled International Labor Defense represented the defendants and won an appeal of the initial guilty verdict. The second, third and fourth trials were rife with CP attempts to bribe witnesses and manipulate the situation. It was the NAACP that prevailed in its work through the legal system to gain limited victories for some of the defendants. Throughout the remainder of the decade, the CP would be at the forefront of the racial struggle.

The New Record Labels

The repeal of the Volstead Act in 1933 meant that Americans could once more legally consume alcoholic beverages, while the rise of the new jukebox industry helped to fuel the revival of the record business. Such race record stalwarts of the 1920s as Paramount and Gennett

The early part of the 1930s was dominated by one major event: the collapse of American financial institutions that led to what is known as the 'Great Depression'. The disaster was underway as the decade began, and hit its lowest point in 1932. Significantly, in the final quarter of that year, there was not a single blues recording session anywhere in

Above
Labourers gamble their cotton money in a juke joint, a place where blues musicians could often find work.

had found it impossible to survive the change in economic conditions; total record sales in 1932 were about six per cent of what they had been in 1920. But the void was quickly filled by Victor's new Bluebird imprint; the revived American Record Corporation (ARC), which by 1934 had consolidated the Vocalion, OKeh and Columbia catalogues; and the brand new Decca label. The vast majority of great blues records would appear on those labels for the remainder of the decade.

Geographically, Chicago became a primary location for blues recording by all three labels. Mississippi artists tended to record there, while Piedmont-area performers were more likely to record in New York; in some cases artists would record in both places. In terms of public performance, much of the country blues was played on street corners or at private functions such as parties, fish fries and picnics; this work was generally done for tips and was described as 'streets and functions'. The pianists tended to work indoors, playing in brothels, barrelhouses, taverns and clubs, and while there would be a kitty jar for tips, they were more likely to be hired. By the end of the decade, brothels and barrel-houses were a less frequent destination and for all blues players of reputation, the tavern and nightclub became more a source of work.

Popular Melody

Kokomo Arnold – 'Milk Cow Blues' (1934)
Agrarian themes were popular among country bluesmen and this track was no exception. Backed by a chunky, slide-guitar sound, Arnold's vocals gradually become more heartrending as the song progresses and the blues take a firmer hold of the unfortunate singer.

The Rise Of Boogie-Woogie

There were new trends in the music of the 1930s. Boogie-woogie, which was heard in the 1920s, developed into a national phenomenon in the 1930s. Its great exponents, such as Albert Ammons (1907–49), Pete Johnson (1904–67) and Meade 'Lux' Lewis (1905–64), would become stars of radio and movies. The style also spread into the jazz market, where it was embraced by big band leaders such as Tommy Dorsey (1905–56), Earl Hines (1903–83) and Count Basie (1904–84). Originally a piano music, it proved easily adaptable to other instruments, especially the guitar.

Most blues artists were recorded with a fairly minimal accompaniment. There were many solo performances and rarely would a recording session involve more than guitar, harmonica, piano and bass. But with the migration to Chicago by so many artists, changes began to occur. Tampa Red (1904–81) was a catalyst for new ideas among Chicago musicians and among those in his circle were Big Bill Broonzy (1893–58), Memphis Minnie (1897–1973), John Lee 'Sonny Boy' Williamson (1914–48) and 'Big Maceo' Merriweather (1905–53). Washboard Sam (1910–66) was the pioneer of blues percussion, but when artists such as Minnie and Broonzy used drums for some of their 1937 recordings, new vistas began to open. Some would be slow to adopt this new sound, but those who did explore it were able to move towards new audiences, such as those attracted to the big-band swing craze that was sweeping America.

The Blues Arrives At Carnegie Hall

In December 1938, record producer John Hammond organized a concert at Carnegie Hall in New York entitled 'From Spirituals To Swing, An Evening Of American Negro Music'. It was dedicated to the memory of Bessie Smith (1894–1937) and was sponsored by a CP magazine, *New Masses*. The concert was a huge success, with almost 3000 people in attendance. While there were jazz and gospel performers featured – including Sister Rosetta Tharpe (1915–73) – the blues was well represented by Sonny Terry (1911–86), Broonzy (a replacement for Robert Johnson, 1911–38), Joe Turner (1911–85) and boogie-woogie piano stars Ammons, Lewis and Johnson. The event generated universal praise in the press and made stars out of most of its participants. It was the first time that any of them had appeared at Carnegie Hall, or before a mostly white audience.

In the aftermath of the concert, a new nightclub called Café Society opened in New York's Greenwich Village, catering to integrated audiences and performances of black jazz, blues and gospel music. Most of the concert's performers appeared there at one time or another. Another 'Spirituals To Swing' concert was held a year later and featured Broonzy, Terry and Ida Cox (1896–1967) as the blues performers. As a result of these concerts, jazz and blues became closely linked, as they had been before, in the jazz accompaniment provided to the vaudeville blues of the 1920s, and would be again.

The Blues Becomes More Citified

By 1939, the big swing bands were at the forefront of American show business. Well-established stars such as Basie and Duke Ellington (1899–1974) had used the blues as a basis for much of what they performed; they were now joined by orchestras led by Erskine Hawkins and Buddy Johnson, who continued that tradition. In the early years of the next decade, Lionel Hampton (1908–2002) and Cootie Williams also led large orchestras following the same trail.

Despite the fact that great country blues would continue to be performed and recorded, it was clear that the momentum in blues music was moving in the direction of a more urban sound. The changes begun in blues in the late 1930s would come to fruition in the next decade; in time, some blues influence would play a part in most styles of American music, including gospel and country.

Far Left
Meade 'Lux' Lewis was among the main exponents of the burgeoning boogie-woogie piano style.

www

Skip James
Devil Got My Woman

musicfirebox.com /Devil

Left
New York's Carnegie Hall – the venue for John Hammond's seminal Spirituals To Swing concert, featuring blues, gospel and jazz music.

Popular Melody

Sonny Boy Williamson – 'Good Morning Little School Girl' (1937)
This song became Williamson's first hit. With original lyrics set to a traditional tune, the track clearly demonstrates Sonny Boy's virtuoso harp playing, as well as the speech impediment that would become a constant source of frustration throughout his career.

Albert Ammons

Right

Albert Ammons (right) with Pete Johnson – two of the great boogie-woogie masters.

Smith, Jimmy Blythe, Cripple Clarence Lofton, Hersal Thomas and Ammons' close friend Meade 'Lux' Lewis. Ammons was the youngest of these men and he learned from all of them. He also drew inspiration from stride-piano great Fats Waller, a major star in black entertainment circles. Lewis and Smith had recorded boogie in the 1920s, and among blues pianists boogie-woogie, with its eight-beats-to-the-bar pattern in the left hand, became an adjunct to the basic style.

Ammons' Big Break

Ammons worked at jobs outside music, led his own swing combos and played with other bandleaders until his big break: a residency at the Club DeLisa, the most important nightspot on Chicago's South Side. This engagement, which began in 1935, led to his discovery by John Hammond and his first recordings, for Decca, in February 1936.

In 1938, Ammons was invited to appear in New York for Hammond's Spirituals To Swing concert at Carnegie Hall. He served as accompanist to Sister Rosetta Tharpe and Big Bill Broonzy, and had his own feature number, 'Boogie Woogie'. He was also teamed with Lewis and Kansas City pianist Pete Johnson for two selections, 'Jumpin' Blues' and 'Cavalcade Of Boogie'. The audience response, which can be heard on the Vanguard recording of the event, was a clear indicator that boogie-woogie had arrived. The occasion also served as a launch-pad for this trio of pianists.

'...I listened to Albert Ammons this morning and it was everything. It was sex, it was life, it was truth. It was marvellous.'

Jools Holland

Albert Clifton Ammons was born in Chicago, Illinois in March 1907. As a young man he learned from Jimmy Yancey, who cast a long shadow over Chicago blues pianists through his work at rent parties, social functions and after-hours jobs. Ammons came to know other pianists and the blues specialists gathered together in Chicago to create a coterie, echoing what was happening with the stride pianists in Harlem. Among the Chicago group, in addition to Yancey, were Clarence 'Pine Top'

Key Track

'Boogie Woogie Stomp' (1939)

This is one of the most powerful boogie-woogie tracks of all time. The rolling boogie in the left hand provides a strong base for the inventive, intricate fingerwork in the right, while the use of tremolo octaves builds into a rousing climax.

The Boogie-Woogie Trio

Ammons, Johnson and Lewis were linked for several years; they appeared in duo or trio settings, occasionally with the addition of vocalist Joe Turner, and recorded for Vocalion, Blue Note and Victor. They toured the US, using Café Society in New York as a base, and also appeared in movies and on radio broadcasts. In the autumn of 1941, Ammons and Johnson had two half-hour radio shows per week on WABC in New York.

The Rhythm Kings

In 1944, during his final extended New York engagement, Albert Ammons recorded two sessions for the Commodore label. One was a solo date, while the other involved an all-star aggregation billed as Albert Ammons & his Rhythm Kings – the same name that Ammons had used on his first recording session. When he returned to Chicago the following year, he signed with the brand-new Mercury

label and began a new series of Rhythm Kings recordings. Until this time, the thematic material used in boogie-woogie was usually the blues or simple, riff-based melodies; Ammons, however, began to adapt his thundering left-hand patterns to pop songs. It is here that we get fresh treatments of standards such as 'Deep In The Heart Of Texas', 'Roses Of Picardy' and 'Swanee River' (the latter was used by Fats Domino as the basis of his 'Swanee River Hop'). Ammons made it clear that, in his hands, a boogie-woogie approach could be applied to any musical source.

Ammons made his final Mercury session just before the start of the second American Federation of Musicians recording ban in January 1948. No doubt the future would have held much for this giant of piano blues but, shortly after appearing at the Inaugural Ball for President Truman, he contracted a mysterious disease – later diagnosed as congestive heart failure – which eventually led to his death in December 1949.

Classic Recordings

Albert Ammons & his Rhythm Kings (1936)
'Boogie Woogie Stomp'

Albert Ammons, Pete Johnson & Meade 'Lux' Lewis (1938)
'Cavalcade Of Boogie'

Albert Ammons (1939)
*'Bass Goin' Crazy',
'Suitcase Blues', 'Boogie Woogie Stomp'*

Albert Ammons & his Rhythm Kings (1946)
'Swanee River Boogie'

Above

Albert Ammons with his band in the Club DeLisa, Chicago in 1936.

Big Bill Broonzy

The parents of William Lee Conley Broonzy were born into slavery. He was born in June 1893 in Scott, Mississippi, one of 17 children. Raised on a farm in Arkansas, Broonzy's first musical instrument was a homemade violin, which he played at church and social functions. In the early teens he was an itinerant preacher, while also working as a country fiddler. He served in the US Army from 1918–19, and shortly after his discharge moved to Chicago. At first he worked as a baggage handler, performing music on a casual basis; it was in Chicago that he first learned to play the guitar.

'As a warm, entertaining blues singer, he had no equal.'
Sam Charters

The Early Recordings

Broonzy worked with Papa Charlie Jackson in 1924 and soon became an accompanist

Right
Blues and folk singer Big Bill Broonzy, during his 1956 tour of the UK.

Key Track

'Just A Dream' (1939)
More than any other artist from the era, Broonzy was not only a great performer but a great songwriter too. 'Just A Dream' contains the memorable stanza: 'I dreamed I was in the White House, sitting in the President's chair/I dreamed he shake my hand ...'. The song became a blues standard covered by dozens of artists.

in demand. He made his recording debut for Paramount in 1927 and by 1930 was recording for Gennett/Champion and Perfect/Banner under a variety of pseudonyms, such as Sammy Sampson and Big Bill Johnson. In 1931, he recorded for Paramount and the resulting tracks were issued by 'Big Bill Broomsley'. By this time, Big Bill Broonzy was a professional entertainer.

Broonzy worked theatres and taverns in Chicago and northern Indiana during this period and toured in a show with Memphis Minnie. Broonzy did not record during 1933 and when he resumed in 1934, for ARC and Bluebird, the records were issued simply as Big Bill. This began a period of prolific recording activity for Broonzy. From 1936, he recorded exclusively for ARC (later Columbia), an arrangement that lasted until the end of 1947. By 1937, performance opportunities had slowed and Broonzy was living on his Arkansas farm, commuting to Chicago three or four times a year to make records.

Spirituals To Swing

In 1938 Broonzy was part of the cast for the John Hammond production 'Spirituals To Swing', a concert held at Carnegie Hall in New York City. He made the most of the opportunity and renewed his career as an entertainer, shortly afterwards appearing at major clubs in New York as well as Chicago. He appeared in the movie *Swingin' The Dream* in 1939, toured with Lil Green during 1941–42 and had theatre dates in New York and Los Angeles in the early 1940s. He released records on a regular basis and by the end of his career he had written and recorded hundreds of songs.

European Tours

For some time, Broonzy's record dates had alternated between the spare accompaniment of piano and bass, and larger ensembles often featuring two horns. As time wore on, the country aspects of his recording sessions were given scant attention. When he signed with Mercury in 1949, his recording began to take on the flavour of the emerging R&B sound. While he continued to record he was, for a time, employed as a janitor at Iowa State University, but things changed markedly when he made

his first overseas tour. He toured England, France and Germany as a solo artist during September and October 1951; he made recordings in each country and proved to be extremely popular.

Another tour in early 1952 came immediately after his final sessions for Mercury. From this point forward, Broonzy would revert to his country blues origins and record prolifically for a variety of European labels. In 1955 his autobiography, *Big Bill Blues*, was published. Further European appearances came during 1955–57 but after the shows Big Bill Broonzy was diagnosed with cancer, from which he died in August 1958 in Chicago.

Classic Recordings

Big Bill (1935)
'Keep Your Hands Off Of Her'

1937
'Louise, Louise Blues'

1939
'Just A Dream (On My Mind)'

1941
'Key To The Highway', 'Keep Your Hand On Your Heart', 'All By Myself'

Big Bill Broonzy (1951)
'Get Back', 'Tomorrow'

Above Left
'Plough Hand Blues', a Big Bill Broonzy track recorded for Melodisc under the pseudonym Chicago Bill.

Big Bill Blues

WILLIAM BROONZY'S STORY

as told to

YANNICK BRUYNOGHE

P.H.O.

with 9 pages of half-tone illustrations and four drawings by
PAUL OLIVER

THE JAZZ BOOK CLUB
by arrangement with
CASSELL & COMPANY LIMITED

Left
Big Bill Blues – Broonzy's autobiography, published in 1955.

Robert Johnson

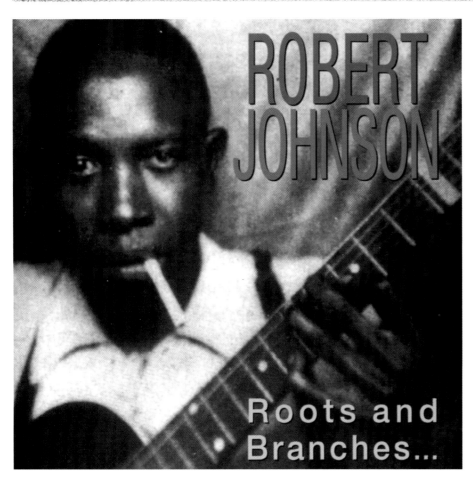

'Amongst all of his peers I felt he was the one that was talking from his soul without really compromising for anybody.' *Eric Clapton*

Key Track

'Hellhound On My Trail' (1937)

This is a prime example of Johnson's work. His anguished vocals express dark, sinister lyrics that confirm contemporary society's view of the blues as 'the devil's music'. With Johnson's exquisite slide-guitar work, backed by his own rhythmic accompaniment on the lower strings, it is a true blues masterpiece.

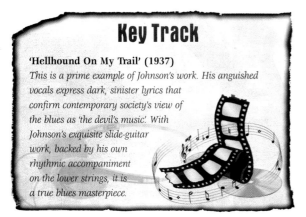

While blues music has produced dozens of great, innovative musicians, vocalists and songwriters, the continuing influence of Robert Johnson over the years has shown that no other performer has succeeded in combining all the elements in quite the exceptional way that he did.

He was born Robert Leroy Johnson in May 1911 in Hazelhurst, Mississippi to Julia Dodds and Noah Johnson. Julia Dodds was the wife of Charles Dodds Jr., a farmer forced to leave Mississippi a few years prior to Robert's birth. Julia had taken up with Johnson in the absence of Charles, who settled in Memphis and adopted the name C.D. Spencer.

Johnson Meets Willie Brown

Julia remarried in 1916, to Willie Willis. Robert lived with them in Robinsonville, Mississippi and was raised as Robert Spencer. It wasn't until his early teens that he was informed about his real father and began to call himself Robert Johnson. Already a keen harmonica player, Johnson began to take an interest in the guitar at this time; he built a rack for his harmonica and was soon picking out accompaniments on the guitar to his harp and voice. He came under the tutelage of Willie Brown, then living in Robinsonville, and Charley Patton, a frequent performer at the area juke joints.

Johnson married Virginia Travis in Penton, Mississippi in February 1929. The couple moved in with Robert's half-sister on a plantation in the Robinsonville area. Robert worked as sharecropper, while continuing his interest in music, and Virginia became pregnant. Who knows which way his life may have turned at this time had his wife not died in childbirth in April 1930.

Music As A Full-Time Occupation

Within weeks of this tragedy, Son House moved to Robinsonville to work with Willie Brown prior to his recording debut for Paramount in late May 1930. During this brief time, Robert became intensely interested in Son House and his music, although the older man regarded Robert as little more than a beginner. Before the end of 1930, Robert Johnson decided to devote himself completely to music, and headed back to Hazelhurst.

Robert met Ike Zinnerman, a bluesman who became his next mentor. The two men worked the area around

Hazelhurst, occasionally encountering artists such as Johnny Temple or Tommy Johnson, and Robert began to blossom. He was working street corners, juke houses, lumber camps – wherever he could make money. In time he returned to the Mississippi Delta area. On a trip back to Robinsonville he encountered Willie Brown and Son House, who were astonished at how well he could play – and so was born the delicious blues legend of how Johnson sold his soul to the devil in return for his guitar-playing abilities. Johnson soon settled in Helena, Arkansas, which remained his main base of operations for the rest of his life.

Rambling Man

By 1934 Robert Johnson had become a constant traveller. His reputation spread and he had a large following throughout Mississippi and Tennessee. He relied on women to care for him in his constant travels, but he longed to make records. His quest led him to H.C. Speir

in Jackson, Mississippi. Speir was a talent scout for ARC records and he passed his recommendation up the line. A recording session was arranged in San Antonio, Texas in November 1936 and Johnson recorded 16 titles in the space of a week. The following June in Dallas, Texas he recorded 13 more.

These 29 songs are the Johnson legacy. 'Terraplane Blues'/'Kindhearted Woman Blues', the first record to be released, was the bestselling track but was still only a modest success. The first LP of this material, *King Of The Delta Blues Singers*, was issued by Columbia in 1961 and inspired a whole new generation of blues musicians. When the CD box-set version, *The Complete Recordings*, was released in 1990, the worldwide public was finally ready for Johnson's genius and it became an enormous hit.

Robert Johnson died of pneumonia in August 1938, following an incident in which he was poisoned at a juke joint near Greenwood, Mississippi.

Far Left
Blues guitar legend Robert Johnson.

Below
Robinsonville, where Johnson grew up.

Leadbelly

Huddie Ledbetter was born in January 1888 in Mooringsport, Louisiana. He was exposed to music from an early age and began playing guitar before he was in his teens. The music he performed was composed of shouts, hollers and Native American songs, as well as ballads, religious songs and dance tunes from a variety of traditions. He became a popular entertainer at functions in his community, which was almost entirely black. By 1901 he had left home and he spent time in the red-light district of Shreveport. It was here that he first encountered early blues songs such as 'The Dirty Dozens'. By the time he was 15, he had his own guitar and his own pistol – both gifts from his father.

In 1910 he was playing in the Deep Ellum area of Dallas and it was probably in 1912 that he met Blind Lemon Jefferson, the Dallas street singer. This is also about the time Huddie acquired his 12-string guitar. Ledbetter and Jefferson worked together over the next three years and Ledbetter absorbed much from the younger man, including his slide guitar technique.

Leadbelly Serves Time

In December 1917, Ledbetter killed his cousin's husband, for which he was convicted and received a sentence of seven to 30 years in jail. He served his time at the Central State Prison Farm, commonly known as Sugarland, near Houston, Texas. During his time in prison, Huddie picked up the nickname 'Leadbelly'. He was frequently called upon to entertain Governor Pat Neff during his visits to Sugarland. On one

Key Track

'The Red Cross Store Blues' (1940)
Leadbelly's powerful vocals strike the listener almost immediately on this track, cutting into the unusually brief guitar introduction. The song features his distinctive use of the bassline throughout, as well as a finger-defying, many-layered guitar break.

'Leadbelly was a man who decided he was going to be a champion in life. Everything he did, he did it with his whole personality: sing, dance, fight, work.'

Alan Lomax

occasion in 1924, Leadbelly created an impromptu blues, which – legend has it – so impressed Neff that he promised to pardon him. He was set free in January 1925, but after his release he continued to exhibit violent behaviour. In January 1930, in Mooringsport, he knifed a white man and was sentenced to six to 10 years' hard labour at Angola State Penitentiary.

Lomaxes To The Rescue

As luck would have it, folklorists John and Alan Lomax visited Angola in July of 1933 as part of John's quest to document American folk songs and ballads using portable disc-recording equipment. Leadbelly recorded for them at Angola; among the songs were 'Ella Speed', 'Frankie And Albert' and a gentle waltz called 'Goodnight Irene'. When it became known that John Lomax was returning to Angola in July 1934, Leadbelly saw an opportunity. As his petition for release was being ignored, he recorded his song 'Governor O.K. Allen'. Lomax brought it to the governor's office and Leadbelly was released in August 1934.

At the end of the year, Lomax arranged for Leadbelly to perform at a dinner given by the Modern Language Association in Philadelphia. Within days, the two visited New York and were written up in the *New York Herald Tribune*. This led to Leadbelly's first commercial recording sessions (for ARC) in early 1935. He also continued to record for John – and later John's son Alan – Lomax for the Library of Congress.

An Acrimonious Split

Financial disagreements caused Leadbelly to split from John Lomax and instead reach an arrangement with Mary Elizabeth Barnicle, a professor who introduced Leadbelly to the liberal and radical community that provided much of his growing audience. He made no commercial recordings from 1936–38 and his last association with John Lomax came when *Negro Folk Songs As Sung By Leadbelly* was published in November 1936. The book received favourable reviews and Leadbelly was profiled in *Life* magazine, after which he appeared on a radio series and began to write new songs.

He was arrested again for felonious assault in 1939. Alan Lomax, trying to raise money for his defence, contacted Musicraft Records to arrange a recording session. The songs Leadbelly recorded were issued on an album titled *Negro Sinful Songs*. He was convicted and served eight months. In 1940 Leadbelly recorded for RCA Victor and by the summer of 1941 he had begun a lengthy association with Moses Asch. With the exception of some 1944 recordings for Capitol, the remainder of his recordings were released on Asch/Stinson/Folkways. He continued to be a popular attraction on the folk circuit until his death in 1949.

Classic Recordings

Leadbelly (1935)
'You Don't Know My Mind',
'Shorty George'

Huddie Ledbetter (1939)
'Frankie And Albert',
'The Bourgeois Blues'

Leadbelly & the Golden Gate Quartet (1940)
'Midnight Special'

Huddie Ledbetter (1940)
'Good Morning Blues',
'New York City'

Huddie Ledbetter (1942)
'Take This Hammer', 'Rock Island Line'

Leadbelly & Guitar (1943)
'Goodnight Irene'

Leadbelly (1944)
'Ella Speed'

Left
Alan Lomax, second-generation American musicologist.

Centre
Huddie 'Leadbelly' Ledbetter – murderer, convict and undisputed blues hero.

Far Left
Leadbelly with session pianist Paul Mason Howard playing the dolceola, a type of fretless zither.

A-Z of artists

A left-handed, bottleneck stylist who had 76 sides issued on Decca, Arnold recorded for the last time in 1938. He mainly worked outside music after 1940, although he did play some Chicago dates during the folk music revival of the early 1960s.

Big Maceo
(Piano, vocals, 1905–53)
Major Merriweather was born in Georgia and taught himself to play piano. He moved to Detroit in 1924 and worked at the Ford Motor Company, also playing jobs, mostly as a soloist, before moving to Chicago. There he developed a friendship with Tampa Red and they recorded for Bluebird in 1941. His 'Worried Life Blues' is a blues standard, while 'Chicago Breakdown' is an instrumental blues masterpiece. He suffered a stroke in 1946, following which his career was sharply curtailed.

Willie Brown
(Guitar, vocals, 1900–52)
An associate of Charley Patton, Brown was a part of the Mississippi blues scene in the early 1920s. While he started out playing with Patton and Tommy Johnson, he teamed

up with Son House in 1926 and accompanied his Paramount session in May 1930, also cutting four songs of his own. Brown played with Robert Johnson frequently in the years prior to Johnson's death. He recorded for the Library of Congress in 1941 but then left the music business.

Above
Pianist Big Maceo, whose 'Worried Life Blues' became a blues standard.

Kokomo Arnold
(Guitar, vocals, 1901–68)
Born and raised in Georgia, James Arnold was taught to play guitar by his cousin. He moved to Buffalo, New York in his late teens and to Chicago in 1929. He worked outside music, making bootleg whiskey, but also played occasional jobs. He first recorded for Victor in 1930 as Gitfiddle Jim and was signed to Decca in September 1934, scoring an instant hit with 'Milk Cow Blues'/'Old Original Kokomo Blues'. The former was a song covered by artists as diverse as Bob Wills, Elvis Presley and George Strait, while the flip side – written about a brand of coffee – provided Arnold with a lifelong nickname.

Right
Sleepy John Estes backstage at London's Royal Albert Hall, 1966.

Sleepy John Estes
(Guitar, vocals, 1899–1977)
John Adams Estes was born in Ripley, Tennessee. He teamed up with mandolinist Yank Rachell to work the area from 1919 until the late 1920s.

His first recordings were made for Victor in 1929 and included his celebrated 'Divin' Duck Blues'. He left Brownsville for Chicago in 1931.

With harmonica player Hammie Nixon, Estes worked medicine shows, fish fries and hobo camps, touring much of the country in the late 1930s. He recorded six sides for Champion in 1935, including 'Drop Down Mama', and he later recorded for Decca from 1937–40. After two sessions for Bluebird in 1941 he returned to Brownsville and left the music scene, with the exception of two recording sessions for Sun in 1952. He had completely lost his sight by 1950. 'Rediscovered' in 1962, he recorded for several labels and began an extensive comeback, which included at least one album of electric blues with younger musicians. He toured the US, Europe and Japan steadily until his death.

Blind Boy Fuller
(Guitar, vocals, 1908–41)
Fuller was born Fulton Allen in Wadesboro, North Carolina and was one of 10 children. He learned to play guitar as a teenager and by the mid-1920s was working for tips around Rockingham, North Carolina. He had lost his sight by 1928. He teamed up with artists such as Gary Davis, Bull City Red and Sonny Terry and worked the area around Durham, North Carolina in the mid-1930s.

He first recorded for ARC in 1935 and, with the exception of two sessions for Decca in 1937, recorded for ARC/Vocalion/OKeh until June 1940. He cut well over 100 sides during that time. Fuller was known for the wide variety of music he played, including pop songs, religious material, ragtime and blues, and because of that range he is considered a unique figure in the pantheon of Carolina blues stylists. He underwent kidney surgery in 1940 and suffered blood poisoning, which ultimately killed him.

Son House
(Guitar, vocals, 1902–88)
The son of a musician, Eddie James House Jr. was born in Riverton, Mississippi. House was preaching sermons by his mid-teens and travelled widely in the 1920s. He did not learn guitar until the age of 25, but soon thereafter was torn between his faith and his love of the blues. After killing a man in a Lyon juke joint and serving two years in jail, House encountered Charley Patton, whose connections at Paramount Records landed him a recording session in 1930.

The intensity and passion of House on songs such as the two-part 'Preachin' The Blues' have rarely been approached in the blues field. However, the records sold poorly and House worked functions in the Delta, often in the company of Willie Brown, for much of the 1930s. He recorded for the Library of Congress in 1941–42, before leaving music in 1943 and moving to Rochester, New York. Rediscovered in 1964, he recorded for a number of labels and toured widely for the rest of the decade.

Below
Son House, whose role in the development of blues in the genre's early days was significant.

'Someone who once heard Caruso sing said that he was so moved that his heart shook. That's the way I felt the first time I heard Son House.'
Martin Scorsese

Skip James
(Vocals, guitar, 1902–69)

Born in Bentonia, Mississippi and raised on a nearby plantation, Nehemiah 'Skip' James played the guitar professionally from a young age and also taught himself to play the piano. His distinctive E-minor guitar tuning, three-finger picking technique and melancholy, high-pitched vocals gave him a unique sound, and his recording session for Paramount in 1931 resulted in some of the most affecting and haunting country blues ever recorded. Songs such as 'Devil Got My Woman', 'I'm So Glad' and '22-20 Blues' still stand out as masterpieces of their genre.

In the 1930s James drifted away from the music scene to concentrate on a career in the church, before being 'rediscovered' in the 1960s, along with Son House and various other blues artists. He performed at the 1964 Newport Folk Festival and recorded a handful of albums for Takoma, Melodeon and Vanguard, while his 'I'm So Glad' was covered by the British blues-rock band Cream. Skip James' revived career was unfortunately cut short by his death from cancer in 1969.

Below

Skip James, whose haunting vocals evoked the desolation of the Mississippi Delta.

Pete Johnson
(Piano, 1904–67)

Born in Kansas City, Missouri, Kermit Holden Johnson teamed up with Joe Turner at the Sunset Café in the early 1930s and went to New York for the Spirituals To Swing concert in 1938. He recorded with Turner for Vocalion (the famous 'Roll 'Em Pete'), as well as alone and with Albert Ammons and Meade 'Lux' Lewis. Beginning in 1944, he recorded for Brunswick, National, Apollo and Swingtime, and was often featured with Turner. He suffered a heart attack in 1958 and was only sporadically active after that.

Meade 'Lux' Lewis
(Piano, 1905–64)

Born in Chicago and inspired by Jimmy Yancey, Meade Anderson 'Lux' Lewis recorded an early boogie-woogie masterpiece, 'Honky Tonk Train Blues', for Paramount in 1927 (the song was also recorded for Parlophone, 1935 and Victor, 1937). He recorded for Decca in 1936 ('Yancey Special') and Vocalion, Blue Note and Solo Art throughout 1941, almost always as a soloist or with Albert Ammons and Pete Johnson. He recorded for many other labels between 1944–61.

John & Alan Lomax
(Folklorists, John Avery Lomax 1867–1948; Alan Lomax 1915–2002)

John Lomax was born in Goodman, Mississippi and raised near Fort Worth, Texas. Although his initial interest lay in cowboy songs, a pre-teen friendship with a servant named Nat Blythe sparked an interest in black music. With the 1910 publication of *Cowboy Songs And Other Frontier Ballads*, his reputation was established. His work on black music took root with a consultancy to the Library of Congress in 1933.

Alan Lomax was 18 when he joined his father to record musicians and singers in their natural habitat. In July 1933, the Lomaxes arrived at Angola Penitentiary, where they discovered Leadbelly. Alan continued his father's essential fieldwork, most notably by finding Son House and discovering Muddy Waters in 1941. Much of Alan's best field recordings were released commercially on Atlantic Records (*The Songs Of The South*, which contained Fred McDowell's first recordings). His 1993 memoir, *The Land Where The Blues Began*, recounts all of these adventures.

Mississippi Fred McDowell
(Guitar, vocals, 1904–72)

Self-taught as a guitarist, music was only a sideline for McDowell for the first 60 years of his life. He worked in the Memphis area before settling in Como, Mississippi to work as a farmer in 1929; he didn't own a guitar until 1940. Discovered and recorded by Alan Lomax in 1959, McDowell's first recordings were issued on Atlantic and Prestige/International.

A bottleneck specialist, McDowell was recorded in 1964 by Chris Strachwitz for Arhoolie Records. This provided a springboard to prominence for McDowell, who soon moved into regular appearances at festivals and on the folk-music circuit. From that point until 1971, he recorded regularly and appeared in three films, including the documentary *Fred McDowell* (1969). He was championed by younger performers such as the Rolling Stones, who covered McDowell's tune 'You Got To Move' on their 1971 album *Sticky Fingers*.

Memphis Minnie
(Guitar, vocals, 1897–1973)

Lizzie Douglas was born in Algiers, Louisiana but was raised in Walls, Mississippi. She learned banjo and guitar at a young age and ran away to Memphis in 1910 to work the music circuit under the name Kid Douglas. She toured with the Ringling Brothers circus for several seasons prior to 1920 and also worked in jug bands, where she met and married 'Kansas' Joe McCoy.

They made their recording debut as Kansas Joe and Memphis Minnie for Columbia in 1929, and recorded for Victor in 1930 and Vocalion during 1930–34. Minnie moved to Chicago in the early 1930s and divorced McCoy in 1935. She recorded for Decca and Bluebird before returning to Vocalion/OKeh/Columbia from 1935–49. She teamed with her third husband, Ernest 'Little Son Joe' Lawlers, in 1939. Minnie then ran a vaudeville company before leaving the music business in the mid-1950s.

Above
Mississippi Fred McDowell, who was an unknown amateur until the blues revival of the 1960s.

Left
Memphis Minnie, one of the finest female blues guitarists of all time.

Little Brother Montgomery
(Piano, vocals, 1906–85)

Eurreal Wilford Montgomery was born in Louisiana and taught himself piano, dropping out of school to work functions and juke joints. He first recorded for Paramount in 1930 ('Vicksburg Blues'/'No Special Rider') and then for Bluebird and ARC in 1935–36. Often featured with traditional jazz bands in addition to his primary work as a soloist, Montgomery settled in Chicago in 1942 and worked as a sideman for other recording artists. He continued to tour and record throughout the 1960s and 1970s.

Below

Tampa Red and Big Maceo enjoyed a relaxed musical dialogue similar to that of Leroy Carr and Scrapper Blackwell in the 1920s.

TAMPA RED & BIG MACEO

THE GREAT PIANO/GUITAR DUO 1941-1946

HISTORIC *RECORDINGS

BLUES COLLECTION

Jimmy Rushing
(Vocals, 1899–72)

James Andrew Rushing was born in Oklahoma City, Oklahoma into a musical family. He worked in California in the mid-1920s as a pianist and vocalist, joined Walter Page's Blue Devils in Oklahoma City in 1927 and made his recording debut with the band in 1929. He played with the Bennie Moten band in Kansas City from 1929, before joining the first Count Basie band in 1935. He remained with Basie until 1950 and recorded more than 50 songs, including his signature song 'Mister Five By Five'.

Right

Sister Rosetta Tharpe, who recorded blues as well as gospel material.

Roosevelt Sykes
(Piano, vocals, 1906–83)

Born in Elmar, Arkansas and raised in St. Louis, Sykes taught himself piano. He made his recording debut for OKeh in 1928 but also recorded for Paramount (as Dobby Bragg) and Victor (as Willie Kelly) from 1929–33. He settled in Chicago in 1931 and created the blues standards '44 Blues', 'Driving Wheel Blues' and 'Night Time Is The Right Time'. Sykes' powerful, lusty style adapted well to modern trends and he remained a prolific recording artist well into his 70s.

Tampa Red
(Guitar, piano, kazoo, vocals, 1904–81)

Hudson Woodbridge was born in Smithville, Georgia; he changed his surname to Whittaker when he went to Tampa, Florida to live with his maternal grandmother. A self-taught musician, he worked juke joints throughout Florida in the early 1920s, before moving to Chicago in 1925. He made his recording debut as Tampa Red for Paramount in 1928. He then teamed with Georgia Tom Dorsey, later a major gospel songwriter, and recorded extensively for Vocalion until 1932, creating blues standards such as 'It's Tight Like That'.

Red also recorded as a soloist, in a successful duo with pianist Big Maceo Merriweather and in jug-band settings. He recorded for Bluebird in 1934 and remained with Bluebird/RCA Victor until 1953, cutting more than 220 titles including the blues standard 'It Hurts Me Too'. Devastated by the death of Frances, his wife and manager, in the mid-1950s, Tampa Red lost interest in music but did make two solo LPs for Prestige/Bluesville in 1960.

Sister Rosetta Tharpe
(Guitar, vocals, 1915–73)

Born in Arkansas, Rosetta Nubin was the daughter of a missionary. She had learned to play guitar by the age of six and accompanied her mother at church functions. The family moved to Chicago and Tharpe signed with Decca in 1938. Sister Rosetta was essentially a gospel performer, but with Lucky Millinder's Orchestra (1941–43) she recorded blues as well as spirituals. In 1944 she teamed up with blues pianist Sammy Price and made hit records including 'Strange Things Are Happening Every Day'.

Sippie Wallace
(Vocals, 1898–1986)

Beaulah Thomas was raised in Houston, Texas. From an early age she sang in church and worked with her pianist brother Hersal Thomas. She moved to Chicago in 1923 and recorded for OKeh, creating blues standards such as 'Up The Country Blues' and 'I'm A Mighty Tight Woman'. She moved to Detroit in 1929 and joined the church, where she played piano and sang. 'Rediscovered' in 1966, she recorded two albums prior to a 1970 stroke. Her final album, *Sippie* (1983), received a W.C. Handy award and a Grammy nomination.

Washboard Sam
(Washboard, vocals, 1910–66)

Robert Brown was born in Walnut Ridge, Arkansas and was the half-brother of Big Bill Broonzy. He left home to play with street singers in the Memphis area in the mid-1920s.

In 1932 he moved to Chicago and teamed up with Sleepy John Estes and Hammie Nixon. He made his recording debut for Bluebird in 1935 and stayed with Bluebird/RCA until 1949; he recorded more than 150 titles, many of which featured Broonzy on guitar.

Peetie Wheatstraw
(Piano, vocals, 1902–41)

William Bunch was born in Tennessee but raised in Arkansas. He played guitar and piano in his youth, left home in the mid-1920s and settled in East St. Louis, Illinois. He made his recording debut in 1930 for Vocalion as Peetie Wheatstraw. A popular and prolific recording artist for Decca and Vocalion until his death, Wheatstraw was billed as 'The Devil's Son-In-Law'. His recordings often also featured a prominent guitarist such as Kokomo Arnold or Lonnie Johnson. He died in an automobile accident less than a month after his final recording session.

Below

Pianist Peetie Wheatstraw recorded with guitarists such as Kokomo Arnold and Lonnie Johnson.

Josh White
(Guitar, vocals, 1908–69)

Joshua Daniel White was born in Greenville, South Carolina to a preacher father and a mother who sang in church. He worked in tandem with street singers such as Blind Blake and Blind Joe Taggart for much of the 1920s. His recording debut was made for Paramount in 1928 but his work for Banner/ARC beginning in 1932 is considered to be his most important. He recorded sacred music (as 'Joshua White, The Singing Christian') in addition to blues under his own name or as 'Pinewood Tom'. After 1940, he was increasingly involved with folk music, where he was promoted to white audiences.

Big Joe Williams
(Guitar, vocals, 1903–82)

Joe Lee Williams was born in Crawford, Mississippi to tenant farmer parents and by the age of five he was playing a homemade guitar. He left home in 1915 to hobo through the South. Williams worked tent shows and medicine

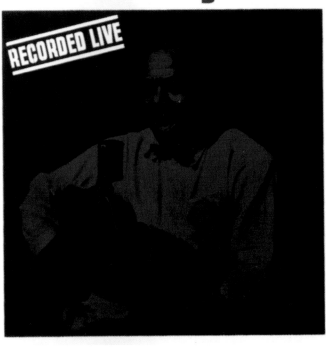

Above

Josh White recorded a variety of blues, gospel and folk music under various pseudonyms.

Right

Big Joe Williams, renowned for his nine-string guitar, was inducted into the W.C. Handy Blues Hall of Fame in 1994.

Far Right

John Lee 'Sonny Boy' Williamson – the first of the great blues harmonica players.

Bukka White
(Guitar, piano, vocals, 1906–77)

Booker T. Washington White was raised on a farm outside Houston, Texas; his father taught him guitar in 1915. Two years later he learned piano and by 1921 he was working barrelhouses and honky tonks in St. Louis. Inspired by a meeting with Charley Patton, he hoboed through the South for much of the 1920s. He made his recording debut for Victor in 1930 as Washington White.

White was athletic and at various times he was a boxer and played baseball for the Birmingham Black Cats. He recorded 'Shake 'Em On Down' for Vocalion in 1937 and the record was a considerable hit. White recorded 12 titles for Vocalion in March 1940, which are among the finest examples of pre-war country blues. He served in the US Navy during the Second World War and retired from music, until being 'rediscovered' in 1963.

shows with a jug band and as a soloist from 1918–24. Often accompanied by Little Brother Montgomery, he played brothels, labour camps and barrelhouses throughout Mississippi and Louisiana during the 1920s.

'Big Joe (Williams) was great to work with and learn from because he was such a character. He was one of the last of the old-time itinerant blues singers.'
Charlie Musselwhite

He made his recording debut for Bluebird in 1935 and one of his early recordings, 'Baby Please Don't Go', became a blues standard. He frequently recorded with Robert Nighthawk and Sonny Boy Williamson on Bluebird sessions in the late 1930s. Although Williams played both six- and 12-string guitars, he is most famous for playing a nine-string instrument of his own construction. He toured constantly and recorded into his late 70s.

Sonny Boy Williamson

(Harmonica, vocals, 1914–48)

John Lee Williamson was born in Jackson, Tennessee. He taught himself harmonica at an early age and left home in his mid-teens to hobo with Yank Rachell and Sleepy John Estes through Tennessee and Arkansas. He settled in Chicago in 1934 and made his recording debut for Bluebird in 1937. His first song, 'Good Morning Little School Girl', became a blues standard.

Williamson was friendly with Big Bill Broonzy and frequently worked Chicago clubs with him. During the years 1939–45 he worked Chicago's Maxwell Street for tips, but in 1947 his record 'Shake The Boogie' became a number-four hit on the Race charts. Williamson was the most gifted and influential harmonica stylist of the pre-war era and was very much in demand to play on recordings by other artists. He was murdered coming home from a job in 1948, after which his name and reputation were taken on by harmonica player Rice Miller – or 'Sonny Boy Williamson II', as he became known.

Jimmy Yancey

(Piano, 1898–1951)

James Edward Yancey was born in Chicago and toured the vaudeville circuit as a dancer in his childhood. He learned piano from his brother Alonzo in 1915 and was soon working rent parties and small clubs around Chicago. He made his recording debut in 1939 for Solo Art and continued to record intermittently, often in the company of his wife, singer Estella Yancey. Yancey was especially adept at slow blues and had a unique ability to develop his own left-hand basslines.

Jazz

Above
During the Great Depression, the American unemployed were forced to queue for their bread.

technique could bring to the music. Louis Armstrong (1901–71) had shown that beautifully wrought high notes, growing out of a carefully plotted emotional logic, could bring stately dramatic power to a simple blues. In the 1930s instinct was inspired by skill, which searched for new hills to climb. Armstrong turned away from the blues and applied himself to the more challenging medium of popular song. The best younger players, previously in awe of Armstrong's technique, promptly mastered it and then extended it. With the high notes achieved, faster and more fluid notes chasing more daring ideas became the norm. In the 1930s the *legato* eighth-note replaced the hammered quarter-note as the centre of jazz phrasing. Roy Eldridge (1911–89) and Harry James (1916–83) showed that one could create a totally original and modern voice within the Armstrong model and take it to new places. Eldridge and Charlie Shavers brought a fresh and ferocious precision to their playing that became the benchmark of virtuosity in the 1940s and formed a technical foundation without which bebop's complexities could not have been mastered.

On piano Art Tatum (1909–56) brought to bear a level of technique so colossal that it would be a generation before others caught up; Teddy Wilson (1912–86) provided a more practical route into the future for most. Tatum and Wilson made their first records in 1933, and each made his right hand the primary focus of his style, playing single-note lines that complemented the rhythmic fluency of swing. But Wilson's gentler, more symmetrical virtuosity made him more accessible and, accordingly, more directly influential.

Jazz entered the 1930s as a clunky, two-cylinder Model A and soared out a stainless-steel zephyr gliding on the wind. Three factors shaped this spectacular transformation: an aggressive quest for virtuosity, the power of mass public acclaim and a conscious spirit of modernity.

'The big bands needed individualists ... we grew up with jazz, felt strongly about our music and each of us developed in his own way, becoming both distinct individuals and soloists. We weren't just another sideman!'
Bud Freeman

The Virtuosos Take Over

Much of the evolution of jazz in the 1930s can be explained in terms of a steeply rising arc of instrumental virtuosity. Jazz players had become conscious during the previous decade of the possibilities that instrumental

The Reign Of The Big Bands

When Benny Goodman (1909–86) combined his clarinet virtuosity with the arranging skills of Fletcher Henderson (1897–1952), big-band jazz became the dominant popular music of the late 1930s. Big bands had occupied a major place in popular music since the end of the First World War but, except those led by Duke Ellington (1899–1974),

Left
*Forward-thinking pianist
Art Tatum stretched the
limits of piano playing
with his innovative style.*

Henderson, Earl Hines (1903–83) and a few others, most were white bands conducted by entertainers who played instruments only incidentally, if at all. Goodman changed

much of that in 1935–36. Perhaps the most fundamental shift he wrought was using jazz to turn popular music towards a true meritocracy. For the first time, the power and the glory began to flow from entertainers towards musicians playing the real thing. By 1939, Goodman had opened the door for a procession of bandleader virtuosos that changed the character of American music. They included Artie Shaw (1910–2004), Count Basie (1904–84), Tommy Dorsey (1905–56), Jimmy Dorsey (1904–57), Harry James, Gene Krupa (1909–73), Benny Carter (1907–2003), Bunny Berigan (1908–42), Chick Webb (1909–39), Woody Herman (1913–87), Teddy Wilson, Glenn Miller (1904–44) and others – all serious, often brilliant players whose names became the great musical brands of the decade.

Left
*Bandleaders such as
Benny Goodman and
Harry James (on
trumpet) were set to
change the character
of American music.*

Popular Melody

Bing Crosby with Joe Sullivan/Mildred Bailey & her Swing Band – 'Someday Sweetheart' (1934)/(1935)

The influence of jazz saturated the best popular singing in the 1930s. No female vocalist personified the sunlit optimism and drive of swing more than Mildred Bailey, while Bing Crosby's loping version of the same song shows that Louis Armstrong's impact was reaching far beyond jazz and deep into mainstream pop singing.

The First Jazz Record Labels

While the big swing units reached mass audiences, a self-proclaimed jazz elite that was distrustful of success held itself apart. Rejecting big bands as commercial distortions of the real thing, they insisted that the only true jazz was improvised small-group music with roots in the style of the late 1920s. Commodore Records became home to this alternative, as well as the first label founded exclusively to record jazz. Formed in 1938 by record store owner Milt Gabler, it concentrated on spirited Dixieland sessions and drew from a stock company that included Eddie Condon (1905–73), Pee Wee Russell (1906–69), Wild Bill Davison, Bud Freeman (1906–91), Bobby Hackett (1915–76), Georg Brunis and Max Kaminsky. A year later Blue Note Records became the country's second jazz-only label, emphasizing traditional black artists such as Sidney Bechet (1897–1959) and Meade 'Lux' Lewis (1905–64). Blue Note remains an important jazz record label to this day.

These labels, with their retro mission, were part of a larger trend – a rising recognition that jazz had a history before 1935. Two music magazines in America (*Down Beat* and *Metronome*) and one in England (*Melody Maker*) became the most influential publications guiding contemporary taste and exploring jazz roots. The first generation of college-educated critics and historians who wrote regularly and articulately about jazz included John Hammond (1910–86), George Simon, George Frazier, Otis Ferguson, Marshall Stearns and Helen Oakley, plus Leonard Feather and Stanley Dance in England and Hughes Panissie in France. *Down Beat* ran a series of articles throughout 1936–38 by Stearns that assembled the first comprehensive (although rough) history of the music. As fans read about jazz history, they grew curious about listening to it as well. At Columbia Records in 1940 George Avakian produced the first series of jazz reissue albums (four 78-rpm records), starting with long out-of-print performances by Armstrong, Henderson, Bessie Smith (1894–1937) and Bix Beiderbecke (1903–31).

Jazz Music Gains Wider Recognition

By 1939 jazz had been performed in Carnegie Hall and was becoming increasingly conscious of itself as a 'serious' art form. Jazz was no longer a simple folk art of self-taught primitives, its (mostly white) promoters argued. Thus, it deserved a place at the table among the higher arts – a claim based partly on the notion that the best jazz

musicians now commanded a level of virtuosity equal to the finest classical players. Mainstream music critics were called upon to recognize jazz on a par with the European masters. At least one classical critic, Winthrop Sargeant of the *New Yorker*, took up the task. His *Jazz, Hot And Hybrid*, published in 1938, was the first serious musicological study of jazz. By the end of the decade, Fred Ramsey and Wilder Hobson had extended jazz's bibliography.

Among the most fundamental changes that made many of these advances possible was an early shift in the rhythm section, which changed the inner clock of jazz and enabled it to swing. By 1932 the banjo and tuba were disappearing, replaced with the more supple sounds of guitar and string bass. Drummers began to untie the rigidity of 1920s two-beat rhythm, giving the pulse a lightness and swiftness that was essential to a swing feel. In the Henderson band, as early as 1932, Walter Johnson began to shift time-keeping from the snare to the elastic swish of the hi-hat cymbal. By the mid-1930s, jazz's rhythm engine was revving out its lumpy two-beat tradition to a driving 4/4 swing, revising the most basic laws of motion in jazz.

The Jazz Age Meets The Machine Age

It is here that we find jazz connecting itself with one of the great controlling sensibilities of the decade, one that touched not only music but also art, architecture, design, cinema and virtually every aspect of the cultural environment. The spirit of the 1930s was dominated by new possibilities of technology and was manifested in notions of speed, structural integration and futuristic, aerodynamic shapes.

Beyond their functions, these technological achievements were also expressions of an empirical technocracy that was irresistibly bright and optimistic. In one brief 18-month period from 1934–36 America saw its first diesel streamliners, the Chrysler Airflow car, the space-age shells that turned steam engines

into projectiles on rails, the DC-3 aircraft, the Golden Gate Bridge and the polished, Brancusian lines of Jean Harlow captured in iconic MGM publicity stills. In the midst of this fixation with stylized modernity and motion, the smooth, rhythmic momentum of swing became an extension of the same spirit of efficiency that found beauty in sleek designs born from the physics of velocity and speed. In jazz terms, swing reached a perfection of form by 1939 with the Count Basie band, particularly in its principal tenor saxophone soloist Lester Young (1909–59) and the drumming of Jo Jones (1911–85), of whom it was said, 'he played like the wind'. It was a fitting allegory for the streamlined 1930s.

If these cultural relationships seem abstract and intangible, they soon assumed more concrete expressions as jazz spilled out into daily life through radio, movies, advertising and the new dance styles created to follow the music. The top white swing bands, in addition to being heard on sustaining broadcasts from hotels, played on their own radio shows sponsored by major advertisers – often cigarette companies eager to reach young audiences. In Hollywood, swing quickly found its way on to the screen. Louis Armstrong appeared in *Pennies From Heaven* (1936), *Artists And Models* (1937) and *Going Places* (1938). Benny Goodman's music mingled with the Art Deco modernism of Paramount's *Big Broadcast of 1937* and Warner Bros.' *Hollywood Hotel* of the same year, and at MGM the link between jazz and the jitterbug dance fad became the basis for Artie Shaw's first film, *Dancing Co-Ed* (1939). In this convergence of modernistic expressions lies perhaps the best explanation of why jazz managed to swiftly become the popular music of America.

Above

Three of the great innovators in jazz during the 1930s – (l–r) Teddy Wilson, Jo Jones and Lester Young – reuniting at a Norman Granz session in 1956.

Popular Melody

Artie Shaw & his Orchestra – 'Carioca' (1939)

Swing not only joined jazz and popular music; it rewrote earlier pop tunes to suit the new standard. Shaw's 'Carioca' takes a pre-swing Latin tune, deconstructs it into a series of riffs and sends it flying like a missile on a joyride of speed and excitement.

Count Basie

'Count is ... just about the best piano player I know for pushing a band and comping for soloists. I mean the way he makes different preparations for each soloist and the way, at the end of one of his solos, he prepares an entrance for the next man.'

Freddie Greene

If swing in its most characteristic form was a hot and hard-driving music, William 'Count' Basie showed that there was a cooler and softer side to the music, an alter ego that even at swift tempos could move with a relaxed, almost serene restraint that subliminally mirrored the streamlined design forms of the Machine Age, in which science and art seemed to mingle.

For Basie this was surely an outcome of chance, not intent. He was born in Red Bank, New Jersey on 21 August 1904 and never finished high school, preferring a life in show business and music. He arrived in New York in 1924 and came to know the

reigning Harlem pianists of the day – James P. Johnson, Willie 'The Lion' Smith and Fats Waller – mastering their dense, two-handed stride style. But for his own style to emerge he needed to escape those powerful influences. Stranded in Kansas City, Basie joined the Blue Devils, led by bassist Walter Page, in 1927.

The Kansas City Scene

The American Southwest was a jazz environment unto itself, alive with regional bands that worked from Chicago to Texas. In the Blue Devils Basie met the core of players who would be with him in Chicago and New York. In 1929 Basie joined the Bennie Moten orchestra. He had recorded nine sessions with Moten by the end of 1932, none of which provide a clue to the pianist that would emerge when he next recorded in 1936.

A lot happened during that four-year blackout. After Moten's sudden death in 1935, Basie took a job at the Reno Club in Kansas City, hiring players from the old Moten unit as well as former Blue Devils. By early 1936 many of the key men were in place, including Walter Page, Jo Jones and Lester Young. Broadcasting nightly from Kansas City, the signals found their way north through the cold night air to Chicago, where they caught the ear of critic John

Key Track

'One O'Clock Jump' (1937)

This Basie theme encapsulates the basic stylistic signatures of the band's music. It is a 12-bar blues; it builds out from the rhythm section. Featuring soloists Evans, Young, Clayton and Basie, the track gathers power through mounting tiers of simple, interlocking riffs. The familiar saxophone theme was first recorded as 'Six Or Seven Times' by the Chocolate Dandies in 1929.

Hammond. Writing in *Down Beat*, he called the band 'far and away the finest in the country' with a rhythm section 'more exciting than any in American orchestral history'.

That summer Hammond drove to Kansas City and was not disappointed. The band was soon on its way to Chicago, where Hammond recorded a small Basie unit featuring Lester Young in the landmark 'Lady Be Good'. Suddenly here was the spacious, minimalist Basie piano style, always implying more notes than were played and allowing the rhythm section to shine through with a transparent clarity.

Basie Rhythm

Rhythm guitarist Freddie Greene joined Jones and Page to complete the unique Basie rhythm team. Page and Greene became the quiet pulse keepers. With a rhythm section so subtle and implicit, the arrangements often held back, offering it space. Many of the band's most characteristic charts would begin softly with a chorus or two of rhythm and Basie's see-through piano, then unfold in steadily expanding layers of riffs (e.g. 'One O'Clock Jump'). The band reached New York in January 1937 and hit its stride in the summer of 1938 during an engagement at the Famous Door. Basie's group recorded more than 60 sides for Decca, then moved to Columbia in 1939 where it remained until after the war. This forms the collective body of work on which the Basie reputation continues to rest.

The Basie Sound Develops

In the early 1950s many of the players who had given the band its voice had left and Basie reformed in 1952 with a new band whose book institutionalized the essence of the Basie sound, but without relying on the cult of the irreplaceable soloist. It became an arrangers' band, in which brilliant writers such as Neal Hefti, Ernie Wilkins, Frank Foster, Thad Jones and Sammy Nestico set the pace. Yet the 'new testament' Basie band would host many fine players and enjoy a steadily growing success from the 1950s through the 1980s. During that time the band recorded extensively for Verve, Roulette and Pablo as Basie watched his fame ascend into legend. The band has continued to tour successfully, under leaders including Thad Jones, Frank Foster, Grover Mitchell and since 2004 Bill Hughes – all alumni of the 1950s Basie bands.

Classic Recordings

Basie Beginnings (1929–32)
'The Count', 'Moten Swing', 'The Blue Room'

America's # 1 Band! (1936–52)
'Lady Be Good', 'Lester Leaps In', 'Taxi War Dance'

The Complete Decca Records (1937–39)
'One O'Clock Jump', 'John's Idea', 'Jumpin' At The Woodside'

Count Basie Live at the Famous Door (1938)
'King Porter Stomp', 'Time Out'

From Spirituals To Swing (1938–39)
'Lady Be Good', 'Swingin' The Blues'

Above Far Left
Accomplished pianist and revolutionary bandleader Count Basie.

Far Left
Kansas City in the 1930s, where Count Basie's band caught the attention of music critic John Hammond.

Left
The Count Basie Band moved to Chicago and then to New York, where they accumulated an extensive following.

Charlie Christian

Far Right
Electric guitar virtuoso Charlie Christian, who found fame with the Benny Goodman quintet.

Charlie Christian was the last great figure to emerge from the jazz scene of the 1930s. He not only brought a perfectly formed approach to his music, but also an entirely new musical platform – the electric guitar. His career in the big time was brief, but Christian was a lighthouse whose beam still illuminates anyone with serious intentions on the instrument.

Charles Henry Christian was born on 29 July 1916 in Dallas, Texas to Clarence and Willie Mae Christian, both professional musicians. When Clarence lost his sight in 1918, he turned to playing the guitar, which he also taught to his three sons. By the time Charlie was 10 his father had died and the family had moved to Oklahoma City, where he began working part-time as a pianist. During his teens his future looked grim: at 15 Christian was a lanky high-school dropout and at 16 he was an unexpected father, trying to get by in the dust bowl of the Great Depression. But beneath the bashful, diffident exterior stirred an emerging savant of whom it was said that he could hear around corners with flawless logic. In Oklahoma City he was able to make his way, landing regular jobs in clubs.

'If Charlie had lived, he would have been real modern.'
Kenny Clarke

Right
Jazz pianist Mary Lou Williams heard Christian play in Oklahoma City and spread the news of his talents.

Christian Joins Benny Goodman

Sometime in the mid-1930s Christian bought a Gibson ES150 electric guitar. No recordings exist by which to chart his development, but there is no question that travelling musicians took notice as Christian worked for $2.50 a night in Oklahoma City. One of the players who heard him while passing through in 1939 was Mary Lou Williams, pianist with the Andy Kirk orchestra.

Meanwhile, Benny Goodman was eager to reinvigorate his band. He was clearly intrigued by the possibilities of the electric guitar and tried out several players on his radio programme, but none was up to the clarinettist's virtuosity. That summer Williams told critic John Hammond about Christian. Hammond flew out to see him, was astonished and shortly afterwards brought him to Los Angeles, where Goodman was playing. In August Christian first sat in with Goodman's quintet. Nothing could have prepared Goodman for what he heard. Christian was immediately hired and for the rest of his short career, the Benny Goodman Sextet and Septet were his professional homes.

He could not have found a more perfect environment. Goodman and vibraphonist Lionel Hampton were brilliant players who recognized one of their own and the Sextet,

Key Track

Benny Goodman Sextet – 'Seven Come Eleven' (1939)

In this track, Christian's consistency as a soloist is augmented by his gift as a composer. The eight-bar bass introduction and the subsequent figure that forms the main theme are the sort of characteristic riffs that Christian would routinely throw off without notice in solos. Here they become the basis of a combo classic still performed today.

with its openness to developing original material, offered an ideal creative mandate. Furthermore, Goodman reached a vast national audience and gave his protégé a generous spotlight. Within weeks, both Christian and the electric guitar were famous. His solos were so inventive in concept and flawless in performance that they seemed to foreclose all future alternatives in one sweeping, inclusive stroke. As 1940 began he stood like a lone colossus on the commanding heights of a dawning, electrified instrumental empire.

Christian's Style

Except for the use of accent chords or recurring triads in his largely set solo on 'Stardust', Christian was a horn-like soloist who played through chords, creating single-note contours that would climb and ebb with a gliding, unbroken flow. He might punctuate with a slicing glissando or unexpectedly riff on a tone pair, i.e. a single note alternating two strings for a variation in timbre.

He was also frighteningly prolific at tossing off concise musical figures, many of which became the basis for the classic pieces originating in the Goodman groups: 'Air Mail Special', 'Seven Come Eleven', 'Shivers', 'A Smooth One' and others.

Away from the Goodman Sextet, Christian's appetite for the jam session was voracious. Several warm-ups were caught during his Columbia sessions, and he took part in a dazzling jam at Carnegie Hall with Count Basie, Lester Young and others in December 1939. He was also recorded playing long solos at Minton's Playhouse in Harlem in 1941, performances that catch him at his most relaxed and unguarded. He died in March 1942 from tuberculosis. Almost immediately, a group of direct disciples emerged: Barney Kessel, Herb Ellis, Remo Palmieri, Irving Ashby and Les Paul. Today, distinguished contemporary players such as Russell Malone and Howard Alden carry on the Christian line.

Classic Recordings

Genius Of The Electric Guitar **(1939–41)**
*'Seven Come Eleven',
'Airmail Special',
'Solo Flight'*

*Solo Flight
Live* **(1939–41)**
*'AC DC Current', 'Soft
Winds', 'Benny's Bugle'*

*First Master Of The
Electric Guitar*
(1939–41)
*'I Got Rhythm', 'Breakfast
Feud', 'Flying Home'*

*The Immortal
Charlie Christian At
Minton's* **(1941)**
*'Swing Yo Bop', 'Up On
Teddy's Hill'*

*Edmond Hall's Celeste
Quartet* **(1941)**
*'Profoundly Blues', 'Jammin'
In Four'*

Roy Eldridge

While Louis Armstrong remained a pre-eminent jazz symbol in the public mind through the 1930s, and inspired many imitators (Taft Jordan, Hot Lips Page, Wingy Manone), younger and better-schooled musicians were coming up who could navigate the trumpet with great agility and dexterity. They would break through the perimeters that Armstrong had established in the 1920s and take the music to new places. In the 1930s no player consolidated those advances or expanded their possibilities more spectacularly than Roy Eldridge, known throughout his career as 'Little Jazz' because of his short stature and high power.

Eldridge's Heroes

Born in Pittsburgh, Pennsylvania on 30 January 1911, David Roy Eldridge came to music with great youthful exuberance, first on drums and then trumpet. In his eagerness to progress, he played by ear at first. It was his older brother Joseph who disciplined his progress and instructed him in matters of theory and the logic of chord sequences, which the young trumpeter acquired by learning the basics of the piano. During his formative years in the late 1920s he avoided the influence of Armstrong, preferring instead to master the speed and precision of saxophonist Coleman Hawkins. Although he began playing professionally around 1927, Eldridge's development as a player is not documented until 1935, when he recorded with Teddy Hill and on three Teddy Wilson-Billie Holiday sessions. Here he emerges as a seasoned player with a big, clean sound and sharp attack.

An Exuberant Playing Style

In 1935 he joined Fletcher Henderson in Chicago and not only showed what he could do, but let loose unimagined possibilities for the trumpet. Starting with Armstrong's sense of dramatic pacing, Eldridge added a wildly exuberant recklessness that threw fast, complex phrasing and penetrating high notes together with meticulous

Key Track

'Heckler's Hop' (1937)

This track is a perfect distillation of the supreme virtuosity jazz enjoyed by the late 1930s – fast, rowdy and brash. Eldridge's first chorus prowls with a poised but cramped rage and then suddenly bursts into a soaring riff, climaxing with an electrifying shriek. While other trumpeters fashioned high notes with lyrical splendour, Eldridge used them as hand grenades.

'When I was growing up, all I wanted to play was swing. Eldridge was my boy. All I ever did was try to play like him but I never quite made it.'
Dizzy Gillespie

precision. Eldridge was a competitive player and thrived on the stimulation of the encounter. The Henderson band gave him his first important foil: tenor saxophonist Chu Berry. On a simple riff piece, 'Jangled Nerves', Berry solos with swift, glancing eighth notes, setting a rapid pace. Then Eldridge bores in with a ferociously suppressed intensity that soon explodes into stabbing high notes, seasoned with a striking dissonance. In the late 1930s it made musicians' heads spin, including that of a young Dizzy Gillespie, who soon showed Eldridge's impact in his first recorded solos.

Faster, Higher!

After leaving Henderson, Eldridge remained in Chicago and formed his own band, which unleashed the full force of his virtuosity. A number of live radio performances from the Three Deuces in Chicago (1937) and the Arcadia in New York (1939) have survived, which offer some of the most breathtaking trumpet solos ever recorded. Interestingly, he performed several Armstrong showpieces, including 'Shine' and 'Mahogany Hall Stomp'. They were homages to the past but also parodies, serving notice that a new generation of elite virtuosos, eager for risk, was now in charge.

Eldridge broke up his band in late 1939, freelanced on record dates, then joined Gene Krupa in 1941, where he gained national prominence (finally topping *Down Beat*'s Readers' Poll in 1942). But he also found his talents restricted to a few showcase numbers. One of them, the beautiful 'Rocking Chair', became one of his most requested pieces. He worked with Artie Shaw in 1944–45 before bebop marginalized him for a period late in the decade. In the 1950s he became part of Norman Granz's Jazz at the Philharmonic tours, recording frequently for Granz's Verve label, and was featured on *The Sound Of Jazz* with Billie Holiday et al. He later recorded with Pablo Records in the 1970s and 1980s, before health problems forced him give up playing. Roy Eldridge died in February 1989.

Classic Recordings

Complete Fletcher Henderson (1927–36)
'Jangled Nerves', 'Shoe Shine Boy', 'Jimtown Blues'

Little Jazz (1935–40)
'Heckler's Hop', 'After You've Gone', 'Rockin' Chair'

Live At The Three Deuces Club (1937)
'After You've Gone', 'Heckler's Hop', 'Chinatown'

At The Arcadia Ballroom (1939)
'Minor Jive', 'Shine', 'Mahogany Hall Stomp'

Original Decca Records (1943–46)
'After You've Gone', 'The Gasser', 'I Surrender Dear'

Roy And Diz (1954)
'I Found A New Baby', 'Limehouse Blues', 'Trumpet Blues'

Far Left
Exuberant trumpeter Roy Eldridge, who battled it out with Louis Armstrong in Fletcher Henderson's band.

Left
Dizzy Gillespie (left) was greatly influenced by the innovative playing of Roy Eldridge.

Benny Goodman

show late that year, and then a record contract with RCA Victor. In 1935 a national tour took him to the Palomar Ballroom in California, where his music finally caught the ear of America and the world.

Benjamin David Goodman was born on 30 May 1909 in Chicago, Illinois and took up the clarinet when he was 10. His progress was so swift that by the age of 13 he had a union card and was soon earning $58 a week playing in the Jules Herbeveaux Orchestra. Goodman's first recordings, made with Ben Pollack's orchestra in December 1926, find him self-assured with a smooth, powerful attack and sparkling sound. Although he was part of the Chicago jazz scene and influenced by its heat, his prodigious technique gave him professional choices that many of his jazz contemporaries lacked. He could rip into raw, hard-driving solos influenced by Johnny Dodds and Frank Teschemacher but also, when the job required, play polite solo interludes with restraint.

'It wasn't just that his own improvisation was marvelous, the spirit, the verve, the vitality, even humor he played with, but the sheer technical mastery. He played that thing like it was a yo-yo.'
Mel Powell

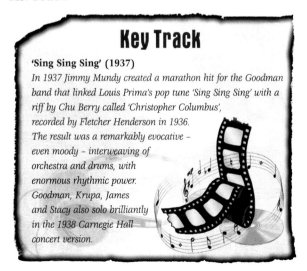

Key Track

'Sing Sing Sing' (1937)
In 1937 Jimmy Mundy created a marathon hit for the Goodman band that linked Louis Prima's pop tune 'Sing Sing Sing' with a riff by Chu Berry called 'Christopher Columbus', recorded by Fletcher Henderson in 1936. The result was a remarkably evocative – even moody – interweaving of orchestra and drums, with enormous rhythmic power. Goodman, Krupa, James and Stacy also solo brilliantly in the 1938 Carnegie Hall concert version.

Benny Goodman was the first of the great bandleader virtuosos of the 1930s to achieve global success. Through a combination of personal connections, nerve, enormous talent and sheer luck, he parlayed a sequence of opportunities in 1934–35 into a payoff that changed American music. After forming his first band in New York in 1934, he won a coveted place on NBC's weekly *Let's Dance* radio

New York Beckons

Moving to New York in 1928, Goodman prospered in radio, theatre and recording work. He was making such a good living by the early 1930s that he had little incentive to fight a growing public indifference to jazz. If Goodman was not committed to 'the cause', however, a young critic and producer named John Hammond was. He approached Goodman in 1933 and provided him with moral support, frequent jazz recording dates and a sense of renewed confidence to pursue the jazz route.

Swing's The Thing

Throughout 1934–35 Benny Goodman became the first white bandleader to bring the swinging spirit of the great black orchestras – Chick Webb, Benny Carter, Duke

Ellington and Fletcher Henderson – to a mass audience. He used the Henderson model, bought many of Henderson's arrangements and sharpened the intonation and attack without suffocating any of the rhythmic energy. To this he added his own brilliant clarinet solos. Suddenly jazz music sounded fresh and new to millions of young dancers, who started to listen. By the time Goodman reached Chicago in December, the whole country was talking about 'swing'.

The arrival of swing awakened a sustained consciousness about jazz and, indirectly, about race. The Goodman tide lifted all boats, black and white, and also became a wedge of direct social progress. More than a decade before Jackie Robinson broke the colour line in baseball, Goodman integrated music by bringing Teddy Wilson (1935), Lionel Hampton (1936) and Charlie Christian (1939) into his small groups. Before the end of the decade Fletcher Henderson joined the full Goodman band on piano, becoming the first black musician ever to play as a regular member of a white orchestra. Although politically liberal, Goodman's instincts were musical, not ideological.

Jazz Goes Legit

In January 1938 Goodman's famous concert in Carnegie Hall seemed to sanctify jazz with a new status and 'legitimacy'. Although Carnegie Hall was the crowning event of Goodman's prime years, other accomplishments would follow: the brilliant sextets and big band of 1939–41 with Charlie Christian and Cootie Williams, innovative new charts by Eddie Sauter and Mel Powell, and the late wartime sextet with Red Norvo. After the Second World War Goodman attempted to embrace bebop and performed a clarinet concerto written for him by Aaron Copeland, before wisely returning to the style in which he was most comfortable. From the 1950s into the 1980s he worked when he liked, in a state of semi-retirement.

As a soloist he never fell into set routines, which led to some inconsistency. But an indifferent performance at one concert was often repaid at the next with inspired solos that seemed to surprise Goodman as much as they did the audience.

Musically active until the end, Benny Goodman died in New York in June 1986. His private papers and recordings are archived at Yale University.

Classic Recordings

The RCA Victor Years **(1935–39)**
'Sing Sing Sing', 'Bugle Call Rag', 'Stompin' At The Savoy'

On The Air **(1937–38)**
'Roll 'Em', 'St. Louis Blues', 'King Porter Stomp'

Famous 1938 Carnegie Hall Jazz Concert **(1938)**
'Sing Sing Sing', 'One O'Clock Jump', 'Avalon'

Genius Of The Electric Guitar by Charlie Christian **(1939–41)**
'Seven Come Eleven', 'Airmail Special', 'Solo Flight'

Plays Fletcher Henderson/Eddie Sauter **(1939–53)**
'Honeysuckle Rose', 'Ramona', 'The Man I Love', 'Superman'

With Benny Goodman: The Complete Recordings 1941–47
'My Old Flame', 'We'll Meet Again, Where Or When'

Together Again **(1963)**
'Seven Come Eleven', 'Four Once More'

Above Far Left
Important bandleader and clarinet virtuoso Benny Goodman (right) jams with Stan Getz and others.

Left
(l–r) Artie Shaw, Benny Goodman, Duke Ellington, Chick Webb (back), George Hall and Raymond Scott.

Lester Young

Right

Tenor saxophone great Lester Young, one of the most influential jazz soloists of the 1930s.

Of all the great solo architects of the 1930s, none personified the smooth, penetrating sweep through space and time more ideally or organically than tenor saxophonist Lester Young. His fluid, unforced phrasing and undulating attack were matched to a cool, satin skin of sound that seemed to dispel all friction by decompressing the emotional density of the prevailing tenors into a piping, almost hollow echo. Young's streamlined contours would have risen to the top in any context, but when joining with the elegant modernity of the Count Basie rhythm section in 1936, Young found his perfect soul-mate; he defined the essence of swing at its most pure and became one of the most influential jazz voices of the decade.

'When Lester plays, he almost seems to be singing; one can almost hear the words.'

Billie Holiday

Above Far Right

Bennie Moten's (seated right) band, shown here in 1929, was where Young met bandleader Count Basie (seated left).

Far Right

Young with his patron and organizer of 'Jazz At The Philharmonic', Norman Granz.

tenor saxophone by 1922. Four years later the Young family relocated to Minneapolis, Minnesota, but Lester grew restless working under his father's hand. When he turned 18 he went out on his own, touring with a variety of regional bands in the upper Midwest. He worked briefly with the Blue Devils in 1930 and with Basie for the first time in the Bennie Moten band in 1934. But Young didn't stay long; he moved through several other groups, then returned to Basie in 1936, just as the bandleader was on the verge of being discovered by John Hammond.

Early Records

Young's career rose swiftly with Basie's, and vice versa. His record debut, made with a small Basie group in October 1936, produced two of the great swing classics of the decade – 'Lady Be Good' and 'Shoe Shine Boy' – and there would be more where that came from. A steady stream of Basie band records poured out, plus many small group sessions, produced by Hammond, that brought Young together with Billie Holiday, Teddy Wilson, Benny Goodman, Charlie Christian and others. The 54 sides made with Holiday between January 1937 and November 1938 carried a particular and persistent fascination – and not merely because the records caught both artists at the peak of their powers. They also seemed to capture a quality of looming melancholy in the relationship of two gentle but

Key Track

'Lester Leaps In' (1939)

Young composed this track and dominates as the soloist in a performance that neatly summarizes the streamlined and aerodynamic unity that jazz had achieved by 1939. Young's highly polished tone seems to float on the soft winds of Basie's rhythmic currents, cutting swiftly through time without any sense of friction or resistance. The simplicity of the theme has made it a jam-session favourite for decades.

A Musical Background

Born in Woodville, Mississippi on 27 August 1909, Lester Willis Young grew up in a musical family that toured and performed together. He experimented with the trumpet, violin and drums as a boy before finally focusing on the

of light-toned players based their style and sound largely on his innovations in the 1930s. Although they continued to revere him, they passed him by to become the stars of the post-war cult of the cool: Al Cohn, Zoot Sims, Alan Eager, Dexter Gordon and above all Stan Getz. Norman Granz became Young's most consistent patron, despite the fact that Young's declining health had an increasingly severe impact on his playing. After the mid-1950s his performances were unquestionably a shadow of their former selves. A final reunion with Billie Holiday in December 1957 on *The Sound Of Jazz*, a CBS Television special, would acquire in the years ahead a special poignancy. Today many feel that they see in the performance the star-crossed character of their brief lives, caught with a touching transparency. Young died on 15 March 1959 in New York.

flawed temperaments, for whom doom due to fragility seemed written on the wind. The music survives in a nimbus of legend.

Young's dry, feathery lyricism and fluid laws of motion immediately set him apart from the flock, as the other musicians recognized a new and original tenor voice. His ideas were oblique and unexpected. He would spread a phrase out over several bars, then suddenly pause over a lingering, out-of-tempo note, or interrupt himself with an impulsive arching swoop. In a broadcast performance of 'I Got Rhythm' from the Southland Café, Young bounces along on a sleek, unbroken F over four continuous bars of rhythmic variations. By the end of the 1930s Young had not only become the first serious alternative to the big-toned, romantic tenor; he also seemed to have opened a door into post-war modernism, where the hot would soon make room for the cool.

Leaving Basie

Young left Basie in 1940, returned briefly in 1944, and was then drafted into the army. During basic training he was caught in possession of marijuana and confined to military prison until December 1945. Although he seemed to recover much of his pre-war form in a series of Jazz At The Philharmonic (JATP) concerts in the spring of 1946, it was soon apparent that Young's sound had taken on a thicker, denser texture. Also, his easy fluency seemed to settle into a series of set signature phrases and figures.

Fans and critics disagree on the merits of Young's later work, but there is little dispute that a younger generation

A-Z of artists

Billy Banks

(Vocals, 1908–67)

A crooner and scat singer, Billy Banks was a protégé of agency impresario Irving Mills. He headlined a handful of legendary records in 1932 by the Rhythmakers – less interesting for his vocals than for the punchy, eccentric work of the all-star band, which included Henry 'Red' Allen, Pee Wee Russell, Fats Waller, Eddie Condon, Pops Foster, Tommy Dorsey and Zutty Singleton. Banks also recorded with the Mills Blues Rhythm band in the 1930s before leaving for Europe in 1952. He later settled in Tokyo, where he ran a club.

Below

Tenor saxophonist Chu Berry (right) with drummer Cozy Cole.

Danny Barker

(Banjo, guitar, educator, 1909–94)

Daniel Moses Barker carried forth the musical traditions of New Orleans, playing with a number of traditional bands in the 1920s and 1930s before marrying Louise Dupont (a.k.a. Blue Lu Barker) in 1930. They recorded several sides together in 1938, including Baker's own song 'Don't You Make Me High', revived in the 1970s by Maria Muldauer. After working with several big bands in the 1930s (including those of Lucky Millinder and Cab Calloway), he was a New Orleans revival activist, leading a youth band that included Wynton Marsalis.

Bunny Berigan

(Trumpet, vocals, 1908–42)

Rowland Bernard Berigan's warm sound and fluent style made him a major figure of the Swing Era. To some extent, his alcohol-related death at 33 has unduly enhanced his legacy, lifting a solid talent to the level of tortured artist-genius. Berigan arrived in New York in 1929 and became a sought-after session player. He played in Benny Goodman's 1935 band, leaving memorable solos on 'King Porter Stomp' and 'Sometimes I'm Happy'.

With Tommy Dorsey in 1937 he scored two more classics – 'Marie' and 'Song Of India'. Berigan assembled his own band and recorded his most famous showpiece, 'I Can't Get Started'. His solo began with a series of reflective breaks and then broke into a majestic high note statement, before falling to a low-register denouement and epilogue. Laid out with strong dramatic pacing, it shows Berigan's debt to Louis Armstrong. In 1939 Berigan dissolved his band, rejoined Dorsey briefly in 1940, and then resumed with his own orchestra.

Chu Berry

(Tenor saxophone, 1908–41)

Inspired by Coleman Hawkins' big sound, Leon 'Chu' Berry honed a more rapid, streamlined tenor attack. He recorded with Benny Carter in 1933 and joined Fletcher Henderson three years later. In 1937 he topped *Down Beat*'s first national poll of leading musicians and joined Cab Calloway's orchestra, where he remained until his death. Berry also participated in numerous small groups. A versatile musician, he was equally at home skating over the beat at fast tempos, surging effortlessly through mid-tempos or playing romantic ballads in the Hawkins tradition.

Cab Calloway
(Bandleader, vocals, entertainer, 1907–94)

Cabell Calloway's orchestra was one of the most successful black bands of the 1930s and by the end of the decade it was home to some of the finest jazz soloists. He arrived in Chicago in the late 1920s and found his niche as a singer, then went to New York, where the band that he fronted replaced Duke Ellington's at the Cotton Club.

He cultivated a jive-talking persona that appealed to a mixed racial audience; in the broad spectrum of American Negro iconography, Calloway represents a key transitional image between nineteenth-century minstrelsy and contemporary hip hop. After 1935 he reflected the trend towards jazz by bringing in a succession of important soloists (Ben Webster, Chu Berry and Dizzy Gillespie), but his vocals remained the focus of the band's sound. From 1939–41 his band was one of the finest in the country, but after the war he gave it up to concentrate on club, theatre and movie work until the end of his life.

Benny Carter
(Alto saxophone, arranger, trumpet, vocals, 1907–2003)

One of the great arrangers and soloists in jazz history, Bennett Lester Carter wrote some of the first big-band music to fully realize the flowing, *legato* ensemble of the coming swing movement. His saxophone ensembles were smooth projections of his solo style. 'Lonesome Nights' and

'The problem of expressing the contributions that Benny Carter has made to popular music is so tremendous it completely fazes me, so extraordinary a musician is he.'
Duke Ellington

'Symphony In Riffs' were so advanced when Carter recorded them in 1933 that they still sounded at home in the late 1930s and early 1940s when Artie Shaw, Tommy Dorsey, Gene Krupa and Cab Calloway recorded their versions.

Carter worked in Europe during 1935–38 and returned to lead a series of excellent bands. He had a rich, poised alto sound that complemented the relaxed elegance of his phrasing, as illustrated in his 1937 versions of 'Crazy Rhythm' with Coleman Hawkins. After settling in California in 1942, Carter prospered in film and worked to integrate musicians in Hollywood. He continued to record and perform at a high level into his 90s.

Doc Cheatham
(Trumpet, vocals, 1905–97)

Adolphus Cheatham played in countless bands and small groups in the 1920s, before settling in the Cab Calloway orchestra in 1931. He remained with Calloway until 1939, after which he resumed work with a variety of bands. He didn't emerge as a soloist until the 1960s, working with George Wein, Benny Goodman and others. His singing style – like the man himself – was polite, courtly and gentle, suited to both cabaret and jazz clubs; he performed regularly in New York throughout the rest of his long life.

Left

Bandleader Cab Calloway, who took over Duke Ellington's slot at the Cotton Club.

Below

Benny Carter, a hugely influential player but a relatively unsung hero of jazz music.

duke ellington ⊚ 66   henry 'red' allen ⊚ 72   coleman hawkins ⊚ 76   tommy dorsey ⊚ 124

Late in 1939, Sy Oliver came over from Jimmie Lunceford as arranger and reinvented the Dorsey band for the 1940s. It became a precision showboat of talent (artists included Frank Sinatra, Jo Stafford, Buddy Rich, Ziggy Elman), which covered everything from hard-swinging originals ('Well Get It') to imaginatively mounted pop tunes ('Without A Song'). In 1953 the Dorsey brothers reunited and combined their books into a single band. Early in 1956 the Dorsey Brothers *Stage Show* introduced Elvis Presley to a national television audience.

Ella Fitzgerald
(Vocals, 1917–96)
Sixteen-year-old Ella Fitzgerald joined Chick Webb's band in 1934 and became its biggest attraction. After Webb's death in 1939 she became titular leader of the orchestra, which continued until 1942; she then worked as a solo artist. After the war Fitzgerald revealed an uncanny talent for bebop scat singing; it drew the attention of Norman Granz, who began adding her to his Jazz At The Philharmonic shows. He became her manager in 1953 and took over her recording career. Under Granz's guidance she rose to become the reigning interpreter of twentieth-century American songs.

Stephane Grappelli
(Violin, piano, 1908–97)
Largely self-taught, Stephane Grappelli's virtuosity came to the attention of the world in 1934 through records with Django Reinhardt and the Quintet of the Hot Club of France. His refined sound was decorative on ballads but could push with an alert and driving attack of formidable power on jazz standards such as 'Tiger Rag', 'Shine' and 'I've Found A New Baby'.

In Paris and London Grappelli recorded with many visiting American players, including violinist Eddie South in 1937. Their repertoire, which ranged from Gershwin to Bach, produced some of the most dazzling and intriguing violin duets ever recorded. The Quintet never appeared in America, although it was heard on several radio broadcasts. Grappelli lived in London during and after the war, but his

Above
Tommy (left) and Jimmy Dorsey (right) with drummer Buddy Rich.

Jimmy Dorsey
(Bandleader, alto saxophone, clarinet, 1904–57)
Thoroughly educated in music as a child, Jimmy Dorsey freelanced in New York in the early 1930s, recording frequently with brother Tommy as the Dorsey Brothers Orchestra. They formed a working band in 1934 but split up in 1935. Jimmy carried on, backing Bing Crosby on radio and recording prolifically for Decca. He came into his own in the 1940s, largely on the popularity of his two vocalists, Bob Eberle and Helen O'Connell. In 1957 he scored an unexpected hit with 'So Rare'.

Tommy Dorsey
(Bandleader, trombone, trumpet, 1905–56)
With the breakup of the Dorsey Brothers Orchestra, Tommy Dorsey quickly hired the Joe Haymes orchestra *en masse* and built a new band to his specifications. For all the talent it would attract, however, it would always be built around the leader's warm trombone sound and flawless perfection on ballads. The Dorsey band of 1935–39 drew its identity from the muscle-loosening swing of drummer Dave Tough, soloists Bud Freeman, Bunny Berigan, Yank Lawson and Johnny Mince, and singers Jack Leonard and Edythe Wright.

Left

The Quintet of the Hot Club of France, with Django Reinhardt (second from left) and Stephane Grappelli (second from right).

John Hammond

(Critic, producer, 1910–86)

John Hammond was the most influential jazz critic, producer and social activist of the politically charged 1930s. A Vanderbilt descendant raised in social prominence and luxury on New York's East Side, Hammond rebelled against his class, producing jazz records and pressing for racial integration. He played a key role in the careers of Fletcher Henderson, Benny Goodman, Billie Holiday, Lionel Hampton, Count Basie and Charlie Christian – bringing them together on occasions – and later Aretha Franklin, Bob Dylan and Bruce Springsteen.

reputation faded. In 1969 George Wein brought him to the Newport Jazz Festival for his American debut. Still at the top of his form, he continued to tour and record for another 28 years.

Bobby Hackett

(Trumpet, cornet, guitar, 1915–76)

After Bobby Hackett was praised in *Down Beat* by Boston critic George Frazier in 1937, he headed to New York and settled into a group of neo-traditional players loosely associated with Eddie Condon. Although a lifelong fan of Louis Armstrong, Hackett's gentle, fluid lyricism made him a more logical descendent of Bix Biederbecke, whom he represented in a historical section of Benny Goodman's 1938 Carnegie Hall concert. Hackett recorded with his own big band in 1939. His association with Condon brought him into an informal stock company of players who recorded for Dixieland-oriented Commodore Records.

He joined Glenn Miller in 1941 and played the famous cornet bridge on 'String Of Pearls'. During the 1940s he divided his time between radio staff work and jazz. Hackett's placid improvisations found a large audience in the 1950s as the featured solo voice on many mood music albums conducted by Jackie Gleason. He also worked prominently with Goodman, singer Tony Bennett and Vic Dickenson in his later years.

Lionel Hampton

(Vibraphone, drums, piano, 1908–2002)

Before jazz became highbrow, musicians were cheered, not censured, for being entertainers; Lionel Hampton embraced that model. The more one did, he believed, the more one made. So Hampton was always doing more. During his early years he worked as a drummer. He began experimenting with the vibraphone around 1930, but few bandleaders wanted its unorthodox sound.

In 1936 Benny Goodman heard Hampton, was impressed and immediately invited him to join Gene Krupa and Teddy Wilson, making the Goodman Trio a quartet. Hampton infused Goodman's groups with enormous inspiration and energy. In 1937 he began a parallel series of remarkable sessions under his own name on Victor that would involve most of the greatest soloists of the period. After leaving Goodman in 1940 Hampton formed his own band, which recorded his definitive version of 'Flying Home' in 1942, featuring tenor saxophonist Illinois Jacquet. He continued leading bands and touring the world well into the 1990s, always a combination of brilliant musician, talent scout and antic showman.

Below

Lionel Hampton playing the vibraphone in Benny Goodman's Quartet.

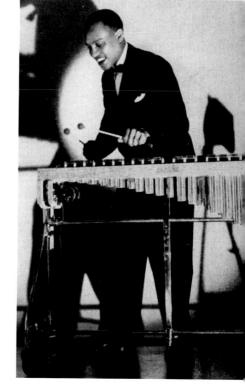

Earl Hines
(Piano, bandleader, 1903–83)

Earl 'Fatha' Hines was the key transitional figure between the early ragtime and stride styles and the essentials of modern piano. He stripped away much of the density of 1920s piano, replacing it with more linear octaves and edgy single-note lines with the right hand – his 'trumpet style' – while softening the rhythmic accompaniment with the left.

Hines established his reputation in Chicago in the late 1920s, recording solos and classics such as 'Weather Bird' and 'West End Blues' with Louis Armstrong. He led the house band at Chicago's Grand Terrace Café from 1928–40. Hines turned it into a first-class orchestra, largely on the basis of arrangements by Jimmy Mundy ('Cavernism', 'Mad House'), whom he discovered and mentored. The band's peak years came on its Victor recordings (1939–42). Hines gave up the band in 1947, toured with Louis Armstrong until 1951 and then fell in to obscurity. In 1964 a New York solo concert returned him to prominence; for the next 19 years he toured and recorded prolifically.

Below

Earl Hines emerged in Louis Armstrong's company, introducing 'trumpet-style' piano.

Johnny Hodges
(Alto and soprano saxophones, 1907–70)

Saxophonist Johnny Hodges was fortunate enough to forge an early relationship with Sidney Bechet; while playing at Club Bechet in New York he won the attention of Duke Ellington, who signed him in 1928. Hodges' sweeping tone and scooping glissandos remained a vital part of Ellington's orchestra for around 40 years, with only a few periods of absence as he experimented with small groups and other ventures. Hodges was admired by many other saxophonists, including Ben Webster and John Coltrane.

Spike Hughes
(Bass, bandleader, critic, 1908–87)

As editor for *Melody Maker* and producer at British Decca, Spike Hughes recorded many dance and novelty sides during 1930–32 but had ambitions in jazz. During a New York visit in 1933 he augmented Benny Carter's band with Coleman Hawkins and recorded 14 of his own arrangements as Spike Hughes & his Negro Orchestra. Notwithstanding Hughes' many excellent solos, John Hammond wrote that he 'could not write music that swung'. At this, Hughes decided to return to journalism and producing, and never recorded again.

Jo Jones
(Drums, 1911–85)

Few players have defined a big band from the drum chair as strongly as Jonathon 'Jo' Jones did with Count Basie. When the first Basie records came out in 1937, their rhythm section was both a revelation and a revolution – and brought jazz drumming into a new, more sleek modernity. A master of the steely hi-hat cymbal, Jones coaxed from it a supple, relaxed whoosh, sliding accents slightly to either side of the beat. It swung with an uncanny crackle and power and became the principle mainspring of his time.

Jones had first worked with Basie in the Blue Devils in 1929. He joined the Basie band in Kansas City and remained during its prime years from 1936–44, during which he also recorded many dates with Teddy Wilson and Billie Holiday. Jones returned to Basie in 1946, by which time new drummers were carrying his innovations into bebop. From the 1950s onwards he freelanced and taught an army of young students, becoming known as 'Papa' Jo Jones in his later years.

Jonah Jones

(Trumpet, vocals, 1909–2000)

By the time Jonah Jones came to prominence on New York's 52nd Street, he had developed a fierce, intense attack that suggested Roy Eldridge without the high notes. He played and recorded with Stuff Smith from 1936–40 and on sessions with Teddy Wilson, Billie Holiday and Lionel Hampton. He worked with Cab Calloway from 1941–52. In 1957 he began recording for Capitol and had several hits, including 'Baubles, Bangles And Beads' and 'On The Street Where You Live', which combined a shuffle rhythm with his muted trumpet.

Gene Krupa

(Drums, 1909–73)

Possibly the most famous jazz drummer, Gene Krupa played in the 'press roll' style of Chicago, where he first recorded in 1927. He was a traditionalist and kept time largely on the snare, with either sticks or brushes, playing two-beat on bass drum. He joined Benny Goodman in 1934 and became a key factor in the band's historic success. Krupa could 'kick' a band in a way that few white drummers had managed before him.

As a soloist, he combined technique, imagination and flash that made him the centre of attention. Much of that technique infused Goodman's trio and quartet pieces. But his *tour de force* would forever be 'Sing Sing Sing', a nine-minute collage of riffs linked by Krupa's rock-solid tom-toms and recurring solo interludes. He left Goodman in 1938 to form his own band, which became a great success in the 1940s with Roy Eldridge and Anita O'Day. Krupa scaled back to a trio in 1951 and worked in that format for the next 20 years.

Jimmie Lunceford

(Bandleader, arranger, 1902–47)

While working as a music teacher in Memphis, Mississippi-born Lunceford formed a band called the Chicksaw Syncopators. They first recorded in 1930 and after four years of touring gained a residency at the Cotton Club and became the Jimmie Lunceford Orchestra. Renowned for its polished stage presence, the band was nevertheless musically tight and trumpeter Sy Oliver's arrangements secured a signature 'Lunceford sound'. Pay disputes split the original line-up in the early 1940s, but Lunceford continued to lead the orchestra until his death.

Wingy Manone

(Trumpet, vocals, 1900–82)

Born in New Orleans, Joseph 'Wingy' Manone's rousing trumpet and gravelly vocals were (as with his fellow Italian-American, Louis Prima) confidently cast from the Armstrong matrix. After scoring a hit with 'Isle Of Capri' in 1935, he became a fixture on New York's 52nd Street before moving to California in 1940 to join Bing Crosby's circle of cronies. His 1930 disc 'Tar Paper Stomp' is the first recorded appearance of the blues riff that would become familiar in 1939 as Glenn Miller's 'In The Mood'.

Irving Mills

(Music publisher, producer, manager, 1884–1985)

Publisher Irving Mills was early to recognize the potential in black music. He formed Mills Music, Inc. with his brother in 1919 and enjoyed a business relationship with Duke Ellington from 1926–39 that brought a procession of Ellington songs into the Mills catalogue. He also formed the Mills Blue Rhythm Band in 1931 and developed it into a fine orchestra before it evolved into the Lucky Millinder band in 1938. Mills Music, Inc. was sold in 1965.

Below
Jimmie Lunceford's band was renowned for its elaborate stage shows.

Above

Hot Lips Page (left) plays with Freddie Moore (back left), Sidney Bechet (right) and Lloyd Phillips (back right) in New York.

Right

Belgian gypsy guitarist Django Reinhardt, who created his own unique playing style.

importance without substantially expanding its time-keeping function. As a component of the unique Count Basie 'all-American' rhythm section from 1936–42, he produced a large, round but never percussive attack, whose ringing tone would remain a Basie hallmark. He also presaged an expanded melodic roll for the bass in 'Pagin' The Devil', made in 1938 with a Basie contingent a year before the arrival of virtuoso bassist Jimmy Blanton.

Django Reinhardt
(Guitar, 1910–53)

One of the reasons that Django Reinhardt dominated conversations about the guitar so completely in the 1930s was his fortunate timing. He arrived on the world jazz scene through the Quintet of the Hot Club of France in 1934 – a year after the death of Eddie Lang and five years before the arrival of Charlie Christian. Belgian by birth, he became a jazz star without ever going to the United States. Reinhardt travelled in a gypsy caravan, yet absorbed American jazz pop and jazz standards, including 'Avalon', 'The Sheik Of Araby' and dozens more.

The Hot Club Quintet had a salonish, continental quality with a tightly packed, chugging rhythm section of two guitars and bass (with no drums). It was an ideal anchor for the improvisations of Reinhardt, whose trajectories had a swift, spun-glass delicacy full of notes

Hot Lips Page
(Trumpet, vocals, 1908–54)

Oran Thaddeus Page surfaced in the Bennie Moten band as a powerful blues player, often using a plunger mute. He was with the as-yet unknown Count Basie in 1936 and might soon have left Kansas City as one of that fabled band of brothers had he not been approached by Joe Glaser. Glaser was Louis Armstrong's personal manager, and he saw in Page's playing and singing another Armstrong; he signed him and took him to New York.

In 1938 Page fronted a band and recorded two sessions for Victor that showcased him as an Armstrong clone. Page's solos were polished, regal and majestic, using many of the spectacular glissandos and dramatic breaks familiar on Armstrong's Decca records. But stardom never came and the band soon broke up. He joined Artie Shaw for five months in 1941–42, reaching his biggest audiences and posting some of his best performances ('There'll Be Some Changes Made'). He freelanced in traditional and small swing groups in the 1940s.

Walter Page
(Tuba, bass, 1900–57)

By the end of the 1930s Walter Page had brought the usually subordinate roll of the bass to a position of critical

quivering with an intense vibrato that was equal parts emotion and ethnic flavouring. After the war he made his only trip to the US, recording with Duke Ellington in 1946.

Luis Russell
(Bandleader, pianist, 1902–63)

Luis Russell first worked in New Orleans, then in Chicago with King Oliver, where he began moving the New Orleans sound towards a big-band format. Between 1929–31 he led one of the best early swing-oriented bands in the country. Its major soloists were J.C. Higginbotham and Henry 'Red' Allen, who also recorded with the band separately under his name in a number of Armstrong-inspired pieces. In 1935 Armstrong himself took over, effectively ending the Russell band as an independent entity.

Pee Wee Russell
(Clarinet, 1906–69)

Great musicians are often judged by the reach of their influence on others, but Charles Ellsworth Russell's clarinet was one of a kind, so personal and eccentric that it offered little to any would-be disciples. He arrived in New York in 1927 from the Midwest, where he had played with Bix Beiderbecke and other Chicago-area musicians. There he built a solid reputation playing a relatively standard hot clarinet with Red Nichols.

By the time he joined Louis Prima on 52nd Street in 1935, however, his tone had taken on a tart growl and his phrasing swung with a lumpy, off-centre quirkiness that seemed to thumb its nose at notions of virtuosity. It gave his playing an 'authentic' quality that appealed to renegade jazz fans in rebellion against the professionalism of swing. From the late 1930s on, he was part of Eddie Condon's stock company of traditionalists. He made his most characteristic records for Commodore from 1938–45.

Artie Shaw
(Clarinet, bandleader, composer, 1910–2004)

If the 1930s comes down to about half a dozen great brand names, Artie Shaw's is surely one of them. After much freelancing in the early 1930s and several years of band-building, Shaw (née Arthur Arshawsky) hit his stride just as Benny Goodman peaked in 1938. But no one ever confused these two unique, clarinet-playing masters. Shaw had a big, broad-shouldered lyricism that could turn diamond-hard in high registers.

His lines were long, bobbing and eloquently fluent. Many clarinettists committed his 'Stardust' solo to memory. When drummer Buddy Rich joined in 1939, the band acquired a supercharged power. But if Shaw loved music and the perquisites of stardom, he disliked the spotlight. He abandoned music in a huff at the end of 1939, returning sporadically between bouts of writing and well-publicized marriages and leading the Gramercy Five in 1953–54. Ultimately, and still in his prime, he disowned the clarinet itself in 1955.

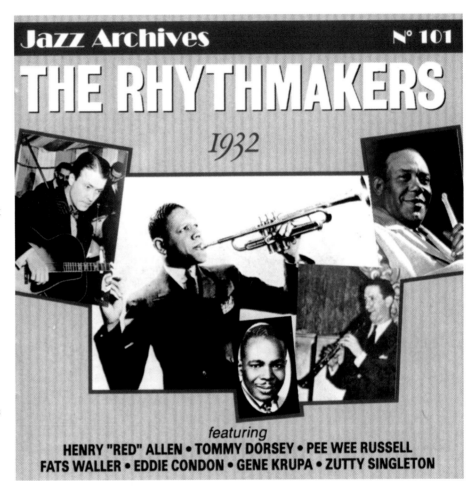

Below

Clarinettist Pee Wee Russell (bottom right) was a member of jazz supergroup the Rhythmakers, who recorded a legendary session in 1932.

Stuff Smith
(Violin, 1909–67)

Inspired by Joe Venuti in the 1920s, Joe Hezekiah Leroy Smith and his sextet (with Jonah Jones) became a sensation on 52nd Street early in 1936. In contrast to the polish of Venuti, Smith turned the violin in a more barrelhouse direction, making it swing with an unremitting swagger. He was also the first to play amplified violin and is remembered for his comic homage to marijuana, 'You'se a Viper'. Norman Granz re-introduced Smith successfully in 1957.

henry 'red' allen ⊙ 72   eddie condon ⊙ 74   count basie ⊙ 112   stephane grappelli ⊙ 124

Willie 'The Lion' Smith
(Piano, 1897–1973)

In the 1920s Willie 'The Lion' Smith was an obscure master of Harlem stride (a virtuoso style that evolved out of ragtime after 1919) whose brilliant technique influenced countless young pianists who heard him in person. His legend began to emerge in 1935 as stride was fading in to nostalgia and he started to record regularly. For the next four decades, he would be celebrated as a living piece of jazz history – derby and cigar intact. His compositions, such as 'Echoes of Spring' and 'Passionette', show an unexpected, impressionistic strain.

Muggsy Spanier
(Cornet, 1906–67)

Francis Joseph Spanier was an early part of the group of young white Chicagoans who in the late 1920s opened up and amended the original New Orleans styles that had come north during the Roaring Twenties. He had a hot, jabbing, poking attack, often coloured by the use of a plunger mute. When Spanier recorded a number of Commodore sessions in 1939–40 with his own Dixieland group, he helped to restore traditional jazz to prominence.

Rex Stewart
(Cornet, 1907–67)

After honing a vocabulary of unorthodox trumpet techniques with Fletcher Henderson between 1926–33, Rex William Stewart switched to cornet and joined Duke Ellington. In an orchestra of distinctive voices, his was among the most unique. He played with a sharp, biting attack in the middle register. His tone had a slightly sour, almost sarcastic attitude, capable of some bizarre extremes. A typical solo on Henderson's 'Underneath The Harlem Moon' (1933) ended with an odd, sub-tone exclamation.

Seven years later, on 'Menelk' with Ellington, he built that into a long, onomatopoeic interlude evoking the sense of a lurking lion. His most famous trademark was squeezing notes through half-depressed valves, which gave his phrasing on 'Boy Meets Horn' (1938) and other pieces an impacted, almost crushed sense of implosion. But he could also swing with a relentless drive, nowhere more so than on his famous exchanges with Cootie Williams on 'Tootin' Through The Roof' (1939). He left Ellington in 1946 for freelancing and a later career as memoirist and critic for *Down Beat*.

Art Tatum
(Piano, 1909–56)

In the arms race of virtuosity that drove jazz in the 1930s, no player was more dazzling than Art Tatum. The piano had a history of virtuosos, but none approached the levels of sheer athletic aptitude that Tatum tossed off with such nonchalance. It came so naturally that he often seemed bored by his own wizardry, hurtling through a procession of sharp contrasts in tempo and style that changed every few bars, under a hail of arpeggios that dropped like confetti.

Tatum, born in Toledo, Ohio with only partial vision, came out of the stride tradition but extended it in so many directions as to create a comprehensive keyboard vocabulary that continues to astonish. His solo showpieces, such as 'Tiger Rag', were intended to intimidate if not terrorize, and in the 1930s he was heard on record and radio mostly in a solo setting. But he was a consummate ensemble player, working with a trio in the 1940s. In the 1950s he recorded a huge body of solo and ensemble work for Norman Granz.

Right

Trombonist Jack Teagarden, who revolutionized the instrument's status within jazz music.

Jack Teagarden

(Trombone, vocals, 1905–64)

Arguably the greatest trombonist in jazz history, Jack Teagarden might have been the dominant player of the 1930s. He made his reputation in the late 1920s with Ben Pollack and Red Nichols, but a lack of ambition and desire for security led him to decline the invitation of an obscure clarinettist launching a new band and choose instead a five-year contract with Paul Whiteman. Within months, Benny Goodman had become destiny's child and Teagarden was watching from the sidelines.

'Through [Jack Teagarden's] completely new style the entire concept of what jazz trombone could sound like was being changed....'
Artie Shaw

His soft sound spoke with a rolling fluidity and ease that no one had ever heard in the trombone, and he was also blessed with one of the best white blues voices of all time, effortlessly singing classics such as 'Basin Street Blues' in a melodic, laid-back drawl. In 1939 he formed his own big band, then in 1940–45 made some of his finest records with small swing groups. He toured with Louis Armstrong from 1947–51 and played with his own groups thereafter.

Chick Webb

(Drums, bandleader, 1909–39)

Associated with the Savoy Ballroom from 1927, the Chick Webb band built a large audience in Harlem. In the 1930s arranger Edgar Sampson became the chief architect of its swinging style, which was propelled by Webb's dynamic drumming and flashy solos, crackling with rim shots. He inspired Gene Krupa, Buddy Rich and other white big-band drummers. When Ella Fitzgerald joined in 1934, she became the band's principal attraction, expanded its audience and took over after Webb's early death.

Teddy Wilson

(Piano, 1912–86)

Although the physical brilliance of Art Tatum may have eluded most pianists in the 1930s, the more practical possibilities offered by Teddy Wilson made him the most influential pianist of the decade. Softening Earl Hines' emphasis on the beat still further, Wilson's style was centred almost wholly in his right hand, which spun smooth, bobbing, single-note lines and tranquil arpeggios, bringing him into perfect alignment with the sleek aerodynamics of swing. This was evident in his first recordings with Benny Carter (1933).

But Wilson found his ideal companionship in the clean rigour of the Benny Goodman Trio and Quartet, which brought him national fame in 1935 and a parallel recording career under his own name that produced a number of jazz classics, several with Billie Holiday. Wilson left Goodman in 1939, formed an excellent but short-lived big band and recorded prolifically during the 1940s, often with Goodman, Edmond Hall and Red Norvo; he continued to perform and record until the end of his life.

Below
Teddy Wilson's accessible yet highly original piano style made him a very influential musician.

Left
Flamboyant drummer Chick Webb's big band introduced singer Ella Fitzgerald to the world.

the forties

t he 1940s encompassed a wide range of musical art, reflecting extremes of economic hardship and recovery, global war and rebuilding. Empowered by necessarily full-tilt production, US industry recovered from the Depression, though the cream of its youth was siphoned off to fight on distant fronts, and returned to a strange new world. Great Britain suffered air strikes, privations and threat of occupation – traumas which took years to heal. Continental Europe, including Russia and on to the Far East, was gripped by government-sanctioned genocide, military invasion and destruction. At the decade's end, the world was divided by victory and defeat.

Blues and jazz, along with all the other popular musical styles and performance arts, were pressed into service during the Second World War as uplifting propaganda and social balm. Trends of the 1930s did not come to a jolting halt, but nothing was immune from change. The draft thinned the ranks of swing bands, and intense experimentation by ambitious youngsters in smaller ensembles filled the jazz air as uncommonly complicated bebop (simultaneous with a counter-restoration of New Orleans traditionalism). The youngest of the Mississippi Delta blues artists headed for Memphis and Chicago, with newly cheap electric gear; adding soulful balladry and urgent rhythms to their folky older country repertoire, they prepared a path for a whole new brand of pop music called rock'n'roll. Rock, R&B and bebop – they were not even dreamt of when the 1940s began.

Key Artists: Blues

John Lee Hooker
Big Joe Turner
T-Bone Walker

Key Artists: Jazz

Dizzy Gillespie
Woody Herman
Billie Holiday
Charlie Parker

Blues

'The Chicago blues is based on the country blues that John Lee Williamson and Big Joe Williams and Robert Nighthawk and all those guys was producing in the late thirties and early forties.'

Billy Boy Arnold

The 1940s was a decade of wrenching, often violent change in America. War clouds were on the horizon as 1939 turned into 1940. In the autumn of 1940, Franklin Delano Roosevelt was elected to his third term as President of the United States; he created the Fair Employment

Practices Committee the following year. The idea was to investigate and report on discrimination in employment. The executive order was largely ignored in the South and where changes were attempted, such as in Mobile, Alabama or Beaumont, Texas, racial violence ensued. The Roosevelt administration offered tepid support and in 1942 the committee was folded into the War Manpower Commission.

America Emerges From The Great Depression

American industry quickly geared up for the war effort. There were no new American automobiles produced between 1942–46 but defence plants were built, modified, adapted and retrofitted with astonishing quickness. Defence plants meant jobs and the nation was finally ridding itself of the yoke of the Great Depression. Defence jobs in California meant the migration of thousands of black people from Texas and Louisiana, while jobs in the Midwest resulted in new arrivals from Mississippi and Arkansas; much of the nation's manpower was in uniform.

The music industry was also undergoing great changes. The American Society of Composers, Authors and Publishers (ASCAP), the performing rights society, had been challenged by a group of radio-station owners protesting the high fees for on-air musical performances. Broadcast Music Incorporated (BMI) was formed in 1940 as an alternative and presented an opportunity for black songwriters who had been largely ignored by ASCAP.

The Record Industry Recovers

James C. Petrillo, the powerful head of the American Federation of Musicians (AFM), called a strike of union musicians against the record labels, effective 1 August 1942. The ban would hold until the autumn of 1943, when Decca Records settled with the union. RCA and Columbia held out for another 14 months, but Decca's agreement meant that other companies could begin (or resume) recording under the same terms. All of a sudden, new labels began to appear at an astonishing pace in New York, Chicago and Los Angeles. BMI, anxious to stockpile compositions for its catalogue, would advance money to labels with BMI-affiliated publishing companies.

One effect of the strike was that singers, once merely a part of an orchestra, now made a move to the front of the stage. Singers were able to record with choirs or small vocal quartets and keep a flow of records coming, so that an artist such as Frank Sinatra (1915–98) could now be as well-known as bandleaders Harry James (1916–83) or Tommy Dorsey (1905–56), his former employers. But the

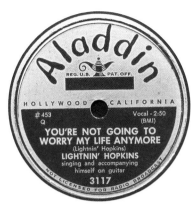

combination of BMI involvement and RCA and Columbia sitting on the sidelines opened the door for jump bands and blues singers as well. Many of the new labels, such as Savoy, Aladdin and Modern, specialized in black jazz, blues and gospel.

Jazz And Blues Part Ways

Jazz and blues, which had been so closely linked at the start of the decade, began to pull apart from one another. Swing was still the dominant musical style of the mid-1940s and was under assault from modern jazz, or bebop, on one hand and a revival of the traditional jazz of New Orleans on the other. The jump band led by saxophonist Louis Jordan (1908–75) was the number one combo in the country. Similar groups led by Roy Milton (1907–83) and Eddie Vinson (1917–88) were finding an audience. Boogie-woogie, once embraced by jazz bands, was now being abandoned but picked up on by those little combos, which utilized the rhythm in very different ways.

Billboard, the record industry trade paper, traced the sales progress of records and its dilemma as to what to call 'black music' was apparent. In 1942 *Billboard* tracked it as the Harlem Hit Parade, changed this name to Race Records in 1945 and in 1949 called it Rhythm & Blues. Finally, they had come up with a term that applied to all secular black music that wasn't bebop or traditional jazz: R&B.

Above
'Landing Blues' by Birmingham Sam (a.k.a. John Lee Hooker) on Savoy; 'You're Not Going To Worry My Life Any More' by Lightnin' Hopkins on Aladdin; John Lee Hooker's 'John L's House Rent Boogie' on Modern.

Far Left
Music fans dance to R&B at a juke joint near Clarksdale, Missouri.

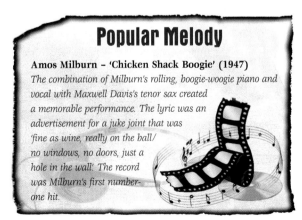

Popular Melody

Amos Milburn – 'Chicken Shack Boogie' (1947)
The combination of Milburn's rolling, boogie-woogie piano and vocal with Maxwell Davis's tenor sax created a memorable performance. The lyric was an advertisement for a juke joint that was 'fine as wine, really on the ball/ no windows, no doors, just a hole in the wall'. The record was Milburn's first number-one hit.

Above

Saxophone honker Big Jay McNeely drives the crowd wild with his stage antics.

Blind Blake
Blind Arthur's Breakdown

musicfirebox.com /Blind

The Golden Age Of The Saxophone

The saxophone really came to prominence during the 1940s. While its use in jazz big bands and combos was not new, the style introduced by Illinois Jacquet with Lionel Hampton's (1908–2002) band and in early 'Jazz At The Philharmonic' concerts, which emphasized rasping, honking and squealing, was quickly adopted by the jump bands. Recording artists such as Hal Singer (b. 1919) and Big Jay McNeely (b. 1927) found an instrumental road directly to the audience, and saxophone-dominated R&B instrumentals became a growth industry.

While all this was going on there were race riots in New York City and Detroit in 1943. President Roosevelt died in 1945 and Vice President Truman ascended to the office. The atom bomb came along in 1945 and while the Axis powers had been defeated, it didn't mean that the free world had no enemies. The theft of atomic secrets in 1948 by Soviet spies made the world aware of the growing threat of Communism, and the closing of defence plants in 1945 sent shockwaves through the US, but a retooling of the domestic economy was immediately ahead. On the music scene, the problems of rationing, shortages and inflation served to make life difficult for big bands and by the end of 1946 many of them had folded.

Shouters And Crooners

Country blues was still being recorded but more and more artists were moving towards a more urban sound. Shouters such as Big Joe Turner (1911–85), Wynonie Harris (1913–69), Jimmy Witherspoon (1922–97) and Roy Brown (1925–81) were an important part of the scene, and smooth blues balladeers such as Charles Brown (1922–99) and Amos Milburn (1927–80) added their abilities to the mix. Vocal groups such as the Ravens and Orioles were very much a part of R&B, as were the big bands of Lionel Hampton, Erskine Hawkins, Buddy Johnson and Lucky Millinder – bandleaders who had been able to keep up with the new trend. Artists such as Sonny Terry (1911–86), Brownie McGhee (1915–96), Memphis Slim (1915–88) and Champion Jack Dupree (1910–92) were being recorded in an R&B context. In time, things would shake out and these artists would return to their original styles. Others that couldn't keep up would be shunted aside by the industry, some to be rediscovered at a later date and others to disappear for good.

R&B Hits The Airwaves

In 1948 President Truman ordered the desegregation of the US military. Between the battle over civil rights and the growing concern with Communism, Truman was challenged by two different factions of his own party when he stood for re-election in the autumn of 1948; he prevailed nonetheless. James C. Petrillo called another strike of the AFM to take effect on 1 January 1948. This one was not as successful, since many of the smaller labels found ways to circumvent the action. Still, there were many small labels, started after the settlement of the 1942 strike, which did not survive 1948. Radio station WDIA in Memphis instituted a black music policy in 1949. It was a huge success and other stations began to play more R&B on the airways. More radio play increased the sales of black records and exposed the music to more people.

In December 1948, Detroit bandleader and saxophonist Paul Williams recorded a song called 'The Hucklebuck'. It was an R&B instrumental that became the biggest black record of 1949. It also started a dance craze and soon people were dancing the hucklebuck in black areas across America. It was the first new dance to come out of the black community during the 1940s. The next decade would have a lot of new dances, a lot more R&B and, right around the corner, rock'n'roll.

Left
Wynonie Harris, one of the great blues shouters of the era.

Popular Melody

Jimmy Witherspoon – 'Ain't Nobody's Business If I Do Pt. 2' (1949)
A laid-back sax sound sets the mood for this calmly self-assured blues track. Witherspoon then sings against a simple rhythm section, giving his vocals a strong, confident feel that is well-suited to the subject matter.

John Lee Hooker

To Memphis And Cincinatti

By 1933, John Lee Hooker had left Mississippi and his family for good. He played some music in Memphis but soon left for Cincinatti, where he stayed for several years. He had a steady job outside music and played parties and functions on weekends. During his time in Cincinnati, he also sang with several different gospel quartets.

In 1943, Hooker moved to Detroit. He found work at clubs on the east side of the city, around Hastings Street, but still had his basic employment outside music until he was discovered by Bernie Bessman. Hooker's first recording for Bessman's Sensation label was in September 1948.

'With one chord, John Lee Hooker could tell you a story as deep as the ocean....' Carlos Santana

John Lee Hooker was born on 22 August 1917 near Clarksdale, Mississippi. He got his first instrument from singer Tony Hollins, but he was taught how to play by his stepfather, Will Moore. Moore would play weekends at jukes and functions in various Delta locations, often in the company of Charley Patton or Son House. Moore's trademark was a rhythmic pattern that his stepson picked up and made his own. He called it the boogie.

'Boogie Chillen' Hits The Chart

The first Hooker record, 'Boogie Chillen', was a huge success. Sensation was a subsidiary of Pan American Record Distributors, a local record wholesaler, and Bessman, recognizing his inability to promote a record nationally, licensed 'Boogie Chillen' to Modern Records in Los Angeles. The record reached number one on *Billboard* magazine's Race Records chart and John Lee Hooker's career as an entertainer was launched.

Within weeks of the Modern release of 'Boogie Chillen', Hooker was recording for a variety of labels under an enormous number of pseudonyms. He was Texas Slim on King, Delta John on Regent, Birmingham Sam on Savoy, Johnny Williams on Prize, Staff and Gotham, the Boogie Man on Acorn and John Lee Booker on Chance and Chess. It didn't seem to affect his sales on Modern, where

Key Track

'Boogie Chillen' (1949)
This track opens with Hooker's percussive boogie beat, interspersed with delicate runs in the bass register. His engaging vocals, together with chordal guitar passages and shifts in rhythm, bring the song together into a curious and refreshingly original take on the post-war electric blues sound.

he had solid sellers such as 'Hobo Blues', 'Crawlin' King Snake Blues' and another number-one hit on the *Billboard* R&B charts, 'I'm In The Mood'. For most of his career, Hooker paid little attention to the exclusivity aspect of recording contracts. Throughout 1948–51, Hooker worked mostly in Detroit. Playing solo or duo, he was very irregular in his patterns, rarely adhering to the 12-bar structure. In the city, Hooker sometimes worked with a small group he called the Boogie Ramblers, where his work followed the more traditional form. His first major roadwork was done in 1952, with Eddie Kirkland on second guitar; they picked up accompanists as needed. It wasn't until 1955 when Hooker signed with Vee Jay that he began recording regularly with a band. Hooker had several hits on Vee Jay, the biggest being 'Boom Boom'.

Reaching New Audiences

As the 1950s turned into the 1960s, Hooker's music began to appear on LP. He performed at both the Newport Folk Festival and Newport Jazz Festival in 1960, gaining exposure to large numbers of white college students for the first time. Beginning in 1962, he became a regular on the European club and concert circuit. At home, he spent much of the early 1960s working coffeehouses and folk-music clubs. He signed a three-year deal with Bluesway in 1966, where he made excellent albums with blues bands until the label folded and was taken over by the parent label, ABC Records, in 1970. He frequently recorded for European labels while overseas. In 1970 Hooker

teamed up with a California rock band, Canned Heat, and the resultant album, *Hooker 'N Heat* (1971), introduced Hooker to rock'n'roll fans. He had brief roles in the movies *The Blues Brothers* (1980) and *The Color Purple* (1985).

The final glorious chapter in John Lee Hooker's career began with an association with the Rosebud Agency, which handled Hooker's bookings from the mid-1980s. Around the same time, Hooker developed a friendship with rock star Carlos Santana and the fruit of that relationship was *The Healer* (1989), an album that was a huge hit and vaulted Hooker back to stardom. In 1990, he recorded the soundtrack for the film *The Hot Spot*, overdubbing tracks with Taj Mahal and Miles Davis. Over time Hooker toured less frequently but continued to record and rack up awards. He died in 2001.

Classic Recordings

1948
'Boogie Chillen'

1949
'Hobo Blues', 'Crawlin' King Snake Blues'

1951
'I'm In The Mood'

1962
'Boom Boom'

John Lee Hooker At Newport (1964)
'Tupelo', 'Bus Station Blues'

Hooker 'N Heat with Canned Heat (1971)
'Whiskey and Wimmen', 'Peavine'

The Healer (1989)
'The Healer', 'I'm In The Mood'

Above Left
Hooker's 'Stutterin' Blues', which was released on the Rockin' label under the pseudonym John Lee Booker.

Left
John Lee Hooker (left) with his first cousin and fellow blues guitarist, Earl Hooker.

Above Far Left
Boogie guitarist John Lee Hooker relaxes in the studio.

Big Joe Turner

'I was sitting up there thinking, "now when is he gonna run out of words?" And then I was thinking "when is he gonna run out of something to play?" But they never ran out of nothing.'

Jay McShann on Big Joe Turner & Pete Johnson

Key Track

'Johnson and Turner Blues' (1945)
The combination of Pete Johnson and Joe Turner exemplifies Kansas City jazz and blues. The perfect tempo of this performance provides inspiration for the singer. Solos from Johnson and trumpeter Frankie Newton sustain the singer's mood. 'Please Mister Johnson, don't play the blues so sad/Please Mister Johnson, don't play the blues so sad/'cause night before last, I lost the best gal I ever had'.

Joseph Vernon Turner was born on 18 May 1911 in Kansas City, Missouri. He dropped out of school after sixth grade and worked with blind singers on the streets. The blues was in the air in Kansas City and when Turner joined in with the street singers he would make up blues lyrics. Turner was functionally illiterate and never learned to read or write properly.

He studied records in his late teens to learn songs and cited Leroy Carr, Lonnie Johnson, Bessie Smith and Ethel Waters as favourites. By

the time he was 17, he had teamed up with Pete Johnson at the Backbiter's Club. There were no microphones at the time and Turner's voice became the stuff of legend as locals told stories of hearing him 10 blocks away. He became the first of a new breed of performer: the blues shouter.

A Fruitful Partnership

In the early 1930s, Turner and Johnson moved to the Black and Tan club, where Turner learned to tend bar. After Prohibition ended in 1933 the pair moved to the Cherry Blossom, a larger spot which had a floor show, including the orchestra of George E. Lee. It was during this time that Johnson and Turner travelled to out-of-town locations such as Omaha, Chicago and St. Louis. In early 1935 the pair moved to the Sunset Café, where they were heard by John Hammond and invited to appear at the Spirituals To Swing concert in New York. A big hit at the concert, Johnson and Turner soon joined forces with Albert Ammons and Meade 'Lux' Lewis, and began a four-year run at a New York nightclub, Café Society, which featured black entertainment. Johnson and Turner made their recording debut for Vocalion (including 'Roll 'Em Pete') but Joe moved over to Decca in 1940. He was a guest vocalist on jazz dates featuring the Varsity Seven, Benny Carter, Joe Sullivan and Art Tatum, and was paired with artists such as pianists Sammy Price and Willie 'The Lion' Smith on his own recordings.

In the summer of 1941, Turner went to Los Angeles to appear in Duke Ellington's musical *Jump For Joy*. Turner was added to the cast after the show had opened but Ellington had written a blues for Turner to perform in the show, 'Rocks In My Bed'. It became Turner's signature song following the show's close in late September, and his return to New York's Café Society.

In 1945, Joe Turner signed with National Records. He was travelling constantly and National managed to record him in New York, Chicago and Los Angeles, backed by small groups that often included horns. In 1947–48 he

recorded sessions in California for Aladdin, Swingtime and MGM. He lived in New Orleans for a time in the late 1940s and early 1950s, and he recorded for Freedom and Imperial during that time, but in 1951 he signed with Atlantic Records; here began the period of his greatest popularity.

Atlantic Years

The Atlantic partners, Ahmet Ertegun and Herb Abrahmson, felt that Turner could thrive in the R&B style that was so popular with black audiences. Turner responded with big hits such as 'Chains Of Love', 'Honey Hush' and 'Shake, Rattle & Roll', forming an important link between the blues and the forthcoming rock'n'roll style. He recorded in Chicago (with electric guitarist Elmore James) and New Orleans, but more often in New York with the arrangements of Jesse Stone. Atlantic also

recorded a jazz album, *The Boss Of The Blues* (1956), which reunited Turner with Pete Johnson. The Atlantic association lasted until 1961 and for the next decade Turner freelanced with various different labels. He settled in southern California in the mid-1950s; by the early 1960s he was a regular at European clubs and festivals. In the US, apart from when touring the festivals, he mainly worked in California. His career was revived by an association with Norman Granz and Pablo records, which produced LPs with top jazz stars such as Count Basie on a regular basis, from 1973 until Turner's death. He was prominently featured in the film *Last of the Blue Devils* (1979), a reunion of Kansas City musicians from the 1930s and 1940s. He earned a Grammy nomination for his Muse album *Blues Train* (1982), recorded with the young New England-based band, Roomful of Blues.

Above
Turner appearing in the 1956 film Shake, Rattle & Rock, *which included footage of Turner and Fats Domino in concert.*

Above Far Left
Powerful blues shouter Big Joe Turner, who provided an essential link between the blues and rock'n'roll music.

T-Bone Walker

Above

T-Bone Walker, electric guitar pioneer and great showman.

'I believe that it all comes originally from T-Bone Walker. B.B. King and I were talking about that not long ago and he thinks so, too.'

Freddie King

Key Track

'T-Bone Shuffle' (1949)

A simple shuffle beat provides the basis for this seductive T-Bone Walker classic. The stunning guitar work is deceptively simple, while the off-the-beat figures and double-stopped passages suggest that a certain Charles Edward Berry may have been a fan.

Aaron Thibeaux Walker was born in Linden, Texas on 28 May 1910, the only child of Rance and Movelia Walker. The family moved to Dallas in 1912 and as a pre-teen Walker would lead Blind Lemon Jefferson around the Dallas streets. He taught himself guitar and worked streets and functions until he toured with various travelling shows in the mid- to late 1920s. He made his recording debut for Columbia in 1929 ('Trinity River Blues'/ 'Wichita Falls Blues') as Oak Cliff T-Bone. The name T-Bone is a phonetic corruption of his middle name.

Walker worked locally with artists as diverse as Cab Calloway and Ma Rainey before moving to the Los Angeles area in 1934, where he worked his own combo at the Little Harlem Club and gradually built a following. He recorded one title ('T-Bone Blues') with the Les Hite orchestra and worked with that band on tours through Chicago and New York for much of 1939–40. He returned to the Little Harlem Club, where he reformed his own group. He played guitar on a record date with Freddie Slack's orchestra in July 1942 and, at the end of the date, recorded two songs ('Mean Old World'/'I Got A Break Baby') for Capitol Records. On the strength of that record he began to tour and to work whites-only clubs in Hollywood. He made frequent stops at the Rhumboogie club in Chicago from 1942–45 and in 1945 he made recordings for the Rhumboogie and Mercury labels.

Black & White

In September 1946, Walker signed an exclusive contract with Black & White Records and worked with producer Ralph Bass. He recorded 49 titles in the next 15 months, among which were all his bestsellers. He had hit records with such well-remembered titles as 'Call It Stormy Monday' and 'T-Bone Shuffle'. He became a national touring attraction and his acrobatic stunts, such as playing the guitar behind his head and doing the splits on stage, helped him to become a major star. Because of the second AFM recording ban, Walker could not make any new recordings during 1948, but the large stockpile of sides he had recorded provided new releases into 1950. Black & White had gone out of business in 1948 and the masters had been acquired by Capitol.

In the spring of 1950, he signed with Imperial Records. Of the 52 titles he recorded over the next four years there were no national hits, but the music is of a high quality. He signed with Atlantic in 1955 and, once again, there were no big sellers but a considerable amount of memorable music. He continued to tour nationally while headquartered in Los Angeles.

An International Star

In 1962, Walker went to Europe with the American Folk Blues Festival and developed a circuit for himself that led to frequent visits overseas; he was now a part of the American festival scene as well. He freelanced his recording deals and recorded for a variety of labels in a numbeer of countries. His Polydor album *Good Feelin'* (1969) won a Grammy award in 1970. He continued to tour and record until shortly before his death.

Walker was a smooth blues singer with some of the qualities of a crooner, but it was his guitar work that made him such an important artist. He was an influence, to some degree, on almost all of the key guitarists of the post-Second World War generation. His sound, his unhurried phrasing and his self-editing ability are hallmarks of his style. T-Bone Walker certainly never overstayed his welcome.

Classic Recordings

Les Hite Orchestra (1940)
'T-Bone Blues'

T-Bone Walker (1942)
'Mean Old World'

1947
*'Call It Stormy Monday',
'T-Bone Shuffle', 'I'm Still
In Love With You'*

1950
'Strollin' With Bones'

1951
'Cold, Cold Feeling'

Left

Walker performing at London's Hammersmith Odeon in December 1970.

Below

A versatile musician, Walker (left) is pictured here with jazz greats Dizzy Gillespie (seated) and James Moody.

A-Z of artists

Above
Vocalist and pianist
Charles Brown was a
legendary performer.

Right
Arthur 'Big Boy' Crudup,
whose compositions were
covered to great effect by
Elvis Presley.

Charles Brown
(Piano, vocals, 1922–99)

Charles Mose Brown was born in Texas City, Texas and had extensive classical piano training as a youth. He moved to Los Angeles in 1943 and by September 1944 had become the vocalist-pianist in Johnny Moore's Three Blazers. The Blazers had several hits before Brown went solo in 1948 and scored success with songs such as 'Trouble Blues' (1949) and 'Black Night' (1951). As a vocalist, Brown was equally at home with ballads and blues. He regained international renown later in his life and continued to record up until his death.

Roy Brown
(Vocals, 1925–81)

Roy James Brown was born in New Orleans and raised in Texas and Louisiana. A strong blues shouter, Brown was one of the first stars of New Orleans R&B. He led his own group, Roy Brown & his Mighty, Mighty Men, and wrote most of the material he recorded. He began recording for DeLuxe in 1947 in New Orleans, and had hit records with 'Long About Midnight' (1948), 'Rockin' At Midnight' (1949) and 'Hard Luck Blues' (1950).

Arthur 'Big Boy' Crudup
(Guitar, vocals, 1905–74)

Arthur William Crudup was born in Forest, Mississippi and did not learn to play the guitar until his 30s. He worked functions in the Clarksdale area before moving to Chicago in 1940, signing with Bluebird in 1941 and finding considerable popularity on record. He returned to Mississippi after the Second World War and worked locally with Rice Miller and Elmore James. Crudup is perhaps best remembered as an outstanding blues songwriter; several of his tunes, such as 'That's All Right' and 'My Baby Left Me', were covered by pop and rock stars, notably Elvis Presley.

Rev. Gary Davis
(Guitar, harmonica, banjo, vocals, 1896–1972)

Gary D. Davis was born in Laurens, South Carolina and

was completely blind by the age of 30. He taught himself harmonica, banjo and guitar and played in string bands throughout the teens, going on to work the Carolinas as a street singer in the 1920s. Ordained as a Baptist minister, he performed mostly religious songs after 1937. Davis began recording regularly in the mid-1950s after a move to New York. His unique guitar playing shows traces of ragtime, blues and other early music. He stands with Blind Blake as the finest of Piedmont-area guitar stylists.

Champion Jack Dupree
(Piano, vocals, 1910–92)

William Thomas Dupree was born in New Orleans. He was raised in the Colored Waifs Home for Boys from infancy. He learned piano at an early age and in the 1920s worked barrelhouses as a soloist, as well as playing with traditional jazz bands. From the early 1930s, he worked as a prizefighter and took occasional music jobs. Dupree was discovered in Chicago and signed to OKeh records in 1940. Among those early sides were the first recordings of 'Junker's Blues' and 'Cabbage Greens'.

After US Navy service, Dupree settled in New York and recorded for several small labels, including Joe Davis, Continental and Apollo, often in the company of Brownie McGhee. He became known for his strong, two-fisted piano and for his humorous songs and vocals. Dupree settled in Switzerland in 1960 and became one of the most visible blues artists in Europe over the next 30 years.

Lloyd Glenn
(Piano, arranger, 1909–85)

Lloyd Colquitt Glenn Sr. was born and raised in San Antonio, Texas. He worked with several southwestern territory bands before joining Don Albert in 1934 in the role of pianist and chief arranger. He moved to California in the early 1940s. Glenn became the prototype of the studio pianist-arranger for blues and R&B record dates while working on sessions for T-Bone Walker, Lowell Fulson and others. A fine blues and boogie-woogie pianist, Glenn recorded hit instrumentals for Swingtime ('Old Time Shuffle Blues' and 'Chica Boo') in 1950–51.

Wynonie Harris
(Vocals, 1913–69)

Raised in Omaha, Nebraska, Wynonie Harris first came to prominence in the Lucky Millinder Orchestra of 1944,

where he had a number-one Race chart hit, 'Who Threw The Whiskey In The Well'. A leather-lunged shouter in the Big Joe Turner tradition, Harris had a long successful run on King records (1947–57), which produced huge hits such as 'Good Rockin' Tonight' and 'All She Wants To Do Is Rock' as well as a wealth of other material of a consistently high standard. He specialized in raunchy, risqué songs, but was rarely active in the last few years of his life.

Above
Rev. Gary Davis's playing style derived from the southeastern Piedmont region.

Helen Humes
(Vocals, 1909–81)

Helen Elizabeth Humes was born in Louisville, Kentucky and made her recording debut for OKeh in 1927. She spent 1938–41 in the Count Basie Orchestra, singing mostly ballads. She moved to California in 1945 and recorded for many different labels while working as a solo artist. She had solid hits with 'Be Baba Leba' in 1945 and 'Million Dollar Secret' in 1950. A versatile singer, Humes had a sweet voice and could adapt to almost any material. She returned to her music in the 1970s after a 10-year absence, and remained active until her death.

Bull Moose Jackson
(Tenor saxophone, vocals, 1919–89)

Benjamin Joseph Jackson was born in Cleveland, Ohio and replaced Wynonie Harris as male vocalist with the Lucky Millinder Orchestra in 1945. From 1947 until the late 1950s he toured with his own group, the Buffalo Bearcats. He recorded for Queen/King from 1945; among his biggest hits were 'I Love You, Yes I Do', 'I Can't Go On Without You', 'Little Girl, Don't Cry' and 'Why Don't You Haul Off And Love Me'. Jackson alternated ballads, jump tunes and risqué novelties, as well as occasionally recording instrumentals featuring his saxophone.

Little Esther
(Vocals, 1935–84)

Esther Mae Washington was born in Galveston, Texas. She moved to the Los Angeles area at the age of five and in 1949 was discovered by Johnny Otis. Her first recording with Otis, 'Double Crossing Blues', was a number-one R&B hit in 1950. In that year the pair had two more number ones on the R&B chart, 'Mistrustin' Blues' and 'Cupid's Boogie'. On her own after 1951, Esther continued to record but her career suffered ups and downs due to her narcotics addiction. As Esther Phillips, she returned in 1962 with yet another R&B number-one, 'Release Me', and other hits.

Brownie McGhee
(Guitar, vocals, 1915–96)

Walter Brown McGhee was born in Knoxville, Tennessee. He learned to play guitar before his tenth birthday and dropped out of school to play throughout the state in the late 1920s. He met Sonny Terry in 1939 and they joined forces almost immediately. McGhee began recording for OKeh in 1940 and moved to New York.

McGhee recorded on his own (without Terry) for several labels, notably Savoy. He was recorded in an R&B context throughout 1948–58, in addition to his own Piedmont-style acoustic blues and duets with Terry. The duo appeared in the Tennessee Williams Broadway drama *Cat On A Hot Tin Roof* from 1955–57 and toured England in 1958, going on to become regular visitors to Europe. McGhee continued to make his own recordings during the folk-blues revival of the early 1960s and the duo continued into the mid-1970s.

Big Jay McNeely
(Tenor saxophone, b. 1927)

Cecil James McNeely was born and raised in Los Angeles. Inspired by Illinois Jacquet, McNeely played in high school with future jazz stars Sonny Criss and Hampton Hawes. He was discovered by Johnny Otis and made his recording debut in 1948 with a number-one hit, 'Deacon's Hop'. He had another hit in 1959 with 'There Is Something On Your Mind'. A stomping, screaming wildman, McNeely was the quintessential showboating saxophonist of the 1950s.

Jay McShann
(Piano, vocals, b. 1916)

James Columbus McShann was born in Muskogee, Oklahoma and moved to Kansas City in 1936. He formed a big band in 1940 and recorded for Decca in 1941–43. The band featured vocalist Walter Brown and alto saxophonist Charlie Parker, and had a big hit with 'Confessin' The Blues'. McShann had a hit record on Vee Jay in 1955 with 'Hands Off' and continued to work in the Kansas City area. Prominently featured in the film *Last of the Blue Devils* (1980), McShann remains a masterful pianist with equal parts jazz and blues in his style.

MEMPHIS SLIM

1940s and mid-1950s, with number-one R&B hits such as 'Chicken Shack Boogie', 'Bewildered' and 'Roomin' House Boogie' (all 1948–49). Beginning in 1949, he toured and recorded with his own band, the Aladdin Chickenshackers, and continued his string of hits with 'Bad, Bad Whiskey' and 'One Scotch, One Bourbon, One Beer'. The success of the latter inspired a series of songs with liquor-related themes.

Milburn was a superb pianist, equally at home with slow blues, rolling boogie-woogie, ballad material, novelties and jump blues. He worked frequently with Charles Brown in the late 1950s but became inactive in music after a stroke in 1970.

Left

Rocking blues pianist Memphis Slim, in a publicity poster for Fontana Records.

Below

Amos Milburn, a supremely talented blues pianist and adaptable singer.

Memphis Slim

(Piano, vocals, 1915–88)

John Len Chatman was born in Memphis, Tennessee. He moved to Chicago in 1937, where he worked with Big Bill Broonzy. He began recording in 1940 and formed his band, the House Rockers, after the Second World War. He had several hits on the Miracle label in 1948–49, including 'Messin' Around' and 'Blue And Lonesome'. A prolific recording artist and first-rate blues pianist, Slim was also a songwriter and wrote most of his own material. He went to Europe in 1962 with the American Folk Blues Festival and settled in Paris.

Amos Milburn

(Piano, vocals, 1927–80)

Joseph Amos Milburn Jr. was born in Houston, Texas, and he began recording in 1946 for Aladdin records. Milburn was an exceptionally popular performer between the late

big bill broonzy ⊙94   charles brown ⊙144   johnny otis ⊙148   sonny terry ⊙149

guitar. He took the name Robert Nighthawk and used it professionally from the early 1940s. Nighthawk had converted to electric guitar by the time he recorded for Aristocrat/Chess from 1948–50. He was a master of the electric slide guitar and his work was influential on future slide stylists such as Muddy Waters and Earl Hooker.

Johnny Otis
(Drums, vibes, vocals, b. 1921)

John Alexander Veliotes, born in Vallejo, California, started as a drummer and formed a big band in 1945. By 1947, Otis had switched to a seven- or eight-piece group. This was one of the earliest R&B combos to tour; the Johnny Otis Rhythm & Blues Caravan included vocalists Little Esther, Mel Walker and the Robins, and scored 10 entries on the R&B charts in 1950 alone. During the 1950s, Otis worked for record labels as an arranger and producer. He introduced Big Mama Thornton, produced vocalist Etta James and recorded with ill-fated singer Johnny Ace.

Roy Milton
(Drums, vocals, 1907–83)

Roy Bunny Milton was born in Wynnewood, Oklahoma. He had his own bands before moving to Los Angeles in 1935, where he formed the Solid Senders combo in 1938 and worked small clubs throughout the city. He began recording in 1945 and had a lengthy relationship with Specialty records throughout 1946–54, which produced such hits as 'R.M. Blues', 'Information Blues' and 'Best Wishes'. The Solid Senders featured pianist Camille Howard and three horns along with the leader's simple yet sincere vocals. The band could handle swing, jump tunes or slow blues.

Robert Nighthawk
(Guitar, vocals, 1909–67)

Robert Lee McCollum was born in Helena, Arkansas. He was taught guitar by his cousin, Houston Stackhouse, in 1930. He moved to St. Louis in 1934, now calling himself Robert McCoy, and first recorded in 1937 on acoustic

Sammy Price
(Piano, 1908–92)

Samuel Blythe Price was born in Honey Grove, Texas. His recording debut came in 1929. In 1938 he moved to New York and became the pianist for Decca Records blues sessions. In this capacity – in addition to making his own recordings – he accompanied Blue Lu Barker, Johnny Temple and Sister Rosetta Tharpe, among others. From 1948 Price played in France on a regular basis and made frequent recordings for European labels – as a piano soloist, with jazz bands and with blues singers.

Hal Singer
(Tenor saxophone, b. 1919)

Harold Singer was born in Tulsa, Oklahoma. He worked with territory bands in the late 1930s and went to New York with Roy Eldridge in 1944. Singer worked around New York, playing on sessions for King and Savoy, during 1946–59. His own recording career began in 1948 and he had a number-one hit with 'Cornbread', the first big record of the honking

R&B tenor style. He frequently toured with his own groups and with R&B shows during 1948–58, and by the late 1950s he was playing jazz as often as R&B. He relocated to Paris in 1965 and has recorded frequently for European labels.

Sonny Terry
(Harmonica, vocals, 1911–86)

Saunders Terrell was born in Greensboro, Georgia and taught himself to play the harmonica at the age of eight. He lost the sight in one eye, aged 10, and the second eye at 16. Terry played mostly in North Carolina from the late 1920s. He teamed up with Blind Boy Fuller in 1934 and recorded with him from late 1937 until Fuller's death. Sonny Terry was featured at the Spirituals To Swing concerts in New York in 1938 and 1939. He recorded for the Library of Congress in 1938 and made his commercial recording debut a few days later.

'Sonny just mystified me. I mean how he did that I'll never know; I STILL don't – it's true! I played with Brownie years later and when I did I never tried to play like Sonny.'
Mark Hummel

He joined forces with Brownie McGhee in 1939 and was present on McGhee's recording of 'The Death Of Blind Boy Fuller' in 1941 – the first time they recorded together. The pair worked in New York with Champion Jack Dupree, Leadbelly and others on the folk-blues circuit of the 1940s, and Terry appeared in the Broadway show *Finian's Rainbow* during 1946–47. The Terry-McGhee team made dozens of duo albums from the mid-1950s through to the mid-1970s.

Eddie 'Cleanhead' Vinson
(Alto saxophone, vocals, 1917–88)

Edward L. Vinson Jr. was born in Houston, Texas. He studied saxophone in high school and played with the Chester Boone and Milt Larkin Orchestras, before touring with a show featuring Lil Green and Big Bill Broonzy in 1941. He joined the Cootie Williams Orchestra in 1942 and recorded hit vocals on 'Cherry Red Blues' and 'Somebody's Got To Go'. He formed his own group in 1945 and had a number-one Race Records hit with 'Old Maid Boogie'. Vinson's influences came from modern jazz, and he also had his own influence on the style, penning the Miles Davis hit 'Four'. Vinson continued to tour and record into the 1980s.

Dinah Washington
(Vocals, 1924–63)

Ruth Lee Jones was born in Tuscaloosa, Alabama and raised in Chicago. She joined Lionel Hampton's band in 1943 and made her first recordings that year. Included were the hits 'Salty Papa Blues' and 'Evil Gal Blues'. She left Hampton in 1945 and signed with Mercury records in 1946. Her recorded output included all kinds of material – and she could handle it all. She had a number-one R&B hit in 1949 with 'Baby, Get Lost' – written by jazz critic Leonard Feather – and crossed over into pop music with 'What A Difference A Day Makes', which was a chart hit in 1959.

Jimmy Witherspoon
(Vocals, 1922–97)

Jimmy John Witherspoon was born in Gurdon, Arkansas. He joined the Jay McShann group in California in 1945. He recorded his own records in late 1947 and among them was 'Ain't Nobody's Business Parts 1 & 2', a huge Race Records hit. Witherspoon toured with his own group until 1952 and had another big hit with 'No Rollin' Blues'/'Big Fine Girl'. As a blues shouter, Witherspoon was influenced by Big Joe Turner; later in his life he developed a smoother, jazz-related ballad style.

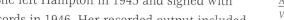

Above
Versatile R&B and jazz artist Eddie 'Cleanhead' Vinson lays down some vocals in the studio.

Above Left
Harmonica player Sonny Terry (right) performs with longtime musical partner Brownie McGhee in 1969.

Jazz

'We often talked in the afternoon [at Minton's]. That's how we came to write different chord progressions and the like.... As for those sitters-in that we didn't want, when we started playing these different changes we'd made up, they'd become discouraged after the first chorus....'

Kenny Clarke

The 1940s plunged the world into a cataclysmic war that left its scars on every aspect of life and precipitated huge changes across the globe. Jazz was also affected; the decade saw the decline of the swing bands that had ruled the roost in the previous decade and

the emergence of a new style of music – bebop. Swing had definitely been king in the 1930s, when the uplifting music of the big bands was seen as an antidote to the miseries of the Great Depression. As it happened, the economic upturn generated by the wartime economy did the big bands little good, but their popularity continued through the 1940s, when bandleaders such as Woody Herman (1913–87), Benny Goodman (1909–86), Glenn Miller (1904–44), Stan Kenton (1911–79) and Harry James (1916–83) remained the pop stars of their day.

Wartime Stringencies Hit The Big Bands

The 1940s took its toll on all of these bands, as well as those led by the great African-American leaders such as Duke Ellington (1899–1974) and Count Basie (1904–84). The drafting of musicians in significant numbers, the closure of dance halls around the country, recording bans called by the American Federation of Musicians in 1942–43, the difficulties of producing records under wartime stringencies, increased transport problems – all of these factors combined to make big bands less and less financially viable as the decade progressed. By its end, most leaders had disbanded and turned to smaller groups, if only temporarily.

At the height of the Swing Era, singers had been largely an adjunct to the big bands, but the 1940s saw the growth of the singer as a popular phenomenon in his or her own right, exemplified by the likes of Bing Crosby, Frank Sinatra (1915–98), Nat 'King' Cole (1917–65), Ella Fitzgerald (1917–96), Sarah Vaughan (1924–90), Dinah Washington (1924–63) and Billie Holiday (1915–59). These figures paved the way for the rise of the modern pop star.

A New Creative Force

The emergence of bebop as a major new creative force in jazz took place against the backdrop of the decline of the swing bands, but the music was essentially an evolution from swing rather than a revolutionary departure. Lester Young (1909–59), Coleman Hawkins

(1904–69), Ben Webster (1909–73), Art Tatum (1909–56), Jimmy Blanton and many others had already laid some of the groundwork for the harmonic and rhythmic rethinking that would become central to bebop.

The new music evolved in after-hours jam sessions at clubs such as Minton's Playhouse and Monroe's Uptown House in New York, and later in the jazz clubs of 52nd Street, dubbed 'Swing Street' in its mid-1940s heyday. The recording ban, wartime shortages of shellac and lack of interest from record companies meant that much of it went unrecorded – a fact that can make the transition between swing and bebop seem artificially abrupt, occurring around 1945.

Charlie Parker (1920–55) and Dizzy Gillespie (1917–93) led the way in launching the new sounds, and the arrival of bebop began a new jazz war immediately after the end of the real one. The late 1940s also saw a Dixieland revival centred around Eddie Condon's (1905–73) club on 52nd Street and a slanging match developed between both the practitioners and the fans, polarized along traditionalist vs modernist lines and conducted in a hail of disparaging remarks that did neither side much credit, but generated a lot of publicity for jazz music.

Above
Minton's Playhouse, where the bebop style began to take shape (l–r Thelonius Monk, Howard McGhee, Roy Eldridge, Teddy Hill).

Left
Dizzy Gillespie on the corner of 52nd Street – the centre of the 1940s New York jazz scene.

Far Left
Swing devotees dance in the Savoy Club, Harlem.

Popular Melody

Duke Ellington/Blanton-Webster Band – 'Cotton Tail' (1940)
This hard-swinging track includes a famous tenor saxophone solo from Ben Webster. The Blanton-Webster Band (1940–42), named after Webster and bassist Jimmy Blanton's groundbreaking experiments at the heart of the rhythm section, epitomized the raucous excitement of swing as the big band era reached its peak, but also looked ahead to more modernist trends and to Ellington's own more ambitious musical developments.

High Art And Low Life

The traditional revival had its counterparts in Europe, notably in England, where jazz groups such as the Crane River Band and Humphrey Lyttelton Band gained ground in the wake of the war. The divisive debates recurred there, although generally a little later as the impact of bebop percolated through to musicians on the other side of the Atlantic, often through the arrival of American musicians looking for a less stressful and less racist way of life.

Bebop brought new harmonic and rhythmic ideas in to jazz and cemented the role of the virtuoso soloist and improviser at the centre of the music. The seedy club-land in which bebop thrived exacerbated the problems with drugs that were all but endemic in its circles, while pervasive racism and police harassment continued to plague the lives of the musicians. However, the clubs on 52nd Street did allow the development of mixed-race audiences in an America that was still heavily segregated, especially in the southern states.

The high artistic demands of the music contrasted vividly with the low esteem in which both the artists' work and their lifestyles were held in many quarters. Parker and Gillespie led the way in establishing the principal musical foundations of bebop. Gillespie claimed that the name came from his habit of singing as yet untitled tunes to the other players using nonsense syllables, although other theories exist – for example, Hot Lips Page (1908–54) claimed that Fats Waller (1904–43) provided the name 'bop' one night at Minton's.

The Rise Of Bebop

The bebop musicians took the 4/4 time signature of swing and added a plethora of new rhythmic accents to it, with drummers such as Kenny Clarke (1914–85) and Max Roach (b. 1924) preferring to 'ride' their cymbals and mark strict time with their hi-hats, rather than state a regular beat on the bass drum. That crucial rhythmic development went hand in hand with a new focus on extended harmonies, using much more complex substitute chords and chromatic intervals as the basic building blocks of improvisations. It afforded great scope for melodic, harmonic and rhythmic invention that was fully exploited by musicians such as Parker, Gillespie, Bud Powell (1924–66), Thelonious Monk (1917–82) and others.

That harmonic expansion was a fundamental strength of bebop, but also its built-in weakness. The musicians tended to use chord structures based on standard tunes or blues as the basis for their new melody lines, and bebop evolved as a music of great sophistication built on a repetitive and limited structure, which ultimately led to musicians exploring more experimental areas a decade later.

New York City, specifically Harlem and midtown from 42nd Street through to 52nd, was very much the crucible for bebop, and musicians gravitated to the city from all over. Bebop also travelled outwards, notably to the West Coast, where musicians including Dexter Gordon (1923–90), Art Pepper (1925–82), Howard McGhee, Hampton Hawes and Charles Mingus (1922–79) made their own contributions to the evolving form in LA's Central Avenue clubs. As in the Swing Era, live radio broadcasts from venues such as the Royal Roost in New York remained an important element in disseminating the music, and also in leaving a legacy of 'live' recordings to supplement the studio fare, where the musicians still worked under the time restraints of the 78-rpm record.

Bebop also touched the swing bands, its influence discernible in the ensembles of Duke Ellington, Woody Herman, Artie Shaw (1910–2004) and Benny Goodman. By the late 1940s, bebop was the new artistic force in jazz, even if it had not won the populist vote – that remained for the wider public with swing, and in the black communities, with the kind of earthy blues and jump music associated with Louis Jordan (1908–75), a forerunner of what would become R&B and then rock'n'roll.

The Birth Of The Cool

Bebop was hip, with its own look, its own argot and its own rather exclusive set of attitudes. The 1950s would see bop move to a more central position, through the emergence of the related forms of hard bop and soul jazz on the jukeboxes of the African-American community.

The end of the decade also saw the first stirrings of another development that would play a key role in the 1950s; the Nonet sessions of 1949–50 under the leadership of Miles Davis (1926–91), later dubbed the 'Birth Of The Cool', took an alternative approach to the by then well-established mores of bebop, using careful arrangements by the likes of Gerry Mulligan (1927–96) and Gil Evans (1912–88), and a less involved interplay of musical textures that would be taken up in the West Coast and cool jazz movements of the coming decade.

Above
Drummers such as Kenny Clarke embellished the 4/4 beat of swing to create new rhythms.

Popular Melody

Louis Jordan – 'Reet, Petite And Gone' (1946)
Jazz in the 1940s is generally described by contrasts between traditional jazz, big-band swing and the newly emerging bebop, but singer and saxophonist Louis Jordan was the figurehead of an even more populist style that proved very influential in the rise of R&B and rock'n'roll. Jordan's raucous, good-time jump-blues style is well-illustrated in this track, and is every bit as emblematic of the decade as any of the swing or bebop classics.

Dizzy Gillespie

John Birks 'Dizzy' Gillespie shares the credit for creating bebop with Charlie Parker, but his place in the history of twentieth-century music rests on a considerably wider achievement. He was born in Cheraw, South Carolina in 1917 and acquired his nickname in the 1930s. He moved to New York and worked in big bands with Teddy Hill, Lionel Hampton and Cab Calloway (the latter relationship ending acrimoniously after a notorious altercation over a spitball).

'Musically, he knows what he is doing backwards and forwards…. So the arranging, the chord progressions and things in progressive music, Dizzy is responsible for.'

Billy Eckstine

He was a prime mover in the jam sessions at Minton's Playhouse in Harlem, which became the forcing ground for the subsequent evolution of bebop. His speed and facility in the high register reflected the influence of Roy Eldridge, but he quickly displayed an increasingly original musical conception that came to fruition in the seminal group that he led with Charlie Parker in 1946.

Right

Dizzy Gillespie's trumpet had a curious, upright bell made to his specification by the Martin company.

Flying With Bird

The collaboration remains one of the crucial episodes in jazz history and laid the template for the new music that would both illuminate and divide the post-war jazz scene. Bebop demanded formidable technical abilities as well as imagination; Gillespie's pyrotechnic brilliance was the perfect foil for Parker's genius, and was underpinned by a more thorough understanding of harmonic theory than many of his contemporaries routinely possessed. Their partnership, which included further recordings and occasional reunions,

such as the famous Massey Hall concert in Toronto in 1953, put bebop on the musical map and assured their joint status as jazz immortals. While Parker burnt himself out and died prematurely, however, Gillespie went on to become a respected elder statesman of the music.

The Cuban Connection

As bebop was coalescing, Dizzy was assembling what would become a celebrated big band – one that made an equally important contribution to the development of modern jazz. Gillespie was a prime mover in the creation of Afro-Cuban jazz (or 'Cubop'), a style that brought Cuban folk and popular idioms into a jazz context. His interest was sparked by Cab Calloway's lead trumpeter Mario Bauzá, who introduced him to percussionist Chano Pozo in 1947. Pozo was fatally shot in a bar in 1948 after contributing to Gillespie's classic Afro-Cuban recordings 'Manteca', 'Guarachi Guaro' and 'Cubana Be, Cubana Bop'. Latin tunes were well-established in jazz, but this was the first band to integrate real Afro-Cuban polyrhythms within

Key Track

'Manteca' (1947)

The immediate impact of the original big-band version of this track lies in its sheer exuberance. Chano Pozo's congas and Al McKibbon's bass lay down the lithe groove as Dizzy chants 'Manteca' (meaning 'grease'). The saxophones enter with a lush counter-statement of the rhythmic figure, and Dizzy comes soaring in with a quicksilver trumpet line. The trumpet section explodes into action, turning the tune's characteristic rhythmic figure into a vibrant mass chorus.

the new bebop idiom, and others followed suit, including Machito, Tadd Dameron, Charlie Parker and Bud Powell.

The Cuban influence remained a strong element in Gillespie's music. He adopted his trademark upturned trumpet bell in 1953 and broke new ground in 1956 by taking jazz bands on State Department-sponsored tours to Africa, the Near East, Pakistan and South America, as well as Europe.

Politics And People

Gillespie became increasingly aware of his African roots and of the civil rights campaigns in America, even running for President in 1964 under a 'politics ought to be a groovier thing' banner. Astute enough to avoid the pitfalls of involvement with the drugs that plagued the bebop community, Gillespie was a natural showman as well as a brilliant musician, and is one of the select band of jazzmen who became household names.

An attempt to join the fashionable jazz-rock fusion movement in the 1970s was a rare lapse of judgement, and was quickly abandoned. He continued to lead both large and small groups throughout the rest of his career, including the United Nation Orchestra (the use of the singular reflected his adherence to the Baha'i faith and their belief in the unity of peoples), which he led from 1988 until his death from cancer in 1993.

Classic Recordings

Dizzy Gillespie Quintet (1945)
'All The Things You Are', 'Dizzy Atmosphere', 'Groovin' High'

Dizzy Gillespie & his All-Star Quintet (1945)
'Salt Peanuts', 'Shaw 'Nuff', 'Lover Man', 'Hot House'

Dizzy Gillespie & his Orchestra (1947)
'Manteca', 'Cubana Be, Cubana Bop', 'Algo Bueno' (a.k.a. 'Woody 'N You'), 'Cool Breeze', 'Good Bait', 'Ool-Ya-Koo', 'Minor Walk'

Dizzy Gillespie with Roy Eldridge (1954)
'Algo Bueno', 'I've Found A New Baby', 'Limehouse Blues'

At Newport (1957)
'Cool Breeze', 'A Night In Tunisia', 'Zodiac Suite'

Sonny Side Up with Sonny Stitt and Sonny Rollins (1957)
'The Eternal Triangle', 'On The Sunny Side Of The Street'

Something Old, Something New (1963)
'Dizzy Atmosphere', 'Good Bait', 'The Cup Bearers'

Left

Gillespie (far left) directs his big band.

Woody Herman

'It was marvellous … to work with Bill and Chubby and Flip, Ralph, Pete, and, of course, Sonny and Davey, too. That was an exciting group to be with. Ideas and whole new tunes sprang out of that group like sparks.'

Woody Herman

Key Track

'Four Brothers' (1947)

Saxophonist Jimmy Giuffre composed and arranged 'Four Brothers' for the recently formed Second Herd. The eponymous saxophone siblings are heard in the order of Zoot Sims, Serge Chaloff (baritone), Herbie Steward and Stan Getz. The tune itself is built on the chord sequence of 'Jeepers Creepers'. It remains a staple of the band's repertoire.

Woodrow 'Woody' Herman (originally Herrmann) led several of the most exciting big bands in jazz history, hitting peaks of achievement in the 1940s that few have equalled. Born in Milwaukee, Wisconsin in 1913 to German immigrants, Herman began his stage career in vaudeville as a child, but his ambition was to lead his own band. He played alto, tenor and baritone saxophone and the clarinet, as well as

singing. He worked for a number of bands before joining Isham Jones in 1934.

He fulfilled his ambition to become a bandleader almost by default in 1936, when Jones unexpectedly broke up his band in Knoxville. The players decided to continue as a co-operative band, and Herman was elected as leader of the group. Known as the Band That Plays The Blues, they began to win a big following. 'Woodchoppers Ball' was a huge hit in 1939, selling some five million copies ('It was great,' Herman said later, 'the first thousand times we played it').

New Directions For The Herd

In the early 1940s, more sophisticated arrangements gradually began to usurp the less formal 'head' structures that had been the band's staple format. Arrangers such as Dave Matthews, Neal Hefti and Ralph Burns had changed the sound of the band by the time it was officially known as Herman's Herd (later referred to as the First Herd) from 1943. By late 1945 the band was regularly winning popularity polls and setting new box-office records. Igor Stravinsky wrote his *Ebony Concerto* for them, and the concerto was premiered at Carnegie Hall in March 1946, alongside Ralph Burns's 'Summer Sequence', later completed by the famous Stan Getz feature 'Early Autumn'.

The Woodchoppers, a small band drawn from the ranks of the orchestra, also achieved success. The band's notable players included trumpeters Conte Condoli, trombonist Bill Harris, saxophonist Flip Phillips, pianist Ralph Burns, and drummers Dave Tough and then Don Lamond. Herman eventually broke up the First Herd at the height of its popularity in December 1946, for domestic reasons.

Four Brothers

The break-up proved a temporary departure. Herman had formed his Second Herd by October 1947 with a new generation of stars in the making, including the famous 'Four Brothers' saxophone section of Stan Getz, Zoot Sims, Herbie Steward (soon to be replaced by Al Cohn) and

Classic Recordings

The Band That Played The Blues (1936–43)
'Trouble In Mind', 'Woodchopper's Ball', 'Blue Flame', 'Woodsheddin' With Woody', 'Blues In The Night', 'Down Under'

Herman's (First) Herd (1944–46)
'Noah', 'I've Got You Under My Skin', 'I Ain't Got Anything But The Blues', 'Laura', 'Apple Honey', 'Caldonia', 'Goosey Gander', 'Northwest Passage', 'I Got The World On A String', 'Bijou', 'Wild Root', 'Your Father's Moustache', 'Blowin' Up A Storm', 'Ebony Concerto', 'Lady McGowan's Dream', 'Summer Sequence'

The Second Herd (1947–49)
'Keen And Peachy', 'Four Brothers', 'The Goof And I', 'Lemon Drop', 'Early Autumn', 'Keeper Of The Flame', 'More Moon', 'Not Really The Blues', 'Tenderly'

The Third Herd (1951–59)
'Blues In Advance', 'Terrissita', 'Stompin' At The Savoy', 'Perdido', 'Blue Lou', 'Four Others', 'The Man From Mars'

Woody Herman's New Big Band At The Monterey Jazz Festival (1959)
'Four Brothers', 'Monterey Apple Tree', 'Skylark'

Encore: Woody Herman (1963)
'That's Where It Is', 'Watermelon Man', 'Caldonia'

Woody's Winners (1965)
'23 Red', 'Opus De Funk'

The Raven Speaks (1972)
'Reunion At Newport', 'The Summer of '42'

40th Anniversary Carnegie Hall Concert (1976)
'Four Brothers', 'Apple Honey', 'Early Autumn'

50th Anniversary Tour (1986)
'Central Park West', 'Pools'

Above Far Left

Woody Herman, a fine reedsman and celebrated bandleader.

Above

The saxophone section from the Second Herd.

Serge Chaloff. Their three-tenors-plus-baritone setup was the Second Herd's distinctive signature sound.

The band reflected a more overt bebop influence than the First Herd, but was also plagued by a less welcome borrowing from bebop – heroin addiction. Moreover, despite the Second Herd's significant musical success, the economies of the music business had turned against big bands and Herman incurred large financial losses. Several key players departed in 1949 and by the end of the year Herman had accepted the inevitable and broken up the band, forming a septet instead.

The Herd Swings On

But Herman could not stay away from big bands for long. The Third Herd ran for much of the 1950s and toured in Europe in 1954 and South America in 1958. The brief Anglo-American Herd made an impact on jazz in the UK in 1959, and the Swinging Herd line-up of the 1960s continued the band's traditions of strong soloists and meaty arrangements. Herman later added soprano saxophone to his roster, dabbled in jazz rock and became involved in the development of formal jazz education, although his bands had been providing a schooling for young musicians from the outset in any case.

His final years were plagued by a long-running dispute with the tax authorities, and eventually all his property and assets were seized by the government. He continued to lead his band until his death in 1987, after which saxophonist Frank Tiberi took over leadership of the Woody Herman Orchestra, which remains active.

jimmy giuffre ◉ 207   zoot sims ◉ 212   stan getz ◉ 249

Billie Holiday

Billie Holiday was entirely untrained as a singer, but drew on the example of popular recording artists such as Bessie Smith and Louis Armstrong in developing her musical approach. She was able to make much of poor songs as well as great ones. Her phrasing, intonation, attention to the weight and nuance of lyrics, and her lightly inflected, subtly off-the-beat rhythmic placement were all highly individual and became widely influential.

Her early life is confusing. Recent biographical research has confirmed that she was born in Philadelphia in 1915 and was known by several names, the most frequently used being Eleanora Fagan. She was known

'What comes out is what I feel. I hate straight singing. I have to change a tune to my own way of doing it.'
Billie Holiday

Right

Jazz and blues singer Billie Holiday, whose distinctive voice was filled with emotion, passion and tragedy.

Key Track

'I Cover The Waterfront' (1941)

Anyone looking for a distillation of the qualities that made Billie Holiday one of the great song interpreters in any genre of music need go no further than her spine-tingling treatment of Heyman and Green's title track for the 1933 film I Cover The Waterfront. Her delicate phrasing and vocal timbre are not yet suffused with the painful anguish of her later material, and she draws out the meaning of the song with artful attention to detail.

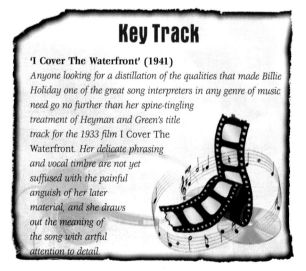

as Billie from childhood, and took the surname Holiday from her largely absent father, guitarist Clarence Holiday. She was jailed for prostitution in New York in 1930, and began her singing career shortly afterwards in clubs in Brooklyn and then Harlem.

Lady Day And Lester

Producer John Hammond heard her perform and arranged for her to record with Benny Goodman in 1933. She made her professional debut at the Apollo Theater in Harlem in 1934, and in 1935–42, with pianist Teddy Wilson, began the series of recordings that made her name, working alongside major jazz musicians such as trumpeters Buck Clayton and Roy Eldridge and saxophonist Lester Young (who bestowed her with the nickname 'Lady Day'). Young was regarded as her closest musical associate, and there was undoubtedly a special chemistry at work in their collaborations.

Her fame was largely confined to the African-American community at that stage, but spells with Count Basie in 1937 and Artie Shaw in 1938 brought her to wider notice and, in the latter case, helped to break the bar on black musicians working with white bands that was still very much in force. Her standing with intellectuals, leftists and radicals was boosted by her appearances at the interracial Café Society in 1939 and her recording of 'Strange Fruit', a song about southern lynchings that quickly attained cult status.

Success Turns Sour

Trademark ballad performances, including 'God Bless The Child', 'I Cover The Waterfront', 'Gloomy Sunday' (all 1941) and 'Lover Man' (1944), had made her a big name by the mid-1940s. She played her only minor acting role on film in 1946, as a maid opposite Louis Armstrong in New Orleans.

Her drug use led to imprisonment on drug charges in 1947 (recent research has suggested that she may have been set up, although her addiction was real enough). Her relationships with men were rarely to her advantage, emotionally or financially. Her career slipped in the wake of her jail sentence, in large part because she could no longer work in clubs in New York without the Cabaret Card, which was automatically denied to musicians convicted of drug charges.

Hard Times

Her health and her voice began to show the ravages of a hard life and drug abuse, but she was still capable of memorable performances in the 1950s, including a treasured clip made for the television special *The Sound Of Jazz* in 1957, in which she sang her 1939 hit 'Fine And Mellow' with a stellar cast of jazzmen, including Lester Young. Her late recordings and performances were often harrowing, but even her final recordings have the power to move the listener profoundly – in some respects, they may even be heard as more powerful emotional testimonies than her classic but sunnier recordings of the 1930s and 1940s.

She died in New York in 1959, having left an auto-biography, *Lady Sings The Blues* (1956), which has been seen as self-serving. Recently, biographer Stuart Nicholson has suggested that the book – but not the 1972 feature film loosely based on it – may be a more accurate depiction of her life than once seemed likely.

Classic Recordings

Billie Holiday & her Orchestra (1936–37)
'Did I Remember?', 'No Regrets', 'Billie's Blues', 'A Fine Romance', 'I've Got My Love To Keep Me Warm', 'Let's Call The Whole Thing Off', 'He's Funny That Way'

1938–39
'Back In Your Own Backyard', 'You Go To My Head', 'The Very Thought Of You', 'I Can't Get Started', 'Strange Fruit', 'Fine And Mellow', 'Some Other Spring', 'Them There Eyes', 'Night And Day', 'The Man I Love'

1940–41
'Ghost Of Yesterday', 'Body And Soul', 'Laughing At Life', 'Loveless Love', 'Let's Do It', 'All Of Me', 'God Bless The Child', 'I Cover The Waterfront', 'Gloomy Sunday'

Billie Holiday (1944–47)
'Lover Man', 'Don't Explain', 'That Old Devil Called Love', 'Good Morning Heartache', 'There Is No Greater Love', 'Easy Living', 'My Man', 'You're My Thrill'

Billie Holiday & her Orchestra (1952–54)
'East Of The Sun', 'These Foolish Things', 'Love For Sale', 'How Deep Is The Ocean?', 'What A Little Moonlight Can Do'

Songs for Distingué Lovers (1956)
'Lady Sings the Blues', 'God Bless The Child', 'Good Morning Heartache'

Lady In Satin (1958)
'You Don't Know What Love Is', 'You've Changed'

Above
Sheet music for Holiday's 1941 hit 'God Bless The Child'.

Charlie Parker

Charlie Parker, also known as 'Yardbird' or 'Bird', was a largely self-taught musical genius with acute self-destructive tendencies. His career exemplified both the creative power and the destructive social ethos of bebop. His music burned as brightly as any in jazz, but his lifestyle sent out the wrong message to too many young musicians, despite his frequent warnings to stay away from drugs.

'The way he got from one note to the other and the way he played the rhythm fit what we were trying to do perfectly.... He was the other half of my heartbeat.'

Dizzy Gillespie

Louis Armstrong had begun the evolution of jazz from an ensemble's to a soloist's music two decades earlier, but bebop brought that process to fruition and Parker was its supreme exponent. His influence was all-pervasive and continues to be so on contemporary musicians, affecting not only saxophonists, but players on every instrument.

Right

Saxophone genius Charlie Parker (third from left) performs among other jazz greats at an All-Stars event organized by Metronome magazine.

Forging The New Sound

Parker was born in Kansas City on 29 August 1920. He played in the city's famous jam sessions, wore out the recordings of Lester Young, picked up basic harmony lessons from local musicians and made remarkable progress after suffering some early slights from established players. He made his recording debut with Jay McShann's band in 1941, before working with Earl Hines and then Billy Eckstine in their seminal swing-into-bop big bands.

His fluency was attracting attention even then, and his development of a new approach to both rhythmic accents and established melodic-harmonic relationships was bearing fruit. He realized that new and radically different sounding melody lines could be created by avoiding the more obvious notes, and developed his use of the upper 'dissonant' intervals beyond the octave. The effect of these experiments was electrifying. His raw materials were ordinary blues and standard AABA tunes, but he transformed them in spectacular fashion. His work with Dizzy Gillespie in 1945–46 and his own recordings of the period formed a benchmark for bebop and seeded the central directions that jazz would explore in the next two decades.

Bird With Strings

He told several people, including the composer Edgar Varese, that he had ambitions to work with more complex musical forms, but never did so. The nearest he got was recording with strings in 1949–52 – sessions that have divided listeners ever since, although they did give him the bestselling 'single' of his career, 'Just Friends'.

Parker had become addicted to heroin sometime in the 1930s and his reliance on the drug is inextricably interwoven with his musical career. An infamous episode in California led to his incarceration in the rehabilitation

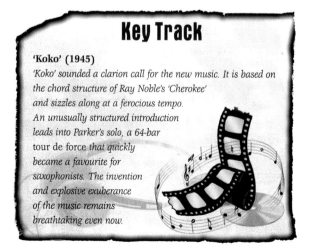

Key Track

'Koko' (1945)

'Koko' sounded a clarion call for the new music. It is based on the chord structure of Ray Noble's 'Cherokee' and sizzles along at a ferocious tempo. An unusually structured introduction leads into Parker's solo, a 64-bar tour de force that quickly became a favourite for saxophonists. The invention and explosive exuberance of the music remains breathtaking even now.

centre at Camarillo in 1947 (memorialized in his 'Relaxin' at Camarillo'), and tales of his addiction and his heavy drinking are endless. He was eventually banned from Birdland, the New York jazz club named in his honour, and the excesses of his life took their predictable toll.

Bird Lives!

Prematurely worn out, Parker died on 12 March 1955 while watching Tommy Dorsey's television show in the Manhattan apartment of Baroness Pannonica de Keonigswarter (known as Nica), a rebellious member of the Rothschild family who became a celebrated patroness of jazzmen. Graffiti proclaiming 'Bird Lives!' began to appear in the streets of New York's Greenwich Village almost immediately, posted by anonymous fans, and the legend continued to grow.

He made his great musical discoveries early and never recaptured the glories of his best work of the 1940s, but he was the supreme creative figure of his era and remained the major influence on a generation of jazz players. His astringent and penetrating sonority became the prevailing model and improvisers everywhere studied and practised every nuance of his inventions, just as he had pored over Lester Young's recordings in the late 1930s. His stylistic pre-eminence would only really be challenged with the emergence of modal jazz and free jazz in the late 1950s.

Left

Parker (left) shares a joke with bebop collaborator Dizzy Gillespie in New York, 1949.

A-Z of artists

Charlie Barnet

(Various saxophones, 1913–91)

Charlie Barnet led a successful big band from 1933
until the late 1940s and was one of the earliest white
bandleaders to employ black musicians, beginning with
Benny Carter as a guest soloist and arranger in 1934. He
introduced singer Lena Horne as an unknown in 1941 and
featured many notable musicians in his line-ups. His style
was based on an energized Basie-like riff formula, but he
was also an undisguised admirer of Duke Ellington, and
attempted to graft elements of the Ellington band's
sophisticated harmonies into his own band arrangements.

He is best remembered for Billy May's arrangement
of the much-covered 'Cherokee' in 1939, but enjoyed a
number of hits with other riff-based favourites, including
'Pompton Turnpike' and 'Redskin Rhumba', both from
1940. Like Harry James, he attempted to move into acting,
and was also involved in the restaurant business, but
continued to perform intermittently until the 1970s.

Mario Bauzá

(Trumpet, 1911–93)

Mario Bauzá takes a large amount of credit for bringing
music from his native Cuba into jazz. He worked with
Noble Sissle and Chick Webb in New York in the 1930s
before teaming up with Machito. While with Cab Calloway
in 1939–40 he sparked Dizzy Gillespie's interest in Cuban
music, which eventually led to 'Cubop'. He was musical
director of Machito's Afro-Cubans for 35 years (1940–75),
after which he formed his own group.

Earl Bostic

(Alto saxophone, 1913–65)

Earl Bostic was a soulful alto saxophonist from Tulsa who
won a wide following in the late 1940s and 1950s for his
accessible but technically accomplished style. He served
a big band apprenticeship as a player and arranger, but

then reinvented himself in more populist mode and made a series of bestselling records in the wake of his big 1951 hit 'Flamingo'. His bands nurtured future stars, including John Coltrane, Benny Golson and Stanley Turrentine.

Big Sid Catlett
(Drums, 1910–51)

Catlett was one of the most well-respected and versatile jazz drummers of the 1930s and 1940s. He played in a variety of ensembles under such luminaries as Benny Carter, Fletcher Henderson, Benny Goodman and Duke Ellington, before going on to join Louis Armstrong's All-Stars. Catlett's remarkable adaptability enabled him to play in a wide range of styles and he also successfully bridged the gap into bebop, contributing to an early Charlie Parker–Dizzy Gillespie session.

George Chisholm
(Trombone, 1915–97)

Scottish-born George Chisholm made his name as a top-class traditional jazz trombone player, but also played piano and several other brass instruments. He started out in Glasgow dance bands before moving to London, where he became an accomplished bandleader and arranger, and a successful television personality in comedy shows in the 1960s. Notable jazz associations included the RAF's famous wartime band the Squadronaires, Kenny Baker's Dozen, the Alex Welsh Band, and his own Gentlemen of Jazz.

Kenny Clarke
(Drums, 1914–85)

Kenny 'Klook' Clarke was a native of Pittsburgh, but made his primary contribution to jazz in New York in the early flowerings of bebop. Clarke, who adopted the Muslim faith as Liaquat Ali Salaam in 1946, is widely credited with developing the new rhythmic concepts that fuelled bebop. His work with Dizzy Gillespie and especially Thelonious Monk at Minton's in Harlem in the early 1940s laid the foundation for the move away from the persistently stated two- and four-beat emphasis on the bass drum.

Swing Era drummers had already experimented with a lighter and more fluid approach to rhythmic accents, but Clarke developed that concept to new heights, using crisp punctuations on bass drum – known as 'dropping bombs' – to accent his rolling ride cymbal. He was drafted to serve in Europe in 1943–46, and eventually settled in Paris in 1956, where his many associations included the acclaimed Kenny Clarke-Francy Boland Big Band.

Nat 'King' Cole
(Piano, vocals, 1917–65)

Nat 'King' Cole (real name Coles) was one of the few jazz artists to become a household name as a popular singer, and was one of the first black American artists to have his own radio show (1948–49), and later television show (1956–57). He was born into a musical family in Alabama, but moved to Chicago at the age of four, where he learned piano by ear, before studying music formally as a teenager.

He formed a trio with Oscar Moore (guitar) and Wesley Prince (drums) that became the model for many subsequent groups, including Oscar Peterson's trio. However, a vocal hit with 'Straighten Up And Fly Right' in 1943 set him on a different career path as a sophisticated pop singer. His fame as a vocalist and his later celebrity have tended to overshadow the fact that he was also a very fine and influential jazz pianist in trio and quartet settings.

Below
Pianist and vocalist Nat King Cole (left) larks about with singer Billy Eckstine.

from 1944–47 that many see as the cradle of bebop, although few recordings survive. He was one of the few black singers to be featured on national radio, largely thanks to his beguiling romantic ballads. He remained a draw on the cabaret circuit in later years.

Dexter Gordon
(Tenor and soprano saxophone, 1923–90)

Dexter Gordon is widely credited as the leading figure in the evolution of bebop on his instrument, the tenor saxophone. The Los Angeles native was influenced initially by stars of the Swing Era, in particular Lester Young, and went on to adapt many of Charlie Parker's alto saxophone innovations to the tenor. He was a notable exponent of the so-called 'chase' form, in which two tenors 'duel' for supremacy; he recorded a famous example with Wardell Gray as 'The Chase' (1947) and was also an inspired interpreter of ballads.

His career took a disastrous drug-induced dip in the 1950s, but he relocated to Europe and returned to music with renewed vigour in the 1960s, in a series of acclaimed recordings for Blue Note Records. He made a triumphal return to America in 1977, and went on to star in Bertrand Tavernier's film *Round Midnight* (1986).

Above

Saxophonists Wardell Gray (left) and Dexter Gordon act out their 1947 hit 'The Chase'.

Buddy DeFranco
(Clarinet, b. 1923)

Buddy DeFranco (Boniface Ferdinand Leonardo) became the leading clarinet player of the post-Swing Era. His liquid sonority and flowing improvisations drew on elements from both swing and bebop, but without settling fully in either camp. He served a big-band apprenticeship with Gene Krupa, Charlie Barnet and Tommy Dorsey in the mid-1940s, but is best known for his work in smaller groups with vibist Terry Gibbs, bands led by George Shearing and Count Basie, and for leading his own groups.

Right

Trumpeter Harry James's admiration of Louis Armstrong and Bunk Johnson was mutual.

Billy Eckstine
(Vocals, 1914–93)

Billy Eckstine's smooth baritone voice and suave manner brought his music to a wide audience. He joined pianist Earl Hines in Chicago in 1939 and then led a big band

Wardell Gray

(Tenor saxophone, 1921–55)

Wardell Gray died in mysterious, drug-related circumstances without fulfilling his immense potential. His control and invention at fast tempos and fluent, swinging style on the tenor saxophone adapted readily to both swing and bebop settings, while his ballad playing was strong in both emotion and tonal warmth. His sadly underweight recorded legacy is largely derived from live club dates and jam sessions, plus the two volumes of studio recordings issued by Prestige as *Wardell Gray Memorial*. Singer Annie Ross (and later Joni Mitchell) made vocalese hits based on his solos.

Harry James

(Trumpet, 1916–83)

Harry James grew up in a circus and went on to become a media celebrity as a bandleader, a fame that only intensified when he married actress Betty Grable in 1943. James made his initial reputation as a formidable trumpet

'Young Harry says to me, "Pops, I don't have to tell you. You and Louis, only men who can play this horn." That was real nice of young Harry, but he play real good trumpet himself. I told him so.'

Bunk Johnson

player with Benny Goodman's band before forming his own group in 1938, but lost some of his credibility with jazz fans when he began to work in a more populist, romantic ballad style in the 1940s.

His playing was admired by his major influences, Louis Armstrong and Bunk Johnson, and his combination of musical invention with bravura technique remained highly impressive throughout his career. He returned to more directly jazz-oriented band arrangements in the 1950s and continued to lead big bands. An inveterate womanizer and compulsive gambler, he worked in Las Vegas for many years from 1963, where his proceeds went straight back into the casinos.

J.J. Johnson

(Trombone, arranger, composer, 1924–2001)

J.J. (James Louis) Johnson was the premier bebop trombonist. His speed of execution and fluent, highly inventive approach to both melody and rhythm essentially devised a new language for an instrument that was not obviously made to suit the wide intervals and rapid

articulation of the style. He took up trombone in high school in Indianapolis, and honed his craft in swing bands before turning to bebop in the mid-1940s.

He worked with virtually all the great jazz names of the bebop era, including Dizzy Gillespie and Charlie Parker. He was part of Miles Davis's so-called 'Birth Of The Cool' project in 1949–50 and the later 'third stream' experiments initiated by John Lewis and Gunther Schuller in the late 1950s. He co-led a very successful group with Danish trombonist Kai Winding (1954–56). He was a fine composer of film and television music as well as jazz.

Below

J.J. Johnson adapted his trombone style to play bebop music with the likes of Dizzy Gillespie.

Louis Jordan

(Alto saxophone, vocals, bandleader, 1908–75)

Louis Jordan & his Tympany Five were major stars in the 1940s, providing energized recordings and exciting live shows. The alto saxophonist began by playing in swing bands, including Chick Webb's, but in 1938 he gambled on the success of his own personality, fronting a small group playing in a more overtly entertaining style. Labelled 'jump blues', this was a precursor of both R&B and rock'n'roll.

He reeled off a succession of jukebox hits through the 1940s, often with novelty titles and lyrics, including 'Five Guys Named Mo', 'Choo Choo Ch'Boogie', 'Ain't Nobody Here But Us Chickens' and 'Saturday Night Fish Fry'. Their appeal, based on melodic good humour and the comic complications of romance, crossed racial boundaries, and his popularity lasted until the early 1950s. Eclipsed by the rise of rock'n'roll, he reverted to more jazz-oriented settings and continued to perform on the cabaret circuit in later years.

in Rhythm Orchestra in 1942. Imaginative arrangements and excellent soloists ensured the band's success. It gave way to the more ambitious Progressive Jazz Orchestra in 1947 and the even more overblown, 43-piece Innovations in Modern Music Orchestra in 1950.

The latter band often featured startling arrangements (notably those by the iconoclastic Bob Graettinger), but fell foul of economic feasibility. Kenton led more standard-sized big bands throughout the 1950s, featuring a galaxy of star players. His expanded groups of the 1960s included the symphonically conceived Los Angeles Neophonic Orchestra. Although uneven in their output, Kenton's bands made a unique contribution to big-band history, and he was also influential as a jazz educator.

Stan Kenton

(Piano, arranger, composer, 1911–79)

Stan Kenton pushed big-band jazz in new directions throughout his career, and in the process divided critical opinion more radically than any other bandleader. He formed his first band in 1940, which became the Artistry

Barney Kessel

(Guitar, 1923–2004)

Barney Kessel took inspiration from his fellow Oklahoman, guitarist Charlie Christian, and developed an electric-guitar style that straddled swing and bop in effective fashion. He was featured in the Oscar-nominated short film *Jammin' The Blues* (1944), and recorded with Charlie Parker in 1947. A stint with the Oscar Peterson Trio in 1952–53 led to recordings as a leader from 1953 onwards. Kessel formed Great Guitars with Herb Ellis and Charlie Byrd in 1973; they toured and recorded until his debilitating stroke in 1992.

Machito
(Vocals, maracas, c. 1912–84)

Frank Raul Grillo was born in Florida of Cuban extraction and took the name Machito in 1940 when his brother-in-law, trumpet player Mario Bauzá, reorganized his year-old band the Afro-Cubans. Their arrangements clothed Cuban melodies and rhythms in jazz harmonies and instrumental voicings. They were highly influential in the emergence of Afro-Cuban jazz (sometimes known as 'Cubop') in the late 1940s, in the mambo craze of the 1950s and the development of modern salsa and Latin jazz.

Glenn Miller
(Trombone, 1904–44)

Glenn Miller was a trombonist of modest accomplishments, but he became one of the most famous big-band leaders in jazz. Although disdained by jazz purists, tunes such as 'In The Mood', 'Moonlight Serenade', 'String Of Pearls' and 'Tuxedo Junction' have remained enduringly popular. Miller's bands played precisely executed riff-based swing tunes and very slow ballads; his signature sound was built on a lead clarinet melody doubled an octave below by tenor saxophone, with the other saxophones, muted trumpets, and trombones all adding soft-focus colour and harmony.

Miller favoured solid, well-disciplined players who could deliver the exact sound that he required on the arrangements, rather than flamboyant jazz soloists. His catchy melodies, intricate but easy-on-the-ear harmonies and swinging rhythms caught the public imagination; his disappearance in a light aircraft over the English Channel *en route* to a concert scheduled for his Allied Expeditionary Force Orchestra only added to the mystique.

charlie christian ⊙ 114   chick webb ⊙ 131   mario bauzá ⊙ 162   oscar peterson ⊙ 210

Gillespie's chair in Billy Eckstine's seminal big band in 1945, and enjoyed a brief but creative relationship with pianist and arranger Tadd Dameron in 1948.

Although curtailed, his career saw him work with most of the major bebop artists, including Kenny Clarke, Coleman Hawkins, Dexter Gordon, Bud Powell and Charlie Parker. His conservative approach to rhythm was balanced by carefully sculpted melody lines and a wealth of harmonic invention, while his burnished tone had a sweetness and richness unusual among the bebop speed merchants. His recordings for Blue Note as a sideman were gathered in two volumes as *The Fabulous Fats Navarro* (1947). He died of tuberculosis, exacerbated by his heroin addiction.

Chico O'Farrill
(Trumpet, composer, arranger, 1921–2001)

Arturo 'Chico' O'Farrill arrived in New York from Havana in 1948 with a self-confessed low opinion of his native Cuban music by comparison with jazz, but found inspiration in the developing Afro-Cuban jazz movement led by Dizzy Gillespie, Machito and Mario Bauzá. He became a key figure in creating what he called the 'very delicate marriage' of Cuban music with jazz. His 'Afro-Cuban Jazz Suite' (1950) is a watershed work and launched a long and successful career. His son, Arturo, is also a major bandleader in Latin jazz.

James Moody
(Tenor and alto saxophone, flute, b. 1925)

James Moody was one of the strongest performers to double on flute in jazz, and was a resourceful and inventive improviser on all his horns. He joined Dizzy Gillespie from the US Air Force in 1946. A recording of 'I'm In The Mood For Love' (1949), made while living in Europe from 1948–51, brought him to a wider audience. He led his own bands in the US from the early 1950s, including a popular septet featuring vocalist Eddie Jefferson (1953–62), in which he often sang a passage of the lyrics in falsetto. Moody continues to tour and record.

Fats Navarro
(Trumpet, 1923–50)

Theodore 'Fats' Navarro died prematurely and left a limited recorded legacy, most of it as a sideman. Nonetheless, he stood alongside Dizzy Gillespie and Miles Davis as one of the most significant trumpeters in bebop. He took over

Sy Oliver
(Trumpet, vocals, arranger, composer, 1910–88)

Sy (Melvin James) Oliver was one of the finest of all big-band arrangers, and a capable instrumentalist and singer as well. His major associations included the bands of

Jimmie Lunceford, Benny Goodman and Tommy Dorsey, and he also led his own bands at various times, from the mid-1940s into the 1980s. He worked as music director and arranger for several record companies, as well as filling that role for the New York Jazz Repertory Orchestra in the mid-1970s.

Chano Pozo

(Drums, percussion, 1915–48)

Cuban percussionist Chano Pozo was Dizzy Gillespie's principal collaborator in melding Cuban music with jazz (a.k.a. 'Cubop'). Their historic 1947 recordings 'Manteca' and 'Cubana Be, Cubana Bop' (co-written with George Russell) were the first to integrate real Afro-Cuban polyrhythms within a bop idiom. Their association proved brief; Pozo was shot dead in a bar in Harlem in mysterious circumstances shortly after the recordings were made, but the Afro-Cuban fusion sound remained a significant element in Gillespie's music throughout his career.

Buddy Rich

(Drums, 1917–87)

Bernard 'Buddy' Rich was a powerhouse drummer with a phenomenal technique, but he was also capable of great delicacy when required. He grew up in the family vaudeville act before joining Joe Marsala's band in 1937. It was the beginning of a series of associations with major Swing Era bandleaders such as Harry James, Artie Shaw, Tommy Dorsey, Benny Carter and – as a deputy for Jo Jones – Count Basie.

He formed his own band in 1945 and also recorded with major bebop artists Charlie Parker, Dizzy Gillespie and Bud Powell. He worked with James again in the 1950s and 1960s, led a small group, and tried unsuccessfully to establish a career as a singer. He formed a new and much more successful big band of his own from the mid-1960s until 1974, then led a small group and ran his own club. Another third big band followed, and Rich enjoyed a high profile, through television appearances, until his death.

Above

Trumpeter Fats Navarro's impressive tonal range was unusual in a bebop player.

Max Roach
(Drums, b. 1924)

Along with Kenny Clarke, Max Roach shares the credit for inventing bebop drumming. When Clarke found himself drafted in 1943, it was Roach who emerged as the leading activist in the search for a drum style to suit the emerging melodic and harmonic complexities of the new music. He developed an approach that was both powerful and flexible enough to match the invention of Charlie Parker or Dizzy Gillespie, while at the same time elevating the drummer to equal status with the front-line soloists for the first time in jazz.

He founded Debut Records with Charles Mingus in 1952 and went on to establish himself as a major bandleader in his own right, beginning in 1954 with a famous group co-led with trumpeter Clifford Brown. He has remained a creative force through decades of stylistic shifts in jazz and has continued to absorb new influences into his ever-evolving music.

Above

Pioneering bebop drummer Max Roach reflects between takes.

George Russell
(Composer, arranger, b. 1923)

Cincinnati-born George Russell is one of a small number of jazz musicians whose primary reputation was earned as a composer and theoretician rather than as an instrumentalist. Initially a student of drums and later a pianist, Russell ultimately limited his onstage contribution to conducting, albeit in the style of a consummate showman. He framed the basic structure of his lifelong work on *The Lydian Chromatic Concept Of Tonal Organization* while hospitalized in 1945–46, and published the first version of that modally based theory in 1953, with several subsequent revisions. Its influence has been vast.

Russell composed and arranged for Dizzy Gillespie, Buddy DeFranco and Lee Konitz in the late 1940s, and began to record as a leader in 1956. His small-ensemble recordings of 1960–62 were followed by equally impressive

Right

Pianist Lennie Tristano explored a variety of styles and was an important jazz educator.

big-band projects. He spent 1963–69 in Europe, mentoring Scandinavian musicians, and then accepted a professorship at the New England Conservatory. He won a prestigious MacArthur Fellowship in 1989.

Lennie Tristano
(Piano, 1919–78)

Lennie Tristano began his career as a performer in promising style in his native Chicago, but later focused much of his time and creative energy on teaching his own musical ideas. He was born weak-sighted and was blind from the age of 10. He gathered a group of important acolytes around him during the late 1940s in New York, including saxophonists Lee Konitz and Warne Marsh and guitarist Billy Bauer, and ran a school of jazz in the city from 1951–56.

He performed and recorded intermittently from the mid-1950s, but continued to teach individual pupils. His musical concept offered an alternative to the prevailing bop orthodoxy of the day, and demanded rigorous discipline and sensitivity to complex nuances of time and tonality. He was an early explorer both of free jazz and of creating multitracked recordings by overdubbing. His own music never found a wide audience and much of it was only released posthumously, but his students ensured that his influence was a significant one.

'Now, take a group like Lennie Tristano's, which added onto that [Dixieland] feeling, made it atonal, the chord progression more intriguing and challenging.'

Dave Brubeck

Sarah Vaughan

(Vocals, 1924–90)

Sarah Vaughan began her career singing in jazz bands
led by Earl Hines and Billy Eckstine, but achieved her
greatest fame singing ballads in more commercial settings
from the late 1940s onwards. She continued to record in
both jazz and popular contexts until 1967, when she took
a five-year break. Her striking control and wide vocal
range established her as a major international star,
and she left an extensive – if sometimes infuriatingly
inconsistent – recorded legacy.

Ben Webster

(Tenor saxophone, 1909–73)

Ben Webster served an initial apprenticeship in 'territory'
bands in the Southwest (including those led by Benny

Moten and Andy Kirk) before moving to New York in
1934. He recorded with Billie Holiday and worked with
a succession of notable bandleaders before joining Duke
Ellington in 1940. He was a key member of Ellington's
legendary band of the time, often referred to as 'the
Blanton-Webster Band' from the influence exerted by
the saxophonist and bassist Jimmy Blanton.

Webster led his own small groups from 1943 and
established a reputation for his warm, lyrical approach
to ballad playing. He rejoined Ellington in 1948, but
problems with alcohol forced him to leave music entirely
from 1950–52. He returned to tour with Norman Granz's
Jazz at the Philharmonic and recorded extensively as
both leader and accompanist. He settled permanently
in Europe from 1964, where he remained active on the
club and festival circuit.

Above

*Sarah Vaughan's
extensive vocal
range ensured her
international success.*

duke ellington ⊙ **66**   **earl hines** ⊙ **126**   **buddy defranco** ⊙ **164**   **clifford brown** ⊙ **205**

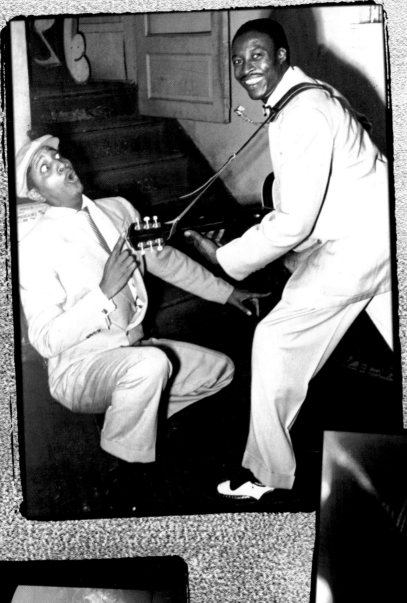

the fifties

The 1950s was a big decade for blues and jazz – arguably, the biggest. In the wake of international triumph and the stirrings of empire, the US enjoyed a boom of babies, cars, television, and urban and suburban development, that trickled down to embolden a stronger movement for civil rights for black people, inspired immigration from Cuba, Puerto Rico and other Caribbean ports, and normalized the spread of its cultural products worldwide. Europe, so much harder hit by the previous decade's war, was in a period of renewal, with the emergence of its first generation since the 1920s that could even imagine itself carefree. There were still conflicts, threats and dangers. The US brewed itself a Cold War with Communism as the bogeyman, Europe was divided by the Iron Curtain, and modernization had not yet arrived fully in Spain, Portugal, Greece and southern Italy as it had in Great Britain, France, Scandinavia, West Germany and the Netherlands.

What did this mean to music? Blues players, backing themselves with loud combos and staunch beats, raised a shout that echoed through the songs of Bo Diddley, Chuck Berry, Ray Charles and Fats Domino to be taken up by white teenagers, including one hip-shaking Elvis Presley. Jazz singers and instrumentalists, ever-more highly regarded for their swinging sophistication and lionized for their bohemian lifestyles, gained self-esteem as well as eager acolytes wherever their newly long-playing records were heard. Blues and jazz had spread wildly and widely since their first recordings in the teens and twenties. In the fifties, blues and jazz stepped out as ambassadors – and wherever they went, their call met with eager, imitative response.

Key Artists: Blues

Ray Charles
Fats Domino
Muddy Waters

Key Artists: Jazz

Miles Davis
Bill Evans
Thelonious Monk
Gerry Mulligan

Blues

'The blues had a baby and they named it rock'n'roll.'
Muddy Waters (song lyric)

The US was at war in 1950, although the Truman administration referred to Korea as a 'police action'. Dwight Eisenhower was elected President in 1952, partly on his promise to 'go to Korea'. He fulfilled this promise and a truce was negotiated, which remains in place more than 50 years later. Eisenhower embarked on a programme of highway development so that the country became more accessible by car, making it much easier for bands to travel. Vast super-highways such as Routes 80, 40 and 10 now went from coast to coast. He also worked to abolish segregation in Washington, DC; this proved slightly more difficult.

Below

Black students enter a racially mixed school in Little Rock, Arkansas under armed escort.

Separate But Not Equal

The country was still largely segregated and the majority white population seemed worryingly comfortable with its racial separation. In 1954 the United States Supreme Court voted to overturn Plessy vs Ferguson, an 1896 ruling that 'segregation was in the natural order of things' and that 'separate but equal' was the law of the land. The Court, in a unanimous verdict, ruled that 'In the field of public education, the doctrine of separate but equal has no place'; this destroyed the legal basis for segregation. However, winning the hearts and minds of many US citizens would take a little longer.

It is significant that this decision came during a time of great glory for the blues. In 1954 Muddy Waters (1915–83) recorded his full band for the first time. The modern Chicago blues sound had arrived and artists such as Howlin' Wolf (1910–76), Sonny Boy Williamson II (Rice Miller, *c.* 1912–65), Jimmy Reed (1925–76) and Little Walter (1930–68) were beginning to have big records and reach a broader public. R&B, that sprawling, inclusive idiom that covered blues shouters, saxophone honkers and crooning vocal groups, was peaking. The biggest selling record of the year was by Guitar Slim (1925–59), and one by Big Joe Turner (1911–85) was fifth. Their success was largely driven by radioplay; in every major city there was now at least one radio station where black music was played every day. Stations such as WLAC in Nashville, with a clear channel signal, could reach as many as 38 states. Radio was colour-blind and was accessible to all; white teenagers were finding black radio stations in ever-increasing numbers.

LITTLE ROCK CEN

Record labels began to produce cover records, with white artists duplicating or sanitizing the arrangements of hit R&B records.

The Role Of The DJ

Celebrity disc jockeys were the key communicators in the world of rock'n'roll radio. One of the most famous was Alan Freed in New York, who insisted on playing the original versions of hit songs. He also insisted on calling the music that he played – whether by black or white artists – rock'n'roll, and is widely credited with coining the term. The small labels that emerged from the carnage of the recording bans of the 1940s were now an industry unto themselves and they were flexing their muscles. Disc jockeys were paid by labels to play specific songs on the air, and black records began to cross over to the pop charts with greater frequency. Rock'n'roll allowed white artists such as Elvis Presley to flourish and be accepted into what had been a blacks-only idiom. Audiences, black and white, loved it.

The establishment, however, were not so enthusiastic, and rock'n'roll was attacked everywhere in the press. The old ASCAP-BMI wars were rekindled and the big record labels began to lose their dominance in the pop field. Before the end of the decade, the establishment seemed to be getting its way; rock'n'roll music, which had at first been so shocking, became bland and commercialized. The blues element, which had been such a key component of the early style, was receding (although still evident in the music of Chuck Berry and Bo Diddley) and R&B was finished. Furthermore, a number of the disc jockeys that had championed R&B – Alan Freed among them – were charged with accepting 'payola'.

Above
Hysterical teenagers cheer Elvis Presley as rock'n'roll fever sweeps the US.

Left
Alan Freed, one of the first broadcasters to grant both black and white artists airplay.

Popular Melody

Elmore James – 'It Hurts Me Too' (1957)
The bluesy piano, warm sax and measured rhythm-guitar playing on this track provide a solid base for James's raw slide guitar and extraordinary vocals, which almost scream out his anguish at the unfairness of the love triangle in which he finds himself.

Singer and songwriter Sam Cooke was one of the first gospel performers to infuriate his fans by moving into secular music.

music', were now routinely venturing into the blues and pop styles. Sam Cooke was one of the first performers to make the move; Johnny Taylor, Aretha Franklin and Lou Rawls would follow. The soul music that flourished in the next decade came alive in the mid-1950s and was gradually forging a place for itself.

Country Blues Is Reintroduced

Country blues artists had been shunted aside in the onrushing march of everything else. Lightnin' Hopkins (1911–82) went almost five years without recording, and many performers had to earn a living outside the music industry. From 1958, however, there was a revival of interest in folk music in the US, which included country blues artists. By the middle of the next decade, many black blues artist who had recorded in the 1920s were being tracked down, 'rediscovered', recorded and made into international stars.

This revival of the blues' popularity resulted in part from the introduction of the long-playing record. In 1950, 78 rpm was the dominant speed of records. The 45- and 33⅓-rpm speeds, introduced in 1948, were slow to gain ground. Atlantic issued its first 45 single in 1951, while Chess did not have any blues LPs until 1958. By the end of the decade, however, 78 rpm had faded completely away and LPs were becoming more important. New country blues recordings were issued in this format.

The Blues Spreads Overseas

Overseas markets were becoming more important for blues artists. The European tours of Big Bill Broonzy (1893–1958) and Muddy Waters in the 1950s would lead to the fully fledged, multi-artist tours of the 1960s. Champion Jack Dupree (1910–92) had settled in Europe; Mickey Baker (b. 1925) and Memphis Slim (1915–88) would follow. Blues artists were welcome all over the globe and this was a trend that would only increase over time. European labels began to produce their own blues recordings, no longer content to license masters from the US.

B.B. King (b. 1925) kept working, averaging more than 300 dates a year from the mid-1950s. He was an artist whose popularity was almost unknown to white audiences, but a steady stream of hit singles and budget-priced LPs kept his name in front of the black public, especially in the South, during the entire decade. Bobby Bland (b. 1930)

Gospel Meets The Blues

Meanwhile, Ray Charles (1930–2004) was on to something different: he was beginning to secularize gospel music. Gospel performers, who had previously been shunned by their fans when they attempted to record 'the devil's

made a breakthrough in 1957, while some stars from the early 1950s, such as Amos Milburn (1927–80) and Charles Brown (1922–99), dropped out of sight. Saxophone honkers such as Hal Singer (b. 1919), Sam 'The Man' Taylor and Big Al Sears were replaced by King Curtis, who assumed much of the New York studio work all by himself. Producers such as Leiber and Stoller, who also wrote songs, became at least as important as the 'professors' such as Jesse Stone and Howard Biggs in guiding record dates.

There was change aplenty in the music of the 1950s, and many of the decisions made during the decade continue to ripple through history. The best music of the period has proved to be exceptionally durable and many of the artists who developed at this time went on to even greater achievements in the decades to come.

Kokomo Arnold
Milk Cow Blues

*musicfirebox.com
/Milk*

Left

Muddy Waters backstage in London; Waters' 1950s UK tours paved the way for the blues tours of the next decade.

Popular Melody

Howlin' Wolf – 'How Many More Years' (1951)
A rolling blues piano and some crashing guitar chords open this track, before Howlin' Wolf's distinctive, gruff vocals take over, together with some highly charged harmonica playing. The lyrics describe the classic blues scenario of the downtrodden male lover - although from the sound of his snarling voice it would take a brave woman to mistreat the Wolf.

Ray Charles

'I do jazz, blues, country music and so forth. I do them all, like a good utility man.'
Ray Charles

A Musical Education

Shortly after his fifteenth birthday, he was expelled and left for Jacksonville, Florida to try to make a living from music. Ray continued his music education at the local union hall in Jacksonville. Within a few months, he was starting to play little jobs around the city. When he was at home, Ray would listen to country music, spirituals and blues on the radio; on his jobs, he heard singers such as Nat 'King' Cole and Charles Brown on the jukebox. Ray listened closely to these two singers and began to use them as his vocal models.

Over the next two years, Ray worked with a variety of different bands. In some cases he wrote arrangements, at other times he played alto sax or wrote songs. He travelled throughout Florida and got his first featured gig in Tampa, playing piano and singing with a combo modelled after that of Nat 'King' Cole.

In March 1948 Ray moved to Seattle, Washington on the advice of G.D. McKee, a guitarist with whom Ray had been working in Tampa. The pair quickly found plenty of work in their new surroundings, and within a few months had been signed by Downbeat Records. 'Confession Blues', one of Ray's tunes, became a hit in the spring of 1949. At this point Ray – who had been known as R.C. Robinson – became Ray Charles. The

Key Track

'I Got A Woman' (1955)
Opening with that legendary 'Weeelll', this understated blues, a celebration of the love of a good woman, is a fine example of Charles' vocal range and ease as a bandleader. His laid-back piano knits together a tight ensemble with impeccable timing to create a great R&B track and an Atlantic classic.

Ray Charles Robinson was born on 23 September 1930 in Albany, Georgia. Blind by the age of seven, he was educated at the Florida School for the Deaf and Blind in St. Augustine, where he studied piano and learned to read music in braille.

Ray Charles: 'The Genius'

Towards the end of the decade, Ray Charles spread his wings. He recorded jazz instrumentals, blues, gospel-inspired material and an album with a large orchestra, *The Genius Of Ray Charles* (1959). At the end of the decade, after more number ones with 'Drown In My Own Tears' and 'What'd I Say', Charles signed with ABC-Paramount. The deal included Ray's ownership of his own masters and complete artistic control.

From this point, Ray Charles rarely looked back. He formed a big band, founded his own record label, Tangerine, and continued to have hits. He recorded a variety of jazz, pop, R&B, soul, and country & western material throughout the 1960s and 1970s, to varying degrees of success, but came back to prominence in the 1980s with a cameo in *The Blues Brothers* (1980) and a USA For Africa single 'We Are The World'. Charles, winner of 12 Grammys and a Lifetime Achievement Award, died on 10 June 2004. His album *Genius Loves Company* (2004), featuring duets with a variety of artists, was released posthumously to huge sales and recieved multiple awards, simultaneous with an Oscar-winning Hollywood biopic, *Ray* (2004).

Classic Recordings

1954
'I Got A Woman'

1955
'A Fool For You', 'Drown In My Own Tears', 'Hallelujah, I Love Her So'

1959
'What'd I Say'

The Genius of Ray Charles (1959)
'Let The Good Times Roll', 'Just For A Thrill'

1960
'Georgia On My Mind'

1961
'Unchain My Heart', 'Hit The Road Jack'

Genius + Soul = Jazz (1961)
'I've Got News For You', 'One Mint Julep'

Modern Sounds In Country & Western Music (1962)
'I Can't Stop Lovin' You', 'You Don't Know Me'

1966
'Let's Go Get Stoned'

Far Left
Gifted pianist and entertainer Ray Charles.

Left
Downbeat Records star Lowell Fulson.

Below
Charles in the 1980 film The Blues Brothers.

owner of Downbeat Records (now Swingtime), Jack Lauderdale, teamed Ray with his number-one act, Lowell Fulson and Ray became a part of Fulson's show, playing piano and singing in the band between 1950–52. The hit 'Baby, Let Me Hold Your Hand' brought Ray more attention, but Lauderdale had entered a dry spell and Charles's contract was sold to Atlantic Records.

A Shaky Start

Ray Charles's first recording session in his own name, in September 1952, was uneventful and follow-ups yielded only one minor hit ('It Should've Been Me'). Meanwhile, Charles was working as a solo artist, picking up musicians along the way. In the summer of 1954 he organized a band to back Ruth Brown on tour, after which the band continued on its own. In November, Ray was ready to call Atlantic Records.

'I Got A Woman', recorded on 18 November 1954, changed everything. The tune was based on a gospel song and, for the first time, all Charles's passion and fervour was captured on record. It was an R&B number one and Ray's biggest hit of the 1950s. His next session produced another number one, 'A Fool For You'. Ray Charles had arrived.

Fats Domino

giving him the advice and encouragement to keep going. He practiced assiduously in his teens and was attracted to the music of boogie-woogie giants Meade 'Lux' Lewis and Albert Ammons, which he heard on jukeboxes, as well as the work of pianist/vocalists such as Charles Brown and Amos Milburn.

Domino Signs With Imperial

He began playing parties and social functions at the age of 16 and the following year joined the combo of Billy Diamond, who christened him 'Fats'. In 1949, he began a regular gig at the Hideaway Club and started to draw crowds and get noticed. New Orleans bandleader Dave Bartholomew, who was serving as a talent scout for Imperial Records, brought the label's owner Lew Chudd to hear Fats at the Hideaway. Domino was signed; Bartholomew worked as producer and the two co-wrote songs together. In the first session, cut on 10 December 1949, Fats and Bartholomew's band recorded 'The Fat Man' – basically Champion Jack Dupree's 'Junker's Blues', dressed up with a new lyric from Bartholomew. It became a smash hit and climbed as high as number two on the *Billboard* magazine Race Records chart.

A Signature Sound

Fats then formed a band modelled on Bartholomew's, which even included some of the same personnel. Much

'When Fats plays that it's magic.... It's something just a little bigger than life, just the way Fats is.'
Allen Toussaint, on the introduction to 'Goin' Home'

Key Track

'Every Night About This Time' (1950)
This track shows Fats' ability to sing a great blues vocal, which is not always so evident in some of his more upbeat numbers. The rhythm of his piano playing pushes against the beat of the band, keeping the song moving along despite its slow tempo.

Antoine Domino Jr. was born on 26 February 1928 in New Orleans, Louisiana, the youngest of eight children. His father played violin and worked at the Fair Grounds Race Track in New Orleans. Young Antoine studied piano and credits Harrison Varrett, a former member of Papa Celestin's band, with

of Fats Domino's sound is based on his vocals and piano, plus tenor saxophone solos; the arrangements on his early records do not differ greatly from those of other blues bands, but the piano's distinctive sound and use of triplets became a Domino trademark after first appearing on 'Every Night About This Time' in 1950.

'Goin' Home' hit number one in 1952 and Fats continued his streak of bestselling singles. He was still working around New Orleans for the most part and recording with the same nucleus of players. He took time out to play piano on 'Lawdy Miss Clawdy' by Lloyd Price, another number-one hit (and yet another lyric grafted on to the 'Junker's Blues' melody). The R&B coming out of New Orleans was beginning to sweep the country and Fats Domino was leading the way. The year 1953 found more hits with 'Please Don't Leave Me' and 'Goin' To The River', which infiltrated the pop chart. Herb Hardesty took most of the tenor sax solos with Fats and began to tour with him, although later on Hardesty tended to split the solos with Lee Allen.

Rock'N'Roll?

Rock'n'roll really arrived in 1955 and Fats was at the head of the pack. He had three consecutive number-one hits with 'Ain't That A Shame', 'All By Myself' and 'Poor Me'. In 1956 he delivered three more: 'I'm In Love Again', 'Blueberry Hill' and 'Blue Monday'. The sound of Fats Domino's band changed little during this period; when people asked him about rock'n'roll, he would tell them that he called it R&B and that he had been playing it for years. Indeed, he still plays that way – complete with triplet rhythms and a large saxophone section – and little has changed in the 50 years since Fats Domino was the talk of the town. He has enjoyed so many successful hit records that he is unable to play them all in any one show.

Classic Recordings

1949
'The Fat Man'

1952
'Goin' Home'

1953
'Goin' To The River', 'Please Don't Leave Me'

1955
'Ain't That A Shame', 'All By Myself', 'Poor Me'

1956
'I'm In Love Again', 'Blueberry Hill', 'Blue Monday'

1957
'I'm Walkin''

1959
'I Want To Walk You Home'

Above Far Left
New Orleans pianist and rock'n'roll superstar Fats Domino.

Left
Dave Bartholomew – bandleader, producer, composer, talent scout, trumpeter and Domino's mentor in the early days.

Muddy Waters

McKinley Morganfield was born in April 1915 in Rolling Fork, Mississippi and was raised by his grandmother Della Jones, a sharecropper on Stovall Plantation in Clarksdale. His education ended with the third grade and he remained illiterate throughout his life. He taught himself harmonica when he was about nine years old.

McKinley Becomes Muddy

Morganfield was a farmer by the time he was 10. On weekends, he was able to hear music in local juke joints and on his grandmother's phonograph. He was 13 when he heard Leroy Carr's 'How Long Blues' and began to play along. He heard Charley Patton, in person and on record, and also caught Big Joe Williams and the Mississippi Sheiks in Clarksdale. Within a few months, he was playing functions in the area; it was around this time that he acquired the nickname Muddy Waters.

In 1932, Muddy bought his first guitar. He became fascinated with Son House, who appeared frequently at area juke joints, and House taught the youngster how to fashion his first slide. Muddy also learned from Patton and his good friend Robert Lee McCollum, later Robert Nighthawk, and saw Robert Johnson play in 1937. Much later, Muddy would declare that his style was a mixture of House and Johnson influences, along with his own innovations.

'Muddy can really sing the blues ... hollering, shouting, crying, getting mad – that's the blues.'
Big Bill Broonzy

Right
Blues great Muddy Waters, whose illustrious recording career was an inspiration to countless blues artists.

From Stovall To Chicago

Muddy was recorded by Alan Lomax on Stovall Plantation in August 1941 and July 1942. In May 1943 he left Mississippi for Chicago

and, encouraged by Big Bill Broonzy, he began to work with Jimmy Rogers. He acquired his first electric guitar in 1945 and in April 1947 he recorded for Aristocrat Records. 'Gypsy Woman'/'Little Anna Mae', Muddy's first record, featured his vocal and guitar with Sunnyland Slim on piano and Big Crawford on bass. A second session in April 1948 produced 'I Can't Be Satisfied'/'I Feel Like Goin' Home', which was only a minor hit but helped Muddy to realize that he could be a successful entertainer. Leonard Chess, Muddy's producer and owner of Aristocrat (soon to become Chess Records), was rather conservative in choosing the supporting cast; Muddy was accompanied only by Crawford up to 1950 and it was December 1951 before Little Walter,

Key Track

'I'm Your Hoochie Coochie Man' (1954)
This Muddy Waters classic epitomizes the post-war Chicago blues sound, with the band sparsely punctuating the verses before launching full-scale into the choruses. A killer guitar break and Muddy's steely vocals, as well as the sexual confidence of the lyrics, ensured the song's durability and it has become a standard of its genre.

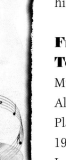

Rogers and Muddy were recorded together. The modern sound of the Chicago blues was beginning to take shape.

Otis Spann was introduced to Muddy by Rogers in 1952 and in January 1954 Muddy, Walter, Rogers, Spann, Willie Dixon and drummer Fred Below went into the studio. The session produced 'I'm Your Hoochie Coochie Man', Muddy's biggest single, and 'Just Make Love To Me', 'I'm Ready' and 'Mannish Boy' followed in quick succession. The personnel in the band turned over with some regularity: Walter left in 1952, although he made most of the record dates; Pat Hare replaced Rogers in 1957; Dixon was used only on record dates, and there were several different drummers. Yet somehow the sound of the Muddy Waters band remained remarkably consistent – he was an exceptional bandleader.

Muddy Reaches New Audiences

In 1958 Muddy Waters was encouraged by British bandleader Chris Barber to tour England. It was his first opportunity to play before large white audiences – at home, his fans were mainly black and were dwindling in numbers due to the popularity of rock'n'roll. Despite some criticism for his use of amplification, Muddy's shows rocked skiffle-mad 1950s England and inspired Cyril Davis and Alexis Korner to branch out into the blues, thereby jump-starting the 1960s blues revival.

Muddy played New York's Carnegie Hall in 1959, and the following year he played the Newport Jazz Festival and was recorded live by Chess. The album was enormously important for Muddy's career – you can hear the largely white, college-age kids responding to Muddy's band. The song 'Got My Mojo Working' gained popularity through this performance and became his signature track.

It had taken him just under 20 years to go from McKinley Morganfield, on Stovall's Plantation in Mississippi, to Muddy Waters, world-famous bandleader and recording artist. He continued to record, tour and collaborate throughout the rest of his career, which was filled with acknowledgements and awards befitting the man who was the source and inspiration of the modern blues sound. He died from heart failure on 30 April 1983.

Above
Muddy Waters' old home on Stovall Plantation, Clarksdale, Mississippi.

Left
Muddy's single 'Evil', recorded for the legendary Chess label.

A-Z of artists

Above
Bobby 'Blue' Bland
performs a slow number
at a crowded dance.

Mickey Baker
(Guitar, b. 1925)

McHouston Baker was born in Louisville, Kentucky. Originally a jazz player, he switched to blues after seeing guitarist Pee Wee Crayton. He began his recording career at Savoy in 1952 and became the first-call guitarist for R&B session work in New York. He teamed with vocalist Sylvia Vanderpool and, as Mickey & Sylvia, they had a huge hit with 'Love Is Strange' in 1956–57. Baker has published several books on guitar instruction. He settled in Paris, France in 1961.

Dave Bartholomew
(Trumpet, producer, composer, b. 1918)

Davis Louis Bartholomew was born in Edgard, Louisiana. He was one of the most prominent bandleaders in New Orleans in the mid-1940s. He recorded for DeLuxe, King and Imperial during the 1940s and 1950s, but is best known as the producer, bandleader and songwriting partner of Fats Domino, whom he produced at Imperial from 1949 into the 1960s. He also produced Smiley Lewis, the Spiders, Snooks Eaglin and dozens of other New Orleans R&B greats.

Bobby 'Blue' Bland
(Vocals, b. 1930)

Robert Calvin Brooks was born in Rosemark, Tennessee. He began recording in 1951 and was associated with B.B. King, Junior Parker, Johnny Ace and others in Memphis. A suave, deep-voiced blues romantic, he signed with Duke Records in 1952 and was one of the most consistent hitmakers in the soul blues idiom from the late 1950s to the 1970s. He had R&B number ones with 'Further On Up The Road' (1957), 'I Pity The Fool' (1961) and 'That's The Way Love Is' (1963).

James Booker
(Piano, organ, vocals, 1939–83)

James Carroll Booker III was born in New Orleans, Louisiana. He studied classical piano from the age of four and made his recording debut for Imperial at 14. He worked as a session musician in New Orleans from the mid-1950s and recorded for many different labels, as well as playing and arranging for the Lloyd Price big band in the early 1960s. Despite some successful European tours, a narcotics addiction slowed his career development, but he is still remembered with deep admiration in his home town.

'[James Booker] would go and do his piano lessons ...and then go and do all these great boogies and stuff.... He was so versatile as a teenager. And he just kept blossoming.'
Dr John

Clarence 'Gatemouth' Brown
(Guitar, violin, vocals, b. 1924)

Clarence Brown Jr. was born in Vinton, Louisiana and raised in Orange, Texas. By the age of 10 he had learned guitar and violin. After the Second World War he settled in the Houston, Texas area. He made his recording debut in 1947 for Aladdin and signed with Peacock Records in 1949. Brown formed his own group, Gate's Express, in 1953 and it continues to this day. He toured Europe in 1971 and became a frequent overseas traveller.

Brown began to freelance his recording opportunities in the 1960s. He expanded his musical palette by adding country, jazz and Cajun material to his repertoire. On guitar, his signature tune 'Okie Dokie Stomp' exemplifies his style of rapid, single notes. He uses his violin more when playing other styles but it can also be very effective on slow blues. Brown was first known as an instrumentalist, although his recordings of recent years have been mostly vocals. He is one of the great modern Texas guitarists, along with T-Bone Walker and Albert Collins.

Nappy Brown
(Vocals, b. 1929)
Napoleon Brown Goodson Culp was born in Charlotte, North Carolina. He sang with a gospel group, the Heavenly Lights, which recorded for Savoy, but was convinced to try blues material in 1954 and had several hits, including 'Don't Be Angry'. He returned to singing gospel in the 1960s but was rediscovered in the late 1970s by the blues community. He recorded several CDs for various labels in the 1980s and 1990s. He continues to tour and record.

Ruth Brown
(Vocals, b. 1928)
Ruth Alston Weston was born in Portsmouth, Virginia. She was heard performing in Washington, DC, where she was recommended to Atlantic Records. Her 1950 R&B number one 'Teardrops From Your Eyes' was followed by four more, including '(Mama) He Treats Your Daughter Mean', and she was so successful that the fledgeling label became known as 'the house that Ruth built'. After a period away from music in the 1960s and 1970s, Brown re-emerged to great acclaim for work on radio, TV, stage and film.

James Cotton
(Harmonica, vocals, b. 1935)
James Henry Cotton was born in Tunica, Mississippi and was inspired by hearing Sonny Boy Williamson II (Rice Miller) on the radio. He worked with his mentor from the late 1940s until 1953, when he made his recording debut for Sun Records. He joined Muddy Waters in 1954 and played with him, on and off, until 1966. He toured Europe with Muddy Waters in 1961 and has been a frequent international traveller. He formed his own group in 1966 and continues to tour and record.

Floyd Dixon
(Piano, vocals, b. 1928)
Floyd Dixon was born in Marshall, Texas and was raised in Los Angeles from the age of 13. He made his recording debut aged 18 for Supreme Records and also recorded for Modern and Peacock before switching to Aladdin in 1950 and releasing his biggest record, 'Call Operator 210'. He continued to record while working primarily on the West Coast. Dixon is a pianist and vocalist in the Charles Brown tradition.

Willie Dixon
(Bass, vocals, songwriter, 1915–92)
Willie James Dixon was born in Vicksburg, Mississippi and moved to Chicago at the age of 11. He learned bass and made his recording debut with the Five Breezes in 1940. After the Second World War he formed the Big Three trio, with whom he worked and recorded until 1952. He began a lengthy working relationship with Chess Records as a studio bassist, talent scout and songwriter, and wrote songs associated with Muddy Waters, Howlin' Wolf, Koko Taylor and Cream, among others. He joined forces with Memphis Slim in 1959 and toured internationally, and later formed his own band, the Chicago Blues All-Stars.

Below

Bassist, songwriter and producer Willie Dixon (centre) plays on a session at Chess Studios with J.B. Lenoir (far left).

Bill Doggett
(Organ, piano, arranger, 1916–96)

William Ballard Doggett was born in Philadelphia, Pennsylvania. The band he led was taken over by Lucky Millinder in 1940 and Doggett stayed on as pianist and arranger. After working with the Ink Spots, he played with Louis Jordan's band from 1947–51. He was active as a studio pianist, organist and arranger until 1953, when he formed the first organ–tenor sax combo. His biggest hit, 'Honky Tonk', was recorded in 1956 for King and was an R&B number one. He continued to tour and record until his death and performed regularly on the festival circuit, often using his concerts to promote civil rights issues.

Panama Francis
(Drums, 1918–2001)

David Albert Francis was born in Miami, Florida. He worked around Florida with saxophonist George Kelly before going to New York in 1938. The following year he made his recording debut with Roy Eldridge, who named him after his choice of hats. Francis worked with Lucky Millinder from 1940–46 and Cab Calloway from 1947–52 but his reputation dates mainly from his session work in New York. He was the first-call drummer on R&B sessions throughout the 1950s and early 1960s, and was an important figure in changing the black swing beat to R&B.

Lowell Fulson
(Guitar, vocals, 1921–99)

Lowell Fulson was born in Tulsa, Oklahoma and began his professional career in Oakland, California. He made his recording debut in 1946 and by 1950 he was a hitmaker for Swingtime Records with such songs as 'Every Day I Have The Blues' and 'Blue Shadows'. His band at this time featured a realatively unknown Ray Charles on piano. He switched to Chess in 1945 and had another hit with 'Reconsider Baby'; his final big record came in 1967 with 'Tramp'. Originally inspired by T-Bone Walker, Fulson managed to stay current with changing blues trends throughout his career.

Rosco Gordon
(Piano, vocals, 1928–2002)

Rosco Gordon was born in Memphis, Tennessee. He won an amateur contest in 1950 and was soon appearing on WDIA radio with his own show. He began recording with Sam Phillips in 1951; Phillips sold the master of 'Booted' to Chess Records and the master of 'No More Doggin'' to Modern. Gordon had two hits, on two different labels, at the same time in 1952. He had a further hit with 'Just A Little Bit' on Vee Jay in 1959.

Gordon was out of music full-time after the 1960s. He moved to New York and operated a dry-cleaning business, before forming his own record label and issuing 45-rpm singles during the 1980s. He was recorded by Stony Plain in 2000 and toured again for the last two years of his life. The idiosyncratic, loping rhythms of Gordon's music was influential on the development of ska and reggae music in Jamaica.

Guitar Slim
(Guitar, vocals, 1925–59)

Eddie Lee Jones was born in Greenwood, Mississippi. He sang in church as a child but had relocated to New Orleans by the age of 17, where he worked with Huey 'Piano' Smith in a small group until 1953. His recording debut was on Imperial in 1951, but his most important recordings were for Specialty during 1954–55 and Atlantic in 1956–58. Guitar Slim had only one hit, but it was an R&B number one: 'Things That I Used To Do', arranged by the pianist on the session, Ray Charles.

Slim was a flamboyant performer, noted for the wild colours of his suits and hair. He was famous for his 'walks':

using a lengthy extension cord he would parade around a room or even out into the street, playing his guitar all the while as the sound continued to come out of his amplifier on stage.

Lightnin' Hopkins
(Guitar, vocals, 1911–82)

Sam Hopkins was born in Centerville, Texas. His father and two brothers were musicians and he learned guitar from an early age. He met and played with Blind Lemon Jefferson at the age of eight. He accompanied his cousin, Texas Alexander, for much of the 1930s, drifting through Texas. He was discovered in Houston by Lola Cullum in 1946 and signed with Aladdin Records. His first record featured pianist Thunder Smith and with that release he became Lightnin' Hopkins. He recorded hundreds of songs from 1948–54, for a variety of different labels.

After a dry patch, Hopkins was 'rediscovered' during the folk blues revival of the late 1950s and from 1959 recorded dozens of albums for various labels. He toured constantly, became a regular on the festival circuit in North America and did considerable film and TV work. Lightnin' Hopkins' great gift was his ability to create songs from the flimsiest suggestion, and to play exquisite country blues guitar even though he lived in a big city for most of his life. He also had an extraordinarily fluid sense of song structure and time.

Earl Hooker
(Guitar, vocals, 1930–70)

Earl Zebedee Hooker Jr., a cousin of John Lee Hooker, was born in Clarksdale, Mississippi. He learned guitar by the age of 10 and moved to Chicago in 1941. Hooker was inspired by Robert Nighthawk and at the end of 1940s returned south, where he played with Rice Miller and Ike Turner. He first recorded in 1952, and from 1959 recorded

a series of singles for small Chicago labels. He recorded and toured internationally in 1965 and 1969. Hooker was a slide guitar player of great originality but was slowed by tuberculosis, which eventually killed him.

Big Walter Horton
(Harmonica, vocals, 1918–61)

Walter Horton was born in Horn Lake, Mississippi. He taught himself harmonica at the age of five and was working the streets shortly thereafter. He moved to Chicago in 1940 but it wasn't until later in the decade that he began to be more active professionally. Horton replaced Junior Wells in the Muddy Waters band in 1953 and worked with Muddy for about a year. One of Chicago's finest harmonica players, he recorded with a variety of different musicians, but was particularly associated with Johnny Shines and Jimmy Rogers.

Left
Texan blues legend Lightnin' Hopkins enjoys a cigarette in the studio.

Below
Slide guitarist Earl Hooker, who played with Rice Miller and Ike Turner, among others.

The inimitable Howlin' Wolf, owner of one of the most distinctive voices in the blues, blows a solo on the harmonica.

Howlin' Wolf
(Guitar, harmonica, vocals, 1910–76)

Chester Arthur Burnett was born in White Station, Mississippi. Inspired by Charley Patton, Wolf earned his living as a farmer in the West Memphis, Arkansas area and was strictly a weekend performer until he was almost 40 years old. He got a radio spot in 1948 and the sound of that band, which was electric rather than acoustic, heightened interest in his work. He began to record in 1951 for Sam Phillips, who sold his masters to both Modern Records and Chess Records. Ultimately, Chess won out and Howlin' Wolf recorded for the label from 1952 until his death.

'When I heard Howlin' Wolf, I said, "This is for me. This is where the soul of man never dies."'
Sam Phillips

While Wolf was a capable guitarist and harmonica player, it was his intense, growling voice that dominated his performances – it was one of the great blues voices of all time. Unlike many of his blues peers, Wolf was a flamboyant entertainer who could rock the house. He was considered a leading light of the Chicago blues scene for many years.

Elmore James
(Guitar, vocals, 1918–63)

Elmore Brooks was born in Richland, Mississippi. He learned guitar at an early age and was playing functions by the age of 14. He often worked with Rice Miller from the late 1930s until he was drafted into the Navy in 1943. He rejoined Miller after the war and was headquartered in West Memphis, Arkansas. James recorded 'Dust My Broom' at the tail end of a Rice Miller session for Trumpet Records in 1951, and it became a surprise hit.

James moved to Chicago, where he formed his own group, the Broomdusters, and recorded for Modern/Flair/Meteor from 1952–56 and Fire/Fury/Enjoy in 1959–62. He was the premier electric slide guitarist of his era and his signature riff, used on 'Dust My Broom', was heard on many of his recordings and copied by countless imitators.

Etta James
(Vocals, b. 1938)

Jamesetta Hawkins was born in Los Angeles, California. She moved to the San Francisco area, where she was discovered by Johnny Otis. She made her recording debut at the age of 16 for Modern, and had a number-one R&B hit with her first record, 'The Wallflower' (a.k.a. 'Roll With Me Henry'). She worked in rock'n'roll package tours throughout the 1950s before signing with Chess Records in 1960 and scoring another big record with 'At Last'. A versatile performer, Etta James can deliver the goods on low-down blues, rockers and tender ballads, and won a blues Grammy in 2005.

Etta James, whose powerful voice suits a wide range of blues material.

Earl King
(Guitar, vocals, 1934–2003)

Earl Silas Johnson IV was born in New Orleans, Louisiana. He was influenced by Guitar Slim and made his recording debut for Savoy, as Earl Johnson, in 1953. Upon switching to Specialty in 1954, he became Earl King. Often associated with New Orleans blues pianist Huey 'Piano' Smith in the 1950s, King scored his biggest hit with 'Those Lonely, Lonely Nights' for Ace Records in 1955. A favoured songwriter among New Orleans R&B artists, King recorded for many small New Orleans labels over the years. He remained an active performer until shortly before his death.

J.B. Lenoir
(Guitar, vocals, 1929–67)

J.B. Lenoir was born in Monticello, Mississippi; his parents were farmers as well as musicians. He learned to play the guitar at the age of eight and left home in the early 1940s to work with Rice Miller and Elmore James, before settling in Chicago in 1949 and making his recording debut in 1951 for Chess Records. He worked around Chicago for most of the decade and recorded for a number of different labels. Lenoir toured Europe with the American Folk Blues Festival in 1965. He is best remembered for his original compositions – many of which explored topical themes – and his distinctive, keening falsetto vocals.

Little Walter
(Harmonica, vocals, 1930–68)

Marion Walter Jacobs was born in Marksville, Louisiana. He taught himself harmonica at the age of eight and was working the New Orleans streets by the time he was 12. He worked in Helena, Arkansas (where he met Rice Miller) and St. Louis before arriving in Chicago in 1946. He was encouraged by guitarists Tampa Red and Big Bill Broonzy and also met Jimmy Rogers. He made his recording debut in 1947 and joined forces with Muddy Waters the following year. He worked with Muddy until 1952 when his own Checker record, 'Juke', became an R&B number-one.

Walter formed his own group with the Aces (David Meyers, Louis Meyers and Fred Below), and toured clubs and concert halls on R&B package tours. He continued to have hit records (including a second number one R&B hit, 'My Babe') throughout the decade. He toured England in 1962 and 1964. Little Walter was an innovative superstar on harmonica, able to create unusually swinging, melodic single-note solos.

Professor Longhair
(Piano, vocals, 1918–80)

Henry Roeland Byrd was born in Bogalusa, Louisiana and formed his first combo, Professor Longhair and the Four Hairs, shortly after the Second World War. His Atlantic sessions in 1949 and 1953 produced his signature songs 'Mardi Gras in New Orleans' and 'Tipitina'. As an ebullient and racy vocalist, and a pianist who employed a characteristic rhumba-boogie, Longhair is the link between older New Orleans pianists and the new arrivals of the 1950s. He enjoyed a comeback after appearing at the 1971 New Orleans Jazz & Heritage Festival, and returned to touring and recording until his death.

Below

J.B. Lenoir performs in the UK during the 1965 American Folk Blues Festival tour.

Earl Palmer
(Drums, b. 1924)

Earl Cyril Palmer was born in New Orleans, Louisiana. As a member of Dave Bartholomew's band, he played drums on the first Fats Domino session in 1949. He soon became the first – and sometimes only – call drummer for New Orleans R&B record dates, recording with a variety of artists that included Little Richard, Smiley Lewis, Bobby Mitchell, the Spiders and Shirley & Lee, and he is generally credited with bringing the New Orleans street beat into the studio. He moved to Los Angeles in 1957 and continued to be a top studio drummer for many years.

Above

Jimmy Reed (right), whose urban Chicago sound was a big influence on the British blues bands of the 1960s.

Little Junior Parker

(Harmonica, vocals, 1932–71)

Herman Parker Jr. was born in Bobo, Mississippi and worked with Howlin' Wolf as early as 1949 in West Memphis. Parker was associated with B.B. King, Bobby Bland and Johnny Ace in the Memphis scene of the early 1950s. He recorded for Sun with his own group, the Blue Flames, in 1953 ('Mystery Train') and signed with Duke Records in December of that year, where he stayed until 1966. Parker was a first-rate harmonica player but an even better singer. He was more of a crooner than a shouter and, as such, his blues ballads were always outstanding.

Piano Red

(Piano, vocals, 1911–85)

Willie Lee Perryman was born in Hampton, Georgia. Perryman was sometimes known as Dr Feelgood, and

his older brother, Rufus, was known as Speckled Red. He worked mainly as a soloist in the Atlanta area before signing with RCA in 1950. His first record, 'Rockin' With Red'/'Red's Boogie' was a two-sided hit. His early records emphasized his piano, but later sessions were in more of an R&B groove, with horns and vocal groups. He continued to tour mostly in Europe, under the name Dr Feelgood, until his death.

Snooky Pryor

(Harmonica, vocals, b. 1921)

James Edward Pryor was born in Lambert, Mississippi. He learned harmonica at the age of 14 and left home in 1937 to work as an itinerant musician. He settled in Chicago in 1940. After Army service during the Second World War he got the idea of amplifying his harmonica, and was the first to develop that sound. He recorded for small Chicago labels throughout the 1950s but left music in the early 1960s, only to be 'rediscovered' in the early 1970s.

Jimmy Reed

(Guitar, harmonica, vocals, 1925–76)

Mathis James Reed was born in Dunleith, Mississippi. His friend Eddie Taylor taught him guitar and harmonica, but he rarely played professionally until he moved to Gary, Indiana in 1948 and gradually worked himself into the Chicago blues scene. He recorded on harmonica with John Brim and, after failing an audition for Chess Records, recorded his own session for Chance Records in 1953. At this point, he reunited with Eddie Taylor.

Reed recorded for Vee Jay from 1953 until the label folded in 1965. His most successful period was 1955–61, when he had seven top 10 R&B hits ('Big Boss Man', 'Bright Lights, Big City' etc.). Reed's formula was simple: a lazy tempo with a boogie figure on the bottom, harmonica solos and his slurred, almost unintelligible vocals. He was the most consistently popular Chicago bluesman, his records routinely making the pop chart, but credit must also go to his faithful guitarist Taylor and his wife, Mama Reed, who helped to write many of his songs.

Huey 'Piano' Smith

(Piano, vocals, b. 1934)

Huey P. Smith was born in New Orleans, Louisiana and worked with Earl King and Guitar Slim in the early 1950s. He made his recording debut for Savoy in 1953 but his on-off tenure with Ace Records from 1955–64 was his most important. His group the Clowns had two huge R&B records in 'Rockin' Pneumonia And The Boogie-Woogie Flu' and 'Don't You Just Know It' in 1957–58. Smith was a fine songwriter, pianist and vocalist, and one of the bright stars of the New Orleans R&B scene of the late 1950s and early 1960s.

Sunnyland Slim
(Piano, vocals, 1906–95)

Albert Luandrew was born in Vance, Mississippi. He was self-taught as a pianist and spent the period 1925–39 in Memphis, playing functions and small clubs. He went to Chicago to find work outside music, but instead fell in with the local blues crowd and worked with Tampa Red, Jump Jackson and Muddy Waters. He began recording in 1947 and recorded for more than two dozen small labels around Chicago. A solid, workman-like performer, Slim was the patriarch of the Chicago blues scene in his later years.

Rufus Thomas
(Vocals, 1917–2001)

Rufus Thomas Jr. was born in Cayce, Mississippi and raised in Memphis, Tennessee. He worked with tent and minstrel shows throughout the 1930s. He recorded for Sun Records in the early 1950s and had the label's first hit with 'Bear Cat' in 1953; he also worked as a disc jockey at WDIA, Memphis. He began recording for Stax in 1959 and had big R&B hits with humorous dance songs such as 'Walkin' The Dog' and 'Do The Funky Chicken'. Billed as the 'World's Oldest Teenager', Rufus Thomas was an ambassador for Memphis blues and is the father of 1960s soul siren Carla Thomas.

Big Mama Thornton
(Harmonica, vocals, 1926–84)

Willie Mae Thornton was born in Montgomery, Alabama. She settled in Houston, Texas in 1948 and began recording for the Peacock label in 1951. She toured with Johnny Otis in 1952–53 and recorded her number-one R&B hit, 'Hound Dog', with his band. The record, famously covered by Elvis Presley, enabled her to branch out on her own. After leaving Peacock in 1957, she settled in the San Francisco area and worked as a solo artist. She recorded albums for Arhoolie, Mercury and Vanguard in the 1960s and 1970s.

Sonny Boy Williamson II (Rice Miller)
(Harmonica, vocals, c. 1912–65)

Alex Ford 'Rice' Miller was born in Glendora, Mississippi. He taught himself the harmonica at the age of five and by his early teens had left home to sing and play as 'Little Boy Blue'. He worked streets, clubs and functions through Mississippi and Arkansas during the 1930s, often playing with Robert Johnson, Elmore James and Robert Lockwood Jr. In 1941 he began a radio programme, *King Biscuit Time*, on KFFA in Helena, Arkansas and billed himself as Sonny Boy Williamson.

Sonny Boy started recording for Trumpet in 1951. He switched to Checker in 1955 and had a big R&B hit with 'Don't Start Me To Talkin'. He toured Europe with the American Folk Blues Festival in 1963 and recorded with the Yardbirds. Rice Miller was an outstanding harmonica player and also had a fantastic blues voice; he was one of the great blues personalities of the 1950s and 1960s.

Below
Sonny Boy Williamson II (Rice Miller) tours with the 1963 American Folk Blues Festival.

Jazz

Above

African-American jazz artists such as Charles Mingus promoted civil rights in their music.

'In New Orleans ... there was the African influence ... from Western Europe came the harmonic sense, the tonal structure, the instruments employed. Today ... there are the newer influences of contemporary serious composers: Bartok, Stravinsky, Milhaud, and others.' **Dave Brubeck**

The 1950s was a period of sharp social and political contrasts. The decade is often regarded as a stultifyingly conservative and rather monochrome one, but the suburbanization and the solidification of middle-class values took place under the looming shadow of the Cold War in America and the physical separation of East and West in Europe. The threat of atomic weapons loomed large, and the 'space race' added further tensions to fraught international relations.

It was also a period of intensifying campaigns to secure civil rights for the African-American population, and the seeds were sowed for the removal of segregationist legislation during the 1960s. That campaign was directly reflected in the music of several major jazz musicians, including Sonny Rollins (b. 1930), Max Roach (b. 1924) and Charles Mingus (1922–79). In Europe, wartime austerity carried on well into the 1950s, and the domination of US culture on a global basis became increasingly apparent – transmitted through media including films, music, Broadway musicals, radio and eventually television.

Rock'N'Roll Revolution

Jazz faced a major new competitor in the quest for listeners – one that was to dominate almost from the outset. Rock'n'roll exploded on to the music scene – the convenient launch point is usually taken to be Bill Haley's 'Rock Around The Clock' in 1954, but the groundwork had already been laid by jazz, blues, country, R&B and gospel music, all of which fed into the new teen-oriented form (the teenager as a distinct – and increasingly marketable – entity was also a new 'invention' of the decade).

Jazz had enjoyed a brief tenure as the principal popular music of America from the 1920s to the early 1940s, but would never regain that position. In the 1950s, though, hard-bop artists enjoyed wide popularity within African-American communities, and jazz was still a mainstay of the neighbourhood jukeboxes and clubs. In Europe, bop began to generate its own adherents, led by the likes of John Dankworth, Ronnie Scott and Tubby Hayes in England; the divisive arguments of the 1940s in America were replicated on the jazz scenes there. As in Hitler's Germany, jazz also came to be seen as an underground symbol of freedom within the Communist bloc, and spawned a clandestine music scene in later decades.

Hard Bop Takes Centre Stage

Hard bop became the 'mainstream' jazz form of the 1950s. It grew out of the new direction pioneered by the bebop artists of the late 1940s, but introduced an earthier feel that drew more overtly on blues and gospel. Art Blakey (1919–90) and Horace Silver (b. 1928) led the way in establishing the genre, while Jimmy Smith (1925–2005) laid down the ground rules for the related form of soul jazz, and paved the way for an eruption of Hammond organ trios.

The music associated with hard bop draws on the rhythmic and harmonic principles laid down in bebop, but with simpler motifs, a greater rigidity in the theme-solos-theme structure and a heavier reliance on 'running' the chord changes. The music had a heavier feel in both instrumental expression and rhythm than the airier registers of bebop, and its more obvious use of blues, gospel and R&B antecedents prompted the 'soul' and 'funk' tags, which quickly became attached to the music. It had a visceral, exciting sound with a distinctly urban ambiance, and it is no accident that many of its principal creators came from the big cities of the Northeast and Midwest – places such as New York, Chicago, Pittsburgh, Detroit and Philadelphia.

Above
Art Blakey helped to form the new hard-bop sound.

Left
'Rock Around The Clock' introduced rock'n'roll.

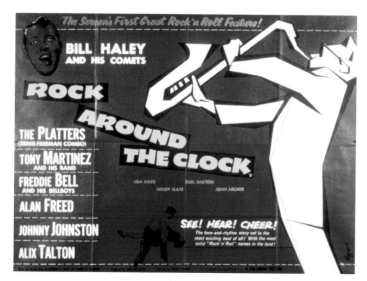

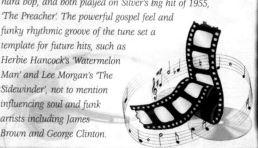

Popular Melody

Horace Silver – 'The Preacher' (1955)
Horace Silver and Art Blakey were the primary progenitors of hard bop, and both played on Silver's big hit of 1955, 'The Preacher'. The powerful gospel feel and funky rhythmic groove of the tune set a template for future hits, such as Herbie Hancock's 'Watermelon Man' and Lee Morgan's 'The Sidewinder', not to mention influencing soul and funk artists including James Brown and George Clinton.

Right
Miles Davis's Kind Of Blue.

Far Right
Trumpeter Chet Baker.

Below
Vocalist Frank Sinatra.

A Complex Mosaic

By the end of the decade, the perceived limitations of the hard-bop format were pushing some musicians into more experimental directions. The emergence of pianist Cecil Taylor (b. 1929) and the arrival of saxophonist Ornette Coleman (b. 1930) in New York in 1959 were crucial turning points in the move towards free jazz in the 1960s, but bop did not relinquish its position immediately and continued to thrive in the hands of young musicians such as Lee Morgan (1938–72), Wes Montgomery (1925–68), Cannonball Adderley (1928–75) and Hank Mobley.

If hard bop was the signature jazz sound of the decade, it was only part of an increasingly complex mosaic within the broad parameters of the music. Louis Armstrong (1901–71) consolidated his position as the most famous of all jazz names with his All-Stars, while traditional jazz still thrived through commercial musicians like Al Hirt, Pete Fountain and numerous others. Many of the big-band leaders had reformed their groups (or never actually halted), including Duke Ellington (1899–1974), Count Basie (1904–84), Woody Herman (1913–87), Benny Goodman (1909–86), Stan Kenton (1912–79), Buddy Rich (1917–87) and Harry James (1916–83).

The developments in popular music since the late 1930s had installed singers as the main focus of teenage devotion; jazz-oriented singers such as Frank Sinatra (1915–98), Ella Fitzgerald (1917–96), Sarah Vaughan (1924–90) and Nat 'King' Cole (1917–65) were all international stars, crossing over to pop audiences with ease. The major names in modern jazz were all musicians who had launched their careers in bebop (or had been strongly influenced by it), but had moved off in diverse directions. They included Miles Davis (1926–91), Thelonious Monk (1917–82), Dizzy Gillespie (1917–93), Charles Mingus, Sonny Rollins and John Coltrane (1926–67) – all of whom helped to shape the development of jazz.

Playing It Cool

Modal jazz was well established by the end of the decade, reflected in the success of Miles Davis's album *Kind Of Blue* (1959). Cool jazz was also a key contributor to the mix. Often seen as a largely white reaction to the mainly black hard-bop mainstream, cool jazz grew out of the arranging experiments of Gerry Mulligan (1927–96) and Gil Evans (1912–88), exemplified in Miles Davis's Nonet recordings of 1949–50 (later dubbed the 'Birth Of The Cool' on their LP release). As the name implies, cool jazz adopted a less frenetic and more arrangement-oriented approach than hard bop, although the forms are clearly related;

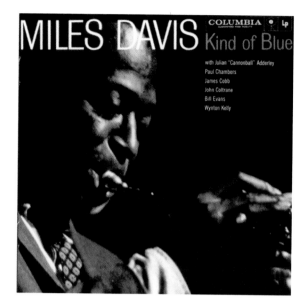

indeed, they are effectively a parallel development from the same harmonic and rhythmic foundations in bebop.

Mulligan's subsequent quartet in Los Angeles with trumpeter Chet Baker (1929–88) proved very popular, and the West Coast became the centre of the cool movement (it is sometimes referred to as 'West Coast' jazz) in the work of artists such as Shorty Rogers, Bud Shank, Shelly Manne, Chico Hamilton and Teddy Edwards. Major names like Dave Brubeck (b. 1920), Stan Getz (1927–91) and Art Pepper (1925–82) often reflected a cooler approach, while Lennie Tristano (1919–78) acolytes Lee Konitz and Warne Marsh also explored related ground.

The Advent Of The LP

The arrival the long-playing (LP) record was a significant development in itself. Up until the early 1950s, all recordings had been made under the strictly imposed time limitations of 78-rpm records. In practice, jazz musicians often played at very extended lengths in live performance, even before the bebop era – especially in club sets or jam sessions.

Broadcasts permitted the players to stretch out, but it was only with the advent of the longer playing time of the LP that they were able to begin reflecting their live work more accurately in the recording studio. That could be a mixed blessing, and many 1950s recordings were little more than loose blowing sessions, but it did allow a more faithful record of a musician's style and abilities to be preserved in the studio environment. The 1950s, then, turned out to be a complex decade, both within jazz and in the wider world, rather than – as they are sometimes depicted – simply the dull, hidebound prelude to the new freedoms and excesses of the 1960s.

Popular Melody

Dave Brubeck Quartet – 'Take Five' (1959)
Pianist Dave Brubeck was one of the most successful jazz artists of the era and scored a major hit with 'Take Five', written by his great saxophonist, Paul Desmond. The pianist liked to experiment with time signatures other than the standard 4/4, and the combination of two memorable melodic hooks and a catchy time signature in 5/4 caught the public's imagination, making it an enduring favourite.

Miles Davis

Miles was brought up in St. Louis and first played music professionally in that city. He moved to New York in 1944, in time to catch the flowering of bebop, and played with Charlie Parker and Dizzy Gillespie in the city's clubs – but the frenetic style of the new music was not his real forte.

Miles Ahead

A lateral shift into a development that had been bubbling under the work of arrangers such as Gil Evans and Gerry Mulligan came with Miles's 1949–50 sessions, later dubbed the 'Birth Of The Cool', which paved the way for cool jazz. That new style quickly came to be seen, despite Miles, as a largely white response to bebop.

In 1954 Davis kicked his heroin addiction and re-launched his flagging career. His use of a Harmon Mute with its stem removed gave him a lyrical, instantly recognizable sound, and perhaps helped him to work around the fact that, by jazz standards, he was not a dazzling virtuoso. The latter half of the 1950s witnessed outstanding peaks of Davis's achievement. In those years, he led his great quintet with saxophonist John Coltrane and also made a series of classic records with Gil Evans, including *Miles Ahead* (1957), *Porgy And Bess* (1958) and *Sketches Of Spain* (1959–60).

Mastering The Modes

The influence of George Russell led Davis towards a modal theory of jazz, in which improvisation was based on a set of scales (modes were originally part of early Greek music) rather than on the chord-based structures of bop. Miles brought these ideas to a wide audience, notably in *Milestones* (1958) and the classic *Kind Of Blue* (1959).

Typically, though, a new decade brought another change of direction. Davis's classic 1960s quintet with saxophonist Wayne Shorter, pianist Herbie Hancock and the rhythm section of Ron Carter and Tony Williams was one of the great units in jazz history. In 1969, he recorded *In A Silent Way* with an electrically-enhanced line-up,

'Don't play what's there, play what's not there.'
Miles Davis

The history of post-war jazz tracked the musical development of Miles Dewey Davis III so closely that it is tempting to see the trumpeter as the orchestrator of each of the most significant stylistic shifts of the era. With the notable exception of free jazz, Miles seemed to trigger a new seismic shift in the music with each passing decade. The reality is inevitably less simple, but there is no question that if Miles did not initiate successive revolutions, he was consistently in the frontline of their development and popularization.

Born into a black, bourgeois family in Alton, Illinois in 1926,

Key Track

'So What' (1959)
This famous track comes from Davis's Kind Of Blue *album. The open (modal) harmonic structure is ideally suited to the trumpeter's characteristic economy of expression, with every note given significant weight and emphasis. The rhythm section floats the music on an airy but strongly defined pulse, and the three horn players respond with lyrical, beautifully wrought soloing.*

Classic Recordings

Birth Of The Cool **(1949–50)**
'Jeru', 'Move', 'Godchild', 'Budo', 'Venus De Milo', 'Rouge', 'Boplicity', 'Israel', 'Deception', 'Rocker', 'Moondreams', 'Darn That Dream'

Miles Davis And The Modern Jazz Giants **(1954)**
'Bemsha Swing', 'The Man I Love'

Cookin', Relaxin', Workin', Steamin' **(1956)**
'Salt Peanuts', 'If I Were A Bell', 'Four', 'When Lights Are Low'

Milestones **(1958)**
'Milestones', 'Two Bass Hit', 'Straight No Chaser'

Porgy And Bess **(1958)**
'Summertime', 'I Loves You, Porgy', 'Gone'

Kind Of Blue **(1959)**
'So What', 'All Blues', 'Blue In Green'

Sketches Of Spain **(1959)**
'Concierto De Aranjuez', 'Saeta', 'Solea'

Miles Smiles **(1966)**
'Orbits', 'Freedom Jazz Dance', 'Footprints'

In A Silent Way **(1969)**
'In A Silent Way', 'Shhh/Peaceful'

Bitches Brew **(1969)**
'Pharaoh's Dance', 'Miles Runs The Voodoo Down'

followed by the dense *Bitches Brew* (1969), generally regarded as the cornerstone of the jazz-rock wave of the 1970s. Many older jazz fans parted company with his music at this point, but Miles was unrepentant in seeking a new, rock-oriented audience.

The textural mass of his music grew increasingly dense with guitars and keyboards, and he himself became progressively more distant from his audience, a move exacerbated by poor health and drug use. He was in the habit of playing with his back to the house, using a trumpet fitted with a modified wah-wah pedal.

Back In Business

He stopped playing altogether throughout 1975–80, but resumed his performing and recording career with a series of pop-funk-oriented bands in the 1980s. Out-of-character reunions in the summer of 1991 with some of his eminent former sidemen at Montreux and in France suggested he was aware that his death in September was imminent.

For four decades Miles had launched the careers of musicians including John Coltrane and Bill Evans in the 1950s, Ron Carter, Wayne Shorter and Herbie Hancock in the 1960s, John McLaughlin, Chick Corea, Jack DeJohnette and Dave Holland in the 1970s, and John Scofield, Mike Stern and Kenny Garrett in the 1980s. He was always open to experiments and brought together diverse influences, ranging from Stockhausen's electronic textures to soul, funk, hip hop and ethnic instruments.

The connecting thread in all of this was Miles himself. His own sound and approach remained largely a constant at the centre of all these changing musical contexts. The abrasive personality, menacing aloofness, foul language and arrogant demeanour that saw him dubbed the 'Prince of Darkness' seemed only to add to his charisma.

Above Far Left

Miles Davis (far right) with Sidney Bechet (far left) at the 1949 Jazz Fair in Paris, France.

Above

The classic quintet of the 1960s: (l–r) Herbie Hancock, Davis, Ron Carter, Wayne Shorter, Tony Williams.

Bill Evans

Bill Evans was one of the most lyrical and romantic of all jazz pianists. His distinctive lightness of touch and singing tone on the piano shone most brightly in his favoured trio settings with compatible bass players and drummers, including famous line-ups that featured Scott LaFaro and Paul Motian, and later Eddie Gomez and Marty Morrell.

Evans was born in Plainfield, New Jersey in 1929 and studied classical piano (and also violin) from the age of six (the trademark hunched position that he later adopted at the keyboard would doubtless have horrified his teacher!). He turned to jazz in his teens and began working professionally in New York in the early 1950s. He came to wider notice through associations with George Russell, Cannonball Adderley and – most significantly – the Miles Davis Sextet of the late 1950s.

> 'He changed forever the way the piano was approached. He opened up so many different possibilities in terms of harmony and rhythm.... He was creating all the time.'
>
> **Joe La Barbera**

Right
Bill Evans played in a small group in the 1970s, a period in which he also experimented with the sound of a Fender Rhodes electric piano.

Rethinking The Piano Trio

Evans' contributions as pianist or composer to all but one track on the classic *Kind Of Blue* was as crucial as anyone's to the success of that famous session. His own recording career as a leader began with *New Jazz Conceptions* (1956). His influences included Bud Powell and Horace Silver, but while his style remained rooted in bop, he developed his approach in an individual fashion that laid heavy stress on the lyrical facets of his music and on original harmonic thinking.

His famous trio with bassist Scott LaFaro and drummer Paul Motian brought a new lustre to one of jazz's most established formats, but the tragic death of LaFaro in a road accident in 1961 brought the group to a premature end. The live recordings that they made at the Village Vanguard in New York are among the highest accomplishments of the trio repertoire in jazz. LaFaro was well-equipped to adopt the kind of interactive accompanying role that Evans favoured, and set a benchmark that the pianist always sought to emulate in his choice of bassists. Later incumbents of that key position included Gary Peacock and Eddie Gomez.

A Pervasive Influence

The pianist's refined sense of melodic inflection and harmonic subtlety proved very influential, not only on his peers but also on a subsequent generation of great jazz pianists, including Herbie Hancock, Chick Corea and Keith Jarrett. That influence remains equally pervasive today. If the trio was his principal vehicle, Evans also explored the use of overdubbing to create multitracked 'solo' piano

Key Track

'Waltz For Debby' (1961)
The version of 'Waltz For Debby' recorded at the Village Vanguard on 25 June 1961 captures Evans' great trio with Scott LaFaro and Paul Motian in a characteristically inventive mood. Their purposeful sense of creative interaction and the energized vitality of their playing illuminates this vibrant take on one of his prettiest tunes.

recordings, as on *Conversations With Myself* (1963). He recorded duo albums with guitarist Jim Hall and singer Tony Bennett, as well as with Eddie Gomez, and sometimes worked with horn players added to his trio. He also recorded with a symphony orchestra in 1965.

Making The Piano Sing

Evans' ability to radically remake standard tunes by the most deft and subtle of alterations was legendary, and his own compositions have stood the test of time. His best-known originals include 'Blue In Green' (jointly credited to Miles Davis), 'Waltz For Debby', 'Comrad Conrad', 'Peace Piece', 'Detour Ahead', 'Funkallero', 'Interplay', 'NYC's No

Lark' (an anagram of the name of pianist Sonny Clark, and a tribute to his memory), 'Laurie', 'Re: Person I Knew' (another anagram, of producer Orrin Keepnews), 'Song For Helen', 'Time Remembered' and 'We Will Meet Again'.

He experimented with a Fender Rhodes electric piano in the 1970s, but his music is inextricably welded to the sonority of the acoustic piano, and his ability to make that instrument sing lay at the heart of his achievement. He acquired a heroin addiction while serving in the US Army, and was plagued with drug problems and ill-health at various times in his career. He died in New York in September 1980, having done much to redefine the art of the piano trio.

Classic Recordings

New Jazz Conceptions (1956)
'Waltz For Debby', 'Speak Low'

Portrait in Jazz (1959)
'Autumn Leaves', 'Come Rain Or Come Shine'

Sunday At The Village Vanguard/Waltz For Debby (1961)
'My Foolish Heart', 'Detour Ahead', 'Waltz For Debby'

How My Heart Sings (1962)
'How My Heart Sings', 'Summertime'

Conversations With Myself (1963)
'How About You', 'Blue Monk', 'Love Theme From Spartacus'

At Shelly's Manne-Hole (1963)
'Isn't It Romantic', 'All The Things You Are'

At The Montreux Jazz Festival (1968)
'One For Helen', 'Nardis', 'Embraceable You'

Blue In Green (1974)
'Blue In Green', 'So What'

Cross-Currents (1977)
'Night And Day', 'Pensativa'

Left
Pianist Bill Evans, whose classical training gave him a romantic sensitivity unusual in jazz performers.

Thelonious Monk

Thelonious Monk was one of the most original and idiosyncratic figures in jazz history. Almost from the start of his long career, the pianist and composer pursued a singular but relentlessly focused path through jazz, playing his own music in his own instantly identifiable way, with a seeming disregard for popular acceptance that was extreme even by jazz standards.

'He'll come in [Minton's] any time and play for hours with only a dim light and the funny thing is he'll never play a complete tune. You never know what he's playing.'
Teddy Hill

Thelonious Sphere Monk Jr. was born in Rocky Mount, North Carolina on 10 October 1917, but lived in New York from the age of six. The Harlem stride pianists of the 1920s became a sublimated but palpable influence on his rhythmic style.

His idiosyncratic approach extended to every element of his music. His angular melodies, unconventional dissonant harmonies and oblique rhythmic patterns all bore his stamp, as did his touch at the keyboard (not to mention his penchant for using his elbow and forearm to crash out huge clusters of notes, or breaking into a little dance around the instrument).

Above Right

A US Post Office stamp featuring Thelonious Monk, from the Jazz Series.

A Unique Artistic Vision

Monk recycled his compositions endlessly in concert and on records, often in rather rigidly demarcated fashion.

He was an introverted, eccentric figure in the colourful world of jazz, but he had a unique artistic vision and a single-minded determination to realize that vision. He was at the centre of the group of musicians who forged the framework for bebop at Minton's Playhouse in the mid-

Key Track

'Blue Monk' (1954)

Monk's trio version of 'Blue Monk' from 22 September 1954 is an excellent example of his concern for structure within a familiar form – the 12-bar blues. His solo reflects his characteristic, clearly delineated structural logic, employing a wide range of his typical techniques, from absolute space, through tellingly placed single notes, all the way to dense harmonic clusters.

1940s, but even there his highly individual style placed him a little to the side of the central flow of the music (Bud Powell, a friend of Monk's, provided the more canonical example of the bebop pianist).

He worked with Coleman Hawkins, Lucky Millinder, Cootie Williams and Dizzy Gillespie in the mid-1940s, and began recording as a leader for Blue Note Records in 1947. His recordings for that label (until 1952), Prestige (1952–54) and Riverside (1954–60) comprise the bulk of his classic music. He signed to Columbia in 1960 and recorded in solo and big-band settings with the label – as well as in the familiar quartet format – but added only 11 new compositions in that time, preferring to rework his classic canon of the 1950s until his departure from the label, and start of total withdrawal, in 1969.

No Compromises Accepted

Monk's music rarely diverged from the structures of the standard 12-bar and 32-bar forms that dominated the era, but they were recast in strange new harmonies and rhythms. He brooked no compromises with his music, and many musicians baulked at the discipline his music required, although others – John Coltrane, Clark Terry,

Steve Lacy and Charlie Rouse among them – embraced its spiky demands. Many of his tunes have entered the jazz repertoire, including "Round Midnight', 'Blue Monk', 'In Walked Bud', 'Rhythm-A-Ning', 'Misterioso', 'Straight No Chaser', 'Well You Needn't' and 'Evidence'.

Monk was featured on the cover of *Time* magazine in 1964 and his increased profile led to his making a tour of Europe in 1961. It had been a long time coming, but he went on to tour abroad regularly throughout the 1960s, mainly with his quartet but also with a nine-piece group in 1969; there are numerous live recordings from Europe and Japan as well as America in that decade.

A Timeless Legacy

His public appearances became increasingly rare in the early 1970s. He made his final studio recordings in London in 1971, and played his last concert at the Newport in New York jazz festival in 1976. His often troubled psychological state and bizarre personal life were overseen by three protective women – his mother, his wife Nellie and his patron the Baroness Pannonica de Koenigswarter. He retired to the Baroness's home in Weehawken, New Jersey in 1976, and there he lived the rest of his life in self-imposed seclusion. He died of a cerebral haemorrhage in February 1982, leaving behind a mysterious, near-mythic reputation and a timeless, unique and endlessly challenging contribution to jazz.

Classic Recordings

Complete Blue Note Recordings (1947–52)
'Well You Needn't', 'In Walked Bud', ''Round Midnight', 'Evidence', 'Misterioso', 'Straight No Chaser', 'I Mean You', 'Crepescule With Nellie', 'Epistrophy'

Complete Prestige Recordings (1952–54)
'Blue Monk', 'Monk's Dream', 'Bemsha Swing', 'Think Of One', 'Nutty', 'Just A Gigolo'

Brilliant Corners (1956)
'Brilliant Corners', 'Ba-lue Bolivar Ba-lues-are', 'Pannonica'

Thelonious Monk With John Coltrane (1957)
'Trinkle Trinkle', 'Nutty', 'Monk's Mood'

Monk's Music (1957)
'Well You Needn't', 'Ruby My Dear', 'Abide With Me'

Thelonious In Action!/ Misterioso (1958)
'Blue Monk', 'Nutty', 'Blues Five Spot', 'Evidence'

Criss-Cross (1962)
'Hackensack', 'Tea For Two', 'Don't Blame Me'

Big Band And Quartet In Concert (1963)
'When It's Darkness On The Delta', 'Played Twice', 'Light Blue', 'Four In One'

Underground (1967)
'Thelonious', 'Ugly Beauty', 'Green Chimneys'

Above Left
Innovative bebop pianist Thelonious Monk.

Left
Monk at New York's Carnegie Hall in his last live appearance, 1976.

Gerry Mulligan

Gerry Mulligan was the leading exponent of the baritone saxophone in jazz, and one of the key instigators of the style that came to be known as cool jazz. Along with trumpeter Chet Baker, Mulligan came to exemplify the cool ethos in the 1950s; he returned to the roots of that style with his *Re-Birth Of The Cool* (1992).

'Mulligan's main contribution was to bring jazz dynamics down to the dynamic range of a string bass – and then to use counterpoint in a natural, unschooled way.'

John Graas

The title and the concept echoed the groundbreaking Nonet sessions of 1949–50, which were led by Miles Davis but fuelled by the arrangements of Mulligan and Gil Evans. The use of French horn and the intricate weave of timbre and texture in the music foreshadowed the later developments of the 'third stream' (the movement's main progenitors, pianist John Lewis and composer Gunther Schuller, were both involved in the sessions), as well as the cool school.

Right
Baritone saxophonist Gerry Mulligan was an important figure in cool jazz, as well as a gifted composer and arranger.

Above Far Right
A performance at the 1955 Newport Jazz Festival featuring (l–r) Percy Heath, Miles Davis and Mulligan.

Far Right
Mulligan with his band at the Capital Jazz Festival in 1982.

Birth Of The Cool

Mulligan was born in New York City in April 1927 and grew up in Philadelphia. He began arranging music in his teens, inspired by the example of the great swing band arrangers such as Duke Ellington, Jimmy Mundy, Fletcher Henderson, Sy Oliver and Gil Evans.

Mulligan wrote arrangements for the Claude Thornhill band in New York in 1946, and was introduced to the textural possibilities of twentieth-century classical music by Evans and drummer Gene Krupa, a devotee of Ravel. Mulligan was an eager learner and quickly began to develop a style that built on his roots in swing but displayed a more contemporary idiom and personal voice.

The 'Birth Of The Cool' recordings of 1949–50 featured his compositions ('Jeru', 'Venus De Milo', 'Rocker') and arrangements. The clarity, control, swing, and rhythmic and harmonic invention of the music were all less frenetic than the bop model, and the cooler approach was ideal for Mulligan.

Quartet And Big Band

Mulligan formed the first of his 'pianoless' quartets in Los Angeles in 1951, featuring Chet Baker's romantic trumpet. The contrapuntal possibilities of two (or more) horns, bass and drums would preoccupy him throughout the 1950s.

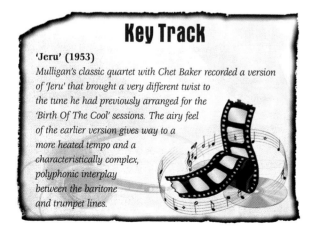

Key Track

'Jeru' (1953)
Mulligan's classic quartet with Chet Baker recorded a version of 'Jeru' that brought a very different twist to the tune he had previously arranged for the 'Birth Of The Cool' sessions. The airy feel of the earlier version gives way to a more heated tempo and a characteristically complex, polyphonic interplay between the baritone and trumpet lines.

Exploring The Big Horn

Mulligan's interest in musical textures extended to his choice of instrument. He began playing tenor saxophone but was seduced very quickly by the deeper sonorities and extended textural possibilities offered by the baritone register. Although he also played soprano saxophone and piano, he was best known for his finely burnished sound on baritone saxophone, and was one of the small group of players who have evolved a genuinely distinctive soloist's voice on that instrument.

The stamp of the Swing Era never left Mulligan's music, both as player and writer. He favoured a lightly textured, flowing style that relied on grace rather than volume, with a special liking for the whispered effects that can be achieved by players who understand the virtues of playing *pianissimo*, but without any sacrifice of intensity.

Given his close link with the cool approach, it is a useful corrective to the typecasting impulse to remember that he also collaborated with the likes of Thelonious Monk and Charles Mingus, and proved himself adaptable to the demands of these two idiosyncratic giants. Despite a long illness, he continued to perform until shortly before his death in January 1996.

Classic Recordings

Gerry Mulligan Quartet (1952–53)
'Line For Lyons', 'My Funny Valentine', 'The Lady Is A Tramp'

California Concerts (1954)
'Blues Going Up', 'Bark For Barksdale', 'Yardbird Suite'

Mulligan Meets Monk (1957)
"Round Midnight', 'Rhythm-A-Ning', 'I Mean You'

Mulligan And Getz And Desmond (1957)
'Line For Lyons', 'Battle Hymn Of The Republic'

Reunion With Chet Baker (1957)
'Ornithology', 'Surrey With The Fringe On Top'

Gerry Mulligan Meets Ben Webster (1959)
'Chelsea Bridge', 'In A Mellotone'

The Concert Jazz Band (1960)
'Bweebida Bobbida', 'My Funny Valentine', 'I'm Gonna Go Fishin''

Re-Birth Of The Cool (1992)
'Godchild', 'Rocker', 'Darn That Dream'

His collaborators included trumpeters Jon Eardley and Art Farmer, valve trombonist Bob Brookmeyer and saxophonist Zoot Sims.

Mulligan began touring with his Concert Jazz Band in 1960, and continued to work on and off in that format throughout the rest of his career. While he made his greatest impact with his smaller groups, where improvisation was the primary element of the music, the large ensemble lent itself well to his particular style of writing and arranging. He revelled in the greater textural possibilities that the big band offered, and he went on to experiment with composing for orchestral ensembles as well, albeit less successfully.

for marijuana possession from 1962–69, resuming his recording career upon his release.

Chet Baker
(Trumpet, 1929–88)

Chet Baker was an icon of cool at the height of his fame in the 1950s. His recording of 'My Funny Valentine' with Gerry Mulligan in 1952 established him as a star of the emerging cool jazz genre; his boyish, film-star looks (later ravaged by drug abuse) and a light, seductively lyrical trumpet style assured his popularity for much of the decade. Baker was born in Yale, Oklahoma but moved to Los Angeles at a young age. He led his own quartet on the West Coast from 1953.

> 'I think we were all secretly happy at the success of Chet Baker, a guy who uses about one octave in a dynamic range of ppp to mf.'
> **John Graas**

Drugs, imprisonment in both the US and Europe, and poor health took a heavy toll from the late 1950s; he also lost some teeth in an assault in 1968, which kept him off the stage until 1973. He worked mainly in Europe from 1975, where he was in demand as a soloist in both small group and orchestral settings, and remained an artful improviser throughout the many vicissitudes of his career. He died after falling from a hotel window in Amsterdam.

Chris Barber
(Trombone, b. 1930)

Chris Barber has been a key figure on the British traditional jazz scene since he broke away from Ken Colyer's band to lead his own group in 1954. The band was one of the leading names in the so-called 'trad boom' of the late 1950s. It became the Chris Barber Jazz & Blues Band – with the addition of electric guitar – in 1968, and brought fresh arrangements and cogent soloing to their venerable traditional jazz and blues repertoire. Barber now tours with his Big Band.

Above
Gene Ammons, big-toned tenor saxophonist and son of boogie-woogie great Albert Ammons.

Gene Ammons
(Tenor saxophone, 1925–74)

The son of pianist Albert Ammons, Gene was equally at home in jazz and R&B settings. He was a prolific recording artist and his hard-hitting, emotionally direct blowing in a blues and funk vein also featured in a popular two-tenor band, co-led by Sonny Stitt. His work in a soul-jazz idiom with organists such as Jack McDuff and Johnny Smith added to his popularity. He served a harsh prison sentence

Acker Bilk

(Clarinet, b. 1929)

Acker Bilk was born in Somerset, England. He took up clarinet in the Army and formed his first band in 1950. His Paramount Jazz Band adopted trademark uniforms of striped waistcoats and bowler hats and was very successful in the UK's trad boom of the late 1950s. Bilk enjoyed a major pop hit with his own 'Stranger On The Shore' in 1961 and remained a popular draw on the international traditional jazz circuit in subsequent decades.

Art Blakey

(Drums, 1919–90)

Art Blakey (also later known as Buhaina or simply Bu after he converted to Islam) led the quintessential hard bop group the Jazz Messengers across four decades from the late 1940s, and was a fervent advocate of the music he loved. He formed his first band in his native Pittsburgh, but moved to New York and played in Billy Eckstine's seminal big band in 1944–47, before relaunching his career as a bandleader with the Seventeen Messengers.

Blakey first used the Jazz Messengers name in collaboration with Horace Silver from 1956. The band had a horns-plus-rhythm set-up in quintet and sextet forms and defined hard bop, spicing bebop with the earthy urgency of blues, gospel and R&B. Blakey's propulsive drumming drove a band whose changing personnel – including trumpeters Lee Morgan, Freddie Hubbard and Wynton Marsalis, saxophonist Wayne Shorter, trombonist Curtis Fuller and pianist Bobby Timmons – was remarkable.

Above
Trumpet star Clifford Brown, who died tragically young in 1956.

Clifford Brown

(Trumpet, 1930–56)

The tragic death of Clifford Brown in a road accident robbed jazz of one of its brightest young stars, but even his truncated legacy has established his standing as a major figure and profound influence. He took up the trumpet at the age of 13, drawing on the influence of bebop stars Dizzy Gillespie and Fats Navarro. The latter's rich sonority and melodic lyricism made a particularly telling impact on the development of Brown's own style.

He recorded with Lou Donaldson, J.J. Johnson and Art Blakey for Blue Note, and cut his own sessions for Pacific Jazz, but his best-known work was recorded in 1954–56, with the quintet he co-led with drummer Max Roach. His technical virtuosity and improvisational flair marked him out as a potential giant. He contributed several much-played compositions to the jazz repertoire, notably 'Joy Spring' and 'Daahoud'.

Left
Chris Barber (far right) with his traditional-style jazz band.

Ken Colyer
(Cornet, trumpet, guitar, 1928–88)

Ken Colyer was a key figure in the UK revivalist movement. He took an infamously purist stance on the New Orleans style of ensemble playing, brooking no departures from orthodoxy. He co-founded the influential Crane River Band in 1949 and formed his own Jazzmen after a visit to New Orleans in 1953, but was ousted when Chris Barber assumed leadership the following year. Colyer formed an influential new band, and then continued to lead his own groups.

Gil Evans
(Arranger, composer, piano, 1912–88)

Gil Evans (born Ian Green) achieved fame through his work with Miles Davis on the seminal recordings *Miles Ahead* (1957), *Porgy And Bess* (1959) and *Sketches Of Spain* (1960). His own output was relatively small, but his influence was much larger. His greatest gift lay in arranging – or more accurately, re-composing – the music of others, elaborately cloaked in his own distinctive manipulations of timbre, colour, texture and shape.

Working with Claude Thornhill in the 1940s allowed him to experiment with unusual instrumentation and distinctive ideas, which came to fruition in the projects with Miles, including his contribution to the 'Birth of the Cool' sessions (1949–50). His own recordings included *Out Of The Cool* (1960) and *The Individualism Of Gil Evans* (1964). His orchestra became an attraction on the international circuit from the mid-1970s; his later music was notably more improvisational in content and allowed the players considerable freedom within looser, sometimes electric and rock-referent structures.

Above

Dave Brubeck (right) with Paul Desmond, the composer of the quartet's biggest hit 'Take Five'.

Right

Gil Evans (right) and Miles Davis, who worked together on the 1949–50 Nonet 'Birth Of The Cool' sessions, among various other projects.

Dave Brubeck
(Piano, b. 1920)

The Dave Brubeck Quartet was one of the most successful jazz groups of all time; Brubeck's fascination with unusual time signatures brought major hits with 'Take Five' (written by saxophonist Paul Desmond) and 'Blue Rondo À La Turk' in 1959. His recording of 'Dialogues For Jazz Combo And Orchestra', composed by his brother Howard, appeared the same year, and the writing of large-scale works became increasingly central to Brubeck's compositions. He has continued to tour with small groups.

João Gilberto

(Vocals, guitar, b. 1931)

João Gilberto came to the notice of the wider jazz public in the wake of saxophonist's Stan Getz's successful *Jazz Samba* (1962). Gilberto had earlier been working with composer Antonio Carlos Jobim on a development of the samba known as 'bossa nova', and Getz translated that form into a popular success. The subsequent *Getz/Gilberto* (1963) album included vocals by his companion, Astrud Gilberto, and spawned a famous hit version of 'The Girl From Ipanema'. Gilberto is a successful international performing artist as well as composer.

Jimmy Giuffre

(Clarinet, baritone, tenor and soprano saxophones, b. 1921)

Jimmy Giuffre composed 'Four Brothers' for Woody Herman's saxophone section in 1947 and later joined the Second Herd. He formed his important trio with Jim Hall (guitar) and Ralph Peña (bass) in 1957, then replaced bass with Bob Brookmeyer's trombone in 1958. A subsequent trio with Paul Bley (piano) and Steve Swallow (bass) in 1961–62 was influential in the rise of free jazz. He remained open to new directions and experimented with electric instruments in the 1980s.

Eddie Harris

(Tenor saxophone, vocals, 1934–96)

Eddie Harris was one of the few jazz musicians to achieve the distinction of a million-selling hit single with his version of the theme from the film *Exodus* (1960). A funky, hard-blowing saxophonist from Chicago, he pioneered the use of electronics with tenor saxophone through the Varitone signal processor and similar devices from the mid-1960s. Harris also played several other instruments and sang; he had an expressive sound and polished technique in straight and exploratory jazz, as well as in crossover settings.

Roy Haynes

(Drums, b. 1925)

Roy Haynes is a major jazz drummer in settings ranging from swing to jazz rock, taking in most genres of the music including free jazz. He spent three years with Charlie Parker (1949–52) and five with Sarah Vaughan (1953–58), and by the mid-1960s had also worked with Bud Powell, Miles Davis, Thelonious Monk, Eric Dolphy and John Coltrane. Later associations include Gary Burton, Chick Corea and Pat Metheny. He has continued to lead his own groups.

Below
João Gilberto's vocalist collaborator Astrud Gilberto performs with two other important figures in the bossa nova movement, Antonio Carlos Jobim (centre) and Stan Getz.

Jimmy Heath
(Tenor and soprano saxophone, flute, b. 1926)
Jimmy Heath's early devotion to Charlie Parker saw him nicknamed 'Little Bird', but he switched from alto to tenor saxophone and developed his own voice. He honed his writing skills with the Dizzy Gillespie Orchestra throughout 1949–50. He spent 1955–59 in prison, but rebuilt his career with a series of recordings for Riverside. Later, he performed with bassist Percy Heath and drummer Albert 'Tootie' Heath in the Heath Brothers. He remains an influential jazz arranger and educator.

Milt Jackson
(Vibraphone, 1923–99)
Milt Jackson diverged from his two great predecessors on vibes, Lionel Hampton and Red Norvo, by developing a linear, rhythmically inflected approach rooted in bebop rather than swing. He preferred the slightly larger vibraharp to the more familiar vibraphone, and adjusted the oscillator to give a trademark rich, warm sound.

He recorded as a leader and worked with many major names, including Coleman Hawkins, John Coltrane, Oscar Peterson and Ray Charles, but was best known as part of the long-running Modern Jazz Quartet, one of the most successful groups in jazz history. That band began as the Milt Jackson Quartet but ran as the MJQ from 1952–74, and occasionally thereafter. Jackson was a gifted soloist, steeped in the earthy pragmatism of gospel and blues; his playing provided a counterweight to the intricate classicism of pianist John Lewis's compositions and arrangements for the group, but without upsetting the balance of the music.

Right
Ahmad Jamal, an inventive improviser who mainly works in jazz trios.

Below
Milt Jackson (right) and Percy Heath perform in the long-lived Modern Jazz Quartet.

Ahmad Jamal
(Piano, b. 1930)
Ahmad Jamal made his name with his very successful trio of the late 1950s and had a hit with his version of 'Poinciana' in 1958. His light touch and use of space has led some to hear too much of the cocktail lounge in his playing, but he is an inventive and influential musician and composer. He experimented with more avant-garde approaches after a break from performing in the early 1960s, and later with electric instruments and symphonic settings; however, he has mostly worked in trios.

Antonio Carlos Jobim
(Composer, piano, guitar, 1927–94)
Jobim was the best known of the Brazilian composers who made an impact on jazz. His international reputation blossomed due to his songs in the film *Black Orpheus* (1959) and with João Gilberto he sparked a bossa nova craze, boosted by Stan Getz and Charlie Byrd's *Jazz Samba* (1962). He led his own band on international tours, and his songs – including 'Girl From Ipamena', 'Desifinado' and

'One Note Stand' – with original lyrics in Portuguese and light, sophisticated harmonies, remain jazz staples.

Quincy Jones
(Trumpet, arranger, b. 1933)

Quincy Jones started out as a trumpet player but first achieved public acclaim as an arranger and subsequently went on to earn an even greater reputation as a record producer for artists including Aretha Franklin and Michael Jackson. He began arranging with Lionel Hampton in 1951 and toured as music director of Dizzy Gillespie's big band in 1956. He wrote for Ray Charles and Frank Sinatra among many others, and produced USA For Africa's 'We Are The World' (1985). He is also a successful film composer and record-company executive.

Steve Lacy
(Soprano saxophone, 1934–2004)

Steve Lacy began his career in Dixieland jazz, sitting in with Henry 'Red' Allen, Rex Stewart and Herbie Nichols, among others, at New York's Café Metronome. However, he quickly shifted tack and became one of the leading figures in the jazz avant-garde. Soprano saxophone is now widely played, but Lacy concentrated on the then-neglected horn from the outset with single-minded focus.

He worked with Cecil Taylor and Thelonious Monk in the late 1950s and Monk's music remained a constant artistic preoccupation, including in later projects with trombonist Roswell Rudd and pianist Mal Waldron. Lacy also began a long musical relationship with Gil Evans at that time and became involved with free jazz in the early 1960s. He began to perform in Europe in 1965 and lived in France from 1970–2002, where he continued to pursue new and experimental musical ideas in a wide variety of contexts. These included his long-running sextet; electronic music; projects involving his wife (singer Irène Aebi); collaborations with poets, dancers and visual artists; and an ambitious improvisational 'opera', *The Cry*.

John Lewis
(Piano, 1920–2001)

John Lewis was an important pianist, composer and educator, but was best known as the musical director of the most successful jazz group of the era, the Modern Jazz Quartet. Over five decades, Lewis was the architect of the group's characteristic fusion of jazz and classical music.

Above
Trumpeter Quincy Jones is also a successful composer, arranger and record producer.

The MJQ's light, spacious, swinging arrangements established them as an international concert draw, while Lewis's compositions amounted to a substantial canon.

His work away from the group was also significant. He worked with Dizzy Gillespie, Charlie Parker and Miles Davis (on the 'Birth Of The Cool' sessions) in the late 1940s and co-founded the jazz-classical fusion movement known as 'third stream' with Gunther Schuller in the late 1950s. He was musical director of the Monterey Jazz Festival from 1958–82, and was leader and director of two ensembles: Orchestra USA (1962–65) and the American Jazz Orchestra (1985–92). Lewis's acclaimed solo album, *Evolution II* (2001), was issued shortly before his death.

collaborations with Miles Davis (1951–52), Charles Mingus (1956, 1958–59) and Art Blakey (1956–57). He recorded a series of albums for Prestige and acted in Jack Gelber's play *The Connection* (1959–61). His powerful recordings for Blue Note in the early 1960s were more experimental. He became an eminent jazz educator in later decades.

Charles Mingus
(Bass, piano, composer, 1922–79)

Charles Mingus had a tempestuous, multi-faceted personality, which is reflected in the almost schizophrenic extremes of his music and the sheer magnitude of his creative aspirations. Early work with Lionel Hampton and Red Norvo brought him in 1951 from California to York, where he worked with Miles Davis, Duke Ellington, Charlie Parker and others.

Mingus formed Debut Records with Max Roach and issued some of his early Jazz Workshop recordings on the label (along with the famous concert from Massey Hall in 1953 with Parker, Gillespie, Powell and Roach). His radical style of ensemble improvisation and his enduring compositions are captured in groundbreaking discs such as *Pithecanthropus Erectus* (1956), *Ah Um* (1959) and the big band album *The Black Saint and the Sinner Lady* (1963). His large-scale work *Epitaph* was only performed in complete form in 1989, a decade after his death.

Art Pepper
(Alto and tenor saxophones, 1925–82)

Art Pepper was a soloist with Stan Kenton (1947–52) and took part in trumpeter Shorty Rogers's first so-called West Coast jazz recordings in 1951. He made a series of classic records for the California-based Contemporary label (1957–60), but was imprisoned at various times for heroin-related offences, culminating in three years' voluntary rehabilitation in Synanon from 1969. He played with the Don Ellis Orchestra in 1975 and enjoyed a triumphant finale to his career as a leader from 1977.

Oscar Peterson
(Piano, b. 1925)

Canadian pianist Oscar Peterson made his name on 'Jazz At The Philharmonic' (JATP) tours in the early 1950s, and formed his own trio in 1952. His most famous line-up (1953–58) featured Herb Ellis (guitar) and Ray Brown (bass); he replaced the guitar with more conventional

Above

British trumpeter Humphrey Lyttelton blows his horn while guitarist Eddie Condon operates the valves.

Humphrey Lyttelton
(Trumpet, clarinet, b. 1921)

Humphrey Lyttelton acquired a passion for jazz as a schoolboy at Eton and developed it in the Grenadier Guards – not a standard jazz background. His professional career began with George Webb's Dixielanders in 1947. He led his own bands from 1948, and courted controversy in the 1950s by bringing bop musicians into his group, to the immense chagrin of traditional purists. His contribution to British jazz as a player, composer, bandleader, historian, broadcaster and writer has been a substantial one.

Jackie McLean
(Alto saxophone, b. 1931)

Jackie McLean worked with Sonny Rollins and practised with Bud Powell as a teenager. His invention and passionate delivery on alto saxophone attracted

Bud Powell
(Piano, 1924–66)

Bud Powell was the pre-eminent bebop pianist. His spare chords and asymmetric accents in the left hand combined with fluid linear inventions in the right hand to establish the foundation of the standard approach to bop piano playing. The mental instability and introverted character that dogged his life are often ascribed to a beating by the police in 1945 but may have preceded it.

He was part of Dizzy Gillespie's seminal bebop quintet in 1945, recorded with Charlie Parker in 1947 and made a series of classic trio recordings from 1949–56 that are his primary legacy. He also took part in the famous Massey Hall concert in 1953 with Parker, Gillespie, Mingus and Roach. He moved to Paris, France in 1959 and continued to perform there (albeit erratically) until 1964, when he made an unsuccessful return to the US. His troubled life in Paris was the major inspiration for the film *Round Midnight* (1986).

Left
Oscar Peterson puts his all into a solo during a 1957 performance.

Below
Highly influential bebop pianist Bud Powell takes a break.

'I believe in using the entire piano as a single instrument, capable of expressing every possible musical idea. I have no one style. I play as I feel.' **Oscar Peterson**

drums from 1958. His extravagant improvisations combined pre-bop and bop elements. He was a virtuoso technician until illness restricted his playing in the 1990s; he recorded voluminously, produced most often by his champion, JATP founder Norman Granz.

Oscar Pettiford
(Bass, cello, composer, 1922–60)

Oscar Pettiford was the first bass player to develop the new melodic and rhythmic concepts of bebop on his instrument and was an accomplished cellist and composer. He was of mixed African-American and Native American extraction and had a famously irascible temperament, frequently falling out with his many collaborators. He worked with Duke Ellington and Woody Herman, and led his own small groups and a big band (1956–57). He spent his final two years in Europe.

Above
Sonny Rollins, one of the most inventive voices on the saxophone since Charlie Parker.

Dannie Richmond
(Drums, 1935–88)

Dannie Richmond's career is inextricably linked with that of Charles Mingus. He played saxophone and piano before taking up drums in 1956, working closely with Mingus until 1979. Richmond's energetic, versatile style was also well-suited to jazz rock; he played with the UK band Mark-Almond (1970–73) and worked with Joe Cocker and Elton John. He co-founded Mingus Dynasty in 1979, and played with bassist Cameron Brown, saxophonist George Adams and pianist Don Pullen until his death.

Sonny Rollins
(Tenor and soprano saxophone, b. 1930)

Sonny Rollins stands alongside John Coltrane as the major bop-rooted stylist on tenor saxophone. He cut his teeth in New York with bop giants including Charlie Parker, Bud Powell, Thelonious Monk and Miles Davis. He was a member of the Clifford Brown–Max Roach Quintet (1955–57), and has led his own bands since then. His late 1950s recordings confirmed his standing as one of the great talents in the music; calypso-based tunes have been a recurring motif since 'St. Thomas' (1956).

He stopped performing to recharge creatively between 1959–61, then recorded with an early hero, Coleman Hawkins (1963), and flirted with the emerging free jazz avant-garde (1965–66). He took his long and discursive soloing to its logical conclusion in *The Solo Album* (1985) and experimented with soprano saxophone, also adding various electric instruments to his group. Rollins is capable of a power and invention that few musicians in jazz have been able to match.

Horace Silver
(Piano, b. 1928)

Horace Silver stands with Art Blakey as the progenitor of the earthier development of bebop, known as hard bop. His Hartford-based trio was hired by Stan Getz in 1950 and he moved to New York the following year. He began recording for Blue Note in 1952, a relationship that would last for 28 years. He formed a band with Art Blakey that became the latter's Jazz Messengers when the pianist left in 1956.

Like the Jazz Messengers, Silver's quintets became a nursery for new talent as well as a vehicle for his own compositions; many of his tunes became part of the standard jazz repertoire. He incorporated the influence of his father's native Cape Verdean folk music, most famously on 'Song For My Father'. His more experimental music of the 1970s was less well-received, but he returned to hard bop from the early 1980s and remains a successful artist, although increasingly hampered by arthritis.

Zoot Sims
(Tenor, soprano and alto saxophones, 1925–85)

John 'Zoot' Sims performed in the family vaudeville act as a child and was a professional musician at 15. His Lester Young-derived tenor sound and artful improvisations were heard to advantage in large and small bands. He worked with Benny Goodman intermittently over four decades, and was part of Woody Herman's famous 'Four Brothers' saxophone section (1947–49). His small groups included stints with Gerry Mulligan (1954–56) and tenor saxophonist Al Cohn, a partnership resumed on many occasions.

Frank Sinatra
(Vocals, 1915–98)

Frank Sinatra was best known as a popular singer and film actor but established his jazz credentials early in his career. He combined the smooth, Italian *bel canto* style with a sure sense of swing, toured with Harry James and learned about breath control from Tommy Dorsey (1940–42). He worked with arrangers Billy May, Gordon Jenkins and Nelson Riddle in his classic years (1953–61). Later projects included collaborations with Count Basie (1962–66) and Duke Ellington (1967).

Jimmy Smith
(Organ, piano, 1925–2005)

Jimmy Smith, a fluent and inventive jazz improviser, is regarded as the greatest of the soul jazz organists; he essentially defined the form in his performances and recordings for Blue Note in the 1950s. His adoption of the Hammond organ to soul jazz's combination of jazz improvisation over blues-rooted grooves opened up a new field. Smith was the genre's most eminent practitioner, although he spawned dozens of imitators and a generation of younger players such as Joey DeFrancesco.

Sonny Stitt
(Alto, tenor and baritone saxophones, 1924–82)

Edward 'Sonny' Stitt was equally proficient on the alto and tenor saxophones. Initially a devotee of Charlie Parker, he developed into a hard-hitting and fluid improviser with a reputation for extreme toughness in 'cutting' contests. He worked with Dizzy Gillespie, Bud Powell, J.J. Johnson and Oscar Peterson, but is best known for his collaborations with fellow tenormen Sonny Rollins, Dexter Gordon, Eddie 'Lockjaw' Davis and Gene Ammons. His prolific discography is uneven, but often brilliant.

Above

Soul jazz organist Jimmy Smith, who recorded extensively for Blue Note in the 1950s.

Left

Saxophonist Sonny Stitt (left of standing group) with Thelonious Monk (seated far left) and (l–r) Clark Terry, Roy Eldridge and Al McGibbon, performing at Monterey, 1971.

the Sixties

the cultural momentum of the 1950s spilled directly into the 1960s – arguably, the change of the decade (and century) in jazz was 1959, when Dave Brubeck, Miles Davis, Ornette Coleman, John Coltrane, Gil Evans, Lambert, Hendricks & Ross, Jackie McLean, Charles Mingus, Thelonious Monk, Wes Montgomery, Sun Ra, Sonny Rollins, George Russell, Dinah Washington and Cecil Taylor all issued or recorded significant and redefining work. In 1960 most blues was issued as disposable 45-rpm singles, but that changed mid-decade, after Columbia Records released the first collection of Robert Johnson recordings from the 1930s, and Chess Records put out LP compilations of hits by Muddy Waters, Howlin' Wolf, Sonny Boy Williamson, Little Walter *et al*.

In that format, the blues hit the UK with a bang, resulting in the birth of the Beatles, the Rolling Stones and the Yardbirds, bands that made the US listen to itself again. Between the British Invasion and the folk-music movement, interest in blues of all eras was rekindled, and rock'n'roll was soon stretching the traditional form into psychedelic shape. In parallel, jazz mainstreamers began to adopt the freedoms, or move towards the market preferences, of younger, larger audiences. Transformation was again the cultural watchword, as assassinations shook the US, civil rights became undeniable and a war in Asia provoked unrivalled discontent. The music of Brazil had its first profound influence, new instruments and studio techniques allowed musicians options beyond imagination and fusions of all styles, from anywhere and everywhere, foreshadowed the shape of things to come.

Key Artists: Blues

Buddy Guy
Albert King
B.B. King

Key Artists: Jazz

Ornette Coleman
John Coltrane
Freddie Hubbard
Sun Ra

Blues

Right

Bob Dylan in his revolutionary electric performance at the 1965 Newport Folk Festival.

'Wolf loved it when he heard the Rolling Stones and Eric Clapton play his songs…. He said, "Hubert, them white boys is gonna make me famous. Then maybe we can make us some money."'

Hubert Sumlin

The seeds for the blues explosion of the 1960s were planted in the previous decade; rock'n'roll resulted from the fusion of African-American blues and R&B with white folk and country music, which was then sped up and amplified in keeping with the pace and technology of the prosperous 1950s.

The Blues Is Reborn

The rock'n'roll revolution did not win everyone over, however; an older generation of folk enthusiasts still pursued their acoustic passions, while some younger listeners began to investigate the roots of the new music. In America, these fans played a crucial role in launching the decade's blues revival. Collectors of 78-rpm discs, such as Gayle Dean Wardlow, travelled to rural southern towns looking for prized acetate recordings by bluesmen of the 1920s and 1930s, and began to turn up surprising bonuses in the form of the artists themselves. Musicologist Alan Lomax (1915–2002), musician John Fahey and Bob Jones, a young hand at the Newport Folk Festival, were all in the thick of rediscovering a whole host of bluesmen and -women previously only embodied by scratched discs. Thus the blues boom of the 1960s truly began.

The old records were reissued as vinyl LPs. The old musicians were dusted off and began to tour. Some, including Son House (1902–88), hadn't held a guitar in years and had to be re-taught some of their own numbers. Others, such as Mississippi John Hurt (1893–1966) and Rev. Gary Davis (1896–1972), emerged with their virtuosity intact. Although Robert Johnson (1911–38) had long been dead, his *King Of The*

Delta Blues Singers collection was issued in 1961, and his razor-edged guitar virtuosity and keening vocal style fired the imaginations of many budding guitarists – Eric Clapton and Keith Richards included, who both went on to cover Johnson songs ('Cross Road Blues' and 'Love In Vain' respectively).

The Great Festivals

The Newport Folk Festival, established in 1959, helped to propel these artists back into the public eye and also drew contemporary blues artists such as John Lee Hooker (1917–2001) and Muddy Waters (1915–83). However, the watershed year for blues at Newport was 1966, when Lomax organized a bill that featured Howlin' Wolf (1910–76), Son House, Skip James (1902–69), Bukka White (1906–77) and others. Newport was the catalyst for the cross-pollination of blues and the singer-songwriter-based original music that was beginning to redefine the folk idiom. Bob Dylan, who had started out with traditional blues numbers, began to take on increasingly modern elements of the genre, culminating in 1965's *Highway 61 Revisited*. Dylan's electric performance that summer at Newport ensured that folk music was no longer a purely acoustic medium; contemporary blues had been given a toe-hold in rock and pop.

Europe also caught festival fever. In 1962, German fans Horst Lippmann and Fritz Rau organized the American Folk Blues Festival. Between the initial tour – which travelled around Europe – and 1964, a veritable who's who of blues stars had appeared on the bill. The main difference between the American Folk Blues Festival and Newport was electricity. Although Waters and Wolf played amplified sets at Newport, traditionalists such as Pete Seeger and Lomax booked mostly acoustic acts – hence why Dylan's electric debut caused such a stir. The travelling European festival offered performances that were not only electric, but often electrifying. Waters had met resistance when he first travelled abroad with his electric guitar in 1958; then, blues audiences comprised vintage recording fans and jazz aficionados. But by 1962 there was a new, younger audience emerging that would permanently change the face of blues music.

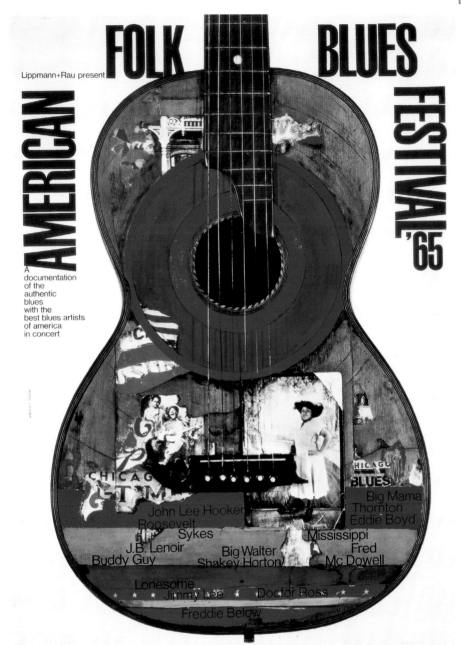

Lippmann+Rau present

AMERICAN FOLK BLUES FESTIVAL '65

A documentation of the authentic blues with the best blues artists of america in concert

Far Left

Keith Richards (far right) of the Rolling Stones was among the many to be influenced by the 1961 release of Robert Johnson's King Of The Delta Blues.

Left

A publicity poster for the 1965 American Folk Blues Festival.

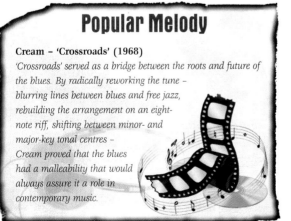

Popular Melody

Cream – 'Crossroads' (1968)
'Crossroads' served as a bridge between the roots and future of the blues. By radically reworking the tune – blurring lines between blues and free jazz, rebuilding the arrangement on an eight-note riff, shifting between minor- and major-key tonal centres – Cream proved that the blues had a malleability that would always assure it a role in contemporary music.

Above

Howlin' Wolf performs at London's Marquee club with Chris Barber's band in 1964.

A New Generation

Alexis Korner (1928–84) was the first white British musician to really seize electrified blues and make it his own. He couldn't find a club in London that would book his group Blues Incorporated, so he opened one. It became a magnet for future English blues players – Mick Jagger, Charlie Watts, Keith Richards, John Mayall and Eric Clapton were among those who haunted the Ealing establishment. When the Rolling Stones, the Yardbirds and the Animals began to make hits, the sound of the blues – albeit filtered through rock'n'roll – echoed back across the Atlantic.

For many young Americans this music seemed novel – but not all. In Chicago, Mike Bloomfield (1943–81), Paul Butterfield (1942–87) and Charlie Musselwhite (b. 1944) had absorbed the blues in the ghetto clubs where black artists reigned seven nights a week. In New York City, Al Kooper and his cohorts in the Blues Project, as well as members of the Lovin' Spoonful, the Young Rascals and other groups, developed their own variations on the blues. Meanwhile, Jimi James & the Blue Flames were holding down a residency at Greenwich Village's Café Wha? that attracted musicians such as Dylan, Bloomfield and John Hammond Jr. (b. 1942); here audiences could catch the group's incendiary guitarist and frontman before he was swept off to England by former Animals bassist Chas Chandler and renamed Jimi Hendrix.

New York was also home to the seminal R&B label Atlantic Records, which – like Chess and other independent blues recording companies – fuelled the imaginations of young white players and listeners with its releases by African-American artists. Although Atlantic had nurtured R&B, it also released sides by blues musicians including T-Bone Walker (1910–75), Jimmy Yancey (1898–1951), Guitar Slim (1926–59), Professor Longhair (1918–80), Otis Rush (b. 1934) and Freddie King (1934–76). More importantly, Atlantic was the distributor of Stax Records, which produced classics by Albert King (1923–92) and Booker T. and the MGs, and was in the vanguard of soul music.

Although the 1960s was an era of prosperity in the US, it also brought great cultural upheaval. The accelerating Vietnam War caused a rift between generations; teenagers and twenty-somethings grew their hair long, donned psychedelic togs and increased their consumption of drugs. Embracing the music of a cultural group that was actively protesting for civil rights – African-Americans – was part of the package. It was not much of a leap to also embrace the people who made that music, and the blues inadvertently became a bridge between races that led to common ground. When the Paul Butterfield Blues Band emerged with an integrated cast in 1965 and when Muddy Waters hired his first white sideman (harmonica player Paul Oscher), these bands sent a message – intentional or not – in support of both youth and racial integration.

The Rise Of The Guitar

The English bluesmen were also sending a message. Much of the success of *Blues Breakers* (1966), the debut album from John Mayall's band, hung on the dazzling playing of guitarist Eric Clapton; this indicated that audiences were ready to listen to blues in a different way. Until then, the style – despite its legacy of great musicians – had been primarily a vocal music. Clapton adopted the techniques of Buddy Guy (b. 1936), Freddie King, B.B. King (b. 1925) and Albert King, and pushed them to a new level of virtuosity. After Clapton, who went on to form the improvisational blues rock supergroup Cream, the blues became associated with the sound of the guitar – particularly that of flattened blue notes and bent, vibrato-coloured strings, teased from an electric instrument.

In 1967 talented blues guitarist Peter Green formed Fleetwood Mac, a group of hardcore blues enthusiasts who gradually developed their own musical style. The early three-guitar line-up cycled through different hues of blues: Green loved stylists such as Elmore James, Jeremy Spencer emulated Chuck Berry and Elvis Presley, and Danny Kirwan leaned towards psychedelia. By 1973 all three had left the band due to personal conflicts and there followed a progressive movement away from the blues.

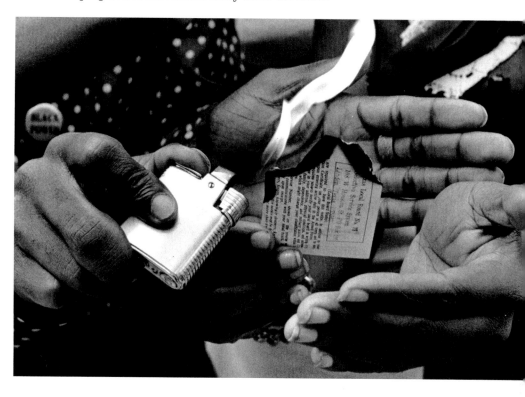

Above
Vietnam War protesters burn draft cards. Social issues such as the war began to divide the generations in the 1960s.

If Clapton did not seal the deal as far as virtuoso electric blues guitarists were concerned, the arrival of Jimi Hendrix did. Hendrix was the musical embodiment of the 1960s – a young black man who became a cultural superstar by pushing the limits of musical freedom. Established bluesmen, including B.B. King and Albert King, suddenly found themselves playing alongside rock stars before racially mixed audiences at large festivals and important venues. The blues seeped throughout the cultural terrain, making the 1960s the greatest period of growth and popularity the genre had experienced since it first emerged on recordings in the 1920s and 1930s.

Popular Melody

Albert King – 'Born Under A Bad Sign' (1967)
This number reflects the influence of other forms of contemporary African-American music, with its heavy funk guitar lick and classic soul groove. Yet it is also connected to the blues' deepest traditions, with King's voice, the guitar riff and the rhythm section setting up three distinct lines of cadence in a manner similar to African group drumming.

Buddy Guy

'When I first heard of the electric guitar, I thought somebody was bullshittin' me,' says George 'Buddy' Guy. 'We lived so far in the country I didn't even know what an acoustic guitar was until my mother started getting mail-order catalogs'. In 2005, Guy, who was born in Lettsworth, Louisiana on 30 July 1936, stands at the pinnacle of modern electric blues. Guy's first instruments were one-stringed contraptions that he made from screen wire, nails and paint cans, before he graduated to a battered acoustic bartered for by his father. He first heard an electric six-string played by Lightnin' Slim at a general store near the plantation where his family sharecropped, and the sound took root. After witnessing Guitar Slim's fiery live act in a Baton Rouge club, Guy's interest in becoming a baseball player vanished. He moved to Baton Rouge himself and began playing professionally, until he earned enough money for a bus ticket to Chicago in 1957.

'He is a consummate blues musician. He's living history.'
Eric Clapton

Right

Electric blues star Buddy Guy performs at London's Marquee club in 1965.

Chicago Blues

The Windy City was less than welcoming. Guy failed to find work on the bandstand or elsewhere, although Chicago's blues scene was at its peak, heightened by Howlin' Wolf, Muddy Waters and many other stars and journeymen, as well as the presence of the Chess, United and Cobra labels. Frustrated and starving, Guy resolved to return home, but Waters intervened and took the young musician under his wing. Guy then became a regular session player at Chess and recorded singles for Chess and Cobra. He supported Waters on the 1963 classic *Folk Singer* and fell into a partnership with vocalist and harmonica player Junior Wells, with whom he recorded *Hoodoo Man Blues* (1965) and *Southside Blues Jam* (1967) on Delmark. Although he could not break out of the Chicago scene, Guy became known for his great live delivery (hanging from rafters and playing with his teeth), his gospel-style testifying and a guitar vocabulary built on explosive dynamics, off-the-neck bends, subtle chromatic lines and uninhibited improvisation.

His Reputation Spreads And Wanes

Guy's reputation reached further than he imagined. His playing influenced guitarists as widespread as Eric Clapton and Jimi Hendrix. Equally impressed, musicologist Samuel Charters produced Guy's first solo albums for the Vanguard label, including the brilliant *A Man & The Blues* (1968), still

Key Track

'First Time I Met The Blues' (1960)
Guy's own visceral style emerged on this track, his first single for Chess Records. His vocal and guitar performances crackle with energy, even if Guy was ultimately unsatisfied with the result. 'Leonard Chess was always saying, "That's a little too much guitar",' Guy recalls. 'I figured he knew better. Now I know he was wrong.'

Classic Recordings

The Complete Chess Studio Recordings (1960–1967)
'First Time I Met The Blues', 'Stone Crazy', 'My Time After Awhile', 'Leave My Girl Alone', 'When My Left Eye Jumps'

Hoodoo Man Blues by Junior Wells' Chicago Blues Band, featuring Buddy Guy (1965)
'Hoodoo Man Blues', 'Snatch It Back And Hold It', 'Chitlin Con Carne'

A Man And The Blues (1967)
'A Man And The Blues', 'One Room Country Shack', 'Sweet Little Angel', 'Jam On A Monday Morning'

Southside Blues Jam with Junior Wells & Otis Spann (1970)
'Blues For Mayor Daley', 'Trouble Don't Last Always'

Drinkin' TNT 'n' Smokin' Dynamite with Junior Wells (1974)
'Ten Years Ago', 'Messing With The Kid'

Damn Right, I've Got The Blues (1991)
'Damn Right, I've Got The Blues', 'Rememberin' Stevie'

Sweet Tea (2001)
'Done Got Old', 'Baby Please Don't Leave Me'

widely considered to be Guy's masterpiece. In 1970 Guy and Wells were invited to tour with the Rolling Stones; they then found themselves on the international festival circuit, together and with their bands, but their fame was fleeting. Guy spent the 1980s without a contract, playing clubs including his own, the Checkerboard Lounge. He later opened Legends in downtown Chicago.

At The Zenith

It took another acolyte, Texan guitarslinger Stevie Ray Vaughan, to propel Guy to the top of the contemporary blues world, where he remains, second only to B.B. King. Vaughan's tireless support won Guy a contract with Silvertone Records, resulting in 1991's *Damn Right, I've Got The Blues* – which was also the title of Guy's 1993 autobiography, co-written by Donald E. Wilcock. The disc, which includes cameos

by Jeff Beck, Mark Knopfler and Eric Clapton, received significant airplay and thrust Guy back to the festival and outdoor amphitheatre circuit, where he continues to play today. Several subsequent CDs found Guy aiming for pop crossover breakthroughs, but their diminishing sales figures indicated that they were eroding his standing among his listeners.

Once again, a prominent fan interceded. Producer Dennis Herring took the reins for 2001's *Sweet Tea*, using vintage amplifier tones and songs culled primarily from the catalogue of modern Mississippi juke blues master Junior Kimbrough. The raw-sounding venture restored Guy's momentum, which he maintained by joining Herring again for 2003's *Blues Singer*, an acoustic country blues homage to Muddy Waters' *Folk Singer* (1964) that returned Guy to his rural roots.

Above
Musicologist Sam Charters, who produced Guy's early albums.

Left
Guy sporting a Stevie Ray Vaughan t-shirt at the launch of his 1991 album Damn Right I've Got The Blues.

Albert King

playing indulged in by so many contemporary blues guitarists. For King, a six-foot-four, 250-pound man possessed of a big, mellow voice and an equally proportional guitar tone, each carefully chiselled note took on the resonance of a life experience.

Born Albert Nelson on 25 April 1923 in Indianola, Mississippi, near the birthplace of B.B. King, Albert King was raised on a plantation in Arkansas, where he occasionally heard Howlin' Wolf perform at parties and roadhouses. He taught himself guitar and began playing local juke joints in 1939. King travelled north and sang lead tenor with the Harmony Kings gospel quartet around South Bend, Indiana for several years before arriving in Chicago, where he played drums with Jimmy Reed, Jackie Wilson, Brook Benton and others.

Guitar Prowess

As a guitarist, King's technique was evolving. He graduated from acoustic to electric guitar, playing in a single-note style based on that of B.B. King, whose surname he also borrowed. These B.B. approximations can be heard on his early singles for the Parrot and Bobbin labels, including his first national hit, 'Don't Throw Your Love On Me So Strong', from 1961. By the time King signed to Stax Records in Memphis in 1966, he had developed his own brawny style. In the late 1950s he had purchased the Gibson Flying V guitar that became his signature instrument. The left-handed musician turned it upside down, tuned it to an open E-minor chord and turned his amplifier's volume up. The resulting sound – round-toned, deliberately squeezed from each string and full of melismatic bent notes – was the soulful equivalent of his gospel-honed voice.

The Stax Years

Featuring a roster of artists and session players that included Booker T. & the MGs, Isaac Hayes and the Memphis Horns, King's Stax singles and albums brought blues into the soul era. The spread of FM radio, along

Key Track

'I'll Play The Blues For You' (1972)

This song is a beautiful summary of Albert King's art. The mellow, burnished tones of his tenor voice, the lyrics about love and devotion with a touch of sadness and the crying, moaning bends and supple yet terse phrasing of his guitar licks make this Stax-era cut a classic.

Albert King's late 1960s and early 1970s recordings for the Stax label remain cornerstones of modern blues. Tunes like 'Born Under A Bad Sign', 'Crosscut Saw' and 'I'll Play the Blues For You' are also an antidote to the over-the-top

Classic Recordings

The Big Blues (1953–1966)
'Let's Have A Natural Ball', 'Don't Throw Your Love On Me So Strong'

Years Gone By (1968)
'Killing Floor', 'The Sky Is Crying'

Live Wire/Blues Power (1968)
'Blues Power'

I'll Play The Blues For You (1972)
'I'll Play The Blues For You', 'Breaking Up Somebody's Home', 'Answer To The Laundromat Blues'

Albert Live (1977)
'Blues At Sunrise', 'Jam In A Flat'

Albert King With Stevie Ray Vaughan (1983)
'Stormy Monday', 'Overall Junction'

Left

King, still brandishing a trademark Gibson Flying V guitar, performs at the Hammersmith Odeon, London in 1983.

with Eric Clapton's incorporation of King's licks and a cover of his 'Born Under A Bad Sign' into Cream's repertoire, introduced King to white listeners. In 1964 King was invited to open a series of shows for Janis Joplin and Jimi Hendrix at San Francisco's Fillmore Auditorium, which solidified his reputation with the rock audience.

King's popularity remained strong until the late 1970s, which was an especially difficult time for blues, as arena rock captured the commercial airwaves and disco claimed clubs that had patronized live music. However, thanks to an association he made with a young guitarist and fan named Stevie Ray Vaughan at the Austin, Texas club Armadillo World Headquarters, King would again experience something of a renaissance. Vaughan continually sang King's praises after his own ascent to

blues and rock stardom in the early 1980s, and invited King to open many important shows. In 1983 they appeared together on Hamilton, Ontario television station CHCH. The ensuing jam and conversation eventually became the CD *Albert King With Stevie Ray Vaughan* (1999).

In Paradise

Although King never regained the level of commercial success he'd achieved with Stax in the 1960s, he toured regularly, playing clubs and blues festivals until he suffered a fatal heart attack in Memphis on 21 December 1992. His body lies beneath a large tombstone at the Paradise Gardens Cemetery in Edmonson, Arkansas bearing a bronze plaque with the epitaph 'I'll play the blues for you'.

Far Left

Albert King, whose clear, sparse sound was a welcome departure.

B.B. King

When the great Mississippi musician Riley King left the cotton fields to seek his fortune in Memphis in 1946, he had $2.50 in his pocket and a battered guitar in his hand.

'Well B.B. was like a hero. You listen to the way that band swings on Live At The Regal, *it's just like a steam roller.'*
Mick Fleetwood

Today, his name is synonymous with the blues. King is probably the most influential guitarist of the past 50 years, with a lush, sustained tone and singing vibrato that has had a vast impact on generations of players across all genres. The soaring phrases of his warm, Delta-accented voice cut right to the emotional core of the blues. Yet his ascendance to the zenith of the blues world has never altered his friendly, downhome nature.

Right
Dynamic guitarist B.B. King, perhaps the most influential blues artist of the post-war era.

King was born on a plantation near Indianola on 16 September 1925. He had a

Key Track

'How Blue Can You Get' (1970)
This song is a valuable snapshot of King's dynamic guitar playing and singing, as well as his warm command of an audience. Each verse builds in intensity and commitment as King sells this song about a mean-spirited woman, working to the punch line 'I gave you seven children / Now you want to give them back' – and letting it strike like a mallet.

difficult childhood, with the intimidations of Jim Crow compounded by his mother's death when he was 10 years old. King was already playing gospel when he left for Memphis to stay for a time with his cousin, bluesman Bukka White. With his bold voice and charisma, and a distinctive guitar style influenced by Lonnie Johnson and T-Bone Walker, King began to win talent shows. In 1948 he secured a daily 10-minute spot on radio station WDIA, which he used to sell patent medicines like Pepticon while also plugging his area gigs. King chose 'The Beale Street Blues Boy' as his radio moniker, which was then abbreviated to 'B.B.' for 'Blues Boy'. The next year he made his debut recordings for the local Bullet label, then signed with Los Angeles-based Modern Records. King's first hit was 'Three O'Clock Blues' (1951), still a staple of the nearly 200 shows he plays each year.

Playing The Chitlin Circuit

King spent most of the 1950s and 1960s expanding his touring base. Initially, he worked at roadhouses within a few hours of Memphis. At a show in Twist, Arkansas in December 1949, he nearly lost his life when he rushed into a burning club to rescue his Gibson L-30 guitar. From that day he has named each of his guitars 'Lucille', after the woman who allegedly started the fire.

When more hit records, including 'You Upset Me Baby' and 'Please Love Me', allowed King to demand $800 a show, he began touring widely in the South. At first he was supported by Memphis bandleader Bill Harvey's group, travelling in a Cadillac and two station wagons to the small theatres and auditoriums where the New York City-based booking agency Universal Attractions secured him shows. In 1955, King assembled his own B.B. King Orchestra and got a loan for his first bus – a used Aero that he dubbed 'Big Red'. His touring route began to include northern African-American population centres, such as Chicago, Los Angeles and Harlem.

King cut many of his finest numbers during this period, 'Sweet Sixteen', 'Rock Me Baby' and 'How Blue Can You Get' among them. The influence of Louis Jordan, another of King's musical heroes, can be heard on many of these sides. In 1962 he switched to ABC-Paramount Records and made the concert album *Live At The Regal* (1964), recorded in a Chicago theatre before a wildly enthusiastic crowd. Although most white fans were listening to acoustic blues at the time, a new generation

of musicians began to sing his praises. Eric Clapton, Mike Bloomfield, Jimi Hendrix and Johnny Winter helped King to reach the rock audience. His star rose, and then soared when the song that would become his signature, 'The Thrill Is Gone', hit number 15 on the American pop charts in January 1970.

Recognition Is Achieved

Since then King has been the blues' top traditional performer, recording several excellent albums including *Indianola Mississippi Seeds* (1970), *Live In Cook County Jail* (1971), *Live In London* (1971) and *Now Appearing At Ole Miss* (1980). He made his home in Las Vegas, which remains his base, but graduated to international touring, playing dozens of countries. King was inducted into the Blues Foundation's Hall Of Fame in 1984 and the Rock And Roll Hall Of Fame in 1987. He also received a Grammy Award for Lifetime Achievement that year. In 1989 he recorded the smash 'When Loves Comes To Town' with U2, which introduced King to a new generation of rock fans. His B.B. King's Blues Club operates nightly on 42nd Street in New York.

Life At The Top

King penned his autobiography *Blues All Around Me* with journalist David Ritz in 1996. Although he has been afflicted by diabetes and arthritis, he remains a gracious and compelling performer and has grown as a guitarist, incorporating more jazz chords and scales into his live improvisations. Since 1991, he has headlined the travelling B.B.

King Blues Festival each summer. Although recent albums such as *Blues On The Bayou* (1998) and *Makin' Love Is Good For You* (2000) are not among his best, *Riding With The King* (2000), a collaboration with his apostle Eric Clapton, won a Grammy Award and hit the top of the pop charts.

Above
King in London with his trusty guitar Lucille.

A-Z of artists

The Animals

(Vocal/instrumental group, 1962–68)

This R&B-influenced UK rock group from Newcastle comprised powerful blues singer Eric Burdon (vocals), Hilton Valentine (guitar), Chas Chandler (bass), Alan Price (keyboards) and John Steel (drums). They backed visiting US bluesmen before releasing their US and UK number-one hit 'House of the Rising Sun' in 1964. A string of blues- and R&B-influenced smashes followed. After the band split, Chandler went on to manage Jimi Hendrix while Burdon moved to California and recorded with War and Night Shift.

Mike Bloomfield

(Guitar, vocals, 1943–81)

Bloomfield apprenticed in Chicago with legends such as Muddy Waters and Howlin' Wolf, as well as among his peers Paul Butterfield, Charlie Musselwhite and Elvin Bishop. He played on classics with the Paul Butterfield Blues Band (1966's *East-West*), Bob Dylan (1965's *Highway 61 Revisited*) and organist Al Kooper (1968's *Super Session*). He helped to form Electric Flag and briefly played in KGB, but then took refuge in acoustic blues in the late 1970s, making virtuoso, instructive recordings until his death from an overdose in 1981.

Below

Los Angeles band Canned Heat covered a selection of 1920s and 1930s blues tracks.

The Blues Project

(Vocal/instrumental group, 1965–71)

The Blues Project was formed around respected session musicians Tommy Flanders (vocals), Danny Kalb (guitar), Steve Katz (guitar, vocals), Al Kooper (organ, vocals), Andy Kulberg (bass, flute) and Roy Blumenfeld (drums). This experimental band, with a love of urban and country blues, quickly rose to the apex of the New York City music scene. By 1967 it had played huge outdoor concerts in Central Park and toured the US, spreading its influence. They recorded three albums, including the excellent debut *Live At The Café Au Go Go* (1966), before Kooper and Katz departed to form Blood, Sweat & Tears.

Paul Butterfield Blues Band

(Vocal/instrumental group, 1963–67)

Harmonica player and singer Butterfield conditioned his band – Jerome Arnold (bass), Elvin Bishop and Mike Bloomfield (guitars), Sam Lay (drums, vocals) and Mark Naftalin (keyboards) – in black Chicago clubs. They backed Dylan's electric debut at the 1965 Newport Folk Festival and helped to usher blues into the psychedelic era, with the groundbreaking *East-West* (1966). After the departure of Bloomfield, Butterfield changed his sound and added a horn section for *The Resurrection Of Pigboy Crabshaw* (1967), considered to be the band's last blues album.

Canned Heat

(Vocal/instrumental group, 1966–present)

Comprising Bob Hite (vocals, harmonica), Al Wilson (guitar, harmonica, vocals), Henry Vestine (guitar), Larry Taylor (bass) and Fito De La Perra (drums), this

Los Angeles band's heyday was between 1966–70, when covers of the Memphis Jug Band's 'On The Road Again' and Henry Thomas's 'Goin' Up The Country' propelled them up the charts. A teaming with John Lee Hooker, *Hooker 'N Heat* (1971), is a highlight in a long slide to the oldies circuit, which began with the fatal overdose of Wilson in 1970 and included the death of Hite in 1981.

Clifton Chenier

(Accordion, vocals, 1925–87)

This Opelousas, Louisiana native cut his teeth on French dance tunes flavoured by Creole blues, as played by his musical forebear Amédée Ardoin. Chenier invented the zydeco style by adding elements of R&B, country and rock'n'roll, combined with a swinging beat. He enjoyed a string of hit singles, including his career-making 1955 US hit 'Eh, Petit Fille'. Chenier's son C.J. joined his band in 1978, and today C.J. carries on his father's musical tradition, updated with a twist of funk. Clifton's blues guitarist cousin Roscoe Chenier also regularly tours.

Albert Collins

(Guitar, vocals, 1932–93)

Collins's highly original and bold, chiselled tone – achieved through an idiosyncratic tuning and high volume – earned

'When I see him I thank God I don't play guitar.'
Kim Wilson

the Texan his nickname 'The Iceman'. The moniker was abetted by a string of chilly-themed, early 1960s instrumental hits that incorporated R&B rhythms, including the million-selling 'Frosty', 'Sno Cone' and 'Thaw Out'. Although his cousin was Lightnin' Hopkins, Collins's aggressive playing style was primarily influenced by T-Bone Walker and Gatemouth Brown. He played almost exclusively on the so-called 'crawfish circuit' in Louisiana and Texas, reaching mostly black audiences.

He crossed over to the mainstream in the late 1960s, when he moved to California and was adopted by San Francisco's psychedelic rock scene. Nonetheless, he achieved his greatest popularity after signing with Chicago-based Alligator Records in 1978, playing the Montreux Jazz Festival and winning a Grammy for 1985's *Showdown!*, a collaboration with Robert Cray and Johnny Copeland. Collins was still among the top attractions in blues when he died from cancer in 1993.

Cream

(Vocal/instrumental group, 1966–68)

In 1966, Eric Clapton (guitar) joined Jack Bruce (bass, vocals, harmonica) and Ginger Baker (drums) to form Cream, the first rock supergroup. These virtuosos fused blues, rock and jazz-like improvisation into a sound that became so popular it altered modern blues from a primarily vocal style into a music dominated by the electric guitar. Their albums *Fresh Cream* (1966), *Disraeli Gears* (1967) and *Wheels Of Fire* (1968) remain dramatic examples of modern blues reinterpretation.

Above

Zydeco accordionist Clifton Chenier plays at London's Albert Hall in 1969.

Left

Texan guitarist Albert Collins, whose hard, cold tone earned him the nickname 'The Iceman'.

henry thomas ⊙57   john lee hooker ⊙138   lightnin' hopkins ⊙187   robert cray ⊙286

Snooks Eaglin
(Guitar, vocals, b. 1936)

Glaucoma and a brain tumour left Eaglin blind at the age of 19 months, but his unorthodox fingerpicking style and a sensibility based on the Crescent City's Caribbean rhythms made him the king of New Orleans guitar. He first performed gospel in churches, before turning to blues and recording his debut album, *New Orleans Street Singer* (1959). Eaglin's music became more sophisticated through associations with Dave Bartholomew and Professor Longhair, and he remains a vital performer, although he rarely tours.

Below

Guitarist Peter Green (centre) gave Fleetwood Mac a blues sound in the band's early days.

Fleetwood Mac
(Vocal/instrumental group, 1968–present)

Many fans who love Fleetwood Mac's string of 1970s hits are unaware of their earlier blues explorations. The band came into being when guitarist Peter Green, drummer Mick Fleetwood and bassist John McVie broke away from John Mayall's Bluesbreakers. In 1968, with Jeremy Spencer on second guitar, Fleetwood Mac debuted on Blue Horizon. A third guitarist, Danny Kirwan, joined in time for the band to gig in Chicago with Willie Dixon and Otis Spann. Their original tunes and covers of blues classics (e.g. 'I Need Your Love So Bad') testified to the band's aptitude.

Right

Slim Harpo, whose 'I'm A King Bee' was covered by the Rolling Stones on their debut album.

In 1970, after the release of the album *Then Play On*, Green became burned out on LSD and was replaced by keyboardist Christine Perfect. Then, during the 1971

tour, Spencer joined the Children Of God cult. The blues content of Fleetwood Mac's music dwindled as they began to lean towards mainstream rock. By the time the band achieved superstar status in 1975, their blues days were over. The band has survived several personnel changes and breakups, remaining a popular concert draw.

John Hammond Jr.
(Guitar, harmonica, vocals, b. 1942)

The son of A&R genius John Hammond, this New York City native left home at the age of 19 to perform professionally. He remains primarily an acoustic player, in the tradition of the classic Delta musicians. Hammond cut a fine series of LPs during 1964–76, encapsulated on 2000's *Best Of The Vanguard Years*. He notably joined Mike Bloomfield and Dr John for *Triumvirate* (1973). Hammond's career also got a boost from *Wicked Grin* (2001), an album of Tom Waits songs that introduced him to a new audience.

Slim Harpo
(Harmonica, guitar, vocals, 1924–70)

Born James Moore in Lobdell, Louisiana, Harpo developed an upbeat style playing juke joints and parties before

signing to Excello Records in 1955, where he was instrumental in defining the label's 'swamp-blues' sound. He had a profound influence on 1960s rockers including Van Morrison, the Kinks and the Rolling Stones, who covered Harpo's 'I'm A King Bee' and 'Shake Your Hips'. Harpo died from a heart attack in Baton Rouge, Louisiana.

Jimi Hendrix

(Guitar, vocals, 1942–70)

This left-handed Seattle, Washington native taught himself to play by flipping over a $5 acoustic guitar and copying licks from blues, R&B and rock'n'roll records. Hendrix apprenticed on the R&B circuit, backing up Little Richard among others, and mastered techniques from the stuttering ninth chords of James Brown sideman Jimmy Nolen to the epic string-bending of Albert King.

Hendrix's solo career ignited when he was discovered at Greenwich Village's Café Wha? by Animals bassist Chas Chandler, who became his manager and moved Hendrix to London.

'Jimi to me was one of the great explorers if you will of the so-called Delta blues....'
B.B. King

The Jimi Hendrix Experience was formed and the group's debut LP *Are You Experienced?* (1967) became an international smash, fortified by Hendrix's flamboyant performing style. Throughout Hendrix's three brief years as an international pop star, his music became increasingly experimental, but even his incendiary version of the 'Star-Spangled Banner', recorded live at Woodstock and full of feedback explosions, showed his unswerving devotion to blues tonality.

Janis Joplin

(Vocals, 1943–70)

Influenced by Bessie Smith, Joplin became a rock star while in San Francisco's Big Brother & the Holding Company, and enjoyed a meteoric solo career before her untimely death from a heroin overdose in Los Angeles. Nonetheless, she was perhaps the most commanding female blues singer of the modern era. Joplin's raw emotional expression and fiery presence overruled complaints about her straying intonation both in concert and on albums like Big Brother's *Cheap Thrills* (1968) and the posthumous *Pearl* (1971).

Freddie King

(Guitar, vocals, 1934–76)

Few bluesmen have possessed the bristling intensity of Freddie King, whose stinging vibrato and energetic, soaring vocal style influenced Eric Clapton. King was born in Gilmer, Texas and learned guitar from his mother at age six. He moved to Chicago in 1950, earning a reputation among peers like Buddy Guy and Otis Rush with his gritty approach.

His 1950s recordings for the Cobra label were not released, but King made his mark after signing with Cincinnati's Federal/King Records in 1960. His Federal/King sides included the oft-covered instrumentals 'Hideaway' and 'San-Ho-Zay', as well as 'Have You Ever Loved A Woman', subsequently made famous by Derek & the Dominos. Waning interest in blues left him without a contract in 1965, but King was soon accepted by white rock audiences and toured England extensively between 1967 and 1969. He played clubs and festivals and recorded for major labels until his heart failed after a Dallas concert.

Above

Guitar legend Jimi Hendrix, whose love of the blues is evident in the blues-tinged rock music he produced.

*Guitarist and blues
promoter Alexis Korner
(right) with harmonica
player Cyril Davies and
drummer Charlie Watts
(seated behind) in Blues
Incorporated.*

Alexis Korner's Blues Incorporated
(Vocal/instrumental group, 1962–67)

Alexis Korner (guitar, piano, vocals), born in Paris, France
in 1928, was considered to be the father of electric British
blues. When he and Cyril Davies (harmonica, vocals)
formed Blues Incorporated in 1962 with Dick Heckstall-
Smith (saxophone), Andy Hoogenboom (bass), Ken Scott
(piano) and Charlie Watts (drums), their amplified line-up
met with resistance. So Korner and Davies opened their
own venue, the Ealing Rhythm & Blues Club, beneath a
London tea shop in 1962; they were soon attracting large
crowds of hipsters including Mick Jagger, Keith Richards
and Brian Jones. Jack Bruce and Ginger Baker replaced
Hoogenboom and Watts, and the group began a residency
at the Marquee Club.

Their debut, the live *R&B From The Marquee* (1962),
was the first British blues album. Yet commercial success
evaded Korner, as the Rolling Stones, Bluesbreakers and
other bands inspired and encouraged by him ascended.
Korner remained musically active in the decades after
Blues Incorporated, before dying of lung cancer in 1984.

Sam Lay
(Drums, vocals, b. 1935)

Shuffle master Lay was an important figure in the racial
integration of 1960s blues. He was born in Birmingham,
Alabama and moved to Chicago, where he played with
Little Walter, Howlin' Wolf and other Chess Records artists.
He joined the Paul Butterfield Blues Band for its first two
albums and played on Bob Dylan's *Highway 61 Revisited*

as well as Dylan's electric debut at Newport in 1965. Lay leads his own band today and has also recently recorded with the Siegel-Schwall Band.

Sammy Lawhorn
(Guitar, 1935–90)
Respected sideman Lawhorn began a nine-year stint with Muddy Waters' band in 1956 after working with harmonica players Sonny Boy Williamson II and Willie Cobbs, among others. Waters fired the Little Rock, Arkansas native in 1973 for excessive drinking. By then his razor-edged tone and imaginative soloing had already left an indelible mark on the blues. Lawhorn subsequently played on sides by James Cotton, Junior Wells and Koko Taylor. His death at the age of 54 was attributed to natural causes.

Little Milton
(Guitar, vocals, b. 1934)
Born to sharecroppers in Inverness, Mississippi, the country music Milton Campbell heard in radio broadcasts from the Grand Ole Opry shaped his soulful sound as much as gospel and blues. After regional success, he signed to the Chess Records subsidiary Checker in 1961 and cut the classics 'If Walls Could Talk', 'Feel So Bad' and 'Grits Ain't Groceries', among others. He remains a major artist on the chitlin circuit, recording for Jackson, Mississippi's Malaco Records.

Robert Lockwood Jr.
(Guitar, harmonica, vocals, b. 1915)
This curmudgeonly survivor is thought to be the only musician given lessons by Robert Johnson, who was infatuated with Lockwood's mother. But Lockwood, who was raised in Helena, Arkansas, also assimilated jazz chords and swinging rhythms to become one of the most sophisticated guitarists to emerge from the Delta. After decades as a sideman and songwriter, Lockwood today resides in Cleveland, Ohio, where he leads a big band, and travels the world playing solo in Johnson's style.

Magic Sam
(Guitar, vocals, 1937–69)
Along with peers Otis Rush and Buddy Guy, Mississippi native Samuel Maghett pioneered the ghetto-born mix of soul singing and guitar pyrotechnics that defined Chicago's West Side sound. 'Easy Baby' and 'All Your Love', cut for Cobra in the 1950s, are his signature tunes, but his Delmark LP *West Side Soul* (1967) is a classic example of raw, open-hearted emotional expression. He died unexpectedly of a heart attack just as his career was gaining momentum.

John Mayall's Bluesbreakers
(Vocal/instrumental group, 1963–present)
Talented bandleader John Mayall (vocals, piano, organ, harmonica), born in Macclesfield, Cheshire in 1933, is largely responsible for igniting the popularity of British blues as well as the careers of famed guitarists Eric Clapton, Peter Green (Fleetwood Mac) and Mick Taylor (the Rolling Stones). Mayall's 1966 debut album *Blues Breakers*, using Chicago blues as a model, established the reputation of Clapton and also featured John McVie (bass) and Hughie Flint (drums). The album reached number six on the UK charts. Powerfully realized, it remains the seminal British electric blues album and began a streak of Bluesbreakers classics, including *A Hard Road* (with Green, 1967) and *Crusade* (with Taylor, 1967).

Mayall began a parallel solo career with the underrated *The Blues Alone* (1968) that peaked the next year, following his relocation to California with *The Turning Point* and its FM-radio staple 'Room To Move'. Mayall continues to perform with a version of his Bluesbreakers and remains one of the few white blues performers whose songwriting equals that of his heroes Muddy Waters and J.B. Lenoir.

Above
Blues Breakers, *the debut album from John Mayall's band, featured the stunning guitar work of Eric Clapton and put British blues on the musical map.*

Pinetop Perkins
(Piano, guitar, b. 1913)
Belzoni, Mississippi's Perkins performed throughout the Delta until 1949, when he relocated to Chicago to play with Robert Nighthawk and Earl Hooker through the 1950s. In 1969 he replaced Otis Spann in Muddy Waters' band. Perkins stayed until 1980, when he, Calvin Jones (bass), Jerry Portnoy (harmonica) and Willie Smith (drums) left Waters to form the Legendary Blues Band. Perkins still works as a solo artist and with the Muddy Waters Tribute Band.

Yank Rachell

(Mandolin, guitar, harmonica, violin, vocals, 1910–97)

Rachell and fellow Brownsville, Tennessee musicians Sleepy John Estes and Hammie Nixon played throughout the mid-South in the 1920s, eventually relocating to Memphis. Rachell and Estes partnered with pianist Jab Jones, recording for Victor as the Three J's Jug Band. During the 1930s and 1940s, Rachell played with John Lee 'Sonny Boy' Williamson. In 1962 he reunited with Estes and Nixon, recording and touring as Yank Rachell's Tennessee Jug-Busters on Chicago's Delmark label.

Rolling Stones

(Vocal/instrumental group 1962–present)

The Rolling Stones' original line-up comprised Mick Jagger (vocals, harmonica), Brian Jones and Keith Richards (guitars), Bill Wyman (bass) and Charlie Watts (drums). The band balanced R&B and blues with pop and psychedelia, releasing the heavily blues-influenced *Beggars Banquet* in 1968. Following the loss of Jones, who drowned in 1969, and the addition of Mick Taylor, the Stones released three more blues rock masterpieces: *Let It Bleed* (1969), *Sticky Fingers* (1971) and *Exile On Main Street* (1972). Now minus Wyman and Taylor, and with Ronnie Wood on guitar, the Stones continue to roll.

Below

Otis Spann, house pianist for Chess Records, pictured at London's 100 Club, 1969.

Otis Rush

(Guitar, vocals, b. 1934)

Rush, who was born in Philadelphia, Mississippi, was – along with Buddy Guy and Magic Sam – part of the defining trinity of Chicago's West Side sound. His 1950s Cobra Records singles 'All Your Love (I Miss Loving)' and 'I Can't Quit You Baby' became standards. Rush is undoubtedly a genius, with a big soulful voice and an unpredictable command of the guitar, but music-business troubles and his own erratic personality have impeded his career.

Siegel-Schwall Band

(Vocal/instrumental group, 1964–present)

College mates Corky Siegel (harmonica, piano) and Jim Schwall (guitar) started out as a duo. They softened the electric blues they heard in Chicago with acoustic guitar and folk-music leanings. They expanded – adding Jos Davidson (bass, vocals) and Russ Chadwick (drums) – and made their debut album for the Vanguard label in 1966. They disbanded in 1974 following a unique blues concerto grosso by William Russo with the Chicago Symphony Orchestra, but reformed in 1988 and released the live *Siegel-Schwall Reunion Concert*.

Otis Spann

(Piano, vocals, 1930–70)

The finest post-war blues pianist, Spann learned to play at churches and parties around his Jackson, Mississippi birthplace. From 1952 until his death from cancer, he was house keyboardist at Chess Records, recording with Muddy Waters, Bo Diddley, Sonny Boy Willliamson, Howlin' Wolf, Little Walter and others. Although Spann made a clutch of fine solo recordings, including the first Candid release, *Otis Spann Is The Blues* (1960) and duets with Robert Lockwood, he is best known as Waters' music director.

Taj Mahal

(Guitar, banjo, bass, harmonica, mandolin, piano, vocals, b. 1942)

Henry Saint Clair Fredericks' concept of the blues was formed partly by his West Indian father's diverse record collection and partly by his coming of age in the collegiate coffeehouses of western Massachusetts. Since Taj Mahal's eponymous debut in 1967, followed in 1968 by a role in *The Rolling Stones' Rock And Roll Circus*, he has challenged purists by employing the sounds and beats of Caribbean, African, Latin and American folk styles. He remains a tireless performer and champion of earlier artists.

Ten Years After

(Vocal/instrumental group, 1967–present)

This UK rock band from Nottingham, comprising Chick Churchill (keyboards), Alvin Lee (guitar, vocals), Ric Lee (drums) and Leo Lyons (bass), emerged as a vehicle for Alvin Lee's speed-demon playing. Their sound was most notably captured on the Woodstock soundtrack in an 11-minute version of the group's signature song, 'Goin' Home'.

They toured the US 28 times and are ably represented by the CD *Anthology 1967–1971*. The classic line-up lasted until 1975, when Alvin Lee left, however the band reformed in 1989.

Johnny 'Guitar' Watson
(Guitar, piano, vocals, 1935–96)

The self-proclaimed 'Gangster Of Love', Watson learned piano from his father in Houston, Texas but became known for his terse, stinging guitar, which influenced Frank Zappa and has been sampled by rappers. Etta James patterned her early singing after Watson's declarative vocals, best immortalized along with his wicked instrumental prowess on King and Federal singles from 1953 to 1963, including 'Motorhead Baby' and 'Space Guitar'. He suffered a fatal heart attack onstage in Japan.

Junior Wells
(Harmonica, vocals, 1934–98)

Amos Blackmore grew up in west Memphis, Arkansas under the sway of Sonny Boy Williamson II and began

recording as a teenager in Chicago, playing with the innovative Four Aces before joining Muddy Waters' band. Wells created a personal style influenced by James Brown. In the mid-1960s he began a long association with guitarist Buddy Guy (who played on Wells's masterful 1965 debut LP *Hoodoo Man Blues*, Delmark Records), which lasted until Wells's death from cancer in 1998.

Above
Johnny 'Guitar' Watson, whose stinging guitar style complemented his declarative vocals.

Yardbirds
(Vocal/instrumental group, 1963–68)

The Chicago blues-inspired Yardbirds, featuring Keith Relf (vocals, harmonica), Eric Clapton and Chris Dreja (guitars), Paul Samwell-Smith (bass) and Jim McCarty (drums), took over the Rolling Stones' residency at London's Crawdaddy Club and backed Sonny Boy Williamson II on tour in 1963. Clapton left after the release of their debut album in 1963 and was replaced by Jeff Beck; a succession of pop hits followed. Guitarist Jimmy Page joined in 1966 and after Beck departed, Page and Dreja formed the New Yardbirds (an ensemble which would eventually develop into Led Zeppelin). A version of the Yardbirds reformed after their 1992 induction into the Rock And Roll Hall Of Fame and continues to tour.

Left
Harmonica ace Junior Wells dances onstage during a 1960s gig.

sonny boy williamson ⊙ 107   sonny boy williamson II (rice miller) ⊙ 191   buddy guy ⊙ 220   led zeppelin ⊙ 267

Jazz

'Jazz is the only music in which the same note can be played night after night but differently each time.'
Ornette Coleman

Above
Cecil Taylor is a great innovator of free jazz and has a distinctive, percussive piano style.

Right
Saxophonist Albert Ayler, who influenced John Coltrane, led his ensembles through several distinct, ecstatic musical styles.

The 1960s was as turbulent a time for jazz as it was for the world's socio-political climate. The American civil rights movement, roots consciousness, the Vietnam War and advances in technology all worked to change the face of jazz. Several major movements arose during the decade, generating balanced waves of controversy and mass popularity.

Running Free

Perhaps the most divisive development of the 1960s was the rise of free jazz, the roots of which had been planted several years before by renegades such as Cecil Taylor (b. 1929), Ornette Coleman (b. 1930) and Sun Ra (1914–93), who had bold new visions about how jazz could evolve in order to stay fresh and relevant. In December 1960 the movement received its name and philosophy from the Atlantic album *Free Jazz: A Collective Improvisation By The Ornette Coleman Double Quartet*. Coleman and seven creative peers improvised with the barest of guidelines,

one-upping each other continually until the final climax of a wild, polyphonic performance unlike anything that had been heard before. *Free Jazz* was the match that lit a searing flame in the musical world for years to come.

Free jazz was an artistic translation of the American civil rights struggle. As black playwrights, poets and authors had spoken their minds about the injustices being inflicted upon their people a century after the Emancipation Proclamation, jazz musicians also took up the call to arms. The music they created was a mirror image of the anguish, bitterness, yearning, resistance, sarcasm and faith inside their collective heart. Their jazz raged, or was introspective and lamenting, or was raw, or, perhaps, free.

A Spiritual Side To Jazz

Coleman was an essential spokesman for the new music, his alto sax a voice crying out for humanity. Cecil Taylor, who reconceived the piano for its percussive potential, was similarly emotional, intellectual and articulate. Bandleader Sun Ra built a complex fantasy world about himself, claiming to be a visitor from Saturn who was seeking a new home in the cosmos for the black race. Ra appealed to both a sense of tradition and community and jazz's self-referential, experimental streak, operating

independently almost beyond commercial society. John Coltrane (1926–67) and Albert Ayler (1936–70) took a different spiritual tack, actively seeking God through free musical expression.

Coltrane made a lasting impression with his 1964 album *A Love Supreme*, his greatest popular achievement, before heading further into extreme freedom. Many critics (especially older and politically conservative ones) hated the new music and labelled it 'anti-jazz'. Although free jazz was a novel, exciting and honest form of music that reflected the turmoil of the era, it never won over the majority of jazz listeners. It has since, however, had a continuing impact on jazz and its major proponents have become revered by critics and honoured with international awards.

Blue Notes And Bossas

While free jazz may have barely made a dent in the music market, hard bop was the sound of the times for most jazz listeners. The soulful, blues-drenched, rhythmically rich style was all the rage on jazz radio and in clubs. A dozen record labels capitalized upon hard bop, none with more success than Blue Note. Founded in the 1930s, Blue Note embraced the hard-bop aesthetic and promoted it with vigour, making stars out of Art Blakey (1919–90), Dexter Gordon (1923–90), Jackie McLean (b. 1932), Horace Silver (b. 1928), Joe Henderson, Lee Morgan (1938–72), Kenny Dorham (1924–72), Wayne Shorter (b. 1933), Herbie Hancock (b. 1940), Freddie Hubbard (b. 1938) and a host of other young jazzmen. Occasionally a top 10 victory was chalked up, as with Lee Morgan's 1964 crossover hit 'The Sidewinder'. For several years Blue Note was the premier label for jazz in the US.

More short-lived, but just as lucrative for a time, was the bossa nova craze. Tenor saxophonist Stan Getz (1927–91), a former member of the Woody Herman Orchestra and star of the 'cool school', collaborated first with guitarist Charlie Byrd and then with the Brazilian musicians João Gilberto

(b. 1931) and Antonio Carlos Jobim (1927–94) on a series of albums which that jazz and Brazilian musical styles together into a captivating new sound. 'The Girl From Ipanema', featuring the warm, distingüe singing of the woman who became known as Astrud Gilberto, was a huge US hit in 1963 and guaranteed the bossa nova a place in jazz history.

Above
Lee Morgan had a 1964 hit with 'The Sidewinder'.

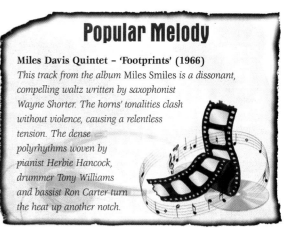

Popular Melody

Miles Davis Quintet – 'Footprints' (1966)
This track from the album Miles Smiles *is a dissonant, compelling waltz written by saxophonist Wayne Shorter. The horns' tonalities clash without violence, causing a relentless tension. The dense polyrhythms woven by pianist Herbie Hancock, drummer Tony Williams and bassist Ron Carter turn the heat up another notch.*

ornette coleman ⊙ **238**   **john coltrane** ⊙ **240**   **sun ra** ⊙ **244**   **cecil taylor** ⊙ **252**

Jimmy Giuffre (b. 1921) and Gerry Mulligan (1927–96), who had made names for themselves in Los Angeles, found more fertile ground in New York City and abandoned much of their cool-jazz interest. Even the Modern Jazz Quartet, mixing hard bop and cool jazz, took frequent hiatuses. One legacy of cool jazz was the so-called 'third stream' of jazz and classical hybrids, in which both Giuffre and the MJQ's John Lewis (1920–2001) took part.

Miles Davis, Revolutionary

The most prominent of the cool jazz pioneers, Miles Davis (1926–91), was perhaps the key innovator of the 1960s. He ushered in the decade with an extension of the modal jazz studies he had championed in 1959's *Kind Of Blue*. Davis's partnership with arranger Gil Evans (1912–88) continued with the triumphant *Sketches Of Spain* (1959–60), including a long, introspective version of the Spanish guitar opus 'Concierto de Aranjuez', and the less accomplished bossa nova venture *Quiet Nights* (1962). With the latter album Davis felt that his experiments with Evans had run their course, so he abruptly changed direction from their orchestral works.

In 1963 Davis gathered what would become the greatest rhythm section of his career. Drummer Tony Williams (1945–97), already a jazz veteran at the age of 18, joined pianist Herbie Hancock and bassist Ron Carter (b. 1937) in backing Davis and a series of tenor saxophonists: first George Coleman, then Sam Rivers (b. 1923) and finally Wayne Shorter, whose innovative compositions gave a bold new sound to the Davis quintet. The trumpeter's modal jazz excursions had been pulling away from the rigour of set chord patterns and now Davis took it one step further. In the quintet's repertoire, chords and traditional improvisation were often abandoned altogether. There were no up-front solos in pieces such as Shorter's 'Nefertiti' – only fully composed passages. At other times, the rhythm section would play ostinatos – repetitive patterns over which Davis would improvise. Hancock, Carter and Williams

www

Louis Armstrong
Orchestra
St. Louis Blues

musicfirebox.com
/Louis

Demise Of The Cool

The 1960s saw the dwindling of cool jazz. Pianist Lennie Tristano (1919–78), who had built a cult following of fanatically devoted young musicians, spent less time onstage and more time teaching at his home. On the West Coast, cool icons such as Shorty Rogers and Bud Shank were fortunate enough to find work in Hollywood's film and television studios as their sounds went out of vogue.

became masters of subtle variation, altering the mood and feeling of tunes almost imperceptibly over the course of several minutes, while the horns had their say in the foreground. This kind of rhythmic and harmonic play was about as close as Davis ever got to free jazz until his 1970s electric works.

Jazz Goes Electric

Later in the decade Davis brought in more young musicians and explored the concept of electric jazz. He initially encouraged Chick Corea, Keith Jarrett (b. 1945) and Joe Zawinul (b. 1932) to play electric piano and organ in a brave first step towards what became known as 'fusion', the union of jazz and rock elements. British electric guitarist John McLaughlin (b. 1942) pushed the envelope further outward with his unprecedented

performances. Eventually Davis plugged his trumpet into a wah-wah pedal to emulate the guitar of Jimi Hendrix (1942–70). Record producer Teo Macero was also a primary factor in the new sound, manipulating the band's tapes into exhilarating collages of music. In 1969 Davis and his troupe made two groundbreaking albums for Columbia, *In A Silent Way* and *Bitches Brew*, which announced the arrival of a fresh new form of jazz. As he had 10 years before with *Kind Of Blue* (1959), Miles Davis had forever altered the course of music.

Above
(l-r) Herbie Hancock, Wayne Shorter and Ron Carter.

Far Left
Rahsaan Roland Kirk played multiple horns.

Popular Melody

Horace Silver – 'Song For My Father' (1964)
An irrepressibly catchy bossa nova, this perennial hard-bop anthem, recorded on Blue Note, features brilliant solo spots by Silver and tenor saxophonist Joe Henderson. In 1974, jazz-rock combo Steely Dan borrowed Silver's piano vamp for 'Rikki Don't Lose That Number'.

Ornette Coleman

Since his emergence in the mid-1950s, alto saxophonist and creative composer Ornette Coleman has risen above controversy to become a respected elder statesman of jazz. Born in 1930 in Fort Worth, Texas, Coleman taught himself the saxophone through trial and error. By avoiding chord structures and set rhythms in favour of melodic experimentation, he developed the new style of 'free jazz'. He dubbed his controversial theory 'harmolodics' – a combination of harmony, motion and melody. Coleman's characteristic tone and his variety of intonation effects often recall a plaintive human voice, touched by the blues.

'Musicians tell me, if what I'm doing is right, they should never have gone to school.'
Ornette Coleman

Breaking New Ground

Coleman received his first saxophone at the age of seven. As he found his way around the horn, Coleman developed notions about music that clashed with traditional practices but remained permanent parts of his artistic philosophy. Four years after beginning his career at the age of 15 with an R&B group, Coleman took to the road and encountered hostility from musicians and audiences who appreciated neither his bebop alterations nor his unkempt appearance. However, bandleaders admired his songwriting abilities and assigned him to refresh their books of blues-related pieces.

In 1956 Coleman found himself unemployed in Los Angeles, where he met some like-minded musicians who were interested in his new concepts. His circle included trumpeters Don Cherry and Bobby Bradford, bassist Don Payne, drummer Billy Higgins and Canadian-born pianist Paul Bley, under whose name they performed at the Hillcrest Club.

Right
Alto saxophonist and composer Ornette Coleman, one of the chief exponents of free jazz.

Far Right
Coleman (centre) performs at Newport in 1977 with Don Cherry (left) and Dewey Redman.

Recordings of those exciting gigs were released years later by Bley's IAI record label.

In 1958 bassist Red Mitchell brought one of Coleman's compositions to Contemporary Records boss Lester Koenig, who signed Coleman to a contract. Coleman and Cherry had developed a loose, intuitive ensemble sound, evident on several Coleman compositions such as 'When Will The Blues Leave' and 'The Blessing', backed somewhat uneasily by Payne and Higgins. Coleman's second Contemporary release featured another sheaf of originals, including 'Tears Inside' and 'Rejoicing'. The session's drummer was big-band veteran and LA jazz-club operator Shelly Manne. Open-minded,

Key Track

'Lonely Woman' (1959)
This track, from The Shape Of Jazz To Come, is often called a 'dirge' due to its slow, lamenting theme. After bassist Charlie Haden and drummer Billy Higgins begin an Eastern-sounding drone, Coleman and trumpeter Don Cherry enter with the freely phrased melody. The mournful, agitated piece is perennially in Coleman's repertoire.

responsive pianist Walter Norris interpreted Coleman's compositions creatively, but the altoist later remarked that the piano's chordal, tempered nature was incompatible with the melody-driven freedom that he sought.

The Birth Of Free Jazz

In 1959 Coleman, Cherry, bassist Charlie Haden and drummer Ed Blackwell moved to New York, where they impressed composer-conductor Leonard Bernstein. Coleman continued to experiment with different ensembles and ideas, few as well-received as his famous quartet. In 1960 he recorded the landmark *Free Jazz: A Collective Improvisation By The Ornette Coleman Double Quartet* for Atlantic Records. It consisted of one long group improvisation, punctuated by a few composed reference points. The performers – Coleman, Cherry, Haden, Blackwell, Higgins, trumpeter Freddie Hubbard, Eric Dolphy on bass clarinet and second bassist Scott LaFaro (who died prematurely in a car accident seven months after the session) – interacted continuously, as individuals and also as an ensemble.

Further Innovations

Following *Free Jazz*, Coleman experimented with a new trio. He took up the violin and trumpet, although these instruments have never been more than ornaments in his overall conception. He dabbled in chamber music, wrote some film scores and arrangements for a posthumous John Coltrane release and often reunited with his former sidemen. Tenorman Dewey Redman became a key associate in that period. In 1966 Coleman controversially began using his 10-year-old son Denardo as his regular drummer. Denardo has

since continued to play drums and act as a producer for both his father and his mother, poet-vocalist Jayne Cortez.

In 1972 Coleman premiered his mammoth *Skies Of America*, a concerto grosso in which his ensemble improvised with a symphony orchestra. After collaborating with Yoko Ono and Morocco's Master Musicians of Jajouka, Coleman assembled the electric band Prime Time and recorded *Dancing In Your Head* in 1976. The group included two drummers (one of them often tabla player Badal Roy), two electric guitarists and electric bass. Later, multi-keyboardist David Bryant further widened Prime Time's scope, culminating in *Tone Dialing* (1995).

Since the late 1990s, Coleman has returned to acoustic groups with pianists. He has also led a quartet with two bassists and his son Denardo. Coleman, who remains a unique saxophone melodicist, an inspiring and world-renowned artist and an enduring composer, has also recorded with Pat Metheny, Jerry Garcia (of the Grateful Dead) and an esoteric range of other musicians.

Classic Recordings

Something Else! (1958)
'When Will The Blues Leave?', 'The Blessing', 'Invisible'

Change Of The Century (1959)
'Ramblin'', 'Free'

This Is Our Music (1960)
'Blues Connotation', 'Embraceable You'

Free Jazz: A Collective Improvisation By The Ornette Coleman Double Quartet (1960)
'Free Jazz'

Science Fiction (1971)
'Street Woman', 'Law Years', 'Civilization Day'

Song X with Pat Metheny (1985)
'Song X', 'Mob Job', 'Kathelin Gray'

In All Languages (1987)
'Peace Warriors'

John Coltrane

From R&B To Bebop

Coltrane was born in 1926 in Hamlet, North Carolina and began playing alto saxophone in high school. He made his first recordings while in the Army and switched to tenor sax at the encouragement of Eddie 'Cleanhead' Vinson. Work in R&B bands led to bebop gigs and in 1949 Coltrane joined Dizzy Gillespie's big band and septet. He continued to grow musically but became addicted to heroin. Coltrane moved on to the bands of Earl Bostic and Johnny Hodges, before meeting Miles Davis in 1955.

The Davis quintet, which included pianist Red Garland, bassist Paul Chambers and drummer Philly Joe Jones, was among the most popular jazz groups. The band cut several albums for Prestige in the mid-1950s with Davis and Coltrane on the front line; however, Davis fired the tenorman in 1957 because of his drug problems. Coltrane returned home to Philadelphia, overcame his addictions, and returned to jazz a new man. He worked with Thelonious Monk before getting his own contract with Prestige.

'Sheets Of Sound'

By the time Coltrane rejoined Davis in 1958, he had developed a technique of playing lengthy cascades of notes in propulsive harmonic extrapolations of complicated chord changes, termed 'sheets of sound' by writer Ira

'He contributed a whole different kind of openness to the music and added a spiritual essence to the music scene.'

Herbie Hancock

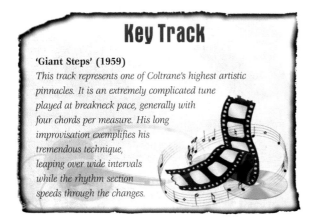

Key Track

'Giant Steps' (1959)

This track represents one of Coltrane's highest artistic pinnacles. It is an extremely complicated tune played at breakneck pace, generally with four chords per measure. His long improvisation exemplifies his tremendous technique, leaping over wide intervals while the rhythm section speeds through the changes.

By the time John Coltrane died in 1967 at the age of 40, he had experienced one of the most remarkable careers in music. 'Trane' was a compelling voice who contributed to some of jazz's greatest innovations, from bebop to free jazz, resulting in both controversy and enduring success through critical and popular acclaim.

albums, as well as with Duke Ellington, cornettist Don Cherry, vibist Milt Jackson and vocalist Johnny Hartman.

In December 1964 Coltrane's basic quartet recorded *A Love Supreme*. The album-length devotional suite offered jazz more exotic than most fans had ever heard. The public embraced it readily, and it became another of the era's hallmark jazz albums.

Ascending To Freedom

Coltrane moved further into free jazz in June 1965, assembling a large ensemble that included trumpeter Freddie Hubbard and saxophonists Pharoah Sanders and Archie Shepp, and recording *Ascension* (1965), two album-length versions of thematically and harmonically unbridled, dense and extremely high-energy improvisation. A few days later Coltrane and Shepp unveiled their somewhat more muted but nonetheless radical new directions at the Newport Jazz Festival.

Although Jones and Tyner followed Coltrane's fearless explorations through frequent sessions that resulted in albums such as *Transition* (1965) and *Meditations* (1966), they were uncomfortable with some of his more free-form, polyphonic and polyrhythmic directions. In 1965 Alice Coltrane, the saxophonist's second wife, became the pianist, and drummer Rashied Ali emerged as a significant player, especially on duet recordings preserved as *Interstellar Space* (1967). John Coltrane continued to explore intense, abstract, progressive and uncompromising jazz until his death from liver disease in July 1967. He stands as a jazz saint to the modern world, a model of musical devotion, authentic discovery and enduring art.

Gitler. The saxophonist joined Davis, altoman Julian 'Cannonball' Adderley and pianist Bill Evans on the classic *Kind Of Blue*, simplifying the music by using modal scales instead of chords. Coltrane responded with his own harmonically complicated *Giant Steps* (1959–60) for Atlantic Records; the title composition remains a test for any jazz musician. In the 1960s Coltrane began playing the soprano saxophone and scored another hit with *My Favorite Things*.

Bassist Jimmy Garrison, pianist McCoy Tyner and drummer Elvin Jones formed the core of Coltrane's early 1960s quartet, which soon became one of the most lauded ensembles in jazz. However, as his career progressed, the artistically restless Coltrane continued to develop his instrumental technique, grounded in what became a deeply spiritual and personal vision. He collaborated with gifted reedman Eric Dolphy, recording dates at New York's Village Vanguard that were later edited into an array of

Classic Recordings

Giant Steps (1959)
'Giant Steps', 'Countdown', 'Naima'

The Avant-Garde with Don Cherry (1960)
'Cherryco'

My Favorite Things (1960)
'My Favorite Things', 'Summertime'

Africa/Brass (1961)
'Africa', 'Blues Minor'

Duke Ellington and John Coltrane (1962)
'In A Sentimental Mood', 'Big Nick'

John Coltrane And Johnny Hartman (1963)
'Lush Life'

A Love Supreme (1964)
'A Love Supreme' Parts 1-4

Ascension (1965)
'Ascension'

Interstellar Space (1967)
'Mars'

Far Left

The controversial and endlessly experimental avant-garde saxophonist John Coltrane.

Above Left

Pianist McCoy Tyner played in Coltrane's hugely popular quartet of the early 1960s.

Below

One of Coltrane's best known albums, 1964's A Love Supreme.

Freddie Hubbard

In the 1960s and early 1970s, trumpeter Freddie Hubbard was the primary alternative to Miles Davis's domination of the field. Hubbard came up in the hard-bop era, blew free jazz with Ornette Coleman and John Coltrane, and established a body of exemplary compositions, recordings and improvisations with the best of the 1960s Blue Note artists: Art Blakey, Herbie Hancock, Wayne Shorter, Andrew Hill, Eric Dolphy, Lee Morgan, Tony Williams, Sam Rivers and many others.

'He had the biggest sound and the most powerful swing out there, on almost any instrument. It was pretty amazing.'

Don Braden

Outward Bound

Born in Indianapolis in 1938, Hubbard drew inspiration from the bebop trumpeters of the early 1950s, particularly Clifford Brown. The Montgomery brothers, guitarist Wes, vibist Buddy and bassist Monk, were quick to hire the young trumpeter because of his stylistic resemblance to Brown. At the age of 20 Hubbard moved to New York City, where he roomed and formed a working relationship with reedsman Eric Dolphy. Hubbard played in the bebop-oriented bands of Sonny Rollins, Philly Joe Jones and J.J. Johnson. 1960 was a banner year: Hubbard made his first album for Blue Note – *Open Sesame* – performed on Dolphy's *Outward Bound* and Ornette Coleman's landmark *Free Jazz* and then went on tour with Quincy Jones.

In 1961 Hubbard made another lasting impression with Oliver Nelson on *Blues And The Abstract Truth*, which resulted in the classic 'Stolen Moments'. That same year he joined tenorman Wayne Shorter and trombonist Curtis Fuller on the front line of Art Blakey's Jazz Messengers, the premier

Right

Trumpeter Freddie Hubbard was inspired by Clifford Brown and played with the Montgomery brothers from a young age.

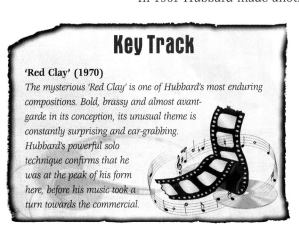

Key Track

'Red Clay' (1970)

The mysterious 'Red Clay' is one of Hubbard's most enduring compositions. Bold, brassy and almost avant-garde in its conception, its unusual theme is constantly surprising and ear-grabbing. Hubbard's powerful solo technique confirms that he was at the peak of his form here, before his music took a turn towards the commercial.

hard-bop ensemble. He remained a Messenger for three years, appearing on some of the band's finest recordings. In 1964 he left the group and contributed to two more enduring sessions, Dolphy's *Out To Lunch* and Herbie Hancock's *Maiden Voyage*. The following year Hubbard ventured deeper into free jazz on John Coltrane's *Ascension*, before joining Max Roach's band.

Rising Star

In 1966 Hubbard took steps to broaden his profile, putting together a quintet that featured alto saxophonist James Spaulding. His next two recordings, *Backlash* – which included his perennially popular composition 'Little Sunflower' (1966) – and *High Blues Pressure* (1967), both for the Atlantic label, garnered more critical acclaim for

Hubbard. His subsequent albums included the politically themed, abstract electronic composition *Sing Me A Song Of Songmy* (1971), and in 1970 he broke new ground on producer Creed Taylor's CTI label. Taylor was a master at reshaping jazz with more popular flourishes such as electric instruments and strings, and Hubbard benefitted greatly from his touch. The soulful albums *Red Clay* (1970), *Straight Life* (1970) and *First Light* (1972) all propelled Hubbard to the top of the jazz record and radio charts.

His triumphs on CTI collapsed when Hubbard signed with Columbia Records in 1972. The label pushed the 'contemporary' angle, dragging the trumpeter into one shallow, poorly conceived session after another. By the mid-1970s Hubbard seemed destined for has-been status. Herbie Hancock helped to rescue Hubbard's career by hiring him for the VSOP repertory group in 1977. The quintet revisited the musicians' 1960s Blue Note

accomplishments and proved that an acoustic setting was where Hubbard shone the brightest.

Welcome Return

Rejuvenated as a player and composer, Freddie Hubbard resumed his climb up the jazz echelon with a triumphant appearance at the 1980 North Sea Jazz Festival in Holland. New records for Pablo, Prestige and Enja led fans to embrace the trumpeter once more, although his stardom was still long past. In 1985 he signed back with the rejuvenated Blue Note, working with the brilliant trumpeter Woody Shaw on a few projects. Unfortunately, Hubbard soon became plagued by lip trouble that ruined his embouchure and required surgery. It took him several more years to return to a point where he could play comfortably again, but he remains on the scene and has recorded with David Weiss's New Jazz Composers Octet.

Classic Recordings

Open Sesame (1960)
'Gypsy Blue', 'All Or Nothing At All'

Mosaic by Art Blakey and the Jazz Messengers (1961)
'Arabia', 'Crisis'

Hub Cap (1961)
'Plexus'

Hub-Tones (1962)
'Hub-Tones', 'You're My Everything'

Backlash (1966)
'Little Sunflower'

High Blues Pressure (1967)
'Can't Let Her Go', 'High Blues Pressure'

Red Clay (1970)
'Red Clay', 'The Intrepid Fox'

Straight Life (1970)
'Straight Life', 'Mr. Clean'

Left

Pianist Herbie Hancock (left), shown here with Ron Carter, helped to resurrect Hubbard's career in the late 1970s.

Sun Ra

'The outer space beings are my brothers. They sent me here. They already know my music.'
Sun Ra

exotic big band blended theatrics with pure jazz and free exploration, crafting a unique brand of 'space jazz' that reflected the mid-century's curiosity about exploring the unknown universe.

Swinging Beginnings

Although Sun Ra claimed to have come to Earth from Saturn, he was in fact born Herman 'Sonny' Blount in Birmingham, Alabama in 1914. He was mostly self-taught as a pianist and performed with his own bands from the age of 20. Later, at Alabama State College, Blount proved to be such an exceptional student that he was permitted to teach from time to time.

Acclaimed as a creative, knowledgeable pianist, young Blount was also an inventive arranger. In 1946 he was hired by bandleader Fletcher Henderson, but his arrangements were so difficult and unusual that the musicians' complaints got him fired within a year. Around this time, Blount had been discussing Egyptian cosmology and science fiction with record producer Alton Abraham. The pair decided to put together a band that combined

Key Track

'Outer Spaceways Incorporated' (1972)
This track, from the Space Is The Place *soundtrack, typifies the Arkestra's style. A bizarre synthesizer introduction precedes upbeat organ sounds and June Tyson's repetitive vocals, coaxing the listener to sign up for an exciting adventure in space travel. Marshall Allen follows with a far-out alto saxophone solo.*

From the 1950s through to the 1990s there was rarely a stranger experience for jazz audiences than witnessing the stage shows of Sun Ra and his Solar-Myth Arkestra. The mysterious, robed keyboardist and his jazz, mythology, black pride and pulp science fiction. At the helm would be Blount, who assumed the persona of 'Sun Ra, Traveler of the Spaceways'. They built up a fantastic backstory for Ra as a sojourner from Saturn who searched the galaxy to find a new home for the mistreated black race on Earth.

Space Is The Place

By the mid-1950s Sun Ra was leading the first incarnation of his big band, called the Arkestra (sometimes augmented with spacy appellations such as 'Solar-Myth' or 'Myth-Science'). Blount's expansive knowledge of jazz history, from Jelly Roll Morton to the modern day, was filtered into his arrangements and compositions for the Arkestra. The band boasted several excellent musicians, among them trombonist Julian Priester, bassist Ronnie Boykins and saxophonists John Gilmore, Marshall Allen and Pat Patrick. Sun Ra used a number of keyboards, including Wurlitzer organ, clavinet and Moog synthesizer. The Arkestra's unusual sonic palette added to the other-worldliness of its music. Ra was a strict enforcer of rules, leading the band as a sort of commune and counselling its members against drug abuse and other unwelcome excesses.

The Arkestra debuted on record in 1957 with *Jazz By Sun Ra* (reissued on Delmark as *Sun Song*). The combination of straight jazz, heavy percussion and far-reaching improvisation heralded a new direction for jazz, but the album received scant distribution and little notice. That same year Ra formed his own record label, Saturn, which issued new Arkestra albums in haphazard form with hand-painted covers and unreliable sound quality. Saturn was one of the earliest labels run completely by musicians, and the enterprise endured even after Ra's death.

Other Worlds Of Sound

However, taut musicianship and consistently interesting music were not sufficient for the Arkestra to be taken seriously by many audiences or music critics, due in part to its outlandish stage costumes and cosmic pretensions. Still, Sun Ra became one of the most recognized, if begrudgingly respected, performers in modern jazz. The psychedelic era was a boon to the bandleader, whose spacey aesthetic was easy for the hippie generation to embrace. In 1972 the band made the movie *Space Is The Place*, based upon Sun Ra's invented mythology.

In the 1980s Sun Ra began to back away from writing original material, preferring to interpret past masters such as Duke Ellington and Fletcher Henderson. In the 1990s he became wheelchair-bound following a series of strokes and died on 30 May 1993, having schooled a further generation of players (including violinist Billy Bang and trombonist Craig Harris). After his death, Evidence Records initiated a reissue programme of Sun Ra's Saturn recordings.

Classic Recordings

Jazz By Sun Ra (a.k.a. *Sun Song*) (1956)
'Call For All Demons', 'Street Named Hell'

Jazz In Silhouette (1958)
'Ancient Aiethiopia', 'Blues At Midnight', 'Saturn'

Holiday For Soul Dance (1960)
'Early Autumn', 'Body And Soul', 'But Not For Me'

The Heliocentric Worlds Of Sun Ra, Volumes 1 & 2 (1965)
'Other Worlds', 'Sun Myth'

Lanquidity (1978)
'Where Pathways Meet'

Far Left
Eccentric keyboard player Sun Ra.

Below
Duke Ellington, a key influence on Sun Ra's later compositions, 1969.

A-Z of artists

Muhal Richard Abrams
(Piano, b. 1930)

Muhal Richard Abrams was one of the principal architects of free jazz in Chicago. After playing with Eddie Harris and the MJT+3, Abrams founded his Experimental Band in 1961 to explore original composition and new directions. In 1965 he founded the Association for the Advancement of Creative Musicians (AACM), which emphasizes creativity, professionalism and social responsibility. Abrams is a gifted composer and bandleader, having recorded many excellent albums with some of Chicago's – and later New York's – finest musicians.

Below
(l–r) Joe Zawinul, Nat Adderley, Sam Jones, Cannonball Adderley and Louis Hayes perform on BBC2's Jazz 625 in 1964.

Cannonball Adderley
(Alto saxophone, 1928–75)

Julian 'Cannonball' Adderley and his brother, trumpeter Nat, presided over one of the 1960s' hippest hard-bop outfits with pianist Joe Zawinul; 'Mercy, Mercy, Mercy' was one of their crossover hits. Adderley had been employed as a Florida school band director when he was overheard at a New York gig and was encouraged by musicans. Besides his own popular groups, Adderley recorded impressively with Miles Davis, John Coltrane, Bill Evans and Gil Evans' Orchestra.

Albert Ayler
(Various saxophones, 1936–70)

Albert Ayler was one of the most controversial free-jazz performers. Eccentric and tirelessly inventive, he shifted ensemble roles in his music so that drummers and bassists were on equal ground with the horns. Ayler influenced John Coltrane and many younger saxophonists, and his recordings gradually moved from free jazz towards rock and soul themes. *Spiritual Unity* (1964) remains one of his most acclaimed albums. Ayler died in mysterious circumstances at the age of 34.

Carla Bley
(Piano, organ, arranger, b. 1938)

Self-taught, Carla Bley is as respected for her compositions and arrangements as for her excellent piano and organ playing. In the 1950s she was briefly married to pianist Paul Bley, who championed her works. In 1965, with her second husband, trumpeter Michael Mantler, Bley co-founded the Jazz Composers Orchestra Association to encourage the creation and distribution of new music in New York. Bley continues to lead a big band and smaller ensembles, often featuring electric bassist Steve Swallow.

Paul Bley
(Piano, synthesizer, b. 1932)

Paul Bley came from Montreal to New York in the early 1950s and worked with Jackie McLean. Later, in Los Angeles, he pioneered free jazz with Ornette Coleman. Throughout his career Bley has performed the compositions of his ex-wives – keyboardist Carla Bley and singer/pianist Annette Peacock – and his own pieces, often ruminative improvisations. Bley helped to popularize the new Moog synthesizer in the early 1970s and has collaborated with Gary Burton, Barre Phillips, Evan Parker, Pat Metheny, Jaco Pastorius, and many others.

Gary Burton
(Vibraphone, b. 1943)

Gary Burton is one of the most impressive vibists in jazz, at times using four mallets in order to harmonize with himself. He began his career in country music with guitarist Hank Garland, played jazz with George Shearing and Stan Getz, and then helped to instigate the jazz-rock fusion movement through his group with guitarist Larry Coryell and drummer Roy Haynes. Burton has made marvellous duet albums with Chick Corea and Paul Bley, and taught at Berklee College of Music from 1971–2002.

Ron Carter
(Bass, piccolo bass, b. 1937)

A consummately professional bassist, Ron Carter possesses a distinctive tone and phenomenal dexterity that place him at the upper level of jazz rhythmists. In the early 1960s Carter joined drummer Chico Hamilton's popular quintet,

then worked with Eric Dolphy, Don Ellis, Thelonious Monk, Cannonball Adderley and Art Farmer. From 1963–68 Carter played in Miles Davis's immortal rhythm section with Herbie Hancock and Tony Williams. He has an equally sturdy background in classical music.

Don Cherry
(Cornet, 1936–95)

Besides serving as the perfect complement for Ornette Coleman in the saxophonist's early quartet, cornettist Don Cherry was a pioneer of the now-popular 'world music' movement. His musician father brought the family to Los Angeles from Cherry's birthplace in Oklahoma, where Cherry played in the Jazz Messiahs before meeting Coleman. After leaving the Coleman group and moving to New York, Cherry co-led the New York Contemporary Five with Archie Shepp and then earned a recording contract with Blue Note, resulting in the classic albums *Complete Communion* (1965) and *Symphony for Improvisers* (1966).

In 1968 he gathered artists from Europe and America, performing music inspired by the Balinese gamelan and Middle Eastern sounds. *Eternal Rhythm*, recorded that year, is a fine early document of his jazz-world music fusions. Cherry continued to investigate sounds inside and outside jazz, working with Turkish musicians, the cross-cultural trio Codona, more mainstream jazz groups, a Coleman repertory quartet called Old and New Dreams, and Coleman himself on occasion. He is the father of pop singers Neneh and Eagle Eye Cherry.

Above

Cornettist Don Cherry, here playing African hunter's harp, helped to introduce music from other cultures into the western world.

Left

Bassist Ron Carter has played in some of jazz's most influential and popular ensembles.

miles davis ⊙**196**   **ornette coleman** ⊙**238**   **john coltrane** ⊙**240**   **joe zawinul** ⊙**281**

Larry Coryell
(Guitar, b. 1943)
Guitarist Larry Coryell got his start in New York with Chico Hamilton. He was a trailblazer of both free jazz and jazz-rock fusion in groups such as the Free Spirits – with saxophonist Jim Pepper and drummer Bob Moses – and in vibist Gary Burton's band. A remarkable technician, Coryell also ventured into free-jazz territory with the Jazz Composers Orchestra Association, dug deeper in to pyrotechnic fusion with the Eleventh House and performed crystalline acoustic jazz in the mid-1970s.

Jack DeJohnette
(Drums, piano, b. 1942)
Few drummers successfully bridge the gap between free jazz and bebop to the same extent as Jack DeJohnette. An intensely intuitive player, young DeJohnette played early on with Jackie McLean and Charles Lloyd. In 1969 he replaced Tony Williams in Miles Davis's electric ensemble, appearing on the essential *Bitches Brew* (1969). After leaving Davis he led the fusion ensemble Compost and the expansive, compositional groups New Directions and Special Edition. He has also recorded many albums in trio with Keith Jarrett and bassist Gary Peacock.

'I hear overtones and chords in the cymbals as well as the drums. I am hearing orchestrally.... I am hearing colors. I consider myself somebody who colors the music.'
Jack DeJohnette

Eric Dolphy
(Alto saxophone, bass clarinet, flute, 1928-64)
In the six years before his untimely death, Eric Dolphy became one of the most beloved and influential musicians in jazz. Brilliant on alto saxophone, he also helped to legitimize the flute and bass clarinet as viable jazz horns. Dolphy worked in relative obscurity until 1958, when he was discovered and hired by popular drummer Chico Hamilton.

He earned positive attention from the jazz press and moved on to work with Charles Mingus in 1960. Dolphy also looked into 'third stream' fusions of jazz and classical music with John Lewis and Gunther Schuller, as well as intense music with Ornette Coleman, John Coltrane and his own groups. Oliver Nelson's 1961 album *Blues And The Abstract Truth* featured the imposing front line of Dolphy and Freddie Hubbard. *Out To Lunch*, recorded in February 1964, is perhaps his most fully realized work. Not long after touring Europe with Mingus, Dolphy died suddenly in Berlin.

Kenny Dorham
(Trumpet, 1924-72)
The star of fame never shone brightly enough upon trumpeter Kenny Dorham, who too often took a back seat to his peers. He played with Dizzy Gillespie, Billy Eckstine and Lionel Hampton before joining Charlie Parker's bebop band in 1948. Dorham was a founding member of Art Blakey's Jazz Messengers in 1954, then replaced Clifford Brown in Max Roach's quartet. He led several fine sessions for Blue Note and Riverside before dying of kidney disease.

Art Farmer
(Trumpet, flügelhorn, 1928-99)
Art Farmer was largely responsible for popularizing the mellow-toned flügelhorn as a solo jazz instrument. A wonderfully lyrical player, he came up in Los Angeles' Central Avenue jazz clubs in the 1940s and worked with Lionel Hampton, Horace Silver, Gerry Mulligan and alto saxophonist Gigi Gryce. In 1959–62 he and tenor saxophonist Benny Golson led the Jazztet, which had a hit with 'Killer Joe'. Farmer was based in Europe from 1968 onwards.

Far Right
Art Farmer (right), pictured with fellow leader of the Jazztet Benny Golson, was jazz music's main exponent of the flugelhorn.

Right
In addition to his skilful saxophone playing, Eric Dolphy raised the profile of the flute and bass clarinet in jazz music.

After leaving the Coleman quartet, Haden began looking into folk music and assembled his politically inspired Liberation Music Orchestra in 1969. Haden has worked in a trio with saxophonist Jan Garbarek and guitarist Egberto Gismonti, and duetted with Pat Metheny; he has also collaborated with pianists Gonzalo Rubalcaba and Hank Jones. In the 1980s he formed his popular Quartet West.

Below
Stan Getz, a distinctive saxophonist and instigator of the early 1960s bossa nova trend.

Stan Getz
(Tenor saxophone, 1927–91)
Stan Getz was one of many white tenor saxophonists influenced by Lester Young, but as he matured he developed a distinctive sound of his own. After working with Jack Teagarden, Stan Kenton, Jimmy Dorsey and Benny Goodman, Getz became one of the 'Four Brothers' in Woody Herman's Second Herd. From the 1950s onwards Getz led his own sessions, heading the massive bossa nova craze of the early 1960s. He initiated many original projects and was widely admired – by John Coltrane among others – for his lyrical virtuosity.

Charlie Haden
(Bass, b. 1937)
Charlie Haden's famed work with Ornette Coleman represents just one small facet of the versatile bassist's career. As a child in Iowa he performed on radio with his family's country and western band. At 15 he took up the bass while recovering from polio, acquiring a novel technique that makes his notes resonate deeply. Haden moved to Los Angeles in 1957 to find jazz work. He met pianist Paul Bley and altoist Ornette Coleman, who were trying out new ideas that formed the roots of free jazz.

In 1961 Kirk worked with Charles Mingus, then continued his solo career with exceptional recordings, such as *Rip, Rig And Panic* (1965). He regularly modified his instruments and took on the mysterious name 'Rahsaan' after a dream. Although partially paralyzed by a stroke at 40, Kirk kept playing his horns until his death in 1977.

Charles Lloyd
(Various saxophones, b. 1938)

Charles Lloyd was an inspirational figure in 1960s jazz and was also enthusiastically embraced by the hippy culture. He moved from playing blues in Memphis to West Coast jazz with Gerald Wilson and Chico Hamilton. His quartet with pianist Keith Jarrett, bassist Ron McClure and drummer Jack DeJohnette was the first American jazz group to tour the Soviet Union. In 1969 he retired to teach transcendental meditation, before returning triumphantly at the 1982 Montreux Jazz Festival. Lloyd has since made a series of excellent albums for ECM.

Herbie Mann
(Tenor saxophone, flute, 1930–2003)

Flautist Herbie Mann was a popularizer of the flute in jazz, an investigator of far-flung ethnic music traditions and a pioneer of jazz-rock fusion. Mann began as a tenor

Above

After working extensively with John Coltrane's quartet, Elvin Jones led his own Jazz Machine band.

Elvin Jones
(Drums, 1927–2004)

Powerhouse drummer Elvin Jones was the engine of John Coltrane's legendary quartet in the 1960s, appearing on most of the saxophonist's most popular recordings. He was the younger brother of pianist Hank and trumpeter Thad Jones and had worked with Bud Powell, Miles Davis, Sonny Rollins and J.J. Johnson prior to joining Coltrane. A masterful innovator of polyrhythms, after a brief stint with the Duke Ellington Orchestra, he formed Elvin Jones Jazz Machine and helmed it until his death. In his last years he also collaborated annually with pianist Cecil Taylor.

Rahsaan Roland Kirk
(Saxophones, clarinet, flute, various invented instruments, 1936–77)

Reeds player Rahsaan Roland Kirk was one of jazz's most colourful figures, an eccentric who developed a method for playing two or three horns simultaneously. Accidentally blinded at the age of two, Kirk taught himself to play several instruments. At 15 he joined an R&B band, and at 20 he made his first record. He modified his unusual pawn-shop horns, the manzello and stritch, with extended keys, developed the skill of circular breathing, enabling him to hold notes indefinitely, and eventually built the discipline to play two separate melodies at once.

Right

Jazz-rock pioneer Herbie Mann was one of the first mainstream jazz players to make the flute his main instrument.

saxophonist but eventually became the most commercially successful of the few jazz players to concentrate exclusively on the flute. He fronted an Afro-Latin group in the late 1950s, then had a major crossover hit with 'Comin' Home Baby' and popular success with *Memphis Underground* (1968). Mann focused upon Brazilian-tinged jazz later in his career, and at the end of his life explored the music of his Central European Jewish ancestry.

Wes Montgomery
(Guitar, 1925–68)

Wes Montgomery was a premier jazz guitarist; his unique guitar sound came from plucking octave figures with his thumb instead of a pick. Born into a musical family, Wes taught himself to play the guitar and toured with Lionel Hampton in the late 1940s. He performed with his brothers, bassist Monk and vibist Buddy, before beginning a solo career that brought him to the top of the jazz sales charts. He moved successfully into pop-jazz crossovers, under the direction of producer Creed Taylor, before his sudden death from a heart attack.

Lee Morgan
(Trumpet, 1938–72)

Born in Philadelphia, trumpeter Lee Morgan led one of the storybook lives in jazz. He joined Art Blakey's Jazz Messengers in 1958, having already worked with Dizzy Gillespie and John Coltrane. A magnificent hard-bop stylist who effectively utilized half-valve techniques and *staccato* blowing, Morgan was a star of the Blue Note Records roster, hitting the R&B top 10 in 1964 with the instrumental 'The Sidewinder'. Tragically, he was murdered by a woman who considered herself his wife outside a jazz club in 1972.

Sunny Murray
(Drums, b. 1937)

James 'Sunny' Murray is one of the quintessential free-jazz drummers. His most enduring legacy may be his many recordings with Cecil Taylor and Albert Ayler, which belie

his beginnings with stride pianist Willie 'The Lion' Smith and Swing Era trumpeter Henry 'Red' Allen. Murray was as melodic on drums as Taylor was percussive on the piano, resulting in a stellar combination. He moved to France in the 1980s and has since led his own sessions.

Joe Pass
(Guitar, 1929–94)

Although drug addiction nearly killed the promising career of Joe Pass, he became one of the most influential and beloved guitarists in jazz. As a young man Pass played with various swing bands, then fell into heroin abuse while in the military. He recorded his first album while in rehabilitation in 1962, showcasing his impressive technique of splitting melodic and accompanying figures. From the mid-1970s until his death from cancer, Pass was a true jazz star, particularly as a solo performer and in recordings with Ella Fitzgerald.

Above

Self-taught guitarist Wes Montgomery created his own unique sound by using his thumb in place of a pick.

Above

Sam Rivers hosted free jazz sessions throughout the 1970s in his Studio RivBea, which served as a launch-pad for the careers of many up-and-coming musicians.

Archie Shepp
(Tenor and soprano saxophones, b. 1937)

Acid-toned saxophonist Archie Shepp was a principal figure in the second wave of free-jazz artists. Also recognized as a playwright and poet, Shepp was an articulate spokesman for Black Power. He emerged in 1960 as a member of Cecil Taylor's group, then collaborated with trumpeter Bill Dixon, Don Cherry and John Coltrane, most notably on Coltrane's powerful *Ascension*. In the late 1970s Shepp moved decisively away from free jazz into more mainstream projects, such as a programme of ballads and gospel songs in duet with pianist Horace Parlan.

Wayne Shorter
(Tenor and soprano saxophones, b. 1933)

Wayne Shorter's most significant early position was in Maynard Ferguson's orchestra in 1958, where he met pianist Joe Zawinul. In 1959 Shorter joined Art Blakey's Jazz Messengers and soon thereafter made his debut as a leader. He gained prominence as a member of Miles Davis's ambitious groups from 1964–70, in which his unusual, compelling compositions were often featured, and as a Blue Note Records leader and sideman. Shorter teamed with Zawinul and bassist Miroslav Vitous in 1970 to form Weather Report, which became one of the world's most popular fusion bands.

Shorter's album *Native Dancer* (1974) introduced Brazilian singer Milton Nascimento to North America, and he was also in the repertory group VSOP with Herbie Hancock and Freddie Hubbard. Shorter left Weather Report in 1985, then toured with rock guitarist Carlos Santana and recorded with Joni Mitchell and Steely Dan. His own projects were intermittent until 1992, when a dying Miles Davis urged him to step forth. Shorter has led his own ensembles since then, acknowledged as a major, if still elusive, jazz voice.

Sam Rivers
(Various saxophones, flute, b. 1923)

Sam Rivers boasts a most impressive resumé: bebop with Tadd Dameron and Dizzy Gillespie, hard bop with Miles Davis, free jazz with Cecil Taylor and Anthony Braxton, and Grammy consideration for his big band. Born in Oklahoma, Rivers played around Florida and Boston in the 1950s before settling in New York City. His 1960s Blue Note records were edgy and impressive. He hosted free jazz sessions at his loft Studio RivBea through the 1970s and helped to launch the careers of bassist Dave Holland and saxophonist Steve Coleman, among others.

Cecil Taylor
(Piano, b. 1929)

Since the late 1950s, pianist Cecil Taylor has maintained a prime position in the pantheon of free jazz. He was one of the first jazzmen to jettison standard chord changes, fixed rhythms and expected ensemble roles in the interest of musical democracy. Taylor developed his unorthodox style while studying at New England Conservatory. Duke Ellington, Thelonious Monk and Lennie Tristano were

the job of house pianist in Ronnie Scott's Soho jazz club. There he accompanied the big names of the day, including Zoot Sims, Stan Getz, Roland Kirk and Sonny Rollins, with whom he recorded the soundtrack for the film *Alfie* (1966). He played solo and in various line-ups ranging from duos to big bands, and had a big hit with his 1965 album *Under Milk Wood*, inspired by Dylan Thomas's audio play and featuring the breathy saxophone playing of Bobby Wellins.

Tracey has released over 45 albums and has received an OBE as well as various music awards. He has continued to compose, tour and record and has also taught for many years at London's Guildhall School of Music. Despite his long career and life in the jazz fast-lane, Tracey has remained refreshingly self-effacing and down-to-earth.

Left
Archie Shepp developed a distinctive tenor saxophone sound that drew inspiration from the jazz of his contemporaries as well as the jazz giants of the 1930s.

'Is Cecil Taylor old? ... when he jumps on that piano, what are you hearing? Are you hearing age or are you hearing a vision that is sharper and sharper and more refined?'
Evan Parker

among his major influences. Taylor debuted in 1956 with *Jazz Advance!*.

He treats the piano as a percussion instrument, hammering out dissonant chords and long, sinuous melody lines, and has been both condemned and praised for his innovations. Besides leading magnificent ensembles – the best of which featured alto saxophonist Jimmy Lyons – and collaborating with artists ranging from Mary Lou Williams and Max Roach to the dancer Mikhail Baryshnikov, Taylor is also a commanding solo performer. He is tirelessly adept at forming beauty out of seeming chaos, and his performances can last for hours.

Stan Tracey
(Piano, accordion, vibraphone, composer, arranger, b. 1926)

Stan Tracey is one of the UK's most original and talented jazz musicians, yet he has always remained underrated by critics; Sonny Rollins is quoted as asking 'Does anyone here realize how good he really is?'. Londoner Tracey was playing professionally from the age of 16, before landing

McCoy Tyner
(Piano, b. 1938)

McCoy Tyner will forever be remembered for his role in John Coltrane's great 1960s quartet. Born in Philadelphia and a member of jazz groups including the Jazztet, Tyner proved to be perfectly compatible with Coltrane until the saxophonist moved into free jazz, at which point the pianist left the band. Tyner worked as a sideman and leader for Blue Note during the rest of the decade, and gained further recognition after signing with Milestone Records. He has continued to lead his own sessions, ranging from solos, trios and larger combos to big bands.

Tony Williams
(Drums, 1945–97)

Aged 14, Boston-born drum prodigy Tony Williams worked professionally with tenor saxophonist Sam Rivers. In 1962 he went to New York, played with Jackie McLean, then became part of one of Miles Davis's greatest bands. A dazzling colourist and dynamic rhythm-maker, Williams recorded two albums for Blue Note and played with many of the label's stars before establishing the breakthrough fusion band Lifetime. After a hiatus, Williams re-emerged in the late 1980s, leading a post-bop quintet of promising young players. He died of a heart attack in 1997 aged 51.

Big Bear Music
Presents

AMERICAN BLUES
LEGENDS 73
HOMESICK JAMES
SNOOKY PRYOR
WASHBOARD WILLIE
BOOGIE WOOGIE RED
LIGHTNIN' SLIM
WHISPERING SMITH

AMERICAN
BLUES LEGENDS
73

TUESDAY 20TH FEBRUARY
100 CLUB
OXFORD ST
LONDON

the seventies

Of the entire century, the 1970s were the years of catching one's breath. Superficially, the promise of the 1960s had faded or failed, the victim of wretched excess and just plain bad taste. America's war in Vietnam sputtered to an end, international relations elsewhere seemed to stalemate in detente and economically the world suffered from stagflation: exhaustion beset with mixed signals.

Blues and jazz also reached some sort of crossroads. Several blues elders were still active, but their best days were behind them and their appearances often amounted to little more than valedictory trots. North American and European blues festivals sought these veterans as if they were holy men, by their presences condoning the appropriation of their lifelong works. A younger wave of true bluesmen had emerged from Chicago's South Side, but they did not gain much notoriety or respect. At the same time US jazz artists, disaffected by the turmoil of politics at home and the public's neglect of their accomplishments in favour of lesser but flashier sounds, sought other avenues in Europe and Japan, where government and corporate funding for jazz ran relatively high. Looking back, great music of the period is identifiable, but at the time such pop genres as progressive rock and disco seemed relatively content-free. The best jazz and blues existed beneath the radar, if not exactly underground. Part of the problem was media-related: FM radio programmed with imagination, but many recording companies had over-extended their investments without adequate gain. The mood was largely: May the seventies end! What's next?

Key Artists: Blues

Allman Brothers Band

Dr John

Key Artists: Jazz

Art Ensemble Of Chicago

John McLaughlin

Blues

*'The stuff they're doin' now –
the disco and everything else –
it's taken from the blues.
The music they call "soul music",
you know, it's the blues. So disco
is not soul; rock'n'roll is not soul.
The blues is soul.'*

John Lee Hooker

In the 1970s, it could be said that the blues took a back seat to its own influence. The root sensibilities and typical three-chord structures of the blues could be detected in the music of hundreds of artists, yet musicians who could genuinely claim the blues as their own territory were all but obscured from the public eye.

Crossing Over

The cross-pollination of blues and rock elements continued as the sounds of the British scene crossed the Atlantic Ocean to re-inspire Americans. The Rolling Stones, the Yardbirds, Cream, John Mayall's Bluesbreakers and a number of other British groups motivated younger artists like Johnny Winter (b. 1944), the Allman Brothers Band and ZZ Top to develop their own distinctive hybrids.

singer named Bonnie Raitt (b. 1949) was turning heads with her slide abilities. Captain Beefheart – a truly idiosyncratic, inspired associate of canny and satirical composer, bandleader and rock-blues guitar virtuoso Frank Zappa – distilled the essence of Howlin' Wolf's (1910–76) gravelly blues into a cocktail of abstract lyrics and avant-garde guitars. Up in San Francisco, bassist Jack Casady and guitarist Jorma Kaukonen broke away from Jefferson Airplane to form Hot Tuna, a group of revolving personnel with a keen interest in acoustic blues traditions.

Hard Times

Despite this resurgence of interest in the *idea* of the blues, many influential players found themselves pushed out of the marketplace altogether and the musicians who inspired the British Invasion now found themselves unable to make a living. At the start of the decade, the Rolling Stones had toured with Buddy Guy (b. 1936), Junior Wells (1934–98) and Bonnie Raitt, temporarily expanding the blues audience. But by 1979, many of their fans were unaware of the primal southern roots of the Stones' beloved music. A number of desperate, neglected blues artists retreated into drug and alcohol abuse, further complicating their declines in popularity.

A few stalwarts kept their careers afloat. B.B. King (b. 1925) seemed to be an unstoppable force in the 1970s: he kicked off the decade with the tremendous hit 'The Thrill Is Gone', collaborated several times with Bobby 'Blue' Bland (b. 1930), and released no fewer than 10 new records before the decade's end. Beloved worldwide and constantly busy, King was a beacon of hope that the bluesmen's stars would someday rise again. He has remained a pre-eminent blues musican into the twenty-first century, guesting with rock stars and appearing in commercials.

American bands blended country and rock'n'roll with their personal takes on the blues, achieving tremendous success. Although Duane Allman and ZZ Top's Billy Gibbons had little in common when it came to guitar techniques, both ranked among the most popular, influential players of the time. By mid-decade, their blues-enriched sounds were hotly competing with disco on the American music market.

Across America, young electric and acoustic blues artists swarmed from the woodwork. So many styles were formulated in so many regions that it was difficult to differentiate between them all. In Austin, Texas, while guitarist Jimmie Vaughan and the Fabulous Thunderbirds were starting down the road to stardom in 1974, little brother Stevie Ray Vaughan (1954–90) was putting together his first band. Around the same time, Roy Buchanan (1939–88) was rocking the house in Washington, DC, Johnny Copeland (1937–97) was club-hopping in New York City and down in New Orleans Dr John (b. 1940) blended traditional jazz, Creole music, blues and voodoo weirdness into a heady, tantalizing stew.

The West Coast of the US boasted an innovative recording-studio blues community. In Los Angeles Ry Cooder (b. 1947) and Taj Mahal (b. 1940), who had played together in the Rising Sons, represented the global side of things as they tied together diverse threads of the blues, jazz, country, gospel and African and Hawaiian music. Elsewhere in town, a young, red-headed guitarist and

Left

The early 1970s was a prosperous time for some black blues artists, who were booked on package tours such as the American Blues Legends, presented by Big Bear music.

Far Left

Slide guitarist Ry Cooder was a key figure on the 1970s Los Angeles blues scene; his music reflected influences from other cultures, including Africa and Hawaii.

Popular Melody

B.B. King – 'The Thrill Is Gone' (1970)
This track soared up the popular music charts in 1970. King's strong, Mississippi-accented voice and distinctively melodic single-string guitar lines, combined with a slightly more contemporary rhythmic base, made an instantly appealing variance on the blues tradition.

Above

Chicago's 1815 club, run by Eddie Shaw (centre, with Frank Weston and Mike Rowe), was an important blues venue in the 1970s.

www

Memphis Minnie
When The
Levee Breaks

musicfirebox.com
/Levee

The Rock Influence

Muddy Waters (1915–83) was moderately active at the time, although it was not until Johnny Winter produced Waters' *Hard Again* in 1977 on Columbia Records that he reclaimed a sizeable portion of his prior high profile. Arthur 'Big Boy' Crudup (1905–74) – an R&B legend who had influenced Elvis Presley – and Albert King (1923–92) experienced rejuvenation in the early 1970s through music festivals and new recording opportunities. And, thanks to a contract with Leon Russell's Shelter label, Freddie King (1934–76) also kept relatively busy until his death in 1976. Howlin' Wolf had not performed much outside of a regular gig at Chicago's 1815 Club due to chronic health problems. His last performance was with

B.B. King at the Chicago Amphitheatre in November 1975, two months before his death.

Around the middle of the decade, some British artists veered sharply away from the blues and headed deeper into mainstream rock. The phenomenon was not universal, as illustrated by the success of Eric Clapton, John Mayall and Rory Gallagher (1949–95), all three of whom stayed relatively faithful to the blues that had been their guiding light. But other influential British blues artists either faded away or irreversibly changed course.

Led Zeppelin was born from the ashes of the Yardbirds when guitarist Jimmy Page put together a 'ghost band' to honour the group's contracts. Its young fans loved the power of Page's sizzling guitar, Robert Plant's banshee voice, John Paul Jones's virtuoso bass licks and John Bonham's thunderous drums, but knew little about the blues covers in Led Zeppelin's set lists. As the band assumed the throne of heavy-metal monarchy, fewer of its songs drew from the blues. A few platinum albums later, the covers of Otis Rush (b. 1934) and the hints of Muddy Waters and Elmore James (1918–63) that seasoned Zeppelin's early work had begun to waft away, although the occasional number, such as 'In My Time Of Dying' on 1975's *Physical Graffiti*, suggested that Led Zeppelin never completely abandoned its blues roots.

Rising Again

A number of promising enterprises arose to keep the blues flame flickering. *Living Blues*, one of the most purist magazines devoted to the music, published its first issue in 1970. It became the principal voice for blues artists and aficionados, touting new releases and reissues with equal zeal. In 1971, when producer Bruce Iglauer failed to get Chicago's Delmark Records to sign Hound Dog Taylor (1917–75) to a contract, he inaugurated his Alligator label specifically to document Taylor's music. Alligator was soon one of the most active blues imprints, issuing impressive albums by artists including Albert Collins (1932–93), Clifton Chenier (1925–87) and Son Seals (1942–2004), and later by Charlie Musselwhite (b. 1944), Johnny Winter and Delbert McClinton (b. 1940).

One of the greatest blessings to grace the blues came from an unlikely source. In 1977, comedians Dan Aykroyd and John Belushi unveiled their Blues Brothers characters on TV's *Saturday Night Live*. The skit was intended to spoof white blues enthusiasts who wore sunglasses and formed their own bands to play classics by Willie Dixon (1915–92), Jimmy Reed (1925–76) and Muddy Waters. Many in the show's audience missed the joke and fell in love with the Blues Brothers, giving birth to an explosive franchise. In 1980 their first feature film employed authentic blues and R&B artists such as Matt Murphy (b. 1927) and Steve Cropper as the Brothers' backing band and showcased performances by Aretha Franklin, Ray Charles (1930–2004), James Brown and Cab Calloway (1907–94), capturing the breadth of inspiration, influence and inherent entertainment imperatives of the blues. This ignited a widespread revival of interest in urban blues. Prior to Belushi's drug-related death they opened integrated blues clubs, from which came the franchise venue House of Blues. The blues had survived its toughest decade, and its future was looking brighter.

Below
Led Zeppelin's 1975 album Physical Graffiti *included some tracks that relied heavily on traditional blues songs.*

Left
The 1980 film The Blues Brothers *sparked a wide revival of interest in blues music.*

Popular Melody

Led Zeppelin – 'In My Time Of Dying' (1975)
The majority of this song's lyrics stem from the earlier Blind Willie Johnson track 'Jesus Make Up My Dying Bed'. The brilliant slide guitar and the frequent blues-rock interludes, charged with energy from John Bonham's drum kit, give a new feel to this traditional song while retaining the original's ominous undertones.

Allman Brothers Band

Muscle Shoals To Macon

Guitarist Duane Allman (1946–71) and his brother, organist/vocalist Gregg Allman (b. 1947), grew up in Daytona Beach, Florida. Their first band, the Escorts, aped the Rolling Stones and the Beatles. They moved further into hard blues and soul with the Allman Joys and the Hour Glass, the latter of which recorded two albums for Liberty Records.

In the late 1960s Duane landed a job as a studio guitarist in Muscle Shoals, Alabama, the famed breeding ground of latter-day soul. He made his name backing King Curtis, Wilson Pickett and Aretha Franklin while framing his own approach to R&B, soul and blues. In 1969 manager Phil Walden urged Allman to put together a band of his own. He hired bassist Berry Oakley, lured guitarist Dickey Betts away from the band Second Coming and selected two drummers: Butch Trucks and Jai Johanny Johanson, a.k.a. Jaimoe. A long jam session proved the concept's viability, and eventually Gregg Allman was brought in on vocals and organ.

Few groups made as powerful an impression on American blues music in the early 1970s as the Allman Brothers Band. Its blend of blues, jazz, rock and country elements was a predominant sound on nascent FM radio and influenced countless bands that followed in their wake. The Allman Brothers Band have endured tragedies, periods of obscurity and personnel shifts to remain active in the new century.

The Allman Brothers Band initially toured Georgia and Florida to build upon its blues-rock template. It first recorded in 1969 for Walden's label, Capricorn. The album did not sell well at first but impressed many of those who did hear it. Word of mouth and solid ticket sales earned the group a good reputation around the South. The Allmans settled in Macon, Georgia, where they worked more acoustic guitar and jazz flavourings into their sound. Duane Allman kept active as a sideman, working with Boz Scaggs, Otis Rush and Johnny Jenkins. He also teamed with Eric Clapton in Bonnie & Delaney, and later Derek & the Dominos.

Key Track

'Whippin' Post' (1969)

The unusual riff that cycles through 'Whippin' Post', from the band's first album, is in 11/8 time. Its urgency and the desperate, blues-drenched passion of Gregg Allman's vocals make for spine-tingling music. Duane Allman's dynamic, absorbing playing shows why he became an idol for electric-guitar players.

'Writing a good instrumental is very fulfilling because you've transcended language and spoken to someone with a melody.'

Dickey Betts,
Allman Brothers Band

Triumph And Tragedy

The group's fame spread on the strength of its second album, the hit tune 'Midnight Rider' and the powerful jam sessions that coloured their live concerts. While the musicians were capable of playing in odd keys and time signatures, their music was still accessible and rock-based enough to maintain its popular momentum.

In March 1971 the band played a series of shows at the Fillmore East, which were documented on its third album. Polydor Records churned up momentum for the record, which turned Duane Allman into America's newest guitar hero. But shortly after *At Fillmore East* was certified gold in October, Duane was killed in a motorcycle accident. Almost exactly one year later, following the success of the follow-up recording, *Eat A Peach*, Berry Oakley also died in a motorcycle crash. Rather than dissolve the group, Gregg Allman and Dickey Betts opted to press on. The first two albums were reissued as a double-LP set, and the next record moved away from the blues underpinnings for a more country-tinged flavour. 'Ramblin' Man' became another huge hit for the band.

The Road Goes On Forever

Around 1974 the group started to fall apart. Gregg Allman's tumultuous marriage to rock singer Cher, his solo career and problems with substance abuse made it hard for the band to stay consistent. Two years later the Allman Brothers Band broke up, with Betts going solo and the other members forming Sea Level. In 1978, cleaned up and ready to roll, Allman reformed the band but faced the spectre of irrelevance as New Wave and punk had staked their claims to rock radio. The band struggled through the 1980s, issuing moderate-selling albums that skirted its prior glory.

In 1989 the band reinvented itself again by bringing in two phenomenal musicians, guitarist Warren Haynes and bassist Allen Woody, whose skills were well beyond anything the Allmans had presented in years. The next album, *Seven Turns* (1990), proved that the band's rock-blues-country fusion was still viable 30 years on. The Allman Brothers Band soon returned to prominence, selling out arenas and concert halls as it has continued to do into the twenty-first century.

Classic Recordings

The Allman Brothers Band (1969)
'Whippin' Post',
'Trouble No More', 'Dreams'

Idlewild South (1970)
'Midnight Rider',
'In Memory Of
Elizabeth Reed', 'Hoochie
Coochie Man'

At Fillmore East (1971)
'Statesboro Blues', 'You
Don't Love Me'

Eat A Peach (1972)
'One Way Out', 'Melissa',
'Mountain Jam'

Brothers And Sisters (1973)
'Ramblin' Man', 'Jessica'

Seven Turns (1990)
'Good Clean Fun',
'Shine It On'

Left

Gifted guitarist Duane Allman, who worked as a session musician and touring sideman in addition to his exquisite slide playing with the Allman Brothers Band.

Dr John

Above

Eccentric New Orleans bluesman Dr John (far left) with his band at London's Roundhouse.

Key Track

'Right Place, Wrong Time' (1973)
Representative of his 'voodoo music', Dr John growls humorous lyrics and pounds out funky keyboard licks while the Meters support him with solid electric bass, female vocal accents and disco-funk guitar. A blues feeling underscores everything, with flattened notes and a brooding spirit sidestepping the absence of a standard blues chord progression.

'When I first came up, the blues I was playing was almost bebop orientated – very hip.... Now it's going back beyond that to some kind of roots....'
Dr John

injury caused him to abandon the guitar in the mid-1960s, and soon he migrated to Los Angeles for studio work.

Voodoo Blues

The Dr John persona emerged in the late 1960s, as Rebennack began to formulate his 'voodoo music', a unique fusion of blues, jazz, R&B and rock elements. His rough, drawling voice, combined with horn licks, deep blues, Mardi Gras funk and electric psychedelia, gave Dr John an instantly recognizable sound. In live performances he draped himself and the stage with coloured beads, feathers, furs and exotic props, conducting a religious/musical ritual of sorts.

His stage theatrics were an amazing blend of authentic voodoo tradition and modern New Orleans hokum, perfectly complementing his otherworldly music; this was exemplified by 'I Walk On Gilded Splinters' and the title track of his debut album *Gris Gris* (1968), which Dr John had recorded during studio time left over from a Sonny and Cher session on which he had worked. This album and its follow-up, *Babylon* (1969), were especially heavy on voodoo symbolism and social commentary, often with the sounds layered so densely that the lyrics were hard to discern. In tuneful, often swinging, sometimes sultry pieces, he drew from the standard New Orleans repertoire of jazz, Cajun, Creole and R&B tunes. He quickly integrated the electric piano and keyboards into his signature sound and challenged his generation of guitarists with the mock-heroic 'Lonesome

Malcolm John 'Mac' Rebennack Jr., a.k.a. 'Dr John the Night Tripper', was born in New Orleans in November 1940. The singer and pianist began his professional career while he was still a teenager. He backed local favourites including Joe Tex and Professor Longhair on guitar and keyboards, produced and arranged sessions at Cosmio Studio, also frequented by Allen Toussaint, and issued a few singles of his own as Mac Rebennack. A hand

John Hammond did not draw much attention. He rose to prominence again in 1981 with an acclaimed solo acoustic album that showed off his authentic, rollicking New Orleans piano style. His debt to pianists such as Professor Longhair and Huey 'Piano' Smith became clearer once the voodoo trappings were removed.

Other Zones

More experiments followed for Dr John: a recording of jazz and pop standards, then another jump into New Orleans history, interpretations of Duke Ellington and several career retrospectives. His more innovative pursuits were followed by rote-sounding returns to his comfort zone, giving Dr John a rather patchy discography during this period.

In 1990 Dr John dug deeper into jazz in the trio Bluesiana Triangle, with saxophonist David 'Fathead' Newman and bebop drummer Art Blakey. At his most ambitious, Dr John collaborated with members of alternative rock bands like Portishead, Squeeze, Primal Scream and Supergrass, upon whom his murky early recordings had been a surprising influence. In 2000 he signed with Blue Note Records and founded his own reissue label, Skinji Brim. His 2001 album, *Creole Moon*, was well-received and saw him continuing to experiment with a melange of musical styles, including jazz, blues and funk.

Classic Recordings

***Gris Gris* (1968)**
'Mama Roux', 'I Walk On Gilded Splinters'

***Dr John's Gumbo* (1972)**
'Iko Iko', 'Junko Partner', 'Tipitina'

***In The Right Place* (1973)**
'Right Place, Wrong Time', 'Such A Night', 'Life', 'Traveling Mood'

***Dr John Plays Mac Rebennack* (1981)**
'Mac's Boogie Woogie', 'Memories Of Professor Longhair', 'Honeydripper'

***Anutha Zone* (1998)**
'I Don't Wanna Know', 'Sweet Home New Orleans'

Left
A youthful Dr John back when he was still known as Mac Rebennack.

Below
(l–r) Dr John, Art Blakey and David 'Fathead' Newman in jazz combo Bluesiana Triangle.

Guitar Strangler'. His approach to music was so unusual and fresh that he built a small but loyal cult following. In the meantime, he also worked in support of artists such as Canned Heat, Jackie DeShannon, B.B. King, Buddy Guy, Albert Collins and John Sebastian.

In The Right Place

In 1972, on *Dr John's Gumbo*, he garnered more attention by interpreting New Orleans standards, including 'Iko Iko' and 'Junko Partner', which had wider public appeal than his prior psychedelic fusions. The following year he broke out on to the mass market with an unlikely hit; on 'Right Place, Wrong Time', Dr John was backed by the Meters, New Orleans' premier funk and soul band. The public ate up the infectious rhythms and his rasping voice, placing the tune high on the charts. It was the most substantial hit of his career and did well enough to seal his legacy.

He attempted to duplicate the winning formula without success on his next few recordings, and even tried a venture into disco. He made an appearance on the Band's *Last Waltz* show in 1977, playing 'Such A Night', but a collaboration with guitarists Mike Bloomfield and

A-Z of artists

Luther Allison

(Guitar, vocals, 1939–97)

Luther Allison was an impressive electric bluesman whose guitar playing at times recalled Jimi Hendrix. After his brother taught him basic guitar techniques, Allison backed artists such as Muddy Waters, Jimmy Dawkins and Howlin' Wolf in Chicago clubs. Early records on Delmark and triumph at the Ann Arbor Festival led to Allison signing with Motown. He lived in France from 1984–94 and died of cancer in the midst of a strong comeback. His son Bernard carries on the family tradition.

Below

J.J. Cale was influential on the 1970s blues scene but has always shied away from the limelight.

Carey Bell

(Harmonica, vocals, b. 1936)

Carey Bell is one of Chicago's most distinctive harmonica players. He began playing with pianist Lovie Lee in Mississippi at the age of 13 and moved to Chicago at 20. Sonny Boy Williamson II and Little Walter were key influences on his harmonica style, while tenures with Willie Dixon and Muddy Waters increased his profile in the business. Bell has led over a dozen sessions since his debut in 1969, some featuring his son, guitarist Lurrie Bell.

Roy Buchanan

(Guitar, vocals, 1939–88)

Roy Buchanan's use of harmonics and his melodic sense were incomparable. Raised on gospel and R&B, he performed with Johnny Otis, Johnny 'Guitar' Watson and Ronnie Hawkins' Hawks as a young man. A 1971 PBS documentary, *The Best Unknown Guitarist In The World*, together with adulation from the likes of John Lennon and Eric Clapton, kick-started Buchanan's rise. He retired in frustration for several years but returned in 1985. Sadly, Buchanan committed suicide while jailed for public drunkenness.

J.J. Cale

(Guitar, vocals, b. 1938)

Cale gigged around his native Tulsa, Oklahoma before moving to LA in 1964. He issued his first record in 1971, after Eric Clapton's hit with Cale's 'After Midnight'. Cale is still known to many only through covers of his songs and has always preferred to stay in the background of the blues scene; this is reflected in his music as he places his vocals way down in the mix, thereby drawing the listener's attention into the record.

'J.J. Cale was so great at making records, I think he really is one of the giants and such a major influence, not just as a writer/ performer, but as a producer.'
Michael Messer

Ry Cooder
(Guitar, mandolin, vocals, b. 1947)

Cooder is one of America's most versatile musicians, equally at home with blues, rock, jazz and various ethnic musics. In the mid-1960s he played guitar with Taj Mahal (in the Rising Sons) and Jackie DeShannon, then did studio work with Paul Revere & the Raiders. Especially gifted as a slide guitarist, he has filled that role on sessions with the Rolling Stones, Captain Beefheart, Little Feat, Randy Newman and other artists.

Cooder has also performed on and/or composed a large number of film scores, including *Performance* (1970), *Paris, Texas* (1984), *Streets Of Fire* (1984), *Cocktail* (1988) and *Steel Magnolias* (1989). On his first album, made in 1970, Cooder interpreted classic blues and folk songs as re-envisioned by arranger Van Dyke Parks. Since that time he has delved into jazz, Hawaiian music, Tex-Mex, Indian sitar music and other styles. Cooder gained particular acclaim for the 1997 album *Buena Vista Social Club*, made with various legendary Cuban musicians, and the subsequent documentary film of the same title.

Jimmy Dawkins
(Guitar, vocals, b. 1936)

Guitarist Jimmy Dawkins came from Mississippi to the West Side of Chicago in 1955, formed a friendship with Luther Allison and slowly built a good reputation with his slow-burning expressiveness. He made his first recording, the award-winning *Fast Fingers*, in 1969 for Delmark Records and followed up with the equally serious *All For Business* (1973). In 1970 Dawkins toured and recorded in Europe with Clarence 'Gatemouth' Brown and Otis Rush. He has been a sideman with many key artists.

Robben Ford
(Guitar, vocals, b. 1951)

Robben Ford was born into a musical family on the coast of northern California. His father,

Charles, was a guitarist who encouraged Robben to teach himself the instrument at the age of 13. Ford has two musical brothers, drummer Pat and harmonica player Mark. Influenced by Mike Bloomfield, Robben and Pat played in the Charles Ford Band in the late 1960s and were hired by Charlie Musselwhite in 1974.

Robben Ford split his allegiances between playing blues with Jimmy Witherspoon, contemporary jazz with Tom Scott and Miles Davis, rock with Joni Mitchell and George Harrison, and leading his own bands. In 1977 his electric backing band, Yellowjackets, became a jazz group in its own right. Ford has continued to skirt the line between jazz and blues. In 1990 he rejoined his brother Pat in the Ford Blues Band, and he formed his acclaimed Blue Line in 1992.

Above
Blues, jazz and rock guitarist Robben Ford, pictured at the 2003 Yellowjackets reunion.

Left
Guitarist Jimmy Dawkins on a 1972 European tour.

Free
(Vocal/instrumental group, 1968–73)

Fronted by charismatic Paul Rodgers, Free was a catalyst in the popular shift from blues-dominated rock to heavy-metal forms. Rodgers left Brown Sugar to form Free with guitarist Paul Kossoff, whose playing on the hit 'All Right Now' sealed its popularity in 1970. Not long thereafter, tensions and drug abuse began to weaken the band. By 1973, Rodgers and drummer Simon Kirke had moved on to Bad Company; Kossoff died of heart failure in 1976.

Rory Gallagher
(Guitar, vocals, harmonica, 1949–95)

Irish blues musician Rory Gallagher fell in love with Delta and Chicago blues as a child, collecting as many records as he could get his hands on. In 1969 he formed the band Taste, receiving moderate acclaim, and a year later he released his own eponymous album to very good reviews. Gallagher became an extremely popular touring artist in the US and Europe and issued 14 albums in his lifetime, all with a strong flavouring of his personal blues sensibility.

Director Tony Palmer's documentary *Irish Tour* captures Gallagher performing live in 1974, while the live albums from the 1970s also successfully represent his energy and subtlety. He performed and recorded with Muddy Waters and Albert King at the height of his career, holding his own with the masters. Aside from a four-year hiatus in the 1980s, Gallagher stayed active as a touring musician until his death at the age of 46, following a failed liver transplant.

Hot Tuna
(Vocal/instrumental group, 1970–present)

Jefferson Airplane's Jorma Kaukonen (guitar, vocals) and Jack Casady (bass) – together with drummer Bob Steeler – formed Hot Tuna in San Francisco in order to satisfy their interest in acoustic blues. After an eponymous debut album, the group went electric, added fiddler Papa John Creach and expanded its range to become a staple of the jam-band scene spearheaded by the Grateful Dead. Many line-ups later, Kaukonen and Casady soldier on at

'I've done songs in all the different styles ... train blues, drinking blues, economic blues.... The music can be very traditional, but you can sort of creep into the future with the lyrics.'

Rory Gallagher

Hot Tuna's fore, blending acoustic blues songs from the 1920s and 1930s with the occasional electric performance.

J.B. Hutto
(Guitar, vocals, 1926–83)

The highly theatrical Joseph Benjamin 'J.B.' Hutto sang in the Golden Crowns Gospel Singers as a child and made his first records with his backup band, the Hawks, in 1954. Hutto then left the music business but returned, rejuvenated, 10 years later. He toured with various incarnations of the Hawks until Hound Dog Taylor's death in 1976, when Hutto briefly took over Taylor's band the Houserockers. He continued to perform with the New Hawks until his own passing.

Led Zeppelin
(Vocal/instrumental group, 1968–80)

In 1968, after all the original members had left the Yardbirds, guitarist Jimmy Page had custody of the band's name and contracts. John Paul Jones, who had produced some of Page's side work, joined on bass, and Page hired singer Robert Plant away from Hobbstweedle. Drummer

John Bonham, a friend of Plant's, rounded out the New Yardbirds to fulfil standing contractual obligations. After Keith Moon, drummer with the Who, quipped that their audacious, harder blues sound would 'go over like a lead zeppelin', the quartet took on a new name.

The group's love of the blues was explicit in its altered cover versions (generally left uncredited), which led to plagiarism charges. Led Zeppelin's self-titled debut album in 1969 was heavy on blues tunes with a psychedelic energy. As Led Zeppelin rose to superstardom it moved further away from the blues but never abandoned it completely. Bonham's death in 1980 effectively brought the premier heavy metal band to an end.

Louisiana Red
(Vocals, harmonica, guitar, b. 1936)

Iverson Minter, a.k.a. Louisiana Red, rose from childhood tragedy to build an impressive career. His mother had died and his father had been murdered by the Ku Klux Klan by the time Red was five years old. He first recorded for Chess in 1949, prior to his military service, and then played with John Lee Hooker before leading his own bands. Louisiana Red is a gifted guitarist, influenced by Elmore James and Muddy Waters.

Above
Louisiana Red first recorded for Chess in 1949 and is equally at home on harmonica and guitar.

Far Left
Blues guitarist Rory Gallagher – an exciting and energetic performer.

Left
J.B. Hutto graces the cover of a 1976 issue of Living Blues.

Above

*Dynamic guitarist
Son Seals performs at
London's Hammersmith
Odeon in 1977.*

Right

*Hound Dog Taylor, for
whom producer Bruce
Iglauer set up Alligator
Records in 1971.*

Delbert McClinton
(Harmonica, vocals, b. 1940)

Delbert McClinton gigged around Fort Worth as a young
man, playing with local acts like the Rondells. He moved
to Los Angeles in the early 1970s, playing and writing songs
with Glen Clark, but returned to Texas in 1975. As both a
performer and songwriter, McClinton smoothly crosses the
dividing lines between blues, country, rock and soul. He
has enjoyed important collaborations with Roy Buchanan,
Bonnie Raitt, Tanya Tucker, B.B. King, Vince Gill and others.

Matt Murphy
(Guitar, vocals, b. 1927)

Matt 'Guitar' Murphy came up in Memphis, playing with
Howlin' Wolf, Little Junior Parker and Bobby 'Blue' Bland
before gaining serious attention with Memphis Slim's band
from 1952 to 1959. In the 1960s Murphy contributed to
sessions by Sonny Boy Williamson II, Chuck Berry and
Otis Rush, and was a crowd favourite while performing
on the 1963 American Folk Blues Festival tour. Murphy's
appearance in *The Blues Brothers* film in 1980 helped to
seal his place in blues history.

Charlie Musselwhite
(Harmonica, vocals, guitar, b. 1944)

Often compared to his contemporary Paul Butterfield,
Charlie Musselwhite has an exceptionally fluid and
melodic harmonica style that places him head and

shoulders above most competitors. He debuted on record
in 1967 and has remained faithful to the Chicago style in
his own projects and in supporting work for Elvin Bishop,
Big Joe Williams, John Hammond Jr., Junior Watson and
others. Musselwhite also gave brothers Robben and Pat
Ford their start in the blues business in 1974. He staged
a comeback in 2004 with a highly promoted album.

Son Seals
(Guitar, vocals, drums, 1942–2004)

In 1973 dynamic guitarist Frank 'Son' Seals became one
of the most exciting artists signed to the fledgling Alligator
Records label. His choppy technique and hard-hitting
vocals on original songs such as 'Your Love Is Like A
Cancer' combine to create an extremely powerful sound.
His finest albums include horn sections, which help to
drive the energy level even higher. In 2000 Seals recorded
Lettin' Go for Telarc, with Hammond organist Al Kooper of
Blood, Sweat & Tears and guitarist Trey Anastasio of the
jam band Phish.

Hound Dog Taylor
(Guitar, vocals, 1915–75)

Many guitarists might sound as if they have extra fingers,
but Theodore 'Hound Dog' Taylor, who did not become a
full-time musician until he was well past 40, actually had

an extra digit on each hand. Producer Bruce Iglauer founded the Alligator label in 1971 expressly to record the guitarist's energetic, raw almost to the point of primitive, 'house-rockin'' style. Taylor and his backing duo, the Houserockers, were among the label's hottest stars for four years until Taylor's death from cancer.

Koko Taylor
(Vocals, b. 1935)

Singer Koko Taylor (née Cora Walton) earned the title 'The Queen of Chicago Blues' due to her no-nonsense, brazen vocal style. She writes much of her own material, songs that resonate with womanly power and assert her claim to blues royalty. Taylor grew up singing gospel in Memphis and switched to the blues after moving to Chicago in 1953. Bassist Willie Dixon signed her to Chess Records and wrote her big hit 'Wang Dang Doodle' in 1964.

After Chess folded in 1975 Taylor moved to Alligator, becoming one of the label's biggest stars. She was managed by her husband, Pops Taylor, who died in 1989 after an auto accident in which Koko was also severely injured. Since her comeback in 1990 Koko Taylor has toured the world constantly, appearing at all the major blues and jazz festivals. Her later bands have often included a number of relatives.

Johnny Winter
(Guitar, vocals, harmonica, b. 1944)

Like his brother, keyboardist and saxophonist Edgar, Johnny Winter is a long-haired Caucasian albino from Texas who reshaped the face of the blues in the 1970s. A phenomenal guitar technician, particularly when using the slide, he rose to prominence in Texas bars and local studios. On his first album for Imperial Records, Winter explored psychedelic blues with middling success. Shortly thereafter he signed with Columbia, for whom he recorded between 1969 and 1974.

His group Johnny Winter And, with guitarist Rick Derringer, had a hit with 'Rock And Roll Hoochie Koo'. Winter is a great interpreter of classic material, covering blues and rock'n'roll tunes by Chuck Berry, B.B. King, Bob Dylan, the Rolling Stones and Van Morrison. *Second Winter* (1969) is one of his best recordings. He is also a gifted producer, working with Muddy Waters in the 1970s on such projects as *Hard Again* (1977). The album *Together – Live* (1976) presents the Winter brothers in fine form.

ZZ Top
(Vocal/instrumental group, 1970–present)

ZZ Top is a perennial blues trio from Houston, Texas, as well known for their sunglasses, furry guitars and long beards as for their signature boogie beats. Guitarist Billy Gibbons, bassist Dusty Hill and drummer Frank Beard specialize in hard, shuffling electric blues, usually tinged with humour and double entendres. Hits like 'La Grange', 'Jesus Just Left Chicago', 'Tush', 'Legs' and 'Sleeping Bag' have kept the band in the studio and on the road since 1970.

Below
Powerful blues singer Koko Taylor, who recorded for Chess Records before signing with the 1970s-founded Alligator label.

Jazz

Above

Trumpeter Miles Davis revolutionized jazz yet again in the 1970s with his jazz-rock fusion.

'Jazz is not dead, it just smells funny.'
Frank Zappa

In many ways, the 1970s can be seen as a transition point in the evolution of jazz. The generational divide became evident with the ascendancy of young artists such as Jaco Pastorius (1951–87), George Benson and Chick Corea, and the deaths of Louis Armstrong (1901–71) and Duke Ellington (1899–74). Jazz musicians were in the pop-music charts for the first time since the 1950s, but this was a new breed of improvisers who were influenced as much by the Beatles or Motown/soul music as by Armstrong or Charlie Parker (1920–55), and used electric instruments to express themselves. The free-jazz movement of the 1960s grew even more politicized and spread its branches to Chicago, St. Louis, Los Angeles and beyond. Artists who trod the middle ground between electricity and the avant-garde found it difficult to get live jobs, yet some still had a productive decade, recording some of their best work.

What Miles Hath Wrought

Trumpeter Miles Davis (1926–91) ushered in the new decade at New York City's Village Gate, in the middle of a month-long residency. The live shows bisected an intensive period of studio work that produced a stunning pair of albums, whose influence would continue to resonate three decades later: *Bitches Brew* (1969) and *Jack Johnson* (1970). While not the first jazz artist to use electric guitar, piano and bass, Davis was the highest-profile leader to adapt the popular approaches of Jimi Hendrix (1942–70), Sly Stone, James Brown and Stevie Wonder to his own ends. His imprimatur cannot be overrated.

Davis had been brewing up his new direction since 1968, and several of his collaborators from the period had ideas of their own about how to fuse elements of rock with jazz. Drummer Tony Williams (1945–97) formed Lifetime,

You checked out 1 item(s) today!

Title:
The Billboard illustrated encyclopedia of jazz &
blues /
Item ID: 38888033385901
Due: 02/17/2022

Account balance: $0.00
Total Items Out: 1

Your current library savings:$30.00

****

Winter Literacy (Dec 1, 2021 - Jan 31, 2022)
This winter, visit your library, curl up with a good
book, and win special prizes along the way using
the Beanstack app:

sequoyahregionallibrary.beanstack.com/reader365

which emulated the guitar-driven power trio sound of Cream and the Jimi Hendrix Experience; saxophonist Wayne Shorter (b. 1933) and keyboardist Joe Zawinul (b. 1932) started Weather Report to explore colour with amplified instruments; pianists Chick Corea and Herbie Hancock (b. 1940) put together their own distinctive electric bands. What these projects had in common was a greater emphasis on volume and individual expression through lengthy solos. Marketing played a more important role, too. Gone was the underplayed artwork of Blue Note Records and Impulse!; in its place were rock-inspired themes and, in the case of Corea's Return To Forever, a series of grandiose sci-fi fantasies that seemed better suited to a British progressive rock band. Instead of nightclubs, the bands played university campuses and outdoor festivals. On FM radio, Weather Report was featured next to rockers like Pink Floyd and the Allman Brothers Band.

Electric Shock

Miles's musical progeny were making improvised instrumental music attractive and commercially viable. *Bitches Brew* and Hancock's *Head Hunters* (1973) set sales records for jazz. Rock artists, including guitarists Carlos Santana and Jeff Beck, blurred the lines between the genres from the opposite direction, while well-established jazz musicians such as Freddie Hubbard (b. 1938) and Donald Byrd, whether because of commercial pressures or artistic

curiosity, began to add electric instruments and broaden their repertoire beyond jazz standards. Even musical iconoclast Ornette Coleman (b. 1930) went electric in the 1970s with his radical septet Prime Time.

However, as with all trends, the fascination wore off for many audiences as the second and third wave of participants arrived, and by the end of the 1970s jazz-rock fusion had become an artistic dead end of overlong solos and overblown imagery. As his former sidemen and acolytes delved into electric jazz rock, Davis moved deeper into dense, pan-cultural music that combined African rhythms, Indian instruments and distorted guitar. All but crippled by leg injuries, sickle-cell anaemia and drug abuse, Davis retreated from music completely in 1975.

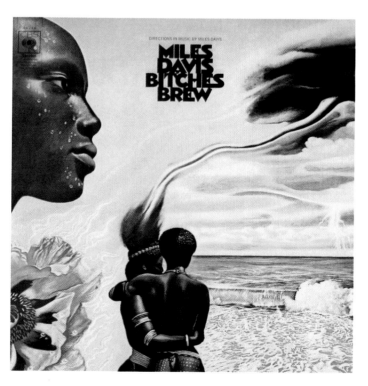

Above
Keyboardist Joe Zawinul, a co-founder of Weather Report – one of the most important electric-jazz combos of the decade.

Left
Davis's 1969 Bitches Brew *album set a new precedent; its influence is still felt in twenty-first century jazz releases.*

Popular Melody

Herbie Hancock – 'Chameleon' (1973)
With its popping bassline, funky drum backbeat and unison sax and synth lead, this song is the archetypal fusion of pop, soul and jazz. Its melody has been used as the basis of many garage-band jam sessions. Sixteen minutes long, it forms a link between 1960s French disco music and the elongated instrumentals of the later 1970s.

Above

Thad Jones (left) jams with Mel Lewis, 1976.

collective that was formed by pianist Muhal Richard Abrams (b. 1930) and others in 1965, Chicago began to develop younger players such as saxophonists Henry Threadgill (b. 1944) and Chico Freeman, trombonist George Lewis and bassist Fred Hopkins, and to attract creative musicians from other Midwest cities, such as St. Louis saxophonists Oliver Lake and Julius Hemphill.

In California, Coltrane's influence also touched two young saxophonists who would make important contributions in the 1970s. Alto saxophonist Arthur Blythe grew up in San Diego and cut his musical teeth with influential pianist Horace Tapscott in Los Angeles. Further north, in Berkeley, David Murray was translating the harmonic freedom of Jimi Hendrix to the saxophone. Studying with Blythe at Pomona College opened Murray's ears to the possibilities inherent in free jazz.

By the mid-1970s, many of these players had made the time-honoured trek to New York City, where they found a common musical outlet in venues that collectively became known as 'the loft scene'. Cross-fertilization became commonplace, with musicians such as Murray, Freeman, drummer Philip Wilson, trumpeter Olu Dara and organist Amina Claudine Myers playing together frequently and influencing one another. In 1976, four of the most prolific reed players – Murray, Hemphill, Lake and Hamiet Bluiett – formed the World Saxophone Quartet. Along with Threadgill's trio Air – which included bassist Hopkins and drummer Steve McCall – Murray's thorny octet, the quartets led by multi-reed player Anthony Braxton and the Art Ensemble of Chicago, the World Saxophone Quartet pointed to a renewed period of creativity for avant-garde jazz.

Mainstream Struggles

While electric jazz-rock dominated live venues and the avant-garde became rejuvenated, the acoustic jazz that had characterized the 1960s was having a rough ride, with the exception of a few well-established names. So enthralled were the jazz media and the record-buying public by the flash and fire of fusion that numerous acoustic recordings gained lustre only in retrospect. Pianist McCoy Tyner (b. 1938) released several superb albums on Milestone – particularly *Sahara* (1972), *Echoes Of A Friend* (1972) and *Enlightenment* (1973) – while saxophone colossus Sonny Rollins (b. 1930), returning from a six-year recording hiatus, explored a range of approaches, from solo

Coltrane's Children

If Davis's followers found commercial fortune in tracking his lead, the influence of John Coltrane (1926–67) was no less powerful. The concept of making music on your own terms and seeking freedom through your instrument was Coltrane's legacy, and there were many younger musicians ready to take up where he had left off. By the 1970s, Chicago had already launched the careers of several distinctive artists, including saxophonist Roscoe Mitchell and trumpeter Lester Bowie. With the Association for the Advancement of Creative Musicians (AACM), a musicians'

World Saxophone Quartet.

improvisation to all-star touring units. Alto player Phil Woods returned from four years in France and formed an outstanding quartet. Tenor giant Dexter Gordon (1923–90) returned to the US more than once, although it was his December 1976 stand in Greenwich Village that garnered the most attention, resulting in one of his best recordings – *Homecoming: Live At The Village Vanguard* (1976) – and a renewed belief in some quarters that acoustic jazz was back on solid ground.

In West Germany, meanwhile, former bassist Manfred Eicher was establishing a hybrid of electric and acoustic music on his nascent ECM label, using a signature crystalline studio sound that would be widely influential. The Canadian expatriate trumpeter Kenny Wheeler released two luminous LPs on ECM – *Gnu High* (1975) and *Deer Wan* (1977) – while Norwegian tenor player Jan Garbarek helped define the 'ECM sound' with his evocative *Witchi-Tai-To* (1974).

Popular Melody

Keith Jarrett – 'In Front' (1971)
The lead track from Jarrett's first solo recording for ECM, Facing You, has the rich harmony, gospel underpinnings and exuberant flights of improvisation that are the pianist's trademarks. Engineer Jan Erik Kongshaug and producer Manfred Eicher set a new standard for the intimate sound of studio recordings.

Art Ensemble Of Chicago

'Jazz is so difficult. A lot of people think once they've learned these licks they can get up and play them for the rest of their life. But that's not being truthful to the music 'cause it's not developing.... I've built a whole career out of making mistakes!' **Lester Bowie**

Key Track

'Uncle' (1980)

Recorded live in Munich at the height of the band's popularity, Roscoe Mitchell's 17-minute 'Uncle' from Urban Bushmen *displays the band's full range and power. From small gestures to grand statements, played on an array of instruments, this typical performance encompasses several decades and genres of jazz history.*

With its tribal masks, arcane percussion instruments and grand sense of theatre, the Art Ensemble of Chicago always seemed to be more than just a jazz band. Indeed, the group grew from the communal activities of the Chicago-based AACM, which quickly became a magnet and laboratory for freedom-seeking African-American musicians in the city, including saxophonists Roscoe Mitchell (b. 1940) and Joseph Jarman (b. 1937), trumpeter Lester Bowie (1941–99) and bassist Malachi Favors (1927–2004). AACM founder Muhal Richard Abrams' Experimental Band (est. 1961) and Mitchell's quartet, which formed two years later, were early models in the sprawling musical vision of the former and the latter's use of unusual timbres created by small percussion instruments.

French Sojourn

In June 1969, as the Roscoe Mitchell Art Ensemble, Mitchell, Bowie, Favors and Jarman travelled to Paris, where they re-christened themselves the Art Ensemble of Chicago. The band's impact was as much visual as musical; Favors and Jarman painted their faces and wore African robes and hats, while Bowie donned a white lab coat. Onstage, multiple saxophones and percussion devices surrounded the quartet. The effect was further heightened when drummer Don Moye (b. 1946) joined in September 1969. Moye called his array of drums, cymbals and hand-crafted instruments 'sun percussion' and liked to climax percussion movements by igniting magician's flash-paper between his fingers.

During its two years in Europe, the band recorded 11 albums and three film scores, and toured widely, frequently accompanied by soul singer Fontella Bass, Bowie's wife. The band's music escaped classification. The first three tracks on the 1969 album *A Jackson In Your House* capture part of the range: anthemic horn statements offset by a bicycle horn; antic vocal effects; melodies reminiscent of the Jazz Age; free-blown horn choruses that defy the shouted order to 'Get in line'; and a waltz performed at half-tempo with the horns stretching the melody line like taffy. The band also integrated Bowie's R&B background, with Moye laying down a backbeat and Favors switching to electric bass.

A Pragmatic Agenda

Returning to the US in 1971, the band's members determined that they would focus on building an audience through performances at jazz festivals, universities and large concert venues. Throughout the 1970s, the Art Ensemble steadily spread its name and its motto: 'Great Black Music, Ancient to the Future'. Two recordings for Atlantic Records exposed them to a broader audience, and a breakthrough commercial contract with ECM initiated the band's most financially successful period. With *Nice Guys* (1978) and *Full Force* (1980) the band achieved a

much higher profile and reached new levels of accessibility. During this period, several members – most notably Bowie and Mitchell – re-established recording and performing careers independent from the band.

Surviving Deaths

The Art Ensemble maintained a relatively high level of creativity and productivity through the 1980s, switching labels to the Japanese DIW company and touring only every other year in order to permit individual projects. In 1993, Jarman left the band to establish a martial arts and Buddhist spiritual centre in New York City, and the others carried on as a quartet. After Bowie's death from cancer in 1999, they re-formed again as a trio. Jarman returned to the fold in 2003, and the group recorded *The Meeting* (2003), as well as announcing an extended concert tour just prior to Favors's death. The remaining members kept the scheduled dates and have plans to continue as a trio or with younger AACM players.

Classic Recordings

A Jackson In Your House (1969)
'A Jackson In Your House', 'Song For Charles'

Les Stances a Sophie (1970)
'Theme De Yoyo', 'Theme Libre'

Live At Mandel Hall (1972)
'Checkmate'

Bap-Tizum (1972)
'Immm', 'Odwalla'

Nice Guys (1978)
'JA', 'Dreaming Of The Master'

Urban Bushmen (1980)
'New York Is Full Of Lonely People', 'Uncle'

The Third Decade (1984)
'Prayer For Jimbo Kwesi', 'The Bell Piece'

The Meeting (2003)
'It's The Sign Of The Times', 'The Train To Io'

Above Far Left
Art Ensemble of Chicago at AACM's twentieth anniversary festival in 1995. (l–r) Roscoe Mitchell, Famodon Don Moye, Lester Bowie, Malachi Favors and Joseph Jarman.

Left
Trumpeter Lester Bowie was a co-founder of the Art Ensemble of Chicago and also led several of his own groups.

John McLaughlin

By turns avant-garde adventurer, high-voltage rocker and Third World explorer, Yorkshire-born guitarist John McLaughlin has seldom repeated himself. Born in 1942, McLaughlin studied piano from the age of nine and taught himself guitar after becoming interested in country blues, flamenco and Django Reinhardt. A gig with Pete Deuchar's Professors of Ragtime in 1958 was his ticket to London, where the storm that would become the British Invasion of the US was brewing. He played with Georgie Fame, Graham Bond and Brian Auger, and picked up studio session jobs – ranging from Petula Clark to David Bowie.

'McLaughlin to me is the most important, certainly the most influential voice in the last decade on the guitar, without a doubt.'
Pat Metheny

Choosing Jazz

By 1967, McLaughlin had tired of session work and moved to Germany to play with vibraphonist Gunter Hampel. Occasionally, he returned to London to jam with musicians such as bassist Dave Holland and drummer Tony Oxley and, eventually, to record the album *Extrapolation* (1969), one of the most exciting debuts in contemporary jazz. Already in place were the remarkably fluid technical facility, diamond-hard tone and harmonic imagination that would set him apart from most jazz guitarists.

Concurrent with this recording, McLaughlin was invited by drummer Tony Williams to join his new band, Lifetime. Within hours of landing in the US, McLaughlin was jamming at Count Basie's club in front of an audience that included Miles Davis. Davis, several months into a two-year period of intensive recording activity, did not waste time; he invited McLaughlin to the studio on 18 February 1969 for what would form part of the seminal *In A Silent Way* (1969). While working with Lifetime, McLaughlin helped shape four other key Davis recordings: *Bitches Brew* (1969), *Jack Johnson* (1971), *Live-Evil* (1971) and *Big Fun* (1974).

Right
Guitarist John McLaughlin, who worked as a session musician before playing with key jazz artists, including Miles Davis.

Following A New Leader

McLaughlin was extraordinarily prolific during his first 18 months in the US. In addition to the work with Davis and the Tony Williams Lifetime albums *Emergency!* (1969) and

Key Track

'The Noonward Race' (1971)
Budding guitarists may well weep with envy when they hear this track, from the Mahavishnu Orchestra's debut album, The Inner Mounting Flame. *It has all the elements – speed, tone and invention – of a classic John McLaughlin solo. Drummers may weep, too, when they hear the mighty Billy Cobham in full flight.*

and advanced dynamics. The band's first recording, *The Inner Mounting Flame* (1971), remains a landmark work of the era. McLaughlin continued to use the Mahavishnu Orchestra name for subsequent bands, but none matched the original for power and invention. The second group is notable for McLaughlin's collaboration with an ensemble conducted by Michael Tilson Thomas, documented on the album *Apocalypse* (1974).

Discovering Other Worlds

In 1976, McLaughlin surprised devotees by releasing *Shakti*, a recording of his acoustic encounter with four traditional Indian musicians. While McLaughlin's trademark lightning arpeggios were still there, the volume was reduced significantly. Never again could fans pin him down to a single style. His subsequent works included renewed interest in jazz rock, *Electric Dreams* (1978) and *Electric Guitarist* (1979); collaborations with classical pianist Katia Labéque, his then-partner; and spirited meetings with guitarists Paco de Lucía and Al DiMeola.

In the 1990s and the early years of the twenty-first century, McLaughlin continued his pattern of going wherever his imagination took him. He recorded and toured with organist Joey DeFrancesco in a trio, continued his occasional forays with De Lucía and DiMeola, and delved back into ragas with Shakti Remembered.

Turn It Over (1970), he recorded the rock-influenced *Devotion* (1970), the adventurous *Where Fortune Smiles* (1970) and the acoustic *My Goal's Beyond* (1970). The title and meditative mood of the latter album pointed to a major turning-point in his life, a spiritual awakening that would find him pledging allegiance to a mystic, re-christening himself Mahavishnu John McLaughlin and launching a band that would set the bar much higher for instrumental prowess in the burgeoning jazz-rock movement.

The Mahavishnu Orchestra debuted in July 1971 and stunned listeners with rapid-fire unison melody lines played between McLaughlin, violinist Jerry Goodman and keyboardist Jan Hammer, unusual time signatures

Classic Recordings

John McLaughlin
***Extrapolation* (1969)**
'Extrapolation',
'Binky's Beam'

***My Goal's Beyond* (1970)**
'Goodbye Pork-Pie Hat',
'Peace One'

The Mahavishnu Orchestra
***The Inner Mounting Flame* (1971)**
'The Noonward Race',
'Meetings Of The Spirit'

***Birds Of Fire* (1972)**
'Birds Of Fire', 'One Word'

Shakti with John McLaughlin
***Shakti* (1976)**
'Joy', 'Lotus Feet'

***Qué Alegría* (1992)**
'Belo Horizonte',
'Qué Alegría'

***The Complete Jack Johnson Sessions* by Miles Davis (2003)**
'Go Ahead John', 'Right Off'

Above Left
McLaughlin (second from left) with the Mahavishnu Orchestra, whose 1971 album The Inner Mounting Flame was a jazz landmark.

Left
McLaughlin (second from left) in Shakti, a group with its roots in traditional Indian music.

A-Z of artists

Gato Barbieri

(Tenor saxophone, b. 1934)

An acerbic-toned saxophonist heavily influenced by John Coltrane, Barbieri is an enigmatic figure, best known for his trademark black borsalino and his successful excursions into commercial music. Argentinean by birth, he first surfaced in Paris as a member of trumpeter Don Cherry's group. After two years with Cherry, Barbieri began to actively seek ways to fuse Latin-American music and jazz. His soundtrack for *Last Tango In Paris* (1972) received widespread acclaim.

Anthony Braxton

(Various saxophones and clarinets, flute, piano, b. 1945)

'I've been isolated and kicked out of jazz as a black man who is not "black" enough, a jazz guy who is not "jazz" enough,' said Chicago native Braxton, looking back on a

highly iconoclastic career that has been documented on more than 130 recordings. After military service, Braxton emerged in 1966 with a musical conception that, while influenced by older saxophonists like Roscoe Mitchell, Warne Marsh and John Coltrane, was wholly original.

His debut recordings as a leader in 1968 – *Three Compositions Of New Jazz* and *For Alto* (both on Delmark) – were stunning in their conceptual maturity. In the 1970s, Braxton's music began to reflect his interest in composers Karlheinz Stockhausen and John Cage, as well as his love of marches by John Philip Sousa. His musical output includes solo works and compositions for massed orchestras of 160 players, but he is best known for his quartets, including the group Circle.

Brecker Brothers

(Randy Brecker, trumpet, flugelhorn, b. 1945; Michael Brecker, tenor and soprano saxophone, EWI, b. 1949)

Philadelphia-born brothers Randy and Michael Brecker were already experienced players when they collaborated with drummer Billy Cobham in 1970 to form Dreams, one of the first groups to attempt combining elements of jazz and rock. In 1975 the siblings formed the Brecker Brothers. Over six years, the band was one of the most popular in jazz, featuring musicians such as David Sanborn, George Duke and Don Grolnick. The brothers reformed briefly in 1992, by which time Michael had established himself as one of jazz's pre-eminent soloists.

Herbie Hancock

(Piano, electronic keyboards, b. 1940)

A classical prodigy in Chicago, Hancock became one of the most versatile and influential jazz pianists of the post-war era. At the age of 20, he moved to New York City to play with trumpeter Donald Byrd. After his debut as a leader, *Takin' Off* (1962), he joined Miles Davis for a high-profile five years. In the 1970s, his Mwandishi sextet and jazz-funk unit Head Hunters were at the forefront of electric jazz,

Below

The Brecker Brothers, who led one of the most popular jazz-rock groups of the 1970s.

and he subsequently alternated between electric and acoustic music, becoming an articulate and much-quoted spokesperson for jazz.

Dave Holland
(Bass, b. 1946)

A professional musician since the age of 13 in his native Wolverhampton, England, Holland became one of jazz's most in-demand bassists after Miles Davis persuaded

> '... [Dave Holland]'s so consistent a group player. He just makes it all possible for you to take it easy. He allowed everyone else to stretch.'
> **John Scofield**

him to emigrate to the US in 1968. Holland performed on two of Davis's seminal studio recordings, *In A Silent Way* (1969) and *Bitches Brew* (1969), before leaving to co-found the quartet Circle. His debut recording as a leader, *Conference Of The Birds* (1972), is one of the era's masterpieces. Having led two quintets and participated selectively in others' projects, he started a distinctive big band in 1999.

Abdullah Ibrahim
(Piano, b. 1934)

Born Adolphe Johannes 'Dollar' Brand in Capetown, South Africa, Abdullah Ibrahim successfully fused African rhythms and lilting melodic lines with the piano styles of Duke Ellington and Thelonious Monk. In 1960, with trumpeter Hugh Masekela and others as the Jazz Epistles, he released the first contemporary South African jazz album. The racial climate in his country forced him and his wife, singer Sathima Bea Benjamin, to seek exile in Switzerland, where he met and recorded for Ellington.

Exposed to a wider audience through extensive jazz-festival work, the pianist played with Elvin Jones after the drummer left John Coltrane, and toured

Europe with Don Cherry and others. Assuming his Muslim name in the 1970s, he worked frequently as a solo artist, but in 1976 he settled in New York City and established the sextet Ekaya; subsequently, he wrote soundtracks for French film director Claire Denis.

Keith Jarrett
(Piano, keyboards, flute, soprano saxophone, percussion, b. 1945)

Few artists are as demanding of themselves and their audiences as Allentown, Pennsylvania native Keith Jarrett. A child prodigy, Jarrett first caused a stir while playing in saxophonist Charles Lloyd's quartet. In 1970, he joined Miles Davis on electric piano and organ. Jarrett soon eschewed electronic keyboards and entered into a long relationship with the German-based label ECM.

In the 1970s he pursued three streams of jazz: improvised solo concerts; knotty, blues- and gospel-inflected works in a quartet with saxophonist Dewey Redman, bassist Charlie Haden and drummer Paul Motian; and more cerebral performances with saxophonist Jan Garbarek, bassist Palle Danielsson and drummer Jon Christensen. In 1983, Jarrett formed a trio with bassist Gary Peacock and drummer Jack DeJohnette to focus on the harmonic and melodic possibilities of the Great American Songbook. Work with this so-called Standards Trio dominated the following two decades, although he continued to pursue other projects, including some recordings of classical works.

Above
Pianist Herbie Hancock has continued to tour, record and explore the boundaries of jazz, electronics, pop music and the classics.

Left
Dave Holland was the pre-eminent bass player of the era, following a stint with Miles Davis.

miles davis ⊙ **196**   **don cherry** ⊙ **247**   **charlie haden** ⊙ **249**   **elvin jones** ⊙ **250**

Above

Steve Lacy brought the straight soprano saxophone back to prominence and inspired John Coltrane to experiment with the instrument.

Volker Kriegel
(Electric guitar, 1943–2003)

As a sociology student in Frankfurt, Germany, Kriegel's playing caught the ears of older musicians, who convinced him to pursue music. After working with visiting US players he joined the nascent Dave Pike Set in 1968. Kriegel's *Spectrum* (1971) was an important step in the development of European jazz rock. In 1973, he formed Spectrum with bassist Eberhard Weber, and in 1976 co-founded the long-running United Jazz and Rock Ensemble.

Steve Lacy
(Soprano saxophone, 1934–2004)

Born Steven Lackritz in New York City, Lacy began his career playing Dixieland music with veterans Henry 'Red' Allen and Rex Stewart, but became best known as a highly lyrical and adventurous champion of the soprano saxophone. His adoption of the straight horn, neglected since the heyday of Sidney Bechet, inspired John Coltrane to double on the instrument. Lacy moved to Paris in 1970 and recorded extensively, often taking inspiration from poets and painters.

Albert Mangelsdorff
(Trombone, b. 1928)

Although he played violin and guitar, Frankfurt native Albert Mangelsdorff did not take up the trombone until the age of 20. However, despite this relatively late start, he became a pioneer of multiphonics on the horn and a leader of the European avant-garde. Recordings with pianist John Lewis and sitarist Ravi Shankar in the 1960s helped to make his name, but it is as a member of the Globe Unity Orchestra, beginning in 1967, that he is perhaps best known.

Thad Jones
(Flugelhorn, cornet, valve trombone, 1923–86)

The middle brother in Detroit's musical Jones family, Thad Jones joined older sibling Hank at age 16 and, after wartime service, played with younger brother Elvin in Billy Mitchell's band. He rose to prominence with Count Basie during a nine-year tenure (1954–63), but he became best known for the 13-year period in which he co-led a big band with drummer Mel Lewis every Monday night at New York's Village Vanguard. In 1979 Jones moved to Denmark, where he formed the Thad Jones Eclipse.

Oregon
(Instrumental group, 1971–present)

The antithesis of the fusion music of the 1970s, Oregon comprised Paul McCandless (oboe, English horn, tenor saxophone, bass clarinet), Glen Moore (bass, violin, piano, flute), Ralph Towner (guitar, piano, French horn, trumpet, flugelhorn) and Colin Walcott (tabla, sitar, clarinet, percussion). In some ways, Oregon resembled a chamber-music quartet more closely than a jazz combo, introducing diverse musical elements from far-flung cultures long before 'world music' came into vogue. After Colin Walcott was killed in a car accident in 1984, the group disbanded, but re-emerged in 1986 with Indian percussionist Trilok Gurtu and an even broader range of influences.

Jaco Pastorius

(Electric bass, piano, 1951–87)

The brash Pennsylvania native burst on to the music scene in 1974 with a debut recording, *Jaco*, which redefined the way in which the electric bass could be played. A veteran of R&B and pop bands in Fort Lauderdale by the age of 24, Pastorius collaborated with his good friend, guitarist Pat Metheny, before being hired to join the band Weather Report. In 1980 he formed his own group, Word of Mouth. Increasingly troubled by mental illness, Pastorius died homeless after being beaten by a bouncer outside a Florida nightclub.

Woody Shaw

(Trumpet, flugelhorn, composer 1944–89)

A lyrical soloist, composer and bandleader, Shaw's career was cut tragically short by illnesses, including deteriorating vision, and a subway accident that cost him an arm. After early work with Willie Bobo and Eric Dolphy, Shaw played extensively in Europe with US expatriates Bud Powell, Kenny Clarke and Johnny Griffin. Returning to America, he worked with Horace Silver, Art Blakey and others. In 1976, he co-led a series of high-profile New York City gigs with Dexter Gordon and thereafter led his own combos, documented by Columbia Records.

Steve Swallow

(Electric bass, b. 1940)

One of a handful of electric-jazz bassists who have shaped the sound of the instrument, Swallow was a student at Yale University when he became attracted to music. An early apprenticeship with pianist Paul Bley grew into a long-term association and the two recorded frequently. Vibist Gary Burton provided another ongoing musical relationship. After a number of years teaching and playing in California, Swallow became involved with pianist-composer Carla Bley, and the pair co-lead numerous projects.

Joe Zawinul

(Piano, electronic keyboards, b. 1932)

Born in Vienna, Josef Zawinul was 27 when he arrived in the US on a music scholarship, but this relatively late start did not prevent him from becoming an enormously influential composer and bandleader. Following brief stints with Dinah Washington and Maynard Ferguson, Zawinul joined Cannonball Adderley's band as musical director and attracted the attention of Miles Davis, to whom he contributed compositions during the transition to electric jazz. In 1970, Zawinul and Wayne Shorter co-founded Weather Report. After 1985 he led a series of bands under the name Zawinul Syndicate.

Below

Jaco Pastorius, who redefined the role of the electric bass in jazz, played with Pat Metheny and Weather Report, among others.

the eighties

as the end of the twentieth century approached, the United States – its culture included – entered a rare period of recapitulation, retrieval and, ultimately, renewal. The election as President of ageing Ronald Reagan, ex-movie star and California governor, introduced unexpected neo-conservatism, an ideology that looked back to a rosy, though mythical, Golden Age. Declaring 'It's morning in America', Reagan spoke for ways of life that had little to do with blues and jazz (or rock, classical and the newly surging rap/hip hop styles). Blues and jazz reacted by themselves, returning to the past. They were aided by the institution of a whole new recording format, the compact disc.

The CD, a palm-sized digital medium developed by German BMG and Japanese Sony corporations and introduced in 1983, re-energized the teetering recording industry as music devotees rushed to replace favourite LPs with the wondrous new product. Reissues of blues and jazz classics outnumbered but also financed new albums by younger artists. Those younger artists, however, also looked back to the glories of the 1950s and early 1960s for inspiration, polishing the past to a streamlined sheen. The new bluesmen still sang of love's pangs, but more often at white college fraternity parties than for black and hipster crowds in low-rent venues. The new jazz instrumentalists were sharply suited 'Young Lions', led by Wynton Marsalis, a virtuoso with classical chops as well as a post-bop background. There were fusion revisionists too – electric guitarist Pat Metheny, and Miles Davis staging a final comeback. Also, jazz voices from overseas announced themselves with a fervour that would not be denied. By the 1980s' end, home computers had transformed how people lived; Communism, the Iron Curtain and the USSR itself were gone, and the global economy had a running start into the contemporary era.

Key Artists: Blues

Robert Cray

Stevie Ray Vaughan

Key Artists: Jazz

Wynton Marsalis

Pat Metheny

Blues

'Ironically, very little [blues today] comes from the radio. It seems to come from other outlets, like commercials and films.' **Roy Rogers**

Texas was a hotbed of rockin' blues in the mid- to late 1970s. Austin-based bands such as the Cobras, featuring guitar sensation Stevie Ray Vaughan (1954–90), and the Fabulous Thunderbirds, formed by Stevie Ray's older brother Jimmie Lee Vaughan, were gathering strong regional followings with their tough brand of roots-oriented roadhouse blues. These potent groups, as well as others

such as the Nightcrawlers, Omar & the Howlers and the Electromagnets, spearheaded a 1980s blues-rock boom that paralleled the trend towards blues rock sparked in the late 1960s by Texas guitarist Johnny Winter (b. 1944).

Stevie Ray Vaughan Arrives

The Fabulous Thunderbirds went on to build a national following in the 1980s in the wake of their major crossover success with 1986's *Tuff Enuff* (the title track was released by Epic Records as a single with accompanying video and

received heavy play on MTV). Stevie Ray Vaughan went on to form his own band, Double Trouble, which quickly became one of the most popular bands in Texas and by 1982 began to receive national recognition. Stevie Ray's appearance with Double Trouble at the Montreux Jazz Festival in the summer of 1982 caught the attention of pop star David Bowie; he recruited the flashy Texan to lay down stinging lead-guitar tracks on his 1982 album *Let's Dance*, bringing Vaughan further into the public eye. Legendary record producer John Hammond (1910–86), who had significantly influenced the careers of everyone from Charlie Christian (1916–42) and Billie Holiday (1915–59) to Bob Dylan and Bruce

Springsteen, signed Stevie Ray to a contract with Epic; his 1983 debut, *Texas Flood*, became an unqualified hit, crossing over to the pop market and earning two Grammy nominations.

The Blues Rock Renaissance

The combined successes of the Vaughan brothers invigorated the blues-rock genre and also led to a renewed appreciation of blues-rock pioneers such as Lonnie Mack (b. 1941), Johnny Winter and Roy Buchanan (1939–88), all of whom signed with Chicago-based Alligator Records in the mid-1980s. The momentum that the Vaughan brothers had created paved the way for 1990s blues-rock players, including Kenny Wayne Sheppard, Jonny Lang, Coco Montoya, Tinsley Ellis (b. 1957), Sonny Landreth, Chris Duarte, Bryan Lee, Little Jimmy King, Larry McCray, Charlie Sexton and British blues-rock guitar hero Gary Moore.

Far Left
A mural in Austin, Texas, which boasted a lively blues scene during the 1980s.

Above Left
The Vaughan brothers Jimmie Lee (left) and Stevie Ray were key figures on the circuit.

Left
Blues-rock artists such as Lonnie Mack enjoyed renewed fame following the Vaughans' success.

Popular Melody

George Thorogood & the Destroyers – 'Bad To The Bone' (1982)
Featuring a raucous riff inspired by John Lee Hooker and driven home by Thorogood's raspy vocals and direct, slashing guitar work, this song received major airplay in 1982–83 and was later revived in 1991 on the soundtrack to the popular Arnold Schwarzenegger film Terminator 2.

Robert Cray

Right

Singer, songwriter and razor-sharp guitarist Robert Cray lets rip onstage during a 1987 UK tour.

Although Robert Cray's clean, good looks, precise guitar lines and slick presentation earned him some knocks from critics early on in his career (hardcore blues aficionados tended to dismiss him as 'blues lite' for yuppies), he later gained their respect for his smart songwriting and razor-sharp guitar licks, along with an intensely passionate vocal style reminiscent of the great 1960s R&B singer O.V. Wright.

A Promising Debut

Born on 1 August 1953 in Columbus, Georgia, Cray moved around frequently until the age of 15, when his family finally settled in Tacoma, Washington. Inspired by Texas guitarslinger Albert Collins (who played at Cray's high-school graduation), he taught himself to play guitar and formed his first band in 1974 with bassist Richard Cousins. After playing around the Pacific Northwest during the 1970s, even joining Collins's backing band on a few West Coast gigs, Cray's band made its recording debut in 1980 with *Who's Been Talkin'* (on Tomato Records). That first album set the tone for Cray's recording career, reflecting an equal allegiance to blues and R&B in his faithful covers of O.V. Wright's 'I'm Gonna Forget About You', Freddie King's 'The Welfare (Turns Its Back On You)' and the Willie Dixon-penned title

> *'I walked into a record store, and they were playing Robert Cray's new record ... the music just grabbed me ... I said, "Man, it's time for me to get back into this music!"'*
>
> **Joe Fonda**

track. But it was Cray's originals 'Nice As A Fool Can Be' and 'That's What I'll Do' that pointed to a future direction for this talented singer, songwriter and guitarist.

Cray followed up with two solid outings on the High Tone label – 1983's *Bad Influence*, which contained the chilling original 'Phone Booth', and 1985's *False Accusations* – before finally breaking through to mainstream acceptance following the release of his superb 1986 Mercury Records debut, *Strong Persuader* (containing his hit original song 'Smoking Gun'). In 1985 Cray appeared on a guitar summit meeting, the aptly-named *Showdown!* (Alligator Records), with fellow blues six-stringers Albert Collins and Johnny 'Clyde' Copeland.

Key Track

'Smoking Gun' (1986)

This smouldering original (co-written with bassist Richard Cousins) is marked by Cray's clean-toned, stinging guitar lines and soulful, gospel-tinged vocals. A minor-key confessional from Strong Persuader, *this track set the tone for Cray's writing through the 1980s and helped him to make the leap from cult act to crossover pop star.*

with a knack for minor-key confessionals. In 1999 he collaborated with drummer Steve Jordan, who produced and played on the Memphis-flavoured *Take Your Shoes Off* (Rykodisc). Also appearing on that retro-soul outing was drummer-producer Willie Mitchell of Hi Records fame; he co-wrote and also created the horn arrangements for the opening track, which has the distinct feel of an early 1970s Al Green number. Elsewhere on the album, Cray offers faithful renditions of Mack Rice's '24-7 Man' and Solomon Burke's 'Won't You Give Him (One More Chance)'.

Time Will Tell

Cray has continued to expertly blend relaxed, good-feeling southern soul and urgent blues on 2001's Stax/Volt-flavoured *Shoulda Been Home* (again produced in Memphis by drummer Steve Jordan) and 2003's *Time Will Tell* (Sanctuary), his thirteenth recording as a leader. That most recent release is easily his most ambitious to date and is in some ways uncharacteristic of his style. Not only does it contain two stridently anti-war songs in 'Survivor' and 'Distant Shore', it also features Cray in an odd turn on electric sitar, playing with the Turtle Island String Quartet on 'Up In The Sky', a psychedelic number that sounds like an outtake from Prince's *Around The World In A Day* (1985). Regardless of the context, however, Cray remains a commanding vocal presence and an assertive six-stringer. After 30 years of constant gigging, he has become one of the seasoned veterans on the contemporary blues scene.

Left
Cray (right) with blues legend B.B. King in 1992.

A Southerly Direction

During the 1990s, Cray took more of a southern soul direction on recordings such as 1990's *Midnight Stroll*, 1992's *I Was Warned* and 1995's *Some Rainy Morning* (all on Mercury), while continuing to blossom as a songwriter

Stevie Ray Vaughan

'I've said that playing the blues is like having to be black twice. Stevie Ray Vaughan missed on both counts, but I never noticed.'
B.B. King

Key Track

'Pride And Joy' (1983)
This introduces many elements of Vaughan's vaunted, six-string vocabulary – the tough Texas shuffle rhythm and lazy, behind-the-beat comping, the ability to shift seamlessly back and forth from rhythm to lead playing, and the Hendrix-inspired 'kiss the sky' crescendo at the peak of his solo.

The premiere torch-bearer for the blues-rock boom of the 1980s, Texan guitar wizard Stevie Ray Vaughan galvanized a generation of players and fans alike with his pyrotechnic licks and flamboyant stage presence. Connecting deeply with both the psychedelic, 'voodoo chile' mystique of Jimi Hendrix and the down-home roadhouse grittiness of his biggest guitar influence, Albert King, Vaughan fashioned a sound that reached out and grabbed listeners with its combination of raucous rock-fuelled abandon, string-bending intensity, gut-level directness and real-deal, bluesy authority.

His meteoric rise to fame during the mid-1980s, over the course of four recordings and countless gigs, was fuelled by self-destructive cocaine-and-alcohol binges that led to a physical collapse and subsequent rehabilitation in 1987. Stevie Ray ultimately mustered the courage to overcome his addictions, returning to the scene in 1988 with a clean bill of health and a renewed sense of conviction. He continued touring and recording and was at his peak when he died in a tragic helicopter crash after a concert in the summer of 1990.

The Vaughan Brothers

Born in the Oak Cliff area of Dallas, Texas on 3 October 1954, Stevie Ray Vaughan grew up under the influence of his older brother Jimmie, an accomplished blues and R&B guitar player and vintage record collector. Stevie Ray got his first guitar at the age of seven and began copying licks from brother Jimmie's records by the likes of Lonnie Mack, Albert King, Freddie King, B.B. King, Buddy Guy, T-Bone Walker, Otis Rush and Jimmy Reed. Although the Vaughan brothers had a competitive relationship, Stevie Ray idolized Jimmie and closely followed his progress through a succession of early bands, including the Swinging Pendulums, the Chessmen and Texas Storm. Stevie Ray formed his own band, Blackbird, in 1970.

In 1971, aged 17, he dropped out of high school to concentrate on music. On New Year's Eve of 1971, Stevie Ray and his Blackbird bandmates all moved to Austin and began working on the thriving blues scene there. In 1973 Steve Ray joined the Nightcrawlers and by the end of 1974 was playing his first gig with Paul Ray's popular Cobras. After leaving the Cobras in July 1977 he formed his own Triple Threat Revue, featuring singer Lou Ann Barton, guitarist W.C. Clark, drummer Freddy 'Pharoah' Walden and keyboardist Mike 'Cold Shot' Kindred. After Triple Threat imploded due to inner bickering between Vaughan and Barton, Stevie Ray formed Double Trouble (named after one of Vaughan's favourite Otis Rush tunes)

in May of 1978. The band built a strong regional following for the next few years, culminating in a triumphant appearance at the Montreux International Jazz Festival on 17 July 1982. Pop stars Jackson Browne and David Bowie were in the audience at that galvanizing performance; Browne later offered his studio to record Double Trouble, while Bowie hired Stevie Ray to play on his recording *Let's Dance* (1983), considerably elevating the guitarist's profile.

A Brilliant Career

Vaughan and Double Trouble were signed to an Epic Records contract by legendary producer and talent scout John Hammond. Stevie Ray's 1983 debut, *Texas Flood*, was an immediate hit and led to a triple award from *Guitar Player* magazine for Best New Talent, Best Electric Blues Guitar Player and Best Guitar Album, as well as W.C. Handy Blues Awards for Entertainer of the Year and Blues Instrumentalist of the Year. Stevie Ray's virtuoso playing and Hendrix-inspired mystique (for a generation of young fans who missed out on the 1960s, he provided a bridge to Jimi through his faithful covers of 'Voodoo Chile [Slight Return]' and 'Third Stone From The Sun', replete with wild guitar-thashing stage antics) helped to fuel subsequent successes with 1984's *Couldn't Stand The Weather* and 1985's *Soul To Soul*. Following an extensive tour in 1986, which yielded the double LP *Live Alive* and culminated in an onstage collapse in London, Vaughan entered a

rehabilitation hospital in Georgia. After taking a year out he returned to the scene, re-energized and with a new outlook on life. By the end of 1988, he had begun writing the material that would make up the bulk of 1989's *In Step*, which went gold (500,000 copies sold) within six months of its release and later won a Grammy Award for Best Contemporary Blues Recording. Vaughan co-headlined a 1989 tour of America with rock guitarist Jeff Beck, and in the spring of 1990 he recorded an album with his brother Jimmie entitled *Family Style*.

An Untimely Death

On 26 August 1990 Stevie Ray and Double Trouble played a gig at the Alpine Valley Music Theater in Easy Troy, Wisconsin. The concert culminated with an all-star encore jam featuring special guests Eric Clapton, Buddy Guy, Jimmie Vaughan and Robert Cray. After the concert, Vaughan boarded a helicopter bound for Chicago; minutes after its 12:30 a.m. takeoff, the helicopter crashed into hills, killing the blues guitar hero instantly. At his funeral in Dallas, Stevie Wonder sang 'Amazing Grace' at the gravesite. Jimmie and Stevie Ray's *Family Style* was released posthumously in October 1990 and won two Grammy Awards for Best Rock Instrumental ('D/FW') and Best Contemporary Blues Recording. Other posthumously released recordings by Stevie Ray Vaughan include 1992's *In The Beginning*, which documents a 1980 concert by Double Trouble, and 2000's four-CD boxed set *SRV*.

Classic Recordings

Texas Flood (1983)
'Love Struck Baby', 'Pride And Joy', 'Rude Mood'

Couldn't Stand The Weather (1984)
'Scuttle Buttin', 'Couldn't Stand The Weather', 'Cold Shot'

Soul To Soul (1985)
'Say What!', 'Lookin' Out The Window', 'Look At Little Sister'

In Step (1989)
'The House Is Rockin', 'Tightrope', 'Wall Of Denial'

Above
Vaughan's well-travelled guitar case.

Far Left
Stevie Ray Vaughan – the greatest guitar virtuoso since Jimi Hendrix – who died tragically young in a helicopter crash.

A-Z of artists

Marcia Ball
(Piano, vocals, b. 1949)

One of the leading exponents of the Professor Longhair school of piano playing, East Texas-born 'Long Tall' Marcia Ball was also greatly influenced by R&B divas Irma Thomas and Etta James, and zydeco king Clifton Chenier. Her infectious blend of modern Texas roadhouse blues, boogie-woogie and Louisiana swamp rock is best exemplified on a series of Rounder recordings, including 1984's *Soulful Dress*, 1986's *Hot Tamale Baby* and 1989's *Gator Rhythms*. Ball still tours continuously and is an annual attraction at the New Orleans Jazz & Heritage Festival.

Below

Piedmont blues exponents John 'Bowling Green' Cephas (right) and 'Harmonica' Phil Wiggins perform in Knoxville, Tennessee in 1982.

Rory Block
(Guitar, vocals, b. 1949)

An interpreter of classic country blues, Block took guitar lessons from Rev. Gary Davis, Mississippi John Hurt and Son House before moving to California and working on the folk-blues coffeehouse circuit. She recorded for small labels before signing with Rounder Records and debuting with 1982's *High Heeled Blues*. She is featured in the Robert Mugge film *Hellhounds On My Trail* (2000), celebrating Robert Johnson's posthumous entry into the Rock And Roll Hall Of Fame. Her most recent recordings are 2003's *Last Fair Deal* and 2004's *From The Dust* (both on Telarc Blues).

The Blues Band
(Vocal/instrumental group, 1979–present)

Blues aficionados Paul Jones (vocals, harmonica), Dave Kelly (vocals, guitar), Tom McGuiness (guitar), Gary Fletcher (bass) and Hughie Flint (drums) formed the Blues Band in 1979, purely for their own enjoyment. Initial success on the pub and club circuit swiftly led to greater things and their first album was released in 1980. Flint was replaced in 1981 by Rob Townsend and the band has continued to perform and record prolifically. Ex-Manfred Mann star Jones also plays an important role in keeping the blues alive as Britain's premier blues DJ.

Cephas & Wiggins
(Vocal/instrumental group, 1978–present)

The W.C. Handy Award-winning duo patterned itself after Sonny Terry & Brownie McGhee. Guitarist John 'Bowling Green' Cephas (b. 1930) and 'Harmonica' Phil Wiggins (b. 1954) met at a jam session in Washington, DC and began performing together in 1978. They toured the globe on a US State Department tour and recorded throughout the 1980s, while their most recent recordings for the Alligator label are 1996's *Cool Down*, 1999's *Homemade* and 2003's *Somebody Told The Truth*. They remain the leading exponents of the Piedmont blues style.

Eddy Clearwater
(Guitar, vocals, b. 1933)

Mississippi-born Eddy Harrington left the South in 1950 and established himself on Chicago's West Side as a Chuck Berry imitator named Guitar Eddy. He later took the stage name Clear Waters as a takeoff on Muddy Waters, but finally settled on Eddy 'The Chief' Clearwater, a nickname he got from his penchant for wearing Native American headdresses on stage. His tough, slashing, southpaw guitar attack is best documented on 1980's Rooster Blues debut, *The Chief*.

Johnny 'Clyde' Copeland
(Guitar, vocals, 1937–97)

The Houston guitarist played with bluesman Joe 'Guitar' Hughes before forming his own band in the late 1950s. Relocating to New York in 1974, Copeland debuted on Rounder Records with 1977's *Copeland Special*. In 1985 he recorded a guitar summit meeting with Albert Collins and Robert Cray (*Showdown!*) and in 1986 recorded *Bringin' It All Back Home*, an adventurous hybrid of African music and blues. He continued this fusion on his last recording – 1996's *Jungle Swing* (Verve), featuring jazz pianist Randy Weston. Singer Shemekia Copeland is his daughter.

Ronnie Earl
(Guitar, b. 1953)

New York City native Ronald Horvath began playing in Boston blues clubs during the 1970s, and in 1980 replaced Duke Robillard in Roomful of Blues. After eight years with the band, he struck out on his own with the Broadcasters, which prominently showcased his passionate Magic Sam meets T-Bone Walker guitar style. One of the jazziest of blues guitarists, he combines finesse and fire on his best outing, 1987's *Smokin'* (on Black Top Blues).

Fabulous Thunderbirds
(Vocal/instrumental group, 1974–present)

Fusing straight blues, early rock'n'roll and classic R&B, the Texas roadhouse band – formed by guitarist Jimmie

Vaughan and harpist/vocalist Kim Wilson – built a cult following throughout the 1970s and early 1980s, before breaking through commercially in 1986 with *Tuff Enuff*. While the band's early Chrysalis recordings appealed mainly to blues and rock'n'roll purists, their late 1980s output for Epic, including 1987's *Hot Number* and 1989's *Powerful Stuff*, brought wider recognition and helped to absorb rock fans into the blues arena.

Lil' Ed & The Blues Imperials
(Vocal/instrumental group, 1975–present)

This Chicago native learned slide guitar from his uncle, renowned bluesman J.B. Hutto. During the early years of the Blues Imperials, flamboyant frontman Ed Williams continued working at his day job in a local car wash, but by the early 1980s the band had established a substantial regional following. Their 1986 Alligator Records debut, *Roughhousin'*, and 1989 follow-up, *Chicken Gravy & Biscuits*, are prime examples of their raucous, rough-edged party music, in the tradition of Hound Dog Taylor.

Above

Guitarist Eddy Clearwater has a distinctive playing style that combines the blues with elements of Chuck Berry's hit songs.

Lonnie Mack
(Guitar, vocals, b. 1941)

Mack's 1964 debut album, *The Wham Of That Memphis Man* – chockfull of lightning-fast licks, vibrato-drenched lines and whammy-bar techniques on his Flying V guitar – captured the imagination of a young Stevie Ray Vaughan growing up in Dallas. Two decades later, Vaughan would produce Mack's 1985 comeback album on Alligator Records, *Strike Like Lightning*. The Indiana native followed up with two offerings on Alligator, before moving to the Epic label with *Road Houses & Dance Halls* (1988).

Magic Slim
(Guitar, b. 1937)

Born Morris Holt in Grenada, Mississippi, Slim began playing on Chicago's West Side in the mid-1960s. In 1976, when Hound Dog Taylor passed away, Slim took over his Sunday afternoon gig at Theresa's on the South Side. Slim's band the Teardrops was featured on the 1970 Alligator anthology series *Living Chicago Blues*. Throughout the 1980s, Slim recorded for the Alligator and Rooster Blues labels, highlighting his stinging licks and gruff vocals.

Bonnie Raitt
(Guitar, vocals, b. 1949)

During the 1960s, while attending college in Cambridge, Massachussetts, Raitt learned the ropes firsthand from slide masters Son House and Mississippi Fred McDowell. She began appearing on the folk and blues festival circuit in the late 1960s, sometimes encouraging elderly, rediscovered blues legends (such as Sippie Wallace) to join her onstage, and in 1971 recorded her self-titled debut for Warner Bros., featuring bluesmen Junior Wells and A.C. Reed. Her blues sensibility has graced gold-selling and Grammy-winning recordings from the 1980s to the present.

Roy Rogers
(Guitar, vocals, b. 1950)

An exponent of acoustic and electric blues, California-based slide guitarist Rogers played with John Lee Hooker's Coast To Coast band from 1982–86, before releasing his debut recording as a leader, *Chops Not Chaps* (1986). He followed up with 1988's *Slidewinder* and in 1990 produced Hooker's Grammy-

winning comeback album *The Healer*. Rogers maintained an acoustic duo in the 1990s with harmonica maestro Norton Buffalo. He is also featured in the Robert Mugge film *Hellhounds On My Trail* demonstrating Robert Johnson's slide-guitar techniques.

Roomful Of Blues
(Vocal/instrumental group, 1967–present)

The nine-piece, horn-based outfit from Westerly, Rhode Island was formed by guitarist Duke Robillard and pianist Al Copley and has been a swinging institution in the Northeast since 1967. The band concentrates on jump blues, boogie-woogie and slow blues numbers. Roomful's self-titled debut on Island Records in 1979 began a rich recorded legacy, which has included Grammy-nominated collaborations with blues greats Big Joe Turner, Eddie 'Cleanhead' Vinson and Earl King. Roomful released its eighteenth album, *Standing Room Only* (Alligator), in 2005.

Right

George Thorogood's energetic guitar playing and gruff vocals gave his band an enduringly popular down'n'dirty blues-rock sound.

'Roy [Rogers] is one of the most authentic interpreters of modern blues. He's a real master man who has spent so much time getting in touch with and really honing in on his craft.'

Bonnie Raitt

1990s – including 1994's *JLW*, 1995's *Blues Of The Month Club* and 1997's *Great Guitars* – and remains active.

Walter 'Wolfman' Washington
(Guitar, vocals, b. 1943)

This New Orleans guitarist started out accompanying R&B singers, but as a leader in the 1970s he developed a strong local following and gradually crossed over to wider audiences through appearances at the New Orleans Jazz & Heritage Festival. He debuted on Rounder Records in 1986 with the funky *Wolf Tracks*, following up with 1988's *Out Of The Dark* and 1991's *Wolf At The Door*. After recording for other labels (Virgin/Pointblank and Artelier), Washington returned to Rounder with 1998's *Funk Is In The House* and 2000's *On The Prowl*. He continues to tour worldwide with his band, the Roadmasters.

Left

Walter 'Wolfman' Washington accompanied R&B artists before branching out as a leader.

Below

Katie Webster's boogie-woogie piano evokes the swamp-blues scene of southern Louisiana.

George Thorogood & The Destroyers
(Vocal/instrumental group, 1973–present)

Thorogood's energetic, Delaware-based band drew inspiration from Elmore James and Hound Dog Taylor. Flash guitarist and raw vocalist Thorogood moved the band to Boston in 1974 and gained popularity on the blues circuit there, leading to its 1978 self-titled debut on Rounder Records. The 1979 album *Move It On Over* was a commercial breakthrough and the band's popularity was further enhanced after opening a Rolling Stones tour in 1981. The band continue to play no-nonsense, rocking boogie into the twenty-first century.

Joe Louis Walker
(Guitar, vocals, b. 1949)

A passionate, gospel-influenced singer, Walker came up in the 1960s on the San Francisco blues scene. In 1975 he began singing with the Spiritual Corinthians, remaining on the gospel circuit until 1985 when he formed his own band, the Boss Talkers. He recorded some strong albums during the 1980s for the High Tone label, such as his 1986 debut *Cold Is The Night* and 1988's *The Gift*. Walker continued to turn out consistently good recordings in the

Katie Webster
(Piano, organ, 1939–99)

This Texas native was active on the southern Louisiana swamp-blues scene in the late 1950s and early 1960s, recording for various regional labels. She spent the 1970s and early 1980s playing her unique brand of boogie-woogie piano around Louisiana – including at the New Orleans Jazz & Heritage Festival – before being 'discovered' by Alligator Records in 1987. She debuted in 1988 with *Swamp Boogie Queen* and followed up with two strong offerings, *Two-Fisted Mama!* (1990) and *No Foolin!* (1991), before suffering a stroke in 1993.

Jazz

By the late 1970s, the jazz-rock fusion movement – which had been ushered in at the outset of the decade with raw, tumultuous abandon by the likes of the Tony Williams Lifetime, Miles Davis and the Mahavishnu Orchestra – had become codified and diluted. Groups and individual artists such as the Crusaders, Chuck Mangione, Bob James, George Benson, Ramsey Lewis, Grover Washington Jr., Spyro Gyra and Jeff Lorber began smoothing off the rough edges, producing a more palatable strain of pop-influenced jazz that sought to cross over to a mainstream audience by appeasing rather than provoking. This tamer brand of fusion from the late 1970s – alternately derided by musicians and critics alike as 'happy jazz', 'fuzak' and 'hot-tub jazz' – paved the way for New Adult Contemporary (NAC) in the 1980s and the smooth-jazz movement of the 1990s.

> 'Whatever avenue you choose, whatever you have to say to the world, it comes down to that basic thing. It's your own voice ... that's what music is – somebody's point of view about the world.'
> *David Sanborn*

Louis Armstrong's
Hot Five
West End Blues

musicfirebox.com
/West

Traditional Vs Modern

Meanwhile, with the rise to prominence in the early 1980s of Wynton Marsalis – a gifted young trumpeter from New Orleans who took an earnest stand to play strictly acoustic jazz in the face of the electrified funk and fusion that dominated the era – a major schism had been set in place in jazz. Marsalis, through the sheer force of his talent and personality, along with his two Grammy Awards for both jazz and classical performance in 1983, quickly became leader of the so-called 'Young Lions' movement, which sought a return to jazz's acoustic roots. Meanwhile, Australian broadcaster and sound engineer Robert

Parker developed a technique of digitally remastering the classic jazz recordings of the 1920s and 1930s, resulting in his *Jazz Classics In Digital Stereo* series and a further surge of interest in the early days of jazz music. This swinging, neo-conservative (neo-con) trend developed in parallel with a trend towards smooth jazz, marked by simpler, more melodious and accessible radio-friendly sounds, and represented by the movement's leader Kenny G (b. 1959), whose 1986 breakthrough album, *Duotones*, became an international multi-million seller.

Right

Pianist Chick Corea (foreground), shown here with tenor saxophonist Bob Berg, was a major force in electronic jazz in the 1980s with his Elektric Band.

Fusion Holds Its Own

A few fusion renegades persisted in the face of both neo-con and smooth-jazz factions during the 1980s, notably drummer and Ornette Coleman disciple Ronald Shannon Jackson, whose Decoding Society accounted for some of the most fiercely uncompromising music of the decade. Alongside him were harmolodic guitarist James 'Blood' Ulmer (b. 1941), alto saxophonist Steve Coleman (b. 1956, founder of the cutting-edge M-Base Collective) and former Weather Report bassist Jaco Pastorius (1951–87), who blended big-band jazz, rock bombast, free-jazz abstractions and Stravinsky-esque dissonance on his 1982 recording *Word Of Mouth*. Fusion pioneers Chick Corea and John McLaughlin (b. 1942) both returned to the electronic arena with a vengeance in the mid-1980s – Corea with his Elektric Band, and McLaughlin with a new edition of his Mahavishnu Orchestra. Another fusion pioneer, Herbie Hancock (b. 1940), scored a massive radioplay hit in 1983 with 'Rock It', a streetwise melding of techno and funk that updated his own early 1970s jazz-funk hit 'Chameleon' while presaging the hip hop–jazz movement of the 1990s.

Another influential and widely imitated musician of the decade was guitarist-composer Pat Metheny (b. 1954), whose refreshingly original sound affected a generation of listeners and players alike. The 1980s also marked the return of Miles Davis (1926–91), who had been in self-imposed retirement since 1975. Davis's comeback band of 1980 included bassist Marcus Miller, guitarist Mike Stern and saxophonist Bill Evans (1929–80), each of whom became a bandleader in his own right later in the decade.

The Stalwarts Of Jazz

Other jazz giants still active on the scene in the 1980s included trumpeter and bebop pioneer Dizzy Gillespie (1917–93), tenor saxophonist and Gillespie protégé James Moody (b. 1925), alto sax burner Jackie McLean (b. 1931), tenor saxophonist Johnny Griffin, drummer Mel Lewis, who continued to lead his orchestra every Monday night at the Village Vanguard through the 1980s, and tenor sax titan Dexter Gordon (1923–90), who appeared in the 1986 film *Round Midnight*. Also significant in this period were vocalist/talent scout Betty Carter – whose band served as a training ground during the 1980s for promising young talent including pianists Benny Green, Marc Cary and Stephen Scott, saxophonists Don Braden and Craig Handy, drummers Winard Harper and Gregory Hutchinson, and

bassists Curtis Lundy and Taurus Mateen – and the great drummer Art Blakey (1919–90), who continued to tour with his Jazz Messengers. The group's ranks during this period included future bandleaders Wynton and Branford Marsalis, trumpeters Terence Blanchard, Philip Harper and Brian Lynch, saxophonists Bobby Watson, Billy Pierce, Donald Harrison and Javon Jackson, pianists James Williams, Donald Brown, Mulgrew Miller and Geoff Keezer, and bassists Charles Fambrough and Lonnie Plaxico. Blakey led his Messengers in typically dynamic fashion right up until his death in 1990.

It was also possible to see legendary jazzmen, such as trumpeters Clark Terry and Doc Cheatham (1905–97), saxophonists Stan Getz (1927–91), Sonny Rollins (b. 1930), Benny Carter (1907–2003) and Jimmy Heath (b. 1926), guitarists Barney Kessel (1923–2004) and Joe Pass (1929–94), trombonist J.J. Johnson (1924–2001), violinist Stephane Grappelli (1905–97), pianists Oscar Peterson (b. 1925), Dave Brubeck (b. 1920) and Eubie Blake (1883–1983), drummers Kenny Clarke (1914–85), Buddy Rich (1917–84) and Max Roach (b. 1924), and bandleaders Count Basie (1904–84), Benny Goodman (1909–86), Cab Calloway (1907–94) and Woody Herman (1913–87).

Above
Tenor saxophone legend Dexter Gordon portrays lonely musician Dale Turner in the 1986 film Round Midnight.

Popular Melody

Miles Davis – 'Jean Pierre' (1981)
This first appeared on Miles Davis's 1981 live album We Want Miles. *Reportedly lifted from a French children's nursery-school rhyme, it would become an audience favourite in Davis's comeback band and an oft-quoted riff in countless other bands on the early 1980s jazz scene in New York.*

Wynton Marsalis

Right

Right

*Wynton Marsalis (right)
and saxophonist brother
Branford were important
figures in the neo-
conservative revival of
traditional jazz values.*

Far Right

*Marsalis's Lincoln
Center Jazz Orchestra,
which is based in
New York but tours
festivals and concert
halls worldwide.*

*'I try to play whatever I'm hearing.
And that's part of jazz music.
That's what it is.'* **Wynton Marsalis**

Key Track

'Knozz-Moe-King' (1983)

*Aged 21, and still in thrall to the Miles Davis-Herbie
Hancock 1960s band, Marsalis displays
compositional ambition, instrumental
ferocity and articulate improvisation
through a multi-faceted theme,
punctuating fanfares and
tempo change-ups, in
quintet with his brother
Branford and explosive
drummer Jeff 'Tain' Watts.*

hot soloist, bandleader, composer and
recording artist, as well as an eager
educator, media charmer and ad-hoc
ambassador of American values.

A Musical Family

Born in New Orleans on 18 October
1961, Marsalis is the second of six sons
of jazz pianist and educator Ellis
Marsalis. His elder brother Branford is
a saxophonist while younger siblings
Delfaeyo and Jason play the trombone
and drums respectively. At the age
of eight Wynton was in the Fairview
Baptist Church band, organized by
veteran jazz banjoist and guitarist
Danny Barker. He also played in
marching bands and classical youth
orchestras, performing the Haydn
Trumpet Concerto with the New
Orleans Philharmonic at the age of 14.
He left his studies in 1980 for the front
line of Blakey's Messengers with

In the 1980s, trumpeter Wynton
Marsalis leapt from jazz-steeped New
Orleans to international artistic
prominence. In 1979
he was enrolled in New
York City's Juilliard
School and was jamming
with Art Blakey's Jazz
Messengers, and 10
years later he had seeded
what has become an
unrivalled international
jazz performance centre.
In between, Marsalis
established himself as a

Branford. In July 1981, Wynton toured Japan with Miles
Davis's famed 1960s rhythm section – pianist Herbie
Hancock, drummer Tony Williams and bassist Ron Carter.
Their recording *Quartet* (1982) was released as Marsalis's
debut on Columbia Records.

The Neo-Conservative Style

Marsalis's youth, energy, technical facility, directness of
expression, breadth of repertoire and articulation of a neo-
conservative aesthetic were in strong contrast with Davis's
flagging health and fading iconoclasm. He was promoted
as king of the Young Lions – a fresh crop of skilled,
musically educated instrumentalists who abjured free jazz
and commercial fusion to stand for the achievements and
ambitions of an African-American middle class. Marsalis

Classic Recordings

Wynton Marsalis (1982)
'Sister Cheryl', 'Hesitation'

Think Of One (1983)
'Knozz-Moe-King', 'Fuchsia', 'Melancholia'

Hot House Flowers (1984)
'Stardust', 'When You Wish Upon A Star', 'I'm Confessin''

Black Codes From The Underground (1985)
'Black Codes', 'Delfeayo's Dilemma', 'Chambers Of Tain'

J Mood (1986)
'Insane Asylum', 'Skain's Domain'

Standard Time, Vol. 1 (1986)
'Caravan', 'Cherokee'

The Majesty Of The Blues (1989)
'The Majesty Of The Blues', 'Hickory Dickory Dock'

Tune In Tomorrow: The Original Soundtrack (1989)
'Crescent City Crawl', 'Sunsettin' On The Bayou (Toonin' Tonight)'

Blue Interlude (1992)
'Blue Interlude (The Bittersweet Saga Of Sugar Cane And Sweetie Pie)'

Citi Movement (1992)
'Cityscape'

In This House, On This Morning (1993)
'Call To Prayer'

Blood On The Fields (1995)
'Follow The Drinking Gourd', 'God Don't Like Ugly', 'Juba And A O'Brown Squaw', 'Calling The Indians Out'

Orion String Quartet (1999)
'At The Octoroon Balls: String Quartet No. 1'

Marsalis Plays Monk, Standard Time Vol. 4 (1999)
'Thelonious', 'Ugly Beauty'

Big Train by Lincoln Center Jazz Orchestra (1999)
'Union Pacific Big Boy', 'Night Train', 'Station Call'

The Marciac Suite by Wynton Marsalis Septet (1999)
'Sunflowers'

The Magic Hour (2004)
'Big Fat Hen', 'The Magic Hour'

proclaimed the primacy of blues, swing, bebop, Louis Armstrong, Duke Ellington, Blakey, mid-period Davis and Thelonious Monk, but he scorned jazz rock, funk and fusion (music Miles was playing at the time).

After leaving Blakey, Marsalis formed a quintet (with Branford, Kenny Kirkland on piano, and Jeff 'Tain' Watts on drums) that expanded on post-bop conventions. Marsalis's *Think Of One* (1983) and his first album of classical trumpet fare both won Grammy Awards, an unprecedented feat he repeated with *Hot House Flowers* and *Baroque Music* in 1984. His *Black Codes (From The Underground)* from 1985 is another early peak. Subsequently, Marsalis recorded two three-volume sets of jazz standards and of original, intertwined material entitled *Soul Gestures In Southern Blues* (1988). As Branford launched his own career (the brothers still appear together, and occasionally *en famille*), Wynton discovered other collaborators, including pianist Marcus Roberts, drummer Herlin Riley and trombonist Wycliffe Gordon.

Marsalis At Lincoln Center

In summer 1987 Marsalis presented a concert series, Classical Jazz, under the auspices of Lincoln Center, New York's premier performing-arts institution. So began a unique collaboration between artist and establishment that has developed far-reaching jazz education programmes, jazz collaborations with chamber-music ensembles, orchestras and ballet troupes, countless radio and television productions, the globe-trotting Lincoln Center Jazz Orchestra, and Wynton himself.

Marsalis is a celebrity, but he has never sold out. He has consistently applied serious efforts to his ensembles, film scores, chamber works and art songs. His oratorio *Blood On The Fields* (1995), featuring vocalists Cassandra Wilson, Miles Griffith and Jon Hendricks, was the first jazz piece awarded the Pulitzer Prize, and he wrote *All Rise* for big band, 100-voice choir and the New York Philharmonic Orchestra to celebrate the turn of the twenty-first century.

In October 2004, Marsalis realized a fondly nurtured dream – the opening of Jazz@Lincoln Center's state-of-the-art Rose Hall, a multi-venue, multi-use facility billed as the first ever specifically designed for jazz. By 1990, Wynton Marsalis was already as he remains today: a tireless advocate for jazz (particularly its African-American strains), a communicator of jazz principles and a virtuoso instrumentalist, credibly interpreting diverse genres and styles, and able to improvise deeply affecting personal statements.

Pat Metheny

Right

*Pat Metheny took jazz
guitar in a new direction
and was refreshingly
open to the influence
of other musical styles.*

Above Far Right

*Vibist Gary Burton, in
whose group Metheny
established his original
playing style.*

*'To me if it's anything, jazz is a verb –
it's more like a process than it is a thing.'*

Pat Metheny

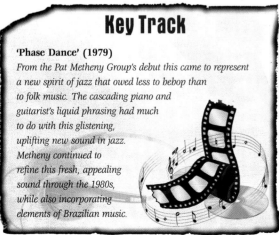

Key Track

'Phase Dance' (1979)

*From the Pat Metheny Group's debut this came to represent
a new spirit of jazz that owed less to bebop than
to folk music. The cascading piano and
guitarist's liquid phrasing had much
to do with this glistening,
uplifting new sound in jazz.
Metheny continued to
refine this fresh, appealing
sound through the 1980s,
while also incorporating
elements of Brazilian music.*

Guitarist Pat Metheny emerged
in the mid-1970s with a fully
realized approach to his
instrument that was
wholly unique for
its time, offering a
refreshing alternative
to both bop and fusion
styles. His sweeping,
warm-toned, reverb-
soaked lines and liquid
phrasing, once described
by *Down Beat* magazine
as 'the sound of wind
through the trees', had
a huge impact on a
generation of guitarists and forged a new direction in jazz
in the late 1970s. Metheny also made a significant impact
as a composer, with original, genre-stretching music that
artfully blended his own folk influences with elements
of rock, Brazilian music, bebop, new age and free jazz.

A Precocious Student

Born on 12 August 1954 in the small midwestern town of
Lee's Summit, Missouri, Metheny started on trumpet aged
eight before switching to guitar at the age of 12. By 15, he
was already a local legend in Kansas City, where he gained
invaluable bandstand experience working with veteran
players on the jazz scene. In 1972 he moved to Florida and
at 18 became the youngest teacher ever at the University
of Miami. In 1973 he joined the faculty at the Berklee
College of Music in Boston and became the youngest

musician ever to be on the staff there (he received an honorary doctorate at Berklee in 1996).

Metheny established his reputation through his work as a sideman with Gary Burton's group – he is featured on Burton's ECM albums *Dreams So Real* (1975) and *Passengers* (1976) – and as a leader of such acclaimed recordings as his 1976 ECM debut, *Bright Size Life* (a trio date with bassist Jaco Pastorius and drummer Bob Moses) and two powerful follow-up recordings for the label: 1977's *Watercolors* (which established his long-running partnership with keyboardist Lyle Mays) and 1978's *Pat Metheny Group* (which introduced the band featuring Mays on keyboards, Mark Egan on electric bass and Danny Gottlieb on drums).

Metheney Meets The Mainstream

Metheny broke into mass-market acceptance with 1979's *American Garage*, a far more rock-oriented recording than the typically introspective and searching ECM fare. He achieved mainstream popularity and attained gold-record status (sales of 500,000 copies) during the 1980s with a string of melodic, Brazilian-tinged albums, including 1983's *Travels*, 1984's *First Circle*, 1987's *Still Life (Talking)* and 1989's *Letter From Home*. And yet he never stopped taking risks and expanding his musical boundaries throughout the decade, as evidenced by such uncompromising side projects as 1980's free-boppish *80/81* with

bassist Charlie Haden, drummer Jack DeJohnette and the twin tenors of Michael Brecker and Dewey Redman; 1981's ethereal duet with keyboardist Mays on *As Falls Witchita, So Falls Wichita Falls*; 1982's abstract *Off Ramp* (which introduces his use of guitar synthesizer); 1983's *Rejoicing*, a subdued guitar-trio setting with bassist Haden and drummer Billy Higgins; 1984's film soundtrack *The Falcon And The Snowman*, which included a collaboration with pop star David Bowie on 'This Is Not America'; and 1986's provocative *Song X*, an historic collaboration with one of his boyhood idols – free-jazz icon Ornette Coleman.

An Experimental Superstar

By the end of the 1980s, Metheny was a bona-fide jazz superstar whose name was on a par with Miles Davis, Keith Jarrett, Herbie Hancock, Joe Zawinul and Wayne Shorter. Through the 1990s, he continued to release recordings of consistently high quality that appealed to his massive fan base (particularly 1992's *Secret Story*, 1994's *We Live Here* and 1997's *Imaginary Day*) while also indulging in purely experimental projects such as 1992's solo guitar synth noise onslaught *Zero Tolerance For Silence* and 1997's *The Sign Of 4*, an edgy free-jazz collaboration with British avant-garde guitar pioneer Derek Bailey, recorded live at New York's Knitting Factory with drummers Paul Wertico and Gregg Bendian.

Over the years, Metheny has won countless polls as 'Best Jazz Guitarist', as well as earning three gold records and 15 Grammy Awards. His Pat Metheny Group, now in its twenty-fifth year, remains one of the longest-standing acts in jazz.

Classic Recordings

Passengers by Gary Burton Quartet with Eberhard Weber (1976)
'The Whopper', 'Claude And Betty', 'B And G (Midwestern Nights Dream)'

Bright Size Life (1976)
'Bright Size Life', 'Omaha Celebration', 'Unity Village'

Pat Metheny Group (1978)
'Phase Dance', 'Jaco', 'Lone Jack'

American Garage (1979)
'American Garage', '(Cross The) Heartland', 'Airstream'

Off Ramp (1982)
'Are You Going With Me?', 'The Bat', 'James'

First Circle (1984)
'Yolanda, You Learn', 'If I Could', 'End Of Game'

Michael Brecker by Michael Brecker (1987)
'Syzygy', 'Original Rays', 'Choices'

Still Life (Talking) (1987)
'Third Wind', 'So May It Secretly Begin', 'Last Train Home'

Letter From Home (1990)
'Beat 70', 'Have You Heard', 'Every Summer Night'

Parallel Realities by Jack DeJohnette (1990)
'Dancing', 'Nine Over Reggae', 'John McKee'

Wish by Joshua Redman (1993)
'Whittlin'', 'Blues For Pat', 'Soul Dance'

I Can See Your House From Here with John Scofield (1993)
'Everybody's Party', 'Say The Brother's Name', 'The Red One'

Te Vou! by Roy Haynes Quintet (1994)
'Trinkle Tinkle', 'If I Could', 'Trigonometry'

Imaginary Day (1997)
'Across The Sky', 'The Awakening', 'Follow Me'

Jim Hall & Pat Metheny (1999)
'Farmer's Trust', 'Falling Grace', 'Summertime'

Left
The line-up for 1986's *Song X* included (l–r) Metheny, Jack DeJohnette and Ornette Coleman.

A-Z of artists

George Adams
(Tenor saxophone, flute, 1940–92)

A passionate voice on tenor sax in Charles Mingus's last band (1973–76), Adams co-led one of the most dynamic quartets of the 1980s with pianist Don Pullen; it also featured Mingus drummer Dannie Richmond and bassist Cameron Brown. In a series of 12 recordings through the 1980s for the Soul Note and Timeless labels, the Adams-Pullen band brilliantly straddled the inside-outside aesthetic, perhaps most successfully on 1983's two-volume *Live At The Village Vanguard*.

Steve Coleman
(Alto saxophone, b. 1956)

Chicago native Coleman worked in funk and R&B bands before switching to jazz and learning under tenor sax great Von Freeman. He moved to New York in 1978 and worked with the Thad Jones–Mel Lewis Orchestra and Sam Rivers. He had a key tenure in the early to mid-1980s with Dave

Holland before forming his own group, Five Elements, which blended solid funk rhythms with odd time signatures and Ornette Coleman-influenced angular lines.

Coleman was also a co-founder (with Greg Osby) of the Brooklyn-based M-Base Collective (short for 'Macro-Basic Array Of Structured Extemporization'), whose ranks included such forward-thinking players as trumpeter Graham Haynes, bassist Lonnie Plaxico, tenor saxophonist Gary Thomas, trombonist Robin Eubanks, keyboardist Geri Allen and vocalist Cassandra Wilson. While enjoying high-profile sideman work with artists such as Sting and Abbey Lincoln, he went on to spearhead adventurous hybrid collaborations with rappers, Cuban percussionists and singers, with his bands Mystic Rhythm Society, Council of Balance and Five Elements.

Paquito D'Rivera
(Saxophone, clarinet, b. 1948)

Growing up in Havana, D'Rivera saw many legendary Cuban musicians, but it was a Benny Goodman recording that inspired him to play jazz. He performed with the National Theater Orchestra of Havana at the age of 10, and in 1973 joined with eight other musicians to form Irakere, which fused jazz, rock and Cuban music in an exhilarating hybrid. In 1981, D'Rivera defected to the US and made his recording debut as a leader with *Paquito Blowin'*. He released a string of recordings during the decade and in 1988 joined Dizzy Gillespie's 15-piece United Nations Orchestra. Since then he has led small group recordings that highlight his virtuosity.

Dirty Dozen Brass Band
(Instrumental group, 1975–present)

Drawing from the age-old parade-band tradition of New Orleans, the Dirty Dozen Brass Band revolutionized the form by drawing on the bebop repertoire and incorporating elements of contemporary R&B into the joyful mix. The innovative group revitalized the brass-band tradition in the

Below

The Dirty Dozen Brass Band combine bebop and contemporary R&B to revitalize a New Orleans tradition.

1980s, inspiring a new generation of brass bands to incorporate popular themes of the day into those infectious grooves. During the 1980s the DDBB recorded for Concord, Rounder and Columbia.

Digby Fairweather
(Cornet, trumpet, b. 1946)

The Essex-born trumpeter worked as both a sideman and a leader in a wide variety of settings throughout the 1970s, before later branching out as a jazz educator, author and radio broadcaster. A key figure in establishing the jazz section of Britain's Musician Union, he also founded the National Jazz Foundation Archive. Fairweather led his own small groups in the 1980s, including the Jazz Superkings, and from 1994 has worked with the Great British Jazz Band.

Kenny G
(Soprano and alto saxophones, b. 1959)

Kenny Gorelick came up as a sideman in Jeff Lorber's fusion band of the 1970s, before releasing his first R&B-

> *'If I ever DO see [Kenny G] anywhere ... he WILL get a piece of my mind, and maybe a guitar wrapped around his head.'*
> **Pat Metheny**

flavoured recordings as a leader in the early 1980s. He hit pay dirt in 1986 with his phenomenally successful *Duotones*, which sold millions on the strength of his huge radioplay hit 'Songbird'. His lyrical, emotive soprano sax playing has come to define smooth jazz, earning him a huge following (as well as hordes of detractors).

Stanley Jordan
(Guitar, b. 1959)

In the early 1980s, Chicago native Jordan developed a revolutionary approach to the guitar, in which he sounded notes by tapping on the fretboard with the fingers of both hands. This technique allowed Jordan to play completely independent lines on the guitar simultaneously. His dazzling polyphony soon captured the attention of Blue Note Records, which released his debut, *Magic Touch*, in 1985. He continued to interpret both jazz and pop standards, recording six more albums for Blue Note before switching to Arista Records in 1994. He continues to perform in solo and trio settings and in 2003 collaborated with the Italian pop group Novecento.

Left

Stanley Jordan's innovations on the guitar allow him to play two lines simultaneously.

Bobby McFerrin
(Vocals, b. 1950)

A vocal gymnast and daring improviser, McFerrin is one of the most distinctive and uncategorizable singers in contemporary music. His remarkable range (he makes uncanny leaps from deep bass tones to the highest falsetto zone), elastic delivery and incredibly open-minded nature allow him to convincingly cover everything from pop, R&B, jazz and rock to demanding classical pieces. His 1982 self-titled debut on Elektra introduced an extraordinary talent, while his 1984 follow-up, *The Voice*, was a milestone in jazz – the first time a singer had recorded an entire album without any accompaniment.

Below

With his vocal range and eclectic musical tastes, Bobby McFerrin carved a unique role for himself in the 1980s jazz scene.

His Blue Note debut, *Spontaneous Inventions* (1986), earned him respect from the jazz community and 1988's *Simple Pleasures* made him a household name on the strength of his surprise hit 'Don't Worry, Be Happy'. McFerrin continued to challenge himself through the 1990s with his vocal group Voicestra and his duet collaborations with classical cellist Yo-Yo Ma and pianist Chick Corea, and has also been a conductor and performer at the BBC Proms in London's Royal Albert Hall.

Courtney Pine
(Tenor and soprano saxophones, bass clarinet, b. 1964)

Starting out in reggae and funk bands in high school, the British saxophonist became interested in jazz in the early 1980s and eventually gravitated towards the music of his biggest influences, Sonny Rollins and John Coltrane. He began playing with John Stevens's Freebop band and by the mid-1980s had formed the Jazz Warriors, an adventurous big band that combined elements of reggae, calypso and ska with jazz.

Pine later formed a sax quartet called the Saxophone Posse and made his recording debut as a leader with 1986's *Journey To The Urge Within* on Island Records. Through his work as a composer-bandleader and virtuosic player – along with his high-profile guest appearances in the UK with the George Russell Orchestra, Art Blakey's Jazz Messengers and the Elvin Jones Jazz Machine – Pine became a role model for a generation of young black jazz musicians in London in the mid-1980s.

David Sanborn
(Alto saxophone, b. 1945)

One of the most instantly recognizable and widely imitated voices in jazz during the 1980s, Sanborn emerged from the New York studio session scene – and a seat in Gil Evans's orchestra – to gain crossover success worldwide on the strength of seven R&B-infused outings for Warner Bros., beginning with 1980's breakthrough album *Hideaway*. His intensely expressive phrasing, marked by leaps into the *altissimo* register, remains a Sanborn signature, while his pungent tone and urgent attack are indebted to Hank Crawford's bluesy alto playing.

John Scofield
(Guitar, b. 1951)

A masterful improviser who is equally adept at funk, fusion, bebop and ballads, Scofield came up in the mid-1970s with the Billy Cobham/George Duke fusion band before recording as a sideman with Charles Mingus, Gary Burton and Dave Liebman. In 1982–85 he worked with Miles Davis, and through the 1980s made six powerhouse recordings as a leader for Gramavision. His 1990s Blue Note recordings established him as one of the premier guitarists in jazz. His sixth recording for Verve, 2005's *That's What I Say*, is a tribute to the late Ray Charles.

Steps Ahead

(Instrumental group, 1979–present)

Originally an acoustic jazz quintet led by vibist Mike
Mainieri and featuring tenor saxophonist Michael Brecker,
pianist Don Grolnick, bassist Eddie Gomez and drummer
Steve Gadd, Steps changed personnel through the early
1980s, changed its name to Steps Ahead in 1983 and by
1985 had become a high-tech fusion outfit, with Mike
Stern on electric guitar and both Brecker and Mainieri
playing MIDI controllers. Mainieri continued to lead the
band with new personnel through the 1990s.

Henry Threadgill

(Alto saxophone, flute, composer, b. 1944)

One of the most prolific and original composers of his
generation, Chicago native Threadgill was a charter
member of the Association for the Advancement of
Creative Musicians (AACM) in the mid-1960s. During the
1970s he collaborated with several AACM colleagues and
also worked with Air, his trio with drummer Steve McCall
and bassist Fred Hopkins. After moving to New York, he
began composing through the 1980s for his acclaimed
Sextet and Very Very Circus. He has also written ambitious
works for symphonic forces and uncategorizable
ensembles such as his Make A Move quintet.

James 'Blood' Ulmer

(Guitar, b. 1941)

Drawing on systems that are both ancient (the blues) and
modern (free jazz), this experimental guitarist forged an
original vocabulary on his instrument that has rarely been
imitated and remains one of the most strikingly individual
approaches in jazz. Ulmer began his career working in

organ bands around the Midwest in the 1960s, before
moving to New York in 1973. Hooking up with Ornette
Coleman that same year introduced him to the harmolodic
theory of musical composition and improvisation, altering
his approach for all time.

Through the 1980s Ulmer led three record dates for
Columbia, which helped to expose his music to a wider
audience. He also worked with tenor saxophonist David
Murray and drummer Ronald Shannon Jackson in the
Music Revelation Ensemble, and then in 1987 formed the
edgy co-operative group Phalanx with tenor saxophonist
George Adams, bassist Sirone and drummer Rashied Ali.

Yellowjackets

(Instrumental group, 1981–present)

Bassist Jimmy Haslip and keyboardist Russell Ferrante
joined drummer Will Kennedy as the backing band for
a 1979 recording by guitarist Robben Ford. By 1981, that
same quartet recorded its fusion debut for Warner Bros.
under the band name Yellowjackets. When Ford left the
band the following year, he was replaced by alto
saxophonist Marc Russo. Through the 1980s they pursued
a Zawinul-influenced sound; saxophonist Bob Mintzer
brought more jazz credibility to the group in the 1990s.

Above
*James 'Blood' Ulmer
has a highly original
approach to jazz music
and plays a blend of
blues and free jazz.*

Far Left
*David Sanborn is
an influential alto
saxophonist with a
distinctive tone and
unusual phrasing.*

Left
*John Scofield (right),
shown here with fellow
guitarist Pat Metheny,
has recorded with many
great jazz artists.*

the contemporary era

b y definition, a contemporary era defies summary. No one living in it has the conclusive perspective to discern the prevailing character of our times, even though we all know what we're going through, and can hear what we hear. The reductive view is: Americans, after a burst stock-market bubble and terrorist attacks, live in uncertainty, tinged with denial. Newly unified Europe, with the UK at some slight distance, is quite possibly on the rise. The large and small states of the former Soviet Union are in disarray, Japan's economy stands still and China has become a production behemoth despite political isolation. Africa remains beset with under-development and internal conflicts. South and Central America, the Caribbean, the South Pacific, including Australia, and Canada exist almost unto themselves. Nice places to visit, they're heard from now and then.

Blues and jazz in the contemporary era, on the other hand, is known everywhere. The musics seem creatively robust, though no more fiscally secure than usual. Blues is the more endangered species, the conditions of its birth fading into history, its fundamental assertions obscured by aggressive and ironic attitudes, digital electronics and the unforgiving beat. As blues is being prepared, we hope prematurely, for museum display, jazz is simultaneously institutionalizing and subverting itself. No one agent is responsible for the tug-of-war: forces of industry, philanthropy, individuals' aesthetics and career choices lead to both jazz classicism and jazz debasement (neither always where you'd expect them), standardization and extreme make-over. Future blues and jazz is unpredictable. The contemporary era is what's happening now.

Blues

We are now in one of the most exciting yet frustrating periods of the blues' long history. The music has become a living continuum, with artists whose ages range from early teens to late-eighties performing everything from field hollers and fife-and-drum band songs to Delta slide guitar, barrelhouse piano, Chicago, Texas and jump blues, improvisational blues rock, blues rap and even more experimental hybrids. At the same time, the proliferation

'If an art form doesn't evolve, it dies.
If blues wants to survive, it's got
to do something fresh and it's got
to reach the youth.'
Otis Taylor

of CD reissues allows listeners to investigate the music of virtually every significant blues artist who ever recorded. It is potentially a Garden of Eden for the genre, but certain factors prevent many musicians from enjoying its rewards.

A worldwide decrease in album sales and opportunities for musicians has occurred in all genres, but the blues' already slim margin has been hit especially hard. At the turn of the millennium, blues CDs accounted for little more than two per cent of overall sales, according to the Blues Music Association (an international trade organization devoted to the style). Since then, that figure has fallen to less than one per cent. Without the emergence of a major crossover artist to spark interest in the music within the mainstream, as Stevie Ray Vaughan (1954–90) did in the 1980s, there is little immediate hope for reversal.

Furthermore, the reissue explosion means that contemporary artists who are lucky enough to hold recording contacts find themselves competing against releases by the likes of Muddy Waters (1915–83) and Robert Johnson (1911–38) for sales, press and airplay. In the US in particular, they do so in an environment that has also been shaken by the closings of many clubs and music shops, declining spending on live entertainment, and commercial radio programming that has been narrowed to the lowest common denominator by corporatization. Internet radio has been a bright spot in the marketplace, with UK programmes such as *Shade Of Blues* on Swindon FM and Paul Jones's BBC Radio 2 show, *Good Time Blues* in Buenos Aires, *Messaround* in Bonn and *Triple R Blues Radio* in the Netherlands bringing blues to a worldwide audience.

Hard Times For Musicians

John Lee Hooker (1917–2001) once said 'When they bury me, they're gonna bury the blues aside of me'. Indeed, as influential labels such as Rooster Blues withdrew from the market and journeyman players scuffled for a living, his words seem like they might have been frighteningly

Right
Guitarist Otis Taylor
blends the roots of blues
music with 1960s-style
psychedelic sounds.

prophetic. Even a chart-topping collaboration between rock star Eric Clapton and the blues' reigning performer B.B. King (b. 1925), *Riding With The King* (2000), failed to produce a trickle-down of interest in other artists. Likewise, the high-profile public television series *Martin Scorsese Presents: The Blues* – composed of six full-length films by major directors including Scorsese himself – had little effect on overall attention for the genre or on record sales, save for the handful of musicians most prominently featured. Both of those events came in 2003, proclaimed the 'Year of the Blues' by the US Congress in order to celebrate the music's centennial.

Yet, as Hooker and many others among the style's elder statesmen have repeated over the decades until it has become a cliché, the blues will never die. The ever-silver lining of the style is its durability and strength, born of its roots in struggle and spirituality. Corey Harris (b. 1969), who was featured in the Scorsese-directed episode of *Presents: The Blues* entitled *From Mississippi To Mali*, has dedicated himself to exploring every traditional avenue of the genre, and spoke not just for himself when he declared in mid-2004, 'It's a sacrifice for me to do this music, but I'm dedicated to its sounds and words and I take my path in it very seriously'. Harris made that statement after a long day at the carpentry job he must work to support his family when he is at home, despite his international standing as a performer.

If anything unites the majority of artists who continue to perform and record blues music in the contemporary era, it is their unswerving dedication to the genre – no matter if they play traditional acoustic or electric forms, cut their lyrics to the urban beats of hip hop or lay slinking slide-guitar lines over tracks played by a band inside a laptop computer and also – for many – no matter the economic consequences.

Traditional Artistry Thrives

There are musicians, such as the New Englanders Duke Robillard (b. 1948) and Ronnie Earl (b. 1953), who can play with the linear eloquence of swinging, single-note guitar soloist T-Bone Walker (1910–75). Others, including Doug MacLeod, who records for the Netherlands' Black and Tan Records, and Louisiana Red (b. 1936), an expatriate American living in Germany, evoke the raw complexity of the Texas acoustic virtuoso Blind Lemon Jefferson (1897–1929) or the early Delta masters Charley Patton

(1891–1934) and Son House (1902–88). Regardless of approach, what the finest of today's traditional blues artists share is a drive for mastery combined with personal expression, including a desire to write original songs that – while in keeping with the sounds and stylistic tics of their chosen idioms – use modern or timeless themes to speak meaningfully to contemporary listeners.

Some are astonishingly eclectic, dipping into every font of the blues with grace and authenticity. A sterling example is Paul Rishell (b. 1950) & Annie Raines (b. 1969), a guitar and harmonica duo from Massachusetts that won the Blues Foundation's W.C. Handy Award for Acoustic Blues Album of the Year in 2000 for *Moving To The Country*. Their repertoire embraces the ballads of Patton, the gospel of Washington Phillips and the laconic playfulness of the Memphis Jug Band, but also extends past that early-twentieth-century music to include Little Walter (1930–68) instrumentals and the Chicago ghetto blues of Magic Sam (1937–69) as well as their own songs, like that album's title track, which celebrates the beauty of modern-day provincial France to a chugging, electric Memphis groove.

Above
Corey Harris, who appeared in Scorsese's 2003 film From Mississippi To Mali, has dedicated himself to keeping the blues alive.

Popular Melody

Otis Taylor – 'Hands on Your Stomach' (2001)
Taylor's ability to make timeless music based on the blues' deepest roots is captured in this track. His repeating guitar figure echoes African rhythms and stringed instruments while a second, effects-laden guitar and a ghostly, digitally enhanced female voice gently brush a psychedelic wash over his growling storytelling to original effect.

Chris Thomas King combines his blues roots with hip hop influences and often samples standard blues records.

Far Right

Elliott Sharp has helped to modernize the blues.

James 'Ironhead'
Baker & Prisoners
Black Betty

musicfirebox.com
/Betty

Keeping The Blues Alive

Otis Taylor (b. 1948) follows tradition even further back, albeit with modern instrumentation. Using digital effects and electric banjos in Appalachian folk tunings, he is able to evoke the sounds of ancient African instruments such as the kora and the n'jarka. Then Taylor, who may be the finest blues lyricist to emerge since Sonny Boy Williamson II (1899–1965) and Willie Dixon (1915–92), ups the ante by returning the blues to the realm of visceral protest music, which it inhabited in the rural South through the era of Jim Crow. His song 'My Soul's In Louisiana', about a lynching, is a blood-chilling example of his art.

Then there are artists who focus on a single type of blues with laser precision. English harmonica virtuoso Paul Lamb (b. 1955), who fronts the King Snakes, and his US counterpart Kim Wilson, who performs both as a solo artist

and with his Fabulous Thunderbirds, are at the forefront of this camp, playing first-generation-style electric blues so authentic that it sounds as if it has been transported from a Chicago steelworkers' bar of the late 1950s.

Blues rock, the brushfire ignited by Cream in the 1960s and swept to all corners of the planet by the likes of Fleetwood Mac, Ten Years After, Savoy Brown, Led Zeppelin, the Rolling Stones and other pioneering British bands, has by now existed long enough to fall into tradition's camp. Many artists who played in those groups, including Peter Green, Alvin Lee, Kim Simmonds (b. 1947), Jimmy Page, Robert Plant and Mick Taylor, are still at the style's forefront. Newcomers Walter Trout (b. 1951), the Black Crowes and Government Mule have carved their place in the subgenre, but overall rock's relationship to blues has become increasingly distant in the past two decades – despite the late crown-prince of grunge Kurt Cobain's penchant for Leadbelly (he covered 'Where Did You Sleep Last Night' and 'They Hung Him On A Cross' with his band Nirvana).

New Directions In Blues

Some of the most interesting musicians in contemporary blues are those nudging it towards its future. Blues industry pundits agree that the music must find a younger audience to gain sales and avoid further marginalization and fossilization. The blues-pop blendings of Keb' Mo' (b. 1951) and Eric Bibb (b. 1951), popular as they are, do not speak to the under-25 or even the under-35 crowd in the same way that John Mayall's Bluesbreakers, to say nothing of the Rolling Stones, did in the 1960s.

A new breed of daring artists are banking their hopes on infusing blues with the electronic rhythms and blunt vocal cadences of hip hop. Foremost among them is Chris Thomas King (b. 1964), who grew up playing traditional electric blues in his father's juke joint in Baton Rouge, Louisiana, but whose imagination was inflamed by the potent words and music of this comparatively new urban sound. Inspired by hip hop's anti-authority stance, King has also delved into the realms of protest music with his stories of hard ghetto life and racial discrimination. Like other rappers, he uses sampling as part of his palette, but on his albums he often samples the likes of Delta pioneer Son House, or his own acoustic slide guitar.

King may become a true touchstone for this hybrid, which has grown in underground popularity to the extent that the Mississippi juke joint label Fat Possum has built hip hop-oriented tracks around its musical patriarch R.L. Burnside (b. 1926) for college audiences. Chuck D., leader of the rap group Public Enemy, dabbled in this arena in 2003 when he led a union of rappers and blues session players into the Chess studios in *Godfathers And Sons* – part of the *Martin Scorsese Presents: The Blues* series – and thrashed John Lee Hooker's 'Boom Boom' in a well-intentioned yet poorly executed performance in the *Lightning In A Bottle* concert film. Other mainstream rappers, notably Arrested Development and Michael Franti of the group Spearhead, have explored blues themes with more satisfying results.

Several years ago Chris Thomas King started his own record label dedicated to the blues. Among his signings is England's Nublues, an interracial group that blends acoustic textures with singing, rapping, sampling and turntable manipulation. There are other smart hybridizers at work, too. The North Mississippi Allstars, for example, have built a niche within the jam-band audience for their live blend of Delta sounds, 1970s blues rock, rap and small cloudbursts of electronic noise. Occasionally, Medeski Martin & Wood and John Scofield (b. 1951), jazz artists who also court the jam-band crowd, make similar excursions. Jazzmen James 'Blood' Ulmer (b. 1941) and Olu Dara took a deeper trip at the end of the 1990s. Ulmer, a six-string expressionist, began collaborating with Vernon Reid, the guitarist in Living Coloür – who is one of the few modern heavy-metal musicians whose playing incorporates blues – while Dara traded cornet for guitar. Both began exploring blues and their native Mississippi roots, without relinquishing their improvisational impulses, in acclaimed albums that have won broad acceptance in Europe.

Out on the very horizon of the music, a few dedicated experimenters are pushing blues further into the digital age while still honouring its deepest traditions. Foremost among them may be Elliott Sharp (b. 1951), who spent years at the front of avant-garde rock. He was a key figure in the downtown Manhattan art-music scene before returning to blues in the early 1990s with his group Terraplane – as well as a laptop computer, deft programming skills and a tonal sensibility that can transform his slide guitar at will into an Arabic musette or a trumpeting elephant.

All of these artists and many others guarantee that the future of the blues will be musically bright. However, whether the style will again enjoy the kind of prominence, economic success and wide appeal that it did in the 1930s, 1960s and, briefly, the 1980s, remains to be seen.

Popular Melody

Chris Thomas King – 'Tha Real' (2002)
Rumbling from the sonic percolations of electronica to a heavy, programmed kick-and-snare-drum beat and slide guitar, this is a gripping example of the new school of potent blues–hip hop fusion. The song's rapped lyrics also define 'the blues' as a part of the emotional landscape of urban struggle, more than simply an idiom from the past, without compromising modernity or tradition.

A-Z of artists

Lurrie Bell
(Guitar, vocals, b. 1958)

Bell grew up among Chicago legends, including his harmonica-playing father Carey Bell. The self-taught guitarist was 17 when he joined Willie Dixon's band and 19 when he toured with Koko Taylor. He had already built a reputation for wiry, envelope-pushing improvisations when he formed Sons of Blues with Billy Branch in the mid-1970s. He has since recorded several solo albums, including 1995's superb *Mercurial Son*, but his career has been interrupted periodically by homelessness and health issues.

Below

Blues harpist Billy Branch (right), with guitarist Kenny Neal.

Eric Bibb
(Guitar, vocals, b. 1951)

Folk-bluesman Bibb blends deep roots with pop influences, occasionally incorporating African and Afro-Cuban sounds. He resides in Sweden but was born in New York City, where his father, Leon, performed in musical theatre and on the folk scene. His uncle was John Lewis of the Modern Jazz Quartet, while Odetta, Pete Seeger and Paul Robeson

Far Right

Blues singer Shemekia Copeland is the daughter of Texas bluesman Johnny 'Clyde' Copeland.

were among his family's friends. Bibb's finest album to date, 2004's *Friends*, features Odetta, Guy Davis, Martin Simpson, Harry Manx and his role model Taj Mahal.

Elvin Bishop
(Guitar, vocals, b. 1942)

This Tulsa, Oklahoma native's return to his roots as a blues player has been characterized by barnstorming live sets and albums for the Alligator label in the Chicago electric tradition, at times approximating the sound of Elmore James's bands. Bishop, who became a charter member of the Paul Butterfield Blues Band while attending college in Chicago in the 1960s, stopped making music for nearly a decade following his Elvin Bishop Group's US number-three pop hit 'Fooled Around And Fell In Love' in 1976. Today he resides in San Francisco.

Billy Branch
(Harmonica, vocals, b. 1951)

Branch began playing harmonica at the age of 10, before polishing his onstage technique in Chicago with Big Walter, James Cotton, Junior Wells and Carey Bell. In 1975 he became a sideman for Willie Dixon and then formed Sons of Blues with Lurrie Bell (guitar). Branch continues to front the band and is a respected blues educator. He also appears in the Robert Mugge-directed concert film *Hellhounds On My Trail: The Afterlife Of Robert Johnson* (1999) and has made cameo appearances in the Hollywood movies *Adventures In Babysitting* (1987) and *Next Of Kin* (1989).

R.L. Burnside
(Guitar, vocals, b. 1926)

Sharecropper Rural 'R.L.' Burnside was inspired to learn guitar by his north Mississippi neighbours Fred McDowell and Ranie Burnette, as well as John Lee Hooker records. He first recorded in the 1960s, but his career ignited after he appeared in the documentary *Deep Blues* (1991) and released *Too Bad Jim* (1994) on Fat Possum, a label based in

whose albums include a disc featuring blues shouter Nappy Brown. Ellis blends the dynamic technique of B.B. King, Freddie King, Albert King, Otis Rush and Magic Sam with the Cream-era pyrotechnics of Eric Clapton. His evolution as a songwriter and musical pluralist, incorporating elements of funk and soul, is captured best on 2000's *Kingpin*.

Left
R.L. Burnside remained relatively unknown until the 1991 documentary Deep Blues.

Burnside's birthplace of Oxford, Mississippi. Along with Junior Kimbrough, this potent rhythm and slide guitarist and singer was responsible for the 1990s juke-blues revival.

John Campbell
(Guitar, vocals, 1952–93)
Campbell, who was born in Louisiana and grew up in Texas, combined the traditional approach of Lightnin' Hopkins with his own swampy, electrified New Orleans hoodoo spiritualism. His debut, the Ronnie Earl-produced *A Man & His Blues* (1988), is a superb summation of his acoustic roots, but its two electric follow-ups, *One Believer* (1991) and *Howlin' Mercy* (1993), which introduced rock flourishes, had him poised for a commercial breakthrough when his heart failed.

Shemekia Copeland
(Vocals, b. 1979)
This Harlem-born daughter of Texas bluesman Johnny 'Clyde' Copeland apprenticed onstage with her father. She emerged as a solo artist in 1997, beginning a run of albums that made her one of the most popular artists in contemporary blues. Nevertheless, it wasn't until 2002's Dr John-produced *Talking To Strangers* that the quality of Copeland's songs matched that of her powerful shouter's voice and live charisma.

Tinsley Ellis
(Guitar, vocals, b. 1957)
Blues rocker Ellis grew up in Florida and emerged in the 1980s from Atlanta, Georgia, where he led the Heartfixers,

Corey Harris
(Guitar, vocals, b. 1969)

Harris was discovered on the streets of New Orleans playing acoustic blues. Soon after his debut, 1995's *Between Midnight And Day*, the Denver, Colorado native began incorporating rock, Afro-Cuban, Afro-Caribbean and African influences into his repertoire, creating a distinctive fusion. The electric *Greens From The Garden* (1999) and *Mississippi To Mali* (2004), a collaboration with musicians from Mississippi and Africa, tied to his appearance in a similarly titled 2003 Martin Scorsese documentary, capture his soulful versatility.

Michael Hill
(Guitar, vocals, b. 1952)

Michael Hill's Blues Mob earned an international cult following with a gritty, aggressive, expansive style well-tailored to Hill's lyrics, which often focus on urban social issues. Born in the south Bronx into a family with roots in North Carolina and Georgia, Hill began playing blues after hearing Jimi Hendrix and Cream. He worked in cover bands and as a sideman before he started making original music in 1987. In 1993 he formed Blues Mob and recorded *Bloodlines*, the first of five strong albums that fuse his rock-fuelled instincts with pop, African and Caribbean flourishes.

Junior Kimbrough
(Guitar, vocals, 1931–98)

Along with Fat Possum labelmate R.L. Burnside, David 'Junior' Kimbrough, from Holly Springs, Mississippi was a leader of the 1990s juke-blues revival and had also played a part in creating the 'Sun sound' by influencing early rockers in the 1950s, including Charlie Feathers. Kimbrough's approach was rooted in traditional African drum groups and he functioned much like a drum master, establishing the band's rhythms on his guitar. His later recordings include *All Night Long* (1993), the first Fat Possum Records release, and he appeared in the documentary *Deep Blues* (1991).

Chris Thomas King
(Guitar, bass, keyboards, drums, vocals, b. 1964)

Multi-talented King began in the footsteps of his father – Baton Rouge, Louisiana juke bluesman Tabby Thomas. King has mastered traditional electric and acoustic blues. He also performs and records rock- and rap-blues hybrids. In 2000 he appeared as Tommy Johnson in *O Brother, Where Art Thou?*. He also played Lowell Fulson in the Ray Charles biopic *Ray* (2004) and Blind Willie Johnson in *The Soul Of A Man*, the Wim Wenders-directed episode of *Martin Scorsese Presents: The Blues*. In 2002 Chris Thomas King established his own New Orleans-based label, 21st Century Blues.

The Kinsey Report
(Vocal/instrumental group, 1984–present)

Gary, Indiana's Kinsey brothers formed the Kinsey Report to support their father, Lester 'Big Daddy' Kinsey. In 1985 they recorded *Bad Situation* as Big Daddy Kinsey & the Kinsey Report. Led by Donald (guitar, vocals), who had been a sideman for Albert King and Bob Marley, the brothers signed with Alligator Records and released *Edge Of The City*, the first of three snarling, blues-rock Kinsey Report albums, in 1987. Big Daddy Kinsey went on to make fine solo recordings, including 1993's *I Am The Blues*, until his death from cancer in 2001.

Below

Blues-rock group the Kinsey Report, pictured in London during a 1993 UK tour.

to blues, he travelled to the Mississippi Delta to study with the late guitarist Eugene Powell. Moore then combined blues with pop hooks and instrumental sweetening, and has released eight easy-listening, semi-acoustic albums, including his eponymous 1994 debut and the 1996 Best Contemporary Blues Grammy-winner *Just Like You*.

John Mooney
(Guitar, vocals, b. 1955)
Born in East Orange, New Jersey, Mooney grew up in Rochester, New York, where he joined Joe Beard's group at 15 and studied slide with Delta giant Son House. In 1976 he moved to New Orleans, where he began to concoct an electric style that blended Crescent City funk rhythms with traditional blues, gelling on his 2000 album *Gone To Hell*. Today Mooney performs and records both with his upbeat band and as a solo acoustic artist.

Left
Harmonica virtuoso Paul Lamb, who tours extensively with his band the King Snakes.

Below
Keb' Mo's accessible, poppy blues style has ensured him several successful albums.

Paul Lamb & The King Snakes
(Vocal/instrumental group, 1989–present)
English harmonica virtuoso Lamb (b. 1955) initially learned to play from recordings, but was mentored by Sonny Terry after they met at the World Harmonica Championships when Lamb was 15. He performed with other blues legends, including Buddy Guy and Junior Wells, before forming the five-piece Paul Lamb & the Kingsnakes in 1989. They released the first of their nine albums in 1990 and play nearly 300 dates annually, faithfully recreating the sound of late 1950s Chicago blues.

Keb' Mo'
(Guitar, vocals, b. 1951)
Songwriter Kevin Moore spent the 1970s and 1980s in his native Los Angeles, playing studio sessions and in mainstream funk and blues bands. Committing himself

Above

The Neville Brothers worked as the house band for Allen Toussaint before going their own way in the 1970s.

Neville Brothers

(Vocal/instrumental group, 1977–present)

The Neville Brothers – Art (keyboards, vocals), Aaron (percussion, vocals), Charles (saxophone, vocals) and Cyril (percussion, vocals) – have been one of New Orleans' foremost musical families since 1954. Art led Allen Toussaint's house band (the Meters) from the late 1960s, before convening his brothers into a unit in 1976. They released the successful *Fiyo On The Bayou* in 1981 and since then have made consistently good albums including *Yellow Moon* (1989), produced by Daniel Lanois. Their album *Walkin' In The Shadow Of Life* (2004) focuses on family ties, cultural heritage and spiritual identity.

Lucky Peterson

(Keyboards, guitar, bass, drums, trumpet, vocals, b. 1963)

Born Judge Kenneth Peterson in Buffalo, New York, this child prodigy keyboardist had played on *The Ed Sullivan Show* by the age of six. His father is soul bluesman James Peterson. At 17, Lucky became Little Milton's bandleader and then played with Bobby Bland. In 1988 he focused on guitar and began a solo career that has

become increasingly experimental, culminating in the racial themes and heavy rock and funk of 2003's visceral *Black Midnight Sun*, produced by Bill Laswell.

Right

Paul Rishell and Annie Raines, who play traditional blues to great critical acclaim.

Paul Rishell & Annie Raines
(Vocal duo, 1993–present)

This Cambridge, Massachusetts-based duo embrace vintage music styles with absolute authenticity. Brooklyn-born Rishell (b. 1950, vocals, guitar) discovered traditional blues in the 1960s and played with Son House and Johnny Shines. He began leading bands and performing solo in 1975, releasing his debut *Blues On Holiday* in 1990. He then met Raines (b. 1969, harmonica, mandolin, vocals), whose influences included Little Walter and Sonny Boy Williamson I. Their first recording together was 1996's *I Want You To Know*, while *Moving To The Country* (2000) won a W.C. Handy Award for Acoustic Blues Album of the Year.

Duke Robillard
(Guitar, vocals, b. 1948)

Robillard's grasp of blues and jazz has kept him in demand since he founded Roomful of Blues in 1967. He was born in Woonsocket, Rhode Island and was influenced by Bill Doggett, T-Bone Walker and many others, absorbing the fine details of playing and arranging. He left Roomful in 1979 for a stint with rockabilly singer Robert Gordon and then ignited his solo career, which he interrupted briefly in 1990 to replace Jimmie Vaughan in the Fabulous Thunderbirds. In the late 1990s he began producing albums for Ruth Brown, Jay McShann, Eddy Clearwater and others.

Mighty Mo Rodgers
(Keyboards, vocals, b. 1942)

Maurice Rodgers grew up sneaking into chitlin circuit clubs in his native Chicago and nearby Gary, Indiana. His distinctive songwriting combines funky arrangements with explorations of the metaphysics of the blues, notably on his 1999 debut *Blues Is My Wailin' Wall*. He began performing in the mid-1960s in Los Angeles with T-Bone Walker, Albert Collins and others; his sound is influenced by the Memphis Stax stable of stars.

Bobby Rush
(Guitar, bass, harmonica, b. 1940)

Rush's mix of vaudeville stage antics and soul-blues grooves has made him the king of the modern chitlin circuit. Born in Homer, Louisiana, Rush moved with his family to Chicago in 1953, already mesmerized by

Muddy Waters and Louis Jordan. He emerged from the West Side blues scene in the 1960s and his career took off with 1971's 'Chicken Heads', after which he spent the next two decades touring and recording. Increasing press coverage and a starring role in an episode of 2003's *Martin Scorsese Presents: The Blues* series have introduced him to a wider audience.

Saffire – The Uppity Blues Women
(Vocal/instrumental group, 1984–present)

Formed in Virginia by virtuoso Ann Rabson (piano, guitar, vocals) and her guitar student Gaye Adegbalola, Saffire burst out internationally in 1990 with the release of their eponymous debut. Andra Faye replaced original bassist Earlene Lewis in 1992. The band has a knack for framing contemporary songs with twists of novelty humour, written from a feminist perspective in traditional acoustic settings reminiscent of Bessie Smith and Ma Rainey. Rabson and Adegbalola also have solo careers.

Below
Mighty Mo Rodgers is a gifted songwriter who has absorbed both blues and soul influences.

Elliott Sharp
(Guitar, bass, reeds, programming, vocals, b. 1951)
Cleveland, Ohio-born Sharp is on the cutting edge, combining his experience as an improviser – he was a cornerstone of Manhattan's 1980s downtown, avant-garde music scene – with deep tradition. Sharp's earliest gigs were with blues bands. After 20 years of sophisticated experimentation with other forms, he formed his own blues band, Terraplane, in 1994. Sharp's playing pushes the envelope of blues tonality and incorporates digital programming and other unconventional elements. It is best heard on 2004's *Do The Don't*, which features guest guitarist Hubert Sumlin.

Below

Howlin' Wolf's erstwhile guitarist Hubert Sumlin plays a gig at London's Borderline club in 2000.

Kim Simmonds
(Guitar, harmonica, piano, vocals, b. 1947)
Simmonds emerged as the leader of early British blues-rock band Savoy Brown in 1965. Although the Welsh-born guitarist's group grew louder and heavier into the 1970s, he never lost his interest in the acoustic country blues that had sparked his playing. Savoy Brown soldiers on, but in 1997 Simmonds began a parallel solo career with the all-acoustic *Solitaire*, and continues to perform and record in that vein.

Angela Strehli
(Vocals, b. 1945)
This raw-edged songstress emerged from the same Austin, Texas scene that yielded Stevie Ray Vaughan, with her 1986 debut *Stranger Blues*. Strehli, who was born in Lubbock, perfected her slow phrasing and dynamic attack at the famed Antone's nightclub, learning from visiting artists Muddy Waters, Otis Rush, Albert Collins and Albert King. She helped to start the influential Antone's record label. In recent years Strehli has incorporated more 1940s and 1950s R&B influences into her music.

Hubert Sumlin
(Guitar, vocals, b. 1931)
Sumlin's distinctive riffs are all over Howlin' Wolf's classic Chess recordings; Wolf plucked the Greenwood, Mississippi innovator from a band he had started with James Cotton, and Sumlin became an integral part of Wolf's sound. After Wolf's death in 1976, Sumlin joined saxophonist Eddie Shaw in his Wolf Gang band and ventured out on his own in 1980, but excessive drinking kept his performances and albums patchy. However, Sumlin sobered up in the late 1990s and has since recorded several successful solo albums, including 2005's brilliant *About Them Shoes*.

Otis Taylor
(Guitar, banjo, mandolin, harmonica, vocals, b. 1948)
Colorado's Otis Taylor is the most inventive blues songwriter to emerge in recent decades. The Chicago native revives the genre's role as protest music, often telling stories of lynchings, racial injustice and homelessness. His use of archaic Appalachian banjo tunings, droning progressions and digital delay creates a sound that reflects the blues' African roots and echoes 1960s psychedelia. It is a wise, timeless combination, best

captured on his potent albums *Respect The Dead* (2002) and *Truth Is Not Fiction* (2003).

Susan Tedeschi
(Guitar, vocals, b. 1970)

Tedeschi was introduced to blues and gospel via her parents' record collection. While singing in the Berklee College of Music gospel choir, she performed at blues jams around her native Boston and formed her own group. Her international debut, 1998's *Just Won't Burn*, was mostly blues rock with hints of emotionalism; it earned her a Grammy nomination and sold 700,000 copies. She seemed poised for a crossover career until the follow-up, 2002's far superior, soul-steeped *Wait For Me*, failed to generate much attention outside blues circles.

Ali Farka Toure
(Guitar, gurkel, n'jarka, vocals, b. 1939)

Toure based his distinctive style on the music of his native Mali and on American blues and R&B – in particular John Lee Hooker, whose simple yet inimitable hypnotic drones are echoed in Toure's songs. Five earlier albums had made Toure a cult favourite when his 1994 Grammy-winning

collaboration with slide guitarist Ry Cooder, *Talking Timbuktu*, elevated him to *éminence grise* of the world music scene. He is now semi-retired from music, devoted to improving his village, Niafunke, near Timbuktu.

Walter Trout
(Guitar, vocals, b. 1951)

In a BBC radio poll, blues rocker Trout was ranked number six among the top 20 guitarists of all time. Not bad for an Ocean City, New Jersey native who worked for decades as a sideman with John Lee Hooker, Big Mama Thornton, Canned Heat and John Mayall before forming his own band in 1990. Since then he has recorded a dozen albums, heavy on guitar, and earned an international reputation for his fiery live performances.

Left
Susan Tedeschi, whose 1998 album Just Won't Burn *earned her a Grammy nomination.*

Below
Mali musician Ali Farka Toure found widespread fame following a 1994 collaboration with guitarist Ry Cooder.

john lee hooker ⊙138   howlin' wolf ⊙188   ry cooder ⊙265   stevie ray vaughan ⊙288

Jazz

In the first decade of the twenty-first century, musical culture is blown every which way and some feel that jazz bears the brunt of the storm. The increased corporate consolidation of the media means that celebrity vocalists mouthing formulaic pop songs rule the airwaves, while vapid, mid-tempo fantasies dominate commercial, 'lite' jazz, also known as instrumental pop. Record companies race to catch up with the changes in how music is captured, heard and sold; they recycle hit songs from eons ago, re-arranged for the latest or the longest-surviving of vocalists, and repackage classic albums with newly added attractions or in new formats, rarely channelling the funds into new artists.

'I've always seen music as interconnected with everything. I feel musicians can ... accomplish certain things that maybe even governments and industries can't accomplish.'

Jack DeJohnette

A Dwindling Audience

At its inception, commercial radio was highly diversified and characterized by local programming; it was perfect for exposing short recordings by regionally known artists to a larger audience. It has since become centrally owned and operated, promulgating a limited playlist. Jazz seldom, if ever, makes that list. Only non-commercial, government-supported 'public radio' in the US and Britain, and the newly burgeoning satellite radio systems (sold to subscribers in a similar way to cable TV networks), seek to serve niche markets, of which the audience for jazz is one. A couple of generations ago, adults on a given night might have danced to a swing band in a ballroom or relaxed at a nightclub; today, their grandchildren are transfixed by home entertainments, watching music videos or downloading favourite songs, often for free. So far, jazz has not proved very telegenic, nor has the downloading of jazz music via the Internet proved particularly popular or profitable.

With each death of a jazz veteran – from the demise of the still-provocative Miles Davis (1926–91) through the close of the Swing Era with the passings of the indefatigable Lionel Hampton (1908–2004) and the scornful, long-retired Artie Shaw (1910–2004) – direct links of jazz to its prior golden ages are lost. At every turn, economic factors and new trends threaten not only the maintenance, but the very growth and development of jazz.

A Global Phenomenon

And yet simultaneously, jazz education at high school and college levels, as well as in prestigious conservatories, has never enjoyed higher enrolment. Jazz has been embraced by musicians and audiences around the globe, with the European Union, West and South Africa, the Caribbean, South America, Russia and the Far East advancing gifted musicians (to name a few: the Scandanavian trio EST; French gypsy guitarist Birelli Lagrene, b. 1966; Cameroonian singer-songwriter-bassist Richard Bona; South African keyboardist Paul Hamner; Mexican drummer Antonio Sanchez; Cuban expatriates trumpeter Arturo Sandoval; reedist Paquito D'Rivera, b. 1948 and pianist Gonzalo Rubalcaba, b. 1963, Brazilian Trio da Paz,

Below

French gypsy guitarist Birelli Lagrene is one of the many bringing new flavours to jazz music.

Above
The New Orleans Jazz & Heritage Festival – proof that the jazz spirit lives on in the city where the music was born.

Japanese pianists Hiromi and Satoko Fujii, and Australian minimalist combo the Necks), as well as stalwart support networks (Jazz Institute of Chicago, San Francisco Jazz, New Orleans Jazz & Heritage Foundation, Monterey Jazz Festival, Earshot Jazz, Northsea Jazz Festival, Umbria Jazz Festival, etc.), which comprise entrepreneurs and semi-professionals alike.

Jazz Raises Its Profile

In autumn 2004 Wynton Marsalis (b. 1961) presided over the opening of the first major performance facility ever designed specifically for jazz. Rose Hall, home of Jazz@Lincoln Center, the world's leading multi-purpose jazz institution, offers three venues (Manhattan nightclub, Greek theatre, Italian opera house), classrooms, rehearsal space, an art gallery and production facilities in a glamorous site in New York City, with an ambitious calendar of staged shows, big band concerts and combo bookings. Jazz – and Wynton himself – was celebrated in a 19-hour series by video documentarian Ken Burns; biographers are publishing volumes on figures as disparate as Django Reinhardt (1910–53) and Wayne Shorter (b. 1933), and jazz's rich, associative legacy has been tapped for literary purposes by the likes of Toni Morrison, Roddy Doyle, Geoff Dyer and Edgardo Vega Yunqué, and in films by Robert Altman, Clint Eastwood, Taylor Hackford and Spike Lee.

Popular Melody

Wayne Shorter – 'Aung San Suu Kyi' (1997)
Honouring the Burmese human-rights activist who was awarded the 1991 Nobel Peace Prize, this track is like a fragment of ancient grandeur that has survived historical onslaught to inspire humanity's efforts in behalf of its highest ideals. Introduced by Shorter on soprano saxophone in duet with pianist Herbie Hancock on 1 + 1, it has generated more expansive, elaborate improvisations.

Neo-conservatives such as the Marsalis brothers canonize the very greatest names of the jazz past, although with selectivity: Duke Ellington (1899–1974) and Count Basie (1904–84), yes; Glenn Miller (1904–44) and Stan Kenton (1912–79), no. Many working musicians pay homage to jazz repertoire by launching outright tribute projects (such as pianist Michael Wolff's Children on the Corner) or by stylistically emulating their heroes, such as alto saxophonist Vincent Herring taking off from Cannonball Adderley (1928–75), and trumpeter Nicholas Payton from Louis Armstrong (1901–71). Direct 'quotes' of historic jazz also proliferate, due to hip hop's rage for digital samples. Turntable artists recycle licks of soul jazz artists of the 1950s and 1960s to make new hits from scraps of the old. British production duo US3 has scored notably, looping the vamp of 'Cantaloupe Island', pianist Herbie Hancock's (b. 1940) Blue Note boogaloo of 1964.

A Brighter Future?

The bland noodlings of soprano saxophonist Kenny G (b. 1959) remain the bestselling recordings by an instrumentalist of all time. The quasi 'chamber jazz' of pianist Bob James's Fourplay, the fleet, light fingerings of fusion-focused guitarists Lee Ritenour and Larry Carlton, the California glitz of put-together studio ensembles such as the Rippingtons, the innocuous effusions of Canadian singer-pianist Diana Krall (b. 1964) and the youthful moxie of British pianist-singer Jamie Cullum all top jazz CD sales lists. However, with purer forms of jazz struggling in the

The Meaning Of 'Jazz' Today

Is jazz a thriving art or a fading pastime? That's a troubling question facing those who love the music, which exhibits both tendencies. Is jazz, in 2005, still fundamentally the realm of black Americans (who are now exploring the much higher profile and higher profit pop-music genres of rap, hip hop and revived old-school soul)? Or does jazz belong to a worldwide elite whose members add their own accents to jazz's trademark themes, rhythms, strategies and variations?

The jazz industries – businesses involved with recording, performing, promoting and marketing the music – can accurately be described as threatened, but jazz itself, the art of a functional culture, may be securing itself through consolidation. Virtuosic saxophonists such as Bobby Watson and Kenny Garrett, steeped in hard swing and deep blues, and sophisticated pianists such as Mulgrew Miller and Bill Charlap (b. 1966) define the young to middle-aged mainstream.

reedsmen Charles Gayle and Roscoe Mitchell and saxophonist-composer John Zorn (b. 1953) continue to test the bounds of their instruments and poke at the lines between structured or spontaneous improvisation. Vocalists including Siberian throat singer Sainkho Namchylak, Czech Iva Bittova, Brooklyn-born Shelly Hirsch and New Jersey's Lisa Sokolow explore the flexiblities of language, while Lawrence Douglas 'Butch' Morris, William Parker (b. 1952) and Walter Thompson conduct large ensembles through instant, scoreless compositions. Folkloric elements from Spain and Latin American settlements in the Western Hemisphere have been embraced as basic to jazz – in the words of Jelly Roll Morton (1890–1941), 'the Spanish tinge' – so Panamanian-born pianist Danilo Perez, Dominican pianist Michel Camilo and Nuyorican trumpeter-conguero Jerry Gonzalez with his *piratas del flamenco* attain full measures of respect and influence.

Jazz continues to mirror contemporary society as does no other art form. Culture is fragmented; so is jazz. Communications are global, and jazz is a worldwide phenomenon. Values everywhere are in dispute; jazz has its internal debates, feuds and competitions. The best news is that the music hasn't been fixed, even for the most comprehensive encyclopedia, or frozen for museum display. Fertile, free of untoward constraints and fighting as always for self-definition, jazz lives!

Left
Musicians such as saxophonist and composer John Zorn continue to question the limits of jazz.

Far Left
Wynton Marsalis at the opening procession for the Rose Hall jazz venue at New York's Lincoln Center.

US but thriving abroad, audiences have been more willing to lend an ear to far-flung ensembles. The Ganelin Trio, darlings of the 1980s Russian avant-garde, have reconvened sporadically since the fall of the Soviet Union, despite the pianist-leader's emigration to Israel. Pierre Dorge's New Jungle Orchestra of Denmark has gained renown, as Denmark has become famous for bestowing the world's most prestigious and remunerative jazz honour, the annual JazzPar Award.

The Effects Of Other Cultures

Individuality, originality and iconoclasm still exist, launched from platforms in jazz. Experimentalists such as British guitarist Derek Bailey (b. 1932) and tenor and soprano saxophonist Evan Parker (b. 1944), American

Popular Melody

'Last Train To Clarksville' – Cassandra Wilson (1996)
There was no predicting that a bubbly novelty number first recorded by the Monkees would reappear in 1996, reinterpreted by sultry, smoky-voiced Cassandra Wilson as a song of adult passion come, gone or awaited. But as heard on New Moon Daughter, this song embodies the baby-boomer generation's nostalgia for times past and realization of where we are now.

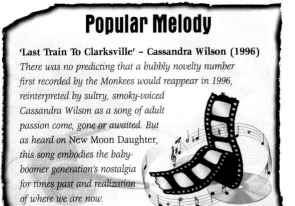

A-Z of artists

Geri Allen
(Piano, b. 1957)

Raised in Detroit, pianist-composer Allen emerged in New York City with older midwestern avant-gardists such as Lester Bowie and Oliver Lake, and hometown colleagues including saxophonist Kenny Garrett. Her albums feature elusive but lyrical compositions for small ensembles. She toured briefly and recorded *Feel The Fire* (1993) with singer Betty Carter, and has worked with her husband, trumpeter Wallace Roney. Allen performed as Mary Lou Williams in Robert Altman's film *Kansas City* (1996).

Below

Trumpeter Steven Bernstein has played in various experimental jazz ensembles.

Fred Anderson Jr.
(Tenor saxophone, b. 1929)

Admired by post-1960s Chicago improvisers as a founding member of the Association for the Advancement of Creative Musicians, tenor saxophonist Fred Anderson's reputation spread after his first trip to Europe in 1977, but he was very sparsely recorded until the 1990s. Since then his huge tone and gutsy, freely associative statements have been captured on numerous albums, and his music club, the Velvet Lounge, has become an internationally renowned venue.

Derek Bailey
(Guitar, b. 1932)

The British guitarist is uncompromisingly, spontaneously cerebral, exploring atonal, anti-melodic, arhythmic yet associative 'sound', abjuring musical conventions. Yet his solos and collaborations with master improvisers of jazz and beyond are compelling. The author of *Improvisation: Its Nature And Practice In Music* (1993), Bailey considers traditions from Africa and India as well as the West. In the early 1990s he produced the television series *On The Edge* for Britain's Channel 4.

Steven Bernstein
(Trumpet, composer, arranger, b. 1961)

A member of several populist-experimental-fun jazz bands since the late 1980s (including Hieroglyphics Ensemble, Kamakazi Ground Crew, Lounge Lizards, Spanish Fly, Sex Mob and the Millennial Territory Orchestra), Bernstein continues to perform on slide trumpet (or soprano trombone), cornet and other standard brass instruments, and to compose and arrange film soundtracks. His projects include adaptations of Jewish folk and liturgical themes with Cuban mambo and New Orleans R&B rhythms.

Dee Dee Bridgewater
(Vocals, b. 1950)

First heard in the 1970s with the Thad Jones-Mel Lewis Orchestra, then in the Broadway musicals *The Wiz* and *Sophisticated Ladies* and later in pop/jazz contexts, Bridgewater relocated to Paris in 1983. Leading a trio, she regained career momentum in the 1990s with tribute projects commemorating Billie Holiday, Horace Silver and Ella Fitzgerald, and has also performed hard-swinging, scat-laden performances of jazz-related standards.

Uri Caine
(Piano, b. 1956)

Born in Philadelphia, Caine pursued classical studies and performances with locally based jazz stars (Philly Joe Jones, Grover Washington Jr.) prior to moving to New York in the late 1980s and commencing an international career. He has productive associations with clarinettist Don Byron and trumpeter Dave Douglas, among others, and his output ranges from mainstream and electric piano trios to neo-klezmer, to post-modern revisions of works by Mahler, Wagner and Bach, and a concept album depicting early-twentieth-century Tin Pan Alley.

James Carter
(Various saxophones, b. 1969)

A musical prodigy from Detroit's Creative Arts Collective, saxophonist James Carter toured Europe at the age of 16, worked with Wynton Marsalis and starred in Julius Hemphill's saxophone opera *Long Tongues*. Since 1990, his New York ensemble has recorded a variety of 'quiet storm' romantic jazz, Django Reinhardt-style gypsy jazz, hard-core fusion and jazz standards. At the fiftieth anniversary Newport Jazz Festival he upped the stakes by improvising 33 choruses of Duke Ellington's 'Diminuendo And Crescendo In Blue' – topping Paul Gonsalves's 1956 benchmark of 26 choruses.

Regina Carter
(Violin, b. 1966)

Violinist Regina Carter has stabilized her instrument's precarious role in jazz after advanced work in classical, jazz-pop and experimental formats. From childhood Suzuki lessons (a method of teaching music that stresses listening over reading skills), she joined the Detroit-based band Straight Ahead, then the String Trio of New York. She was a featured soloist in Wynton Marsalis's Pulitzer Prize-winning *Blood On The Fields* oratorio (1995) and was the first jazz musician, person of colour or woman to play and record on Paganini's Stradivarius, 'the Cannon'.

Above

The violin has made a comeback on to the jazz scene in the hands of Regina Carter.

Bill Charlap
(Piano, b. 1966)

The son of Broadway composer Moose Charlap and singer Sandy Stewart, Bill Charlap was inducted into professional jazz by Gerry Mulligan and has been critically acclaimed for his deft playing, superb taste and unfailing swing feel. In 2004 he succeeded pianist Dick Hyman as director of the long-established, prestigious jazz series at New York's 92nd Street Y (Young Men's and Young Women's Hebrew Association).

Left

Dee Dee Bridgewater has lent her vocals to jazz groups, Broadway musicals and tribute projects.

gerry mulligan ⊙202   art ensemble of chicago ⊙274   thad jones ⊙280   wynton marsalis ⊙296

Ravi Coltrane
(Tenor and soprano saxophones, b. 1965)

Ravi Coltrane, the son of John and Alice Coltrane, faces problematic expectations to which he has responded with modesty and genuine accomplishment. Raised by his spiritually devout mother, Ravi joined Coltrane drummer Elvin Jones's band in his early 20s. The loosely organized Brooklyn M-Base Collective supported his individuality and, while touched by the influence of his parents, he mines a progressive rather than radical musical style.

Above

Inspired by Wes Montgomery, Bill Frisell (right) is one of the most sought-after jazz guitarists of his generation.

Joey DeFrancesco
(Organ, b. 1971)

The son of jazz organist Papa John DeFrancesco, Joey's keyboard skill and enthusiasm were well-recognized even before 1987, when he was a finalist in the annual Thelonious Monk Competition. Indebted in style to Jimmy Smith, DeFrancesco played with Miles Davis and recorded on Columbia Records prior to his graduation from high school. His prodigious youthful energy has attracted audiences and revitalized an interest in jazz organ.

Dave Douglas
(Trumpet, b. 1963)

Dave Douglas spans musical abstraction and gutsiness in acclaimed albums and a busy, international touring schedule. After attending Berklee School of Music, New England Conservatory and New York University, he studied with classical trumpeter Carmine Caruso and toured with Horace Silver. He has recorded for a variety of

Right

Roy Hargrove plays both ballads and funk tracks in a clean, hard-bop-influenced trumpet style.

small labels, as well as BMG-RCA Victor, and is known for his Tin Hat Trio (jazzing Balkan music) and John Zorn's Sephardic-tinged jazz quartet Masada. In 2005 Douglas introduced his own record label with *Mountain Passages*.

Bill Frisell
(Guitar, b. 1951)

A distinctive electric guitar stylist, Frisell evokes longing and wonder through melodic selectivity, *legato* attack and strategic outbursts. Originally a clarinettist, then inspired by Wes Montgomery, he studied at Boston's Berklee School of Music and with Jim Hall. He recorded for ECM and won fame in the New York noise/improv scene, exploring pastoral Americana imagery in his own projects. Besides playing in Paul Motian's trio with Joe Lovano, Frisell has recorded colouristic accompaniments for rock and pop singers.

Roy Hargrove
(Trumpet, b. 1969)

Encouraged by Wynton Marsalis while in high school in Dallas, Texas, Hargrove has a jauntier approach to trumpet than his mentor. He principally employs hard-bop vocabulary, but has also led the Latin jazz band Crîsol with Cuban pianist Chucho Valdés, recorded with hip hop/soul singer D'Angelo, and co-starred in Herbie Hancock's New Standards quintet with saxophonist Michael Brecker. In his own programmes, Hargrove plays both tender ballads and R&B/funk hits.

Shirley Horn
(Vocals, piano, b. 1934)

Shirley Horn was successful from 1954 through the mid-1960s

in her hometown of Washington, DC. She was promoted by Miles Davis and Quincy Jones and owned a club called the Place Where Louie Dwells, but gradually turned full attention to her family. She returned with records, club dates and concert tours in the mid-1980s, and is admired for her unadorned, expressive ballad singing and self-accompaniment. Horn suffered a diabetic foot amputation in 2004 but continues to perform.

Charlie Hunter
(Guitar, b. 1967)

The leading exponent of briefly trendy 'acid jazz', guitarist Charlie Hunter has learned to emulate the organ-bass runs of his inspiration, Larry Young, on a customized guitar. Raised in Berkeley, California, the son of a guitar repairer, he was a street musician in Europe prior to founding Disposable Heroes of Hiphoprisy in the early 1990s – the first of his series of popular combos, which draw on the R&B, soul, alternative rock and reggae repertoires. His fingerpicking is ingenious and his melodic playing intrigues young audiences.

Vijay Iyer
(Piano, composer, b. 1971)

Raised in Rochester, New York, Vijay Iyer started Suzuki violin lessons at the age of three and taught himself to play piano. He performed professionally while pursuing advanced studies at Yale and the University of California, Berkeley and moved to New York in 1998, having released two albums and toured with saxophonist Steve Coleman. Iyer incorporates socio-political concerns and South Asian musical elements into his cross-genre projects, frequently in collaboration with saxophonist Rudresh Mahanthappa.

Norah Jones
(Vocals, piano, b. 1979)

An overnight sensation, Norah Jones's debut album *Come Away With Me* (2002) won numerous Grammy Awards and its sales revitalized Blue Note Records. Introduced by her mother to Billie Holiday's music, Jones won *Down Beat* Student Music Awards in 1996 and 1997 and studied jazz piano at North Texas State University prior to arriving in New York City in 1999. Her warm voice and intimate delivery lend compelling inflections to pop, folk and country songs in basic arrangements with 'jazz' content from sidemen.

Diana Krall
(Vocals, piano, b. 1964)

From western Canada, Diana Krall attended Berklee School of Music, was encouraged to sing by Los Angeles-based pianist-singer Jimmy Rowles and was mentored by bassist Ray Brown. Her first trios, co-led by guitarist Russell Malone, emulated Nat 'King' Cole's; her accessible stylings led to international festival tours, bestselling recordings and increasingly nuanced vocal shadings. In 2004 Krall married British singer-songwriter Elvis Costello and released her first album of all-original material.

Above

Charlie Hunter is a flexible guitarist and was a key figure in the acid-jazz movement.

Birelli Lagrene
(Guitar, b. 1966)

A French gypsy, Lagrene was hailed as Django Reinhardt's heir upon the release of his first album at the age of 13. He has performed gypsy jazz in the company of swing veterans Benny Carter, Benny Goodman and Stephane Grappelli, but has also developed a personal, fusion-oriented style and mixes both approaches in collaborations with guitarists John McLaughlin, Al Di Meola, Paco de Lucia, Larry Coryell, Philip Catherine, Christian Escoudé and Stanley Jordan, among others.

Abbey Lincoln
(Vocals, composer, b. 1930)

Right

Joe Lovano is one of the most prolific saxophonists on the current jazz scene.

Lincoln caps her long, diversified singing and acting career as an iconic songwriter and performer. Her first record, in the 1950s, was with Benny Carter's orchestra; in the 1960s she recorded politicized material with then-husband Max Roach. In the mid-1980s she re-emerged, paying tribute to Billie Holiday and embodying an African-American feminism. Employing top younger instrumentalists in her bands, she has also become a model for younger vocalists such as Cassandra Wilson, Erika Badhu and Lizz Wright.

Below

Abbey Lincoln has become a mentor for younger musicians and vocalists.

Joe Lovano
(Various saxophones, clarinet, drums, b. 1952)

The son of Cleveland saxophonist Tony 'Big T' Lovano, Joe Lovano attended Berklee School of Music before working in organ groups. He was in Woody Herman's 1970s Thundering Herd and Mel Lewis's Vanguard Jazz Orchestra, freelanced extensively and joined drummer Paul Motian's trio with Bill Frisell in 1990. He has become a leading voice of mainstream modernism, applying himself to diverse contexts. He has collaborated with his vocalist wife, Judi Silvano, various saxophonists and rhythm sections, and composer Gunther Schuller.

Medeski, Martin & Wood
(Instrumental group, 1991–present)

In the 1990s John Medeski (keyboards, b. 1965), Billy Martin (drums, b. 1963) and Chris Wood (bass, b. c. 1969) established an energized form of lengthy improvisations over powerful grooves, playing student venues and festivals. All three members have impressive resumés, including conservatory training and experience with experimental jazz leaders. Their recordings have taken increasing liberties with the basic jam band formula, adding DJs, vocalists, compositional complexity and collage effects.

Arturo O'Farrill
(Piano, orchestra leader, b. 1960)

Arturo O'Farrill is the pianist and music director of the Latin jazz orchestra his father, Cuban-born Chico O'Farrill, organized upon his comeback in the mid-1990s; he has also worked with keyboardist-composer-bandleader Carla Bley, trumpeter Lester Bowie and the Fort Apache Band. Upon Chico's death in 2000, Arturo inherited his bandbook and legacy. In 2003 he was named leader of Jazz@Lincoln Center's Afro-Latin Jazz Orchestra.

Greg Osby

(Alto and soprano saxophones, b. 1960)

After playing in R&B bands in St. Louis, Greg Osby studied at Washington, DC's Howard University, with classmates including pianist Geri Allen. He quit Berklee School of Music to tour with Dizzy Gillespie, then moved to New York City and joined Steve Coleman's M-Base Collective. At first their styles were mirror images, but Osby gradually found a unique voice based on phrase displacements. He has recorded with Cassandra Wilson, older iconoclasts and acoustic groups with new talents such as pianist Jason Moran.

Evan Parker

(Tenor and soprano saxophones, b. 1944)

Bristol-born Evan Parker has been an important experimentalist in the UK and continental Europe for 40 years with the Spontaneous Music Ensemble, Music Improvisation Company, London Jazz Composer's Orchestra, Brotherhood of Breath, Dutch-based ICP and Globe Unity Orchestra. His mastery of circular breathing and alternate fingerings have resulted in inimitable, multi-levelled, atonal improvisations. Live shows by his Electro-Acoustic Ensemble feature interactive electronics.

William Parker

(Bass, b. 1952)

William Parker apprenticed with major bassists in New York City's Jazzmobile programme, studied privately with Jimmy Garrison and Wilber Ware, and performed with Cecil Taylor's group at the age of 21. He has anchored many ensembles, including the David S. Ware Quartet. His prodigious work ethic, instrumental steadiness, dependability and selflessness have made Parker central to activities that culminate annually in a week-long interdisciplinary Vision Festival, produced by his wife, dancer-choreographer Patricia Parker.

Chris Potter

(Various saxophones, b. 1971)

A Chicago native, Chris Potter emerged professionally in bebop trumpeter Red Rodney's combo, before moving on to featured roles in the Mingus Big Band and bassist Dave Holland's quintet and big band. Potter became the youngest musician to win Denmark's prestigious and financially valuable Jazzpar Prize in 2000. Personally self-effacing, Potter is a virtuosic instrumentalist with an adventurous frame of melodic mind, equal to any musical challenge.

Enrico Rava

(Trumpet, b. 1939)

Raised in Turin, Italy and taught piano by his conservatory-graduate mother, Rava began playing traditional jazz on trombone as a teenager but, inspired by Miles Davis, switched to trumpet. He worked with expatriate American jazzmen in Rome and travelled throughout Europe and around South America and New York. Through broad perspective and international experience he has arrived at a distinctive sound, with a melodic style that embraces both conventional and radical gestures.

Below

Chris Wood, from the improvisational jazz-rock combo Medeski, Martin & Wood.

Above
Like his father Dewey, Joshua Redman is a versatile and successful jazz reedsman.

Clark Terry. She sang in Los Angeles studio sessions in the late 1970s and 1980s, and with pop/jazz groups Caldera, Night Flight and Sergio Mendes's troupe. Her albums blend jazz, gospel, African and Brazilian accents with pop-music production. She has recorded a tribute to Sarah Vaughan and in 2002 was appointed Creative Chair for Jazz by the Los Angeles Philharmonic, to curate jazz bookings and educational workshops at the Hollywood Bowl and the Walt Disney Concert Hall.

Gonzalo Rubalcaba
(Piano, keyboards, b. 1963)

A pianist with Romantic sensibilities, Rubalcaba is from a revered musical family and studied at Havana's Amadeo Roldan Conservatory. He led an electric Grupo Proyecto on tours of Europe and Asia in the 1980s, representing triumphs of Castro-era Cuba, but the US denied him entry until 1993. Bassist Charlie Haden sponsored his first Blue Note Records albums and remains an important collaborator, while Rubalcaba has continued to compose lush yet abstract works for trio, quartet and quintet, occasionally employing electronics.

Maria Schneider
(Composer, arranger, bandleader, b. 1960)

Schneider studied several instruments and composition prior to an internship with arranger Gil Evans in New York City in 1985. After further work with Bob Brookmeyer and Mel Lewis, she established a jazz orchestra that performed weekly in Greenwich Village from 1993–98 and recorded three albums. In 2004 she self-produced *Concert In The Garden* and distributed it over the Internet. She has written for orchestras in Paris, Denmark and Stockholm, and for the Pilobolus Dance Theater company.

Joshua Redman
(Tenor and soprano saxophones, b. 1969)

Joshua Redman neé Shedroff grew up in Berkley, California and played reeds throughout high school. He was accepted by Yale Law School, but his victory at the 1991 Thelonious Monk competition persuaded him to take up music professionally. He was quickly accepted by jazz elders, peers and audiences due to his strong, blunt tone, populist taste, articulate manner and voracious style. In 2000 he was appointed artistic director and artist-in-residence of the San Francisco Jazz Festival, and continues to record and tour widely.

Dianne Reeves
(Vocals, b. 1956)

Dianne Reeves's parents were musicians and her cousin, pianist George Duke, encouraged her, as did trumpeter

Matthew Shipp
(Piano, b. 1960)

A prolific recording artist, Shipp considers himself to be a follower of bassist William Parker, with whom he has worked on many projects including the David S. Ware's Quartet. His keyboard style is rhythmically propulsive; he lays dense harmonic accompaniments for single-note instruments. In 1999 he contracted with Thirsty Ear Records to produce his own imprint, Series Bleu, featuring himself with associates including hip hop DJs and punk-rock bands.

Chucho Valdés
(Piano, b. 1941)

Chucho remained in Cuba after his father, pianist Bebo Valdés, defected in the late 1950s. In his mid-20s Chucho established Orquesta Cubana de Musica Moderna, which became the much-recorded, internationally touring jazz showband Irakere; he turned it over to his son in 1998. A large man with huge hands, Valdés is capable of sweeping ballads as well as dazzling fast display. He teaches at Havana's Beny Moré School of Improvised Music and at the Banff Center for the Arts in Canada, and directs the annual Cuban Jazz festival.

Ken Vandermark
(Tenor saxophone, clarinet, b. 1961)

Ken Vandermark studied film before turning to music with a trio in Boston in the mid-1980s. He moved to Chicago in 1989, playing reeds with a flinty, aggressive sound. His investigations of free improvisation won him a five-year MacArthur Foundation 'genius' grant in 1999 and he has used the funding to invest in further recordings and his international career, including membership in saxophonist Peter Brotzmann's high-energy Tentet.

Jeff 'Tain' Watts
(Drums, b. 1960)

Watts played timpani in the Pittsburgh Youth Symphony Orchestra during his teens and vibraphone at Berklee School of Music, where he met the Marsalis brothers. He recorded with Wynton Marsalis from 1981 and then with Branford, following him into the house band of the televised *Tonight Show*. An explosive polyrhythmist who can also provide restrained accompaniment, 'Tain' is much in demand for sessions by many jazz modernists.

Cassandra Wilson
(Vocals, composer, b. 1955)

Raised in Mississippi, smoky contralto Wilson sang R&B and folk music, but emerged in New York City in the early 1980s as a member of

the M-Base Collective and with Henry Threadgill's band. Her breakout album *Blue Skies* (1988) reprised jazz standards and she starred in Wynton Marsalis' oratorio *Blood on the Fields*, but the cornerstone of her mature style is *Blue Light 'Til Dawn* (1993), in which she performs original songs, famous blues and unusual rock/pop choices with interesting arrangements.

Above
Cassandra Wilson's mellow vocals are ideally suited to jazz- and blues-tinged material.

John Zorn
(Alto saxophone, composer, b. 1953)

New Yorker John Zorn deconstructed bebop themes in the late 1970s and created musical games that dictated improvisational structures. He plays assertively in bands such as Masada, purveying electric funk, Japanese pop and punk rock. Zorn has encouraged other renegade musicians by establishing music policies at venues and curating international festivals. As principal of Tzadik Records, he jump-started the avant-garde klezmer and 'Radical Jewish Culture' movements. He remains a prolific composer and has also branched into film soundtracks and chamber music.

Left
Jeff 'Tain' Watts started out playing with the Marsalis brothers and has become one of the foremost drummers of his generation.

instruments & equipment

the instruments used to play blues and jazz have ranged from the jew's harp to the bagpipes, but convention has favoured a fairly set group of brass, reed, string and percussion instruments. While the instruments originated largely in Europe in the early decades, blues and jazz musicians distinguished themselves by emphasizing vocal and rhythmic aspects with roots in African traditions, funnelled through the unique American slave and pre-jazz experiences.

Vocal emulation and rhythmic variation have dominated the evolution of both blues and jazz, whether the music has been played on the bottleneck guitars of the earliest Mississippi Delta bluesmen or on the turntables of contemporary jazz improvisers. Another constant has been innovation; since the earliest years, blues and jazz musicians have demonstrated their ability to push instruments past their traditional limits in search of personal expression. This experimentation encompasses the entire span of the music – from the rips and slurs that marked Louis Armstrong's repertoire of trumpet techniques to Little Walter Jacobs's amplification of the harmonica, and from Cecil Taylor's percussive approach to piano to Bobby McFerrin's use of the human body itself in making music.

Blues musicians and, to a greater extent, jazz musicians have also been responsible for exposing some new or neglected instruments to a wider audience. Examples include the electric guitar and its cousin the electric bass in blues, and the bottom-most members of the saxophone family in avant-garde jazz. Beginning in the 1970s, jazz players also helped to broaden the interest in instruments from other cultures, particularly those from India, Africa and South America.

From washtub bass to djembe drum, and from kazoo to iBook, the language of blues and jazz is spoken in many ways.

Blues

Bass

Early blues bands often utilized large earthenware jugs or an upturned metal washtub, broom handle and baling twine to create a rudimentary bassline. In his role as A&R man and house songwriter for Chess Records, Willie Dixon made the double bass a dominant instrument in Chicago blues. The invention of the electric bass made it a standby for blues combos beginning in the early 1950s.

Drum Kit

Like the bass, drum kits were little used in early blues groups. Rudimentary kits began to appear in the 1930s, and drummers such as Fred Below, Elga Evans and Francis Clay provided propulsive drive and rhythmic accents to the electric-blues movement based in Chicago.

Guitar

Cheap, portable and highly expressive – particularly when played with a glass or metal slide – the guitar was the itinerant bluesman's meal ticket. Many southerners bought their instruments from mail-order catalogues, although some, like Bukka White, preferred metal-bodied resonator guitars manufactured by National, for their volume and sturdiness. The electric guitar gained dominion when blues players moved north and formed bands, with Muddy Waters setting the pace. In the 1950s, T-Bone Walker and B.B. King popularized horn-like *legato* lines that utilized the sustained capability of modern amplification.

Harmonica

Invented by a German clockmaker in 1821, the harmonica – or 'blues harp' – was first mass-produced in the US in 1857. The diatonic harmonica, with reeds that produce the natural notes of a single scale, lends itself well to the bent notes, slurs and other vocal effects of blues. Players like Little Walter Jacobs and Sonny Boy Williamson II (Rice Miller) also used the larger chromatic harmonica, which contains complete 12-note octaves. Amplified, the harmonica offers a wide range of tonal effects.

Organ

Although musicians like Jimmy Smith and Johnny Hammond popularized bluesy jazz playing on the Hammond B-3 and other lesser-known models, the organ is something of a rarity in true blues settings. Robert Hooker and Gregg Allman are notable exceptions.

Piano

Blues songs were a key part of the repertoire for pianists who spanned ragtime and the early jazz era. The canon expanded with the compositions of W.C. Handy, and pianists held a prominent place as accompanists of blues singers such as Bessie Smith in the 1920s. Leroy Carr and Jay McShann were among the first to introduce a more urban style of blues piano, and artists such as Memphis Slim (Peter Chatman) and Big Maceo (Major Merriweather) were major forces on the Chicago blues scene. Otis Spann redefined the role of blues piano as the longtime sideman of Muddy Waters. In New Orleans, players such as Professor Longhair (Henry Roy Byrd) and James Booker were pioneering other styles still.

Saxophone

Although primarily used in ensemble settings in blues, particularly in the jump-blues bands that dominated on the US West Coast, the saxophone did find a few standout solo performers in tenorists J.T. Brown – a frequent sideman with Elmore James – and his protégé A.C. Reed, as well as alto player Eddie 'Cleanhead' Vinson.

Trumpet

While almost every jazz trumpeter has played blues forms, and the trumpet has often been featured in larger blues ensembles, few trumpet soloists have worked in traditional blues settings. One notable exception is Olu Dara, a Mississippi-born New Yorker who also plays guitar and sings.

Jazz

Brass

Cornet: Pitched in B♭, or occasionally in C, the three-valved cornet was invented in 1830 and adapted by New Orleans brass bands later in the century. Manuel Perez is credited by some as the first jazz cornettist, although Buddy Bolden may have in fact preceded him. The dominant brass instrument in jazz until the late 1920s, the cornet has continued to be favoured by some players, including Bobby Bradford and Graham Haynes.

Trumpet: Usually pitched in B♭, the trumpet supplanted the slightly smaller cornet thanks largely to Louis Armstrong's use of the instrument on his revolutionary recordings of 1926–27 and, along with the tenor saxophone, has become jazz's dominant solo instrument. It has been the voice of many of the genre's leading improvisers – including Armstrong, Dizzy Gillespie, Fats Navarro, Clifford Brown, Miles Davis and Freddie Hubbard – and an expressive tool for stylists such as Bubber Miley, Maynard Ferguson and Lester Bowie. Major advancements include King Oliver's use of mutes, Don Ellis's experiments with electronics and extra valves for microtonality, and Davis's popularization of amplification and processing.

Flugelhorn: Pitched in B♭, the flugelhorn (with a bell and bore that are slightly larger than the trumpet's) is favoured as an alternate instrument by many trumpeters for its dark, burnished tone. Joe Bishop introduced the flugelhorn to jazz with Woody Herman's band in 1936, and Miles Davis helped to popularize it on *Miles Ahead* (1957). Chuck Mangione is one of the few musicians to concentrate on flugelhorn alone, but others such as Kenny Wheeler, Art Farmer and Thad Jones have used it extensively.

Trombone: The B♭, tenor slide trombone became the most commonly used in jazz, although some players prefer the B♭/F or B♭/F/E instruments, which have valves to alter the pitch. Various models also have trumpet-like valves or a combination of valves and slide. Capable of a wide range of vocal effects, the trombone was a standby in the early New Orleans bands, where its function was largely rhythmical or as a supporter of the lead instruments, at least until the advent of Jack Teagarden and his virtuoso solo playing. The trombone then went on, in the hands of Joe 'Tricky Sam' Nanton, to become a staple of Duke Ellington's orchestra in the Swing Era. During the bebop revolution, J.J. Johnson introduced a new dexterity and fluidity to the trombone, and avant-gardists such as Albert Mangelsdorff and George Lewis created new techniques to expand the instrument's sound.

Tuba: A carryover from marching bands, this large, valved instrument carried the bassline in early jazz groups. Subsequently supplanted by the double bass, the tuba fell from popularity until being revived by Gil Evans in arrangements for Claude Thornhill and Miles Davis, usually played by Bill Barber for the latter. In the 1980s, Howard Johnson and Bob Stewart brought the tuba back to prominence as a solo instrument.

Keyboards

Clavichord: Developed as early as the fourteenth century, the clavichord features metal tangents that strike the strings from below and stay in contact as long as the keys are depressed. This design allows the player to alter the pitch of notes or produce a narrow *glissando* or controlled vibrato. Oscar Peterson – *Porgy & Bess* (1976) – and Keith Jarrett – *Book Of Ways* (1986) – have used the instrument to good effect.

Electric Piano: Earl Hines recorded on an early version of the electric piano in 1940, but it was not until the late 1950s that artists such as Sun Ra and Joe Zawinul began to incorporate the Wurlitzer electric piano. The invention of the highly portable Fender Rhodes piano in 1965 coincided with the growing interest in tonal variation, and the sound of the instrument dominated the 1970s. Interest waned in the 1980s, but the distinctive sound of the vintage instruments made a comeback in the late 1990s.

Organ: Until 1935, when Hammond created its first electronic organ, the use of the instrument was limited to recordings using church-based pipe organs or theatre organs. Fats Waller recorded extensively on organ in the 1920s and Count Basie included organ on some recordings and live performances in suitably equipped venues. Waller adopted the Hammond organ immediately, taking it on tour in the late 1930s. Glenn Hardman, Wild Bill Davis and Milt Buckner were also early converts, but it was Jimmy Smith who used the electronic organ to change the sound of jazz when he formed his first trio in 1955. The organ-guitar-drums trio became a standby in nightclubs in the 1950s and 1960s. Larry Young adapted the organ for use in free jazz, and latter-day players such as John Medeski and Larry Goldings continued to keep it in the forefront in to the twenty-first century.

Piano: From James P. Johnson to Art Tatum to Bud Powell to Cecil Taylor to Keith Jarrett, the piano has constantly been in the vanguard of change and innovation in jazz. The diversity of other major influential pianists, including Earl Hines, Duke Ellington, Oscar Peterson, Thelonious Monk and Herbie Hancock, shows the range that jazz piano can cover.

Synthesizer: Developed by electronics engineers in the early 1950s, synthesizers cover a very broad range of devices that generate and process sound, from keyboard-triggered systems that emulate strings to touchpad-controlled digital samples of actual sounds. Sun Ra and Paul Bley were early proponents of the synthesizer in jazz, and various versions became a standby during the jazz-rock fusion era. As advances in digital technology occurred, synthesizers became much more flexible. They continue to be used extensively by many players, including Herbie Hancock, Joe Zawinul and Lyle Mays.

Percussion

African, Asian, Indian and Latin Percussion:
One of the major innovations in jazz after the Second World War was the integration of elements of music from other parts of the world, and nowhere was this more evident than in the rhythm section. The rise in interest in Afro-Cuban music that Dizzy Gillespie and Chano Pozo spearheaded in 1947 introduced congas to jazz, and opened the way for a range of Caribbean and Central and South American percussive devices, such as bongos, maracas and the cuica, or Brazilian friction drum. In the 1970s and 1980s some musicians, such as trumpeter Don Cherry, began introducing various ancient African instruments, for example the berimbau and various talking drums. Indian devices like the tabla also gained prominence with bands and musicians, including Oregon and Miles Davis in the 1970s. Drummers have long sought out exotic sounds, for instance Chinese gongs; in the 1980s, this expanded to include instruments such as traditional gamelan gongs from Bali and unusually pitched cymbals and bells from other parts of Asia.

Drum Kit: The drum kit, or trap set (from 'contraption'), evolved to serve the needs of orchestral percussionists during the late-nineteenth century. The main elements – bass (or kick) drum mounted with a foot pedal, snare drum, floor- or rack-mounted tom tom, foot-controlled hi-hat cymbals and assorted other accent cymbals – have not changed beyond advancements in materials. But, from the early years of jazz, drummers have augmented their kits with other percussive devices, including cowbells, wooden blocks and drums of various sizes. Sonny Greer had an extensive kit – featuring timpani, tubular bells and Chinese gongs – when he was in Duke Ellington's orchestra, and in the 1970s jazz-rock drummers added double-bass drums and a wide array of cymbals. Techniques have evolved to encompass hand drumming and the use of chopsticks and multi-pronged wooden sticks. In the 1980s, synthesizers were incorporated into drum kits, allowing the drummer to alter the sound of his instruments or trigger a variety of digitized sounds. Major advances in technique were introduced by Papa Jo Jones, Kenny Clarke, Max Roach, Ed Blackwell, Han Bennink and Gerry Hemingway.

Reeds

Bassoon: The double reed bassoon is relatively rare in jazz. Used as early as 1928 by Frankie Trumbauer in Paul Whiteman's band, it held a very small role until the 1960s, when Yusef Lateef began to incorporate it into his work. More recently, Karen Borca has become a prominent soloist in avant-garde music.

Clarinet: Like saxophones, clarinets cover the musical range from the E♭ sopranino to the B♭ contrabass, but it is the B♭ soprano that is most commonly used by jazz musicians. The clarinet was the dominant woodwind in jazz until it was supplanted by the saxophone in the 1930s; however the instrument remained in the forefront because of its use by high-profile players such as Benny Goodman, Artie Shaw and Buddy DeFranco. Jimmy Giuffre and John Carter used the clarinet in more modern types of improvised music, and Anthony Braxton, Marty Ehrlich and Don Byron have ensured that it remains a highly contemporary instrument.

Bass Clarinet: Among the clarinet family, the B♭ bass version is the other reed to gain prominence in jazz, largely for its warm, woody tonal quality. Eric Dolphy alternated bass clarinet with flute and alto saxophone, and helped to extend the range normally associated with the instrument. Anthony Braxton, David Murray and Marty Ehrlich are other important proponents.

Oboe: This double reed woodwind is rarely used in jazz, although players from Don Redman in the 1920s to Paul McCandless in the 1970s have found effective uses for it.

Sopranino Saxophone: The highest pitched of Adolphe Sax's family of single reed instruments, the sopranino's range is about an octave above the alto saxophone. Little used in jazz until the 1960s, it gained some popularity when avant-gardists Joseph Jarman and Anthony Braxton played it.

Saxello/Manzello: A variant of the B♭ soprano saxophone, the saxello was invented in the 1920s. Forty years later, Rahsaan Roland Kirk modified the horn and renamed it the manzello.

Soprano Saxophone: Manufactured as either a straight or curved horn, the soprano was popularized by Sidney Bechet and used widely as a secondary instrument in the big bands of the 1930s and 1940s. Steve Lacy revived interest in the soprano, but it was John Coltrane who made it a featured solo instrument again with his recording of 'My Favorite Things' (1960).

Alto Saxophone: Popularized by Jimmy Dorsey, Frankie Trumbauer and Johnny

Hodges in the 1920s, the alto was frequently used by big-band arrangers as the lead voice in the saxophone section. In the 1940s, Charlie Parker revolutionized the sound of the alto with his speed, dexterity and harmonic sophistication. Ornette Coleman and Eric Dolphy introduced subsequent innovations on the instrument.

Stritch: A variation of the straight E♭ alto horn, developed by Rahsaan Roland Kirk.

Tenor Saxophone: All things considered, the tenor remains the dominant saxophone voice of jazz. In the hands of Coleman Hawkins, Lester Young, Sonny Rollins, John Coltrane and Joe Lovano – to name a few of the instrument's many outstanding virtuosos through the ages – the tenor has shown itself to be remarkably versatile and expressive.

C-melody Saxophone: Pitched in C, this version of the tenor saxophone was the principal horn used by Frankie Trumbauer in the 1920s, but it faded from use until revived in the 1980s by Bob Wilber and Kenny Davern.

Baritone Saxophone: Used primarily for colour in large ensembles until the 1950s, the baritone was popularized as a solo instrument by Gerry Mulligan and Pepper Adams. Latter-day players Hamiet Bluiett, John Surman and James Carter extended the upper range of the horn by using the technique called 'overblowing'.

Contrabass Saxophone: An octave below the baritone, the contrabass saxophone was little used until Anthony Braxton began to feature it on recordings in the 1970s.

Bass Saxophone: Something of a novelty when played by Adrian Rollini in the 1920s, the largest of the saxophone family continued to be employed by musicians such as Charlie Ventura in the post-war era, often to supplement or replace the double bass. In the 1960s and 1970s, Roscoe Mitchell, Anthony Braxton and Vinny Golia took up the unwieldy instrument – which

stands approximately 5 ft (1.52 m) high – and James Carter featured it on a 2000 tribute to Django Reinhardt.

Strings

Banjo: This five-string fretted instrument was popular in ragtime and fulfilled a rhythm role in early jazz bands. Banjoist Johnny St. Cyr was a prominent member of Louis Armstrong's Hot Five and Hot Seven bands. Briefly revived in the 1940s with the renewed interest in New Orleans jazz, the banjo is now only occasionally used as a textural device by string musicians such as Vernon Reid.

Bass: The double (string, or upright) bass was prominently featured in ragtime and early jazz groups, although frequently as a bowed, rather than plucked, instrument. John Lindsay and Pops Foster were two of the earliest stars of the instrument, introducing various effects such as slapping the strings for percussive effect. Later developments were introduced by Jimmy Blanton with Duke Ellington, Oscar Pettiford and Ray Brown. Charles Mingus, Scott LaFaro and Charlie Haden have been important for their contribution in moving the bass beyond its traditional role in the rhythm section. The introduction of the Fender Precision electric bass in 1951 gave the instrument more tonal variety and volume, but major developments that separated the electric and acoustic instruments did not occur for more than 20 years, when players such as Jaco Pastorius, Stanley Clarke, Steve Swallow and Jamaladeen Tacuma revolutionized the electric bass through advancements in electronics and extended playing and improvisational techniques.

Cello: As the string instrument pitched closest to the human voice, the cello has grown in popularity in improvised music. Bassist Oscar Pettiford used the instrument occasionally in the 1950s, as did Ron Carter in the 1970s. In the later years of the twentieth century artists such as Hank Roberts, Tom Cora, Diedre Murray, David Eyges, Erik

Friedlander and Peggy Lee helped to make the cello a legitimate jazz instrument.

Guitar: Largely a rhythm instrument in the hands of many of jazz's early players, with notable exceptions including Lonnie Johnson, Eddie Lang and Django Reinhardt, the guitar gained prominence when amplification was introduced. Charlie Christian popularized flowing *legato* lines and Wes Montgomery expanded the vocabulary through his expressive use of octaves. From the 1970s onwards, the guitar became one of the genre's dominant instruments, in the hands of players like George Benson, John McLaughlin, Pat Metheny, John Scofield and Bill Frisell.

Violin: Prominent in the society orchestras of New Orleans, the violin was used sparingly in jazz until the late 1920s. Among the early US standouts on the instrument were Joe Venuti, Stuff Smith, Ray Nance and Claude 'Fiddler' Williams, while in Europe Stephane Grappelli played a key role in the Quintet of the Hot Club of France. Players such as Leroy Jenkins and Billy Bang have made important contributions to free jazz, and Ornette Coleman used the violin as a textural device beginning in the early 1960s. The violin's amplification gave it a prominent spot in the jazz-rock fusion movement, with Jean-Luc Ponty, Jerry Goodman and Michal Urbaniak making notable contributions.

Wind

Flute: Despite Wayman Carver's work with Benny Carter and Chick Webb in the 1930s, the flute was a rarity in jazz, more often heard soloing in Latin dance bands, until the 1950s, when Frank Wess (also a talented saxophonist) became a featured soloist in Count Basie's band and several California-based composers began to utilize the instrument. Although several other saxophonists have doubled on flute effectively – particularly Eric Dolphy, Charles Lloyd and Jane Bunnett – it was the specialists, such as like Herbie Mann, Hubert Laws and James Newton, who legitimized the instrument as a solo voice.

Glossary

African-American Also known as Afro-Americans or Black Americans; an ethnic group in the United States of America whose ancestors, usually in predominant part, were indigenous to Sub-Saharan and West Africa.

Arrangement The reworking or recomposing of a musical **composition** or some part of it (such as the **melody**) for a medium or **ensemble** other than that of the original; also the resulting version of the piece.

Ballad Properly, a sentimental love song; also used in reference to any slow piece.

Barrelhouse A bar, originating in the late 1800s, serving liquor straight from the barrel; also, the loud, rough style of piano-playing initially practised in these establishments.

Bebop Style of **jazz** developed in the 1940s and characterized by jagged **rhythms**, asymmetric phrases and fast **tempi**.

Blue note A **note** that is flattened for expressive effect; most commonly the third or seventh degree of the **scale**.

Blues Most commonly, a musical **form** consisting of a repeated 12-bar pattern with standardized **harmony**; also a **melodic** style and a particular mood.

Boogie-woogie Originally a style of dance performed to piano accompaniment; later the style of piano-playing itself, characterized by continuous, repeated patterns in the left hand and **blues harmonies**.

Break A **solo** passage played during a break in the accompaniment, most often occurring at the end of a phrase.

Bridge Generally applied to a passage of music that links two sections of a piece. In **jazz** it often refers to the contrasting middle section of a **tune** (the B section of an AABA **form**, for example).

Burlesque A humorous piece involving parody through exaggeration. In late-nineteenth- and early-twentieth-century America, it referred to a variety show in which the main attraction was striptease.

Cadence A recognizable **harmonic progression** or **melodic** formula occurring at the end of a phrase or piece, which indicates whether the piece is to continue or has concluded. It also establishes the tonality of a section or piece.

Chase A competition between two or more **soloists** playing in turn.

Chord A group of two or more **notes** sounded simultaneously. There are many descriptors that can be attached to 'chord' to indicate the **notes** included, for example 'added sixth chord').

Chorus In **jazz**, one complete cycle of a **tune** or of the harmonies that make up that **tune**. More generally a chorus is the section of a song that is repeated with identical words and **melody** in between verses.

Chromatic Based on an **octave** divided into 12 **semitones**, as opposed to the seven-**note diatonic scale**. Chromatic has its root in the Greek word 'chromatikos' meaning 'coloured'.

Composition The act of creating a piece of music, and the product of that process. In **jazz**, the product is generally referred to as a '**tune**'.

Cool Applied to many styles of **jazz** that focus on simplicity and understated lyricism. Particularly used in reference to musicians in the late 1940s and early 1950s that followed the examples of Miles Davis and Lester Young.

Creole Ill-defined term often referring to descendants of French and Spanish settlers in the southern United States and Louisiana in particular. Used by several early **jazz** bands made up of Creole musicians from **New Orleans**.

Dectet See *Ensemble*

Diatonic Based on an **octave** divided into seven steps of **tones** and **semitones** in various configurations, as opposed to **chromatic**. The major, natural minor **scale**, and Church modes are diatonic. Diatonic **harmony** is, most loosely, that which contains only **notes** from the **scale** on which a piece is based.

Ditty A short, simple song; also a short poem, often humorous in nature.

Dixieland The original **form** of **jazz** as appeared in **New Orleans** in the early 1900s. Also referred to as **New Orleans jazz** and **trad jazz**.

Duo See *Ensemble*

Ensemble From the French meaning 'together'. A group of two or more instrumentalists and/or singers performing together. Various sizes of ensemble have specific names, e.g. duo (2 musicians), trio (3), quartet (4), quintet (5), sextet (6), septet (7), octet (8), nonet (9), dectet (10). In **jazz** the instrumental line-up of an ensemble is not fixed.

Fake book A collection of **tunes** made illegally (hence 'fake'). Most often sold by word of mouth, or belonging to a particular band for use of the members only. Better presented, legal collections were later published as 'real books'.

Folk music A term that has no clear definition but essentially refers to the traditional music of an indigenous population. Generally lacks an identifiable composer, is passed on aurally (i.e. not notated) and is performed by non-professionals.

Form The structure or organization of a piece of music; usually related to recognizable sections of **melody** and/or **harmony**.

Free jazz A style of **jazz** typified by Ornette Coleman and late-era John Coltrane and characterized by a lack of predetermined **harmonic** and **melodic** structures and a focus on both individual and group **improvisation**. Very often high-octane in mood.

Fusion Loosely describes a musical style begun in the 1960s that combined the **harmonic** language and **improvisatory** techniques of **jazz** with the instrumentation and idioms of rock music. Well-known exponents include Wayne Shorter, Herbie Hancock and Chick Corea. The style was originally known as '**jazz** rock'; the term 'fusion' was only applied from the mid-1970s.

Gospel music Religious song deriving from evangelical Protestant groups in the United States, both white and **African-American**, that came to prominence in the early twentieth century. African-American gospel music had a profound impact on **jazz** both musically and spiritually.

Groove A regular, repeated pattern. Also an aesthetic judgement; a piece that is said to 'groove' has an instinctive feeling of 'rightness'.

Harmony The combining of a succession of **chords** to produce a harmonic **progression**. There are systems governing such **progressions** which are help to create recognizable harmonic structures.

Hot jazz Used to describe any **jazz** but particularly early jazz and **swing** that is energetic and vigorous in character.

Improvise To invent with little or no preparation. In **jazz**, improvisation generally takes place over an existing **harmonic** structure and often uses **melodic** shapes and ideas from a set **tune**.

Jam session An informal gathering of **jazz** musicians playing for their own pleasure, free from the constraints of public performance. Jam sessions came to be organized for audiences in the 1930s, thus losing their essence, but in the 1970s the original jam session made a comeback.

Jazz A style of music characterized by **rhythmic syncopation**, repeated **harmonic** structures and **improvisation** that has its roots in performing conventions brought to the United States by **African-Americans**.

Jazz rock See *Fusion*

Jug band An instrumental **ensemble** developed amongst **African-Americans** in the early twentieth century consisting of a variety of homemade instruments, such as kazoos and washboards. The jug of the name was used as a bass instrument.

Key In western tonal music, describes an arrangement of **pitches** and the relationships between them.

Latin Applied to **jazz** in which elements of Latin-American music are conspicuous, particularly dance **rhythms** and percussion instruments such as claves, bongos and cowbells.

Lyrics The words written for a song.

Mainstream Loosely refers to the type of **jazz** using **solos improvised** over a set **harmonic** structure. Specifically coined by Stanley Dance in the 1950s to refer to the **swing** music of the 1930s and 1940s.

Melody An organized group of **pitches**, each sounded subsequently.

Metre Generally, a **rhythmic** pattern of stressed and unstressed sounds. In music it is used as a way of organizing sounds to create a framework in time. Also used to refer to time signature.

Minstrel show An indigenous **form** of American entertainment consisting of comic sketches and songs performed by actors in blackface.

Modern jazz Used to describe collectively the **jazz** styles developed between the 1940s and 1960s.

Mouldy fig Used derisively by practitioners of bebop to describe fans of older styles of **jazz**; one whose tastes are out-of-date.

New Orleans See *Dixieland*

Nonet See *Ensemble*

Notation A means of describing musical sounds visually through symbols representing instructions to the performer.

Note Specifically, the graphical representation of a sound; also used in reference to the sound itself.

Obbligato Refers to an essential line in a **composition** that is not the principal **melody**.

Octave The interval between two **pitches** 12 **semitones** apart. Acoustically these **pitches** are very similar, seeming to differ only in **register**, and as such have played a central role in the development of tonal systems.

Octet See *Ensemble*

Pentatonic Literally, 'five **tones**'. Applied to **scales** constructed of five different **pitches**. Most commonly used for the **scale** C-D-E-G-A.

Pitch The quality of a sound that fixes its position in a **scale**. Sounds that do not belong in a **scale** (usually percussive sounds) are said to be unpitched.

Pop Applied a particular group of musical styles that are popular. As a result, the term is subject to constant redefinition.

Progression See *Harmony*

Pulse A regular, **rhythmic** beat related to but not necessarily the same as the time signature.

Quartertone See *Tone*

Quartet See *Ensemble*

Quintet See *Ensemble*

Ragtime A style music popular in America between the 1890s and 1920s. Most often played on the piano, it is distinguished by a **syncopated** (or 'ragged') **melody** set against a straight-moving bass.

Real book See *Fake book*

Recording Used to mean any method for storing visual images and/or sound. Audio recording was invented in 1877 by Thomas Edison.

Register Relative height of a pitch or group of pitches. The violin, for example, plays in a higher register than the cello.

Rhythm The variation in the duration of sounds in time. The perception of rhythm in music is related to the use of metre and **pulse**.

Riff A short, recognizable phrase. Also, a pre-prepared **melodic** phrase used in **improvisation**.

Scale A sequence of **notes** arranged in ascending or descending order of **pitch**.

Semitone The smallest commonly used division, a 12th, of the **octave**. A step comprising two semitones is known as a tone. The division of the semitone in half is known as a quartertone.

Septet See *Ensemble*

Sextet See *Ensemble*

Solo In jazz, a continuous **improvisation** by one player, normally over several repetitions of a **tune's harmony**.

Standard A **tune** that has become established in the repertory.

Stride A style of piano-playing that developed from **ragtime**, particularly associated with Harlem, New York. Takes its name from the distinctive 'stride bass', characterized by strong leaping left-hand figures. Typified by Fats Waller and, later, Theolonius Monk.

Swing A style of **jazz** from the 1930s characterized by big bands, **solo improvisation** and strong **rhythmic pulse**. A **rhythmic** manner of playing first heard in the swing style. Also, an indefinable quality associated with great **jazz** perhaps best described as having the x-factor.

Syncopation The effect of **rhythmic** displacement through accents on weak beats or in between beats.

Tailgate A style of trombone-playing typical of **New Orleans jazz** and characterized by *glissandi* (sliding **notes**). Bands at the time played on wagons and the only place with enough room for the trombonist was the tailgate.

Tempo The speed at which a piece is played. In the plural 'tempi'.

Third stream Term coined by Gunther Schuller for a type of music that synthesized elements of classical music and **jazz**.

Timbre The tonal quality of an instrument or voice.

Tone See *Semitone*

Traditional, trad A style of **jazz** practised in the UK in the 1950s and 1960s that revived the style and instrumentation of turn-of-the-century **New Orleans jazz**, typified by Acker Bilk and Kenny Ball. Also, the original **jazz** style of the early 1900s, otherwise known as **Dixieland**.

Trio See *Ensemble*

Tune A **jazz composition** or performance.

Vamp A short, simple passage of accompaniment repeated freely until the **soloist** is ready to begin or continue.

Vaudeville Originally a satirical French song. In the nineteenth century it came to indicate a musical comedy or music hall variety show.

Virtuoso An instrumentalist or singer (or indeed any craftsman) of extraordinary technical skill.

Jazz Artists

1980s–	3 Mustaphas 3	World Fusion	Various instruments	Balkan
1950s–	Aaltonen, Juhani	Modern Jazz; Jazz Rock	Flute, saxophones	Finnish
1940s–1950s	Aaron, Alvin (Abe)	Big Band	Clarinet, saxophones	Canadian
1950s–1980s	Aarons, Al	Modern Jazz; Bebop	Flugelhorn, trumpet	American
1940s–1960s	Abadie, Claude	Modern Jazz; Big Band	Clarinet	French
1970s–1990s	Abarius, Gintautas	Modern Jazz; World Fusion	Piano	Lithuanian
1970s–1990s	Abate, Greg	Fusion	Saxophone	American
1920s–1960s	Abbey, Leon	Traditional Jazz; Big Band	Violin, bandleader	American
1970s–1990s	Abdullah, Ahmed	Modern Jazz	Trumpet	American
1950s–1980s	Abdul-Malik, Ahmed	Bebop; Hard Bop; World Fusion	Bass	American
1970s	Abe, Kaoru	Free Jazz	Saxophone	Japanese
1950s–1990s	Abene, Mik	Modern Jazz	Piano	American
1970s–	Abercrombie, John	Modern Jazz	Guitar	American
1960s–	Aberg, Lennart	Modern Jazz; Jazz Rock; Free Jazz	Saxophones, bandleader	Swedish
1940s–1980s	Abney, Don	Swing; Modern Jazz	Piano	American
1980s–	Abou-Khalil, Rabih	World Fusion	Ud, composer	Lebanese
1980s–	Abrahams, Chris	World Fusion; Jazz Rock; Free Jazz	Piano	Australian
1960s–	Abrams, Muhal Richard	Free Jazz	Piano, clarinet, composer	American
1980s–	Actis Dato, Carlo	Free Jazz; World Jazz	Saxophones, clarinet, bandleader	Italian
1970s–	Adaker, Ulf	Jazz Rock; Latin Jazz	Trumpet, composer, bandleader	Swedish
1950s–1990s	Adams, George	Hard Bop; Modern Jazz	Saxophone, flute	American
1950s–1980s	Adams, Pepper	Hard Bop	Saxophone	American
1950s–1970s	Adderley, Cannonball	Hard Bop; Soul Jazz	Saxophone	American
1950s–1990s	Adderley, Nat	Hard Bop; Soul Jazz	Trumpet	American
1930s–1990s	Addison, Bernard	Swing; Traditional Jazz	Guitar	American
1970s–	Aebi, Irene	Free Jazz	Vocals, cello, violin	Swedish
1990s–	Affif, Ron	Hard Bop; Jazz Rock	Guitar	American
1980s–	Afrika, Mervyn	World Fusion; Soul Jazz	Piano, composer, arranger	African
1920s–1970s	Ahola, Sylvester	Traditional Jazz	Trumpet	American
1970s–1980s	Air	Free Jazz	Various instruments	American
1980s–	Akagi, Kei	Modern Jazz	Piano, keyboard	Japanese
1950s–	Akiyoshi, Toshiko	Big Band; Modern Jazz; Hard Bop	Piano, composer, bandleader	Chinese
1970s–	Aklaff, Pheeroan	Free Jazz	Drums	American
1940s–2000s	Albam, Manny	Big Band; Cool Jazz; Bebop	Arranger, composer, saxophone	American
1940s–1970s	Albany, Joe	Modern Jazz; Bebop	Piano	American
1990s	Albion Jazz Band	Dixieland Revival	Various instruments	Canadian
1980s–	Albright, Gerald	Smooth Jazz; Jazz Pop	Saxophone	American
1950s–1970s	Alcorn, Alvin	New Orleans Jazz	Trumpet	American
1980s–	Alden, Howard	Swing; Big Band; Traditional Jazz	Guitar, bandleader	American
1960s	Alegre All Stars	Latin Jazz	Various instruments	American
1930s–1960s	Aleman, Oscar	Swing; Traditional Jazz	Guitar	Argentinian
1990s–	Alexander, Eric	Modern Jazz	Saxophone	American
1960s–	Alexander, Monty	Modern Jazz; Hard Bop	Piano, bandleader	Jamaican
1940s–1980s	Alexander, Mousey	Big Band; Swing	Drums	American
1960s–1990s	Alexander, Roland	Modern Jazz; Bebop; Free Jazz	Saxophone	American
1950s–1990s	Alexandria, Lorez	Swing; Bebop	Vocals	American
1960s–	Ali, Muhammad	Free Jazz	Drums	American
1960s	Ali, Rashied	Free Jazz	Drums	American
1960s–	Alias, Don	Modern Jazz; Fusion	Drums	American
1950s–	Allan, Jan	Modern Jazz; Free Jazz	Trumpet	Swedish
1960s	Allen, Byron	Free Jazz	Saxophone	American
1980s–	Allen, Carl	Modern Jazz	Drums, bandleader	American
1920s–1960s	Allen, Ed	New Orleans Jazz; Traditional Jazz	Trumpet	American
1980s–	Allen, Eddie	Free Jazz; Jazz Rock; Big Band	Trumpet	American
1980s–	Allen, Geri	Free Jazz; Modern Jazz	Piano	American
1980s–	Allen, Harry	Swing; Modern Jazz	Saxophone	American
1920s–1960s	Allen, Henry 'Red'	New Orleans Jazz; Swing; Chicago Jazz; Dixieland	Trumpet, vocals, composer	American
1950s–	Allen, Marshall	Free Jazz	Saxophone, flute	American
1940s–1990s	Alley, Vernon	Swing	Bass	American
1950s–	Allison, Mose	Hard Bop	Piano, vocals, composer	American
1950s–1990s	Almeida, Laurindo	Brazilian Jazz; Latin Jazz	Guitar	Brazilian
1950s–1990s	Alphonso, Roland	Swing; Jamaican Jazz	Saxophone	Cuban
1970s–	Altena, Maarten	Free Jazz; Modern Jazz	Bass, bandleader	Dutch
1960s–	Altschul, Barry	Free Jazz	Drums	American
1990s–	Alvim, Cesarius	Modern Jazz	Bass, piano, composer	Brazilian
1920s–1950s	Alvin, Danny	Traditional Jazz	Drums, bandleader	American
1940s–	Ambrosetti, Flavio	Bebop	Saxophone, vibraphone	Swedish
1960s–	Ambrosetti, Franco	Hard Bop; Modern Jazz	Trumpet, flugelhorn	Swedish
1940s–1970s	Ammons, Gene	Bebop; Hard Bop	Saxophone	American
1950s–1990s	Amram, David	World Fusion; Latin Jazz; Bebop	French horn, composer	American
1980s–	Amsallem, Frank	Modern Jazz	Piano, composer	Algerian
1960s–2000s	Amy, Curtis	Soul Jazz; Modern Jazz	Saxophone, bandleader	American
1940s–1970s	Anderson, Cat	Swing; Big Band	Trumpet	American
1980s–	Anderson, Clifton	Hard Bop; Big Band	Trombone	American
1940s–	Anderson, Ernestine	Cool Jazz	Vocals	American
1960s–	Anderson, Fred	Free Jazz	Saxophone	American
1930s–1940s	Anderson, Ivie	Swing; Big Band	Vocals	American
1970s–	Anderson, Jay	Modern Jazz; Big Band	Bass	American
1970s–	Anderson, Ray	Free Jazz; Modern Jazz	Trombone, bandleader	American
1980s–	Anderson, Wessell	Hard Bop; Modern Jazz; Swing	Saxophone	American
1970s–	Andersson, Krister	Hard Bop; Big Band	Saxophone, clarinet	Swedish
1940s–	Andrews, Ernie	Bebop; Swing	Vocals	American
1940s–	Anthony, Ray	Big Band	Trumpet, bandleader	American
1950s–	Antolini, Charly	Big Band; Swing	Drums	Swedish
1980s–	Aoki, Tatsu	Free Jazz	Bass	Japanese
1930s–1960s	Archey, Jimmy	Swing; Traditional Jazz	Trombone	American
1940s–1960s	Archia, Tom	Bebop	Saxophone	American
1920s–1970s	Armstrong, Louis	New Orleans Jazz; Swing; Chicago Jazz	Trumpet, vocals	American
1940s–1960s	Arnold, Harry	Big Band	Saxophone, arranger, bandleader	Swedish
1950s–	Arnold, Horacee	Modern Jazz	Drums	American
1960s–	Aronov, Ben	Modern Jazz; Swing	Piano	American
1990s–	Arriale, Lynne	Modern Jazz	Piano, bandleader	American
1960s–	Art Ensemble of Chicago	Free Jazz	Various instruments	American
1980s–	Ascione, Joe	Swing	Drums	American
1950s–1990s	Ashby, Harold	Swing; Traditional Jazz	Saxophone	American
1940s–1970s	Ashby, Irving	Swing; Bebop	Guitar	American
1930s–	Asmussen, Svend	Swing; Traditional Jazz	Violin, vocals	Danish
1990s	Assad, Badi	Brazilian Jazz	Guitar	Brazilian
1960s–	Atkinson, Lisle	Modern Jazz	Bass	American
1950s–1980s	Attenoux, Michel	Traditional Jazz; Swing	Saxophone	French
1960s–	Auger, Brian	Jazz Rock; Fusion	Keyboards, vocals	British
1930s–1980s	Auld, Georgie	Swing; Big Band; Bebop	Saxophone, bandleader	Canadian
1950s–1980s	Austin, Claire	Swing; Dixieland; Traditional Jazz	Vocals	American
1920s–1960s	Austin, Lovie	Swing; Traditional Jazz	Piano	American
1930s–1970s	Autrey, Herman	Swing; Traditional Jazz	Trumpet, vocals	American
1930s–	Avakian, George	All Jazz Styles	Producer, critic	Armenian
1990s–	Avery, Teodross	Modern Jazz	Saxophone	American
1960s–	Ayers, Roy	Soul Jazz; Fusion; Jazz Funk	Vibraphone	American
1960s–1970s	Ayler, Albert	Free Jazz	Saxophone	American
1970s–1990s	Azymuth	Brazilian Jazz; Fusion	Various instruments	Brazilian
1970s–	Baars, Ab	Free Jazz	Saxophone	Dutch
1940s–1980s	Babasin, Harry	Cool Jazz; Bebop; Modern Jazz	Bass, cello	American
1940s–	Babs, Alice	Swing; Modern Jazz	Vocals	Swedish
1980s–	Back Bay Ramblers	Dixieland Revival	Various instruments	American
1970s–	Backer, Steve	Modern Jazz	Producer	American
1920s–1940s	Bacon, Louis	Swing; Traditional Jazz	Trumpet	American
1940s–1980s	Bacsik, Elek	Swing; Traditional Jazz	Guitar, violin	Hungarian
1960s–	Baden Powell, Roberto	Brazilian Jazz	Guitar	Brazilian
1950s–	Badini, Gerard	Swing; Modern Jazz	Saxophone, clarinet, piano, composer, bandleader	French
1940s–	Bailey, Benny	Swing; Big Band; Modern Jazz; Hard Bop	Trumpet	American
1920s–1960s	Bailey, Buster	Big Band; Swing; Traditional Jazz	Clarinet, saxophone	American
1950s–	Bailey, Dave	Modern Jazz	Drums	American
1960s–	Bailey, Derek	Free Jazz	Guitar	British
1950s–	Bailey, Donald	Modern Jazz	Drums	American
1970s–	Bailey, Judy	Modern Jazz	Piano, composer	New Zealander
1920s–1950s	Bailey, Mildred	Swing	Vocals	American
1980s–	Bailey, Victor	Modern Jazz	Electric bass	American
1950s–1980s	Baker, Chet	Cool Jazz	Trumpet, vocals, flugelhorn	American
1950s–	Baker, David	Big Band; Modern Jazz	Trombone, cello, composer	American
1970s–	Baker, Ginger	Jazz Rock; Fusion	Drums	British
1940s–1990s	Baker, Kenny	Traditional Jazz; Swing; Big Band	Trumpet	British
1930s–1960s	Baker, Shorty	Swing; Modern Jazz	Trumpet	American
1980s–	Bakr, Rashid	Free Jazz	Drums	American
1970s–	Balke, Jon	Jazz Rock; Modern Jazz	Piano, composer, arranger	Norwegian

1950s–1990s	Ball, Kenny	New Orleans Jazz; Chicago Jazz; Dixieland	Trumpet, vocals, bandleader	British
1980s–	Ballamy, Iain	Modern Jazz; Big Band	Saxophone	British
1950s–	Balliett, Whitney	All Jazz Styles	Author, critic	American
1960s–	Baltazar, Gabe	Hard Bop; Bebop; Big Band	Saxophone	American
1980s–	Balzar, Robert	Modern Jazz	Bass, bandleader	Czech
1970s–	Bang, Billy	Free Jazz; Fusion	Violin, composer	American
1910s–1940s	Baquet, George	Traditional Jazz; New Orleans Jazz	Clarinet	American
1940s–1960s	Barbarin, Paul	New Orleans Jazz	Drums	American
1940s–1990s	Barber, Chris	New Orleans Jazz; Chicago Jazz; Dixieland	Trombone, vocals, bandleader	British
1960s–1990s	Barbieri, Gato	Latin Jazz; Jazz Pop	Saxophone, flute, percussion, vocals	Argentinian
1930s–1960s	Barbour, Dave	Traditional Jazz; Big Band	Guitar	American
1930s–1970s	Barefield, Eddie	Swing; Big Band	Saxophone, clarinet	American
1970s–	Barefield, Spencer	Free Jazz	Guitar	American
1930s–1990s	Barker, Danny	New Orleans Jazz; Swing	Guitar, banjo, composer	American
1980s–	Barker, Guy	Modern Jazz; Big Band	Trumpet	British
1980s–	Barlow, Dale	Hard Bop; Fusion	Saxophone	Australian
1940s–	Barnard, Bob	Traditional Jazz	Trumpet	Australian
1980s–	Barnes, Alan	Modern Jazz	Saxophone, clarinet	British
1930s–1970s	Barnes, George	Swing	Guitar	American
1950s–	Barnes, John	Modern Jazz	Clarinet, flugelhorn	British
1920s–1970s	Barnes, Polo	Traditional Jazz; Swing; New Orleans Jazz	Clarinet, saxophone	American
1930s–1960s	Barnet, Charlie	Swing; Big Band	Saxophone, vocals	American
1970s–	Baron, Joey	Free Jazz; Big Band	Drums	American
1960s–	Barone, Gary	Modern Jazz; Big Band	Trumpet, flugelhorn	American
1960s–	Barone, Mike	Big Band; Modern Jazz	Trombone, composer, arranger	American
1980s–	Barrett, Dan	Swing; Dixieland; Big Band	Trombone, cornet, bandleader	American
1990s–	Barretto, Carlos	Modern Jazz	Bass, composer	Portuguese
1950s–	Barretto, Ray	Latin Jazz	Percussion	American
1950s–1980s	Barron, Bill	Hard Bop; Modern Jazz	Saxophone	American
1950s–	Barron, Kenny	Hard Bop; Modern Jazz	Piano	American
1930s–1970s	Barroso, Ary	Brazilian Jazz; Latin Jazz	Composer	Brazilian
1980s–	Barth, Bruce	Modern Jazz	Piano	American
1970s–	Barthelemy, Claude	Modern Jazz; Big Band	Guitar, composer	French
1960s–	Bartkowski, Czeslaw	Modern Jazz; Jazz Rock	Drums	Polish
1960s–	Bartz, Gary	Modern Jazz	Saxophone	American
1930s–1960s	Bascomb, Dud	Modern Jazz; Swing; Big Band	Trumpet	American
1930s–1980s	Bascomb, Paul	Swing; Big Band	Saxophone	American
1920s–1980s	Basie, Count	Swing; Big Band	Piano, bandleader	American
1960s–	Bass, Mickey	Modern Jazz	Bass	American
1980s–	Bates, Django	Free Jazz; Fusion	Piano, keyboards, trumpet, composer, bandleader	British
1980s–1990s	Batish, Ashwin	World Fusion; Fusion	Sitar	Indian
1950s–	Batiste, Alvin	Free Jazz	Clarinet	American
1990s–	Battaglia, Stefano	Free Jazz; Modern Jazz	Piano, bandleader	Italian
1970s–	Battle, Bobby	Modern Jazz	Drums, saxophone	American
1990s	Batuque, Grupo	Brazilian Jazz	Various instruments	Brazilian
1920s–1980s	Bauduc, Ray	New Orleans Jazz; Big Band	Drums	American
1940s–1950s	Bauer, Billy	Cool Jazz	Guitar	American
1970s–	Bauer, Conrad	Free Jazz	Trombonist	German
1980s–	Bauer, Johannes	Free Jazz	Trombonist	German
1980s–	Bauer, Stefan	Free Jazz	Vibraphone, marimba	German
1930s–1990s	Bauza, Mario	Latin Jazz	Trumpet, saxophone, arranger	Cuban
1950s–1960s	Bean, Billy	Modern Jazz	Guitar	American
1980s–	Beard, Jim	Modern Jazz; Jazz Rock	Piano, keyboards	American
1920s–1950s	Bechet, Sidney	Chicago Jazz; New Orleans Jazz	Clarinet, soprano saxophone	American
1960s–	Beck, Gordon	Modern Jazz	Piano	British
1950s–	Beck, Joe	Fusion	Guitar	American
1970s–	Beckerhoff, Uli	Modern Jazz	Trumpet	German
1960s–	Beckett, Harry	British Jazz; Big Band	Trumpet, flugelhorn	Barbadian
1920s–1930s	Beiderbecke, Bix	New Orleans Jazz; Traditional Jazz	Cornet, piano	American
1980s–	Beier, Chris	Free Jazz	Piano, composer	German
1970s–	Beirach, Richard	Free Jazz; Modern Jazz	Piano, composer	American
1970s–	Belden, Bob	Big Band; Modern Jazz	Saxophone, arranger, record producer	American
1950s–	Belgrave, Marcus	Modern Jazz; Big Band	Trumpet	American
1970s–	Bell, Kelvyn	Free Jazz	Guitar, vocals	American
1940s–1990s	Bellson, Louie	Swing; Bebop	Drums	American
1980s–	Belmondo, Lionel	Modern Jazz; Big Band	Saxophone, clarinet, composer, bandleader	French
1980s–	Belmondo, Stephane	Modern Jazz; Big Band	Trumpet, flugelhorn, trombone, bandleader	French
1970s–	Bem, Ewa	Modern Jazz	Vocals	Polish
1920s–1980s	Benford, Tommy	Swing; Traditional Jazz	Drums	American
1980s–	Benita, Michel	Modern Jazz	Bass, composer	French
1960s–	Benjamin, Sathima Bea	Modern Jazz	Vocals	South African
1960s–	Benko, Sandor	Dixieland	Clarinet, saxophone, bandleader	Hungarian
1930s–1940s	Bennett, Buster	Swing; Traditional Jazz	Saxophones, piano, bandleader	American
1960s–1990s	Bennett, Lou	Modern Jazz; Hard Bop	Organ, bandleader	American
1950s–	Bennett, Max	Swing; Big Band	Bass, composer	American
1950s–	Bennett, Tony	Swing; Cool Jazz	Vocals	American
1960s–	Bennink, Han	Free Jazz	Percussion	Dutch
1970s–	Benoit, David	Fusion; Jazz Rock	Piano, producer	American
1960s–	Benson, George	Smooth Jazz; Hard Bop	Guitar, vocals	American
1980s–	Bentzon, Nikolaj	Funk Jazz; Hard Bop; Modern Jazz	Keyboards, arranger, composer	Danish
1940s–1990s	Berendt, Joachim-Ernst	All Jazz Styles	Producer, author, concert promoter	German
1970s–	Beresford, Steve	Free Jazz	Piano, trumpet, trombone, guitar, violin	British
1970s–	Berg, Bob	Modern Jazz; Hard Bop	Saxophone	American
1970s–	Bergalli, Gustavo	Modern Jazz; Big Band	Trumpet	Argentinian
1980s–	Bergcrantz, Anders	Hard Bop; Modern Jazz	Trumpet	Swedish
1960s–	Berger, Karl	Free Jazz	Vibraphone	German
1970s–	Bergin, Sean	Hard Bop; Modern Jazz; Big Band	Saxophones, composer, bandleader	South African
1970s–	Bergman, Borah	Free Jazz	Piano	American
1970s–	Bergonzi, Jerry	Hard Bop; Bebop; Modern Jazz	Saxophone	American
1930s–1940s	Berigan, Bunny	Swing	Trumpet, vocals	American
1960s–	Berk, Dick	Modern Jazz	Drums	American
1970s–	Berlin, Jeff	Jazz Rock	Electric Bass	American
1940s	Berman, Sonny	Swing; Big Band	Trumpet	American
1970s–	Berne, Tim	Free Jazz	Saxophones	American
1930s–1980s	Bernhardt, Clyde	Swing; Traditional Jazz; Big Band	Trombone, vocals, bandleader	American
1960s–	Bernhardt, Warren	Modern Jazz	Keyboards, composer	American
1940s–	Bernhart, Milt	Big Band	Trombone	American
1980s–	Bernstein, Peter	Modern Jazz	Guitar	American
1950s–	Berry, Bill	Swing; Big Band	Trumpet, cornet, bandleader	American
1930s–1940s	Berry, Chu	Swing	Saxophone	American
1930s–1970s	Berry, Emmett	Swing; Big Band	Trumpet	American
1940s–	Bert, Eddie	Bebop; Big Band	Trombone	American
1960s–	Bertles, Bob	Jazz Rock; Free Jazz	Saxophones	Australian
1920s–1940s	Berton, Vic	Big Band; Traditional Jazz	Drums	American
1960s–	Bertoncini, Gene	Cool Jazz; Modern Jazz	Guitar	American
1940s–1960s	Best, Denzil	Swing; Modern Jazz	Drums	American
1970s–	Betsch, John	Free Jazz	Drums	American
1940s–	Betts, Keter	Swing; Bebop; Modern Jazz	Bass	American
1980s–	Beuf, Sylvain	Modern Jazz; Bop; Big Band	Saxophones, composer	French
1980s–	Bex, Emmanuel	Free Jazz; Modern Jazz	Piano, organ, composer, bandleader	French
1950s–	Bey, Andy	Hard Bop; Soul Jazz; Modern Jazz	Vocals	American
1980s–1990s	Bhatt, Vishwa Mohan	World Fusion	Guitar	Indian
1950s–	Bickert, Ed	Cool Jazz; Modern Jazz	Guitar	Canadian
1920s–1970s	Bigard, Barney	New Orleans Jazz; Swing	Clarinet, saxophone	American
1980s–	Bijma, Greetje	Free Jazz	Vocals	Dutch
1950s–1990s	Bilk, Acker	New Orleans Jazz; Traditional Jazz	Clarinet, vocals, bandleader	British
1950s–1960s	Billbeg, Rolf	Modern Jazz; Big Band	Saxophone	Swedish
1970s–	Bingert, Hector	World Fusion, Big Band	Saxophone	Uruguayan
1970s–	Biscoe, Chris	Free Jazz; Big Band; Modern Jazz	Saxophone, clarinet	British
1920s–1980s	Bishop, Wallace	Swing; Traditional Jazz; Bebop	Drums	American
1960s–1990s	Bishop, Walter Jr	Bebop; Hard Bop	Piano	American
1980s–	Bisio, Michael	Modern Jazz; Free Jazz	Bass	American
1980s–	Bjorkenheim, Raoul	Free Jazz	Guitar, composer	Finnish
1950s–	Bjorksten, Hacke	Modern Jazz	Saxophone, bandleader	Finnish
1950s–1990s	Blackburn, Lou	World Fusion, Big Bands,	Trombone	American
1980s–	Blackman, Cindy	Hard Bop; Big Band	Drums, bandleader	American
1950s–1990s	Blackwell, Ed	Free Jazz	Drums	American
1990s–	Blade, Brian	Modern Jazz; Jazz Rock; Fusion	Drums	American
1970s–	Blades, Reuben	Latin Jazz	Vocals, composer	Panamanian
1970s–	Blake, Alex	Latin Jazz; Modern Jazz; Free Jazz; Jazz Rock	Bass	Panamanian
1910s–1980s	Blake, Eubie	Ragtime	Piano, composer	American
1970s–	Blake, John	Modern Jazz; Smooth Jazz	Violin, bandleader	American
1960s–	Blake, Ran	Free Jazz; Modern Jazz	Piano, composer	American
1980s–	Blake, Ron	Free Jazz; Modern Jazz	Saxophone	Puerto Rican

1990s–	Blake, Seamus	Hard Bop; Modern Jazz	Saxophone	Canadian
1990s–	Blakeslee, Rob	Free Jazz	Trumpet, flugelhorn, clarinet	American
1940s–1990s	Blakey, Art	Hard Bop	Drums	American
1980s–	Blanchard, Terence	Hard Bop; Modern Jazz	Trumpet, composer	American
1920s–1940s	Bland, Jack	Traditional Jazz;	Guitar, banjo	American
1930s–1940s	Blanton, Jimmy	Swing; Big Band	Bass	American
1940s–1980s	Blesh, Rudi	Traditional Jazz; Swing; Ragtime	Producer, author, critic	American
1960s–	Bley, Carla	Free Jazz; Big Band; Modern Jazz	Keyboards, composer, bandleader	American
1950s–	Bley, Paul	Free Jazz	Piano, keyboards, composer	Canadian
1970s–	Bloom, Jane Ira	Free Jazz; Modern Jazz	Saxophone, composer, arranger, bandleader	American
1970s–	Bluiett, Hamiet	Free Jazz; World Fusion	Saxophone	American
1960s–	Blythe, Arthur	Free Jazz; Modern Jazz; World Fusion	Saxophone, bandleader	American
1920s–1930s	Blythe, Jimmy	Traditional Jazz	Piano	American
1950s–1980s	Bobo, Willie	Latin Jazz	Percussion	Spanish
1900s–1960s	Bocage, Peter	Dixieland; Big Band; New Orleans Jazz; Big Band	Cornet, violin	American
1960s–	Bohanon, George	Big Band; Jazz Rock	Trombone, euphonium	American
1970s–	Boiarsky, Andres	Latin Jazz; Big Band; World Jazz	Saxophone	Argentinian
1950s–	Boland, Francy	Big Band; Swing; Bebop	Piano, arranger, composer, bandleader	Belgian
1980s–	Bolberg-Pedersen, Henrik	Big Band; Bebop	Trumpet	Danish
1900s–1930s	Bolden, Buddy	Traditional Jazz; New Orleans Jazz	Cornet, bandleader	American
1980s–	Bollenback, Paul	Soul Jazz; Fusion	Guitar	American
1940s–	Bolling, Claude	Swing; Big Band	Piano, composer, bandleader	French
1980s–	Bolognesi, Jacques	Big Band	Trombone, piano, accordion, bandleader	French
1980s–	Bonafede, Salvatore	Modern Jazz	Piano	Italian
1920s–1960s	Bonano, Sharkey	Chicago Jazz	Trumpet, vocals, bandleader	American
1950s–	Bond, Jimmy	Modern Jazz; Bebop	Bass, composer	American
1990s–	Boney James	Fusion; Smooth Jazz	Saxophone	American
1950s–1990s	Bonfá, Luiz	Brazilian Jazz	Guitar, composer	Brazilian
1970s–	Boni, Raymond	Free Jazz	Guitar	French
1970s–	Bonner, Joe	Modern Jazz; Big Band	Piano	American
1960s–	Booker, Walter	Modern Jazz	Bass	American
1960s–	Boone, Richard	Modern Jazz; Big Band	Trombone, vocals	American
1920s–1950s	Bose, Stirling	Traditional Jazz; Big Band; Chicago Jazz	Trumpet, cornet	American
1920s–1930s	Boswell Sisters, The	Swing	Various instruments	American
1990s–	Botti, Chris	Smooth Jazz	Trumpet	American
1950s–	Botschinsky, Allan	Big Band; Fusion Jazz	Trumpet, flugelhorn, arranger, composer	Danish
1970s–	Bottlang, Rene	Modern Jazz; Big Band	Piano, composer	Swedish
1980s–	Bourde, Herve	Modern Jazz; Big Band	Saxophone, flute, composer	French
1980s–	Bourelly, Jean-Paul	Free Jazz; World Fusion; Jazz Rock	Guitar	American
1980s–	Boussaguet, Pierre	Modern Jazz	Bass, composer	French
1960s–1990s	Bowie, Lester	Free Jazz	Trumpet, flugelhorn, vocals, percussion	American
1930s–1960s	Bowman, Dave	Dixieland; Traditional Jazz	Piano	American
1950s–1970s	Boykins, Ronnie	Free Jazz; Big Band	Bass	American
1990s–	Braam, Michiel	Modern Jazz	Piano, bandleader	Dutch
1960s–	Brackeen, Charles	Free Jazz	Saxophone	American
1960s–	Brackeen, JoAnne	Modern Jazz	Piano, composer	American
1980s–	Braden, Don	Hard Bop; Modern Jazz	Saxophone, flute	American
1950s–	Bradford, Bobby	Free Jazz; Modern Jazz	Cornet, trumpet, composer	American
1910s–1930s	Bradford, Perry	Traditional Jazz	Piano, composer, producer	American
1930s–1950s	Bradley, Will	Swing; Big Band; Boogie Woogie	Trombone, bandleader	American
1950s–	Bradshaw, Sonny	Jamaican Jazz; Big Band	Trumpet, flugelhorn, arranger, bandleader	Jamaican
1940s–2000s	Braff, Ruby	Dixieland Revival; New Orleans Jazz; Swing	Trumpet	American
1960s–	Braith, George	Modern Jazz; Soul Jazz	Saxophone	American
1970s–1980s	Brand, Dollar (Abdullah Ibrahim)	World Fusion	Piano	South African
1990s–	Brand New Heavies	Acid Jazz	Various instruments	British
1920s–1960s	Braud, Wellman	Big Band; Swing	Bass	American
1960s–	Braxton, Anthony	Free Jazz	Saxophones, clarinet, flute, percussion, vocals	American
1970s–	Breakstone, Joshua	Cool Jazz; Modern Jazz	Guitar	American
1960s–1980s	Breau, Lenny	Modern Jazz	Guitar	American
1990s	Breaux, Zachary	Soul Jazz	Guitar	American
1960s–	Brecker, Michael	Fusion	Saxophones, flute	American
1960s–	Brecker, Randy	Fusion; Hard Bop	Trumpet, piano, drums	American
1950s–1960s	Bregman, Buddy	Big Band	Producer	American
1940s–1960s	Brehm, Simon	Traditional Jazz; Swing	Bass, bandleader	Swedish
1970s–	Brennan, John Wolf	Jazz Rock; Fusion Jazz; Big Band	Piano, organ, keyboards, composer	Irish
1960s–	Breuker, Willem	Big Band; Free Jazz	Saxophone, clarinet, composer	Dutch
1950s–	Brewer, Teresa	Swing; Big Band	Vocals	American
1960s–	Bridgewater, Cecil	Hard Bop; Modern Jazz	Trumpet, flugelhorn, arranger, composer	American
1970s–	Bridgewater, Dee Dee	Modern Jazz	Vocals	American
1920s–1940s	Briggs, Arthur	Traditional Jazz; British Jazz	Trumpet	American
1950s–	Bright, Ronnell	Modern Jazz; Big Band	Piano, composer	American
1950s–2000s	Brignola, Nick	Hard Bop; Modern Jazz; Big Band	Saxophone, flute	American
1950s–	Brisker, Gordon	Modern Jazz; Big Band; Australian Jazz	Saxophone, arranger	American
1960s–	Broberg, Bosse	Big Band; Bebop; World Fusion	Trumpet, composer	Swedish
1950s–	Brodie, Hugh	Modern Jazz	Saxophone	American
1940s–1990s	Brom, Gustav	Modern Jazz; Swing; Dixieland; Big Band	Clarinet, bandleader	Czech
1980s–	Bromberg, Brian	Hard Bop; Modern Jazz; Fusion	Bass	American
1950s–	Brookmeyer, Bob	Cool Jazz	Valve trombone, piano, arranger	American
1950s–2000s	Brooks, Bubba	Swing	Saxophone	American
1980s–	Brooks, Cecil	Modern Jazz; Soul Jazz	Drums, bandleader	American
1960s–	Brooks, Roy	Modern Jazz; Hard Bop	Drums	American
1950s–1960s	Brooks, Tina	Hard Bop	Saxophone	American
1980s–	Broom, Bobby	Jazz Funk; Jazz Rock; Modern Jazz	Guitar	American
1960s–	Brötzmann, Peter	Free Jazz	Saxophones, clarinet	German
1980s–	Brown, Ari	Free Jazz	Saxophone, piano	American
1930s–1950s	Brown, Boyce	Big Band; Traditional Jazz	Saxophone, clarinet	American
1950s–	Brown, Brian	Free Jazz; World Fusion	Saxophone, composer, bandleader	American
1990s–	Brown, Carlinhos	Brazilian Jazz	Percussion	Brazilian
1930s–1980s	Brown, Cleo	Swing; Traditional Jazz	Piano, vocals	American
1950s	Brown, Clifford	Hard Bop; Bebop	Trumpet	American
1980s–	Brown, Donald	Modern Jazz; Hard Bop	Piano, composer	American
1970s–	Brown, Gerry	Modern Jazz; Jazz Rock	Drums, bandleader	American
1990s–	Brown, Jeri	Bebop; Modern Jazz	Vocals	American
1930s–1980s	Brown, Lawrence	Big Band; Swing	Trombone	American
1930s–2000s	Brown, Les	Big Band	Bandleader, arranger, composer	American
1960s–1990s	Brown, Marion	Free Jazz	Saxophone	American
1950s–1980s	Brown, Marshall	Swing; Big Band; Modern Jazz	Trombone, bandleader	American
1950s–	Brown, Oscar Jr.	Modern Jazz; Soul Jazz	Vocals, composer	American
1930s–1960s	Brown, Pete	Bebop; Swing	Saxophone, bandleader	American
1940s–2000s	Brown, Ray	Bebop	Bass, cello	American
1980s–	Brown, Rob	Free Jazz	Saxophone	American
1980s–	Browne, Allan	Traditional Jazz; Modern Jazz	Drums, bandleader	Australian
1970s–	Brubeck, Darius	Modern Jazz; World Fusion	Piano, keyboards	American
1950s–	Brubeck, Dave	Cool Jazz; West Coast Jazz	Piano, composer	American
1960s–	Bruford, Bill	Jazz Rock; Jazz Funk	Drums	British
1920s–1960s	Brunies, Abbie	New Orleans Jazz; Traditional Jazz; Dixieland Jazz	Cornet	American
1920s–1970s	Brunies, Georg	New Orleans Jazz; Traditional Jazz; Dixieland Jazz; Ragtime	Trombone	American
1920s–1960s	Brunies, Merritt	New Orleans Jazz; Traditional Jazz; Dixieland Jazz	Cornet, trombone	American
1980s–	Bruning, Uschi	Free Jazz	Vocals	German
1970s–	Bruninghaus, Rainer	Jazz Rock; Free Jazz	Piano, synthesizer	German
1960s–	Brunious, Wendell	New Orleans Jazz; Latin Jazz; Big Band; Traditional Jazz	Trumpet, bandleader	American
1930s–1950s	Brunner, Eddie	Traditional Jazz; Swing	Saxophone, clarinet	Swiss
1980s–	Bruno, Jimmy	Modern Jazz	Guitar	American
1960s–1990s	Bryant, Bobby	Big Band; Modern Jazz	Trumpet, saxophone	American
1950s–	Bryant, Ray	Soul Jazz; Swing; Bebop	Piano	American
1950s–1980s	Bryant, Rusty	Soul Jazz; Hard Bop	Saxophone	American
1980s–	Buck, Tony	Free Jazz; Jazz Rock	Drums, composer	Australian
1960s–1970s	Buckley, Tim	Jazz Rock	Vocals, composer	American
1940s–1970s	Buckner, Milt	Big Bands; Swing	Piano, organ, arranger	American
1930s–1980s	Buckner, Teddy	Dixieland; Chicago Jazz	Trumpet, flugelhorn, vocals	American
1950s–	Buddle, Errol	Modern Jazz; Big Band	Bassoon, saxophone	Australian
1950s–	Budimir, Dennis	Big Band; Modern Jazz	Guitar	American
1950s–1990s	Budwig, Monty	Cool Jazz; Bebop	Bass	American
1990s–	Buena Vista Social Club	Latin Jazz	Various instruments	Cuban
1970s–	Bukovsky, Mike	Modern Jazz; Big Band	Trumpet, composer, bandleader	Czech
1960s–1980s	Bull, Sandy	World Fusion	Guitar, banjo, vocals	American
1970s–	Bullock, Hiram	Jazz Rock	Guitar	Japanese
1950s–	Bunch, John	Swing	Piano	American
1920s–1970s	Bunn, Teddy	Swing; Traditional Jazz	Guitar	American
1980s–	Bunnett, Jane	Bebop; World Fusion; Latin Jazz	Saxophone, flute, bandleader	Canadian
1940s–1970s	Burbank, Albert	New Orleans Jazz; Dixieland	Clarinet, vocals	American
1960s–	Burnap, Campbell	British Jazz; Traditional Jazz	Trombone, vocals	British
1960s–	Burnett, Carl	Modern Jazz	Drums	American
1940s–	Burns, Dave	Bebop; Hard Bop	Trumpet, flugelhorn, piano	American
1940s–2000s	Burns, Ralph	Swing; Bebop; Big Band	Piano, arranger, composer	American
1950s–	Burns, Roy	Swing; Modern Jazz	Drums	American
1970s–	Burr, Jon	Modern Jazz; Big Band	Bass	American
1980s–	Burrage, Ronnie	Modern Jazz	Drums	American
1960s–	Burrell, Dave	Free Jazz	Piano	American
1950s–	Burrell, Kenny	Bebop; Hard Bop; Cool Jazz	Guitar, vocals	American
1960s–	Burrowes, Roy	Jamaican Jazz; Hard Bop; Bebop	Trumpet	Jamaican
1950s–	Burrows, Don	Modern Jazz; Swing; Cool Jazz	Clarinet, saxophone, flute,	Australian
1990s–	Burton, Abraham	Hard Bop; Modern Jazz	Saxophone, bandleader	American
1960s–1980s	Burton, Ann	Modern Jazz	Vocals	Danish
1960s–	Burton, Gary	Modern Jazz	Vibraphonist, bandleader	American
1960s–	Burton, Rahn	Hard Bop; Free Jazz	Piano, composer	American
1970s–	Busch, Sigi	Modern Jazz	Bass	German
1930s–2000s	Bushkin, Joe	Traditional Jazz; Swing	Piano, trumpet	American
1950s–1980s	Butler, Frank	Bebop; West Coast Jazz; Hard Bop	Drums	American
1980s–	Butler, Henry	Modern Jazz; Rhythm & Blues	Piano	American
1930s–	Butler, Jacques	Swing	Trumpet, vocals	American
1980s–	Butman, Igor	Modern Jazz	Saxophone	Russian
1930s–1980s	Butterfield, Billy	Chicago Jazz; Swing	Trumpet, flugelhorn	American
1940s–1990s	Byard, Jaki	Free Jazz	Piano, saxophones, arranger	American
1930s–1970s	Byas, Don	Swing; Bebop	Saxophone	American
1950s–1990s	Byers, Billy	Big Band	Trombone, arranger	American
1950s–1990s	Byrd, Charlie	Brazilian Jazz; Latin Jazz	Guitar	American
1950s–	Byrd, Donald	Fusion; Hard Bop	Trumpet, flugelhorn	American
1990s–	Byron, Don	Free Jazz; Modern Jazz	Clarinet, bandleader	American
1970s–	Cables, George	Hard Bop; Modern Jazz	Piano, keyboards, composer	American
1930s–1970s	Caceres, Ernie	Swing	Clarinet, saxophone	American
1940s–	Cachao	Latin Jazz	Bass	Cuban
1980s–	Cain, Michael	Free Jazz; Modern Jazz	Piano, keyboards	American
1990s–	Caine, Uri	Free Jazz; Modern Jazz	Piano, composer	American
1980s–	Calderazzo, Joey	Modern Jazz	Piano, keyboards	American
1970s–	Cale, Bruce	Modern Jazz; Big Band	Bass, composer	Australian
1920s–1930s	California Ramblers	Traditional Jazz	Various instruments	American
1960s–	Caliman, Hadley	Hard Bop; Modern Jazz	Saxophone	American
1940s–1980s	Callender, Red	Cool Jazz; Swing; Bebop	Bass, tuba	American
1920s–1970s	Calloway, Blanche	Swing	Vocals, bandleader	American
1920s–1980s	Calloway, Cab	Swing	Vocals, bandleader	American
1950s–	Cameron, Jay	Swing; Modern Jazz	Saxophone	American
1970s–	Camilo, Michel	Latin Jazz; Hard Bop	Piano, composer, bandleader	Dominican
1970s–	Campbell, John	Modern Jazz	Piano	American
1970s–	Campbell, Roy	Hard Bop; Modern Jazz	Trumpet	American
1980s–	Campbell, Tommy	Modern Jazz; Big Band; Hard Bop	Drums	American
1950s–	Candido	Latin Jazz	Drums	Cuban
1940s–1990s	Candoli, Conte	Cool Jazz; Bebop	Trumpet	American
1940s–	Candoli, Pete	Swing; West Coast Jazz; Big Band	Trumpet	American
1960s–	Capon, Jean-Charles	Free Jazz; Modern Jazz	Bass	French
1950s–	Capp, Frank	Modern Jazz; Swing; Big Band	Drums, bandleader	American
1980s–	Caratini, Patrice	Swing; Big Band	Bass, composer, bandleader	French
1990s–	Cardenas, Steve	Modern Jazz	Guitar	American
1910s–1940s	Carey, Mutt	New Orleans Jazz	Trumpet	American
1940s–1990s	Carisi, Johnny	Cool Jazz; Big Band; Jazz Rock	Trumpet, composer, arranger	American
1970s–	Carl, Rudiger	Free Jazz	Saxophone, clarinet, accordion	German
1940s–1960s	Carle, Frankie	New Orleans Jazz	Piano, bandleader	British
1930s–1950s	Carlisle, Una Mae	Swing	Piano, vocals, composer	American
1960s–	Carlsson, Rune	Modern Jazz	Drums, vocals	Swedish
1960s–	Carlton, Larry	Fusion; Hard Bop; Soul Jazz; Smooth Jazz	Guitar	American
1920s–1960s	Carmichael, Hoagy	Traditional Jazz	Piano, vocals, composer	American
1980s–	Carmichael, Judy	Swing	Piano	American
1920s–1970s	Carney, Harry	Swing; Big Band	Saxophone	American
1960s–	Carr, Ian	Modern Jazz; Jazz Rock; Fusion	Trumpet, flugelhorn, composer, bandleader	Scottish
1960s–	Carr, Mike	Hard Bop; Modern Jazz	Organ	British
1980s–	Carrington, Terri Lyne	Hard Bop; Funk	Drums	American
1970s–	Carroll, Baikida	Free Jazz	Trumpet, flugelhorn	American
1940s–	Carroll, Barbara	Bebop; Modern Jazz	Piano, vocals	American
1940s–1980s	Carroll, Joe 'Bebop'	Bebop	Vocals	American
1950s–1990s	Carson, Ernie	Dixieland Revival	Cornet	American
1920s–1990s	Carter, Benny	Swing	Saxophone, trumpet, arranger, composer	American
1950s–1990s	Carter, Betty	Bebop	Vocals	American
1970s–	Carter, Daniel	Free Jazz	Saxophone, clarinet, flute, trumpet	American
1990s–	Carter, James	Hard Bop	Saxophones	American
1960s–1990s	Carter, John	Free Jazz	Clarinet, saxophone, composer, bandleader	American
1960s–	Carter, Kent	Free Jazz; Modern Jazz	Bass, violin, keyboards, percussion	American
1990s–	Carter, Regina	Jazz Funk; Modern Jazz	Violin	American
1960s–	Carter, Ron	Hard Bop	Bass, cello	American
1930s–1960s	Carver, Wayman	Swing	Saxophone, flute	American
1960s–	Carvin, Michael	Modern Jazz; Jazz Rock; Hard Bop	Drums	American
1940s–1990s	Cary, Dick	Traditional Jazz; Swing	Piano, trumpet, arranger, alto horn	American
1990s–	Cary, Marc	Modern Jazz	Piano	American
1920s–1960s	Casa Loma Orchestra	Swing; Big Band	Various instruments	American
1930s–	Casey, Al	Swing	Guitar	American
1970s–	Castellucci, Bruno	Modern Jazz; Big Band; Bebop	Drums	Belgian
1930s–1980s	Castle, Lee	Big Band; Swing	Trumpet, bandleader	American
1950s–	Castro, Joe	Swing; Hard Bop; Bebop	Piano, bandleader	American
1950s–	Castro-Neves, Oscar	Brazilian Jazz; Modern Jazz	Guitar, composer, arranger	Brazilian
1970s–	Catherine, Philip	Modern Jazz; Jazz Rock	Guitar	Belgian
1930s–1950s	Catlett, 'Big' Sid	Swing	Drums	American
1990s–	Catney, Dave	Modern Jazz	Vocals, piano	American
1980s–	Caumont, Elisabeth	Swing; Modern Jazz	Vocals, composer	French
1970s–	Ceccarelli, Andre	Modern Jazz	Drums, bandleader	French
1980s–	Celea, Jean-Paul	Free Jazz	Drums	Algerian
1910s–1950s	Celestin, Papa Oscar	New Orleans Jazz	Trumpet, bandleader	American
1970s	Centipede	Jazz Rock	Various instruments	British
1950s–	Cerri, Franco	Modern Jazz; Swing; Bebop	Guitar, bass	Italian
1940s–1970s	Cesari, Umberto	Swing; Modern Jazz	Piano	Italian
1970s–	Chadbourne, Eugene	Free Jazz; Fusion	Guitar, banjo, vocals	American
1960s–	Chaix, Henri	Big Band; Swing	Piano, trombone, arranger, bandleader	French
1920s–1980s	Challis, Bill	Traditional Jazz; Swing	Arranger	American
1940s–1950s	Chaloff, Serge	Bebop	Saxophone	American
1970s–	Chambers, Dennis	Fusion; Jazz Funk	Drums	American
1960s–	Chambers, Joe	Free Jazz; Modern Jazz	Drums, vibraphone, composer	American
1950s–1960s	Chambers, Paul	Hard Bop	Bass	American
1940s–	Chamblee, Eddie	Swing; Big Band	Saxophone, bandleader	American
1970s–	Chancey, Vincent	Free Jazz	French horn	American
1980s–1990s	Chapin, Thomas	Free Jazz; Modern Jazz	Saxophone, flute, bandleader	American
1980s–	Charlap, Bill	Modern Jazz	Piano	American
1950s–1990s	Charles, Dennis	Free Jazz	Drums	American
1950s–1990s	Charles, Teddy	Cool Jazz	Vibraphone, composer	American
1980s–	Chase, Allan	Free Jazz	Saxophone, bandleader	American
1950s–1970s	Chase, Bill	Swing; Jazz Rock; Big Band	Trumpet	American
1920s–1990s	Cheatham, Doc	Swing; Chicago Jazz	Trumpet	American
1980s–	Cheatham, Jeannie	Swing	Piano, vocals	American
1980s–	Cheatham, Jimmy	Swing	Trombone, bandleader	American
1990s–	Cheek, Chris	Free Jazz; Fusion	Saxophone	American
1970s–	Chekasin, Vladimir	Free Jazz	Saxophone, keyboards, composer	Russian
1950s–1990s	Cherry, Don	Free Jazz; World Fusion	Trumpet, keyboards, vocals	American
1980s–	Cherry, Ed	Soul Jazz; Big Band	Guitar	American
1990s–	Chestnut, Cyrus	Hard Bop; Modern Jazz	Piano	American
1970s–	Chiasson, Warren	Bebop	Vibraphone	Canadian
1940s–	Childers, Buddy	Big Band; Swing	Trumpet	American
1970s–	Childs, Billy	Modern Jazz	Piano, keyboards, composer	American
1950s–	Chilton, John	Swing; Traditional Jazz	Trumpet, flugelhorn, composer, bandleader, author	British
1930s–1990s	Chisholm, George	Traditional Jazz; Big Band; British Jazz	Trombone	Scottish
1920s–1960s	Chittison, Herman 'Ivory'	Traditional Jazz	Piano	American
1960s–	Christensen, Jon	Modern Jazz; Big Band; Jazz Rock	Drums	Norwegian
1980s–	Christi, Ellen	Free Jazz	Vocals	American
1920s	Christian, Buddy	New Orleans Jazz	Banjo	American
1930s–1940s	Christian, Charlie	Swing; Bebop	Guitar	American
1910s–1960s	Christian, Emile	Traditional Jazz; New Orleans Jazz	Trombone	American
1960s–	Christian, Jodie	Hard Bop; Free Jazz; Modern Jazz	Piano, bandleader	American
1950s	Christie Brothers Stompers	New Orleans Jazz; Chicago Jazz	Various instruments	British
1940s–1970s	Christie, Keith	Swing; Big Band; Traditional Jazz	Trombone	British
1970s–	Christlieb, Pete	Bebop	Saxophone	American
1970s–	Christmann, Gunter	Free Jazz	Trombone, bass	Polish
1940s–1980s	Christy, June	Cool Jazz	Vocals	American
1960s–	Cicero, Eugen	Free Jazz; Modern Jazz	Piano	Romanian
1970s–	Cinelu, Mino	Modern Jazz; Jazz Rock; Fusion	Percussion, keyboards, vocals	French
1950s–1970s	Cirillo, Wally	Modern Jazz	Piano, composer	American
1930s–1940s	Claes, Johnny	Traditional Jazz	Trumpet	British
1950s–	Clark, Buddy	Modern Jazz; Bebop; Big Band	Bass, arranger	American
1970s–	Clark, Curtis	Free Jazz	Piano	American
1940s–1950s	Clark, Gus	Big Band; Swing	Piano	Belgian
1970s–	Clark, John	Free Jazz; Modern Jazz; Big Band	French horn, bandleader	American
1940s–1980s	Clark, Mahlon	Swing; West Coast Jazz	Clarinet	American
1960s–	Clark, Mike	Modern Jazz; Jazz Rock	Drums	American
1950s–1960s	Clark, Sonny	Bebop; Hard Bop	Piano	American
1940s–1980s	Clarke, Kenny	Bebop	Drums, composer	American
1960s–1990s	Clarke, Stanley	Fusion	Bass	American
1960s–1970s	Clarke-Boland Big Band	Big Band	Various instruments	German
1990s–	Clarvis, Paul	Free Jazz	Percussion	British
1970s–	Clausen, Thomas	Hard Bop; Modern Jazz	Piano, composer, arranger	Danish
1950s–1990s	Clay, James	Hard Bop	Saxophone, flute	American
1920s–1960s	Clay, Sonny	Traditional Jazz	Piano, drums, bandleader	American
1930s–1990s	Clayton, Buck	Swing	Trumpet, arranger, composer	American

1970s–	Clayton, Jay	Free Jazz	Vocals	American
1980s–	Clayton, Jeff	Swing; Big Band	Saxophone	American
1920s–	Clayton, John	Big Band; Swing	Bass, composer, arranger, bandleader	American
1990s–	Cleaver, Gerald	Free Jazz; Modern Jazz	Drums	American
1930s–1940s	Cless, Rod	Traditional Jazz	Clarinet	American
1940s–	Cleveland, Jimmy	Modern Jazz; Big Band	Trombone	American
1970s–	Cliff, Dave	Modern Jazz; Swing	Guitar	British
1980s–	Cline, Alex	Free Jazz; Modern Jazz	Percussion	American
1980s–	Cline, Nels	Free Jazz; Modern Jazz	Guitar	American
1930s–1940s	Clinton, Larry	Traditional Jazz; Big Band	Trumpet, arranger, composer, bandleader	American
1950s–	Clooney, Rosemary	Traditional Jazz; Swing	Vocals	American
1950s–	Clyne, Jeff	Swing; Big Band; Modern Jazz	Bass	American
1950s–	Coates, John Jr.	Cool Jazz	Piano	American
1930s–1980s	Cobb, Arnett	Soul Jazz	Saxophone	American
1950s–	Cobb, Jimmy	Hard Bop	Drums	American
1920s–1960s	Cobb, Junie	Big Band; Traditional Jazz	Clarinet, saxophone, banjo, piano, violin	American
1970s–	Cobham, Billy	Fusion	Percussion	American
1970s–	Cochrane, Michael	Free Jazz; Modern Jazz	Piano	American
1970s–1980s	Codona	World Fusion; Free Jazz	Various instruments	American
1950s–	Coe, Tony	Hard Bop; Modern Jazz	Saxophone, clarinet	British
1970s–	Coetzee, Basil	World Fusion; Free Jazz	Saxophone	South African
1950s–2000s	Coggins, Gil	Modern Jazz	Piano	American
1970s–1980s	Cohelmec	Free Jazz	Various instruments	French
1990s–	Cohen, Avishai	Hard Bop; Modern Jazz; Fusion	Bass	Israeli
1980s–	Cohen, Greg	Free Jazz; Jazz Rock	Bass	American
1940s–1980s	Cohn, Al	Bebop; Cool Jazz	Saxophone	American
1980s–	Cohn, Joe	Modern Jazz	Guitar	American
1980s–	Coke, Alex	Free Jazz; Modern Jazz	Saxophone, flute	American
1950s–1980s	Coker, Dolo	Bebop	Piano	American
1960s–1990s	Cola, Kid Sheik	New Orleans Jazz; Traditional Jazz	Trumpet, bandleader	American
1970s–	Colaiuta, Vinnie	Jazz Rock; Modern Jazz	Drums	American
1930s–1970s	Cole, Cozy	Swing	Drums	American
1950s–	Cole, Freddy	Swing	Vocals, piano	American
1980s–	Cole, Holly	Swing; Traditional Jazz	Vocals	Canadian
1930s–1960s	Cole, Nat 'King'	Swing	Piano, vocals	American
1970s–1990s	Cole, Richie	Bebop	Saxophones	American
1980s–	Coleman, Anthony	Modern Jazz	Piano, keyboards, composer	American
1920s–1980s	Coleman, Bill	Traditional Jazz; Swing	Trumpet	American
1940s–1990s	Coleman, Earl	Swing; Bebop	Vocals	American
1950s–	Coleman, George	Hard Bop	Saxophones	American
1950s–1990s	Coleman, Ornette	Free Jazz	Saxophones, composer	American
1980s–	Coleman, Steve	Modern Jazz; Free Jazz; Big Band	Saxophone, bandleader	American
1950s–1990s	Coles, Johnny	Hard Bop	Trumpet, flugelhorn	American
1980s–	Colianni, John	Modern Jazz	Piano	American
1930s–1950s	Colignon, Raymond 'Coco'	Traditional Jazz	Piano	Belgian
1950s–	Collette, Buddy	Cool Jazz	Saxophone, clarinet, flute	American
1980s–	Colley, Scott	Modern Jazz	Bass	American
1950s–	Collie, Max	New Orleans Jazz	Trombone, vocals	Australian
1960s–	Collier, Graham	British Jazz; Big Band	Composer, bass, author	British
1950s–	Collier, James Lincoln	All Jazz Styles	Author	American
1970s–2000s	Collins, Cal	Swing; Modern Jazz	Guitar	American
1940–	Collins, Dick	Swing; Big Band	Trumpet	American
1930s–2000s	Collins, John	Swing; Modern Jazz	Guitar	American
1950s–	Collins, Joyce	Hard Bop	Piano, vocals	American
1920s–1950s	Collins, Lee	New Orleans Jazz; Traditional Jazz	Trumpet, bandleader	American
1970s–	Colombo, Eugenio	Free Jazz; Modern Jazz	Saxophone, flute, composer	Italian
1960s–	Colon, Willie	Latin Jazz	Trombone, bandleader	American
1960s–1980s	Coltrane, Alice	Free Jazz	Piano, organ, harp	American
1950s–1960s	Coltrane, John	Modal Jazz; Free Jazz; Hard Bop	Saxophones, composer	American
1990s–	Coltrane, Ravi	Hard Bop; Modern Jazz	Saxophone	American
1940s–1980s	Colyer, Ken	New Orleans Jazz	Trumpet, vocals, bandleader	British
1940s–1980s	Combe, Stuff	Swing; Bebop	Drums	Swiss
1930s–1970s	Combelle, Alix	Swing	Saxophone, clarinet	French
1970s–1990s	Concord Allstars	Swing; Bebop	Various instruments	American
1920s–1970s	Condon, Eddie	Chicago Jazz; Swing; Big Band	Guitar, banjo, bandleader	American
1970s–	Connick, Harry Jr.	Swing; Traditional Jazz; Big Band	Piano, vocals, bandleader	American
1930s–	Conniff, Ray	Big Band	Trombone, arranger, bandleader	American
1900s–1920s	Connolly, Dolly	Ragtime	Vocals	American
1950s–	Connor, Chris	Cool Jazz	Vocals	American
1970s–	Connors, Bill	Modern Jazz; Fusion	Guitar	American
1970s–	Connors, Norman	Fusion	Vocals, composer, producer	American
1970s–	Conte, Luis	Fusion; Latin Jazz; Cuban Jazz	Percussion	Cuban
1950s–1990s	Cook, Junior	Hard Bop	Saxophone	American
1960s–	Cook, Marty	Free Jazz	Trombone	American
1940s–2000s	Cook, Willie	Swing; Big Band	Trumpet	American
1990s–	Coolbone Brass Band	Acid Jazz	Various instruments	American
1950s–	Coon, Jackie	Traditional Jazz	Flugelhorn	American
1920s–1930s	Coon-Sanders Nighthawks	Traditional Jazz	Various instruments	American
1930s–1940s	Cooper, Al	Swing	Saxophone, clarinet, bandleader	American
1940s–1990s	Cooper, Bob	Cool Jazz; Hard Bop	Saxophone, oboe	American
1950s–	Cooper, Buster	Swing	Trombone	American
1920s–1940s	Cooper, Harry	Swing	Trumpet	American
1970s–	Cooper, Lindsay	Jazz Rock; Free Jazz	Saxophone, bassoon, composer	British
1970s–	Copland, Marc	Hard Bop; Modern Jazz	Piano, saxophone	American
1970s–1990s	Cora, Tom	Free Jazz	Cello	American
1940s–1990s	Corb, Morty	Swing; Traditional Jazz	Bass	American
1940s–1970s	Corcoran, Corky	Big Band	Saxophone	American
1990s–	Corduroy	Acid Jazz	Various instruments	British
1960s–	Corea, Chick	Fusion; Free Jazz	Piano, keyboards, composer	American
1960s–	Coryell, Larry	Fusion	Guitar, composer	American
1980s–	Coscia, Gianni	Swing	Accordion, composer	Italian
1950s–1960s	Costa, Eddie	Bebop	Piano, vibraphone	American
1950s–1990s	Costa, John	Swing	Piano	American
1970s–1990s	Costa, Paulinho Da	Brazilian Jazz; Latin Jazz; World Fusion	Percussion	Brazilian
1970s–	Coster, Tom	Free Jazz; Fusion; Jazz Rock	Piano, organ, keyboards	American
1980s–	Cottle, Laurence	Jazz Rock; Big Band	Bass, composer	Welsh
1930s–1970s	Cottrell, Louis	New Orleans Jazz; Traditional Jazz	Clarinet, saxophone	American
1930s–1970s	Coughlan, Frank	Swing	Trombone, trumpet, arranger, vocals, bandleader	Australian
1940s–1960s	Counce, Curtis	Hard Bop	Bass	American
1980s–	Courtois, Vincent	Modern Jazz	Cello, composer	French
1990s–	Courvoisier, Sylvie	Free Jazz	Piano	Swiss
1960s–	Cowell, Stanley	Hard Bop; Modern Jazz	Piano, composer, bandleader, producer	American
1980s–	Cox, Anthony	Free Jazz; Hard Bop	Bass	American
1990s–	Cox, Bruce	Jazz Funk; Free Jazz	Drums	American
1960s–	Coxhill, Lol	Free Jazz	Saxophone	British
1960s–1990s	Cranshaw, Bob	Hard Bop	Bass	American
1950s	Crawford, Hank	Soul Jazz; Hard Bop	Saxophone, piano	American
1940s–1990s	Crawford, Ray	Hard Bop; Soul Jazz	Guitar	American
1970s–	Crispell, Marilyn	Free Jazz	Piano, bandleader	American
1940s–1970s	Criss, Sonny	Hard Bop	Saxophones	American
1970s–	Critchinson, John	Jazz Funk	Piano	British
1980s–	Croft, Monte	Modern Jazz	Vibraphone	American
1950s–1990s	Crombie, Tony	Swing; Jazz Rock; Bebop	Drums, composer	British
1970s–	Crook, Hal	Modern Jazz; Big Band	Trombone, piano	American
1920s–1970s	Crosby, Bing	Swing; Traditional Jazz	Vocals	American
1920s–1990s	Crosby, Bob	Swing; Traditional Jazz; Big Band; Dixieland	Vocals, bandleader	American
1980s–	Crosby, Gary	Jamaican Jazz	Bass, bandleader	Jamaican
1930s–1960s	Crosby, Israel	Cool Jazz; Swing	Bass	American
1960s–1980s	Cross, Earl	Free Jazz	Trumpet, cornet, flugelhorn, mellophone	American
1970s–	Crothers, Connie	Free Jazz; Modern Jazz	Piano	American
1960s–	Crouch, Stanley	All Jazz Styles	Author, critic, drums	American
1960s–	Crusaders, The	Hard Bop; Soul Jazz; Fusion	Various instruments	American
1950s–	Cruz, Celia	Latin Jazz	Vocals	Cuban
1950s–1970s	Cuba, Joe	Latin Jazz	Percussion	American
1960s–	Cuber, Ronnie	Hard Bop	Saxophone	American
1930s–1960s	Cugat, Xavier	Latin Jazz	Violin, bandleader	Spanish
1980s–	Cugny, Laurent	Big Band; Modern Jazz; Jazz Rock	Piano, arranger, author	French
1960s–1990s	Cullum, Jim Jr	Dixieland Revival	Cornet	American
1980s–	Cunliffe, Bill	Hard Bop; Modern Jazz; Fusion Jazz	Piano, arranger, composer	American
1950s–1990s	Cuppini, Gil	Swing; Big Bands	Drums, bandleader	Italian
1970s–	Curnow, Bob	Modern Jazz	Arranger, bandleader	American
1960s–	Curson, Ted	Hard Bop	Trumpet	American
1960s–	Cuscuna, Michael	Modern Jazz; Hard Bop;	Producer, author	American
1970s–	Cutler, Chris	Jazz Rock; Fusion	Drums	American
1970s–	Cuypers, Leo	Free Jazz	Piano, composer	Dutch
1960s–	Cyrille, Andrew	Free Jazz	Drums, composer	American
1990s–	D*Note	Acid Jazz	Various instruments	British
1980s–	D'Agaro, Daniele	World Fusion; Free Jazz	Saxophone, clarinet	Italian
1970s–	D'Ambrosio, Meredith	Cool Jazz	Vocals	American
1930s–1960s	D'Amico, Hank	Swing	Clarinet, saxophone	American
1960s–	D'Andrea, Franco	Hard Bop; Free Jazz; Jazz Rock; Modern Jazz	Keyboards	Italian
1970s	D'Earth, John	Modern Jazz; Big Band	Trumpet	American
1990s–	D'Influence	Acid Jazz	Various instruments	British
1970s–	D'Rivera, Paquito	Latin Jazz	Saxophones, clarinet, flute	Cuban
1970s–	Dagradi, Tony	Jazz Rock; Modern Jazz	Saxophone, bandleader, author	American
1990s–	Dahl, Carsten	Modern Jazz; Hard Bop	Piano	Danish
1950s–	Dahlander, Bert	Modern Jazz; Swing	Drums	Swedish
1960s–1980s	Dailey, Al	Hard Bop	Piano, composer	American
1930s–1970s	Daily, Pete	Big Band; Dixieland Revival	Cornet, saxophone, tuba	American
1980s–	Dalla Porta, Paolino	Modern Jazz	Bass, composer	Italian
1940s–	Dallwitz, Dave	Traditional Jazz	Piano, trombone, arranger, bandleader	Australian
1980s–	Dalseth, Laila	Modern Jazz	Vocals	Norwegian
1940s–1960s	Dameron, Tadd	Bebop	Piano, composer, arranger	American
1970s–	Damiani, Paolo	Free Jazz; Modern Jazz	Bass, cello, composer, bandleader	Italian
1930s–1990s	Dance, Stanley	All Jazz Styles	Author, critic	British
1960s–	Daniel, Ted	Free Jazz	Trumpet	American
1960s–	Daniels, Eddie	Hard Bop	Saxophone, clarinet	American
1980s–	Danielsson, Lars	Free Jazz	Bass, cello, composer, bandleader	Swedish
1970s–	Danielsson, Palle	Modern Jazz	Bass	Swedish
1970s–	Danko, Harold	Hard Bop; Modern Jazz	Piano	American
1940s–	Dankworth, John	Bebop; Big Band; British Jazz	Saxophone, arranger, composer, bandleader	British
1960s–1990s	Dapogny, James	Dixieland Revival; Swing	Piano, bandleader	American
1980s–	Dara, Olu	Free Jazz	Trumpet, cornet	American
1940s–1980s	Darensbourg, Joe	Traditional Jazz; Dixieland; New Orleans Jazz	Clarinet, saxophone	American
1970s–	Darling, David	Modern Jazz; Fusion	Cello, composer	American
1980s–	Darriau, Matt	World Fusion; Modern Jazz	Saxophone, clarinet	American
1960s–	Dasek, Rudolf	Modern Jazz	Guitar	Czech
1930s–1970s	Dash, Julian	Swing	Saxophone, composer	American
1970s–	Dato, Carlo Actis	Hard Bop; Free Jazz	Saxophone, clarinet, bandleader	Italian
1960s–	Dauner, Wolfgang	Modern Jazz; Jazz Rock	Piano, composer, bandleader	German
1950s–2000s	Davenport, Wallace	Swing; Bebop	Trumpet, bandleader	American
1950s–	Davern, Kevin	Dixieland Revival; Swing	Clarinet, saxophones	American
1950s–2000s	Davies, John R.T.	Traditional Jazz	Saxophones, guitar, banjo, drums, producer, discographer	British
1970s–	Davis, Anthony	Free Jazz; Modern Jazz	Piano, composer	American
1950s–	Davis, Art	Hard Bop; Modern Jazz	Bass	American
1950s–	Davis, Charles	Hard Bop	Saxophone	American
1940s–1980s	Davis, Eddie 'Lockjaw'	Bebop; Hard Bop	Saxophone	American
1950s–	Davis, Jackie	Soul Jazz	Organ	American
1980s–	Davis, Jesse	Hard Bop	Saxophone	American
1940s–	Davis, Lem	Bebop; Swing	Saxophone	American
1940s–1950s	Davis, Martha	Swing; Bebop	Piano, vocals	American
1940s–1990s	Davis, Miles	Bebop; Hard Bop; Cool Jazz; Jazz Rock; Fusion	Trumpet, flugelhorn, composer	American
1960s–	Davis, Nathan	Hard Bop; Free Jazz	Saxophone	American
1950s–	Davis, Richard	Hard Bop	Bass	American
1970s–	Davis, Stanton	Free Jazz	Trumpet	American
1960s–1980s	Davis, Steve	Bebop; Hard Bop	Drums	American
1940s–1970s	Davis, Tiny	Swing	Trumpet, vocals	American
1950s; 1970s–1980s	Davis, Walter Jr	Bebop; Hard Bop	Piano	American
1940s–	Davis, Wild Bill	Swing	Organ, piano, arranger	American
1990s–	Davis, Xavier	Modern Jazz	Piano	American
1920s–1980s	Davison, Wild Bill	Dixieland Revival	Cornet	American
1970s–	Dawkins, Ernest	Free Jazz; Modern Jazz	Saxophone, flute	American
1950s–1990s	Dawson, Alan	Hard Bop	Drums	American
1960s–	Dean, Elton	Free Jazz; Modern Jazz	Saxophone, saxello, bandleader	British
1970s–	Dean, Roger	Free Jazz	Keyboards, bass, composer	British
1940s–	DeArango, Bill 'Buddy'	Bebop; Hard Bop	Guitar	American
1950s–	Dearie, Blossom	Bebop	Vocals, piano	American
1990s–	DeBethmann, Pierre	Modern Jazz	Piano	French
1930s–	DeBoeck, Jeff	Traditional Jazz; Swing	Drums	Belgian
1980s–	Debriano, Santi	Free Jazz; Latin Jazz	Bass	Panamanian
1940s–	Dedrick, Rusty	Swing; Traditional Jazz	Trumpet, arranger, composer	American
1960s–	Dee, Brian	Modern Jazz	Piano	British
1930s–1990s	Deems, Barrett	Swing	Drums	American
1980s–	Deffaa, Chip	All Jazz Styles	Author, critic	American
1980s–	DeFrancesco, Joey	Soul Jazz; Hard Bop	Organ, piano, trumpet	American
1940s–1990s	DeFranco, Buddy	Bebop	Clarinet, saxophone	American
1960s–	Degen, Bob	Modern Jazz; Hard Bop	Piano	American
1970s–	DeGraaff, Rein	Modern Jazz; Hard Bop	Piano	Dutch
1960s–	DeJohnette, Jack	Fusion	Drums, piano, composer	American
1930s–1950s	DeKers, Robert	Traditional Jazz; Swing	Trumpet, bandleader	Belgian
1990s–	Delbecq, Benoit	Free Jazz; Modern Jazz	Piano, keyboards	French
1980s–	DelFra, Riccardo	Modern Jazz	Bass, composer, arranger, bandleader	Italian
1990s–	Delius, Tobias	Modern Jazz	Saxophone	British
1930s–1950s	Deloof, Gus	Swing	Trumpet, composer, arranger	Belgian
1980s–	Demierre, Jacques	Free Jazz; Modern Jazz	Piano	Swiss
1940s–	Deniz, Frank	Swing; British Jazz	Guitar, bandleader	British
1980s–	Denley, Jim	Free Jazz	Saxophone, flute	Australian
1970s–	Dennard, Kenwood	Jazz Rock; Funk Jazz; Free Jazz	Drums	American
1980s–	Dennerlein, Barbara	Hard Bop; Modern Jazz	Organ	German
1960s–	Deodato	Brazilian Jazz; Soul Funk	Piano, arranger	Brazilian
1920s–1960s	DeParis, Sidney	Chicago Jazz	Trumpet, tuba, vocals	American
1920s–1970s	DeParis, Wilbur	Traditional Jazz; Dixieland	Trombone, bandleader	American
1970s–	Derome, Jean	Free Jazz; Jazz Rock	Saxophone, flute, composer	Canadian
1940s–1970s	Desmond, Paul	Cool Jazz	Saxophone	American
1950s–1990s	Deuchar, Jimmy	Bebop; British Jazz	Trumpet, flugelhorn	Scottish
1980s–	Dial, Garry	Modern Jazz	Piano, keyboards	American
1970s–	Dibango, Manu	World Fusion	Saxophone, piano, vibraphone	African
1990s–	DiBattista, Stefano	Modern Jazz; Hard Bop	Saxophone	Italian
1980s–	DiCastri, Furio	Modern Jazz	Bass	Italian
1980s–	Dick, Robert	Free Jazz; Modern Jazz	Flute	American
1930s–1980s	Dickenson, Vic	Swing	Trombone, vocals	American
1970s–	Dickerson, Dwight	Modern Jazz	Piano	American
1960s–	Dickerson, Walt	Modern Jazz	Vibraphone	American
1990s–	Dickey, Whit	Free Jazz	Drums	American
1970s–	Dikker, Loek	Free Jazz	Piano, composer	Dutch
1970s–	DiMeola, Al	Fusion; Jazz Rock; World Fusion	Guitar	American
1960s–1990s	Din, Hamza el	World Fusion	Ud	African
1940s–	DiNovi, Gene	Swing; Bebop; Modern Jazz	Piano	American
1960s–	Diorio, Joe	Modern Jazz	Guitar	American
1980s–	Dirty Dozen Brass Band	New Orleans Jazz	Band	American
1970s–1990s	Dissidenten	World Fusion	Various instruments	German
1950s–2000s	Distel, Sacha	Modern Jazz; Bebop	Guitar, vocals	French
1960s–	Dixon, Bill	Free Jazz	Trumpet, flugelhorn, composer	American
1950s–1980s	Dixon, Eric	Big Band; Bebop; Hard Bop	Saxophone	American
1990s	DJ Greyboy	Acid Jazz	DJ, producer	American
1990s–	DKV Trio	Free Jazz	Various instruments	American
1990s–	Dobbins, Bill	Modern Jazz	Piano	American
1920s–1950s	Dodds, Baby	New Orleans Jazz	Drums	American
1920s–1940s	Dodds, Johnny	New Orleans Jazz	Clarinet	American
1990s	Doky Brothers	Hard Bop	Various instruments	Danish
1970s–	Doldinger, Klaus	Modern Jazz; Fusion	Saxophone, bandleader	German
1950s–1960s	Dolphy, Eric	Free Jazz	Saxophone, flute, clarinet	American
1990s–	Domancich, Sophia	Free Jazz	Piano, composer	French
1960s–	Domanico, Chuck	Modern Jazz	Bass	American
1920s–1950s	Dominique, Natty	New Orleans Jazz	Trumpet	American
1940s–	Domnerus, Arne	Swing; Bebop	Saxophone, clarinet, bandleader	Swedish
1930s–1970s	Donahue, Sam	Swing; Big Band	Saxophone, bandleader	American
1980s–	Donald, Barbara	Free Jazz	Trumpet	American
1950s–1970s	Donaldson, Bobby	Swing; Bebop	Drums	American
1950s–	Donaldson, Lou	Bebop; Hard Bop	Saxophone	American
1960s–1970s	Donato, João	Brazilian Jazz	Piano, vocals, trombone	Brazilian
1970s–	Donato, Michel	Modern Jazz	Bass	Canadian
1990s–	Doneda, Michel	Free Jazz	Saxophone, bandleader	French
1940s–1990s	Donegan, Dorothy	Swing; Bebop	Piano, vocals	American
1950s–2000s	Donegan, Lonnie	Traditional Jazz	Vocals, guitar, banjo	Scottish
1970s–	Doran, Christy	Free Jazz; Modern Jazz	Guitar	Irish
1960s–	Dorge, Pierre	Free Jazz; Modern Jazz; Big Band	Guitar, bandleader, composer	Danish
1940s–1970s	Dorham, Kenny	Hard Bop	Trumpet, composer	American
1940s–	Dorough, Bob	Cool Jazz; Bebop; Swing	Piano, vocals, composer	American
1920s–1950s	Dorsey, Jimmy	Swing; Big Band	Clarinet, saxophone, trumpet	American
1990s–	Dorsey, Leon Lee	Modern Jazz	Bass	American
1920s–1950s	Dorsey, Tommy	Swing; Big Band	Trombone, trumpet	American
1990s–	Douglas, Dave	Free Jazz; Modern Jazz	Trumpet, bandleader	American
1930s–1950s	Douglas, Tommy	Traditional Jazz; Big Band	Clarinet, saxophone, arranger	American
1970s–	Downes, Wray	Modern Jazz; Bebop	Piano	Canadian
1970s–	Drake, Hamid	Free Jazz; Cuban Jazz	Drums, tabla	American
1950s–1980s	Draper, Ray	Hard Bop	Tuba	American
1990s	Dread Flimstone	Acid Jazz	DJ, producer	American
1980s–	Dresch, Mihaly	Free Jazz	Reeds, composer, bandleader	Hungarian
1970s–	Dresser, Mark	Free Jazz; Modern Jazz	Bass, composer	American
1950s–1990s	Drew, Kenny	Hard Bop	Piano	American
1990s–	Drew, Kenny Jr.	Hard Bop; Modern Jazz	Piano	American
1970s–	Drew, Martin	Bebop; Swing; Modern Jazz	Drums	British
1990s	Drummond, Billy	Hard Bop	Drums	American
1980s–	Drummond, Ray	Hard Bop	Bass	American
1970s	Dubin, Larry	Free Jazz	Drums	Canadian
1990s–	Ducret, Marc	Free Jazz	Guitar	French
1960s–	Dudas, Lajos	Modern Jazz	Clarinet, saxophone, composer, arranger, bandleader	Hungarian
1960s–	Dudek, Gerd	Free Jazz	Saxophone, clarinet, flute	German
1970s–	Dudziak, Urszula	Modern Jazz; Fusion	Vocals	Polish
1960s–	Duke, George	Fusion; Jazz Pop	Keyboards, composer, producer	American

1950s–	Dukes of Dixieland	Dixieland Revival	Various instruments	American
1980s–	Dulfer, Candy	Smooth Jazz	Saxophone	Dutch
1970s–	Dulfer, Hans	Free Jazz	Saxophone	Dutch
1960s–	Dunbar, Ted	Soul Jazz; Hard Bop	Guitar	American
1910s–1930s	Dunn, Johnny	Traditional Jazz	Trumpet, bandleader	American
1950s–	Duran, Eddie	Cool Jazz	Guitar, bandleader	American
1960s–	Durham, Bobby	Soul Jazz; Modern Jazz	Trombone, vibraphone, bass	American
1920s–1980s	Durham, Eddie	Swing; Big Band	Trombone, guitar, arranger	American
1950s–	Dutch Swing College Band	Dixieland; Swing; Big Band	Various instruments	Dutch
1990s–	Duval, Dominic	Free Jazz; Modern Jazz	Bass	American
1950s–1990s	Duvivier, George	Swing; Big Band; Bebop	Bass, arranger	American
1970s–	Dvorak, Jim	Fusion	Trumpet	American
1960s–1980s	Dyani, Johnny	Free Jazz	Bass, vocals	South African
1990s–	Dyer, Ann	Free Jazz	Vocals	American
1980s–	Eade, Dominique	Modern Jazz	Vocals, composer	British
1940s–2000s	Eager, Allen	Cool Jazz; Bebop	Saxophone	American
1950s–1970s	Eardley, Jon	Cool Jazz; Bebop	Trumpet	American
1960s–1990s	Earland, Charles	Soul Jazz; Hard Bop	Keyboards	American
1970s–	Easley, Bill	Hard Bop	Clarinet, saxophone	American
1970s–1990s	Eça, Luiz	Brazilian Jazz	Piano	Brazilian
1970s–	Ecklund, Peter	Traditional Jazz	Cornet, trumpet, whistle	American
1940s–1980s	Eckstine, Billy	Bebop	Vocals, trumpet, guitar	American
1940s–1980s	Edelhagen, Kurt	Big Band	Bandleader, piano	German
1940s–1990s	Edison, Harry 'Sweets'	Swing	Trumpet	American
1970s–	Eduardo, Ze	Modern Jazz	Bass, piano, composer, arranger, bandleader	Portuguese
1920s–1970s	Edwards, Cliff 'Ukulele Ike'	Traditional Jazz	Vocals, ukulele	American
1970s–	Edwards, Marc	Free Jazz	Drums	American
1940s–2000s	Edwards, Teddy	Bebop; Hard Bop	Saxophone, arranger	American
1970s–	Egan, Mark	Modern Jazz; Fusion	Bass, composer	American
1970s–	Ehrlich, Marty	Free Jazz; Modern Jazz	Saxophone, clarinet, bandleader	American
1970s–	El'Zabar, Kahil	Free Jazz	Drums	American
1930s–1980s	Eldridge, Roy	Swing	Trumpet, flugelhorn, vocals	American
1980s–	Elf, Mark	Modern Jazz; Bebop	Guitar	American
1960s–	Elgart, Billy	Free Jazz; Bebop	Drums	American
1970s–	Elias, Eliane	Brazilian Jazz; Latin Jazz	Piano, vocals	Brazilian
1990s–	Elling, Kurt	Modern Jazz	Vocals	American
1920s–1970s	Ellington, Duke	Swing	Piano, arranger, composer	American
1940s–1990s	Ellington, Mercer	Swing	Trumpet, arranger, composer	American
1970s–	Elliot, Richard	Smooth Jazz	Saxophone	Scottish
1950s–1970s	Elliott, Don	Cool Jazz; Swing; Fusion	Mellophone, vibraphone, vocals, composer	American
1960s–1970s	Ellis, Don	Free Jazz; Modern Jazz; Big Band	Trumpet, composer, bandleader	American
1940s–1990s	Ellis, Herb	Swing; Bebop	Guitar	American
1980s–	Ellis, Lisle	Free Jazz; Modern Jazz	Bass	Canadian
1930s–1980s	Elman, Ziggy	Swing; Big Band	Trumpet	American
1970s–	Emborg, Jorgen	Fusion; Big Band	Piano, composer, bandleader	American
1970s–	Emery, James	Free Jazz; Modern Jazz	Guitar	American
1980s–	Endresen, Sidsel	Jazz Rock; Modern Jazz	Vocals, composer	Norwegian
1980s–	Eneidi, Marco	Free Jazz	Saxophone	American
1950s–	Enevoldsen, Bob	Cool Jazz; West Coast Jazz	Trombone, saxophone, bass	American
1970s–	Engels, John	Modern Jazz; Hard Bop	Drums	Dutch
1970s–1990s	Enriquez, Bobby	Cuban Jazz	Piano	American
1940s–1990s	Ericson, Rolf	Swing; Bebop	Trumpet, flugelhorn	Swedish
1970s–	Erquiaga, Steve	Modern Jazz; Hard Bop	Guitar	American
1970s–	Erskine, Peter	Cool Jazz; Bebop; Fusion	Drums	American
1960s–	Erstrand, Lars	Swing	Vibraphone	Swedish
1950s–1960s	Ervin, Booker	Hard Bop	Saxophone, composer	American
1950s–1980s	Erwin, Pee Wee	Swing	Trumpet	American
1970s–	Eschete, Ron	Modern Jazz	Guitar	American
1960s–	Escovedo, Pete	Latin Jazz; Fusion	Percussion, vibraphone	American
1980s–	Eskelin, Ellery	Free Jazz; Modern Jazz	Saxophone	American
1970s–	Etheridge, John	Jazz Rock; Swing	Guitar	British
1920s–1950s	Etting, Ruth	Traditional Jazz	Vocals	American
1970s–	Eubanks, Kevin	Hard Bop; Modern Jazz	Guitar, bandleader	American
1980s–	Eubanks, Robin	Hard Bop; Modern Jazz	Trombone, bandleader	American
1940s–1980s	Evans, Bill	Cool Jazz; Modal Jazz	Piano, composer	American
1980s–	Evans, Bill	Jazz Rock; Fusion	Saxophone	American
1940s–1970s	Evans, Doc	Traditional Jazz; Dixieland	Cornet	American
1940s–1980s	Evans, Gil	Cool Jazz; Fusion	Piano, arranger, composer	Canadian
1980s–	Evans, Sandy	Fusion; Free Jazz	Saxophone, composer	Australian
1940s–1980s	Ewell, Don	Traditional Jazz; Swing	Piano	American
1970s–1990s	Faddis, Jon	Bebop	Trumpet, flugelhorn	American
1950s–2000s	Fagerquist, Don	Cool Jazz; Bebop	Trumpet	American
1970s–	Fahn, Mike	Swing; Big Band	Trombone	American
1970s–	Fairweather, Digby	British Jazz	Cornet, author	British
1990s–	Falay, Maffy	Bebop; World Fusion	Trumpet	Turkish
1970s–	Fambrough, Charles	Hard Bop; Modern Jazz	Bass	American
1950s–1990s	Farlow, Tal	Bebop; Cool Jazz	Guitar	American
1950s–1990s	Farmer, Art	Bebop; Hard Bop; Cool Jazz	Trumpet, flugelhorn	American
1980s–	Farnham, Allen	Hard Bop; Modern Jazz	Piano, producer	American
1990s–	Farnsworth, Joe	Hard Bop	Drums	American
1960s–1980s	Farrell, Joe	Hard Bop	Saxophones, flute	American
1970s–	Fasoli, Claudio	Modern Jazz; Jazz Rock	Saxophone, composer, bandleader	Italian
1970s–	Fasteau, Zusaan Kali	World Fusion; Free Jazz	Vocals, various instruments	American
1930s–1990s	Fatool, Nick	Swing; Big Band; Dixieland	Drums	American
1980s–	Fattburger	Smooth Jazz	Various instruments	American
1990s–	Faulk, Dan	Hard Bop	Saxophone	American
1960s–2000s	Favors, Malachi	Free Jazz	Bass, banjo, zither, percussion	American
1960s–	Favre, Pierre	Hard Bop; Free Jazz	Drums, bandleader	Swiss
1980s–	Fay, Rick	Dixieland	Saxophone, clarinet	American
1930s–1940s	Fazola, Irving	New Orleans Jazz; Traditional Jazz	Clarinet, saxophone	American
1930s–1990s	Feather, Leonard	Swing; Bebop	Author, piano, critic, composer, arranger	British
1980s–	Felder, Dale	Modern Jazz	Saxophone	American
1960s–	Felder, Wilton	Hard Bop; Soul Jazz; Fusion	Saxophone, bass	American
1980s–	Feldman, Mark	Free Jazz	Violin	American
1950s–1980s	Feldman, Victor	Cool Jazz	Vibraharp, percussion	British
1950s–1990s	Ferguson, Maynard	Hard Bop	Trumpet, flugelhorn, bandleader	Canadian
1970s–	Ferguson, Sherman	Hard Bop; Modern Jazz	Drums	American
1960s–	Ferre, Boulou	Swing; Bebop; Modern Jazz	Guitar	French
1980s–	Ferrell, Rachelle	Modern Jazz	Vocals	American
1970s–	Ferris, Glenn	Jazz Rock; Big Band; Hard Bop	Trombone	American
1960s–1990s	Fest, Manfredo	Brazilian Jazz; Latin Jazz	Piano, bandleader	Brazilian
1960s–	Few, Bobby	Hard Bop; Free Jazz	Piano	American
1960s–1970s	Feza, Mongezi	World Fusion	Trumpet	South African
1980s–	Fields, Brandon	Modern Jazz	Saxophone	American
1930s–1960s	Fields, Ernie	Swing; Big Band	Trombone, bandleader	American
1940s–1950s	Fields, Herbie	Swing	Clarinet, saxophone	American
1990s–	Fields, Scott	Free Jazz	Guitar, composer	American
1980s–	Filiano, Ken	Free Jazz	Bass	American
1970s–	Fine, Milo	Free Jazz	Piano, clarinet, percussion, critic	American
1980s–	Fioravanti, Ettore	Hard Bop; Free Jazz	Drums, composer	Italian
1940s–1960s	Firehouse Fire Plus Two	Dixieland Revival	Various instruments	American
1960s–	Fischer, Clare	Hard Bop; Latin Jazz	Piano, composer, arranger, bandleader	American
1970s–	Fischer, John	Free Jazz	Piano, composer, bandleader	Belgian
1930s–1990s	Fitzgerald, Ella	Swing; Bebop	Vocals	American
1940s–2000s	Flanagan, Tommy	Bebop; Hard Bop	Piano	American
1970s–	Fleck, Bela	Modern Jazz; Fusion	Banjo	American
1950s–	Florence, Bob	Modern Jazz	Piano, arranger, composer, bandleader	American
1950s–	Flores, Chuck	Swing; Modern Jazz; Big Band	Drums, bandleader	American
1980s–1990s	Flores, Luca	Free Jazz	Piano	Italian
1970s–	Flory, Chris	Swing	Guitar	American
1950s–	Flory, Med	Big Band; Bebop; Swing	Saxophone, arranger, bandleader	American
1940s–1970s	Fol, Raymond	Traditional Jazz; Bebop	Piano	French
1970s–	Folds, Chuck	Traditional Jazz; Swing	Piano	American
1950s–1990s	Fonatana, Carl	Cool Jazz; Bebop	Trombone	American
1950s–	Fonseque, Raymond	Traditional Jazz	Trombone, arranger, bandleader	French
1970s–	Ford, Joe	Free Jazz; Modern Jazz	Saxophone, flute	American
1970s–	Ford, Ricky	Hard Bop; Modern Jazz	Saxophone	American
1970s–	Ford, Robben	Fusion	Guitar	American
1970s–	Forman, Bruce	Bebop	Guitar, bandleader	American
1980s–	Forman, Mitchel	Modern Jazz; Fusion	Piano, keyboards	American
1990s–	Formanek, Michael	Free Jazz; Modern Jazz	Bass, composer	American
1940s–1980s	Forrest, Jimmy	Hard Bop	Saxophone	American
1960s–	Fortune, Sonny	Free Jazz; Modern Jazz	Saxophone	American
1960s–	Foster, Al	Hard Bop; Jazz Rock	Drums	American
1950s–1990s	Foster, Frank	Hard Bop; Swing	Saxophone, arranger	American
1960s–	Foster, Gary	Bebop; Cool Jazz	Saxophone, flute	American
1910s–1940s	Foster, Pops	New Orleans Jazz	Bass	American
1970s–	Foster, Ronnie	Soul Jazz	Piano, keyboards, organ	American
1940s–1990s	Fountain, Pete	Dixieland Revival	Clarinet, saxophones	American
1990s–	Fourplay	Smooth Jazz	Various instruments	American
1970s–1990s	Frampton, Roger	Free Jazz	Piano, saxophone, composer	British
1970s–	Francioli, Leon	Free Jazz	Bass, cello	Swiss
1980s–	Franck, Tomas	Hard Bop	Saxophone	Swedish
1970s–	Franklin, Henry	Hard Bop; Modern Jazz	Bass	American
1980s–	Fraser, Hugh	Free Jazz; Modern Jazz; Hard Bop; Big Band	Trombone, piano, composer, bandleader	Canadian
1990s–	Freelon, Nnenna	Modern Jazz	Vocals	American
1920s–1980s	Freeman, Bud	Swing	Saxophone, clarinet, composer	American
1970s–	Freeman, Chico	Modern Jazz	Saxophone, clarinet, flute, bandleader	American
1940s–1980s	Freeman, Russ	Cool Jazz; Bebop	Piano	American
1950s–1960s	Freeman, Stan	Cool Jazz; Swing; Bebop	Piano, composer	American
1960s–	Freeman, Von	Modern Jazz	Saxophone, bandleader	American
1990s–	Fresu, Paolo	Free Jazz	Trumpet, flugelhorn, composer, bandleader	Italian
1990s–	Friedlander, Erik	Free Jazz	Cello	American
1970s–	Friedman, David	Hard Bop; Modern Jazz	Vibraphone, marimba	American
1950s–	Friedman, Don	Hard Bop; Modern Jazz	Piano	American
1970s–	Friesen, David	Modern Jazz	Bass	American
1940s–	Frigo, Johnny	Swing	Violin, bass	American
1970s–	Frisell, Bill	Fusion	Guitar	American
1960s–	Frishberg, Dave	Swing; Bebop	Piano, vocals, composer	American
1970s–	Frith, Fred	Free Jazz	Guitar, composer	British
1990s–	Froman, Ian	Modern Jazz; Hard Bop	Drums	Canadian
1950s–1960s	Fruscella, Tony	Cool Jazz	Trumpet	American
1990s–	Fryland, Thomas	Modern Jazz; Big Band	Trumpet	Danish
1990s–	Fujii, Satoko	Free Jazz; Big Band	Piano	Japanese
1950s–1990s	Fuller, Curtis	Hard Bop	Trombone	American
1940s–1990s	Fuller, Gil	Big Band; Bebop	Arranger	American
1980s–	Futterman, Joel	Free Jazz	Piano	American
1980s–	G, Kenny	Smooth Jazz	Saxophone	American
1930s–2000s	Gabler, Milt	Swing	Producer	American
1970s–	Gadd, Steve	Jazz Rock; Modern Jazz	Drums	American
1930s–1950s	Gaillard, Slim	Swing	Vocals, piano, guitar, composer	American
1950s–	Galbraith, Barry	Swing; Soul Jazz; Hard Bop	Guitar	American
1960s–	Gale, Eddie	Free Jazz	Trumpet	American
1970s–1990s	Gale, Eric	Jazz Funk; Soul Jazz	Guitar	American
1960s–	Gales, Larry	Hard Bop	Bass	American
1990s	Galliano	Acid Jazz	Various instruments	British
1970s–	Galliano, Richard	Modern Jazz	Accordion, composer	French
1960s–	Galloway, Jim	Swing; Dixieland	Saxophone, clarinet	Canadian
1970s–	Galper, Hal	Modern Jazz	Piano, bandleader	American
1980s–	Gambale, Frank	Fusion	Guitar	Australian
1970s–1990s	Ganelin Trio	Free Jazz	Various instruments	Russian
1970s–	Gannon, Oliver	Swing; Jazz Rock; Modern Jazz	Guitar	Canadian
1960s–	Garbarek, Jan	Free Jazz	Saxophone, composer	Norwegian
1920s–1970s	Garber, Jan	Big Band	Violin, bandleader	American
1980s–	Gardony, Laszlo	Modern Jazz	Piano, composer	Hungarian
1950s–1980s	Garland, Red	Hard Bop	Piano	American
1940s–1970s	Garner, Erroll	Bebop; Swing	Piano	American
1960s–	Garnett, Carlos	Free Jazz; Hard Bop; Modern Jazz	Saxophone	Panamanian
1980s–	Garrett, Kenny	Modern Jazz	Saxophone	American
1950s–	Garrick, Michael	Free Jazz	Piano, organ, composer	British
1960s–1980s	Garrison, Jimmy	Free Jazz	Bass	American
1970s–	Garson, Mike	Modern Jazz	Piano, keyboards	American
1990s–	Garzone, George	Modern Jazz	Saxophone	American
1940s–	Gaslini, Giorgio	Free Jazz	Piano, composer	Italian
1980s–	Gatto, Roberto	Fusion; Hard Bop	Drums	Italian
1980s–	Gayle, Charles	Free Jazz	Saxophone, clarinet, piano	American
1950s–1990s	Gaynair, Wilton 'Bogey'	Modern Jazz; Hard Bop	Saxophone	Jamaican
1980s–	Gebbia, Gianni	Free Jazz	Saxophone, bandleader	Italian
1940s–	Geller, Herb	Hard Bop; Bebop	Saxophone	American
1900s–1930s	Gershwin, George	Ragtime	Piano, composer	American
1980s–	Gertz, Bruce	Free Jazz	Bass	American
1960s–	Getz, Jane	Hard Bop; Modern Jazz	Piano	American
1940s–1990s	Getz, Stan	Cool Jazz; Hard Bop	Saxophone	American
1980s–	Gewelt, Terje	Fusion; Jazz Rock; Modern Jazz	Bass	Norwegian
1980s–	Ghiglioni, Tiziana	Free Jazz	Vocals	Italian
1970s–	Giammarco, Maurizio	Free Jazz; Fusion; Hard Bop	Saxophone	Italian
1960s–	Gibbs, Mike	Free Jazz; Fusion	Trombone, composer, arranger, bandleader	Rhodesian
1950s–1990s	Gibbs, Terry	Bebop	Vibraphone, drums	American
1970s–1990s	Gibson, Banu	Dixieland Revival	Vocals	American
1940s–1990s	Gibson, Harry 'The Hipster'	Swing	Vocals, piano	American
1970s–	Giddins, Gary	All Jazz Styles	Author, critic	American
1960s–	Gilberto, Astrud	Brazilian Jazz	Vocals	Brazilian
1950s–	Gilberto, João	Brazilian Jazz	Vocals, guitar	Brazilian
1930s–1990s	Gillespie, Dizzy	Bebop	Trumpet, vocals, composer	American
1950s–1990s	Gilmore, John	Free Jazz; Bebop	Saxophone, drums	American
1970s–	Gilmore, Steve	Modern Jazz	Bass	American
1980s–1990s	Giordano, Vince	Dixieland Revival	Bass, tuba, saxophone	American
1930s–1990s	Girard, Adele	Swing; Dixieland	Harp	American
1950s	Girard, George	Chicago Jazz	Trumpet, vocals	American
1960s–1990s	Gismonti, Egberto	Brazilian Jazz; World Fusion	Guitar, piano, keyboards, vocals	Brazilian
1950s–	Gitler, Ira	All Jazz Styles	Author, critic	American
1940s–	Giuffre, Jimmy	Bebop; Cool Jazz	Clarinet, saxophones, flute	American
1990s–	Gjerstad, Frode	Free Jazz	Saxophone	Norwegian
1930s–1970s	Gleason, Ralph	All Jazz Styles	Author, critic	American
1930s–1970s	Glenn, Tyree	Swing; Big Band	Trombone, vibraphone	American
1980s–	Glerum, Ernst	Free Jazz	Bass, piano	Dutch
1960s–	Globe Unity Orchestra	Free Jazz; Big Band	Various instruments	German
1990s–	Goldberg, Ben	Hard Bop; Free Jazz	Clarinet, bandleader	American
1950s–1990s	Goldie, Don	Dixieland	Trumpet	American
1980s–	Goldings, Larry	Modern Jazz	Piano, organ	American
1920s–1960s	Goldkette, Jean	Traditional Jazz	Bandleader	French
1970s–	Golia, Vinny	Free Jazz	Saxophone, clarinet, flute, bassoon, arranger, composer	American
1950s–	Golson, Benny	Hard Bop	Saxophone, arranger, composer	American
1960s–	Gomez, Eddie	Modern Jazz	Bass	Puerto Rican
1920s–1970s	Gonella, Nat	Dixieland	Trumpet, vocals	British
1940s–1970s	Gonsalves, Paul	Swing; Bebop	Saxophone, guitar	American
1940s–1970s	Gonzales, Babs	Bebop	Vocals	American
1980s–	Gonzales, Ruben	Latin Jazz	Piano	Cuban
1970s–	Gonzalez, Dennis	Free Jazz; Modern Jazz	Trumpet, flugelhorn	American
1970s–	Gonzalez, Jerry	Latin Jazz; Cuban Jazz	Trumpet, flugelhorn, congas, bandleader	American
1920s–1970s	Goodman, Benny	Swing; Big Band	Clarinet, saxophone, bandleader	American
1970s–	Goodrick, Mick	Modern Jazz	Bass	American
1960s–	Goodwin, Bill	Modern Jazz; Bebop	Drums	American
1970s–	Goodwin, Jim	Traditional Jazz; Dixieland	Cornet	American
1940s–1950s	Gordon, Bob	Cool Jazz	Saxophone	American
1960s–	Gordon, Bobby	Swing	Clarinet	American
1940s–1980s	Gordon, Dexter	Bebop; Hard Bop	Saxophones	American
1940s–1960s	Gordon, Joe	Hard Bop	Trumpet	American
1970s–	Gottlieb, Danny	Modern Jazz	Drums	American
1890s	Gottschalk, Louis Moreau	Ragtime	Piano, composer	American
1950s–	Gourley, Jimmy	Bebop; Hard Bop; Modern Jazz	Bass, author	American
1960s–	Goykovich, Dusko	Hard Bop	Flugelhorn, trumpet	Slovenian
1950s–	Graas, John	Cool Jazz	French horn	American
1930s–1940s	Grace, Terry	Swing	Vocals	American
1980s–	Graewe, Georg	Free Jazz; Big Band	Piano	German
1960s–2000s	Graillier, Michel	Free Jazz	Piano, composer	French
1980s–	Granelli, Jerry	Modern Jazz	Drums, bandleader	American
1940s–1990s	Granz, Norman	Bebop	Producer	American
1930s–1990s	Grappelli, Stephane	Swing	Violin	American
1990s	Grassy Knoll, The	Acid Jazz	Various instruments	American
1960s–	Graves, Milford	Free Jazz	Percussion	American
1940s–1950s	Gray, Wardell	Bebop; Swing	Saxophone	American
1980s–	Green, Benny	Modern Jazz	Piano	American
1950s–1960s	Green, Bennie	Swing; Bebop	Trombone	American
1940s–1980s	Green, Bunky	Hard Bop	Saxophone	American
1920s–1930s	Green, Charlie 'Big'	Traditional Jazz	Trombone	American
1940s–1980s	Green, Freddie	Swing	Guitar	American
1950s–1970s	Green, Grant	Hard Bop	Guitar	American
1940s–	Green, Urbie	Swing; Bebop	Trombone	American
1960s–	Greene, Burton	Free Jazz; Modern Jazz; World Fusion	Piano, composer	American
1970s–	Greenwich, Sonny	Free Jazz	Guitar	Canadian
1920s–1940s	Greer, Sonny	Swing	Drums	American
1960s–	Gregorio, Guillermo	Free Jazz	Saxophone, clarinet	Argentinian
1980s–	Gress, Drew	Free Jazz; Modern Jazz	Bass, pedal steel	American
1940s–1990s	Grey, Al	Bebop; Swing	Trombone	American
1990s	Greyboy Allstars	Acid Jazz	Various instruments	American
1940s–	Griffin, Johnny	Bebop; Hard Bop	Saxophone	American
1960s	Grimes, Henry	Free Jazz; Hard Bop	Bass	American
1940s–1970s	Grimes, Tiny	Bebop	Guitar, vocals	American
1960s–1990s	Grolnick, Don	Modern Jazz; Jazz Rock; Fusion	Piano, keyboards	American
1990s–	Groove Collective	Acid Jazz	Various instruments	American
1980s–	Grossman, Richard	Free Jazz	Piano	American
1960s–	Grossman, Steve	Hard Bop	Saxophone	American
1950s–1990s	Grosz, Marty	Dixieland Revival	Guitar, banjo, vocals	American
1960s–	Gruntz, George	Modern Jazz; Big Band	Keyboards, composer, bandleader	Swiss
1960s–	Grusin, Dave	Fusion	Piano, producer, composer	American
1970s–	Grusin, Don	Smooth Jazz	Keyboards	American
1950s–1970s	Gryce, Gigi	Hard Bop	Saxophone, flute, composer	American
1950s–1970s	Guaraldi, Vince	Cool Jazz	Piano, composer	American
1930s–1980s	Guarnieri, Johnny	Swing	Piano, composer	American
1930s–1960s	Guesnon, George	Swing; New Orleans Jazz	Banjo, guitar, vocals	American
1950s–1990s	Gulda, Friedrich	Free Jazz	Piano, flute, saxophone, composer, vocals	Austrian
1950s–1970s	Gullin, Lars	Cool Jazz; Bebop	Saxophone, composer, arranger	Swedish

1970s–	Gurtu, Trilok	World Fusion; Fusion	Percussion	Indian
1980s–	Gustafsson, Mats	Free Jazz	Saxophone	Swedish
1970s–	Guy, Barry	Free Jazz	Bass, composer	British
1930s–1980s	Guyer, Bobby	Swing; Chicago Jazz	Trumpet	American
1930s–1970s	Hackett, Bobby	Chicago Jazz; Swing	Cornet, trumpet, guitar	American
1950s–	Haden, Charlie	Free Jazz; Hard Bop	Bass	American
1940s–1990s	Hafer, Dick	Cool Jazz	Saxophone	American
1970s–	Hagans, Tim	Hard Bop	Trumpet, flugelhorn	American
1930s–1990s	Haggart, Bob	Swing; Dixieland	Bass, composer, arranger	American
1960s–	Hahn, Jerry	Modern Jazz	Guitar	American
1940s–1980s	Haig, Al	Bebop	Piano	American
1940s–1980s	Hakim, Sadik	Bebop	Piano	American
1920s–1940s	Hall, Adelaide	Swing	Vocals	American
1930s–1960s	Hall, Edmond	New Orleans Jazz; Swing	Clarinet, saxophone	American
1950s–	Hall, Jim	Cool Jazz	Guitar	American
1950s–	Hallberg, Bengt	Bebop; Cool Jazz	Piano, composer, arranger	Swedish
1970s–1990s	Halliday, Lin	Hard Bop	Saxophone	American
1950s–	Hamilton, Chico	Cool Jazz; Hard Bop	Drums	American
1970s–	Hamilton, Jeff	Bebop	Drums	American
1950s–1990s	Hamilton, Jimmy	Bebop; Swing	Clarinet, saxophone, arranger	American
1970s–	Hamilton, Scott	Swing; Modern Jazz	Saxophone	American
1960s–	Hammer, Jan	Fusion	Piano, keyboards, drums	Czech
1930s–1980s	Hammond, John	All Jazz Styles	Producer, author, critic	American
1960s–	Hampel, Gunter	Free Jazz	Vibraphone, piano, flute, clarinet	German
1920s–1990s	Hampton, Lionel	Swing; Big Band	Vibraphone, drums, piano, vocals, bandleader	American
1950s–	Hampton, Slide	Bebop; Hard Bop	Trombone, arranger, composer	American
1960s–	Hancock, Herbie	Modal Jazz; Hard Bop; Fusion	Keyboards, composer	American
1950s–	Handy, John	Modern Jazz	Saxophone	American
1950s–	Hanna, Jake	Swing	Drums	American
1950s–2000s	Hanna, Roland 'Sir'	Swing; Hard Bop; Modern Jazz	Piano	American
1980s–1990s	Hanrahan, Kip	World Fusion; Fusion	Bandleader	American
1920s–1930s	Hanshaw, Annette	Traditional Jazz	Vocals	American
1980s–	Haque, Fareed	Modern Jazz; Fusion	Guitar	American
1980s–	Hardcastle, Paul	Fusion	Keyboards	British
1950s–1960s	Harden, Wilbur	Hard Bop	Trumpet, flugelhorn	American
1920s–1970s	Hardin Armstrong, Lil	Swing; Traditional Jazz; Swing	Piano, vocals, composer	American
1950s–1990s	Hardman, Bill	Hard Bop	Trumpet, flugelhorn	American
1980s–	Hardy, Craig	Hard Bop	Saxophone	American
1960s–1970s	Hardy, John 'Captain John'	New Orleans Jazz	Saxophone	American
1940s–1960s	Harewood, Al	Bebop	Drums	American
1980s–	Hargrove, Roy	Hard Bop	Trumpet	American
1960s–	Harley, Rufus	Hard Bop; Soul Jazz	Saxophone, flute, bagpipes	American
1890s–1900s	Harney, Ben	Ragtime	Piano, composer	Austrian
1970s–	Harrell, Tom	Hard Bop; Big Band	Trumpet	American
1950s–1970s	Harriott, Joe	Free Jazz; Modern Jazz; World Fusion	Saxophone	Jamaican
1990s–	Harris, Allan	Swing	Vocals	American
1950s–	Harris, Barry	Bebop	Piano	American
1960s–1990s	Harris, Beaver	Free Jazz, Modern Jazz	Drums, bandleader	American
1950s–	Harris, Benny	Bebop	Trumpet	American
1940s–1970s	Harris, Bill	Swing; Bebop	Trombone	American
1970s–	Harris, Craig	Free Jazz	Trombone	American
1960s–1990s	Harris, Eddie	Soul Jazz; Hard Bop	Saxophone, keyboards, vocals	American
1950s–1990s	Harris, Gene	Soul Jazz; Hard Bop; Fusion	Piano, keyboards	American
1990s–	Harris, Stefon	Free Jazz; Modern Jazz	Vibraphone	American
1980s–	Harrison, Donald	Modern Jazz	Saxophone	American
1940s–1990s	Harrison, Lou	World Fusion	Composer	American
1970s–	Harrison, Wendell	Bebop	Saxophone, clarinet	American
1960s–	Harrow, Nancy	Modern Jazz	Vocals	American
1990s–	Hart, Antonio	Hard Bop; Modern Jazz	Saxophone	American
1960s–	Hart, Billy	Modern Jazz	Drums	American
1980s–	Hart, John	Hard Bop; Modern Jazz	Guitar	American
1940s–1980s	Hartman, Johnny	Modern Jazz	Vocals	American
1980s–	Haslam, George	Free Jazz	Saxophone	British
1940s	Hasselgard, Stan	Swing; Bebop	Clarinet	Swiss
1980s–	Hauser, Fritz	Free Jazz; World Fusion	Drums	Swiss
1950s–1970s	Hawes, Hampton	Bebop; Hard Bop	Piano	American
1920s–1960s	Hawkins, Coleman	Swing; Bebop	Saxophone	American
1930s–1970s	Hawkins, Erskine	Swing	Trumpet, bandleader	American
1920s–1930s	Hayes, Clifford	Traditional Jazz	Violin, bandleader	American
1950s–	Hayes, Louis	Hard Bop	Drums	American
1950s–1970s	Hayes, Tubby	Big Band; Hard Bop; Modern Jazz	Saxophone, flute, vibraphone, arranger, composer	British
1980s–	Haynes, Graham	Modern Jazz	Cornet	American
1980s–	Haynes, Phil	Free Jazz	Drums, bandleader	American
1940s–	Haynes, Roy	Bebop; Hard Bop	Drums	American
1980s–	Hays, Kevin	Modern Jazz	Piano	American
1940s–1980s	Heard, J.C.	Swing; Bebop	Drums	American
1940s–1990s	Heath, Albert 'Tootie'	Hard Bop	Drums	American
1940s–1990s	Heath, Jimmy	Hard Bop	Saxophone, flute, composer	American
1940s–1990s	Heath, Percy	Bebop; Hard Bop; Cool Jazz	Bass	American
1940s–1960s	Heath, Ted	Big Band; Swing	Trombone, bandleader	British
1980s–	Hedges, Chuck	Swing; Dixieland	Clarinet	American
1940s–1990s	Hefti, Neal	Swing; Big Band	Trumpet, arranger, composer	American
1970s–	Helias, Mark	Free Jazz; Modern Jazz	Bass	American
1940s–1990s	Helm, Bob	Dixieland Revival	Clarinet	American
1970s–	Hemingway, Gerry	Free Jazz; Modern Jazz	Drums, composer, bandleader	American
1960s–1990s	Hemphill, Julius	Free Jazz	Saxophone, composer	American
1950s–	Henderson, Bill	Modern Jazz	Vocals	American
1970s–	Henderson, Eddie	Modern Jazz; Fusion	Trumpet	American
1920s–1950s	Henderson, Fletcher	Swing; Big Band	Piano, arranger, bandleader, composer	American
1930s–1950s	Henderson, Horace	Swing; Big Band	Piano, arranger, bandleader	American
1960s–1990s	Henderson, Joe	Hard Bop	Saxophone, flute, composer	American
1980s–	Henderson, Scott	Fusion	Guitar	American
1960s–	Henderson, Wayne	Hard Bop; Soul Jazz; Fusion	Trombone, producer	American
1940s–	Hendricks, Jon	Bebop	Vocals	American
1960s–1970s	Henry Cow	Jazz Rock	Various instruments	British
1940s–1950s	Henry, Ernie	Hard Bop	Saxophone	American
1940s–	Hentoff, Nat	All Jazz Styles	Author, critic	American
1930s–1980s	Herman, Woody	Swing; Big Band; Cool Jazz	Clarinet, saxophone, vocals, bandleader	American
1980s–	Herring, Vincent	Hard Bop; Modern Jazz	Saxophone	American
1970s–	Hersch, Fred	Modern Jazz	Piano	American
1980s–	Herwig, Conrad	Latin Jazz; Modern Jazz	Trombone, bandleader	American
1920s–1980s	Heywood, Eddie	Swing	Piano, composer	American
1960s–	Hicks, John	Hard Bop; Modern Jazz	Piano, bandleader	American
1980s–1990s	Hidalgo, Giovanni	Latin Jazz; World Fusion	Percussion	Puerto Rican
1920s–1960s	Higginbotham, J.C.	Swing; New Orleans Jazz	Trombone	American
1950s–1990s	Higgins, Billy	Hard Bop; Free Jazz	Drums	American
1950s–	Higgins, Eddie	Hard Bop; Modern Jazz	Piano	American
1950s–	Hill, Andrew	Modal Jazz	Piano, composer	American
1950s; 1970s–	Hill, Buck	Hard Bop	Saxophone	American
1920s–1980s	Hines, Earl	Swing; Big Band	Piano, vocals, composer	American
1960s–	Hino, Terumasa	Hard Bop; Fusion	Trumpet, cornet, flugelhorn, bandleader	Japanese
1930s–1990s	Hinton, Milt	Swing	Bass	American
1950s	Hipp, Jutta	Hard Bop; Cool Jazz; Bebop	Piano	German
1970s–1990s	Hiroshima	World Fusion	Various instruments	American
1950s–1990s	Hirt, Al	Dixieland Revival	Trumpet	American
1980s–	Ho, Fred	World Fusion	Saxophone, composer	American
1990s–	Hobgood, Laurence	Free Jazz; Modern Jazz	Piano	American
1930s–1990s	Hodes, Art	Chicago Jazz	Piano	American
1920s–1960s	Hodges, Johnny	Swing	Saxophone, composer	American
1890s–1900s	Hogan, Ernest	Ragtime	Composer	American
1970s–	Hoggard, Jay	Free Jazz	Vibraphone	American
1970s–	Holdsworth, Allan	Jazz Rock; Fusion	Guitar, violin, composer	British
1930s–1950s	Holiday, Billie	Swing	Vocals	American
1970s–	Holland, Dave	Free Jazz	Bass, cello, composer	British
1950s–1990s	Holley, Major 'Mule'	Swing; Bebop	Bass	American
1950s–	Holloway, Red	Soul Jazz; Swing; Bebop	Saxophones	American
1980s–	Holloway, Ron	Hard Bop	Saxophone	American
1980s–	Hollyday, Christopher	Hard Bop	Saxophone	American
1950s–	Holman, Bill	Hard Bop; Modern Jazz; Big Band	Saxophone, arranger, composer, bandleader	American
1950s–1990s	Holmes, Richard 'Groove'	Soul Jazz; Hard Bop	Organ	American
1960s–	Hooper, Stix	Hard Bop; Soul Jazz; Fusion	Drums, bandleader	American
1940s–1960s	Hope, Elmo	Hard Bop; Bebop	Piano, composer	American
1940s–1990s	Hope, Stan	Hard Bop; Big Band	Piano	American
1930s–1980s	Hopkins, Claude	Swing	Piano, bandleader	American
1970s–1990s	Hopkins, Fred	Free Jazz	Bass	American
1980s–1990s	Horiuchi, Glenn	Free Jazz; World Fusion	Piano, keyboards	American
1950s–	Horn, Paul	World Fusion; Hard Bop	Flute, saxophone, clarinet	American
1950s–	Horn, Shirley	Traditional Jazz	Piano, vocals	American
1980s–	Horvitz, Wayne	Free Jazz; Jazz Funk; Modern Jazz	Organ, piano, keyboards	American
1990s–	Houle, Francois	Free Jazz	Clarinet	Canadian
1970s–1990s	Howard, George	Smooth Jazz	Saxophones	American
1960s–	Howard, Noah	Free Jazz	Saxophone	American
1960s–	Hubbard, Freddie	Hard Bop; Fusion	Trumpet, flugelhorn, composer	American
1940s–1990s	Hucko, Peanuts	Chicago Jazz; Swing	Clarinet, saxophone	American
1930s–1970s	Hug, Armand	New Orleans Jazz; Dixieland	Piano	American
1970s–1990s	Humphrey, Bobbi	Soul Jazz; Fusion	Flute	American
1950s–1990s	Humphrey, Percy	New Orleans Jazz; Dixieland	Trumpet	American
1990s–	Hunter, Charlie	Jazz Rock; Fusion	Guitar	American
1980s–	Hurst, Robert	Hard Bop	Bass	American
1960s–	Hussain, Zakir	World Fusion	Percussion	Indian
1960s–	Hutcherson, Bobby	Hard Bob	Vibraphone, marimba	American
1940s–	Hyman, Dick	Swing	Piano, composer	American
1990s–	Ibarra, Susie	Free Jazz	Drums	American
1980s–	Incognito	Acid Jazz	Various instruments	British
1970s–	Ingham, Keith	Swing; Dixieland Revival; Traditional Jazz	Piano	British
1970s–	Irakere	Latin Jazz	Various instruments	Cuban
1950s–	Israels, Chuck	Cool Jazz, Modern Jazz	Bass	American
1940s–2000s	Jackie & Roy	Bebop; Modern Jazz	Vocals	American
1940s–2000s	Jackson, Chubby	Swing; Bebop	Bass	American
1920s–1970s	Jackson, Cliff	Swing	Piano	American
1990s–	Jackson, D.D.	Modern Jazz	Piano, bandleader	Canadian
1930s–	Jackson, Franz	Swing; Dixieland; Traditional Jazz	Saxophone, clarinet	American
1980s–	Jackson, Javon	Hard Bop	Saxophone	American
1970s–	Jackson, Michael Gregory	Free Jazz; Jazz Rock	Guitar	American
1940s–1990s	Jackson, Milt	Bebop; Hard Bop	Vibraphone, piano	American
1920s–1930s	Jackson, Preston	New Orleans Jazz	Trombone	American
1970s–	Jackson, Ronald Shannon	Free Jazz; Hard Bop; Fusion	Drums, bandleader	American
1940s–1980s	Jackson, Willis 'Gator'	Soul Jazz; Hard Bop	Saxophone	American
1940s–1990s	Jacquet, Illinois	Swing; Bebop	Saxophone	American
1950s–	Jamal, Ahmad	Cool Jazz	Piano	American
1970s–	Jamal, Khan	Free Jazz; Modern Jazz	Vibraphone	American
1960s–	James, Bob	Fusion	Piano, composer	American
1930s–1970s	James, Harry	Swing	Trumpet	American
1990s–	Jamiroquai	Acid Jazz	Various instruments	British
1970s–	Jang, Jon	Free Jazz; World Fusion	Piano, composer	American
1960s–1990s	Jarman, Joseph	Free Jazz	Saxophones, reeds	American
1960s–	Jarreau, Al	Jazz Rock, Modern Jazz	Vocals	American
1960s–	Jarrett, Keith	Fusion	Piano, composer	American
1960s–1990s	Jarvis, Clifford	Free Jazz	Drums	American
1950s–1960s	Jasper, Bobby	Hard Bop; Cool Jazz	Saxophone, flute	Belgian
1940s–1980s	Jazz at the Philharmonic	Swing; Bebop	Various instruments	American
1960s	Jazz Crusaders, The	Soul Jazz; Acid Jazz	Various instruments	American
1980s–	Jazz Passengers	Modern Jazz	Group	American
1980s	Jazz Warriors, The	Acid Jazz	Various instruments	British
1950s–1970s	Jefferson, Eddie	Bebop	Vocals, composer	American
1930s–	Jeffries, Herb	Swing	Vocals	American
1930s–1990s	Jenkins, Gordon	Swing; Cool Jazz	Composer	American
1950s–	Jenkins, John	Hard Bop	Saxophone	American
1970s–1990s	Jenkins, Leroy	Free Jazz	Violin, viola, composition	American
1950s–	Jensen, Arne Papa Bue	New Orleans Jazz; Dixieland	Trombone	Dutch
1990s–	Jensen, Ingrid	Hard Bop	Trumpet	Canadian
1990s	Jhelisa	Acid Jazz	Vocals	British
1950s–1990s	Jobim, Antonio Carlos	Brazilian Jazz; World Fusion; Latin Jazz	Guitar, piano, composer	Brazilian
1960s–	Johansson, Sven-Ake	Free Jazz	Drums, accordion, vocals	Swedish
1930s–1980s	Johnson, Budd	Swing; Bebop	Saxophones, clarinet, arranger	American
1910s–1940s	Johnson, Bunk	New Orleans Jazz	Trumpet	American
1940s–1950s	Johnson, Dink	New Orleans Jazz	Piano, clarinet, drums	American
1940s–1990s	Johnson, J.J.	Bebop; Hard Bop	Trombone, arranger, composer	American
1910s–1950s	Johnson, James P.	Ragtime	Piano, arranger, composer	American
1970s–	Johnson, Marc	Modern Jazz	Bass	American
1930s–1960s	Johnson, Pete	Boogie Woogie	Piano	American
1950s–	Johnson, Plas	Swing; Hard Bop; Soul Jazz	Saxophone	American
1980s–	Johnston, Phillip	Free Jazz; Modern Jazz	Saxophone	American
1950s–2000s	Jolly, Pete	Cool Jazz; Bebop	Piano	American
1970s–1980s	Jones, Bobby	Hard Bop	Saxophone, flute	American
1960s–2000s	Jones, Elvin	Hard Bop	Drums, composer	American
1940s–2000s	Jones, Etta	Modern Jazz	Vocals	American
1950s–1990s	Jones, Hank	Swing; Bebop	Piano	American
1920s–1940s	Jones, Isham	Traditional Jazz	Saxophones, bass	American
1940s–1980s	Jones, Jimmy	Swing	Piano, arranger, composer	American
1930s–1970s	Jones, Jo	Swing	Drums	American
1960s–1970s	Jones, Joe 'Boogaloo'	Soul Jazz	Guitar	American
1930s–1990s	Jones, Jonah	Swing; Dixieland	Trumpet, bandleader	American
1940s–1990s	Jones, Max	All Jazz Styles	Author, critic	British
1980s–	Jones, Oliver	Bebop	Piano	Canadian
1950s–1980s	Jones, Philly Joe	Hard Bop	Drums, piano	American
1950s–	Jones, Quincy	Swing; Bebop	Trumpet, arranger, composer	American
1920s–1940s	Jones, Richard M.	New Orleans Jazz	Piano, vocals, composer, arranger	American
1970s–	Jones, Rodney	Modern Jazz; Fusion	Guitar	American
1950s–1980s	Jones, Sam	Hard Bop	Bass, cello	American
1950s–1980s	Jones, Thad	Bebop; Hard Bop	Trumpet, arranger, composer	American
1900s–1910s	Joplin, Scott	Ragtime	Piano, composer	American
1950s–1990s	Jordan, Clifford	Hard Bop	Saxophone	American
1940s–1990s	Jordan, Duke	Bebop; Hard Bop	Piano, composer	American
1930s–1970s	Jordan, Louis	Swing	Saxophone, vocals, bandleader	American
1990s–	Jordan, Ronny	Acid Jazz	Guitar	British
1960s–	Jordan, Sheila	Free Jazz; Modern Jazz	Vocals, composer	American
1980s–	Jordan, Stanley	Modern Jazz; Jazz Bop	Guitar	American
1970s–	Jorgensmann, Theo	Free Jazz	Clarinet	German
1970s–	Juris, Vic	Hard Bop; Modern Jazz	Guitar	American
1940s–1990s	Kaminsky, Max	Dixieland	Trumpet	American
1950s–1970s	Kamuca, Richie	Cool Jazz	Saxophone	American
1990s–	Karayorgis, Pandelis	Free Jazz	Piano	Greek
1950s–	Katz, Dick	Swing; Modern Jazz	Piano, arranger	American
1940s–1990s	Kay, Connie	Cool Jazz	Drums	American
1950s–	Keepnews, Orrin	Modern Jazz	Producer, author	American
1980s–	Keezer, Geoff	Hard Bop	Piano	American
1960s–	Kellaway, Roger	Hard Bop; Bebop	Piano, arranger, composer	American
1990s–	Keller, Sue	Ragtime	Piano	American
1950s	Kelley, Peck	Traditional Jazz	Piano	American
1950s–1970s	Kelly, Wynton	Hard Bop	Piano	American
1930s–1970s	Kenton, Stan	Big Band	Piano, composer	American
1960s–2000s	Kenyatta, Robin	Free Jazz; Hard Bop; World Fusion	Saxophone, flute	American
1920s–1930s	Keppard, Freddie	New Orleans Jazz	Cornet	American
1940s–1990s	Kessel, Barney	Bebop; Cool Jazz	Guitar	American
1990s–	Kessler, Siegfried	Free Jazz	Piano	German
1970s–	Khan, Steve	Modern Jazz; Fusion	Guitar	American
1980s–	Kibwe, Talib Qadir	Modern Jazz	Saxophone, flute	American
1980s–	Kilgore, Rebecca	Swing	Guitar, vocals	American
1980s–	Kimbrough, Frank	Modern Jazz	Piano	American
1950s–	King Pleasure	Bebop	Vocals	American
1990s–	King, Nancy	Modern Jazz	Vocals	American
1930s–1950s	Kirby, John	Swing	Bass, tuba	American
1920s–1950s	Kirk, Andy	Swing; Big Band	Saxophones, tuba	American
1950s–1970s	Kirk, Rahsaan Roland	Free Jazz; Modern Jazz	Saxophone, flute, clarinet, bandleader	American
1980s–1990s	Kirkland, Kenny	Modern Jazz; Latin Jazz	Piano, keyboards	American
1980s–	Kisor, Ryan	Trumpet; Modern Jazz	Trumpet	American
1950s–	Klein, Oscar	New Orleans Jazz; Dixieland	Trumpet, guitar	Austrian
1960s–	Klemmer, John	Smooth Jazz; Hard Bop; Modern Jazz; Fusion	Saxophone, flute, kalimba, keyboards, composer	American
1960s–	Kloss, Eric	Hard Bop; Modern Jazz	Saxophone, bandleader	American
1970s–	Klugh, Earl	Fusion	Guitar	American
1940s–	Knepper, Jimmy	Hard Bop; Big Band	Trombone	American
1950s–2000s	Koffman, Moe	Bebop; Jazz Pop	Saxophone, flute	Canadian
1970s–	Koglmann, Franz	Free Jazz	Flugelhorn, trumpet, composer	Austrian
1940s–	Konitz, Lee	Cool Jazz	Saxophones	American
1960s–	Kowald, Peter	Free Jazz	Bass	German
1950s–1970s	Kral, Irene	Modern Jazz	Vocals	American
1990s–	Krall, Diana	Swing	Vocals, piano	Canadian
1920s–1960s	Kress, Carl	Swing; Traditional Jazz	Guitar	American
1960s–	Krivda, Ernie	Modern Jazz	Saxophone	American
1920s–1970s	Krupa, Gene	Swing; Big Band	Drums	American
1960s–	Kuhn, Joachim	Modern Jazz; Hard Bop; Free Jazz	Piano, composer	German
1950s–	Kuhn, Rolf	Swing, Modern Jazz	Clarinet, bandleader	German
1960s–	Kuhn, Steve	Modern Jazz	Piano, composer, bandleader	American
1960s–1970s	Kynard, Charles	Soul Jazz	Organ	American
1970s–	LA Four	Cool Jazz	Various instruments	American
1960s–	LaBarbera, Pat	Hard Bop; Big Band	Saxophone	American
1950s–	Lacy, Steve	Free Jazz	Soprano saxophone, composer	American
1920s–1930s	Ladnier, Tommy	Traditional Jazz	Trumpet	American
1980s–	Lagrene, Bireli	Swing; Modern Jazz; Fusion	Guitar	French
1970s–	Lake, Oliver	Free Jazz	Saxophone, flute, composer	American
1980s–	Lalama, Ralph	Hard Bop	Saxophone, flute	American
1950s	Lamb, Joseph	Ragtime	Piano, composer	American
1950s–1960s	Lambert, Henricks & Ross	Bebop	Vocals	American
1960s–	Lancaster, Byard	Free Jazz; Modern Jazz	Saxophone, flute	American
1950s–2000s	Land, Harold	Hard Bop	Saxophone, flute	American
1970s–	Lande, Art	Free Jazz; Fusion	Piano, percussion, bandleader	American
1920s–1930s	Lang, Eddie	Swing	Guitar	American
1940s–2000s	Lanphere, Don	Modern Jazz; Bebop	Saxophone	American
1940s–2000s	LaPorta, John	Cool Jazz	Saxophone, clarinet	American
1950s–2000s	Larkins, Ellis	Swing	Piano	American
1950s–	LaRoca, Pete	Hard Bop; Latin Jazz	Drums	American
1960s–	Lasha, Prince	Free Jazz	Flute	American
1980s–1990s	Last Exit	Free Jazz	Various instruments	American
1970s–	Laswell, Bill	Free Jazz; Fusion	Guitar, producer	American
1950s–	Lateef, Yusef	Hard Bop	Saxophone, flute, reeds	American

1960s–	Ponder, Jimmy	Soul Jazz; Hard Bop	Guitar	American
1960s–	Ponty, Jean-Luc	Fusion	Violin	American
1970s–	Pope, Odean	Modern Jazz	Saxophone	American
1960s	Porter, Bob	Soul Jazz	Producer, author	American
1940s–1950s	Potter, Tommy	Bebop	Bass	American
1960s–	Powell, Baden	Latin Jazz	Guitar, composer	Brazilian
1940s–1960s	Powell, Bud	Bebop	Piano, composer	American
1940s–1960s	Powell, Mel	Swing	Piano, composer	American
1940s	Pozo, Chano	Latin Jazz	Percussion, vocals	Cuban
1950s–	Preservation Hall Jazz Band	Dixieland Revival	Various instruments	American
1940s–	Previn, André	Cool Jazz; Bebop	Piano	French
1980s–	Previte, Bobby	Free Jazz	Drums, bandleader	American
1950s–	Priester, Julian	Free Jazz; Modern Jazz	Trombone	American
1960s–	Priestley, Brian	All Jazz Styles	Piano, author, critic	British
1960s–1970s	Pucho & his Latin Soul Brothers	Latin Jazz	Various instruments	American
1940s–1990s	Puente, Tito	Latin Jazz	Percussion, vibraphone	American
1960s–1990s	Pukwana, Dudu	Free Jazz	Saxophone	South African
1960s–1990s	Pullen, Don	Free Jazz	Piano, organ, composer	American
1940s–2000s	Puma, Joe	Modern Jazz	Guitar	American
1960s–	Purdie, Bernard 'Pretty'	Soul Jazz	Drums	American
1970s–	Purim, Flora	Brazilian Jazz; Latin Jazz; Fusion	Vocals, guitar, percussion	Brazilian
1940s–1960s	Quebec, Ike	Hard Bop; Soul Jazz; Swing	Saxophone	American
1940s–1980s	Quinichette, Paul	Swing	Saxophone	American
1930s–1940s	Quintet of the Hot Club of France	Swing	Band	French
1940s–1950s	Raeburn, Boyd	Bebop	Saxophones	American
1960s–	Rainey, Chuck	Soul Jazz; Hard Bop	Bass	American
1930s–1990s	Ramirez, Ram	Swing	Piano, organ, composer	Puerto Rican
1970s–	Ramzy, Hossam	World Fusion	Drums	Egyptian
1970s–	Raney, Doug	Cool Jazz	Guitar	American
1950s–1990s	Raney, Jimmy	Cool Jazz	Guitar	American
1960s–	Ranglin, Ernest	Jamaican Jazz	Guitar, arranger, composer	Jamaican
1960s–	Rava, Enrico	Free Jazz; Modern Jazz	Trumpet	Italian
1990s–	Red Snapper	Acid Jazz	Various instruments	British
1950s–1970s	Red, Sonny	Hard Bop	Saxophone	American
1950s–1990s	Redd, Freddie	Hard Bop	Piano, composer	American
1960s–1990s	Redman, Dewey	Free Jazz	Saxophones, clarinet	American
1920s–1950s	Redman, Don	Swing	Saxophones, vocals, arranger, composer	American
1990s–	Redman, Joshua	Modern Jazz	Saxophone, bandleader	American
1950s–	Reece, Dizzy	Hard Bop	Trumpet	Jamaican
1990s–	Reed, Eric	Modern Jazz	Piano	American
1960s–1980s	Reed, Waymon	Hard Bop	Trumpet, flugelhorn	American
1970s–	Reeves, Dianne	Modern Jazz	Vocals	American
1970s–	Reid, Rufus	Modern Jazz	Bass, bandleader	American
1970s–	Reid, Steve	Free Jazz	Drums	American
1970s–	Reijseger, Ernst	Free Jazz	Cello	Dutch
1920s–1950s	Reinhardt, Django	Swing	Guitar	Belgian
1970s–1990s	Remler, Emily	Swing; Modern Jazz	Guitar	American
1970s	Return to Forever	Fusion	Various instruments	American
1980s–	Ribot, Marc	Free Jazz; Jazz Rock	Guitar	American
1940s–1980s	Rich, Buddy	Swing; Bebop; Big Band	Drums, vocals	American
1940s–1960s	Richards, Johnny	Latin Jazz	Composer	Brazilian
1950s–1990s	Richardson, Jerome	Cool Jazz; Hard Bop	Saxophones, flute	American
1950s–1980s	Richmond, Dannie	Modern Jazz	Drums	American
1960s–	Richmond, Kim	Big Band; Modern Jazz	Saxophone, clarinet, flute, arranger, composer	American
1960s–	Riley, Ben	Hard Bop	Drums	American
1980s–	Rippingtons, The	Smooth Jazz	Various instruments	American
1970s–1990s	Ritenour, Lee	Fusion	Guitar	American
1960s–	Rivers, Sam	Free Jazz	Saxophones, flute, piano	American
1960s–1970s	Roach, Freddie	Soul Jazz	Organ	American
1940s–1990s	Roach, Max	Bebop; Hard Bop	Drums, composer	American
1980s–	Roberts, Hank	Free Jazz	Cello	American
1950s–1990s	Roberts, Howard	Cool Jazz	Guitar	American
1980s–	Roberts, Marcus	Hard Bop; Modern Jazz	Piano	American
1920s–1990s	Robinson, Ikey	Traditional Jazz	Banjo, guitar, vocals	American
1990s–	Robinson, Reginald R.	Ragtime	Piano	American
1980s–	Robinson, Spike	Swing; Cool Jazz	Saxophone	American
1950s–1990s	Roca, Pete la	Latin Jazz; Hard Bop	Drums	American
1940s–1990s	Rodney, Red	Bebop; Hard Bop	Trumpet	American
1950s–1990s	Rogers, Shorty	Cool Jazz	Trumpet, flugelhorn	American
1920s–1950s	Rollini, Adrian	Traditional Jazz	Saxophone	American
1940s–	Rollins, Sonny	Bebop; Hard Bop	Saxophones, composer	American
1970s–	Romao, Dom Um	Latin Jazz; Brazilian Jazz; World Fusion	Drums, percussion	Brazilian
1980s–	Roney, Wallace	Hard Bop; Modern Jazz	Trumpet	American
1930s–1990s	Rose, Wally	Dixieland; Ragtime	Piano	American
1980s–	Rosnes, Renee	Hard Bop; Modern Jazz	Piano	Canadian
1940s–1970s	Rosolino, Frank	Bebop; Big Band	Trombone	American
1970s–	Rothenberg, Ned	Free Jazz; World Fusion	Saxophone, clarinet, bandleader	American
1940s–1980s	Rouse, Charlie	Hard Bop	Saxophone	American
1950s–1990s	Rowles, Jimmy	Bebop; Swing	Piano, vocals	American
1940s–1980s	Royal, Ernie	Bebop; Swing; Big Band	Trumpet	American
1940s–1990s	Royal, Marshal	Swing	Saxophone, clarinet	American
1980s–	Rubalcaba, Gonzalo	Latin Jazz	Keyboards	Cuban
1950s–	Rudd, Roswell	Free Jazz	Trombone, composer	American
1950s–1990s	Ruff, Willie	Hard Bop; Bebop	Bass, French horn	American
1950s–1990s	Rugolo, Pete	Swing	Arranger, bandleader	American
1970s–1990s	Ruiz, Hilton	Latin Jazz; Bebop	Piano	Cuban
1950s–1960s	Rumsey, Howard	Cool Jazz; Bebop	Bass, bandleader	American
1960s–	Rusch, Bob	All Jazz Styles	Author, critic	American
1970s–	Rushen, Patrice	Smooth Jazz; Modern Jazz	Vocals, keyboards, arranger, composer	American
1920s–1970s	Rushing, Jimmy	Swing	Vocals, piano	American
1940s–1950s	Russell, Curly	Bebop	Bass	American
1950s–	Russell, George	Free Jazz; Modern Jazz; Big Band	Piano, composer, arranger,	American
1950s–1990s	Russell, Hal	Free Jazz	Saxophone, trumpet, vibraphone, drums, bandleader	American
1920s–1940s	Russell, Luis	Swing	Piano, bandleader	American
1920s–1960s	Russell, Pee Wee	Swing; Chicago Jazz	Clarinet, saxophones	American
1960s–	Rutherford, Paul	Free Jazz	Trombone	British
1970s–1990s	Rypdal, Terje	Fusion	Guitar, flute	Norwegian
1940s–1970s	Safranski, Eddie	Swing; Bebop; Big Band	Bass	American
1950s–1990s	Salvador, Sal	Cool Jazz; Bebop	Guitar	American
1960s–	Sample, Joe	Hard Bop; Fusion; Soul Jazz	Piano	American
1970s–	Sanborn, David	Smooth Jazz	Saxophone, flute	American
1970s–	Sanchez, Poncho	Latin Jazz	Percussion, bandleader	American
1990s	Sandals	Acid Jazz	Various instruments	British
1960s–	Sanders, Pharaoh	Free Jazz; Hard Bop	Saxophones	American
1970s–	Sandoval, Arturo	Latin Jazz	Trumpet, flugelhorn, keyboards, percussion	Cuban
1950s–1990s	Santamaria, Mongo	Latin Jazz	Percussion	Cuban
1960s–	Schiano, Mario	Free Jazz; Modern Jazz	Saxophone, vocals, bandleader	Italian
1950s–	Schifrin, Lalo	Bebop	Piano, composer	Argentinian
1960s	Schlippenbach, Alex	Free Jazz	Piano, composer, bandleader	German
1990s–	Schneider, Maria	Big Band	Piano, composer, arranger, bandleader	American
1960s–	Schuller, Gunther	Ragtime; Modern Jazz	French horn, arranger, composer, author	American
1980s–	Schulz, Bob	Dixieland Revival	Cornet	American
1980s–	Schuur, Diane	Modern Jazz	Vocals, piano	American
1950s–	Schweizer, Irene	Free Jazz	Piano, bandleader	Swiss
1950s–1960s	Scobey, Bob	Chicago Jazz	Trumpet	American
1970s–	Scofield, John	Fusion	Guitar, composer	American
1940s–1990s	Scott, Clifford	Swing	Saxophone, flute	American
1940s–1950s	Scott, Hazel	Cool Jazz	Piano	American
1940s–1990s	Scott, Ronnie	Bebop; Big Band; Modern Jazz	Saxophone, bandleader	British
1950s–1990s	Scott, Shirley	Soul Jazz; Hard Bop	Organ	American
1960s–	Scott, Tom	Jazz Pop; Fusion	Saxophone, flute, bandleader	American
1950s–1990s	Scott, Tony	Cool Jazz	Clarinet, saxophones, piano, arranger	American
1970s–	Scott-Heron, Gil	Modern Jazz; Jazz Rock	Vocals, composer, keyboards	American
1960s–	Sebesky, Don	Hard Bop; Jazz Rock	Trombone, arranger, composer	American
1940s–	Severinsen, Doc	Swing; Big Band	Trumpet, bandleader	American
1970s	Shakti	World Fusion; Fusion	Various instruments	American
1950s–	Shank, Bud	Cool Jazz; Hard Bop	Saxophones, flute	American
1970s–1990s	Shankar, Lakshminarayana	World Fusion; Fusion	Violin, composer	Indian
1980s–	Sharpe, Avery	Free Jazz	Bass	American
1960s–1990s	Sharrock, Sonny	Free Jazz	Guitar, composer	American
1930s–1970s	Shavers, Charlie	Swing	Trumpet, vocals, composer	American
1930s–1950s	Shaw, Artie	Swing	Clarinet, saxophones, composer	American
1960s–	Shaw, Marlena	Modern Jazz; Soul Jazz	Vocals	American
1960s–1980s	Shaw, Woody	Hard Bop	Trumpet, flugelhorn, composer	American
1930s–1990s	Shearing, George	Cool Jazz; Bebop	Piano	British
1950s–	Sheldon, Jack	Bebop	Trumpet	American
1960s–	Shepp, Archie	Free Jazz; Hard Bop	Saxophones, piano, vocals, composer	American
1980s–	Sheppard, Andy	Modern Jazz	Saxophone, flute, composer, bandleader	British
1960s–	Shew, Bobby	Hard Bop; Big Band	Trumpet, flugelhorn	American
1950s–1990s	Shihab, Sahib	Bebop; Hard Bop	Saxophones, flute	American
1980s–	Shipp, Matthew	Free Jazz	Piano, composer	American
1950s–1970s	Shirley, Don	Cool Jazz	Piano, arranger, composer	Jamaican
1930s–1980s	Shirley, Jimmy	Swing; Bebop	Guitar	American
1960s–	Shoemake, Charlie	Hard Bop; Bebop	Vibraphone	American
1950s–	Shorter, Wayne	Modern Jazz; Hard Bop; Fusion	Saxophone	American
1970s–	Sidran, Ben	Smooth Jazz; Cool Jazz	Piano, vocals	American
1960s–	Silva, Alan	Free Jazz	Bass, cello, violin, piano	American
1990s	Silva, Robertinho	Brazilian Jazz	Drums, percussion	Brazilian
1980s–1990s	Silveira, Ricardo	Brazilian Jazz; Fusion	Guitar	Brazilian
1950s–	Silver, Horace	Hard Bop; Fusion	Piano, composer	American
1920s–1950s	Simeon, Omer	New Orleans Jazz; Swing	Clarinet	American
1960s–	Simmons, Sonny	Free Jazz	Saxophone	American
1950s–2000s	Simone, Nina	Smooth Jazz	Vocals, piano	American
1940s–1980s	Sims, Zoot	Bebop; Cool Jazz	Saxophones	American
1930s–1990s	Sinatra, Frank	Swing	Vocals	American
1920s–1970s	Singleton, Zutty	Swing; Big Band	Drums	American
1910s–1970s	Sissle, Noble	Traditional Jazz	Vocals, bandleader	American
1990s	Slide Five	Acid Jazz	Various instruments	American
1920s–1990s	Smith, Buster	Swing	Saxophone, arranger, composer	American
1920s–1970s	Smith, Jabbo	Bebop	Trumpet, trombone, vocals	American
1950s–2000s	Smith, Jimmy	Hard Bop	Organ, piano, vocals	American
1950s–1990s	Smith, Johnny	Cool Jazz	Guitar	American
1950s–1990s	Smith, Johnny 'Hammond'	Hard Bop; Soul Jazz	Organ	American
1950s–	Smith, Keely	Swing	Vocals	American
1960s–	Smith, Lonnie	Soul Jazz; Hard Bop	Organ	American
1970s–1990s	Smith, Lonnie Liston	Fusion	Piano, keyboards	American
1950s–	Smith, Louis	Hard Bop	Trumpet	American
1980s–	Smith, Marvin 'Smitty'	Hard Bop; Modern Jazz	Drums	American
1940s–	Smith, Paul	Swing; Cool Jazz; Bebop	Piano, arranger	American
1920s–1960s	Smith, Stuff	Swing	Violin, vocals	American
1940s–1950s	Smith, Tab	Swing	Saxophones	American
1970s–	Smith, Wadada Leo	Free Jazz	Trumpet, flugelhorn, flute	American
1960s–	Smith, Warren	Free Jazz	Percussion	American
1930s–1960s	Smith, Willie	Swing	Saxophone, clarinet	American
1920s–1970s	Smith, Willie 'The Lion'	Traditional Jazz	Piano, vocals, composer	American
1920s–1960s	Snowden, Elmer	Traditional Jazz	Guitar, banjo, bandleader	American
1960s–1990s	Soft Machine, The	Jazz Rock	Various instruments	British
1950s–	Solal, Martial	Modern Jazz	Piano, composer, arranger, bandleader	North African
1970s	Soprano Summit	Swing	Various instruments	American
1950s–1990s	South Frisco Jazz Band	Dixieland Revival	Various instruments	American
1920s–1950s	South, Eddie	Swing	Violin	American
1950s–1960s	Southern, Jeri	Cool Jazz	Vocals	American
1920s–1960s	Spanier, Muggsy	Chicago Jazz	Trumpet	American
1960s–	Sparks, Melvin	Hard Bop; Soul Jazz	Guitar	American
1950s–	Spaulding, James	Hard Bop; Modern Jazz	Saxophone, flute	American
1970s–	Spyro Gyra	Smooth Jazz; Fusion	Various instruments	American
1920s–1930s	St. Cyr, Johnny	New Orleans Jazz	Banjo, guitar	American
1930s–1990s	Stacy, Jess	Swing	Piano	American
1960s–	Stanko, Tomasz	Free Jazz	Trumpet	Polish
1920s–1930s	State Street Ramblers	Traditional Jazz	Various instruments	American
1950s–	Staton, Dakota	Modern Jazz	Vocals	American
1970s–	Steely Dan	Jazz Rock	Various instruments	American
1940s–	Stein, Lou	Swing; Bebop	Piano	American
1970s–	Steps Ahead	Modern Jazz; Fusion	Group	American
1980s–	Stereo MCs	Acid Jazz	Various instruments	British
1990s–	Stern, Peggy	Hard Bop	Piano	American
1960s–1990s	Stevens, John	Free Jazz	Drums, cornet, trumpet	British
1960s–	Stewart, Louis	Swing; Modern Jazz	Guitar	Irish
1920s–1960s	Stewart, Rex	Chicago Jazz; Swing	Trumpet	American
1940s–1980s	Stewart, Slam	Swing	Bass, vocals	American
1940s–1980s	Stitt, Sonny	Bebop	Saxophones	American
1970s–	Stivin, Jiri	Free Jazz	Flute, saxophone, composer	Czech
1930s–1960s	Strayhorn, Billy	Chicago Jazz	Piano, composer, arranger	American
1950s–	Strozier, Frank	Hard Bop; Modern Jazz	Saxophone, flute, clarinet, piano	American
1960s–	Stubblefield, John	Free Jazz; Hard Bop; Modern Jazz	Saxophone	American
1940s–2000s	Sulieman, Idress	Hard Bop; Bebop	Trumpet, flugelhorn	American
1950s–	Sullivan, Ira	Modern Jazz; Bebop	Saxophone, trumpet, flute	American
1930s–1960s	Sullivan, Joe	Chicago Jazz; Swing	Piano	American
1930s–1980s	Sullivan, Maxine	Swing	Vocals	American
1940s–1990s	Sun Ra	Free Jazz	Keyboards, composer	American
1960s–	Sunshine, Monty	New Orleans Jazz; Chicago Jazz	Clarinet	British
1970s	Supersax	Bebop	Saxophones	American
1960s–	Surman, John	Free Jazz; Jazz Rock	Saxophone, clarinet	British
1940s–2000s	Sutton, Ralph	Traditional Jazz	Piano	American
1970s–	Suzuki, Yoshio	Hard Bop	Bass, piano	Japanese
1970s–	Swainson, Neil	Modern Jazz	Bass	Canadian
1960s–	Swallow, Steve	Modern Jazz	Bass, composer	American
1980s–	Swanton, Lloyd	Fusion	Bass, composer	Australian
1970s–	Swartz, Harvie	Modern Jazz	Bass	American
1960s–	Szabo, Gabor	Modern Jazz; Pop Jazz	Guitar, composer, arranger, bandleader	Hungarian
1960s–	Tabackin, Lew	Hard Bop	Saxophone, flute	American
1970s–	Tacuma, Jamaaladeen	Free Jazz; Free Funk	Bass	American
1970s–	Takase, Aki	Free Jazz; Modern Jazz	Piano, bandleader	Japanese
1960s–1990s	Takayanagi, Masayuki	Free Jazz	Guitar	Japanese
1960s–1990s	Tapscott, Horace	Free Jazz; Big Band	Piano, arranger, composer, bandleader	American
1930s–1970s	Tate, Buddy	Swing	Saxophone	American
1950s–1990s	Tate, Grady	Hard Bop	Drums, vocals	American
1920s–1950s	Tatum, Art	Swing	Piano	American
1950s–1990s	Taylor, Art	Bebop; Hard Bop	Drums	American
1940s–	Taylor, Billy	Bebop; Hard Bop; Swing	Piano	American
1950s–	Taylor, Cecil	Free Jazz	Piano, composer	American
1950s–	Taylor, Creed	American Jazz	Producer	American
1980s–	Taylor, James	Acid Jazz; Soul Jazz	Keyboards	British
1960s–	Taylor, John	Free Jazz	Piano	British
1970s–	Taylor, Martin	Swing; Cool Jazz; Bebop	Guitar	British
1960s–	Tchicai, John	Free Jazz	Saxophones, flute	Danish
1920s–1960s	Teagarden, Jack	Swing; Chicago Jazz	Trombone, vocals	American
1950s–	Temperley, Joe	Swing; Hard Bop	Saxophone, clarinet, flute	Scottish
1970s–	Termos, Paul	Free Jazz	Saxophone, composer	Dutch
1990s–	Terrasson, Jacky	Modern Jazz	Piano, keyboards, bandleader	German
1950s–	Terry, Clark	Bebop; Swing	Trumpet, flugelhorn	American
1920s–1930s	Teschemacher, Frank	Traditional Jazz	Clarinet, saxophone	American
1960s–	Texier, Henri	Hard Bop; Modern Jazz; Bebop	Bass	French
1950s–	Thielemans, Toots	Brazilian Jazz; Latin Jazz; Swing; Bebop	Harmonica, guitar, composer	Belgian
1950s–1990s	Thigpen, Ed	Bebop; Hard Bop	Drums	American
1960s–1990s	Thomas, Leon	Free Jazz; Modern Jazz	Vocals	American
1970s–1990s	Thompson, Barbara	Free Jazz; Fusion	Saxophones, flute	British
1960s–	Thompson, Butch	Traditional Jazz, Ragtime	Piano, clarinet	American
1960s–	Thompson, Don	Modern Jazz;	Bass, piano	Canadian
1940s–1970s	Thompson, Lucky	Bebop; Hard Bop	Saxophones	American
1970s–	Thompson, Malachi	Free Jazz; Modern Jazz	Trumpet, bandleader	American
1940s–	Thompson, Sir Charles	Swing; Bebop	Piano, organ, composer	American
1930s–1950s	Thornhill, Claude	Cool Jazz	Piano, arranger	American
1970s–	Threadgill, Henry	Free Jazz	Saxophone, flute, composer, bandleader	American
1950s–1960s	Three Sounds, The	Soul Jazz; Hard Bop	Various instruments	American
1970s–	Tibbetts, Steve	Fusion	Guitar	American
1950s–1960s	Timmons, Bobby	Soul Jazz; Hard Bop	Piano, vibraphone, composer	American
1960s–1990s	Tippett, Keith	Free Jazz; Fusion	Piano, composer	British
1970s–1990s	Tiso, Wagner	Brazilian Jazz; Latin Jazz	Piano, keyboards, arranger, composer	Brazilian
1930s–1960s	Tizol, Juan	Swing; Big Band	Valve trombone, arranger, composer	Puerto Rican
1950s–1980s	Tjader, Cal	Cool Jazz; Latin Jazz	Vibraphone, percussion	American
1960s–	Togashi, Masahiko	Free Jazz; Hard Bop	Drums, composer, bandleader	Japanese
1960s–1980s	Tolliver, Charles	Hard Bop	Trumpet, flugelhorn	American
1980s–	Tommaso, Bruno	Free Jazz; Big Band; Modern Jazz	Bass	Italian
1960s–	Tompkins, Ross	Swing; Bebop; Cool Jazz	Piano	American
1980s–	Tonolo, Pietro	Free Jazz	Saxophone	Italian
1980s–	Tononi, Tiziano	Free Jazz; Modern Jazz; Big Band	Drums, composer, bandleader	Italian
1940s–1990s	Tormé, Mel	Swing; Bebop	Vocals, percussion	American
1970s–	Towner, Ralph	Modern Jazz	Guitar	American
1970s–	Toyama, Yoshio	New Orleans Jazz; Dixieland	Trumpet, vocals, bandleader	Japanese
1950s–	Tracey, Stan	Free Jazz; Hard Bop; Modern Jazz	Piano, composer	British
1990s–	Tramontana, Sebi	Free Jazz	Trombone	Italian
1940s–1960s	Tristano, Lennie	Cool Jazz; Bebop	Piano, composer	American
1970s–	Tucker, Mickey	Hard Bop; Modern Jazz	Piano	American
1920s–1960s	Tucker, Sophie	Ragtime	Vocals	American
1980s–	Tuncboyaciyan, Arto	World Fusion	Percussion	Armenian
1930s–1990s	Turner, Joe	Boogie Woogie	Piano	American
1940s–2000s	Turney, Norris	Swing	Saxophone, flute	American
1890s	Turpin, Tom	Ragtime	Composer	American
1970s–	Turre, Steve	Latin Jazz; Hard Bop; Bebop	Trombone	American
1960s–1990s	Turrentine, Stanley	Hard Bop; Fusion	Saxophone	American
1960s–	Tusques, Francois	Free Jazz	Piano, composer, bandleader	French
1960s–1990s	Tyler, Charles	Free Jazz	Saxophone	American
1960s–	Tyner, McCoy	Modern Jazz; Hard Bop	Piano, composer, bandleader	American
1950s–2000s	Ulanov, Barry	All Jazz Styles	Author	American
1970s–	Ulmer, James Blood	Free Jazz	Guitar, flute, vocals	American
1990s–	United Future Organization	Acid Jazz	Various instruments	Japanese
1970s–	Urbani, Massimo	Free Jazz	Saxophone	Italian
1970s–	Urbaniak, Michal	Fusion	Violin, saxophones, composer	Polish
1970s–	Vache, Warren Jr	Swing; Chicago Jazz	Cornet, flugelhorn	American
1950s–	Valdes, Carlos 'Patato'	Latin Jazz	Percussion	Cuban
1970s–	Valdes, Chucho	Latin Jazz	Piano	Cuban
1970s–	Valente, Gary	Free Jazz; Big Band	Trombone	American
1920s–1970s	Valentine, Kid Thomas	New Orleans Jazz	Trumpet	American

1970s–	VanDeGeyn, Hein	Bebop; Big Band; Modern Jazz	Bass	Dutch
1970s–	VanDenBroeck, Rob	Free Jazz; Jazz Rock	Piano	Dutch
1980s–	Vandermark, Ken	Free Jazz	Saxophones, clarinet	American
1930s–1990s	VanEps, George	Swing	Guitar	American
1950s–	VanGelder, Rudy	Modern Jazz	Recording engineer	American
1960s–	VanHove, Fred	Free Jazz	Piano	Belgian
1960s–	VanManen, Willem	Free Jazz	Trombone, composer, bandleader	Dutch
1970s–	Vasconcelos, Nana	Latin Jazz; World Fusion	Percussion	Brazilian
1940s–1980s	Vaughan, Sarah	Bebop; Cool Jazz	Vocals	American
1940s–1990s	Ventura, Charlie	Swing; Bebop	Saxophone, bandleader	American
1920s–1970s	Venuti, Joe	Swing	Violin	American
1960s–1980s	Vick, Harold	Soul Jazz; Hard Bop	Saxophones	American
1950s–1990s	Vinnegar, Leroy	Cool Jazz	Bass	American
1940s–1980s	Vinson, Eddie 'Cleanhead'	Bebop	Saxophone, vocals, composer	American
1960s–	Vitet, Bernard	Modern Jazz; Free Jazz	Trumpet, composer	French
1960s–	Vitous, Miroslav	Free Jazz; Modern Jazz; Fusion	Bass	Czech
1980s–1990s	VonEssen, Eric	Free Jazz; Modern Jazz	Bass, cello	American
1960s–	VonSchlippenbach, Alexander	Free Jazz; Big Bang	Piano, bandleader	German
1960s–	Vuckovich, Larry	Modern Jazz	Piano	Montenegran
1980s–	Vukan, George	Modern Jazz	Piano, composer, arranger, bandleader	Hungarian
1980s–	Vysniauskas, Petras	Free Jazz	Saxophone, clarinet	Lithuanian
1970s–	Wadud, Abdul	Free Jazz	Cello	American
1970s–1980s	Walcott, Colin	World Fusion	Sitar, percussion, vocals	American
1970s–1980s	Waldo, Terry	Ragtime	Piano, vocals, arranger	American
1950s–2000s	Waldron, Mal	Hard Bop	Piano, composer	American
1970s–	Wallace, Bennie	Modern Jazz	Saxophone	American
1920s–1940s	Waller, Fats	Swing	Piano, vocals	American
1940s–1960s	Wallington, George	Bebop	Piano, composer	American
1970s–	Walrath, Jack	Modern Jazz	Trumpet, composer, arranger, bandleader	American
1950s–	Walton, Cedar	Hard Bop	Piano, composer	American
1970s–	Ware, David S.	Free Jazz	Saxophone	American
1950s–1970s	Ware, Wilbur	Hard Bop	Bass	American
1960s–1990s	Washington, Grover Jr	Soul Jazz	Saxophones, clarinet, bass, piano	American
1970s–	Wasserman, Rob	Fusion	Bass	American
1960s–	Watanabe, Sadao	Jazz Pop	Saxophone	Japanese
1940s–1990s	Waters, Benny	Swing	Saxophones, clarinet, arranger	American
1920s–1960s	Waters, Ethel	Swing	Vocals	American
1950s–1970s	Watkins, Julius	Hard Bop	French horn	American
1960s–	Watrous, Bill	Bebop	Trombone, composer	American
1970s–	Watson, Bobby	Hard Bop; Modern Jazz	Saxophone, bandleader	American
1930s–1960s	Watters, Lu	Chicago Jazz	Trumpet	American
1960s–	Watts, Ernie	Modern Jazz; Jazz Rock	Saxophone, flute	American
1990s–	Watts, Jeff 'Tain'	Modern Jazz	Drums	American
1940s–1990s	Wayne, Chuck	Swing; Modern Jazz	Guitar	American
1970s–1980s	Weather Report	Fusion	Various instruments	American
1920s–1930s	Webb, Chick	Big Band; Swing	Drums, bandleader	American
1970s–	Weber, Eberhard	Modern Jazz; World Fusion	Bass, cello, composer, bandleader	German
1930s–1970s	Webster, Ben	Swing	Saxophones, arranger	American
1950s–	Wein, George	Dixieland; Traditional Jazz	Piano, vocals, promoter	American
1920s–1980s	Wells, Dicky	Swing	Trombone	American
1950s–1980s	Wellstood, Dick	Traditional Jazz; Ragtime	Piano	American
1970s–	Werner, Kenny	Modern Jazz	Piano	American
1940s–	Wess, Frank	Cool Jazz; Swing; Bebop	Saxophones, flute	American
1990s	West Coast All Stars	Traditional Jazz	Various instruments	American
1980s–1990s	West Jemond Rhythm Kings	Dixieland Revival	Various instruments	American
1980s–	Westbrook, Mike	Free Jazz; Big Band	Piano, bandleader	British
1950s–1990s	Weston, Randy	Hard Bop	Piano, composer	American
1920s–1950s	Wettling, George	Chicago Jazz	Drums	American
1980s–	Whalum, Kirk	Smooth Jazz	Saxophone	American
1960s–	Wheeler, Kenny	Free Jazz; Modern Jazz	Trumpet, flugelhorn	Canadian
1970s–	White, Andrew	Fusion; Hard Bop	Saxophone	American
1980s–	White, Michael	Dixieland Revival; New Orleans Jazz	Violin	American
1920s–1960s	Whiteman, Paul	Big Band; Traditional Jazz	Bandleader, violin	American
1950s–1990s	Wiggins, Gerald	Swing; Bebop	Piano	American

1940s–	Wilber, Bob	Traditional Jazz	Clarinet, soprano saxophone, arranger, composer	American
1940s–	Wilder, Joe	Swing	Trumpet, flugelhorn	American
1930s–1970s	Wiley, Lee	Swing, Modern Jazz	Vocals	American
1970s–	Wilkerson, Ed	Hard Bop; Free Jazz	Saxophone, clarinet, piano, composer, bandleader	American
1950s–1990s	Wilkins, Ernie	Bebop; Swing	Saxophones	American
1960s	Willette, Baby Face	Soul Jazz; Hard Bop	Organ	American
1960s–	Williams, Buster	Hard Bop	Bass	American
1920s–1940s	Williams, Clarence	Swing	Piano, vocals, arranger, bandleader, composer	American
1920s–2000s	Williams, Claude 'Fiddler'	Swing	Violin, guitar, vocals	American
1930s–1970s	Williams, Cootie	Swing	Trumpet	American
1960s–	Williams, Jackie	Swing	Drums	American
1970s–2000s	Williams, James	Modern Jazz; Hard Bop	Piano, composer	American
1970s–	Williams, Jessica	Modern Jazz	Piano	American
1930s–1990s	Williams, Joe	Swing	Vocals	American
1940s–1960s	Williams, John	Swing	Saxophone	American
1950s–1990s	Williams, Martin	All Jazz Styles	Author, critic	American
1920s–1970s	Williams, Mary Lou	Swing; Bebop	Piano, arranger, composer	American
1960s–1990s	Williams, Tony	Fusion; Hard Bop	Drums, composer	American
1950s–1990s	Williamson, Claude	Cool Jazz; Bebop	Piano	American
1950s–1990s	Williamson, Stu	Cool Jazz	Trumpet, trombone	American
1960s–	Willis, Larry	Fusion	Pianist, arranger, composer, producer	American
1960s–	Wilmer, Val	Jazz	Author, photographer, critic	British
1980s–	Wilson, Cassandra	World Fusion	Vocals	American
1940s–1990s	Wilson, Gerald	Bebop	Trumpet, arranger, composer	American
1960s–	Wilson, Nancy	Modern Jazz	Vocals	American
1960s–1990s	Wilson, Phillip	Free Jazz	Drums	American
1960s–1990s	Wilson, Reuben	Soul Jazz; Hard Bop; Fusion	Organ	American
1930s–1980s	Wilson, Teddy	Swing	Piano, arranger	American
1940s–1970s	Winding, Kai	Bebop	Trombone	American
1960s–	Winter, Paul	World Fusion	Saxophones, producer	American
1980s–	Winterschladen, Reiner	Free Jazz	Trumpet, flugelhorn	German
1960s–	Wofford, Mike	Modern Jazz	Piano	American
1990s–	Wong, Francis	Modern Jazz	Saxophone	American
1980s–	Woodard, Rickey	Hard Bop; Swing	Saxophone	American
1950s–	Woode, Jimmy	Modern Jazz; Hard Bop; Bebop	Bass	American
1940s–2000s	Woodman, Britt	Swing; West Coast Jazz	Trombone	American
1950s–	Woods, Phil	Bebop; Hard Bop	Saxophone, clarinet	American
1950s–	Workman, Reggie	Hard Bop; Free Jazz	Bass	American
1970s–	World Saxophone Quartet	Free Jazz	Saxophones	American
1960s–1970s	World's Greatest Jazz Band	Dixieland Revival	Various instruments	American
1950s–1970s	Wright, Eugene	Cool Jazz; Swing	Bass	American
1960s–1990s	Wright, Frank	Free Jazz	Saxophone	American
1950s–	Wyands, Richard	Hard Bop; Modern Jazz	Piano	American
1920s–1940s	Yancey, Jimmy	Boogie Woogie	Piano	American
1980s–1990s	Yellowjackets, The	Smooth Jazz; Fusion	Various instruments	American
1960s–1990s	Yoshizawa, Motoharu	Free Jazz	Bass	Japanese
1960s–	Young, Dave	Modern Jazz	Bass	Canadian
1960s–1970s	Young, Larry	Soul Jazz; Hard Bop; Fusion	Organ, piano	American
1930s–1950s	Young, Lester	Swing; Cool Jazz	Saxophone, clarinet	American
1950s–1990s	Young, Snooky	Swing	Trumpet	American
1930s–1960s	Young, Trummy	Swing	Trombone, vocals	American
1950s–1960s	Young, Webster	Cool Jazz	Trumpet	American
1960s–1990s	Zappa, Frank	Jazz Rock; Fusion	Guitar, composer	American
1950s–1990s	Zawinul, Joe	Fusion; World Fusion; Soul Jazz; Hard Bop	Piano, keyboards, composer	Austrian
1960s–	Zeitlin, Denny	Hard Bop; Modern Jazz	Piano	American
1940s–2000s	Zentner, Si	Swing; Big Band	Trombone, bandleader	American
1970s–	Zingaro, Carlos	Free Jazz; Fusion	Violin	Portuguese
1960s–1990s	Zoller, Attila	Modern Jazz	Guitar	Hungarian
1970s–	Zorn, John	Free Jazz	Saxophone, composer, bandleader	American

Blues Artists

1960s–1970s	AB Skhy	Blues Rock	Various instruments	American
1970s–1990s	Abrahams, Mick	Blues Rock; Rhythm & Blues	Guitar	British
1950s	Ace, Johnny	Rhythm & Blues	Guitar, vocals	American
1960s–1970s	Acklin, Barbara	Rhythm & Blues	Vocals, composer	American
1950s–	Adams, Alberta	Rhythm & Blues	Vocals	American
1970s–1990s	Adams, Arthur	Modern Electric Blues	Guitar, vocals	American
1950s–1960s	Adams, Faye	East Coast Blues; Jump Blues; Rhythm & Blues	Vocals	American
1950s–1990s	Adams, Johnny	Rhythm & Blues	Vocals	American
1950s–1990s	Adams, Marie	Rhythm & Blues	Vocals	American
1950s–1970s	Agee, Ray	West Coast Blues	Vocals	American
1920s–1930s	Akers, Garfield	Delta Blues	Guitar, vocals	American
1930s	Alabama Shiekhs	Country Blues	Various instruments	American
1960s–1970s	Alexander, Arthur	Rhythm & Blues	Vocals, composer	American
1950s–1960s	Allen, Annisteen	Jump Blues	Vocals	American
1940s–1980s	Allen, Lee	Rhythm & Blues	Saxophone	American
1960s–1990s	Allison, Luther	Chicago Blues; Modern Electric Blues	Guitar	American
1950s–	Allison, Mose	Country Blues	Piano, vocals, composer	American
1960s–	Allman Brothers Band	Blues Rock	Various instruments	American
1960s–1970s	Allman, Duane	Blues Rock	Guitar	American
1970s–1990s	Allman, Gregg	Blues Rock	Keyboards, vocals	American
1930s–1940s	Altheimer, Joshua	Country Blues	Piano	American
1920s–1940s	Ammons, Albert	Boogie-Woogie	Piano	American
1970s–1980s	Anderson, Little Willie	Modern Electric Blues; Chicago Blues	Harmonica	American
1960s–1990s	Anderson, Miller	Blues Rock	Guitar, vocals	British
1930s–1960s	Anderson, Pink	Country Blues	Guitar	American
1950s; 1980s–	Andrews, Ernie	West Coast Blues	Vocals	American
1960s–1980s	Animals, The	British Blues; Blues Rock	Various instruments	British
1990s	Arc Angels, The	Blues Rock	Various instruments	American
1920s–1930s	Ardoin, Amadie	Country Blues	Vocals, accordion	American
1930s–1990s	Armstrong, Howard 'Louie Bluie'	Country Blues; Swing	Vocals, mandolin, fiddle, guitar	American
1990s–	Armstrong, James	Modern Electric Blues	Vocals, guitar, composer	American
1950s–	Arnold, Billy Boy	Chicago Blues	Harmonica, vocals	American
1930s–1940s	Arnold, Kokomo	Chicago Blues	Guitar, vocals	American
1960s–1970s	Ashton, Gardner & Dyke	Blues Rock	Various instruments	British
1950s–1990s	August, Joseph 'Mr. Google' 'Mr. G.'	Rhythm & Blues	Vocals	American
1950s–1970s	Austin, Sil	East Coast Blues; Jump Blues	Saxophone	American
1970s	Bacon Fat	West Coast Blues	Various instruments	American
1970s–1990s	Bad Company	Blues Rock	Various instruments	British
1920s	Bailey, Deford	Country Blues	Harmonica	American
1920s–1950s	Bailey, Mildred	Country Blues	Vocals	American
1970s	Baker Gurvitz Army	Blues Rock	Various instruments	British
1920s	Baker, Edythe	Boogie-Woogie	Vocals	American
1950s; 1980s–1990s	Baker, Etta	Country Blues	Guitar	American
1970s–	Baker, Ginger	Blues Rock	Drums	British
1950s–1960s; 1980s–1990s	Baker, Lavern	Rhythm & Blues; Jump Blues	Vocals	American
1950s–1970s	Baker, Mickey	Rhythm & Blues; East Coast Blues	Guitar	American
1950s–	Baldry, Long John	British Blues; Blues Rock	Vocals	British
1970s–	Ball, Marcia	Modern Electric Blues	Piano	American
1950s–1990s	Ballard, Hank	Rhythm & Blues	Vocals, composer	American
1930s	Barbee, John Henry	Country Blues; Delta Blues	Vocals	American
1920s–1930s	Barbeque Bob	Country Blues	Guitar	American
1930s–1980s	Barker, Blue Lu	East Coast Blues	Vocals	American
1970s–1990s	Barnes, Roosevelt 'Booba'	Modern Electric Blues	Guitar, harmonica	American
1940s–1990s	Bartholomew, Dave	Rhythm & Blues	Producer, composer, bandleader, trumpet	American
1980s–	Barton, Lou Ann	Blues Rock; Texas Blues	Vocals	American
1960s–1970s	Bass, Fontella	Rhythm & Blues	Vocals	American
1940s–1970s	Bass, Ralph	West Coast Blues; Rhythm & Blues Chicago Blues	Producer	American
1960s–	Bastin, Bruce	Country Blues; East Cost Blues	Author, producer	British
1920s	Beale Street Sheiks	Delta Blues	Various instruments	American
1950s	Beasley, Jimmy	Rhythm & Blues	Vocals, piano	American
1960s–	Beck, Jeff	British Blues; Blues Rock	Piano, guitar	British
1990s	Bedard, George	Blues Rock	Vocals, guitar	American
1960s–1990s	Bell, Carey	Modern Electric Blues; Chicago Blues	Harmonica	American

1980s–1990s	Bell, Lurrie	Modern Electric Blues; Chicago Blues	Guitar	American
1970s–1980s	Bell, Maggie	Blues Rock	Vocals	British
1990s	Bell, T.D.	Texas Blues; Modern Electric Blues	Guitar	American
1950s–1960s	Below, Fred	Chicago Blues	Drums	American
1950s	Belvin, Jesse	Rhythm & Blues	Vocals, composer	American
1960s–1970s	Bennett, Duster	British Blues; Blues Rock	Vocals, harmonica	British
1960s–1980s	Bennett, Wayne	Rhythm & Blues; Texas Blues	Guitar	American
1990s–	Benoit, Tab	Modern Electric Blues	Guitar, vocals, composer	American
1920s–1940s	Bentley, Gladys	Country Blues	Vocals, piano	American
1950s–1970s	Benton, Brook	Rhythm & Blues	Vocals	American
1960s–1990s	Benton, Buster	Modern Electric Blues; Chicago Blues	Guitar, vocals	American
1950s–1990s	Berry, Chuck	Rhythm & Blues	Vocals, guitar, composer	American
1950s–1960s	Berry, Richard	Rhythm & Blues	Vocals, composer	American
1990s–	Bibb, Eric	Folk Blues; Modern Acoustic Blues	Vocals, guitar, composer	American
1970s–1990s	Big Bad Smitty	Modern Electric Blues	Vocals, guitar	American
1960s–1990s	Big Brother & the Holding Company	Blues Rock	Various instruments	American
1990s	Big Dave & the Ultrasonics	Blues Rock; Modern Electric Blues	Various instruments	American
1940s–1960s	Big Maybelle	East Coast Blues; Jump Blues; Rhythm & Blues	Vocals	American
1940s–1950s	Big Three Trio, The	Chicago Blues	Vocals, guitar	American
1970s–	Big Time Sarah	Modern Electric Blues	Vocals	American
1970s–1990s	Binder, Roy Book	Country Blues	Guitar	American
1960s–	Bishop, Elvin	Modern Electric Blues	Guitar	American
1960s	Bizor, Billy	Texas Blues	Vocals	American
1920s–1940s	Black Ace	Country Blues; Texas Blues	Guitar	American
1950s–1960s	Blackwell, Francis 'Bumps'	Rhythm & Blues	Producer, arranger	American
1950s–1970s	Blackwell, Otis	East Coast Blues	Voclas, piano, composer	American
1920s–1930s; 1950s–1960s	Blackwell, Scrapper	Chicago Blues	Guitar, vocals	American
1950s–	Bland, Bobby 'Blue'	Texas Blues; Rhythm & Blues	Vocals	American
1920s–1930s	Blind Blake	Country Blues	Guitar, vocals	American
1960s	Blind Faith	Blues Rock; British Blues	Artist	British
1960s–	Block, Rory	Country Blues, Delta Blues	Vocals, guitar	American
1960s–1990s	Blodwyn Pig	Blues Rock	Various instruments	British
1960s–1980s	Bloomfield, Michael	Modern Electric Blues; Chicago Blues	Guitar	American
1950s–1980s	Blue, Little Joe	West Coast Blues; Modern Electric Blues	Vocals	American
1990s–	Bluebirds, The	Blues Rock	Various instruments	American
1960s	Blues Incorporated	British Blues	Various instruments	British
1960s–1970s	Blues Project, The	Blues Rock	Various instruments	American
1990s–	Blues Traveler	Blues Rock	Various instruments	American
1980s	Bluesbusters, The	Blues Rock	Various instruments	American
1950s–	Bo, Eddie	Rhythm & Blues	Piano, vocals	American
1920s–1930s	Bogan, Lucille	Country Blues	Vocals	American
	Bogan, Ted	Country Blues	Guitar, vocals	American
1980s	Bollin, Zuzu	Texas Blues	Guitar	American
1960s–1970s	Bond, Graham	British Blues; Blues Rock	Saxophone, keyboards	British
1920s–1940s	Bonds, Son	Country Blues	Guitar	American
1950s–1970s	Bonner, Juke Boy	West Coast Blues; Texas Blues	Guitar, vocals	American
1940s–1970s	Boogie-Woogie Red	Boogie-Woogie	Piano	American
1950s–1980s	Booker, James	Boogie-Woogie; Rhythm & Blues	Piano	American
1930s–1960s	Bostic, Earl	Rhythm & Blues	Saxophone	American
1980s–	Bourelly, Jean-Paul	Blues Rock	Guitar	American
	Bowman, Priscilla	Rhythm & Blues	Vocals	American
1980s	Box of Frogs	Blues Rock	Various instruments	British
1940s–1980s	Boyd, Eddie	Chicago Blues	Guitar, piano, composer	American
1940s–1950s	Boze, Calvin	Jump Blues	Vocals, trumpet	American
1920s–1930s	Bracey, Ishman	Delta Blues	Guitar	American
1930s–1950s	Bradshaw, Tiny	Jump Blues; Rhythm & Blues	Vocals, drums	American
1980s–1990s	Bramhall, Doyle	Texas Blues; Modern Electric Blues	Drums, vocals, composer	American
1970s–	Bramlett, Bonnie	Blues Rock	Vocals	American
1970s	Bramlett, Delaney	Blues Rock	Vocals	American
1970s–	Branch, Billy	Chicago Blues	Vocals, harmonica	American
1940s–1960s	Brenston, Jackie	Jump Blues; Rhythm & Blues	Saxophone	American
1950s–1960s; 1990s	Brim, John	Chicago Blues	Guitar	American
1970s–	Brooks, Elkie	Blues Rock	Vocals	British
1940s–1960s	Brooks, Hadda	Boogie-Woogie	Piano	American
	Brooks, Leon 'Big'	Chicago Blues	Harmonica	American

1950s–1990s	Brooks, Lonnie	Modern Electric Blues	Guitar	American
1920s–1950s	Broonzy, Big Bill	Country Blues; Chicago Blues	Vocals, guitar	American
	Brown, Andrew	Chicago Blues	Guitar	American
1940s–1990s	Brown, Charles	West Coast Blues	Piano, vocals	American
1940s–	Brown, Clarence 'Gatemouth'	Texas Blues; Country Blues	Guitar	American
1940s–1950s	Brown, J.T.	Chicago Blues	Vocals, saxophone	American
1950s–	Brown, James	Rhythm & Blues	Vocals, composer	American
1930s–1940s	Brown, Lee	East Coast Blues; Boogie-Woogie	Guitar	American
1960s–1970s	Brown, Maxine	Rhythm & Blues	Vocals	American
1950s–1960s; 1980s–1990s	Brown, Nappy	Jump Blues; Rhythm & Blues	Vocals	American
c. 1900s–1930s	Brown, Richard 'Rabbit'	New Orleans Blues	Vocals	American
1940s–1970s	Brown, Roy	Jump Blues; West Coast Blues	Vocals, composer	American
1940s–1960s; 1980s–1990s	Brown, Ruth	Jump Blues; Rhythm & Blues	Vocals	American
	Brown, Texas Johnny	Rhythm & Blues; Texas Blues	Guitar, vocals, composer	American
1940s–1950s	Brown, Walter	Jump Blues; Rhythm & Blues	Vocals	American
1920s–1930s	Brown, Willie	Delta Blues	Guitar	American
1980s–	Brozman, Bob	Country Blues	Guitar	American
1960s–	Bruce, Jack	British Blues	Bass	Scottish
1970s–1980s	Buchanan, Roy	Blues Rock; Modern Electric Blues	Guitar	American
1930s	Bull City Red	Country Blues; East Coast Blues	Washboard, guitar	American
1930s–1950s	Bumble Bee Slim	Country Blues; West Coast Blues	Guitar, vocals	American
1990s–2000s	Burks, Eddie	Modern Electric Blues	Vocals, harmonica	American
1950s–	Burns, Eddie	Chicago Blues; Detroit Blues	Vocals, guitar, harmonica	American
1960s–	Burnside, R.L.	Delta Blues; Modern Electric Blues	Guitar, vocals	American
1950s–1960s	Burrage, Howard	Rhythm & Blues; Chicago Blues	Vocals, composer, producer	American
1960s–1980s	Burris, J.C.	Country Blues	Vocals, harmonica	American
1990s–2000s	Butler Twins	Modern Electric Blues	Various instruments	American
1950s–1980s	Butler, Billy	Jump Blues; Rhythm & Blues	Guitar	American
1970s–2000s	Butler, George 'Wild Child'	Modern Electric Blues	Vocals, harmonica	American
1950s–1990s	Butler, Jerry	Rhythm & Blues	Vocals	American
1920s–1930s	Butterbeans & Susie	Country Blues	Various instruments	American
1960s–1980s	Butterfield, Paul	Chicago Blues; Blues Rock	Harmonica	American
1950s–1960s	Cadets, The	Rhythm & Blues	Various instruments	American
1950s	Caesar, Harry 'Little'	Rhythm & Blues	Vocals	American
1980s–	Cain, Chris	Modern Electric Blues	Vocals, guitar	American
1970s–1990s	Cale, J.J.	Blues Rock	Guitar, vocals, composer	American
1930s; 1960s	Callicott, Joe 'Mississippi'	Country Blues	Vocals, guitar	American
1960s–	Campbell, Eddie C.	Modern Electric Blues	Vocals, guitar	American
1920s–1930s	Campbell, Gene	Country Blues	Vocals, guitar	American
1980s–1990s	Campbell, John	Modern Electric Blues	Vocals, guitar	American
1960s–	Canned Heat	Blues Rock; Modern Electric Blues	Various instruments	American
1920s–1960s	Cannon, Gus	Country Blues	Banjo	American
1920s–1930s	Cannon's Jug Stompers	Country Blues	Various instruments	American
1960s–1980s	Captain Beefheart	Blues Rock	Vocals, harmonica	American
1940s–19550s	Carolina Slim	Country Blues	Vocals, guitar	American
1960s–	Carr, Barbara	Rhythm & Blues	Vocals	American
1920s–1930s	Carr, Leroy	Boogie-Woogie	Piano, vocals, composer	American
1950s	Carr, Sister Wynona	Jump Blues; Rhythm & Blues	Vocals, composer	American
1920s–1940s	Carter, Bo	Country Blues	Guitar, vocals	American
1960s–2000s	Carter, Levester 'Big Lucky'	Modern Electric Blues; East Coast Blues	Vocals, guitar	American
1940s–1980s	Caston, Leonard 'Baby Doo'	Country Blues; Jump Blues	Vocals, piano, guitar	American
1980s–	Cephas & Wiggins	East Coast Blues	Various instruments	American
1940s–2000s	Charles, Ray	Rhythm & Blues	Vocals, piano, composer	American
1960s–	Charters, Samuel B.	Country Blues	Author, producer, folklorist	American
1930s–1980s	Chatmon, Sam	Delta Blues	Guitar	American
1950s–1980s	Chenier, Clifton	Rhythm & Blues	Vocals, accordion, harmonica	American
1960s–1980s	Chicken Shack	British Blues; Blues Rock	Various instruments	British
1960s–	Clapton, Eric	British Blues; Blues Rock	Guitar, vocals, composer	British
1950s–1980s	Clark, Dave	Rhythm & Blues	Producer, composer	American
1950s–1980s	Clark, Dee	Rhythm & Blues	Vocals	American
1980s–1990s	Clark, W.C.	Texas Blues; Modern Electric Blues	Guitar	American
1970s–	Clarke, Mick	British Blues; Blues Rock	Guitar	British
1970s–1990s	Clarke, William	Modern Electric Blues	Harmonica	American
1960s–	Clay, Otis	Rhythm & Blues	Vocals	American
1920s	Clayborn, Reverend Edward	Country Blues	Vocals, guitar	American
1930s–1940s	Clayton, Peter 'Doctor'	Chicago Blues	Vocals, composer	American
1970s–	Clayton, Willie	Rhythm & Blues	Vocals, composer	American
1950s–	Clearwater, Eddy	Modern Electric Blues; Rhythm & Blues; Chicago Blues	Guitar, vocals	American
1960s–1990s	Climax Blues Band	Blues Rock	Various instruments	British
1940s–1950s	Clovers, The	Rhythm & Blues	Vocals	American
1950s–1970s	Coasters, The	Rhythm & Blues	Vocals	American
1930s–1980s	Cobb, Arnett	Jump Blues	Saxophone	American
1950s–	Cobbs, Willie	Country Blues; Modern Electric Blues	Vocals, harmonica, guitar	American
1960s–	Cocker, Joe	Blues Rock	Vocals	British
1960s–	Cohn, Larry	Country Blues	Producer, author	American
1990s–	Coleman, Deborah	Modern Electric Blues	Guitar, vocals	American
1980s–1990s	Coleman, Gary 'B.B.'	Modern Electric Blues	Vocals, keyboards, bass, producer	American
1920s–1930s	Coleman, Jaybird	Country Blues	Harmonica	American
1980s–	Coleman, Michael	Modern Electric Blues; Chicago Blues; Rhythm & Blues	Vocals, guitar	American
1950s–1990s	Collins, Albert	Texas Blues; Modern Electric Blues	Guitar, vocals, composer	American
1920s–1940s	Collins, Sam	Country Blues	Guitar	American
1980s–	Connor, Joanna	Modern Electric Blues	Guitar, vocals, composer	American
1970s–1990s	Cooder, Ry	Blues Rock	Guitar	American
1950s–1960s	Cooke, Sam	Rhythm & Blues	Vocals, composer	American
1960s–1990s	Copeland, Johnny 'Clyde'	Modern Electric Blues; Texas Blues	Guitar, vocals	American
1990s–	Copeland, Shemekia	Modern Electric Blues	Vocals	American
1950s–1980s	Cotten, Elizabeth	Rhythm & Blues	Guitar, vocals, composer	American
1950s	Cotton, James	Modern Electric Blues; Chicago Blues	Guitar, harmonica	American
1930s	Council, Floyd 'Dipper Boy'	Country Blues	Vocals, guitar	American
1940s–1980s	Cousin Joe (Pleasant Joseph)	Rhythm & Blues; Swing	Vocals, composer, piano	American
1920s–1960s	Cox, Ida	Country Blues	Vocals	American
1950s–1960s	Crawford, James 'Sugar Boy'	Rhythm & Blues	Vocals, piano	American
1970s–	Cray, Robert	Modern Electric Blues	Guitar, vocals	American
1940s–1980s	Crayton, Pee Wee	West Coast Blues; Texas Blues	Guitar	American
1950s–1990s	Creach, John 'Papa'	Jump Blues	Vocals, violin	American
1960s	Cream	British Blues; Blues Rock	Various instruments	British
1960s	Crockett, G.L.	Rhythm & Blues	Vocals, guitar	American
1970s	Crowbar	Rock Blues	Blues band	Canadian
1940s–1970s	Crudup, Arthur 'Big Boy'	Delta Blues; Rhythm & Blues	Vocals, guitar	American
1990s–	Cusic, Eddie	Country Blues	Vocals, guitar	American
1950s–1960s	Dale, Larry	East Coast Blues; Rhythm & Blues	Guitar	American
1950s–	Dane, Barbara	Folk Blues	Vocals, guitar, piano	American
1920s–1930s	Darby, Blind Teddy	Country Blues	Guitar	American
1920s–1950s	Davenport, Charles 'Cow Cow'	Boogie-Woogie	Piano	American
1960s	Davies, Cyril	British Blues	Vocals, harmonica	British
1980s–	Davies, Debbie	Modern Electric Blues	Vocals, guitar	American
1930s–1950s	Davis, Blind John	Boogie-Woogie	Piano	American
1960s–1980s	Davis, Geater	Rhythm & Blues	Vocals	American
1990s	Davis, Guy	Country Blues; Folk Blues	Vocals, guitar, harmonica	American
1950s–1980s	Davis, James 'Thunderbird'	Modern Electric Blues	Vocals	American
1950s–1990s	Davis, Larry	Texas Blues	Drums, guitar	American
1940s–1960s	Davis, Maxwell	Rhythm & Blues	Saxophone, producer, arranger	American
1960s–1980s	Davis, Maxwell St. Jimmy	Country Blues	Vocals, guitar	American
1930s–1970s	Davis, Rev. Gary	East Coast Blues	Guitar, vocals	American
1960s–2000s	Davis, Tyrone	Rhythm & Blues	Vocals	American
1920s–1940s	Davis, Walter	Country Blues	Vocals, piano	American
1960s–1990s	Dawkins, Jimmy	Modern Electric Blues; Chicago Blues	Guitar	American
1960s–1970s	Delaney & Bonnie	Blues Rock	Vocals	American
1980s–	Delay, Paul	Modern Electric Blues	Vocals, harmonica	American
1970s	Derek & the Dominoes	British Blues; Blues Rock	Various instruments	American
1960s–	Detroit Junior	Modern Electric Blues	Vocals, piano	American
1950s–	Diddley, Bo	Rhythm & Blues; Chicago Blues	Guitar, vocals, composer	American
1950s–1960s	Dillard, Varetta	Rhythm & Blues	Vocals	American
1940s–1970s; 1990s	Dixon, Floyd	Jump Blues; Rhythm & Blues; West Coast Blues	Guitar, vocals	American
1960s–	Dixon, R.M.W.	Country Blues	Author	British
1940s–1990s	Dixon, Willie	Jump Blues; Chicago Blues	Bass, composer, producer	American
1950s–1990s	Doctor Ross	Delta Blues	Guitar, vocals, harmonica	American
1940s–1990s	Doggett, Bill	Rhythm & Blues	Piano, organ, composer	American
1940s–1980s	Domino, Fats	Rhythm & Blues	Piano, vocals	American
1950s–1960s	Dominoes, The	Rhythm & Blues	Vocals	American
1950s–1960s	Don & Dewey	Rhythm & Blues	Vocals	American
1940s–1990s	Donegan, Dorothy	Boogie-Woogie	Piano	American
1920s–1930s	Dorsey, Georgia Tom	Country Blues	Piano, composer	American
1960s–1980s	Dorsey, Lee	Rhythm & Blues	Vocals	American
1950s–1970s	Douglas, K.C.	Delta Blues	Guitar, composer	American
1970s–	Downchild Blues Band	Modern Electric Blues; Jump Blues; Chicago Blues	Blues Band	Canadian
1960s–	Dr John	Rhythm & Blues	Piano, vocals, composer	American
1920s	Dranes, Arizona	Country Blues	Vocals, piano	American
1950s–1990s	Drifters, The	Rhythm & Blues	Vocals	American
1950s	Du Droppers, The	Rhythm & Blues	vocals	American
1990s–	Duarte, Chris	Blues Rock	Guitar, vocals	American
1990s–2000s	Dupree, Big Al	Modern Electric Blues	Vocals, piano, saxophone	American
1940s–1990s	Dupree, Champion Jack	Chicago Blues; Rhythm & Blues	Piano, vocals, composer	American
1960s–	Dupree, Cornell	Modern Electric Blues; Rhythm & Blues	Guitar	American
1940s–1980s	Duskin, Big Joe	Boogie-Woogie	Piano	American
1950s–2000s	Dyer, Johnny	Delta Blues; Chicago Blues; West Coast Blues	Vocals, harmonica	American
1950s–	Eaglin, Snooks	Rhythm & Blues	Guitar, vocals	American
1980s–1990s	Ealey, Robert	Texas Blues	Drums, vocals	American
1970s–	Earl, Ronnie	Blues Rock; Modern Electric Blues	Guitar	American
1950s–1960s	Easy Baby (Alex Randle)	Rhythm & Blues: Modern Electric Blues	Vocals, harmonica	American
1980s	Edwards, Archie	Modern Electric Blues	Guitar	American
1940s–2000s	Edwards, Frank	Country Blues	Vocals, guitar, harmonica	American
1940s–	Edwards, Honeyboy	Modern Electric Blues	Guitar, harmonica	American
1920s–1960s	Edwards, Susie	Country Blues	Vocals	American
1950s	Egan, Willie	Boogie-Woogie	Piano, vocals	American
1960s–1970s	Electric Flag	Blues Rock	Various instruments	American
1980s–	Ellis, Tinsley	Modern Electric Blues	Guitar	American
1990s–	Erickson, Craig	Modern Electric Blues	Guitar	American
1950s	Esquerita (Eskew Reeder)	Rhythm & Blues	Vocals, piano	American
1930s; 1960s–1970s	Estes, Sleepy John	Country Blues	Vocals, guitar	American
1960s–	Evans, David	Country Blues	Author, producer	American
1960s–	Evans, Margie	Rhythm & Blues; West Coast Blues	Vocals	American
1950s–1970s	Everett, Betty	Rhythm & Blues	Vocals	American
1970s–	Fabulous Thunderbirds, The	Blues Rock	Various instruments	American
1950s–1990s	Fahey, John	Country Blues; Delta Blues	Guitar, composer, author	American
1990s–	Farr, Deitra	Modern Electric Blues; Jump Blues; Chicago Blues	Vocals	American
1950s–1990s	Ferguson, Robert 'H-Bomb'	Rhythm & Blues; Jump Blues	Vocals, piano	American
1950s–1960s	Five Keys, The	East Coast Blues; Rhythm & Blues	Vocals	American
1950s–1960s	Five Royales, The	Rhythm & Blues	Vocals	American
1960s–	Fleetwood Mac	British Blues; Blues Rock	Various instruments	British
1990s–	Flynn, Billy	Modern Electric Blues	Guitar	American
1990s–	Foley, Sue	Modern Electric Blues	Vocals, guitar	Canadian
1950s–	Ford, Frankie	Rhythm & Blues	Piano, vocals	American
1940s–1950s	Forest City Joe	Chicago Blues	Harmonica, composer	American
1950s	Foster, 'Baby Face' Leroy	Chicago Blues	Vocals, drums, guitar	American
1950s	Fowler, T.J.	Jump Blues,	Piano, bandleader	American
1950s–	Fran, Carol	Rhythm & Blues	Vocals, piano	American
1940s–1980s	Francis, Panama	Rhythm & Blues; Swing	Drums, bandleader	American
1950s–1990s	Frank, Edward	Rhythm & Blues	Piano	American
1950s	Frazier, Calvin	Jump Blues	Vocals, guitar	American
1960s–1970s	Free	Blues Rock	Various instruments	British
1950s–1990s	Frost, Frank	Modern Electric Blues	Keyboards, guitar	American
1930s–1940s	Fuller, Blind Boy	East Coast Blues	Guitar, vocals	American
1950s–1960s	Fuller, Jesse	Country Blues; West Coast Blues	Bass, guitar, harmonica	American
1950s–1980s	Fuller, Johnny	Rhythm & Blues; West Coast Blues	Guitar	American
1940s–1990s	Fulson, Lowell	West Coast Blues; Texas Blues	Guitar, vocals	American
1980s–	Funderburgh, Anson	Modern Electric Blues	Guitar	American
1950s–1990s	Gaddy, Bob	Rhythm & Blues	Vocals, piano	American
1950s	Gaines, Earl	Rhythm & Blues	Vocals	American
1950s–	Gaines, Grady	Jump Blues; Texas Blues; Rhythm & Blues	Saxophone	American
1970s–	Gaines, Roy	Modern Electric Blues	Guitar	American
1930s–1940s	Gaither, Bill 'Leroy's Buddy'	Country Blues	Vocals, guitar	American
1970s–1980s	Gallagher, Rory	British Blues; Blues Rock	Guitar	Irish
1940s–1950s	Gant, Cecil	West Coast Blues; Rhythm & Blues	Piano, vocals	American
1950s	Garlow, Clarence 'Bon Ton'	Rhythm & Blues	Vocals, guitar	American
1990s–	Garner, Larry	Modern Electric Blues	Vocals, guitar, composer	American
1960s–	Garon, Paul	Blues	Author	American
1950s–1990s	Gayles, Billy	Jump Blues; Rhythm & Blues	Vocals, drums	American
1940s–1960s	Gayten, Paul	Rhythm & Blues	Vocals, piano, composer, producer	American
1960s–	Geremia, Paul	Country Blues	Vocals, guitar	American
1920s–1930s	Gibson, Clifford	Country Blues	Guitar	American
1960s–	Gibson, Lacy	Modern Electric Blues; Chicago Blues	Vocals, guitar	American
1930s–1940s	Gillum, Bill 'Jazz'	Country Blues	Harmonica	American
1950s	Gilmore, Boyd	Country Blues	Vocals, guitar	American
1940s–1950s	Glenn, Lloyd	West Coast Blues; Jump Blues	Piano, producer	American
1940s–1960s	Glover, Henry	Rhythm & Blues	Producer, composer, trumpet	American
1960s–1990	Godrich, John	Country Blues	Author	Australian
1990s–	Gogo, David	Modern Electric Blues	Vocals, guitar	Canadian
1950s–1990s	Gordon, Rosco	Rhythm & Blues	Vocals, piano, composer	American
1980s–	Grand, Otis	Modern Electric Blues	Guitar, band leader	British
1920s–1940s	Grant, Coot	Country Blues	Vocals	American
1920s–1930s	Graves, Blind Roosevelt	Country Blues	Guitar, vocals	American
1950s–1990s	Gray, Henry	Chicago Blues	Vocals, piano	American
1950s	Great Gates (Edward White)	Jump Blues; Rhythm & Blues	Vocals, piano, organ	American
1960s–	Green, Al	Rhythm & Blues	Vocals	American
1950s–1990s	Green, Clarence	Texas Blues	Piano	American
1950s	Green, L.C.	Detroit Blues	Vocals, guitar	American
1920s–1930s	Green, Leothus Lee	Country Blues	Piano	American
1940s–1950s	Green, Lil	Country Blues	Vocals	American
1970s–	Green, Peter	British Blues; Blues Rock	Guitar	British
1950s–1960s	Greene, Rudy	Rhythm & Blues	Vocals	American
1940s–1950s	Greer, Big John	East Coast Blues	Vocals, saxophone	American
1960s; 1980s	Grey Ghost	Texas Blues	Piano	American
1960s	Griffin, Shirley	Country Blues	Vocals, guitar	American
1940s–1970s	Grimes, Tiny	Jump Blues	Guitar	American
1960s–	Grossman, Stefan	Country Blues	Vocals, guitar, author	American
1960s–1990s	Groundhogs, The	Blues Rock	Various instruments	British
1960s	Guitar Junior (a.k.a. Lonnie Brooks)	Chicago Blues	Vocals, guitar	American
1950s–	Guitar Shorty	Modern Electric Blues	Guitar	American
1950s	Guitar Slim	Rhythm & Blues	Guitar	American
1950s	Gunter, Arthur	Rhythm & Blues	Vocals, guitar	American
1970s–	Guralnick, Peter	Rhythm & Blues	Author	American
1960s–	Guy, Buddy	Modern Electric Blues; Chicago Blues	Guitar, vocals	American
1980s–	Guy, Phil	Modern Electric Blues	Vocals, guitar	American
1990s–	Haddix, Travis	Modern Electric Blues	Vocals, guitar	American
1950s–1970s	Hall, Rene	Rhythm & Blues; Jump Blues	Guitar, producer, arranger	American
1960s–	Hammond, John Jr.	Blues Rock; Rhythm & Blues	Producer	American
1900s–1920s	Handy, W.C.	Delta Blues	Vocals, composer	American
1950s–1960s	Hare, Pat	Modern Electric Blues	Guitar	American
1930s	Harlem Hamfats	East Coast Blues	Various instruments	American
1980s–	Harman, James	Modern Electric Blues	Vocals, harmonica	American
1950s–1960s	Harmonica Slim	West Coast Blues	Harmonica	American
1970s	Harney, Richard 'Hackshaw'	Country Blues	Guitar	American
1950s–1960s	Harper, Toni	Boogie-Woogie; Rhythm & Blues	Vocals	American
1950s–1960s	Harpo, Slim	Jump Blues	Guitar, harmonica	American
1990s–	Harris, Corey	Delta Blues; Modern Electric Blues	Vocals, guitar	American
1950s–1990s	Harris, Don 'Sugarcane'	Rhythm & Blues	Vocals, violin, guitar	American
1960s	Harris, James 'Shakey Jake'	Modern Electric Blues	Vocals, harmonica	American
1940s–1970s	Harris, Peppermint	Jump Blues; West Coast Blues	Vocals	American
1940s–1960s	Harris, Wynonie	Jump Blues; Rhythm & Blues	Vocals, drums	American
1950s–1970s	Harrison, Wilbert	Rhythm & Blues	Vocals	American
1990s–	Hart, Alvin Youngblood	Country Blues	Vocals, guitar,	American
1990s–2000s	Hatch, Provine Little	Modern Electric Blues	Vocals, harmonica	American
1950s–1990s	Hawkins, Screamin' Jay	Rhythm & Blues	Vocals, piano, saxophone	American
1940s–1950s	Hawkins, Roy	West Coast Blues; Rhythm & Blues	Piano, vocals	American
1950s–1980s	Hawkins, Ted	Rhythm & Blues	Guitar, vocals	American
1950s–1990s	Heartsman, Johnny	Rhythm & Blues; Modern Electric Blues	Vocals, guitar, flute	American
1960s–	Hemphill, Jessie Mae	Country Blues; Delta Blues	Vocals, guitar	American
1940s–1950s	Henderson, Duke	West Coast Blues	Vocals	American
1960s–1970s	Hendrix, Jimi	Blues Rock	Guitar, composer	American
1950s–1960s	Henry, Clarence 'Frogman'	Rhythm & Blues, vocals	Piano, trombone	American
1940s–1990s	Hibbler, Al	Jump Blues	Vocals	American
1920s	Hicks, Edna	Country Blues	Vocals	American
1950s	Higgins, Chuck	Jump Blues	Saxophone	American
1920s	Hill, Bertha 'Chippie'	Country Blues	Vocals	American
1960s–1970s	Hill, Jessie	Rhythm & Blues	Drums, vocals	American
1960s–1980s	Hill, Z.Z.	Modern Electric Blues	Vocals	American
1970s–1990s	Hinton, Eddie	Rhythm & Blues	Vocals, guitar, composer	American
1990s–	Hoax, The	British Blues; Blues Rock	Various instruments	British
1960s–1990s	Hogan, Silas	Modern Electric Blues; Louisiana Blues	Vocals, guitar, harmonica	American
1940s–1950s	Hogg, Smokey	Country Blues; Rhythm & Blues	Vocals, guitar	American
1990s–	Hole, Dave	Modern Electric Blues	Vocals, guitar	Australian
1980s–	Holland, Jools	Boogie-Woogie	Piano, bandleader	British
1940s	Hollis, Tony	Country Blues	Vocals, guitar	American
1970s	Hollywood Fats Band	Modern Electric Blues	Various instruments	American
1980s–	Holmes Brothers	Modern Electric Blues	Various instruments	American
1950s–1970s	Hooker, Earl	Delta Blues; Chicago Blues	Guitar	American
1940s–1990s	Hooker, John Lee	Delta Blues; Country Blues	Guitar, composer	American
1950s–1970s	Hopkins, Lightnin'	Texas Blues	Vocals, guitar	American
1950s–1980s	Hopkins, Linda	East Coast Blues; Jump Blues	Vocals	American
1990s–	Hornbuckle, Linda	Modern Electric Blues	Vocals	American
1940s–1980s	Horton, Big Walter 'Shakey'	Chicago Blues	Harmonica	American
1930s–1960s	House, Son	Work Songs; Delta Blues	Guitar, vocals, composer	American
1950s–1980s	Houston, Bee	Texas Blues	Guitar	American
1950s–	Houston, Joe	Jump Blues	Vocals, saxophone	American
1970s	Hovington, Fred	Country Blues	Guitar	American
1930s–1940s	Howard, Rosetta	East Coast Blues	Vocals	American
1920s–1930s	Howell, Peg Leg	Country Blues	Vocals, composer	American
1930s–1970s	Howlin' Wolf	Chicago Blues	Vocals, guitar	American
1930s–1940s	Hudson, 'Black Bob'	Country Blues	Piano	American
1950s–	Hughes, Joe 'Guitar'	Texas Blues; Modern Electric Blues	Guitar	American

1960s–1980s	Humble Pie	Blues Rock; British Blues	Various instruments	British
1920s–1970s	Humes, Helen	Country Blues; Jump Blues	Vocals	American
1920s–1980s	Hunter, Alberta	Rhythm & Blues	Vocals	American
1930s–1970s	Hunter, Ivory Joe	West Coast Blues; Rhythm & Blues	Piano, composer	American
1960s–1990s	Hunter, Long John	Modern Electric Blues; Texas Blues	Guitar, vocals	American
1920s–1940s; 1960s	Hurt, Mississippi John	Country Blues; Work Songs	Guitar, vocals, composer	American
1960s–1980s	Hutto, J.B.	Chicago Blues	Guitar, vocals	American
1950s–	Isley Brothers, The	Rhythm & Blues	Vocals	American
1970s–1980s	J. Geils Band	Blues Rock	Various instruments	American
1950s–1960s	Jacks, The	Rhythm & Blues	Various instruments	American
1960–	Jackson, Big Jack	Modern Electric Blues	Vocals, guitar	American
1940s–1950s	Jackson, Bull Moose	Jump Blues; Rhythm & Blues	Saxophone	American
1970s–1980s	Jackson, Chuck	Rhythm & Blues	Vocals	American
1990s–	Jackson, Fruteland	Country Blues	Vocals, guitar	American
1970s–	Jackson, George	Rhythm & Blues	Vocals, piano, composer, producer	American
1950s–1990s	Jackson, Grady 'Fats'	Rhythm & Blues	Vocals, saxophone	American
1910s–1930s	Jackson, Jim	Country Blues	Guitar	American
1960s–1990s	Jackson, John	Country Blues	Guitar	American
1940s–1960s	Jackson, Melvin 'Lil' Son'	Texas Blues	Guitar, vocals	American
1920s–1930s	Jackson, Papa Charlie	Country Blues	Banjo	American
1980s–1990s	Jacque, Beau	Modern Electric Blues	Vocals, accordion	American
1990s–	James, Colin	Modern Electric Blues; Jump Blues	Vocals, guitar	Canadian
1950s–1960s	James, Elmore	Chicago Blues	Guitar, vocals, composer	American
1950s–	James, Etta	Rhythm & Blues	Vocals	American
1930s; 1960s	James, Skip	Delta Blues; Country Blues	Guitar, vocals, composer	American
1920s–1940s	Jaxon, Frankie 'Half Pint'	East Coast Blues	Vocals	American
1920s	Jefferson, Blind Lemon	Country Blues; Texas Blues	Guitar, vocals	American
1970s–1990s	Jelly Roll Kings, The	Modern Electric Blues	Artist	American
1950s–1960s	Jenkins, Bobo	Modern Electric Blues; Detroit Blues	Vocals, guitar	American
1950s	Jenkins, Gus	Rhythm & Blues	Vocals, piano	American
1920s–1940s	Johnson, Blind Willie	Texas Blues	Guitar, vocals	American
1930s–1960s	Johnson, Buddy	Jump Blues; Rhythm & Blues	Pianist, bandleader, composer	American
1950s–2000s	Johnson, Conrad	Jump Blues; Texas Blues	Saxophone, bandleader	American
1940s–1950s	Johnson, Ella	Jump Blues; Rhythm & Blues	Vocals	American
1960s–	Johnson, Jimmy	Modern Electric Blues	Vocals, guitar	American
1950s–1990s	Johnson, Johnnie	Boogie-Woogie; Rhythm & Blues	Piano	American
1960s–1970s	Johnson, Larry	Modern Electric Blues	Guitar, vocals	American
1920s–1960s	Johnson, Lonnie	Country Blues	Guitar, vocals, banjo	American
1960s–1970s	Johnson, Luther 'Georgia Boy' 'Snake'	Modern Electric Blues	Vocals, guitar	American
1960s–	Luther 'Guitar Jr.' Johnson	Chicago Blues	Guitar, vocals	American
1990s–	Johnson, Luther 'Houserocker'	Modern Electric Blues	Guitar, vocals	American
1950s–1960s	Johnson, Marv	Rhythm & Blues	Vocals, composer	American
1920s–1960s	Johnson, Pete	Boogie-Woogie	Piano	American
1950s–	Johnson, Plas	Jump Blues; Rhythm & Blues	Saxophone	American
1930s	Johnson, Robert	Delta Blues; Country Blues	Guitar, vocals, composer	American
1960s–	Johnson, Syl	Rhythm & Blues	Vocals	American
1920s–1930s	Johnson, Tommy	Delta Blues; Country	Guitar, vocals, composer	American
1960s–	Jones, Andrew 'Jr. Boy'	Modern Electric Blues; Texas Blues	Vocals, guitar	American
1930s–1960s	Jones, Curtis	Country Blues	Vocals, piano	American
1920s–1930s	Jones, Dennis 'Little Hat'	Country Blues	Vocals, guitar	American
1960s	Jones, Eddie 'One String'	Delta Blues	Guitar	American
1950s–1960s	Jones, Floyd	Chicago Blues	Guitar, composer	American
1940s–1960s	Jones, Little Johnny	Chicago Blues; Boogie-Woogie	Piano	American
1990s–	Jones, Tutu	Modern Electric Blues	Guitar, drums	American
1960s–1970s	Joplin, Janis	Blues Rock	Vocals	American
1920s–1940s	Jordan, Charley	Country Blues	Vocals, guitar	American
1930s–1970s	Jordan, Louis	East Coast Blues; Jump Blues	Vocals, saxophone	American
1950s–1970s	Julian, Don	Rhythm & Blues	Vocals	American
1960s–1990s	K-Doe, Ernie	Rhythm & Blues	Vocals, composer	American
1990s–	Keb' Mo'	Blues Rock	Guitar, songwriter	American
1960s–1990s	Kelly, Jo Ann	British Blues	Vocals	British
1960s–	Kelly, Paul	Rhythm & Blues	Vocals, composer	American
1990s–	Kelly, Vance	Modern Electric Blues; Chicago Blues	Vocals, guitar	American
1950s	Kennedy, Tiny	East Coast Blues; Jump Blues	Vocals	American
1950s–1960s	Kenner, Chris	New Orleans Blues	Vocals, composer	American
1970s–	Kent, Willie	Modern Electric Blues	Vocals, electric bass	American
1960s–1990s	Kimbrough, Junior	Modern Electric Blues; Delta Blues; Country Blues	Guitar, composer	American
1970s–2000s	King Biscuit Boy	Modern Electric Blues; Chicago Blues	Vocals, harmonica	Canadian
1950s–1970s	King Curtis	Rhythm & Blues; East Coast Blues	Saxophone	American
1960s–1980s	King, Albert	Modern Electric Blues; Rhythm & Blues	Vocals, guitar	American
1940s–	King, B.B.	Modern Electric Blues; Rhythm & Blues	Vocals, guitar	American
1980s–	King, Chris Thomas	Modern Electric Blues; Louisiana Blues	Vocals, guitar	American
1950s–	King, Earl	Rhythm & Blues	Vocals, guitar	American
1980s–	King, Eddie	Modern Electric Blues	Vocals, guitar	American
1950s–1970s	King, Freddie	Texas Blues; Rhythm & Blues; Modern Electric Blues	Vocals, guitar	American
1990s–2000s	King, Little Jimmy	Modern Electric Blues	Vocals, guitar	American
1940s–1960s	King, Saunders	Jump Blues	Vocals, guitar	American
1990s	King, Shirley	Modern Electric Blues	Artist	American
1980s–	Kinsey Report	Modern Electric Blues; Chicago Blues	Various instruments	American
1980s–2000s	Kinsey, Lester 'Big Daddy'	Modern Electric Blues	Vocals, guitar, harmonica	American
1960s–1990s	Kirkland, Eddie	Modern Electric Blues	Guitar	American
1950s–1960s	Kittrell, Christine	Rhythm & Blues	Vocals, piano	American
1990s–	Knock-Out Greg & Blue Weather	Modern Electric Blues; Chicago Blues; Delta Blues	Various instruments	Swedish
1960s–1990s	Koerner, Ray & Glover	Country Blues; Folk Blues	Various instruments	American
1950s–1960s	Kolax, King	Jump Blues	Trumpet, bandleader	American
1960s–1980s	Korner, Alexis	British Blues; Blues Rock	Guitar	Greek
1990s–	Kubek, Smokin' Joe	Modern Electric Blues	Guitar	American
1920s	Lacy, Rube	Country Blues	Vocals, guitar	American
1990s–	Lang, Jonny	Modern Electric Blues	Vocals, guitar	American
1960s–	LaSalle, Denise	Rhythm & Blues	Vocals, composer	American
1960s–	Latimore, Benny	Rhythm & Blues	Vocals, piano	American
1980s–	Laws, Johnny	Modern Electric Blues; Rhythm & Blues	Vocals, guitar, composer, producer	American
1950s–	Lazy Lester	Modern Electric Blues	Vocals, harmonica	American
1960s–1970s	Leadbitter, Mike	Country Blues; Rhythm & Blues; Delta Blues	Author	British
1960s	Leake, Lafayette	Boogie-Woogie	Piano	American
1960s–1980s	Led Zeppelin	British Blues; Blues Rock	Various instruments	British
1920s–1940s	Ledbetter, Huddie 'Leadbelly'	Country Blues	Vocals, guitar	American
1990s–	Lee, Bonnie	Chicago Blues	Vocals	American
1940s–1950s	Lee, Julia	Jump Blues	Vocals, piano	American
1970s–	Lee, Little Frankie	Rhythm & Blues	Vocals	American
1980s–1990s	Lee, Lovie	Chicago Blues; Modern Electric	Vocals, piano	American
1980s–	Legendary Blues Band	Modern Electric Blues	Various instruments	American
1950s–1960s	Lenoir, J.B.	Chicago Blues	Guitar	American
1970s–	Levy, Ron	Modern Electric Blues	Piano, organ	American
1920s; 1960s–1970s	Lewis, Furry	Delta Blues	Guitar, vocals	American
1930s–1960s	Lewis, Meade 'Lux'	Boogie-Woogie	Piano	American
1920s–1960s	Lewis, Noah	Country Blues	Harmonica	American
1950s	Lewis, Pete 'Guitar'	Jump Blues; Rhythm & Blues	Vocals, guitar	American
1940s–1960s	Lewis, Smiley	Rhythm & Blues	Piano, vocals	American
1940s–1950s	Liggins, Jimmy	Jump Blues; Rhythm & Blues	Guitar	American
1940s–1950s	Liggins, Joe	Jump Blues; Rhythm & Blues	Piano, arranger	American
1950s	Lightfoot, Alexander 'Papa George'	Rhythm & Blues	Vocals, harmonica	American
1950s–1970s	Lightnin' Slim	Chicago Blues	Guitar	American
1980s–	Lil' Ed & the Blues Imperials	Modern Electric Blues	Various instruments	American
1920s–1930s	Lincoln, Charley	Country Blues	Guitar	American
1970s–	Linden, Colin	Modern Electric Blues	Guitar, composer	Canadian
1950s–1970s	Lipscomb, Mance	Country Blues	Guitar, vocals	American
1950s–1960s	Little Anthony & the Imperials	Rhythm & Blues	Vocals	American
1960s–	Little Buster	Rhythm & Blues	Vocals, guitar	American
1980s–1990s	Little Charlie & the Nightcats	Modern Electric Blues	Various instruments	American
1970s–	Little Feat	Blues Rock	Various instruments	American
1950s–	Little Milton	Modern Electric Blues; Rhythm & Blues	Guitar	American
1940s–1950s	Little Miss Cornshucks	Rhythm & Blues	Vocals	American
1950s–1990s	Little Richard	Rhythm & Blues	Vocals, piano	American
1960s–	Little Sonny	Modern Electric Blues	Vocals, harmonica	American
1940s–1960s	Little Walter	Chicago Blues	Harmonica, composer	American
1950s–1960s	Little Willie John	Rhythm & Blues	Vocals	American
1940s–1990s	Littlefield, Little Willie	Jump Blues; West Coast Blues; Boogie-Woogie; Rhythm & Blues	Piano, vocals	American
1960s–1990s	Littlejohn, John	Chicago Blues; Modern Electric Blues	Guitar, vocals	American
1930s–	Lockwood, Robert Jr.	Delta Blues; Chicago Blues	Guitar, vocals	American
1930s–1940s	Lofton, Cripple Clarence	Country Blues	Vocals, piano	American
1930s–1990s	Lomax, Alan	Work Songs	Producer	American
1930s–1940s	Lomax, John A. Sr	Country Blues	Producer, folklorist	American
1950s–1970s	Lonesome Sundown	Chicago Blues	Piano, guitar	American
1970s–1990s	Long, Joey	Texas Blues	Guitar	American
1960s–1980s	Lornell, Kip	Country Blues	Producer, author, folklorist	American
1990s	Louis, Big Joe, & his Blues Kin	British Blues	Various instruments	British
1940s–1950s	Louis, Joe Hill	Delta Blues	Guitar, harmonica	American
1950s–	Louisiana Red	Country Blues; Rhythm & Blues	Vocals, guitar	American
1960s–1970s	Love Sculpture	Blues Rock	Various instruments	British
1950s	Love, Billy	Delta Blues	Vocals	American
1950s–	Love, Clayton	Rhythm & Blues	Vocals, piano	American
1950s–2000s	Love, Preston	Jump Blues	Saxophone, producer	American
1950s	Love, Willie	Delta Blues; Rhythm & Blues	Vocals, piano	American
1970s–	Lowery, Robert	Country Blues, Delta Blues	Vocals, guitar	American
1960s–1970s	Lowry, Pete	Country Blues	Producer, folklorist	American
1950s–1980s	Lucas, Bill 'Lazy'	Chicago Blues	Vocals, piano	American
1940s–1950s	Lutcher, Joe	Rhythm & Blues	Saxophone	American
1950s–1960s	Lutcher, Nellie	Jump Blues	Vocals, piano	American
1960s–1990s	Lynn, Barbara	Rhythm & Blues; Modern Electric Blues	Guitar, vocals	American
1970s–	Lynn, Trudy	Rhythm & Blues	Vocals	American
1950s–1980s	Mabon, Willie	Chicago Blues; Rhythm & Blues	Vocals, piano, harmonica	American
1960s–	Mack, Lonnie	Modern Electric Blues; Rhythm & Blues	Guitar	American
1990s	Madcat & Kane	Rhythm & Blues	Harmonica, guitar	American
1990s	Magic Dick	Blues Rock; Modern Electric Blues	Harmonica	American
1950s–1960s	Magic Sam	Modern Electric Blues; Chicago Blues	Guitar, vocals	American
1970s–	Magic Slim	Modern Electric Blues	Guitar	American
1960s–2000s	Malone, J.J.	Modern Electric Blues	Vocals, guitar, keyboards	American
1990s–	Manfreds, The	Blues Rock; Rhythm & Blues	Various instruments	British
1960s–	Margolin, Bob	Modern Electric Blues	Guitar	American
1930s–1970s	Martin, Carl	East Coast Blues	Guitar	American
1920s–1930s	Martin, Sara	Country Blues	Vocals	American
1970s–	Mason, Dutch	Modern Electric Blues	Vocals, guitar	Canadian
1960s–	Mayall, John	British Blues; Blues Rock	Vocals, guitar, harmonica, keyboards	British
1950s–1990s	Mayfield, Curtis	Rhythm & Blues	Vocals, guitar, composer	American
1940s–1970s	Mayfield, Percy	West Coast Blues; Rhythm & Blues	Vocals, composer	American
1950s–1990s	Mayweather, George 'Earring'	Chicago Blues	Vocals, harmonica	American
1950s–1960s; 1980s–	McCain, Jerry 'Boogie'	Modern Electric Blues	Harmonica, composer	American
1960s–	McCall, Cash	Rhythm & Blues	Vocals, guitar, composer	American
1960s–	McClain, Mighty Sam	Rhythm & Blues	Vocals	American
1930s–1940s	McClennan, Tommy	Delta Blues	Guitar, vocals	American
1960s–	McClinton, Delbert	Blues Rock; Modern Electric Blues	Harmonica, guitar, vocals, composer	American
1920s–1930s	McCoy, Charlie 'Mississippi Muddler'	Country Blues, Delta Blues	Vocals, guitar, mandolin	American
1960s–1970s	McCoy, Ethel & George	Country Blues	Vocals, guitar	American
1920s–1930s	McCoy, Joe	Country Blues	Guitar, vocals	American
1920s–1930s	McCoy, Viola	Country Blues	Vocals	American
1950s–1990s	McCracklin, Jimmy	West Coast Blues; Rhythm & Blues	Vocals	American
1990s–	McCray, Larry	Modern Electric Blues	Vocals, guitar	American
1950s–1970s	McDowell, Mississippi Fred	Delta Blues	Guitar, vocals	American
1940s–1990s	McGhee, Brownie	East Coast Blues; Country Blues	Guitar,	American
1950s–1960s	McGhee, Sticks	Country Blues; East Coast Blues	Vocals, guitar	American
1940s–1990s	McNeely, Big Jay	Jump Blues; Rhythm & Blues; West Coast Blues	Saxophone	American
1950s–1960s	McPhatter, Clyde	Rhythm & Blues	Vocals	American
1930s–	McShann, Jay	Jump Blues	Piano	American
1920s–1950ss	McTell, Blind Willie	East Coast Blues; Country Blues	Guitar, vocals	American
1940s–1960s	McVea, Jack	Jump Blues	Saxophone, clarinet	American
1960s–1970s; 1990s	Medicine Head	British Blues	Artist	British
1930s–1940s	Melrose, Lester	Country Blues; Chicago Blues	Producer	American
1920s–1930s	Memphis Jug Band	Country Blues	Various instruments	American
1920s–1950s	Memphis Minnie	Country Blues; Chicago Blues	Guitar, vocals	American
1990s	Memphis Sheiks	Country Blues	Various instruments	American
1930s–1980s	Memphis Slim	Boogie-Woogie	Piano, vocals	American
1930s–1950s	Merriweather, 'Big Maceo'	Chicago Blues	Piano, vocals	American
1960s–1990s	Meters, The	Rhythm & Blues	Various instruments	American
1950s–1960s	Mickey & Sylvia	Rhythm & Blues	Guitar, vocals	American
1940s–1960s	Milburn, Amos	Jump Blues; West Coast Blues; Rhythm & Blues	Piano, vocals	American
1920s–1930s	Miles, Lizzie	Country Blues	Vocals	American
1950s–1960s	Miller, Jay D.	Jump Blues; Swamp Blues	Producer, composer	American
1940s–1980s	Milton, Roy	Jump Blues; West Coast Blues; Rhythm & Blues	Vocals, drums	American
1920s–1930s	Mississippi Sheiks	Country Blues	Various instruments	American
1960s–1970s	Mitchell, George	Country Blues	Producer, folklorist	American
1960–1970s	Mitchell, McKinley	Rhythm & Blues	Vocals	American
1960s–	Mitchell, Willie	Rhythm & Blues	Producer, arranger, composer	American
1930s–1970s	Montgomery, Little Brother	Boogie-Woogie	Piano	American
1970s–	Mooney, John	Delta Blues	Guitar	American
1950s	Moonglows, The	Rhythm & Blues	Vocals	American
1920s–1980s	Moore, Alex 'Whistling'	Country Blues; Texas Blues	Vocals, piano, composer	American
1940s–2000s	Moore, Arnold 'Gatemouth' '	Rhythm & Blues; Jump Blues	Vocals	American
1940s–1950s	Moore, Johnny & the Three Blazers	Jump Blues	Various instruments	American
1980s–	Moore, Johnny B.	Chicago Blues; Modern Electric Blues	Vocals, bass	American
1950s–1970s	Moore, Merrill	Boogie-Woogie; Rhythm & Blues	Piano, vocals	American
1940s–1980s	Moore, Oscar	Cool Blues; Jump Blues	Guitar	American
1990s–	Morgan, Mike	Modern Electric Blues; Texas Blues	Guitar	American
2000s–	Morganfield, 'Big' Bill	Chicago Blues	Vocals, guitar	American
1930s–1940s	Moss, Buddy	East Coast Blues; Country Blues	Guitar, harmonica	American
1940s–1980s	Muddy Waters	Delta Blues; Chicago Blues	Guitar, vocals	American
1950s–	Murphy, Matt 'Guitar'	Modern Electric Blues	Vocals, guitar	American
1960s–	Musselwhite, Charlie	Modern Electric Blues	Harmonica	American
1950s–1990s	Myers, Louis	Modern Electric Blues	Vocals, guitar, harmonica	American
1950s–	Myers, Sam	Modern Electric Blues	Vocals, harmonica	American
1960s–	Naftalin, Mark	Modern Electric Blues	Piano, producer	American
1960s–1970s	Napier, Simon	All Blues Styles	Author	British
1980s–	Neal, Kenny	Modern Electric Blues; Louisiana Blues	Vocals, guitar, harmonica	American
1950s–1960s	Neal, Raful	Modern Electric Blues	Harmonica	American
1950s–1960s	Nelson, Jimmy	Jump Blues; Rhythm & Blues	Vocals	American
1920s	Nelson, Romeo	Country Blues	Vocals, piano	American
1960s–	Neville Brothers, The	Rhythm & Blues	Various instruments	American
1960s–	Neville, Aaron	Rhythm & Blues	Keyboards, vocals	American
1920s	Newbern, 'Hambone' Willie	Country Blues	Guitar, vocals	American
1950s–1990s	Newborn, Calvin	Rhythm & Blues	Guitar	American
1930s	Newman, Jack	Country Blues	Artist	American
1960s–1970s	Nicholls, Billy	British Blues	Vocals, composer	British
1930s–1960s	Nighthawk, Robert	Chicago Blues	Guitar, vocals	American
1940s–1970s	Nix, Willie	Chicago Blues	Vocals, drums	American
1920s–1980s	Nixon, Hammie	County Blues	Vocals, mandolin, guitar	American
19090s–	Nocturne, Johnny Band	Jump Blues; Modern Electric Blues	Various instruments	American
1990s–	Nulisch, Darrell	Texas Blues; Modern Electric Blues	Vocals, harmonica	American
1960s–1990s	Numbers Band, The	Blues Rock	Various instruments	American
1970s–	O'Neal, Jim	All Blues Styles	Author	American
1930s–1960s	Oden, 'St. Louis' Jimmy	Country Blues	Vocals, composer, piano	American
1950s–	Odetta	Country Blues	Vocals, guitar	American
1960s–1990s	Odom, Andrew 'Big Voice' 'B.B.'	Chicago Blues	Vocals	American
1950s–1990s	Oliver, Paul	Country Blues; Delta Blues	Author, producer, folklorist	British
1950s–1960s	Olympics, The	Rhythm & Blues	Vocals	American
1980s–	Omar & the Howlers	Modern Electric Blues; Blues Rock	Various instruments	American
1940s–1960s	Orioles, The	Rhythm & Blues	Vocals	American
1970s–	Oscher, Paul	Modern Electric Blues	Vocals, harmonica, guitar, piano	American
1940s–1990s	Otis, Johnny	Jump Blues; West Coast Blues; Rhythm & Blues	Producer, songwriter, drums	American
1960s–	Otis, Shuggie	Modern Electric Blues; Blues Rock	Guitar	American
1960s–1970s	Owens, Jack	Delta Blues; Country Blues	Guitar	American
1980s–	Page, Jimmy	British Blues	Guitar, composer, producer	British
1950s–	Palmer, Earl	Rhythm & Blues	Drums	American
1970s–1990s	Palmer, Robert	All Blues Styles	Author, producer	American
1950s–	Parker, Bobby 'Barber'	Rhythm & Blues	Vocals, guitar	American
1950s–1970s	Parker, Junior	Rhythm & Blues	Vocals	American
1940s–`1950s	Parker, Sonny	Jump Blues; Rhythm & Blues	Vocals	American
1990s	Parrish, Michael	Country Blues	Piano, guitar	American
1920s–1930s	Patton, Charley	Delta Blues; Country Blues	Guitar, vocals, composer	American
1960s–	Peebles, Ann	Rhythm & Blues	Vocals	American
1920s–1930s	Peer, Ralph	Country Blues	Producer	American
1930s–1970s	Peg Leg Sam	Country Blues	Harmonica	American
1970s; 1990s	Pena, Paul	Rhythm & Blues	Vocals, piano, guitar	American
1940s–	Perkins, Pinetop	Boogie-Woogie; Chicago Blues	Piano	American
1960s–	Peterson, Lucky	Modern Electric Blues	Vocals, guitar, keyboard	American
1940s	Petway, Robert	Country Blues	Vocals, guitar	American
1950s–1970s	Phillips, Esther	Rhythm & Blues	Vocals	American
1940s–1950s	Phillips, Gene	West Coast Blues; Jump Blues	Guitar	American
1920s	Phillips, Washington	Country Blues	Vocals, dulceola	American
1950s–1960s	Piano Red	Boogie-Woogie	Piano, keyboards	American
1960s–	Piazza, Rod	West Coast Blues; Modern Electric Blues	Vocals, harmonica	American
1970s–	Piccolo, Greg	Jump Blues	Saxophone, vocals	American
1950s–1960s	Pickens, Edwin 'Buster'	Country Blues	Vocals, piano	American
1930s	Pickett, Charlie	Country Blues	Guitar	American
1940s–1950s	Pickett, Dan	Country Blues	Vocals, guitar	American
	Pitchford, Lonnie	Country Blues	Vocals, guitar	American
1940s–1990s	Pomus, Doc	Rhythm & Blues	Vocals, composer	American
1960s–	Porter, Bob	Rhythm & Blues	Producer	American
1970s–	Portnoy, Jerry	Country Blues; Chicago Blues	Vocals, harmonica, guitar, piano	American

1930s–1990s	Powell, Eugene 'Sonny Boy Nelson'	Country Blues	Vocals, guitar	American
1950s–1970s	Presley, Elvis	Rhythm & Blues	Vocals, piano, guitar	American
1950s–	Price, Big Walter	Rhythm & Blues	Vocals, piano	American
1950s–1960s; 1980s	Price, Lloyd	Rhythm & Blues	Piano, vocals, producer	American
1920s–1980s	Price, Sammy	Boogie-Woogie; Jump Blues	Piano, bandleader	American
1930s–1970s	Prima, Louis	Jump Blues; Rhythm & Blues	Vocals, trumpet, bandleader	American
1970s–	Primer, John	Modern Electric Blues	Guitar	American
1990s–	Primrich, Gary	Modern Electric Blues	Vocals, harmonica	American
1940s–1980s	Professor Longhair	Rhythm & Blues	Piano, vocals, composer	American
1940s–1990s	Pryor, Snooky	Chicago Blues	Vocals, harmonica	American
1940s–1990s	Prysock, Arthur	Rhythm & Blues	Vocals	American
1950s–1960s	Prysock, Red	Jump Blues; Rhythm & Blues	Saxophone	American
1930s	Pullum, Joe	Country Blues	Vocals	American
1990s–2000s	Qualls, Henry	Texas Blues; Modern Electric Blues	Guitar	American
1930s–1980	Rachell, Yank	Country Blues	Guitar, harmonica	American
1920s–1930s	Rainey, Ma	Delta Blues	Vocals	American
1970s–	Raitt, Bonnie	Blues Rock	Guitar, vocals, composer	American
1980s	Rascoe, Moses	Country Blues	Vocals, guitar	American
1950s–	Rawls, Lou	Rhythm & Blues	Vocals	American
1960s–2000s	Reed, A.C.	Rhythm & Blues; Modern Electric Blues	Vocals, saxophone	American
1950s–1970s	Reed, Jimmy	Chicago Blues; Rhythm & Blues	Vocals, guitar, composer	American
1980s–	Rey, Del	Country Blues	Vocals, guitar	American
1960s–	Rhodes, Sonny	Rhythm & Blues; Modern Electric Blues	Vocals, guitar, composer	American
1950s	Rhodes, Todd	Jump Blues	Piano, bandleader	American
1950s–	Rice, Sir Mac	Rhythm & Blues	Vocals, composer	American
1970s–	Ricks, Jerry 'Philadelphia'	Country Blues; Folk Blues	Vocals, guitar	American
1950s–1990s	Ridgley, Tommy	New Orleans Blues; Rhythm & Blues	Vocals, piano	American
1980s–	Rishell, Paul & Annie Raines	Country Blues	Guitar, vocals, harmonica	American
2000s	Roach, Michael	Country Blues; Folk Blues	Vocals, guitar	American
1970s–	Robertson, Sherman	Modern Electric Blues	Vocals, guitar	American
1970s–	Robillard, Duke	Modern Electric Blues	Vocals, guitar	American
1940s–1950s	Robins, The	Rhythm & Blues	Vocals	American
1960s–1980s	Robinson, Fenton	Texas Blues	Guitar, vocals	American
1960s–2000s	'Robinson, Jimmie Lee	Modern Electric Blues; Rhythm & Blues	Vocals, guitar, composer	American
1950s–1970s	Robinson, L.C. 'Good Rockin''	Modern Electric Blues	Vocals, guitar, violin	American
1920s–1930s	Rodgers, Jimmie	Country Blues	Vocals, guitar, composer	American
1950s–1990s	Rogers, Jimmy	Chicago Blues	Drums	American
1970s–	Rogers, Roy	Blues Rock	Guitar, producer	American
1930s	Roland, Walter	Boogie-Woogie; Country Blues	Piano, vocals	American
1960s–	Rolling Stones, The	Blues Rock	Various instruments	British
1970s–	Roomful of Blues	Jump Blues; Modern Electric Blues	Various instruments	American
1950s–	Rush, Bobby	Rhythm & Blues	Vocals, guitar, harmonica	American
1950s–	Rush, Otis	Chicago Blues	Guitar, vocals	American
1920s–1970s	Rushing, Jimmy	East Coast Blues; Jump Blues	Vocals	American
1990s–	Saffire – The Uppity Blues Women	Country Blues	Various instruments	American
1950s–1990s	Sahm, Doug	Country Rock; Blues Rock	Guitar, arranger, composer	American
1950s–2000s	Sain, Oliver	Rhythm & Blues	Saxophone, composer, producer, bandleader	American
1980s–	Salgado, Curtis	Modern Electric Blues	Vocals, harmonica	American
1920s–1930s	Sane, Dan	Country Blues	Guitar	American
1960s–	Santana, Carlos	Blues Rock	Guitar	American
1980s–	Satan & Adam	Modern Acoustic Blues; Folk Blues	Vocals, guitar, harmonica	American
1950s–1960s	Saunders, Red	Rhythm & Blues; Jump Blues	Drums, bandleader	American
1960s–	Savoy Brown	Blues Rock; British Blues	Various instruments	British
1950s–1990s	Scott, Buddy	Modern Electric Blues; Chicago Blues	Vocals, guitar	American
1990s–	Scott, E.C.	Soul Blues; Rhythm & Blues; Modern Electric Blues	Vocals	American
1940s–	Scott, Jimmy Little	Rhythm & Blues	Vocals	American
1950s–1970s	Scott, Joe	Rhythm & Blues	Trumpet, arranger, composer	American
1960s–	Scott-Adams, Peggy	Modern Electric Blues	Vocals	American
1970s–2000s	Seals, Son	Modern Electric Blues	Guitar, vocals, composer	American
1950s–1960s	Sears, Big Al	Jump Blues; Rhythm & Blues	Saxophone	American
1990s–	Sease, Marvin	Rhythm & Blues	Vocals, composer	American
1940s–1960s	Sellers, John 'Brother'	Country Blues; Folk Blues	Vocals, guitar	American
1920s–1960s	Shade, Will	Country Blues	Harmonica, vocals, guitar	American
1990s–	Shannon, Mem	Modern Electric Blues	Vocals, guitar	American
2000s–	Shannon, Preston	Modern Electric Blues; Rhythm & Blues	Vocals, guitar	American
1960s–	Shariff, Omar	Texas Blues	Piano, vocals	American
1990s	Sharpe, B.J.	Blues Rock	Vocals	American
1950s	Sharpe, Ray	Texas Blues	Guitar, vocals	American
1960s–	Shaw, Eddie	Jump Blues; Modern Electric Blues	Vocals, saxophone, bandleader	American
1930s; 1960s–1980s	Shaw, Robert	Boogie-Woogie	Piano	American
1930s–1940s	Shepard, Ollie	Country Blues	Vocals, piano, composer	American
1990s–	Shepherd, Kenny Wayne	Modern Electric Blues	Vocals, guitar	American
1990s–	Shields, Lonnie	Modern Electric Blues, Rhythm & Blues	Vocals, guitar	American
1960s–1990s	Shines, Johnny	Delta Blues; Chicago Blues	Guitar, vocals	American
1950s–1960s	Shirley & Lee	Rhythm & Blues	Vocals	American
1930s–1960s	Short, J.D.	Country Blues	Piano, guitar, clarinet	American
1960s–1980s	Siegel-Schwall Band	Modern Electric Blues	Various instruments	American
1960s–1990s	Simmons, Little Mack	Rhythm & Blues; Chicago Blues	Vocals, harmonica	American
1940s–1960s	Sims, Frankie Lee	Country Blues	Guitar	American
1950s–	Singer, Hal 'Cornbread'	Jump Blues; Rhythm & Blues	Saxophone	American
1940s–1950s	Slack, Freddie	Boogie-Woogie	Piano, bandleader	American
1940s–1980s	Slim, Sunnyland	Chicago Blues	Piano	American
1950s–1970s	Slim, Tarheel	Rhythm & Blues	Guitar, vocals	American
1950s–1960s	Slim, T.V.	Country Blues; Rhythm & Blues	Guitar	American
1920s–1930s	Smith, Bessie	Country Blues	Vocals	American
1960s–	Smith, Byther	Modern Electric Blues	Vocals, guitar	American
1920s–1930s	Smith, Clara	Country Blues	Vocals	American
1930s	Smith, Funny Paper	Texas Blues	Guitar	American
1940s–1980s	Smith, George 'Harmonica'	Modern Electric Blues	Harmonica	American
1950s–1960s	Smith, Huey 'Piano'	Rhythm & Blues	Piano	American
1920s–1930s	Smith, Ivy	Country Blues	Vocals	American
1930s	Smith, J.T. 'Funny Paper'	Country Blues	Vocals, guitar	American
1920s	Smith, Laura	Country Blues	Vocals, composer	American
1920s	Smith, Mamie	Country Blues	Vocals	American
1960s–1970s	Smith, Moses 'Whispering'	East Coast Blues; Louisiana Blues	Vocals, harmonica	American
1920s	Smith, Pinetop	Boogie-Woogie	Piano	American
1920s–1930s	Smith, Trixie	Country Blues	Vocals	American
1990s–	Smith, Willie 'Big Eyes'	Modern Electric Blues	Drums	American
1960s	Smokey Babe	Country Blues	Guitar, vocals	American
1960s–1990s	Smothers, Otis 'Big Smokey'	Modern Electric Blues; Rhythm & Blues	Vocals, guitar	American
1950s–2000s	Solomon, Clifford	Jump Blues; West Coast Blues	Saxophone	American
1980s–	Sons of Blues	Chicago Blues	Various instruments	American
2000s	Spady, Clarence	Modern Electric Blues	Vocals, guitar	American
1920s–1930s	Spand, Charlie	Country Blues	Vocals, piano	American
1950s–1970s	Spaniels, The	Rhythm & Blues	Vocals	American
1950s–1960s	Spann, Otis	Chicago Blues	Piano	American
1920s–1930s	Speckled Red	Boogie-Woogie	Piano	American
1980s–	Specter, Dave	Modern Electric Blues; Jump Blues	Guitar	American
1920s–1930s	Speir, H.C.	Delta Blues; Country Blues	Talent scout	American
1960s	Spellman, Benny	Rhythm & Blues	Vocals	American
1970s	Spencer, Jeremy	British Blues; Blues Rock	Guitar	British
1920s–1930s	Spivey, Victoria	Country Blues	Vocals	American
1920s–1930s	Spruell, Freddie	Country Blues	Vocals, guitar	American
1960s–1970s	Stackhouse, Houston	Country Blues; Delta Blues	Vocals, guitar	American
1960s	Steampacket	British Blues	Various instruments	British
1940s–1960s	Stidham, Arbee	Jump Blues	Vocals, guitar	American
1910s–1920s	Stokes, Frank	Country Blues	Guitar	American
1940s–1950s	Stone, Jesse	Rhythm & Blues	Producer, composer, piano	American
1980s–	Strehli, Angela	Modern Electric Blues	Vocals	American
1950s–1960s	Strong, Nolan	Rhythm & Blues	Vocals	American
1970s–	Strother, Percy	Modern Electric Blues	Vocals, guitar, harmonica	American
1970s–1990s	Sugar Blue	Modern Electric Blues	Harmonica	American
1950s–1990s	Sumlin, Hubert	Chicago Blues; Modern Electric Blues	Guitar	American
1920s–1980s	Sykes, Roosevelt	Chicago Blues	Piano	American
1920s–1930s	Taggart, Blind Joe	Country Blues	Guitar	American
1960s–	Taj Mahal	Country Blues	Vocals, piano, guitar, harmonica	American
1970s–	Talley, James	Country Blues; Modern Electric Blues	Guitar, vocals, composer	American
1920s–1960s	Tampa Red	Chicago Blues	Guitar	American
1940s–1950s	Tarrant, Rabon	Jump Blues	Vocals, drums	American
1950s–1980s	Taylor, Eddie	Modern Electric Blues; Rhythm & Blues	Guitar	American
1920s–1940s	Taylor, Eva	Country Blues	Vocals	American
1960s–1970s	Taylor, Hound Dog	Chicago Blues	Guitar, vocals	American
1950s–2000s	Taylor, Johnnie	Rhythm & Blues	Vocals	American
1960s–	Taylor, Koko	Modern Electric Blues; Chicago Blues; Rhythm & Blues	Vocals	American
1950s–1990s	Taylor, Little Johnny	Rhythm & Blues	Vocals	American
1990s	Taylor, Melvin, & the Slack Band	Modern Electric Blues	Various instruments	American
2000s	Taylor, Otis	Folk Blues; Modern Acoustic Blues	Vocals, guitar, banjo, harmonica, composer	American
1990s	Taylor, Sam	Jump Blues	Guitar, composer	American
1950s–1980s	Taylor, Ted	Rhythm & Blues	Vocals	American
2000s	Tedeschi, Susan	Modern Electric Blues	Vocals, guitar	American
1930s–1950s	Temple, Johnnie 'Geechie'	Delta Blues; Chicago Blues	Guitar, bass	American
1960s–1990s	Ten Years After	British Blues; Blues Rock	Various instruments	British
1930s–1980s	Terry, Sonny	East Coast Blues; Country Blues	Harmonica, vocals	American
1920s–1940s	Texas Alexander	Country Blues	Vocals, composer	American
1970s–	Thackery, Jimmy	Modern Electric Blues	Vocals, guitar	American
1930s–1960s	Tharpe, Sister Rosetta	Jump Blues	Vocals, guitar	American
1970s–	Theesink, Hans	Folk Blues; Modern Electric Blues	Vocals, guitars, mandolin, harmonica	Dutch
1960s	Them	British Blues; Blues Rock	Various instruments	British
1990s–	Thomas, Earl	Rhythm & Blues	Vocals, composer	American
1920s–1930s	Thomas, Henry 'Ragtime Texas'	Country Blues	Guitar, vocals, composer	American
1920s–1940s	Thomas, Hociel	Country Blues	Vocals	American
1960s–	Thomas, Irma	Rhythm & Blues	Vocals	American
1960s–1980s	Thomas, James 'Son'	Delta Blues	Guitar	American
1930s–1990s	Thomas, Jesse	Texas Blues	Piano, guitar	American
1950s–1960s	Thomas, Lafayette 'Thing'	Modern Electric Blues; West Coast Blues	Vocals, guitar	American
1920s–1930s	Thomas, Ramblin'	Country Blues	Guitar	American
1950s–1990s	Thomas, Rockin' Tabby	Chicago Blues	Guitar, vocals	American
1950s–1990s	Thomas, Rufus	Rhythm & Blues	Vocals, composer	American
1970s–1980s	Thompson, Ron	Modern Electric Blues	Piano, bandleader	American
1950s–1960s	Thompson, Sonny	Jump Blues	Piano, composer, bandleader	American
1970s–1990s	Thorogood, George	Blues Rock	Guitar	American
1940s–1970s	Thornton, Big Mama	Texas Blues; Rhythm & Blues	Vocals	American
1970s–	Toure, Ali Farka	Modern Electric Blues	Guitar, vocals, percussion	Malinese
1950s–1990s	Toussaint, Allen	Rhythm & Blues	Artist	American
1920s–1980s	Townsend, Henry	Country Blues	Guitar	American
1960s–1970s	Tramp	British Blues	Various instruments	British
1940s–1980s	Treniers, The	Jump Blues; Rhythm & Blues	Various instruments	American
1940s–1960s	Trice, Richard & Willie	Country Blues	Vocals, guitar	American
1920s	Tucker, Bessie	Country Blues; Delta Blues	Vocals	American
1960s–1990s	Tucker, Luther	Modern Electric Blues, Chicago Blues	Guitar	American
1930s–1980s	Turner, Big Joe	Jump Blues; Rhythm & Blues	Artist	American
1940s–	Turner, Ike	Rhythm & Blues	Piano, guitar, vocals, bandleader, producer	American
1930s–1980s	Turner, Big Joe	Jump Blues; Boogie-Woogie	Vocals	American
1950s–1970s	Turner, Titus	East Coast Blues; Jump Blues; Rhythm & Blues	Vocals, composer	American
1940s–1950s	Turner, Zeb	Boogie-Woogie	Guitar	American
1960s	Twice as Much	British Blues	Modern Electric Blues	British
1950s–1990s	Tyler, Alvin 'Red'	Rhythm & Blues	Saxophone	American
1970s	Tyson, Willie	Country Blues	Piano	American
1950s–	Upchurch, Phil	Rhythm & Blues	Guitar	American
1950s–2000s	Van Ronk, Dave	Folk Blues	Vocals, guitar	American
1940s–1990s	Van Walls, Harry 'Piano Man'	Rhythm & Blues	Piano	American
1980s–	Vaughan, Jimmie	Modern Electric Blues; Blues Rock	Guitar	American
1980s–1990s	Vaughan, Stevie Ray	Texas Blues; Modern Electric Blues; Blues Rock	Guitar	American
1980s–	Vaughn, Maurice John	Chicago Blues	Vocals, guitar, saxophone	American
1940s–1980s	Vinson, Eddie 'Cleanhead'	Jump Blues; West Coast Blues; Rhythm & Blues	Saxophone	American
1920s–1940s; 1960s–1970s	Vinson, Walter	Delta Blues	Guitar	American
1980s–	Walker, Joe Louis	Modern Electric Blues	Guitar	American
1950s–1990s	Walker, Johnny 'Big Moose'	Chicago Blues	Vocals, piano	American
1950s–1990s	Walker, Jr. & The All-Stars	Rhythm & Blues	Vocals, saxophone	American
1970s–1990s	Walker, Philip	Modern Electric Blues	Vocals	American
1920s–1970s	Walker, T-Bone	Texas Blues	Guitar, vocals, composer	American
1920s–1940s	Wallace, Sippie	Country Blues	Vocals	American
1940s–1960s	Walton, Mercy Dee	West Coast Blues	Piano	American
1950s	Ward, Billy	Rhythm & Blues	Vocals	American
1960s–	Ward, Robert	Modern Electric Blues; Rhythm & Blues	Guitar	American
1950s–1960s	Warren, Baby Boy	Detroit Blues	Vocals, guitar	American
1930s–1950s	Washboard Sam (Robert Brown)	Chicago Blues	Vocals, washboard	American
1960s–1990s	Washington, Albert	Rhythm & Blues; Modern Electric Blues	Vocals, guitar, keyboard	American
1940s–1960s	Washington, Dinah	Rhythm & Blues; Swing	Vocals	American
1960s	Washington, Leroy	Chicago Blues	Vocals	American
1970s–	Washington, Toni Lynn	Rhythm & Blues	Vocals	American
1950s–1980s	Washington, Tuts	Boogie-Woogie	Piano	American
1970s–	Washington, Walter 'Wolfman'	Rhythm & Blues, Modern Electric Blues	Vocals, guitar	American
1940s–	Waterford, Charles 'Crown Prince'	Rhythm & Blues	Vocals	American
1960s–	Waterman, Dick	Blues	Photographer, promoter, manager, author	American
1920s–1960s	Waters, Ethel	Country Blues	Vocals	American
1950s–1990s	Watson, Johnny 'Guitar'	Modern Electric Blues; Texas Blues; Rhythm & Blues	Guitar, vocals	American
1990s	Watson, Junior	West Coast Blues	Guitar, vocals	American
1950s–1990s	Watts, Noble	East Coast Blues; Jump Blues	Saxophone	American
1990s–	Weathersby, Carl	Modern Electric Blues	Guitar	American
1920s–1930s; 1950s	Weaver, Curley	Country Blues	Guitar	American
1920s	Weaver, Sylvester	Country Blues	Guitar, vocals	American
1950s–1980s	Webb, Boogie Bill	Rhythm & Blues; Country Blues	Guitar	American
1960s; 1980s–1990s	Webster, Katie	Rhythm & Blues	Piano	American
1920s–1940s	Weldon, Casey Bill	Country Blues	Guitar, vocals	American
1980s–1990s	Wellington, Valerie	Modern Electric Blues	Vocals, piano	American
1950s–1990s	Wells, Junior	Chicago Blues; Modern Electric Blues	Harmonica	American
1930s–1940s	Wheatstraw, Peetie	Country Blues	Piano, guitar, vocals	American
1970s	Whispering Smith	Rhythm & Blues	Harmonica, vocals	American
1970s–	White, Artie 'Blues Boy'	Rhythm & Blues	Vocals	American
1930s–1940s; 1960s–1970s	White, Bukka	Country Blues	Guitar, piano, vocals	American
1990s–	White, Charles	West Coast Blues	Vocals	American
1930s–1940s	White, George	Country Blues; Jump Blues	Vocals	American
1930s–1960s	White, Josh	Country Blues	Vocals, guitar, composer	American
1970s–1980s	White, Josh Jr.	Country Blues	Vocals, guitar, composer	American
1970s–	White, Lynn	Rhythm & Blues	Vocals	American
1930s	Wiley, Geechie	Country Blues	Vocals, guitar	American
1950s–1970s	Wilkins, Joe Willie	Country Blues; Delta Blues	Vocals, guitar	American
1920s–1930s	Wilkins, Rev. Robert	Country Blues	Guitar, vocals	American
1950s–1970s; 1990s–	Williams, Andre	Rhythm & Blues	Vocals	American
1930s–1980s	Williams, Big Joe	Delta Blues	Guitar, vocals, composer	American
1920s–1940s	Williams, J. Mayo 'Ink'	Country Blues; Chicago Blues	Producer	American
1950s–1960; 2000s	Williams, Jody	Rhythm & Blues; Chicago Blues	Vocals, guitar	American
1940s–1990s	Williams, Joe	Jump Blues	Vocals	American
1940s–1950s	Williams, L.C.	Texas Blues	Vocals, drums	American
1950s–1970s	Williams, Larry	Rhythm & Blues	Vocals, piano, composer	American
1960s–	Williams, Lee 'Shot'	Modern Electric Blues	Vocals, guitar	American
1940s–1950s	Williams, Lester	Rhythm & Blues	Guitar	American
1940s–1960s	Williams, Paul 'Hucklebuck'	Jump Blues; Rhythm & Blues	Saxophone, bandleader	American
1950s–1970s	Williams, Robert Pete	Country Blues	Guitar, vocals	American
1930s–1990s	Williamson, Homesick James	Chicago Blues	Guitar	American
1930s–1940s	Williamson, Sonny Boy (I)	Chicago Blues	Guitar, harmonica, vocals	American
1930s–1960s	Williamson, Sonny Boy (II)	Delta Blues; Chicago Blues	Harmonica, vocals	American
1980s–	Willis, Chick	Modern Electric Blues	Vocals, guitar	American
1950s	Willis, Chuck	Rhythm & Blues	Vocals	American
1940s–1950s	Willis, Ralph	Country Blues	Guitar	American
1990s–	Willson, Michelle	Jump Blues	Vocals	American
1920s–1960s	Wilson, Edith	Country Blues	Vocals	American
1950s–1970s	Wilson, Hop	Texas Blues	Guitar	American
1950s–1970s	Wilson, Jackie	Rhythm & Blues	Vocals	American
1950s	Wilson, Jimmy	Rhythm & Blues; West Coast Blues	Vocals	American
1980s–	Wilson, Kim	Modern Electric Blues	Vocals, harmonica	American
1990s–2000s	Wilson, U.P.	Texas Blues; Modern Electric Blues	Vocals, guitar	American
1920s	Winston, Edna	Country Blues	Vocals	American
1960s–	Winter, Johnny	Blues Rock; Modern Electric Blues	Guitar	American
1940s–1990s	Witherspoon, Jimmy	Jump Blues	Vocals, guitar	American
1980s–	Woods, Mitch	Boogie-Woogie; Jump Blues	Piano	American
1940s	Woods, Oscar 'Buddy'	Country Blues	Vocals, guitar	American
1940s–1950s	Wright, Billy	Jump Blues	Vocals	American
1950s–1970s	Wright, O.V.	Rhythm & Blues	Vocals	American
1930s–1950s	Yancey, Jimmy	Boogie-Woogie	Piano	American
1960s	Yardbirds, The	British Blues; Blues Rock	Artist	British
1940s–1960s	Young, Johnny	Modern Electric Blues; Chicago Blues	Vocals, mandolin, guitar	American
1960s–1990s	Young, Mighty Joe	Chicago Blues	Guitar	American
1990s–	Young, Zora	Modern Electric Blues	Vocals	American
1970s–1980s	Zwingenberger, Axel	Boogie-Woogie	Piano	German
1970s–1990s	ZZ Top	Blues Rock	Various instruments	American

Further Reading

Roots and Teens Blues

Abbott, L. & Seroff, D., *Out of Sight: The Rise of African American Popular Music, 1889-1895*, University of Missouri Press, 2003
Brooks, T., *Lost Sounds: Blacks and the Birth of the Recording Industry 1890-1919*, University of Illinois Press, 2004
Cohn, L. (ed.), *Nothing But the Blues: The Music and the Musicians*, Abbeville Press, 1993
Dixon, R.M.W., Godrich, J. & Rye, H. (eds.), *Blues & Gospel Records, 1890-1943*, Clarendon Press, 1997
Handy, W.C. (ed.), *Blues: An Anthology*, Applewood Books, 2001
Handy, W.C., *Father of the Blues*, Da Capo Press, 1991
Lomax, A., *The Land Where the Blues Began*, Random House USA Inc., 1993
Lotz, R.E., *Black People: Entertainers of African Descent in Germany and Europe*, Birgit Lotz Verlag, 1997
O'Neal, J. & van Singel, A. (eds.), *The Voice of the Blues*, Routledge, 2002
Odum, H.W. & Johnson, G.B., *The Negro and His Songs: A Study of Typical Negro Songs in the South*, Greenwood Press
Oliver, P., *Songsters & Saints: Vocal Traditions on Race Records*, Cambridge University Press, 1984
Oliver, P., *The Story of the Blues*, Pimlico, 1997
Roberts, J.S., *Black Music of Two Worlds*, Allen Lane, 1973
Titon, J.T., *Early Downhome Blues: A Musical and Cultural Analysis*, Atlantic Books, 1995
Wondrich, D., *Stomp and Swerve: American Music Gets Hot 1843-1924*, A Capella Publishing, 2003

Roots and Teens Jazz

Badger, R., *A Life in Ragtime: A Biography of James Reese Europe*, American Philological Association, 1995
Blesh, R. & Janis, H., *They All Played Ragtime*, Schirmer, 1974
Brunn, H.O., *The Story of the Original Dixieland Jazz Band*, Louisiana State University Press, 1960
Charters, S.B. & Kunstadt, L., *Jazz: A History of the New York Scene*, Da Capo Press, 1981
Chilton, J., *Sidney Bechet: Wizard of Jazz*, Da Capo Press, 1996
Kimball, R., *Reminiscing with Sissle and Blake*, Cooper Square Books, 2000
Morgan, T. & Barlow, W., *From Cakewalks to Concert Halls: An Illustrated History of African-American Popular Music from 1895 to 1930*, Black Belt Press, 1992.
Schafer, W.J. & Reidel, J., *The Art of Ragtime*, Louisiana State University Press, 1973
Schuller, G., *Early Jazz*, Oxford University Press, 1986

1920s Blues

Barlow, W., *Looking Up At Down*, Temple University Press, 1989
Charters, S., *Sweet As The Showers Of Rain*, Oak Publications, 1977
Davis, F., *The History Of The Blues*, Hyperion, 1995
Gurlanick, P., *Lost Highway*, Harper & Row, 1979
Harris, S., *Blues Who's Who*, Da Capo Press, 1978
Oliver, P., *The Story Of The Blues*, Chilton, 1979
Rowe, M., *Chicago Blues*, Da Capo Press, 1982
Santelli, R., *The Big Book Of Blues*, Pavilion, 1994
Silvester, P.J., *A Left Hand Like God*, Da Capo Press, 1988

1920s Jazz

Balliett, W., *Jelly Roll, Jabbo & Fats*, Oxford University Press, 1983
Gara, L., *The Baby Dodds Story*, Louisiana State University Press, 1992 (revised edition)
Mongran, N., *The History of the Guitar in Jazz*, Oak Publications, 1983
Reich, H. & Gaines, W., *Jelly's Blues*, Da Capo Press, 2003
Sallis, J. (ed.), *The Guitar in Jazz: An Anthology*, University of Nebraska Press, 1996
Sallis, J., *The Guitar Players*, University of Nebraska Press, 1982
Waller, M. & Calabrese, A., *Fats Waller*, Schirmer Books, 1997

1930s Blues

Berry, P., *Up From the Cradle of Jazz*, University of Georgia Press, 1986
Brovan, J., *Walking To New Orleans*, Blues Unlimited, 1974
Charters, S., *The Country Blues*, Da Capo Press, 1975
Wolfe, C. & Lornell, K., *The Life and Legend of Leadbelly*, HarperCollins, 1992
Wardlow, G.D., *Chasin' That Devil Music*, Miller Freeman Books, 1998
Lomax, A., *The Land Where The Blues Began*, Pantheon Books, 1993
Page, C.I., *Boogie Woogie Stomp: Albert Ammons & His Music*, Northeast Ohio Jazz Society, 1997

1930s Jazz

Appel, A., *Jazz Modernism*, Alfred A. Knopf, 2002
Basie, C. & Murray, A., *Good Morning Blues*, Random House, 1985
Berger, M. & E. & Patrick, J., *Benny Carter, A Life in American Music*, Scarecrow Press, 1982
Dance, S., *The World of Swing*, Scribner's, 1974
Daniels, D.H., *Lester Leaps In: The Life and Times of Lester 'Pres' Young*, Beacon Press, 2002
Ferguson, O. et al, *The Otis Ferguson Reader*, December Press, 1982
Firestone, R., *Swing Swing Swing: The Life and Times of Benny Goodman*, W.W. Norton & Co., 1993
Giddins, G., *Visions of Jazz: The First Century*, Oxford University Press, 1998
Hammond, J., *John Hammond On Record*, Summit Books, 1977
Kirchner, B. (ed.), *The Oxford Companion to Jazz*, Oxford University Press, 2000
Sargeant W., *Jazz, Hot and Hybrid*, E.P. Dutton & Co. 1938
Schuller, G., *The Swing Era*, Oxford University Press, 1989
Simon, G.T., *The Big Bands (4th ed.)*, Schirmer Books, 1981
Simosko, V., *Artie Shaw: A Musician Biography and Discography*, Scarecrow Press, 2000
Stowe, D.W., *Swing Changes: Big Band Jazz in New Deal America*, Harvard University Press, 1994
Wilder, A., *American Popular Song: The Great Innovators, 1900-50*, Oxford University Press, 1972

1940s Blues

Cohodas, N., *Spinning Blues Into Gold: The Chess Brothers and the Legendary Chess Records*, St. Martin's Press, 2000
Dance, H., *Stormy Monday: The T-Bone Walker Story*, Louisiana State University Press, 1987
Edwards, D., *The World Don't Owe Me Nothing*, Chicago Review Press, 1997
Murray, C.S., *Boogie Man: The Adventures of John Lee Hooker in the American Twentieth Century*, St. Martin's Press, 2000
Palmer, R., *Deep Blues*, Viking Press, 1981
Rowe, M., *Chicago Breakdown*, Drake Publishers, 1975

1940s Jazz

Britt, S., *Long Tall Dexter: A Critical Musical Biography*, Quartet Books, 1989
DeVeaux, S., *The Birth of Bebop: A Social and Musical History*, University of California Press, 1997
Gillespie, D. & Fraser, A., *Dizzy: To Be Or Not To Bop*, Doubleday, 1979
Gitler, I., *Jazz Masters of the 40s*, Macmillan Press, 1966
Gelly, D. (ed), *Masters of Jazz Saxophone*, Balafon Books, 2000
Lees, G., *Leader of the Band: The Life of Woody Herman*, Oxford University Press, 1995
Levinson, P., *Trumpet Blues: The Life of Harry James*, Oxford University Press, 1999
Mathieson, K., *Giant Steps: Bebop and the Creators of Modern Jazz, 1945-65*, Payback Press, 1999
Nicholson, S., *Billie Holiday*, Gollancz, 1995
Owens, T., *Bebop: The Music and Its Players*, Oxford University Press, 1995
Russell, R., *Bird Lives!*, Charterhouse, 1972
Shipton, A., *Groovin' High: The Life of Dizzy Gillespie*, Oxford University Press, 1999
Woideck, C., *Charlie Parker: His Music and Life*, University of Michigan Press, 1996

1950s Blues

Gordon, R., *Can't Be Satisfied: The Life & Times of Muddy Waters*, Little, Brown and Company, 2002
Lydon, M., *Ray Charles: Man and Music*, Riverhead Books, 1998
Salem, J., *The Late, Great Johnny Ace*, University of Illinois Press, 1999
Segrest, J. & Hoffman, M., *Moanin' at Midnight: The Life and Times of Howlin' Wolf*, Pantheon Books, 2004

1950s Jazz

Alexander, C. (ed.), *Masters of Jazz Guitar*, Balafon Books, 1999
Catalano, N., *Clifford Brown: The Life and Art of the Legendary Jazz Trumpeter*, Oxford University Press, 2000
Carr, I., *Miles Davis: The Definitive Biography*, Harper Collins, 1998
Crease, S. S., *Gil Evans: Out of the Cool*, A Cappella, 2002
Davis, M. & Troupe, Q., *Miles: The Autobiography*, Simon and Schuster, 1989
Gavin, J., *Deep in a Dream: The Long Night of Chet Baker*, Chatto & Windus, 2002
Goldberg, J., *Jazz Masters of the 50s*, Macmillan Press, 1965
Gourse, L., *Straight, No Chaser: The Life and Genius of Thelonious Monk*, Schirmer Books, 1997
Kahn, A., *Kind of Blue: The Making of the Miles Davis Masterpiece*, Da Capo Press, 2000
Keepnews, O., *The View From Within: Jazz Writings, 1948-1987*, Oxford University Press, 1987
Klinkowitz, J., *Listen: Gerry Mulligan*, Schirmer Books, 1991
Maggin, D., *Stan Getz: A Life in Jazz*, William Morrow, 1996
Mathieson, K., *Cookin': Hard Bop and Soul Jazz, 1954-65*, Canongate, 2002
Nisenson, E., *Open Sky: Sonny Rollins and His World of Improvisation*, St. Martin's Press, 2000
Pepper, A., *Straight Life*, Schirmer Books, 1979
Peterson, O., *A Jazz Odyssey*, Continuum, 2002
Pettinger, P., *Bill Evans: How My Heart Sings*, Yale University Press, 1998
Porter, L., *John Coltrane: His Life and Music*, University of Michigan Press, 1998
Rosenthal, D., *Hard Bop: Jazz and Black Music*, 1955–1965, Oxford University Press, 1992
Santoro, G., *Myself When I Am Real: The Life and Music of Charles Mingus*, Oxford University Press, 2000
Szwed, J., *So What: The Life of Miles Davis*, Heinemann, 2002

1960s Blues

Brunning, B., *Blues: The British Connection: The Stones, Clapton, Fleetwood Mac and the Story of Blues in Britain*, Helter Skelter, 2003
Clayson, A., *The Yardbirds*, Backbeat Books, 2002
Friedman, M., *Buried Alive: the Biography of Janis Joplin*, Harmony, 1973
Henderson, D., *'Scuse Me While I Kiss the Sky: The Life of Jimi Hendrix*, Doubleday, 1978
Hotchner, A.E., *Blown Away: the Rolling Stones and the Death of the Sixties*, Simon and Schuster, 1990
King, B.B. with Ritz, D., *Blues All Around Me: The Autobiography of B.B. King*, Avon Books, 1996
Kooper, A., *Backstage Passes & Backstabbing Bastards*, Billboard, 1998
Obrecht, J., *Rollin' and Tumblin': The Postwar Blues Guitarists*, Backbeat Books, 2000
Sawyer, C., *B.B. King: the Authorized Biography*, Quartet Publishing, 1982
Schumacher, M., *Crossroads: the Life and Music of Eric Clapton*, Hyperion, 1995
Tisserand, M., *The Kingdom of Zydeco*, Avon Books, 1998
Waterman, D., *Between Midnight and Day: the Last Unpublished Blues Archive*, Thunder's Mouth Press, 2003
Wein, G. with Chinen, N., *Myself Among Others: a Life in Music*, Da Capo, 2003
Wexler, J. & Ritz, D., *Rhythm and the Blues: a Life in American Music*, Alfred A. Knopf, 1993
Wilcox D.E. & Guy, B., *Damn Right I've Got the Blues/Buddy Guy and the Blues Roots of Rock-and-Roll*, Woodford Press, 1993
Wolkin, J.M. & Keenom, B., *Michael Bloomfield: If You Love These Blues*, Miller Freeman Books, 2000

1960s Jazz

Ekkehard, J., *Free Jazz*, Da Capo Press, 1981
Jenkins, T.S., *Free Jazz and Free Improvisation: An Encyclopedia*, Greenwood Press, 2004
Kofsky, F., *Black Nationalism and the Revolution in Music*, Pathfinder Press, 1970
Litweiler, J., *The Freedom Principle: Jazz After 1958*, William Morrow and Co., 1984
Wilmer, V., *As Serious As Your Life*, Serpent's Tail, 1992 (2nd ed.)

1970s Blues

Cook, B., *Listen to the Blues*, Charles Scribner's Sons, 1973

1970s Jazz

Litweiler, J., *The Freedom Principle*, Quill, 1984
Lyons, L., *The 101 Best Jazz Albums*, William Morrow, 1980
Nicholson, S., *Jazz-Rock: A History*, Schirmer Books, 1998
Tingen, P., *Miles Beyond: The Electric Explorations of Miles Davis, 1967–1991*, Billboard Books, 2001

1980s Blues and Jazz

Fraher, J., *The Blues Is A Feeling: Voices and Visions of African-American Bluesmen*, Face To Face Books, 1998
Milkowski, B., *Rockers, Jazzbos & Visionaries*, Billboard Books, 1998
Patoski, J.N. & Crawford, B., *Stevie Ray Vaughan: Caught in the Crossfire*, Little, Brown and Company, 1993

Contemporary Blues

Eyre, B., *In Griot Time: An American Guitarist in Mali*, Temple University Press, 2000
Neville, A. & Ritz, D., *The Brothers: An Autobiography*, Da Capo, 2001
Nicholson, R., *Mississippi the Blues Today!*, Da Capo Press, 1999
Raccuglia, D., *Darker Blues*, Fat Possum Records, 2003
Santelli, R., *The Big Book of Blues: a Biographical Encyclopedia*, Penguin, 1994
Tipaldi, A., *Children of the Blues: 49 Musicians Shaping a New Blues Tradition*, Backbeat Books, 2002

Contemporary Jazz

Davis, F., *Bebop and Nothingness: Jazz and Pop at the End of the Century*, Schirmer Books, 1996
Mandel, H., *Future Jazz*, Oxford University Press, 1999
Mercer, M., *Footprints: The Life and Work of Wayne Shorter*, Tarcher/Penguin, 2004
Santoro, G., *Highway 61 Revisited: The Tangled Roots of American Jazz, Blues, Rock & Country Music*, Oxford University Press, 2004
Szwed, J., *Jazz 101: A Complete Guide to Learning and Loving Jazz*, Hyperion, 1999
Zabor, R., *The Bear Comes Home*, Norton, 1998
Zorn, J. (ed.), *Arcana: Musicians on Music*, Granary Books, 2000

Author Biographies & Picture Credits

Howard Mandel
(General Editor; chapter openers; Jazz Contemporary)
Howard Mandel is a writer and editor specializing in jazz, blues, new and unusual music. Born in Chicago, now living in New York City, he is a senior contributor for *Down Beat*, produces arts features for National Public Radio, teaches at New York University, is president of the Jazz Journalists Association and edits its website www.Jazzhouse.org. Mandel's *Future Jazz* (Oxford University Press, 1999) ranges from the AACM to John Zorn; he has written for *Musical America*, *The Wire* (UK), *Swing Journal* (Tokyo), *Bravo* (Rio de Janeiro), and many other periodicals.

Ted Drozdowski (Blues 1960s; Blues Contemporary)
Ted Drozdowski is a freelance journalist and musician living in Boston, Massachusetts. He writes about popular culture, specializing in music. His writing has appeared internationally in a wide variety of publications including *Tracks*, *Rolling Stone* and *Musician*. He is co-author of *The Best Music CD Art and Design* and appears on television and radio offering commentary on music. He was a research consultant for Martin Scorsese's PBS-TV series *The Blues* and has been awarded the Blues Foundation's Keeping the Blues Alive Award for Journalism. He leads the Mississippi-informed blues band Scissormen.

James Hale (Jazz 1970s; Instruments)
Based in Ottawa, Canada, James Hale is a feature writer, Critics Poll jury member and a frequent CD reviewer for *Down Beat*. He is also a frequent feature and review contributor to *Coda*, *Planet Jazz* and the *Ottawa Citizen*, and his work has appeared in *Jazziz*, *Pulse!*, *The Jazz Report*, *Modern Drummer*, *Words & Music* and *RhythmMusic*. In 2002 and 2003, he was nominated for a Canadian National Jazz Award as Best Journalist. A member of the Jazz Journalists Association, Hale is managing editor of the organization's website – Jazzhouse.org – and associate editor of their newsletter, *JazzNotes*.

Todd Jenkins (Jazz 1960s; Blues 1970s)
Todd S. Jenkins is a contributor to *Down Beat*, *All About Jazz*, *Signal To Noise*, *The ZydE-Zine* and *Route 66* magazines. He is the author of *Free Jazz and Free Improvisation: An Encyclopedia* (Greenwood Press), *Eclipse: The Music of Charles Mingus* (Praeger), and an upcoming biography of pianist Jimmy Rowles. A resident of San Bernardino, California, Todd is a member of the American Jazz Symposium and the Jazz Journalists Association.

Kenny Mathieson (Jazz 1940s; Jazz 1950s)
Kenny Mathieson lives and works in Boat of Garten, Strathspey, Scotland. He studied American and English Literature at the University of East Anglia, graduating with a BA (First Class) in 1978 and a PhD in 1983. He has been a freelance writer on various arts-related subjects since 1982, specializing in music, primarily jazz, classical and folk. He contributes to *The Herald*, *The Scotsman*, *The List*, *Times Educational Supplement Scotland*, *Jazzwise* and other publications. He has contributed to a variety of reference books. He is the author of two books on jazz, *Giant Steps* and *Cookin'* (both Canongate), and edited and co-wrote *Celtic Music – A Listener's Guide* (BackbeatUK). He writes on arts for the *Inverness Courier*, and is the commissioning editor for the HI-Arts online arts journal (www.hi-arts.co.uk).

John McDonough (Jazz 1930s)
John McDonough has been critic and contributing editor at *Down Beat* since 1968, and a contributor on jazz and other cultural topics to *The Wall Street Journal* since 1986. A three-time Grammy nominee for Best Album Notes, he has written biographies on Lester Young, Pee Wee Russell and Coleman Hawkins for Time-Life Books as well as the book accompanying the Grammy winning *The Complete Ella Fitzgerald Song Books* on Verve. He has also contributed other notes for Mosaic, Pablo, Columbia, Victor, et al. McDonough is also editor of The

Encyclopedia of Advertising (2003) and a long-time contributor to *Advertising Age* and National Public Radio, for which he writes and produces historical pieces in partnership with former CBS anchor Walter Cronkite. He lives near Chicago with his wife and son.

Bill Milkowski
(Jazz 1920s; Blues 1980s; Jazz 1980s)
Bill Milkowski is a regular contributor to *Jazz Times*, *Jazziz*, *Bass Player*, *Modern Drummer*, *Guitar Club* (Italy) and *Jazzthing* (Germany) magazines. He was named the Jazz Journalists Association's Writer of the Year for 2004. He is also the author of *JACO: The Extraordinary Life of Jaco Pastorius* (Backbeat Books), *Rockers, Jazzbos & Visionaries* (Billboard Books) and *Swing It! An Annotated History of Jive* (Billboard Books).

Jim O'Neal (Blues Early Years)
Jim O'Neal is based in Kansas City and is founding editor of *Living Blues*, America's first blues magazine. He co-edited *The Voice of the Blues: Classic Interviews from Living Blues Magazine* (Routledge 2002), and he collects and sells soul, R&B, funk, jazz, country, folk, world/ethnic, gospel, soundtrack and rock'n'roll records as well as blues. His website, BluEsoterica.com, is a research forum for discussing new, obscure or overlooked details on blues.

Bob Porter
(Blues 1930s; Blues 1940s; Blues 1950s)
Bob Porter is a discographer, record producer and award-winning broadcaster and writer based in New Jersey. His syndicated blues program *Portraits in Blue* began its 24th year in autumn 2004. As well as serving on the board of directors of the Blues Foundation and being on the nominating committee for the Rock And Roll Hall of Fame, he has won two Grammies for his liner notes and produced more than 150 jazz and blues albums for artists such as Big Joe Turner and Illinois Jacquet. Porter has written for *Jazz Times Magazine*, *Down Beat*, *Jazz Journal* and *Discographical Forum*, amongst others. He contributed to the *Oxford Companion to Jazz*, and in 1992 was awarded the New Jersey Jazz Society's Outstanding Service Award.

William Schafer (Jazz Early Years)
Since gaining a Phd as the University of Minnesota, William Schafer has worked as editor and publications designer for the military and USDA, and taught at Berea College, Kentucky, where he is Chair of the English Department and head of the humanities program. His many publications include *The Art of Ragtime* (with Johannes Reidel, LSU Press), *Rock Music* (Augsburg Press), *Brass Bands and New Orleans Jazz* (LSU Press), *The Truman Nelson Reader* (ed., University of Massachusetts Press) and *Mapping the Godzone* (University of Hawaii Press). William has also contributed to *Contemporary Novelists* (St. Martin's Press), *Contemporary Short Stories* (St. Martin's Press), *The Encyclopedia of Southern Culture* (University of North Carolina Press) and Grove's dictionaries of American Music and Jazz. He is also a contributing editor of *Mississippi Rag*.

David Whiteis (Blues 1920s)
David Whiteis, an internationally published critic and journalist with over 25 years of experience writing about blues, jazz, and other essential issues, currently writes on a regular basis for the *Chicago Reader*, *Down Beat*, *Living Blues*, *Juke Blues*, and others. He is the recipient of the Blues Foundation's 2001 Keeping the Blues Alive Award for Achievement in Journalism. His book, *I Mean It From The Heart: Stories and Portraits in Chicago Blues*, is due to be published by University of Illinois Press in 2005.

Index